Ford's Illustrated Guide to

WINES, BREWS, & SPIRITS

Ford's Illustrated Guide to

WINES, BREWS, & SPIRITS

Gene Ford

wcb

Wm. C. Brown Publishers
Dubuque, Iowa

Cover photo: Bob Coyle
Designer: Kevin Pruessner

Since this page cannot legibly accommodate all copyright
notices, pages 371–72 constitute an extension of the
copyright page.

To The Brothers of the Christian Schools

Just over three hundred years ago, in the rolling hills of the Champagne country of northern France, nobleman John Baptiste de la Salle established a new teaching order dedicated to educating the poor.

Just over 100 years ago, members of this teaching group founded a small winery north of San Francisco to support their schools.

This book salutes the 18,000 Brothers of the Christian Schools worldwide and, in particular, the many who have guided the fortunes of the Christian Brothers Winery in its first 100 years.

Finally, this book is dedicated to that gentle giant of a cellar master, Brother Timothy Deiner, F. S. C., whose unerring sense of proportion has guided the winery through nearly half of those first hundred years.

Alcohol: The Anomaly of Anomalies

Alcohol is the king of potables, and carries to the nth degree the excitation of our palates; its diverse preparations have opened up to us many new sources of pleasure . . . it gives to certain medicaments . . . a strength which they would not have without it; it has even become in our hands a powerful weapon, for the nations of the New World have been almost as much conquered and destroyed by brandy as by firearms.

Jean Anthelme Brillat-Savarin

. . . if it be the design of Providence to extirpate these savages in order to make room for the cultivation of the earth, it seems not improbable that rum may be the appointed means.

Benjamin Franklin

It is true that even then it was known and acknowledged that many were greatly injured by it; but none seemed to think the injury arose from the use of a bad thing, but from the abuse of a very good thing.

Abraham Lincoln

Contents

Tables

Preface

During six years of writing a syndicated newspaper feature and of teaching college courses in the field of wine and spirits, I have had the unusual and pleasurable experience of rummaging through dozens of new and used book stores in as many cities looking for new material. This pleasant exercise soon revealed a curious anomaly.

While there exists a prodigious literature on wines and their making, and a few scattered texts and coffee table tomes on brews, precious few works for a general audience that cover the historical and cultural aspects of spirits and liqueurs have turned up. Books and pamphlets on the evils of drink abound, as do medical studies about the ravages of abuse. But, few books can be found with more than cursory treatment of the brews and distilled spirits so universally ingested. A specious gentility seems to cloak their presence in society.

In the United States, more than one hundred million individuals consume some form of potable alcohol on a regular basis. The vast majority of these drinkers are both temperate in manner and eclectic in their choice of beverages. Gone is the day of the single drink drinker. Modern consumers move freely between types and styles, from the cooling brew at Miller Time to an elegant Chardonnay with the fowl and, finally, to a smooth and delicious Bailey's Irish Cream with dessert.

In this book, each potable alcohol is considered in terms of the ingredients from which it is made, its method of production and its popular uses. The alcohols are presented, more or less, in the historical sequence of their use. They are also presented in considerable technical detail because this detail unlocks the mysteries of our favorite, as well as least liked, alcoholic beverages.

Part 1 considers the effects of alcohol on humans and details the development of alcoholic beverages throughout history. Part 2 provides descriptions of the originally fermented major alcohols, while Part 3 describes distilled beverages in the same manner.

Tasting guides for each of the beverages covered in Parts 2 and 3 are included for use either in a class setting or by individuals. (When using the tasting guides on an individual basis, enlist six or eight other people to share the expense—and the fun!)

This book has been written as a primer both for the professional in the hospitality industry and for the curious in that vast population of drinkers who wonder about the origins, the manufacture, and the uses of their favorite wines, brews, and spirits. There are tasting guides that can lead the adventurous step-by-step through the entire realm. There are brief discussions of the physiology of alcohol and of both the historical and the current patterns of consumption that will surprise many readers. Finally, for the more than curious, there are ample reading lists, arranged by topic and located as follows:

For this writer, the book is an effort to redress the anomaly, to tie together in some cohesive manner the lore and the fact of alcohol consumption—a universal at least as certain as death and taxes!

ACKNOWLEDGMENTS

My gratitude extends to individuals too numerous to encompass in a conventional acknowledgment page. Many firms and publications are credited throughout the book. But these few must be thanked in a public way. My appreciation extends to Dr. H. A. Divine, who hired me to teach the Washington State University course on which this book rests. My colleagues at The Christian Brothers—John Hoffman, Dave Cofran, Gordon Pilone, Ron Hanson and Joe Kelley—have patiently seen me through the intricacies of wine and brandy making, correcting and advising all the while.

As early readers and critics of the first drafts, I deeply appreciate the advice of University of Washington history professor Dr. W. J. Rorabaugh and Seattle University's expert on alcoholism, Dr. James E. Royce, S. J., both of whom also returned to the task with evaluations of the final manuscript. Longtime brewmaster and vice president of the Rainier Brewing Company, John H. Lindsay, provided essential expertise and encouragement.

Final readers added a broader perspective than I could possibly attain, including D. V. S. Burroughs of England's Wine and Spirit Education Trust, Cal Hoerneman, Midwest wine writer, and Peter M. F. Sichel of H. Sichel Sohne, Inc.

A special and familial note of thanks to Lisa Marie Ford who, fresh from her Masters in English, gave six months to researching, copyediting and entering the manuscript onto floppy disks—monumental achievements all. To Kathy Loy, my thoughtful editor, immense gratitude for the gradual taming of the manuscript to appropriate dimensions. To Patricia Schmelling, production editor, and Kevin Pruessner, designer, I owe abiding thanks for making the melange manageable. Finally, to Karleen Redle, my gratitude for her learned and perspicacious copyediting of the final work. Thanks, one and all.

Ford's Illustrated Guide to

WINES, BREWS, & SPIRITS

PART ONE

INTRODUCTION TO ALCOHOL

Alcohol and Humans

*P*otable alcohol came into being without the aid of mankind. Airborne microflora called yeast have caused the breakdown of natural sugar in grapes and in honey from beehives as long as these ingredients have existed. Wine making is simply a natural process in the plant kingdom.

Among alcohol's attributes are its powers to intoxicate, to release the consumer from the cares of the day, and to bring about sociability amid strife—to elevate and exhilarate. Despite the euphoria it may produce, it can also heighten aggressive tendencies and lead to trouble and dissension among ordinarily compatible individuals and groups.

A CERTAIN FOCUS

In order truly to comprehend the role of alcohol in human society, one must have at least rudimentary knowledge of its chemistry as well as an historical overview of its use. Unfortunately, as Chandler Washburne notes in *Primitive Drinking* (1961), his study of the use of alcohol in tribal societies: "There is hardly any such thing as a thorough study of a society which presents a more or less complete picture of the meaning, uses and functions of alcoholic beverages within that society."

This is not to imply that alcohol remains unstudied in terms of its chemical dimensions or its impact on humans and their societies in medical and social contexts. Indeed, there is a prodigious amount of medical literature focusing on alcoholism and its physical ravages. But what is missing is a correlation of these clinical and therapeutic disciplines with an understanding of the dynamics of the societies themselves.

*T*herefore God give thee of the dew of heaven, and the fatness of the earth, and plenty of corn and wine.

Genesis 27:28

*T*he U.S. systems of alcohol controls are chaotic relics. They provide little support in mitigating alcohol problems and may induce a counterproductive ambivalence among the public.

Second Report on Alcohol and Health (HEW)

There is new hope and promise because of support from both governmental and private agencies for this kind of interdisciplinary approach. Some diverse perspectives form the first section of this book, and they provide at least a framework within which people can make rational decisions about the sale and consumption of beverage alcohols.

Most leading authorities and researchers are as yet unwilling to state with certainty that there are biological bases for the abuse of, and the addiction to, alcohol. Yet there is high probability that some susceptibility is passed from generation to generation of abusers as in northern Europe where large numbers of people in diverse populations have great difficulty

The Fields of the Blest *from the tomb of Sen-Nuden depicts the abundance of Ancient Egypt with wheat, dates, olives and other fruits.*

handling alcohol. For them, genetic predisposition could be a factor. However, it is not considered fact at present. It is only a theory now, but one which must be considered seriously.

Conversely, there is little dispute that cultural influences play a major role in fostering abusive consumption practices within a society, for alcohol and many other substances. It is the consistent and insistent point of view of this book that these debasing habits may be altered, thereby reducing the numbers of people affected by harmful abuse, or the disease of alcoholism. It is also important to recognize that for the alcoholic no one alcohol is better or worse than another. There is no intrinsically "better or worse" alcohol. All of the claims and counterclaims to that end are absurdly specious. To the abuser, ethanol is ethanol no matter its source, whether it is hair oil or single malt Scotch. Every potable alcohol has been abundantly abused, no matter its origin.

Those of us who perceive the glorious varietal complexity of a fine Cabernet must join forces with the single-malt-Scotch lovers first by recognizing that although all alcoholic beverages are appropriate to certain circumstances and to partisan users, the way they are used is paramount. Only then can we penetrate the welter of conflicting data and reach some reasonable national consensus about how to teach our young to cope with this potentially dangerous drug.

The problem, of course, is that any debate is subject to partisanship. Those who feel evil incarnate lurks in the bottle

TABLE 1.1 Economics of the Alcohol Industry, 1979

Expenditures	Dollars	
Non-agricultural supplies & services	31.50	billions
Taxes and levies	13	billions[a]
Agricultural purchases	1.29	billions
Barrels, cases, labels, etc.	850	millions
Shipping	910	millions

Source: DISCUS Facts Book 1979 (Washington D.C.: Distilled Spirits Council of the United States, Inc., 1980).
[a]Estimated

do not want to be bothered with other relevant facts. They are willing to ignore the fact that the economic well-being of quite a considerable segment of our population is dependent upon the production and sale of potable alcohols. A tremendous amount of money was pumped into the economy in 1979 by 616,000 firms that employed over 1.7 million workers (see table 1.1).

THE GREAT MONEY-MAKER

No doubt about it. All major public agencies have a budgetary interest in alcohol consumption, especially since repeal of Prohibition. Nearly $11 billion is raised through licensing and from federal, state, and local taxes when the alcohol is made, transported, and sold respectively, as well as another $2 billion in corporate and personal taxes that are associated with alcohol. Over half of the cost of each bottle of liquor is siphoned off to public revenue.

These statistics are taken from a publication of the Distilled Spirits Council of the United States, *DISCUS Facts Book 1979*. Public revenues from distilled spirits alone constitute a daily $19 million bonanza. With the recent sudden increase in per capita wine consumption, distilled spirits are near the bottom of the barrel in terms of total consumption and yet that barrel is a veritable tax cornucopia. The *Facts Book* sums it up:

> Distilled spirits rank behind soft drinks, coffee, beer, wine, and tea in gallons consumed per capita, yet their sale yields a greater amount of tax revenue than all other beverages combined. The taxes on distilled spirits accounted for 70.5% of the total Federal revenue collections from all beverage alcohol in 1979.

According to Dr. Robert Dupont of the National Institute on Drug Abuse, "The drugs we do not prohibit are far more used than the drugs we prohibit." Although in gross tonnage legal drugs may well lead the parade, it appears that many more dollars are invested in the illicit market. Marijuana, for example, which is used by a distinct minority, apparently exceeds $20.5 billion in sales compared to less than $16 billion in cigarette sales. Since alcohol is openly distributed, we can more readily trace its uses and abuses, and any ensuing calamitous consequences.

However, although some of our fellow citizens with varying degrees of insecurity use alcohol only, some use it in combination with an assortment of potentially life-endangering substances. Therefore, many of the consequences attributed to alcohol use and abuse must be at least qualified, if not discounted. It is often the combination of alcohol and human misery, valium, marijuana, or some other substance that should be considered. The federal government places the annual cost of alcohol abuse above $40 billion which includes statistics on lost production, motor accidents, violent crimes and other costs attributed to alcohol use. The argument that there may be other contributing factors is not presented to vitiate the accuracy of these statistics, but to qualify them in the interest of greater accuracy though the loss of even a single life through alcohol-induced starvation or the maiming of a single person in an alcohol-related traffic accident is unacceptable. Rather than playing a numbers game and fixing blame through sensationalism, it is necessary to examine the costs as well as the benefits of alcohol use from a wider perspective.

Drink We Will

Figures from the *Third Special Report to Congress on Alcohol and Health* (1978) demonstrate conclusively that Americans choose to consume alcohol, no matter the ultimate consequences (see table 1.2).

TABLE 1.2 Americans Who Drink, 1978

	Men (%)	Women (%)	Total Age 21 and over[a] (%)
Light drinkers	30	33	31
Moderate drinkers	24	12	18
Heavy drinkers	15	4	9
Abstainers	31	51	42

Source: Adapted from U.S. Department of Health, Education, and Welfare. *Third Special Report to Congress on Alcohol and Health* (Washington: Government Printing Office, 1978).
[a] Harris Survey

TABLE 1.3 Percent Who Drink, 1939–1982

Date	%
Latest (August 13–16)	65
January, 1982	67
1981	70
1979	69
1978	71
1976	71
1974	68
1969	64
1966	65
1964	63
1960	62
1958	55
1957	58
1956	60
1952	60
1951	59
1950	60
1949	58
1947	63
1946	67
1945	67
1939	58

Source: The Gallup Poll, statistics released 30 September 1982.

Statistics drawn from the *Third Report* do provide important insights. To no one's surprise, more women than men abstain. But it may surprise some to learn that heavy drinkers, among the young, constitute a minority, only 9 percent according to the Harris Survey. These data are not meant to imply that the heavy-drinking minority is responsible for all drinking problems. An infrequent drinker may easily kill himself or others if he gets behind the wheel of an automobile while intoxicated.

Another verification of our predilection to drink is found in the results of a series of surveys by the Gallup organization (see table 1.3). Responses indicate a curious drop in total

TABLE 1.4 Percent Who Drink by Group

	1981 (%)	1982 (%)	Point Change
National total	70	65	−5
Men	75	69	−6
Women	66	61	−5
College education	81	79	−2
High school	70	66	−4
Grade school	52	29	−23
18–29 years	76	77	+1
30–49 years	74	71	−3
50 years & older	63	52	−11
East	77	72	−5
Midwest	75	69	−6
South	58	52	−6
West	72	69	−3
Protestants	62	58	−4
Catholics	82	76	−6
Family income			
$15,000 and over	78	77	−1
Under $15,000	62	51	−11

Source: The Gallup Poll, statistics released 30 September 1982.

The Cooper.

drinkers halfway through a forty-year period. However, in the 1970s, the number of consumers of alcohol in our society has remained relatively constant.

The 1982 Gallup Survey sought to determine, according to area, education, and religion, who was doing the drinking (see table 1.4). Age, geographical location, and religion all apparently influence whether one drinks. These figures are sufficient to demonstrate how universal but variable alcoholic consumption is, and how dangerous it is to generalize about it. Evaluation of these data is best left to experts in the field of social behavior. It is sufficient for us to recognize that if regional, religious, and other cultural differences are factors in the choice to drink, they may be factors in one's choice of alcoholic beverages and the amounts consumed. Many of these external influences can be moderated, which suggests we can alter drinking patterns.

Therefore, there is great value in shedding some historical light on beverage alcohol consumption. Chapters 3 and 4 provide a review of alcohol consumption by other national groups and in other times; alcohol consumption by contemporary Americans may be measured against this panorama.

Alcohol is, in a moral sense, neither good nor evil. It is, rather, a substance which, when used properly, contributes to our well-being and, when misused, contributes to our stress. It is a chemical abundantly available in nature, as are aspirin, sugar, and many other chemicals we consume for relief, pleasure or sustenance. So alcohol problems arise not from the substance itself, but from our misuse of it.

Since a majority of us choose to consume alcohol, it is our collective responsibility to educate ourselves and those around us in the hope that heavy drinkers will see how important it is to adopt more temperate habits. For true temperance is not abstinence, but reasonable moderation in satisfying passions and desires.

DRINKING BY THE YOUNG

There is clear danger of misinterpretation and subsequent sensationalizing of basic data with regard to the young because parents are concerned with their children's welfare. From reading the *Third Report,* one might come to believe that drinking among the young is getting out of hand. While total consumption of alcohol by the young may be increasing, this phenomenon may be totally unrelated to abuse and alcoholism.

Drinking alcohol is clearly a visible celebration of the rite of passage to adulthood in our society. It is a peer group practice which is influenced by the "older generation," as suggested by North and Orange in *Teenage Drinking:*

> For many teenagers, drinking and smoking represent symbols [*sic*] of approaching adulthood. In much the same way that many of us imitated our parents by dressing up in their clothes, many teenagers begin to drink to feel "grown up". . . . True, no one knows for certain why teenagers are increasingly abusing alcohol; but we do know that the two greatest influences on adolescents are their peers and parents.

There is abundant empirical evidence that people of all ages and all classes as well as both sexes, tend, when under stress, to abuse alcohol, tobacco, and coffee, sugar, and other foods, along with a host of pills. Alcohol, of all these substances, simply provides a quick and legal escape from the web of anxiety and depression. In fact, there is considerable evidence that we teach our young that a quick "fix" is always attainable whether in the form of sugar, caffeine, "uppers" or an alcoholic drink.

In recognition of the contradiction between our expressed concern about alcohol abuse and the example we set of "acceptable" misuse, one professional in the field of alcoholism has suggested a novel approach. Bill Saunders, director of the Alcohol Study Center at Paisley College of Technology in Scotland, believes that education can prevent alcohol abuse, if one's mentors treat drinking like a skill and begin instruction early, for example, when young people reach age twelve.

As farfetched as this suggestion might seem, it should be weighed against the rather good evidence that we have for years been teaching our youth, by example, how they can abuse. Even if subsequent research verifies the reported increases in alcohol consumption by the young, we must recognize that the creature comforts we proffer to our offspring are also increasing. We are a nation of spenders who cater to our young with wanton abandon.

Since alcohol is a legal beverage, it can and should be considered apart from the host of illegal drugs. There is a real difference between overconsumption and alcoholism, a distinction most difficult to grasp amid the swamp of propaganda. While both are offensive, the former does not necessarily lead to the latter. A person may abuse alcohol every weekend for thirty years and not be alcoholic according to the classic definition of the disease. Reform in the behavior of those who abuse alcohol can be achieved apart from finding the solution to the perplexing problem of alcoholism.

AMERICAN DRINKING IN PERSPECTIVE

What follows is a patchwork quilt of historical tidbits. Defining the historical pattern of alcohol consumption in our country is undertaking a complex task because of the multiplicity of our originating cultures. We are not a relatively homogeneous mass like the population of Italy or France. We are Philippine, Nordic, Spanish, and African, as well as Indo-European and

*F*or when we quaff the gen'rous bowl
Then sleeps the sorrows of the soul.
Anacreon

a conglomeration of other nationalities, each with a unique history of drinking. The approach here is simply to trace the development of drinking in western society from its roots in the Sumerian civilization through the Colonial Period and Prohibition into contemporary times. For the most part, immigrants have been assimilated gradually into our drinking culture which, to a large degree, is our heritage from western European societies.

How much are Americans drinking today? The average American annually consumes the equivalent of one case each of liquor and wine, plus twelve cases of beer. That is a considerable amount of alcohol. But our average American also ingests 105 pounds of sugar (a potentially lethal substance placed in nearly all prepared foods), a prodigious number of aspirin and other pain killers, and a significant number of marijuana cigarettes for which there is no accurate estimate. The composite American is a trained consumer with a sufficient expendable income to sate a wide range of appetites.

A recent article ranked nations according to their demonstrated comparative alcohol consumption (see table 1.5). In 1981 the United States placed eighth among western nations in distilled spirits, twelfth in beer and did not even appear on the wine chart.

Two important facts are revealed by these rankings. One, the United States ranks very high in spirit consumption, up with those Eastern European nations traditionally considered heavy consumers. Second, the United States does not even rank among the first twenty in per capita wine consumption. It is fair to say that our nation ranks in the middle in total consumption.

In the sixth of a continuing series of annual surveys of affluent American households, Mendelsohn Media Research presents some mind-boggling statistics to American wine sellers. The reports, titled *The Dimensions of the Affluent Market,* track households that have combined incomes of $40,000 or more.

This study shows an interesting phenomenon—only two years ago the affluent group totaled 15,800,000; in 1982 it reached 29,850,000. Even when inflation is taken into account, this group is the fastest growing segment of our population. These reports demonstrate the very real discretionary income these people, who comprise 14 percent of the total number of households, spend. Table 1.6 excerpts the consumption of alcohol by the affluent.

These statistics become really impressive when you multiply them by fifty-two weeks and convert the ounces to gallons.

TABLE 1.5 Nations Ranked according to Alcohol Consumption, 1981

Rank	Spirits	Gal.	Beer	Gal.	Wine	Gal.
1	Luxembourg	6.3	W. Germany	38.8	France	23.8
2	E. Germany	6.3	Czech.	37.0	Portugal	20.3
3	Hungary	3.0	E. Germany	36.3	Italy	19.5
4	Poland	2.8	Australia	35.4	Argentina	19.3
5	Czech.	2.4	Belgium	32.8	Spain	15.8
6	Canada	2.3	Luxembourg	32.5	Switz.	12.8
7	U.S.S.R.	2.2	Denmark	32.3	Greece	11.9
8	U.S.	2.0	N. Zealand	32.2	Chile	11.5
9	Peru	2.0	Ireland	30.7	Luxembourg	10.6
10	Spain	2.0	England	29.5	Austria	9.3
11	W. Germany	1.9	Austria	27.7	Hungary	9.2
12	Finland	1.8	U.S.	24.6	Rumania	7.6
13	Netherlands	1.7	Netherlands	23.6	Yugoslavia	7.4
14	Sweden	1.6	Hungary	23.0	Uruguay	6.6
15	Iceland	1.5	Canada	22.5	W. Germany	6.5
16	Belgium	1.4	Switz.	18.6	Bulgaria	5.8
17	Switz.	1.4	Venezuela	16.5	Belgium	5.5
18	Cyprus	1.4	Bulgaria	16.1	Australia	4.8
19	N. Zealand	1.3	Finland	15.1	Denmark	4.2
20	France	1.3	Spain	14.8	Czech.	4.2

Source: IMPACT (1 November 1982), 10.

TABLE 1.6 Selected Examples of Beverage Alcohol Consumption; Households of Adults Earning $40,000 and Above

Type	Number of Drinks (Average per Week)
Whiskey	3.1
Scotch	1.3
Vodka	1.3
Gin	0.8
Wine	4.6
All types	11.1

Source: adapted from *The Dimensions of the Affluent Market: 1982 Survey of Adults and Markets of Influence* (New York: Mendelsohn Media Research, Inc., 1982), 1–11.

Rough estimates show that this group consumed a tidy 12.5 million cases of Scotch, about half of the total number consumed. Figuring six ounces of wine per drink, the group consumed an astounding 361 million gallons of wine, nearly 70 percent of all wine consumed. Indeed, wine is a privileged beverage in America.

However, generalizing about any statistics, the parlor game of partisans, can lead to almost any conclusion. The important factor is not the *total consumption* of raw alcohol but the *means* of consumption. From a purely quantitative point of view, it can be asserted that we are generally a temperate nation of imbibers.

Indeed, we are consuming substantially less than our forefathers. In a remarkable book based on his doctoral research Professor W. J. Rorabaugh (1979) presents a chrono-logical picture of early American drinking, focusing on the socially and industrially explosive period from the Revolutionary War through 1830. Through his research, Rorabaugh identified one period of extremely concentrated consumption: "I began to suspect that the temperance movement had been launched in the 1820s as a response to a period of exceptionally heavy drinking. The truth was startling: Americans between 1790 and 1830 drank more alcoholic beverages per capita than ever before or since." He attributes their intemperance to unrest stemming from social and industrial change. The scarcity of records concerning the production of alcohol during the period suggests an almost conspiratorial ambivalence toward drinking on the part of both past and present historians. Gathering the data necessary for a statistical analysis of the production and consumption of alcohol during the nation's history was an extraordinary research accomplishment (see table 1.7).

CONSUMPTION MODERATING

Consumption of total absolute alcohol is shown as a function of the total drinking population, persons fifteen and over. According to Rorabaugh's table, total consumption in 1970 was a scant tenth of a percent lower than in 1910. By contrast, the 1970 figure is only about one-third of the shocking 7.1 gallons per person ingested in 1830. The most significant figures, however, are those that pertain to the second half of the last century. Moderation in drinking seemed to parallel the transition from a pre-industrial society to a highly successful industrial one.

The gradual increase in consumption of beer and wine was responsible for the increase in the *total amount* of raw alcohol consumed. Total per capita consumption of *hard* spirits

TABLE 1.7 Alcoholic Beverage Consumption, 1710–1975

Year	Spirits		Wine		Cider		Beer		Total
	Bev.	Abs. Alc.	Bev.	Abs. Alc.	Bev.	Abs. Alc.	Bev.	Abs. Alc.	Abs. Alc.
1710	3.8	1.7	.2	<.05	34.	3.4	-	-	5.1
1770	7.0	3.2	.2	<.05	34.	3.4	-	-	6.6
1785	5.7	2.6	.6	.1	34.	3.4	-	-	6.1
1790	5.1	2.3	.6	.1	34.	3.4	-	-	5.8
1795	5.9	2.7	.6	.1	34.	3.4	-	-	6.2
1800	7.2	3.3	.6	.1	32.	3.2	-	-	6.6
1805	8.2	3.7	.6	.1	30.	3.0	-	-	6.8
1810	8.7	3.9	.4	.1	30.	3.0	1.3	.1	7.1
1815	8.3	3.7	.4	.1	30.	3.0	-	-	6.8
1820	8.7	3.9	.4	.1	28.	2.8	-	-	6.8
1825	9.2	4.1	.4	.1	28.	2.8	-	-	7.0
1830	9.5	4.3	.5	.1	27.	2.7	-	-	7.1
1835	7.6	3.4	.5	.1	15.	1.5	-	-	5.0
1840	5.5	2.5	.5	.1	4.	.4	2.3	.1	3.1
1845	3.7	1.6	.3	.1	-	-	2.4	.1	1.8
1850	3.6	1.6	.3	.1	-	-	2.7	.1	1.8
1855	3.7	1.7	.3	.1	-	-	4.6	.2	2.0
1860	3.9	1.7	.5	.1	-	-	6.4	.3	2.1
1865	3.5	1.6	.5	.1	-	-	5.8	.3	2.0
1870	3.1	1.4	.5	.1	-	-	8.6	.4	1.9
1875	2.8	1.2	.8	.1	-	-	10.1	.5	1.8
1880	2.4	1.1	1.0	.2	-	-	11.1	.6	1.9
1885	2.2	1.0	.8	.1	-	-	18.0	.9	2.0
1890	2.2	1.0	.6	.1	-	-	20.6	1.0	2.1
1895	1.8	.8	.6	.1	-	-	23.4	1.2	2.1
1900	1.8	.8	.6	.1	-	-	23.6	1.2	2.1
1905	1.9	.9	.7	.1	-	-	25.9	1.3	2.3
1910	2.1	.9	.9	.2	-	-	29.2	1.5	2.6
1915	1.8	.8	.7	.1	-	-	29.7	1.5	2.4
1920	2.1	.9	-	-	-	-	-	-	.9
1925	2.0	.9	-	-	-	-	-	-	.9
1930	2.0	.9	-	-	-	-	-	-	.9
1935	1.5	.7	.4	.1	-	-	15.0	.7	1.5
1940	1.3	.6	.9	.2	-	-	17.2	.8	1.6
1945	1.5	.7	1.1	.2	-	-	24.2	1.1	2.0
1950	1.5	.7	1.1	.2	-	-	24.1	1.1	2.0
1955	1.6	.7	1.3	.2	-	-	22.8	1.0	1.9
1960	1.9	.8	1.3	.2	-	-	22.1	1.0	2.0
1965	2.1	1.0	1.3	.2	-	-	22.8	1.0	2.2
1970	2.5	1.1	1.8	.3	-	-	25.7	1.2	2.5
1975	2.4	1.1	2.2	.3	-	-	28.8	1.3	2.7

Source: From *The Alcoholic Republic: An American Tradition* by W. J. Rorabaugh. Copyright © 1979 by Oxford University Press, Inc. Reprinted by permission.
Note: Absolute alcohol for each beverage, per capita of drinking-age (15+) population, in U.S. gallons.

dropped from 4.3 gallons of absolute alcohol in 1830 to 1.1 gallons in 1975. Spirit consumption leveled at about 2 gallons per person in 1980.

Historian Fernand Braudel, in *The Structures of Everyday Life* (1981), reconstructs many of the drinking patterns in the sixteenth to the eighteenth centuries. His figures validate those found by Rorabaugh.

But a Parisian consumed an average of 121.76 litres [32 gallons] of wine between 1781 and 1786, 8.96 [2.3 gallons] of beer and 2.73 [1 gallon] of cider. . . . Drunkenness increased everywhere in the sixteenth

century. Consumption in Valladolid reached 100 litres per person [26 gallons per year] in the middle of the century; in Venice, the Signoria was obliged to take new and severe action against public drunkenness in 1598; in France Laffermas was quite positive on that point at the beginning of the seventeenth century . . . In fact wine, principally low quality wine, had become a cheap foodstuff. Its price even fell relatively every time grain became too expensive.

While there is no "ideal" for total consumption of alcohol, except the unrealistic goal of total abstention proposed by the drys, it is fair to conclude that not only did total per

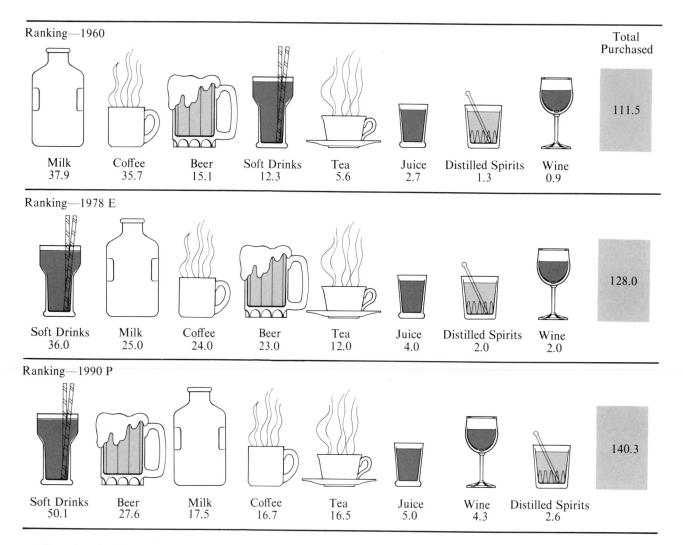

Ranking—1960

								Total Purchased
Milk 37.9	Coffee 35.7	Beer 15.1	Soft Drinks 12.3	Tea 5.6	Juice 2.7	Distilled Spirits 1.3	Wine 0.9	111.5

Ranking—1978 E

								Total Purchased
Soft Drinks 36.0	Milk 25.0	Coffee 24.0	Beer 23.0	Tea 12.0	Juice 4.0	Distilled Spirits 2.0	Wine 2.0	128.0

Ranking—1990 P

								Total Purchased
Soft Drinks 50.1	Beer 27.6	Milk 17.5	Coffee 16.7	Tea 16.5	Juice 5.0	Wine 4.3	Distilled Spirits 2.6	140.3

Figure 1.1 *The changing world of beverage consumption in the United States (per capita consumption in gallons). Of the approximately 170 gallons of fluid each person needs for survival in a year, Americans purchase a larger portion of those fluids each year.*

capita consumption decrease during the last century, but per capita consumption of the stronger distilled spirits has also moderated considerably in our own century.

Professor Rorabaugh's figures are presented to demonstrate the unrealistic base of 1850 chosen for the various federal reports on alcohol and health. In fact, the earlier the period for which figures can be reconstructed, the heavier the per capita consumption seems to have been. It is much fairer to state that by 1860, most Americans had abandoned the abusive patterns of their forefathers. However, there is still much to be done to aid those who currently abuse alcohol.

In any attempt to understand why people drink, we must first recognize that the body loses about 6 percent of its water daily, which requires replacement by any water-based fluids. An article appearing in *IMPACT* included a chart showing most of the fluids we ingest to stay alive (fig. 1.1). Consumption quantities of each fluid for the selected years—1960, 1978,

and a projection into 1990—suggest a veritable revolution in taste.

Some interesting conclusions can be drawn from this graphic depiction of beverage consumption trends. The most significant finding is that quantities of *purchased fluids* continue to increase even though water would obviously replace lost fluid. Per capita consumption of purchased beverages totaled 111.5 gallons in 1960, increased to 128 gallons in 1978 and is projected to rise to a whopping 140.3 gallons in 1990. This tells us two things: Americans have enough expendable income to purchase beverages, and beverage alcohols will constitute an increasing proportion of replacement fluid.

America's love affair with soft, light, medium sweet, usually carbonated beverages is obvious. The 1978 soft drink consumption of 35 gallons per person is 12.8 ounces daily. If the 1990 projection is accurate, each and every one of us will drink 17.5 ounces daily. Does anyone wonder at the increasing

Vindemia (The Vintage). *By an anonymous eighteenth century artist.*

consumption of light spirits and light, bubbly wines when the young have been raised on Pepsi and Coke? Per capita consumption of all three of the major alcoholic beverages is projected to increase substantially with wine realizing the greatest proportional increase. These generally dependable trends are not necessarily flags of danger; they are indicators of how easily we can satisfy distinct thirsts. The projected changes in both quantities and beverages consumed may well point to a more temperate era ahead, despite the fears of those who view any increase as a signal of drug abuse.

CONSIDERATION OF ALCOHOL AS A DRUG

A perplexing difficulty arises from the very definition of drugs. Most dictionaries concur that drugs are either substances used as medicines or chemical substances that alter one's state of mind. Clearly, some potable alcohols have served both uses. Dictionaries that define *drug* as "a narcotic" only increase our difficulty because being soothed or feeling relieved are anticipated effects of using drugs. What does this mean when we consider sugar, caffeine or nicotine? Does the relief experienced after eating a candy bar, smoking a cigarette, or drinking a soda pop or a blessed cup of coffee alter one's state of mind?

In the broadest sense, sugar is the most abused drug in our society. It is estimated that 12 percent of the caloric intake of adults is in the form of processed sugar and the estimate is a horrendous 20 percent for our young people. Although it is a carbohydrate that is completely utilized by the body, sugar is of little primary use and does much secondary harm.

The problem with sugar commanding such a significant portion of our diets—one the magnitude of four or five times that of a hundred years ago—is its secondary effects. On an average, an American eats over *ten pounds of sugar each month!* The sellers of products containing it never explain that sugar contains no vitamins, no minerals, nothing by way of fiber or enzymes, the stuff on which bodies thrive. As a consequence, we are to some degree starving ourselves in a manner not dissimilar to the true alcoholic who feels little hunger since his daily dose of alcohol runs to thousands of calories. While the effects of excessive amounts of sugar may not be immediately apparent, the long range effects most certainly include premature mortality.

While it is a bit unfair to blame addiction to sugar entirely on soda producers, it is fair to say that they encourage the fondness through artful, and unrelenting, promotion. Perhaps it is time to take a pause and refresh our perceptions of which drugs do the most harm, the long-criticized alcohol, the more recently censured nicotine, or the caffeine in coffee and colas or, of course, sugar.

The tobacco industry spends over $1 billion on advertising and sells 622 billion cigarettes annually. Laws prohibiting sales to minors are but loosely enforced. One can sympathize with those in the quandary Dr. Emboden describes in *Narcotic Plants* (1979).

Profits to the tobacco industry that well exceed ten billion dollars annually permit extravagant advertising, with a minimum of caution, and permit the legal purchase of influence in the form of governmental lobbyists. It is perplexing to find a society with a deadly national narcotic that is under federal subsidy, hitting hard at persons smoking milder euphoriants that are relatively harmless. We have legislated the death penalty for persons selling *Cannabis* to minors in some states, and at the same time we have supported with tax dollars the tobacco aristocracy that was built in the eighteenth century and persists today. It will present an enigma to the social anthropologist of the future.

Marijuana was, of course, a substance that could be freely purchased until 1937. Other substances that were once widely advertised and freely used have had their sales, and even production, affected by increased knowledge and/or legislation. As few as three cups of coffee have enough caffeine to elevate the blood pressure a dozen or more degrees. Colas, of course, often have both caffeine and sugar. One of the venerable symbols of American enterprise began its corporate life with a patent medicine that contained cocaine and continued to contain it well into this century.

In *The Cola Wars* (1980), a penetrating study of the role of soda pop in our society as seen through the two giant companies, Louis and Yazijian commented on what preceded the recent acquisition by Coca-Cola of Taylor and several other wineries.

> The Coca-Cola Company got its start on cocaine, made its mark with caffeine, and now was reaching for alcohol. A break with Coke's tradition as a wholesome and upstanding alternative to spirits, the Taylor acquisition was all part of a "master plan." Said Al Killeen, head of the Coca-Cola wine division, "We want to be the Great American Wine Company."

Alcohol Statistics Often Mislead

Humans have always formed a drug culture in the sense that they have taken relief when and where it was available. While keeping its dangers in true perspective, we must free alcohol from being the lone whipping boy. In the *DISCUS Facts Book 1979,* Ira H. Cisin of the Social Research Group of George Washington University decries the unreliability of figures on alcoholism.

> I was a reluctant midwife at the creation of the by-now-famous nine million problem drinkers (who have now grown to ten million alcoholics in the popular press). Can one . . . seriously contemplate development of a new discipline in such an atmosphere of game playing?

In another article in *Facts Book,* Dr. Robin Room of the Berkeley School of Public Health at the University of California makes the reasonable suggestion that alcohol doesn't create all of the problems which are attributed to abuse.

> When people go out there and reel off that list of things that are due to alcohol—in terms of the casualties on the road and the crime that's due to it, and so forth, we have to say there is a difference between causation and association . . . that even if alcohol were causally involved, the causes are undoubtedly multiple . . . and it is misleading to start off this list, as we always do, in trying to sell bigger budgets to the society by implying that all of these problems, these economic costs of alcohol abuse . . . if you just took away the alcohol abuse . . . would just disappear.

Despite the tendency in the past to hold stereotyped views about those who have problems handling alcohol, at long last a considerable amount of interdisciplinary research is now underway. Typical of this thoughtful research is *Ethnic Drinking Subcultures* (1979) by Andrew M. Greeley, William C. McCready, and Gary Thiesen. They surveyed various peoples and found there were patterns of drinking behavior associated with certain ethnic groups.

> In summary, then, there is overwhelming evidence of differences among American ethnic groups and drinking patterns, particularly among the Italians, the Jews, and the Irish. There seems to be some reason for expecting these differences to persist from generation to generation. However, there is also evidence that among drinkers, the incidence of alcoholism among the Irish is not abnormally high but rather that among the Italians and Jews the incidence is abnormally low.

This study isolates circumstances in the day-to-day life of respondents which precondition them to remain a unique subculture amid the mainstream of American life. Ethnic group attitudes and everyday activities are responsible for Irish and Jewish drinking habits.

> We have suggested that much of the explanation can be found by looking at the subtle interactions with one's role opposites, parents, spouses, friends, both in direct imitation of their behavior and in the use of power and affection in that relationship. . . . Precisely because they are both subtle and unperceived, these patterns of expectations and interactions are absorbed early, internalized rather completely, and transmitted to the next generation quite unself-consciously.

The findings of this study are akin to those established by Washburne as described in *Primitive Drinking.* Much of our drinking behavior is determined by what is expected of us. And, to the degree that learned habits predominate, there is hope for change. With a good deal of education and effort, we can deliberately alter these subtle transmissions from one generation to the next. In *Alcoholic Beverages in Clinical Medicine* (1966), Leake and Silverman concur that our attitudes towards drinking are learned.

> In most high-risk groups, both in Europe and in the United States, excessive drinking and public intoxication are socially acceptable. No matter what the social class involved, heavy drinking by a man is viewed as a sign of virility . . . In low-risk groups, especially among the Italians, Chinese and Jews, intoxication is not acceptable. It's traditionally considered to be slovenly, boorish and disgusting . . .

STUDY OF BEHAVIOR PATTERNS

While much more research is necessary, there have already been significant studies identifying ethnic behavioral patterns that dictate not only how much and how fast one is expected to drink

FESTE EN L'HONNEUR DE BACCHUS.

Whether depicted as a merry cherub or a fun-loving adult, the great wine god Bacchus nearly always hovers near the edge of abandonment.

but also how to behave while drinking. Any serious researcher or professional concerned with alcohol use should refer to *Beliefs, Behaviors, and Alcoholic Beverages: A Cross Cultural Survey* (1979), a series of papers by sociologists and anthropologists. Mac Marshall, who edited the work, provides some important general conclusions, including the following:

1. Solitary, addictive, pathological drinking behavior does not occur to any significant extent in small-scale, traditional pre-industrial societies; such behavior appears to be a concomitant of complex, modern, industrialized societies. . . .

3. When members of a society have had sufficient time to develop a widely shared set of beliefs and values pertaining to drinking and drunkenness, the consequences of alcohol consumption are not usually disruptive for most persons in that society. . . .

4. The amount of pure ethanol in the beverage consumed bears little or no direct relationship to the kind of drunken comportment that results; i.e., one cannot assert that the stronger the beverage the more disruptive the comportment. . . .

7. Socially disruptive drinking occurs only in secular settings. . . .

8. Beverage alcohol is used for festive, ceremonial, or ritual celebrations the world over. . . .

10. Typically, alcoholic beverages are used more by males than females and more by young adults than by preadolescents or older persons. . . .

14. When alcoholic beverages are defined culturally as a food and/or a medicine, drunkenness is seldom disruptive or antisocial. . . .

16. Once alcoholic beverages have become available in a society, attempts to establish legal prohibition have never proven completely successful. . . .

The two final conclusions are thought-provoking. Our society's slavish adherence to the "liquor is evil" position may well be the foundation for disruptive and antisocial behavior even though it is an obvious reality that legal sanctions will never completely restrict the availability of alcohol or, for that matter, any other drug.

The integrative, harmonious use of the chemical alcohol appears to be a definite cultural attribute. Articles in *Beliefs, Behaviors, and Alcoholic Beverages* reveal some common patterns arising from mutual respect and harmony among such disparate peoples as the Kofyars of Africa, Orientals who live by the Confucian philosophy of personal propriety, ruddy Bavarians, traditional Mexican Indians who have not yet adapted to urban behavior patterns, and Jews of any nationality.

A more reasonable attitude toward alcohol will not emerge without tremendous birth pains. That attitude will include a recognition that the effects of using alcohol as a dependency vehicle when under stress differ vastly from the effects of using alcohol in perfectly harmonious and controlled situations. Leake and Silverman (1966) provide one key to instilling a healthy attitude.

> In low-risk groups . . . children are generally introduced to alcohol beverages relatively early in life and under conditions which are apparently crucial in fostering safe drinking habits . . . at this introduction, the child is given no particular indication that the beverage is of any importance . . . but merely a food which happens to be served in liquid form . . . Thereafter the child is served the beverage more or less regularly . . . almost always the beverage is served with meals.

NEED FOR NATIONAL STUDY

In addition to public ignorance about alcohol abuse and mass confusion because of conflicting regulations from state to state, we have a federal enforcement agency playing stern policeman. And yet there is no realistic national policy on alcohol consumption. The real question in this cacophony is whether alcohol abuse can be alleviated. The answer is a resounding yes! Other nations have had success, and so can we. But we must first engage in a serious, realistic national discussion about drinking. We must disregard the abundant prejudices of the extremists in order to accomplish something.

In an excellent book, *Alcohol Problems and Alcoholism,* Father James Royce of the Seattle University Alcohol Studies Program refers to often acrimonious debate between the hereditarians and the behaviorists, and reminds us that it is impossible to distinguish, in any absolute sense, which behaviors are determined by heredity and which by environment. It is, therefore, not only useless to look for a single cause, but it is also a devastating waste of energy. Royce calls for an openmindedness on the part of researchers and health practitioners:

> Rather than a naive acceptance that "everybody says" it is a disease, alcoholism must be understood in the

Dinner of the Four in Hand Club at Salthill, *done in 1811 by George Cruikshank, clearly demonstrates the inebriety of the day.*

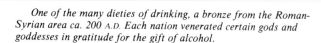

One of the many dieties of drinking, a bronze from the Roman-Syrian area ca. 200 A.D. Each nation venerated certain gods and goddesses in gratitude for the gift of alcohol.

full light of its many-faceted nature and complex etiology. We need not choose between heredity and environment or between medical model and psychological approach. A holistic view takes into account all aspects. (1981)

This holistic approach encompasses the new research by undertaking the practical, down-to-earth task of educating the offspring of groups that have traditional patterns of abuse and disease. Royce refers to data that demonstrates the importance of keeping an open mind:

Behaviorism, in its stress on environmental conditioning, had scoffed at the exaggerated hereditarianism of early evolutionary theory. It was not until the invention of the electron microscope and discovery of the DNA molecule, along with other advances in the science of genetics, that there has been a renaissance of emphasis on heredity. As this has moved into the alcoholism field, the attitude is not one of hopelessness but rather "forewarned is forearmed."

It is also necessary to recognize that it is not only the level of consumption that leads to abuse or its attendant problems. Italians drink twice as much total alcohol per capita as do citizens of the United States, yet Italy does not have the significant alcohol abuse problems that we do. Though scientists are still arguing over which is dominant, both environment and genetics play roles in determining what and how we drink. For our purposes, it is sufficient to accept the premise that *learned cultural habits do play a significant role.*

DRINKING PATTERNS AND ALCOHOLISM

What follows is a very brief discussion of a complicated topic. Our progenitors were mighty drinkers indeed. This is known, but not often do history books report that nearly all of the western cultures had wine and beer in the diet as well as in the medical pharmacopoeia. Our founding fathers consumed prodigious amounts of wine, cider, rum and, eventually, bourbon whiskey. From the time of the first farmers in Mesopotamia through six thousand years to the American of today there has been steady, widespread use of alcohol.

For alcohol, the discovery stage is over. Berton Roueché has written one of the shortest chapters in literature—literally just four sentences—to make this point in *Alcohol: The Neutral Spirit* (1960).

The age of alcoholic innovation expired with the nineteenth century. Its final accomplishment was the application of the Scottish principle of blending to Kentucky bourbon and Pennsylvania rye. By 1900, all the forms of alcohol now known had been discovered, tried, and appraised. The chief concern of the twentieth century has been to appraise the nature of alcohol itself.

According to Roueché the attempts to appraise the nature of spirits have produced a "popular mythology of alcohol":

As a compendium of ageless error, of phantom fears and ghostlier reassurances, it probably has no equal. It

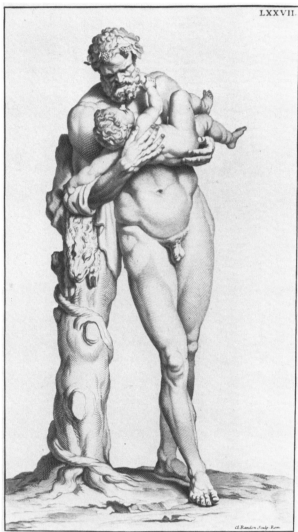

LXXVII.

SILENO CORONATO DI PAMPINI CON BACCO FANCIVLLO COMMESSO ALLA SVA CVRA IN BRACCIO IN POSITVRA D'ACCAREZZARLO. Petron. Arbit in Satyr.
Negl'orti Borghesi. Cl.Randon Sculp.Rom

The god Silenus, foster father of Bacchus, the god of wine, is shown in a French engraving titled Silenus Holding the Infant Bacchus. *Silenus counseled moderation despite his own reputation for drinking.*

I hear many cry, "Would there were no wine! O folly! O madness!" Is it the wine that causes this abuse? No. For if you say, "Would there were no wine!" because of drunkards, then you must say, going on by degrees, "Would there were no night!" because of the thieves, "Would there were no light!" because of the informers, and "Would there were no women!" because of adultery.

St. John Chrysostom

Some facts about alcoholism appeared in the American Medical Association's *Manual on Alcoholism,* published in 1973. Authorities were noted as agreeing "there is *no single cause,* but rather a *complicated interplay of physiological, psychological and sociological factors which leads to the origin and development of alcoholism.*" The pamphlet contained other crucial conclusions which have not been widely circulated:

> *Alcohol by itself does not cause alcoholism.* . . . The
> argument of its being the *causative* agent . . .
> seems to investigators to be no more logical than
> saying sugar causes diabetes. . . .
> *Alcoholism does not result from drinking a particular
> beverage.* Alcoholics and non-alcoholics alike may
> drink any and all forms of beverage alcohol, and no
> particular one of them predisposes the individual to
> alcoholism. . . .
> *Alcoholism is not an allergic manifestation.* . . .
> There is no similarity between the signs and
> symptoms of alcoholism and those of known
> allergies. . . .
> *Alcoholism is not due to an alcoholic
> personality.* . . . . Descriptions of the "typical
> alcoholic" are highly variable, frequently
> misleading and, as a rule, ambiguous.

Family history and sociological and cultural patterns are discussed as possible predisposing factors in the disease. These are factors that should be discussed in every school, in every home, and in every medical and therapeutic facility so that those of us with predisposing tendencies can at least be forewarned. The manual defines alcoholism as

> *an illness characterized by preoccupation with alcohol
> and loss of control over its consumption such as to
> lead usually to intoxication.* . . . It is not known with
> certainty whether the incidence of alcoholism is
> increasing or decreasing, although many are convinced
> of its steadily progressive rise.

is, perhaps, the classic text in the illiterature [*sic*] of medicine. . . . The opinions of science, the pronouncements from the pulpit, and the dialectics of the tavern, though elaborately conceived and infinitely varied, were all rooted in fancy.

From the beginning of organized societies, wine has been a food, a necessary part of social and religious celebrations, and a predominant article of commerce. The early deities of Sumer, Greece, and Rome included patrons of grape and grain. Praised or reviled, promoted or restricted, but always consumed, wines and liquors are part of the very fabric of our existence. How could it be otherwise with so common a substance? Why, then, are some of us unable to drink without abusing alcohol?

The Nippur tablet (Sumer) shows formulas for treatment of diseases with wines and herbs, ca. 2100 B.C.

relationship to alcohol abuse. The studies found that in certain areas of the United States and in parts of France virility is associated with drinking.

Although France has the dubious distinction of having the highest alcohol-related death rate per hundred thousand, the Rutgers studies isolate some interesting facts not evident from these tragic figures. First, a minuscule 2 percent of the French consume an astounding 43 percent of the hard spirits. Of even greater significance is evidence, reported by Sadoun, that alcohol abuse occurs predominantly in the northern regions. In *Drinking in the French Culture* (1965) he says, "The highest death rates are reported for those regions—especially Normandy and Brittany in the Northwest in which wine is the least frequently used but is replaced by other alcoholic beverages and in which drinking between meals is most prevalent." In contrast, the Midi area has the fewest alcohol-related deaths, although they actually consume more total alcohol than people in the rest of France. Awareness of these extremes in drinking habits in Languedoc and Normandy is important because many believe the myth that *all* Frenchmen die from cirrhosis of the liver. As will be shown, it is no surprise to the historian that the Normandy and Brittany farmers or, for that matter, Americans of Irish and Nordic stock are heavy drinkers. It is a heritage that probably predates written history.

The real question, then, is whether we and the northern French predispose our young to eventual drinking problems. Like the French, Americans consume about half as much absolute alcohol as Italians, but we have eight times as many alcohol problems. If our public education system and our private religious and social agencies did nothing but help us locate their future clients by means of what is already known about predisposing factors, they would be performing a great public service. The Rutgers researchers are quite optimistic about the potential of education to change well-established cultural patterns.

> In the U. S. A. as a whole, drinking is typical behaviour, both abstinence and heavy drinking, (especially for escape from life's problems) are atypical.
>
> The level of drinking (as distinct from heavy drinking or problem drinking) varies according to the position of the individual in society; but in most social status groups a much higher proportion of men and younger persons drink than do women and older people.
>
> If the cloak of social acceptance is removed from inebriety, and individuals learn to drink under physiological and psychological conditions which prevent inebriety, a major step toward the eventual prevention of alcoholism will have been taken.

The reasons we drink and the patterns chosen seem to influence the intensity of consumption. Americans, to varying degrees, follow all four of the classic patterns of consumption—religious, ceremonial, utilitarian and hedonistic. Wine is an integral part of worship. Hardly a major feast or event occurs without a toast or communal drinking rite. Wines and liquors are taken as food and medicine, nor do we lack opportunities for hedonism. In any of these situations dangerous indulgence can occur; however, as the AMA manual reminds us: "It becomes obvious that the purposes for which alcohol is used will greatly influence the drinking pattern and can figure prominently in the origin and development of alcoholism."

Purposes for Drinking Important

A series of monographs researched and written at the Rutgers University Center of Alcohol Studies support the AMA conclusion that the *purpose of consumption* has a direct causal

LIVING UP TO EXPECTATIONS

The conclusions of the Rutgers researchers are not the generalizations of amateurs, but rather the findings of the experts on alcoholism. They say that we obtain what we expect in behavior. It has probably always been so if the societies studied by Chandler Washburne accurately reflect early drinking patterns of certain ethnic groups.

> Thus, by the time an individual starts drinking he has a whole series of expectations in mind about his behavior when drinking, and his behavior when drunk will follow the pattern laid down in his society. . . . Another factor encourages aggression when drinking in many societies. A person is not punished as severely for doing forbidden things while drunk. . . . In a sense, society is encouraging the discharge of aggressions (and other inhibited or suppressed behavior) when drinking, as the consequences will then be less unpleasant. (1961)

Washburne reports that some peaceable tribes, such as the Tarahumara in Central America, deliberately emphasize the social and communal aspects of drinking as do the Italians. The morale-building and euphoric aspects of drinking are stressed. Naturally, these peoples experience little alcohol-induced aggression.

In contrast, in much of North America, drinking and becoming intoxicated are rites of passage into adulthood. Legally, alcohol is restricted to persons over a certain age, but in practice the law is often ignored. A Gallup Poll recently revealed that 71 percent of those over eighteen consume alcohol, and a scant 15 percent of young drinkers consume 70 percent of the alcohol consumed by their age group. As with the northern French, we can trace problem drinking to a very small, identifiable minority, rather than malign all young drinkers.

Recall the American Medical Association's finding that the *purpose* for which alcohol is consumed is a strong determinant in alcohol abuse. If the purpose for drinking is to demonstrate manhood and power, one's conduct when intoxicated will inevitably be hostile and disruptive. Contrast the behavior arising from alcohol being associated with a "macho" image (all too prevalent an association in the United States) with Mexican drinking behavior reported by Madsen and Madsen: *Belief Behaviors and Alcoholic Beverages* (1979).

> Since preconquest times, Indian drinking behavior has been structured by the assumption that drinking is a form of corporate communion among men and between men and gods. Pulque drinking is defined as a rite of sharing that signifies identification with the group and acceptance of all its members as social equals.

Laws Instead of Programs

For a moment, contrast the rite of passage attitude with the confused and wild gyrations in lawmaking from sovereign state to sovereign state in our nation regarding drinking comportment for our youth. Over the last decades, the age for legal consumption has been lowered in many jurisdictions with the

apparent result a rise in automobile accidents and social disruptions. The current trend is to raise those minimum ages but with no programs designed to teach the *civility* and *responsibility* involved in social drinking. While we move to reduce the likelihood of drunk driving by high school seniors, there is little to allay the confusion in the minds of youngsters of 19 to 21 years. Perhaps we need something like the ancient wisdom of the Mexican Indians to help in instilling healthful attitudes about alcohol.

Confusion reigns. Perhaps the folly of topsy-turvydom was most fully revealed during a session of the Virginia legislature in 1981 when it was decided that an eighteen year old would be allowed to *drink beer* on the premises, but could *not purchase beer to go* until his or her nineteenth birthday! It would seem more constructive for legislatures to establish some kind of uniformity in laws governing the sale of wines, brews, and spirits to young people. We must not only require that one be of sufficient age to make wise decisions about alcohol but also recognize the tendency of *some groups* to abuse drugs. A 1980 Gallup Poll found that teenage drinking mirrored to an exacting degree parental attitudes toward alcohol and parental drinking behavior. Willingness to educate ourselves and our young people about predisposing factors—be they genetic, cultural or social—would at least remove the onus of being headed for alcoholism from any youth who enjoys an occasional drink.

What this opening section has sought to encourage is a more open attitude toward drinking and a healthy scepticism about how badly or how well we are doing. No sane person could be anything but appalled at the human and economic waste that results from alcohol abuse. Many of the abusers are so heavily beset with emotional problems that alcohol is simply the most readily available, relatively inexpensive relief. Others, who abuse it periodically, are simply fulfilling the expectations of some members of our society. These overacting individuals can easily be reached and helped.

STEPS TOWARD PREVENTION OF ALCOHOLISM

It is quite clear that something must be done to control alcoholism. Roueché, in his penetrating study (1960) gives us the alternatives:

> The uncertain results of therapy have persuaded most investigators that the eventual control of alcoholism lies not in treatment but in prevention. There are two ways this may be brought about. One is through a quickened public comprehension of the causes, symptoms, and the essential nature of the disease. The other is through the abolition of alcohol. The latter has always been the vehement choice of emotion. Reason prefers the other.

It is historical fact, from the attempts of the ancient Chinese to America's shameful "noble experiment," that prohibition rarely works. Education often does. Total consumption apparently increased under the Volstead Act, the law which

State	21	20	19	18	State	21	20	19	18
Alabama			●		Montana			●	
Alaska			●		Nebraska⁵		●		
Arizona			●		Nevada	●			
Arkansas	●				New Hampshire				●
California	●				New Jersey				●
Colorado	●			▲	New Mexico	●			
Connecticut				●	New York				●
Delaware		●			North Carolina	●			
Dist. of Columbia	●			■	North Dakota	●			
Florida¹			●		Ohio	●			
Georgia²			●		Oklahoma	●			
Hawaii				●	Oregon	●			
Idaho			●		Pennsylvania	●			
Illinois	●		○		Rhode Island			●	
Indiana	●				South Carolina	●			○
Iowa			●		South Dakota				▲
Kansas	●			▲	Tennessee				●
Kentucky	●				Texas				●
Louisiana				●	Utah	●			
Maine		●			Vermont				●
Maryland	●				Virginia	●			□
Massachusetts				●	Washington	●			
Michigan³	●				West Virginia				●
Minnesota⁴			●		Wisconsin				●
Mississippi	●				Wyoming			●	
Missouri	●								

Legend

■ Wine N/O 14% vol. and Beer

● All Beverages   □ Beer N/O 4% wt.

▲ 3.2 Beverages   ○ Beer and Wine

Footnotes
¹Effective Oct. 1/80 (presently 18)

²Effective Sept. 1/80 (presently 18)

³18 Permitted to sell/serve

⁴18 Permitted to serve

*Excluding military, which is still 18

**Legislation pending to 19

⁵Those 19 before/on July 18, '80 legal age; those 19 *after* have to wait until 20

Figure 1.2 Legal drinking age by state, 1980.

defined alcohol and aided the enforcement of Prohibition, just as the use of marijuana hasn't decreased at all under the relentless pressure of criminal sanctions. Startling evidence of the latter failure was revealed in a Drug Enforcement Agency newsletter which claimed marijuana has become the top cash crop in Florida and California, eclipsing the nearly billion dollar grapefruit and cotton harvests.

In addition, "pot moonshining" is infiltrating the once famous illicit whiskey areas of the southern United States, according to the Oklahoma Bureau of Narcotics.

In terms of quantity and quality, these operations have improved in the last two or three years. These fields are intensively cultivated, fertilized, and tended almost constantly. There are armed guards posted. It's like trying to sneak up on a moonshine still.

In Tennessee, rural raiding parties found marijuana plants worth over $100 million at street price. Why not, when the going price is about $120 per pound? If this is the current status of an illegal substance, one is hardly surprised to learn there is *ever-decreasing* support for prohibition of alcohol (see table 1.8).

The Drug Abuse Council, an agency independent of federal and state governments, completed an exhaustive seven-year study of drug abuse. The Council's report, *The Facts about Drug Abuse,* is uniquely objective and free from partisan influences and politics. It clearly corroborates the distinction between abuse and addiction that has been the theme of this section. The report (1980) includes these conclusions:

Despite progress in a number of areas, more Americans use and misuse more psychoactive drugs

TABLE 1.8 Return to Prohibition?

Year	Voting Dry (%)
1979	19
1976	19
1966	22
1960	26
1957	28
1956	33
1954	34
1952	33
1948	38
1945	33
1944	37
1942	36
1940	32
1938	36
1936	38

Source: *The Gallup Poll*, statistics released 19 August 1979.

than ever. . . . Psychoactive substances have been available for use since the beginning of recorded time and will predictably remain so. Man will undoubtedly continue to use such substances for a variety of reasons: to relax, to escape, to enjoy, to worship, to delude, to destroy. . . . *While the use of psychoactive drugs is pervasive, misuse is much less frequent.* A failure to distinguish between the misuse and the use of drugs creates the impression that all use is misuse or "drug abuse."

This valuable addition to current literature in the field states that well-intentioned, popularly supported, and generously funded governmental programs prohibiting drug use have been monumental flops. The report recommends reality in place of subterfuge: "To state it plainly, the challenge facing America regarding drugs is to determine how best to live with the inevitable availability of psychoactive drugs while mitigating the harmful aspects of their misuse."

The U. S. government generates over $9 billion annually in alcohol taxes and returns a scant 3 percent to be used to find a solution to alcohol problems. Much more attention and research funding must be directed toward alcohol abuse. While both vascular disease and cancer are frightening and expensive, their ultimate costs, emotional and financial, to organized society are not greater than the cost of alcohol abuse.

NEW CONSENSUS NEEDED

In their 1981 book *Drinking in America*, Lender and Martin describe the over 300 years of the "drink is good, drink is evil" syndrome that has developed American ambivalence on the subject. Lender and Martin conclude that, for all practical purposes, America has determined to stay wet despite the pullings, pushings and indecisions of the agencies charged with seeking solutions to alcohol abuse.

Thus, at this juncture, there are no uniform standards—either acceptable drinking behavior or of alcohol use in general—to guide national efforts against alcohol problems. Whether the energies at work in treatment, prevention, research, the liquor industry can produce any agreement will remain an open question into the foreseeable future . . . but for the present, ambivalence and division are the standing orders of the day.

If there is an identifiable attitude for this book, which is the culmination of three years of intensive research and reading, it is related to that found in *The Alcoholic Republic*. Rorabaugh's well-argued theories seem both rational and hopeful, as an appendix, "Review of Drinking Motivation Literature," demonstrates.

Social scientists thus far have suggested that drinking is a function of a culture's social organization. When social systems fail to meet individual needs, a high intake of alcohol and drinking to excess may occur. In particular, a high level of drunkenness is likely in cultures that are anxiety-ridden, structurally disintegrating, or incompetent in providing individuals with a sense of effectiveness. . . . In any event, drinking mores cannot be separated from, and are functions of, ideologies, customs, and social processes. (1979)

The key to eliminating abusive and addictive consumption of alcohol lies first in recognizing why it is being used, and then in developing a more structured, meaningful social system in which individuals can live and grow effectively. The forging of what used to be called a public consensus may result from widespread discussion of many social issues, ranging from divorce to abortion. Whether or not we can ever resolve deeply felt social divisions, we can at least begin teaching our young the facts about alcohol rather than perpetuating the myths.

Dr. Sidney Cohen, psychiatrist and author of *The Drug Dilemma*, implores us to avoid repeating the mistakes of our checkered and vitriolic past in attempts at drug control that have already proved ineffective.

Controls over the abuse of chemicals are necessary, but simply passing laws is rarely a final solution. The abuse of alcohol was not solved by the Volstead Prohibition Act . . . the Harrison Narcotics Act . . . reduced the number of cocaine and opiate users but created a criminal hierarchy supported by those locked into heroin . . . The amount of public support is one part of the answer. Whether the substance is culture-alien or culturally accepted is another. The third part of the answer involves a major task of our day. *It is to teach the young how to live in a changing world and how to establish new goals when the old ones become threadbare and irrelevant.* [Italics mine]

Amen! Amen!

The Physiological Effects of Alcohol

There is at present much confusion and debate about why some individuals drink to excess. What happens to the alcohol ingested into our systems can be quite clearly delineated.

Ethyl alcohol, or ethanol as it is known to the chemist, is formed by the combustion or fermentation of sugars by minute plant cells called yeasts. Curiously, the process involves one plant life consuming another. In addition to ethanol, fermentation creates numerous higher alcohols in small proportions and a host of other chemicals. The complexity of wines and liquors derives largely from these by-products of the yeast ferments. Our primary concern is the ethyl alcohol, since it is the intoxicant present in all of the alcoholic drinks we imbibe. Ethyl alcohol is also produced naturally in our own bodies at levels up to .003 percent from the starches we eat. In rare (and extreme) manifestations this internal fermentation can evolve into systemic candidosis, a disease in which internal yeast populations produce sufficient alcohol from a normal diet to inebriate the victims, even those who are teetotalers.

Fermentations produce many types of alcohol. The human body can tolerate small portions of ethanol since it is of light toxicity. One alcohol called methyl or methanol, obtained primarily from wood, is deadly poisonous. Another, called isopropyl, also slightly toxic, has no intoxicating effect on the brain; it constitutes most antifreezes for automobiles. But for our purposes it is sufficient to limit discussion to ethyl alcohol, the primary potable or consumable alcohol.

ALCOHOL AS FOOD AND MEDICINE

Before 1842, it was generally believed that alcohol departed the body unchanged, and abundant but deceptive visual evi-

Good wine is an aid to digestion and a promoter of good cheer. I don't think anyone will find a sound argument against the moderate use of it.

George Ade

Wine makes daily living easier, less hurried, with fewer tensions and more tolerance.

Benjamin Franklin

dence supported this belief. The German chemist Justus von Liebig discovered in the mid-nineteenth century that ethanol is actually reduced within the body by another combustion, similar to fermentation, called oxidation. Later studies revealed that this reduction is made possible by the absorption of alcohol into the bloodstream directly from the stomach and the small intestines. Of this absorbed amount, 90 percent is eventually metabolized by fusion with oxygen to become carbonic acid which leaves the body as carbon dioxide and water. The remaining 5 to 10 percent is expelled unchanged by the lungs and kidneys and through the skin, hence the familiar drinker's breath and body odor.

The method of consumption determines the rate of absorption. Food, particularly protein, delays absorption. Carbonation relaxes the pylorus, the passage from the stomach to

In this 1617 etching by Jacob de Gheyn III, Fortuna is shown with a horn of plenty signifying a good harvest of grain and grape.

the intestine, and tends to speed up the process. Thus, a glass of champagne drunk as a wedding toast is generally felt more quickly than bourbon and water taken with hors d'oeuvres. However, once in the bloodstream, alcohol is metabolized by the liver at the steady rate of 15 milliliters per hour which is about one-third of an ounce of pure alcohol.

Caloric Values

Because alcohol has calories, about seven per gram, this oxidation produces a release of energy. An ounce of 100 proof alcohol contains approximately the same calories as a lamb chop or twelve bluepoint oysters (see table 2.1). As a result, alcoholic drinks can be considered a rudimentary sort of food. The pure alcohol calories are often called "empty calories" since the body burns them immediately and they cannot be stored as body fat. However, some beverage alcohols such as beer, wine, and mead contain considerable concentrations of vitamins, minerals, and carbohydrates in addition to the ethanol (table 2.2). Although wine alone cannot sustain life, it does contain most of the vitamins and minerals necessary to our existence.

TABLE 2.1 Calorie Comparison of Popular Beverages

	Ounces	Approx. Calories
Glass of milk	8	160
Dry martini	2	160
Liqueur or cordial	2	200
Glass of beer	12	150
Glass of dry wine	4	96
Glass of dry sherry	3	99
Glass of cream sherry	3	120
Glass of champagne	3	75
Daquiri	2	150
Shot of bourbon	1¼	120

Source: Gene Ford, *The ABC'S of Wine, Brew and Spirits* (Seattle: Murray Publishing Co., 1980), 119.

A glass of dry table wine equals in caloric energy a slice of roast beef, one sausage link, an ear of corn, or two tablespoons of granulated sugar. Beer and wine have definite food value, and one can find the average calories and solids in various classes of wine listed in tables such as that of Leake and Silverman (see table 2.2).

24

TABLE 2.2 Average Caloric Content of Beers and Wines

Beverage	Alcohol			Total Solids		Total Cal/ 100cc	Total Cal/ oz	"Typical Serving," oz	Total Cal/ Serving
	% Vol	GM %	Cal %	GM %	Cal%				
Beers, avg	4.6	4.6	32.2	4.6	18.4	50.6	15.2	8.0	122
Lager	3.8	3.8	26.6	4.5	18.0	44.6	13.5	8.0	108
								12.0	162
Malt liquor	5.1	5.1	35.7	3.9	15.6	51.3	15.4	8.0	123
								12.0	185
Ale	3.8	3.8	26.6	4.8	19.2	45.8	13.7	8.0	110
								12.0	165
Stout	5.6	5.5	38.5	5.0	20.0	58.5	17.6	8.0	141
								12.0	211
Cider, avg	6.5	5.2	36.4	1.0	4.0	40.4	12.1	8.0	96
Table wines, avg	12.2	9.7	67.9	3.4	13.6	81.5	24.4	4.0	98
Red	12.2	9.7	67.9	2.9	11.6	79.5	23.8	4.0	95
Rosé	12.2	9.7	67.9	2.6	10.4	78.3	23.5	4.0	94
Dry white	11.9	9.4	65.8	2.4	9.6	75.4	22.6	4.0	90
Sweet white	12.4	9.8	68.6	5.7	22.8	91.4	27.4	4.0	110
Champagne	12.5	9.9	69.3	3.3	13.2	82.5	24.8	4.0	99
Kosher wine	12.5	9.9	69.3	10.0	40.0	109.3	32.8	4.0	131
Dessert wines, avg	19.8	15.7	109.9	10.4	41.6	151.5	45.4	2.0	91
Dry sherry	20.0	15.9	111.3	4.7	18.8	130.1	39.0	2.0	78
Sweet sherry	19.8	15.7	109.9	10.7	42.8	152.7	45.8	2.0	92
Port	19.8	15.7	109.9	12.6	50.4	161.3	48.4	2.0	97
Muscatel	19.7	15.6	109.2	13.5	54.0	163.2	49.0	2.0	98
Vermouths, avg	17.4	13.8	96.6	8.8	35.2	131.8	39.6	3.0	119
French type	17.7	14.0	98.0	3.8	15.2	113.2	34.0	3.0	102
Italian type	17.1	13.6	95.2	13.8	55.2	150.4	45.1	3.0	135

Source: Reproduced with permission from Leake, C. D., and Silverman, M.: ALCOHOL BEVERAGES IN CLINICAL MEDICINE. Copyright © 1966 by Year Book Medical Publishers, Inc., Chicago, 74.

The Therapeutic Value of Wine

One of the more knowledgeable and prolific writers on the medical and therapeutic roles of wine in history is Salvatore P. Lucia, Professor Emeritus of Preventative Medicine at the University of California. In a popular text, *Wine and Your Well Being* (1971), Lucia eloquently presents his position:

> Water, milk, fruit juices and fermented beverages—especially those derived from the grape—are among the most natural and essential dietary accompaniments to solid food in human nutrition. Wine was appraised by Louis Pasteur—one of the greatest scientific minds of the nineteenth century—as the most healthful, the most hygienic dietary beverage of all.

Very dramatic support for this attitude is emerging from current research. For example, Janet McDonald and Sheldon Margen conducted an experiment at the Human Nutrition Laboratory at the University of California in which six male subjects were studied over a seventy-five day period. Signifi-cantly greater amounts of calcium, zinc, magnesium, and iron were utilized by the body when Zinfandel wine or "dealcoholized" wine, rather than spiritous alcohol or deionized water, accompanied the subjects' food. Though uncertain of what caused extra mineral absorption, the researchers theorized that the natural acidity of wine was the probable cause. There are, of course, minerals in wine. According to Dr. Lucid (1971), "Modern wines contain in some degree all of the mineral elements necessary for the maintenance of human life, i.e., potassium, magnesium, sodium, calcium, iron, phosphorus, chlorine, sulfur, copper, manganese, zinc, iodine, and cobalt." Not only does wine increase the body's utilization of minerals but it is more slowly absorbed than other alcohols.

Paul Scholten, addressing the Society of Medical Friends of Wine in 1980 used the graph developed by Leake and Silverman (see fig. 2.1) to demonstrate the differences in rate of absorption of wine and other alcohols. Dr. Scholten stressed that "the policy of treating all alcoholic beverages alike may perhaps be explained by what it deliberately conceals: the evidence that identifies light mealtime wine as the least intoxicating and therefore the most temperate of all alcoholic drinks."

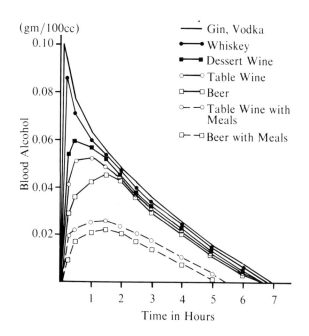

(gm/100cc)

——— Gin, Vodka
●——● Whiskey
■——■ Dessert Wine
○——○ Table Wine
□——□ Beer
○- -○ Table Wine with Meals
□- -□ Beer with Meals

Blood Alcohol

Time in Hours

Figure 2.1 *This graph depicts blood absorption levels from the consumption of various types of beverage alcohols. The same amount of alcohol in vodka will produce twice the intoxication as from wine. When taken with food, wine is indeed the beverage of moderation both in a chemical and a cultural sense.*

Scholten decries—as do the Wine Institute, the many who love wine and those who write about it—the tendency of the government and the spirit industry to lump all drinks together as "alcoholic beverages" or "beverage alcohols." And while there is rationale for segregation of wine and brews from the ardent spirits, to some degree such semantics beg the question. Regardless of the beverage, an abuser will ingest sufficient quantities with sufficient speed to reach the desired level of intoxication. To emerge a truly temperate nation, we must change our attitudes about all types of alcoholic beverages. Although wine has had a unique food role throughout history, to most Americans wine is just another alcoholic beverage.

Several years ago, in *The New Physician,* Dr. Robert Stepto blamed our lack of appreciation of wine's food and medicinal properties on attitudes formed during the years of Prohibition:

> If wine does not today appear in the U.S. Pharmacopoeia, we can only blame that experiment known as Prohibition . . . Like many medicines dispensed in the hospital, wine has alcohol as an important constituent. Alcohol has its own effects on the body, of course, but it also interacts with other ingredients in wine, some of which serve to retard its absorption from the digestive tract, thus providing for the relatively low blood-alcohol concentrations characteristic of this dietary beverage.

Effects of Wine on Heart Disease

A series of medical research projects on the relationship of alcohol to heart disease has been conducted on several continents in recent years. A perspective on these widely separated studies was provided in the May 1979 issue of *The Beverage Analyst.* The following items were reported: the *Second Report on Alcohol and Health* (1974) revealed that moderate drinkers usually live longer than teetotalers, former drinkers and alcoholics; the report by William J. Darby of the Nutrition Foundation that three drinks or less per day might reduce the risk of heart attacks, lessen exhaustion and encourage healthy psychosocial attitudes; another study of 91,656 patients that nondrinkers have more fatty tissue than drinkers of five drinks per day; the study by Katsuhiko Yano of 7,705 Japanese men living in Hawaii that drinkers had fewer heart attacks than nondrinkers; the Kaiser-Permanente Medical Center studies by Dr. Arthur L. Klatsky that there was a large population of teetotalers among 500 heart attack victims as well as a study of 120,000 other patients which revealed a 30 percent reduction in likelihood of heart attacks in moderate drinkers.

The magazine reported some uncertainty by the doctors conducting the studies as to the specific reasons why heart attack danger lessens in moderate drinkers. Major theories are the lower intake of artery-damaging saturated fats by moderate drinkers, the lowering of the adverse effects of stress by alcohol, and the production of HDL—high density lipoproteins. The Kaiser-Permanente study concluded that a high HDL in the blood is related to lower risk of heart attack.

A correlation of the HDL theory research was reported in the Autumn 1982 issue of the Society of Wine Educators *Chronicle.* The newsletter reported on a convention presentation by D. June Forkner, which told of research in Europe and in the United States over the last quarter of a century designed to identify in wine the substances which reduce cholesterol levels, thereby reducing incidence of heart attack. That research indicates that the high density lipoproteins help to eliminate the harmful low density lipoproteins which tend to clog the arterial walls. One study of 18 developing countries by scientists at the University of Bordeaux found the protective cardiac substance was the polyphenols or the red pigments originating in wine skins, stems and seeds. One of these, procyanidin, was found to work synergistically with vitamin C in breaking down cholesterol, and wine is the only palatable form of procyanidin in the diet. Forkner reported a 200 percent increase in wine consumption in the past twenty years and a corresponding drop of 34 percent in heart disease. Two four-ounce glasses of wine daily were reported to increase removal of harmful low density lipoproteins from the body.

Another Klatsky study reported in the September 1981 issue of the *NABCA Newsletter* included 8,000 people carefully selected to eliminate variances in age, sex, race, and tobacco use from skewing study results. In this group, subjects who drank one or two drinks per day had the lowest mortality. Total abstainers had a death rate 40 percent higher than that of these moderate drinkers. However, those who drank three

- Alcohol is a natural by-product of the interaction of plant forms.
- Alcohol has been used both as medicine and therapy from the earliest recorded times.
- People in social or emotional distress and those between 18 and 24 drink more, and more often, than others.

- "Alcohol by itself does not cause alcoholism"—the American Medical Association.
- Alcohol is defined as a food because it releases energy.
- Moderate drinkers apparently live longer than do teetotalers, former abusers who now refrain, and alcoholics.

to five drinks or more had a mortality rate 50 percent higher than that of the moderate group. Suffice it to say that there is much medical research being done on drinking and how it affects our health, both negatively and positively. One should note, however, that *every credible source stresses the importance of moderation.*

Wine has qualities that make it a particularly appropriate beverage for older people. In *Alcohol and Old Age,* Mishara and Kastenbaum acknowledge the special relationship between reverence for wine and reverence for the aged. Often, in a very special way, libations are encouraged because the tranquilizing and sedative effects are particularly important to the elderly. Wine contributes in a special way to the diets of older citizens. "Sensory acuity tends to diminish with age. The gustatory and olfactory senses are included as a part of the general decline, which probably contributes to the observed reduction of appetite in old people." By its stimulation of the salivary glands, wine helps stimulate a desire for food. The slow absorption rate of wine is especially important for people whose weight, as well as appetite, may have decreased with age:

> One of the important physiological differences between wine and hard liquors is associated with their respective nonethanol components. Wines are relatively rich in tannins . . . the tannins and solids seem to be operative in maintaining a relatively slow absorption rate of alcohol. The alcohol in whiskey, brandy, vodka and gin is absorbed more rapidly. This means that the classes of beverages that have higher concentrations of alcohol to begin with also tend to have faster rates of absorption. (1980)

Several hundred years ago, this kind of knowledge, though intuitive, was nonetheless common. In his seventy-sixth year, Jefferson wrote, "I have lived temperately, eating little animal food and that not as an aliment, so much as a condiment to the vegetables which constitute my principal diet. I double, however, the doctor's glass and a half of wine and even treble it with a friend . . ." During his two terms as president, Thomas Jefferson ran up a wine bill double the amount of his food bill.

Physical Effects of Alcohol

Wisdom previously accepted on the grounds of people's own observation and experience is now grounded in research results and statistics. Morris Chafetz, M.D., founding director of the National Institute on Alcohol Abuse and Alcoholism, has written a question and answer book entitled *Why Drinking Can Be Good for You* (1976). In it, the former government expert dispels the major myths perpetrated in the name of reform. He advises how one can avoid inebriation by understanding the impact of method and rate of consumption on the system.

> Besides sipping slowly, how can you keep your system from overreacting to alcohol? You can dilute the alcohol with plenty of ice to further slow the rush into the bloodstream. Food in your stomach, preferably protein or fatty foods, taken before you drink is most effective in slowing alcohol's invasion of the bloodstream and brain. An experienced drinker knows that, all things being equal, the same dose of alcohol taken with food in the stomach will provide a different, more pleasant outcome than alcohol on an empty stomach.

It is the brain that is the target of all of our drinking. Man drinks to change his mood. Although scientists are unsure of the exact process, they know alcohol inhibits the normal transmissions of the neurons in the brain. Alcohol does them no apparent injury, within reasonable doses, and does no permanent damage.

The immediate impact is a relaxation of emotional and autonomic controls. This is the pleasurable release that the drinker seeks. Judgment and memory are the first to go. Inhibitions disappear and variable emotional changes occur. Thoughts tumble out in rushed speech, and general euphoria appears. As the concentration of alcohol in the bloodstream increases, depression also increases, and the loss of physical control occurs. Eventually, with rapid overconsumption, the brain cuts out altogether, and the body is comatose until the liver eliminates the overdose.

Figure 2.2 *A guide used to calculate blood alcohol concentration according to body weight and number of drinks.*

Number of Drinks*		1	2	3	4	5	6	7	8
Alcohol % in Blood at Various Weights	100 lbs	.029	.058	.088	.117	.146	.175	.204	.233
	140 lbs	.021	.042	.063	.083	.104	.125	.146	.166
	180 lbs	.017	.033	.049	.065	.081	.097	.113	.130
	200 lbs	.015	.029	.044	.058	.073	.087	.102	.117

Physical Abilities Impaired for Driving or Other Functions

Legally Drunk Concentration

*One drink equals a shot of liquor, a beer, or a glass of wine.

The Depressant That Seems to Enliven

Pharmacologically speaking, alcohol always acts as a depressant, in the class of barbituates and sedatives. Ironically, it often appears to the consumer and to the observer to be quite the opposite. At low dosages, the *release* phenomenon results in animation and increased social activity. The key to maintaining this happy level lies in understanding the *blood alcohol concentration,* commonly called the BAC. The Washington State Liquor Control Board distributes a guide which gives the BAC in relation to weight (see fig. 2.2).

The effects of alcohol on the human system turn out not to be all depressing. In fact, Leake and Silverman (1966) found that relaxation, appetite stimulation, and enhanced gastric function derive from alcohol's impact on the system. They stress the tremendous difference in absorption rate when one takes food and alcohol together: "When it is taken with food, absorption is conspicuously slowed and the blood alcohol peak is reduced from 15 to as much as 50%." The cocktail canapé may well be your best friend.

Leake and Silverman emphasize the positive nature of the release afforded by alcohol:

In the cortex, alcohol depresses both sensory and motor centers . . . There is usually an easing of tensions and anxieties. Performance of such manual tasks as typing or target shooting may be adversely affected, but the ability to solve complex intellectual problems may be improved. . . . Probably the most striking is the use of alcoholic beverages to reduce emotional tension . . . In discussing alcohol as a tranquilizer, Greenberg emphasizes that it is undoubtedly the oldest in use, and probably the safest.

Among a medley of other physical effects Leake and Silverman list the following: antiseptic actions; skin cooling when used externally; increased blood flow; stimulation of digestive enzymes; slowing of respiration; and in natural evacuation, dilation of arterioles and capillaries which probably reduces hypertension; raising of blood sugar levels; increased flow of bile; increased diuretic action in the kidneys; and, if a male has taken an excessive amount, a decrease in potency. In a jocular aside, the authors cite *Macbeth:*

Macduff: What three things does drink especially provoke?
Porter: Marry, sir, nose-painting, sleep and urine. Lechery, sir, it provokes and unprovokes: it provokes the desire, but it takes away the performance.

It is manifestly obvious that alcohol ingested in moderate amounts with food can be a positive element in a normal diet. It is equally and starkly evident that hundreds of maladies, both physical and mental, occur from consumption that exceeds one's level of tolerance.

From whatever source, and in whatever amount, once ingested into the system, ethyl alcohol travels relentlessly around the circulatory system until the liver completely oxidizes it. A healthy liver can dispatch about one drink per hour, no more. As long as there is alcohol in the system, the depressing and intoxicating effects will be felt, showers, coffee, and bracing air notwithstanding.

It should be understood that the larger the body, the greater the capacity for alcohol. The bloodstream accounts for the difference. While the body steadily burns the alcohol, no matter the weight, the larger frame simply has more tubing to hold the substance. This is basic information that should be presented in schools and homes.

TABLE 2.3 Some Effects of Alcoholic Beverages

Amount of Beverage	Concentration of Alcohol Attained in the Blood (%)	Effects		Time Required for All Alcohol to Leave the Body
1 highball (1½ oz. whisky) *or* 1 cocktail (1½ oz. whisky) *or* 3½ oz. fortified wine *or* 5½ oz. ordinary wine *or* 2 bottles (24 oz.) beer	0.03	Slight changes in feeling		2 hrs.
2 highballs *or* 2 cocktails *or* 7 oz. fortified wine *or* 11 oz. ordinary wine *or* 4 bottles beer	0.06	Increasing effects with variation among individuals and in the same individual at different times	Feeling of warmth—mental relaxation—slight decrease of fine skills—less concern with minor irritations and restraints	4 hrs.
3 highballs *or* 3 cocktails *or* 10½ oz. fortified wine *or* 16½ oz. (1 pt.) ordinary wine *or* 6 bottles beer	0.09		Buoyancy—exaggerated emotion and behavior—talkative, noisy or morose	6 hrs.
4 highballs *or* 4 cocktails *or* 14 oz. fortified wine *or* 22 oz. ordinary wine *or* 8 bottles (3 qts.) beer	0.12		Impairment of fine coördination—clumsiness—slight to moderate unsteadiness in standing or walking	8 hrs.
5 highballs *or* 5 cocktails *or* 17½ oz. fortified wine *or* 27½ oz. ordinary wine *or* ½ pt. whisky	0.15	Intoxication—unmistakable abnormality of gross bodily functions and mental faculties		10 hrs.

Source: Reprinted by permission from Journal of Studies on Alcohol. From: Greenberg, L. A., *What the Body Does with Alcohol.* (Popular pamphlets on Alcohol Problems, No. 4) New Brunswick, N.J.; Rutgers Center of Alcohol Studies; 1955.
Note: Based on a person of "average" size (150 pounds). For those weighing considerably more or less, the amounts would have to be correspondingly more or less to produce the same results. The effects indicated at each stage will diminish as the concentration of alcohol in the blood is reduced by being oxidized and eliminated.

Blood Alcohol Concentrations

Among the brilliant publications on the effects of alcohol is Leon A. Greenberg's pamphlet *What the Body Does with Alcohol.* He considers different types of alcohol and indicates in detail the effects of increasing blood alcohol concentrations (see table 2.3). A 1977 Department of Transportation booklet *You . . . Alcohol and Driving* shows the correlation of the BAC to the risk of an automobile accident (see fig. 2.3). This suggests a direct relationship between motor response and alcohol concentrations. It is important to note the risk pertains to all individuals with a given blood alcohol concentration; neither the experience that comes with age nor the supposedly quicker reflexes of the young give any advantage.

This section has stressed both the obvious and the inevitable. A few moments studying the charts will be sufficient to convince the boldest that we are indeed equal when under the influence of alcohol. While knowing this will not in itself keep everyone from abusing or misusing alcohol, certainly broadcasting the facts could dispel some of the abysmal myths about being "macho."

The latest evidence of the human's limitless capacity for self-deception occurred in 1979 in the small Wisconsin town of Wind Lake. A nineteen-year-old youth boasted of his ability to break a presumed record for rapid alcohol consumption. He is reported as having consumed forty-six shots of brandy, whiskey, and rum throughout the evening. While drinking a soda about midnight, he toppled from the bar stool and died—a tragic, needless death.

The rules are simple but ineluctable. Stay within the maximum BAC according to your weight, and drinking can be a joy forever. Stray above, and you invite, at the very least, the painful mornings after.

The Hangover

In Italy, it is called *stonato*—out of tune. The French call it *gueule de bois*—wood in the mouth. Whatever its name, the physical and psychological debilitation from overindulgence knows only one sure cure. Time!

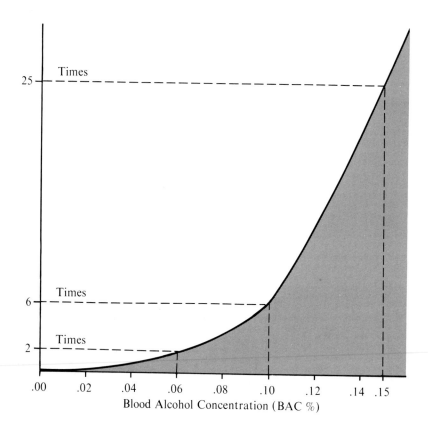

Figure 2.3 *This graph on blood alcohol and accident risks demonstrates that at .06% alcohol concentration there is twice the risk of accidents as when sober and that at the .10% legal inebriation level the risk is six times as great.*

O God, that men should put an enemy in their mouths to steal away their brains! That we should, with joy, pleasance, revel, and applause, transform ourselves into beasts!

Shakespeare

There is fairly common medical agreement about the causes of hangovers. First, there is simple exhaustion. All too often, excessive drinking is accompanied by late hours and extreme physical activity such as dancing or standing endless hours in animated conversation on already fatigued legs. The drinker simply overdoes it and suffers lassitude the next day.

Equally important, alcohol is an irritant, particularly to the gastrointestinal tract. In too great a concentration it ravages the stomach lining, eventually ulcerating the heavy drinker. In the process of oxidizing alcohol, the liver produces excessive amounts of a by-product, acetaldehyde, which foments nausea

and vertigo. Finally, remorse, a purely psychological factor, compounds the physical discomforts.

The common headache is generated both by the fuming stomach acids and by vascular irritation. Alcohol acts as a vasodilator, which means it dilates the blood vessels as the brain becomes anesthetized. Through these distended vessels, and into the brain cells, pass the minute chemical components called congeners. These are the substances responsible for the distinctive and desirable tastes and smells of our favorite liquors. Unfortunately, though pleasurable at ingestion, when combined with the effects of excess acid and irritated brain cells, they produce a nagging head pain. Finally, we overindulge in one other way in a vain effort to achieve relief. Alcohol in the bloodstream releases water from body cells and creates the impression of thirst. Deluded into thinking we are thirsty, we flood the system with water.

Of all of these chemical consequences, the effect of the congeners is believed to be the most mischievous. It is easy to understand the current trend to light and white drinks after noting the average concentrations of congeners in popular liquors (see table 2.4). Both gin and vodka are neutral spirits, free of the devilish congeners.

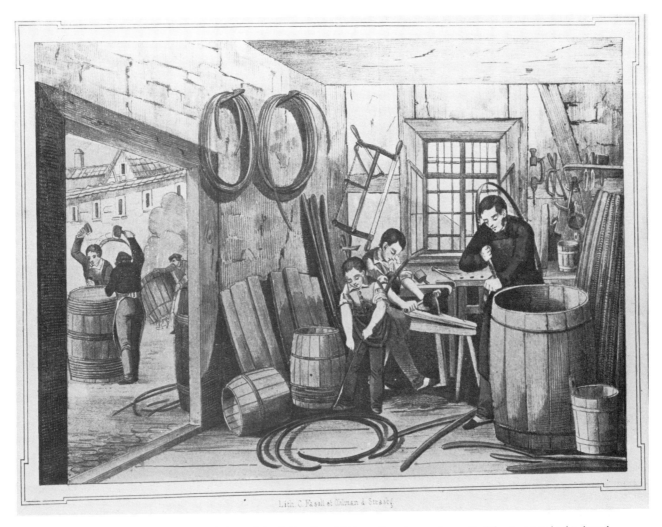

Tonnelier (The Cooper). *This handsome lithograph by C. Fasoli and Ohlman, Strasbourg, shows all of the steps involved in barrel production.*

TABLE 2.4 Average Congeneric Concentrations of Popular Liquors

Liquor	Percentage
Bourbon	.309
Whiskey	.292
Rum	.292
Cognac	.239
Scotch	.160
Blended whiskey	.116
Canadian whisky	.085
Wines	.04
Beer	.01
Vodka	.00
Gin	.00

AROMATICS AND TASTINGS

We Americans are in dire need of remedial education in eating and drinking. The tendency to bolt food and drink may well be a root cause of obesity and alcohol abuse. Although it is deemed a necessity to tuck away three square meals each day, little thought is given to the niceties of this process.

Over one hundred years ago the guru of gastronomers, Jean Anthelme Brillat-Savarin, wrote that "gastronomy is the intelligent knowledge of whatever concerns man's nourishment." In his unique treatise, *The Physiology of Taste* (1949), he ascribes an imaginative dimension and even responsibility to the sense of taste. In his opinion, taste is the fundamental magnetism that draws humans together and assures the continuation of the species. Admittedly, that may be reaching a trifle since we would probably continue to procreate even if we had less sensitive taste organs. Yet Brillat-Savarin was correct

31

Wine measurably drunk, and in season, bringeth gladness to the heart, and cheerfulness to the mind.

Ecclesiastes

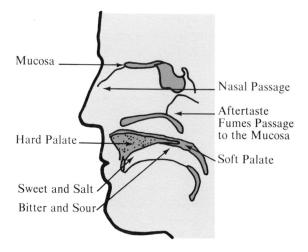

Figure 2.4 *Smelling and tasting are often used but little understood human functions. Scientists have determined that while there are only four natural tastes, there are up to thirty natural smells that combine and recombine to make at least ten thousand distinctive aromas. Flavor, or food appreciation, comes predominantly from these odors. Tiny olfactory mucosa in the nasal passage transmit to the brain with greater intensity than any other human sensory system.*

in noting the uniqueness of humans' sense of taste compared to that of all the other creatures on earth. The range of his treatise is evident in the following excerpts:

> Men who eat quickly and without thought do not perceive the taste impressions . . .
> . . . of all the creatures who walk, swim, climb, or fly, man is the one whose sense of taste is the most perfect. . . .
> In physical man it is the apparatus by which he distinguishes various flavors.
> . . . there is no full act of tasting without the participation of the sense of smell, but I am also tempted to believe that smell and taste form a single sense, of which the mouth is the laboratory and the nose is the chimney . . .
> . . . taste causes sensations of three different kinds: *direct, complete,* and *reflective.*

These random quotes reflect the power and dynamism of Brillat-Savarin's thinking. His book is an absolutely essential text for professionals in the food industry.

Man is a sensual being, and he can remember and then anticipate what his senses have previously experienced. He can judge food or other objects in terms of standards adopted personally or established by his society. This is man's critical dimension. Since we all have essentially the same physical equipment, cultivated eating and drinking are within the grasp of almost everyone.

First, the physical apparatus should be understood. Man is born with five to ten thousand minute papillae or taste buds on the tongue. Individuals possessing the greater number of taste buds will be more sensitive to particular tastes. So the perception level varies with individuals. Also, there is the theory that the buds diminish in sensitivity with advancing age, so that added stimuli are necessary to elicit taste response.

According to Gorman in *Flavor, Taste and the Psychology of Smell* (1978), "Definite atrophy of the taste buds begins at forty-five, but progresses markedly after seventy." Gorman indicates the position of greatest acuity for each of the four tastes: "Sweet, sour, salt and bitter. The perception of sweet and salt is most acute at the tip of the tongue, sour is best at the sides and bitter is best tasted posteriorly." In addition, Gorman describes a *chemical sense* similar to the

body's sense of pain and cold: "The specific chemical sense perceives stinging and acridity and produced reflex reactions such as salivation and sneezing."

Until relatively recent times lists of tastes included some merely descriptive words such as pungent, harsh, and insipid, which have now been discarded. In *The Human Senses* (1972) Geldard suggests that

> It was doubtless the demonstration, just about as the twentieth century was being ushered in, that salt, sour, sweet, and bitter have their own individual modes of distribution that tended to establish these four (which had always been present in all lists) as the fundamental taste qualities.

Geldard also points out what may be obvious, that most foods, although strikingly different, do contain elements of all four tastes. He uses the term *gust* to mean a unit of psychological intensity for perception of the four tastes (see table 2.5). On a scale of 100, only honey exceeds the 50 percent intensity level of the sweet taste. This suggests that most of our foods are within relatively narrow taste ranges, but our imagination and memory can amplify tastes to the exquisite and the sublime depending on the circumstances of our earlier experiences of them. Coffee and ale are rated remarkably bitter, and grapefruit definitely sour. But for the most part we react to the four tastes in various foodstuffs as more mild than might be expected.

TABLE 2.5 Taste Characteristics of Common Foods, in Gusts

	Sweet	Bitter	Sour	Salt	Sum for all Qualities
Cola drink	11.2	2.2	5.0	1.3	19.7
Ale	2.5	28.2	10.0	1.3	42.0
Unsw. grapefr. juice	3.2	2.0	35.5	2.0	42.7
Consommé	1.4	1.3	4.5	7.9	15.1
Tokay wine	10.0	4.2	4.2	1.8	20.2
Riesling wine	1.0	7.5	6.7	1.3	16.5
"Root" tonic	4.2	1.3	3.2	1.3	10.0
Coffee, unsw.	1.0	42.3	3.2	1.0	47.5
Coffee, 5% sucr.	3.2	23.8	3.2	1.3	31.5
Anchovy fillet	1.3	23.8	5.6	10.0	40.7
Sweet pickles	3.2	3.2	13.4	3.2	23.0
Sour pickles	1.0	1.8	18.0	3.2	24.0
Raspberry jam	23.8	1.8	10.0	1.3	36.9
Honey	56.4	2.4	1.8	1.3	61.9
RANGES	1–56.4	1.3–42.3	1.8–35.5	1–10.0	10–61.9
MEANS	8.8	10.4	8.9	2.7	

Source: Beebe-Center, J. G. "Standards for Use of the Gust Scale." *Journal of Psychology* 28(1949), 417.

Taste Perceptions Vary Widely

Note particularly gust qualities in sweetened and unsweetened coffee to recognize how the addition of a sweetener changes the sweet and bitter responses. With 5 percent sucrose added, the sweet perception triples while the bitter perception is reduced by nearly one-half. This is only one indication that individuals vary widely in perception or thresholds of sugar sensation, which explains the wide variations of opinion at wine tastings. Thresholds are distinct levels of taste reaction which vary for the four tastes in different individuals. Some may perceive sugar when there is as little as .8 of 1 percent, while others will not perceive it until the concentration is well over 1 percent. Some people frequently talk "dry" while describing wines which contain up to 1½ percent sugar. These individuals evidently perceive sugar only in higher concentrations, which should confirm your healthy skepticism about the inviolable correctness of published results of professional wine tasters and writers on the subject. Perception is a singular and personal entity. Quite simply, we may react differently to the same stimuli.

Similarly, the concentrations of fixed acids and tannins in wines, spirits, and other food may well stimulate varied physical reactions once they are ingested because they tend to produce excessive hydrochloric acid in the stomach. It is well known that coffee, tea, and brews, wines, and any other alcohols stimulate the production of stomach acids. Other foods such as strawberries, anchovies, and chocolate bars do the same. *Consequently, the flavor perceived in the first moment of sensation and the flavor perceived during continuing ingestion may also be quite different.* Tasting, then, is a terribly complex function involving literally all of the senses as well as judgments and prejudices entrenched in the mind. Geldard's table of taste intensities indicates, in his words, "the relative bland-

ness of many foods notable for distinctive 'flavor' and points up a conclusion, arrived at much earlier on the basis of other considerations, that flavor is largely a matter of odor, not taste."

The importance of these findings to those involved in tasting wines, brews, and spirits cannot be too strongly emphasized. Tasting, when referring to beverages, involves more than a simple tactile and mouth reaction. Other elements, particularly the odors which proliferate at wine and other spirits tastings, are prominent. The *idea* of what the wine *should be,* the product's temperature as well as the time of the day at which the tasting occurs, the presence of other odoriferous foods or substances nearby and one's state of mind—all of these come into play.

This helps us understand how a person of relatively advanced age with presumably weaker taste reactions can still savor and identify fine wines. The recognition depends almost entirely on the odors—provoking remembrances of things past. As Gorman (1978) suggests, "Flavor is not a quality of an object but is a subjective sensation. The sensations which comprise flavor are taste, smell and the chemical sense. The chemical sense . . . permits us to perceive such sensations as astringency or sharpness." We must keep this in mind when participating in corporate wine and spirit tastings, as well as private tastings at home or in restaurants. Be patient and open for you may not know what you are missing.

Smelling

The olfactory bulb in the cranial cavity receives and then transmits to the brain the sensations we call smells. The capability of this organ is immense, apparently limited only by lack of exposure. We seem to be able to remember smells longer

*M*yrtle, orange and the blushing rose.
Each seems to smell the flavor which the
other blows.

John Dryden

than we remember what we see and hear. Ten thousand or more odors may be catalogued and sorted by the memory bank into favorable or repulsive, merely pleasing or absolutely delicious. Odors emanating from the objects about us pass through the nostrils, stimulate the olfactory organ which transmits stimuli to the brain. The brain interprets stimuli and categorizes them in terms of desirability, repugnance, etc. In describing odors, we reach for extremes, often approaching the poetic. Some terms describing particular smells are *spicy, fruity, resinous, flowery, putrid,* and *burnt.*

The ability to remember and imagine sensory experience, to contrive arbitrary scales and respond to them, to make fine distinctions is what differentiates humans from apes, from the limited sensory experience of a child to the Elysian heights of a Brillat-Savarin. One definition of taste recognizes that it is stimulation by food, drink, etc., of the sense of taste combined with the senses of touch and smell. The combination of tasting and smelling is automatic; it is, in fact, preceded by other sensations. When we see an apple on the counter, our memory of past apples may stimulate the juices in the mouth, and the stomach may begin secretion. The idea of "apple" is sufficient to evoke a sort of taste. By the time the apple nears the nose, the fingers have already registered an appealing firmness. The particular odors released from the skin confirm value just seconds before the first bite explodes with sweetness, fruity acidity, and a tang of bitterness from the skin. At this point, smell and taste have already merged, constituting a *flavor* of which probably *75 percent is determined by smell.*

When a child is repelled by a certain food, he artlessly pinches his nostrils to avoid the taste. When one is afflicted with a cold and stuffy nose, the response to food is invariably, "I can't taste a thing," indicating, of course, the effect a loss of the sense of smell has on the sense of taste. Onions and apples are remarkably similar in the mouth if one cannot see and smell. An imbalance in, or dysfunction of, this delicate chemical-sensing mechanism can lead to devastation. Often a result of some terrible accident, loss of the sense of smell can make all foods taste like unappealing cardboard or lead to negative reactions to the most common of foods.

Tasting is an organoleptic function; that is, for most of us it involves all five of the senses simultaneously. The taste may be only a ravenous gulp, or it can involve a loving, patient process that develops into a revelation of the complex mingling of taste, texture, appearance, aroma and, even, sound of the food. Most often, we compromise and experience taste somewhere between the two extremes. As with any other talent, practice in truly tasting is required to approach mastery.

Maynard Amerine and Edward Roessler in *Wines and Their Sensory Evaluation* (1976), like Brillat-Savarin, consider tasting in its nonphysical dimensions. They view it as an artistic, aesthetic activity and describe our initial reaction to food as subjective, an automatic response akin to the conditioned responses of Pavlov's dog. Our secondary response is an objective, thoughtful evaluation based on remembered criteria. Is this particular Chardonnay better or worse than other Chardonnays experienced? Does this particular lasagna compare favorably with the idea of lasagna in my mind? No other animal possesses this exalted dimension of criticism. The capacity to appraise food enriches the purely animalistic act of assuaging hunger.

> Aesthetics has to do with the subjective and objective appraisal of works of art: music, art, architecture, literature—and wine. The properties that we associate with aesthetic appreciation are symmetry, balance, harmony, complexity, etc. We believe that the full appreciation of an aesthetic object requires some degree of formal training, or at least conscious study. Our enjoyment of wine is thus essentially a learned response. . . . it has overtones of sensual pleasure and is obviously related to social customs.

Those societies in which the young are taught to savor food and drink seem to have no need of warnings about the "dangers of drink." In his studies Dr. Chafetz found an interesting cultural phenomenon regarding hangovers.

> I heard no easy familiarity with the hangover in China, Israel, Spain, Italy, or Lebanon. Interestingly, the countries that focus on them are the countries with big or growing alcohol problems. . . . In societies that place drink in the proper perspective and drink sensibly, there are few drinking problems and hangovers are rare. (1976)

There are ground rules for enhancing one's perception of flavors. Speed in consumption destroys the opportunity for objective evaluation. If we gulp Chateau Lafite in great drafts, it will provide about the pleasure of Annie Greensprings or a soda pop. This would be a waste of taste. If we ingest chilled beverages or foods, we reduce our capacity to recognize the nuances in taste. Only vodka is tolerable at 32° F since it is devoid of redeeming taste. We should take advantage of opportunities to enjoy our perception of taste since it is a variable perception. As we age, our sense of taste diminishes. In times of sorrow or great joy, there is little appetite or enjoyment of the things we taste. Nutritional deficiencies, dentures, and anemia also impair sensory responses.

Brillat-Savarin, Amerine and Roessler, and other writers tell us how to increase our sensory capability. Serious students of wine tasting should attend training sessions whenever possible. No matter the grouping, there inevitably emerges a complete spectrum of reactions. The levels of perception for elements such as sugar, sulfur, tannin, and acid are incredibly diverse. As the Romans often said, *De gustibus non est disputandum*— "there's no accounting for taste!"

Suggested Readings

Braudel, Fernand. *The Structures of Everyday Life: The Limits of the Possible.* New York: Harper & Row, Publishers Inc., 1981.
> The first and, in many ways, the foremost in my lexicon of suggested readings—a novel historical approach to the realities of life including those things we eat, drink and wear.

Brillat-Savarin, Jean Anthelme. *The Physiology of Taste or Meditations on Transcendental Gastronomy.* Translated by M. F. K. Fisher. New York: Harcourt Brace Jovanovich, Inc., 1949.
> Absolutely charming treatise on the good life.

Cahalan, Don; Cisin, Ira H.; and Crossley, Helen M. *American Drinking Practices.* New Brunswick, N.J.: Rutgers Center of Alcohol Studies, 1969.
> The who, what, and why of alcohol consumption in America.

Chafetz, Morris, M.D. *Why Drinking Can Be Good For You.* New York: Stein and Day Publishers, 1976.
> Presented in a question/answer format—sensible and informative.

DISCUS Facts Book 1979. Washington, D.C.: Distilled Spirits Council of the United States, Inc., 1980.
> All the 1979 statistical and financial information about spirit consumption, as well as reference sources.

The Drug Abuse Council. *The Facts About "Drug Abuse."* New York: The Free Press, 1980.
> Reasoned and authoritative report on drug abuse by an independent, scholarly agency.

Emboden, William. *Narcotic Plants.* New York: Collier Books, 1979.
> A scientist's manual of the origins and uses of all mind-altering plants.

Lamb, Richard B., and Mittelberger, Ernest G. *In Celebration of Wine and Life.* San Francisco: The Wine Appreciation Guild, 1980.
> A veritable treasure trove of pictorial, artistic endeavors about the wine world with abundant historical text.

Leake, Chauncey D., and Silverman, Milton. *Alcoholic Beverages in Clinical Medicine.* Chicago: Year Book Medical Pubs. Inc., 1966.
> The chemistry of alcohols we consume and their medical ramifications.

Louis, J. C., and Yazijian, Harvey Z. *The Cola Wars.* New York: Everest House, 1980.
> Thorough study of the titanic battles between Coke and Pepsi for the stomachs of the world.

Lucia, Salvatore Pablo, M.D. *Wine and Your Well-Being.* New York: Popular Library, 1971.
> After reading this, you will become a connoisseur and put wine in your medicine cabinet.

Marshall, Mac, ed. *Beliefs, Behaviors, and Alcoholic Beverages: A Cross-Cultural Survey.* Ann Arbor: University of Michigan Press, 1979.
> An anthology of articles by anthropologists and sociologists. A must book for cross-cultural data on alcohol consumption.

Maury, E. A., M.D. *Wine Is the Best Medicine.* Kansas City: Sheed Andrews and McMeel, Inc., 1977.
> A French doctor prescribes wines for everything from flatulence to tonsillitis.

Mishara, Brian L., and Kastenbaum, Robert. *Alcohol and Old Age.* New York: Grune and Stratton, Inc., 1980.
> Thorough review of wine in relation to the aged.

National Institute on Drug Abuse. *Marijuana and Health, Eighth Annual Report to the U.S. Congress From the Secretary of Health and Human Services.* Washington, D.C.: U.S. Government Printing Office, 1980.
> The latest research on marijuana use and its effects.

North, Robert, and Orange, Richard, Jr. *Teenage Drinking: The #1 Drug Threat to Young People Today.* New York: Collier Books, 1980.
> Excellent advice for parents of teenagers.

Rorabaugh, W. J. *The Alcoholic Republic: An American Tradition.* New York: Oxford University Press, Inc., 1979.
> The first really dispassionate study of alcohol consumption in post-revolutionary America.

Roueché, Berton. *Alcohol: The Neutral Spirit.* New York: Berkley Publishing Corp., 1960.
> The most reasonable and thorough discussion of alcohol I have ever read.

Royce, James E. *Alcohol Problems and Alcoholism.* New York: The Free Press, 1981.
> An invaluable, reasoned, and comprehensive survey of the many and diverse problems arising from excessive drinking and of programs which attempt to correct the disease.

Sadoun, Roland; Lolli, G.; and Silverman, M. *Drinking in French Culture.* New Brunswick, N.J.: Rutgers Center of Alcohol Studies, 1965.
> Statistical study of alcoholism patterns in France.

Shearer, Robert J., M.D., ed. *Manual on Alcoholism.* 3d rev. ed. Chicago: American Medical Association, 1973.
   A must for every professional.

U.S. Department of Health, Education, and Welfare. *Second Special Report to the U.S. Congress on Alcohol and Health.* Prepared by Morris E. Chafetz, M.D. Washington, D.C.: U.S. Government Printing Office, 1974.
   Basic research on alcoholism and programs for prevention.

————. *Third Special Report to the U.S. Congress on Alcohol and Health.* Ernest P. Noble, M.D., ed. Washington, D.C.: U.S. Government Printing Office, 1978.
   An updated compendium of statistics from alcohol studies.

————. *Fourth Special Report to the U.S. Congress on Alcohol and Health.* John R. DeLuca, ed. Washington, D.C.: U.S. Government Printing Office, 1981.
   The latest in this series of reports especially indicates the progress made in combating and treating alcoholism.

U.S. Department of Transportation. *You . . . Alcohol and Driving.* Washington, D.C.: U.S. Government Printing Office, 1977.
   Well-illustrated and easily read compendium of information on the automobile and alcohol.

Washburne, Chandler. *Primitive Drinking: A Study of the Uses and Functions of Alcohol in Preliterate Societies.* New York: College and University Press Publishers, 1961.
   Scholarly research on drinking patterns of sixteen tribes from Africa, the Americas, Asia, and the Pacific.

Wasson, R. Gordon; Ruck, Carl A. P.; and Hoffman, Albert. *The Road to Eleusis.* New York: Harcourt Brace Jovanovich, Inc., 1978.
   Scholarly research on the Eleusinian rites of ancient Greece.

Alcohol in History

*F*rom rock paintings and burial objects it seems evident that even before written history, people over the earth produced potable alcoholic concoctions from available sources of sugar. For example, the Chagga and Azande tribes in Africa fermented beer from Eleusine grain. The Tarahumara in Central America were fond of a corn beer called *tesquina* and another variation from the maguey cactus called *pulque*. In the Pacific, island tribes such as the Dusun created a rice beer called *topai*. And a favorite of the Asian Mongols was *kumiss*, fermented from mare's milk.

The earliest written record of alcohol dates from about 5000 B.C. A tablet found at the Temple of Erech near the Persian Gulf indicates wages of "bread and beer for the day" for the laboring temple workers. Beer, bread, and onions formed the common diet of the day. The practice of using alcoholic beverages as staples seems to have emerged independently in cultures all over the world.

However, what we now term the *wine culture* had specific origins coinciding with the birth of western civilization. And that occurred as a result of the cross-fertilization of Persian and Semitic cultures in Mesopotamia. The wild ferments of nature were tamed by fledgling societies and were, eventually and systematically, propagated throughout all of the western societies.

Anthropological studies confirm the probability of widely dispersed discoveries of ferments across the entire globe. Simple fermented beverages were produced wherever there were fruits and grains (see table 3.1).

In general, fermentation, as practice, followed the growth of agriculture. Peoples with no native agriculture were introduced to intoxicating drinks, usually with dire consequences,

*A*nd Noah often said to his wife, when he sat down to dine, "I don't care where the water goes, if it doesn't get into the wine."
G. K. Chesterton

*T*hree cups of wine will settle everything and a drinking bout will dissipate a thousand cares.

Chinese proverb

by conquering visitors. The Eskimos, many roving Indian tribes of North America, the aborigines of New Guinea, and the Polynesians suffered cultural disintegration because of their introduction to alcohol. As A. P. McKinley noted in an article in the *Quarterly Journal of Studies on Alcohol* from December, 1948, "when a folk of primitive culture came into contact with wine, drunkenness usually followed and repeatedly did such indulgence end in catastrophe."

The history of use and abuse is varied throughout the Mediterranean basin, northern Europe, and the Pacific Islands. In general, the more sophisticated the culture, the greater the degree of inebriety. McKinley argues that less urban communities exhibited, for the most part, more temperance:

In general, the inhabitants of the west and south are rated by most writers as somewhat restrained in the

TABLE 3.1 Ancient Ferments

Name of Alcohol	Food Source	Locale
Aguamiel, pulque	Maguey plant	Mexico, South America
Awamari	Sweet potatoes	Japan
Beer	Millet	Central Africa
Beer	Wheat, barley	Egypt, Asia Minor, Sumer
Broga	Millet	Romania
Busa	Millet	Scythia
Chicha	Corn	South America, Mexico
Hydromel, mead	Honey	Wherever there were bees
Kaniog	Raspberries and blueberries	Northern Europe
Koumiss, kumiss	Mare's milk	Asia
Sabaia	Grain and honey	Iceland, Norway
Saki	Rice	India, Japan, China
Soma	Palm stalks or milkweed	Indonesia
Tibe	Figs and raisins	Switzerland
Tuwak	Palm stalks	Indonesia
Wine	Grapes and other fruits	Asia Minor, Europe
Wine	Palm sap	Africa, India, Asia
Zythos	Emmer, barley	Gaul

Philip Galle's Autumn, *ca. 1600, shows every aspect of a very ordered vineyard and winery down to the nude but "chapeaud" men treading the grapes to burst the skins.*

use of alcoholic beverages; whereas the peoples of the Near East, of central Europe, and of the Balkans were contrariwise minded . . . the more simple the state of the society among a people, and the farther away it was from well developed centers of population, the more likely it was to have a reputation for sobriety.

The association of sobriety with a simpler way of life should be kept in mind when examples of heavy drinking are cited in ensuing pages. McKinley found evidences of abstemiousness among early Spanish and Italian peoples, just as he found widespread drunkenness among the Egyptians, Scythians (Russians), Persians, Carthaginians, and Celts.

A RELIGIOUS MATTER

According to Charles Seltman in *Wine in the Ancient World,* we can infer liberal drinking in early pagan societies because of the many gods associated with grapes or grape products. One of the earliest divinities, the Hittite peasant god, was represented in stone—a huge fellow clutching both grapes and grains. Likewise, Priapus, a Greco-Roman god, harbors grapes in his belt. And most widely known, Dionysus, the beloved son of Zeus, was the patron of orgiastic, drunken bacchanals. Wine may well have been used in early religious rites, according to Seltman, as a substitute for blood sacrifice.

Christianity and wine are, of course, historically inseparable. Over 150 references to wine are found in the Old Testament, ranging from favorable to pejorative. Oddly, there are

but few in the New Testament; one wonders if the feeling was that the subject had already been thoroughly covered! "Drink a little wine for thine stomach's sake, and thine often infirmities," from 1 Timothy is typical of biblical comments about wine, as is this admonition from Ecclesiastes, "There is joy for the heart and the soul in wine when it is drunk without excess." The twin themes of physical benefit and the need to avoid the dangers of excess are seen throughout the Bible.

The circumstances that made possible the spread of Christianity, Clarence Patrick suggests in *Alcohol, Culture and Society* (1952), were involved in the spread of wines:

> . . . it is interesting to note that the spread of viticulture and of Christianity in Western Europe were concomitant. Christianity became the established religion of the Roman Empire about the first decade of the fourth century. It was at that time that the culture of the grape began to spread throughout Gaul, and St. Martin of Tours was found preaching the Gospel and planting vineyards at the same time.

In many of the earliest cultures, both pagan and Christian, drinking was a communal activity. There are few reports of solitary drinking, the hallmark of the alcoholic. When there were natural hallucinogens available, they contributed to the festivities as well. One function of such substances was surely to enhance the communal nature of celebrations. Drinking released members of the tribes from tensions and encouraged sociability. It is difficult to socialize by oneself.

THE DELICATE BALANCE

The ready availability of alcohol led inevitably to abuse. The Latin *intoxicare* means "to drug or poison." Over the years, a secondary meaning developed—"to exhilarate." Throughout the literature of western civilization, the need to be aware of

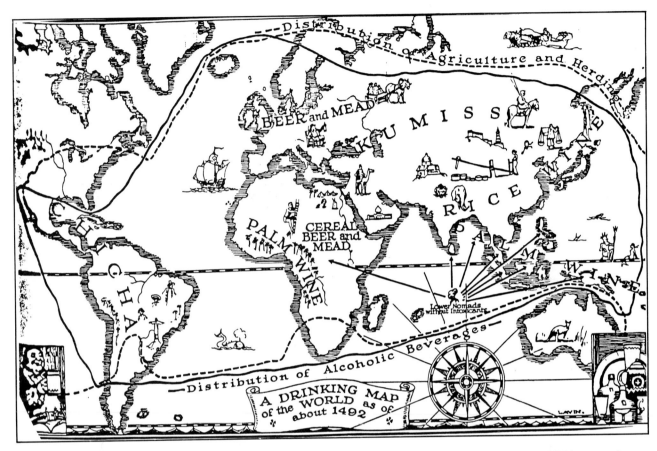

Figure 3.1 *This drinking map of the world of 1492, the time of Columbus, shows how the beverages reflected the available sources from milk,* kumiss, *in the Mongol lands to maize,* chicha, *in South America. (Source unknown.)*

There are no admission fees to the more than five hundred wine festivals held in the historic German wine towns. The ultimate in appreciation and promotion, the festivals include wines, cheeses and breads.

the delicate balance between ecstasy and stupor is endlessly repeated.

For example, Hammurabi developed the first comprehensive code of laws for the first Babylonian dynasty, which includes an astonishing number of rules and regulations (about three hundred) among them some regarding alcohol. Penalties for offenders ranged from loss of a limb to loss of life itself. Genghis Khan warned his soldiers to be drunk no more than once a week. In the Middle Ages the Roman Church imposed on both the clergy and the laity severe penances for alcohol abuse. American Puritans used wooden stocks and fines to penalize offenders and to discourage misuse. Finally, America made a massive attempt to eliminate consumption altogether by establishing Prohibition.

I went to Frankfurt and got drunk
With the most learn'd Professor Brunk.
I went to Worms and got more drunken
With the more learn'd Professor Ruhnken.
Richard Porson

*D*rink not the third glass, which thou
canst not tame when once it is within thee.
George Herbert

Perhaps we should have scrutinized more carefully our philosophers' attitudes through the centuries, for example, that of Euripedes who encouraged drinking: "Wine removes the cares pressing upon the minds of sorrowing mortals who when filled with this juice of the grape no longer need sleep and no longer remember their daily miseries. There is no other cure for all their troubles." Or that of our own William James who found that alcohol "tends to stimulate mystical faculties of human nature usually crushed to earth by the cold facts and dry criticisms of the sober hour. Sobriety diminishes, discriminates and says no. Drunkenness expands, unites and says yes." So it is now, and always will be, the legacy of western societies to have to walk that tightrope between the extremes of cold sobriety and senseless inebriation. It is a paradox that Homer puzzled over when he ruminated: "Inflaming wine, pernicious to mankind, Unnerves the limbs, and dulls the noble mind . . . The weary find new strength in generous wine."

Drinking was common to our ancient progenitors and was commonly excessive. It is curious that even though the same natural ferments were discovered in widely separated places, ingenuity also seemed to proliferate. In places as remote from each other as Japan and India, the chewing of select plant materials initiated fermentation with enzymes found in the mouth. In India milkweed was fermented in this way to make soma, as were rice for wines in Japan and millet for beer in Africa. Brews were created from sugar-rich, water-soaked bread crusts in Babylonia, Egypt, and in areas now part of Russia.

Sanctions against Abuse Universal

Excessive consumption generated governmental sanctions in nearly every recorded society, including those of the Aztecs, Incas, Chinese, Hindus and Mongols, as well as religious sanctions such as the total abstinence demanded of the Moslems. However, what is lacking is a complete body of research on drinking and how it has been controlled. Donald Horton commented, in the *Quarterly Journal of Studies on Alcohol* (1943) on how little has been done:

> There is little precedent for anthropological study of alcohol. Even distribution studies in this field are rare, and relatively little historical work has been reported . . . The subject has scarcely been touched, even on the descriptive historical side.

Against this somewhat clouded background, the following pages suggest, through historical vignettes, the tumultuous pattern of alcohol consumption in western civilization. Horton advises that

> Culture is to be understood as a set of normative patterns of habitual behaviors; that the behavior of human beings in society consists of a set of interrelated habits learned under the influence of the transmitted cultural imperatives.

Some rather grim and shocking stories follow; they are necessary if we are to grasp the "normative patterns of habitual behavior" that have been handed down to us through the centuries.

THE DEVELOPMENT OF WINE MAKING

As far as history is concerned, wines and brews were born in Mesopotamia in the famed valley formed by the Tigris and Euphrates rivers. Between 9000 and 6000 B.C., the art of pottery had developed leading to the critical invention of a vessel for storage of perishable fruit wines. While the existence of wines and brews in deep antiquity has been conjectured, it is fact that the ingenious Sumerians developed agriculture in the rich bottom land of the Persian Gulf. The nearby Egyptians developed the 365 day calendar, probably based on their growing seasons. As the years passed, vines and grains were propagated to the rich Egyptian delta, to Syria, to India, and even to far away China.

According to Tannahill in *Food in History* (1973), the Greek god of wine Dionysus fled the land of Mesopotamia in disgust because of so much beer being consumed, indulgence being the practice of the day:

> . . . it appears that forty percent of the Sumerian grain yield was used for beer production. An ordinary temple workman received a ration of about 1.75 Imperial or 2.2 American pints a day, and senior dignitaries five times as much, some of which they probably used as currency.

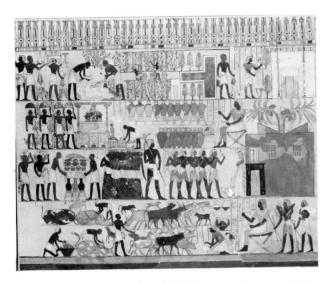

Neb-Amun's Gratitude for His Wealth, *a painting on a wall of his tomb, shows the elaborate wine-making procedures and the pillared and trellised vineyards of his era (1500–1450 B.C.).*

These gold, glass and silver wine vessels from the Eighteenth Dynasty of Thebes, each engraved with the owner's name, demonstrate the importance placed on the consumption of wine.

The Egyptians developed thriving vineyards in huge walled estates. Throughout the ancient dynasties, wine was mainly the beverage of the upper classes. There was ample brew for the workers. Viticulture was advanced considerably with systems for irrigation and with trellising which kept the fruit out of the hot sun. In the colder climates in the North, where the grape vines would not grow, brews and honey wines satisfied humans' desire for drink. However, it was the vine and its product that were to be the essence of trade in western societies.

The Phoenicians and the Semites of North Africa became the first great traders and navigators of the Mediterranean. Along with spices and other foods, they carried not only the wines but also the vines of Mesopotamia to Greece, Spain, and even to the Bordeaux region of France. They developed a particularly fortuitous trade with Greece when it was reaching its Olympian heights.

The vines grew tolerably well in the arid Greek soils, but what really interested the Phoenicians and the Egyptians were the superlative, water-tight clay amphorae from Greece. Since the invention of the wooden barrel would not occur for centuries, the clay pottery of the time served as the universal vessel of transport. Amphorae held up to 9 gallons and could be utilized to ship everything from grain to water, of particular importance in desert country. Millions of these jars were used in Mediterranean commerce.

The thoughtful Greeks advanced the science of agriculture and grape growing considerably. Their soil produced harsh acidic wines that required much doctoring with additives, which ranged from sea water to marble dust. Their search for more desirable land led eventually to the propagation of cultivated wines in the Italian boot.

Around 750 B.C., Greek immigrants planted their highly cultivated grapes in Italy. No more harmonius or fruitful ag-

ricultural advance could be imagined. The Greek cuttings of *vitis vinifera* sprang to life, a life flourishing to this day. But as H. Warner Allen notes in *A History of Wine* (1961), there were wines native to Italy. "The vine was doubtless indigenous to Italy. Fossils show that it flourished far away to the north in Champagne [France] during the Tertiary Period when time ticked happily away without man to take account of it." However, it was the varieties propagated from ancient Sumer that were destined to make this mountainous country the paragon of wine making.

Natural innovators, the Romans carefully cultivated the precious new varieties of berries and rapidly advanced the science of viticulture. The pruning knife still in use today was developed then as well as the critical practice of pruning back the fruit wood to maximize production. Records indicate that Roman farmers produced up to 2,000 gallons of wine per acre, more than double the average yield in California today.

Rain makes the vines grow. The vines make the wine flow. Oh, Lord! Let it rain!
Anonymous

Overindulgence: A Roman Trait

Soon there was a significant divergence in the manner of consumption of the Greeks and the Romans. Although wine production had developed in Greece to the point that the masses could imbibe, a spirit of temperance discouraged abuse. Solon, the great lawgiver quoted by Allen (1961), set the tone: "Such, you see, is the Greek way of drinking. Taking their wine in moderation, they enjoy conversation and fun." Allen also quotes his contemporary, Alexis, who wrote, "My reason is not drunk, but only just so drunk that I carefully enunciate every syllable I utter." A worthy standard yet! The Romans, in contrast, developed abusive drinking habits almost from the beginning of the wine culture.

By the first century B.C., Roman wine culture had begun to spread throughout the European continent. Amphorae by the millions floated down the rivers and across the Mediterranean in a vain effort to satisfy the unquenchable thirst of Rome's citizenry. The city of Rome had become the first great consumer metropolis. The population depended upon the thousands of ships which delivered grains, fruits, spices, and wines from all the reaches of the known world.

The practice of flavoring wines dominated early vintages. Gradually, however, there developed the kind of unadulterated wine worthy of consumption. The Greek practice of aging wines was carried over to finer Roman harvests with superlative results and gave rise to sometimes judging a wine by its label, as a passage from Petronius *Satyricon* quoted by Seltman (1957) attests:

> Falernian of Opimius's Vintage one hundred years in the bottle [circa 121 B.C.] and as we were reading the labels Trimalchio clapped his hands and cried, "Alas that wine lives longer than wretched man! So, let us wet our whistles, for wine is life!"

During the several hundred years before Christ's birth, as the Romans swarmed over Europe, they developed the unique winegrowing regions which serve the world today. Special strains of grapes were developed for particular soils and climates. While serving the Roman legions, these ancestral vines and grapes created a priceless, timeless legacy for us all.

*I*t was a time of confusion, of brigandage, of crimes unpunished and universal insecurity. . . . No solitary man was safe.
H. G. Wells

To some degree, the Romans' cravings and carnal desires contributed to the demise of their empire. In particular, the cost of spices and silks from the East drained their meager treasuries, particularly, Tannahill suggests, from the beginning of the first millennium: "Roman cooks used large quantities of spices. The spice trade was of considerable antiquity. . . . but the full flood of the spice trade did not come until the first century A.D." (1973)

As soon as the first really large city separated itself from agrarian pursuits, prodigious amounts of food had to be warehoused and distributed in Rome. Because there was no refrigeration at this time, rancidity and spoilage of all sorts could be masked only by ever-increasing amounts of spices and condiments. When Rome eventually succumbed to the spirited and determined barbarians who had gnawed at the fringes of their empire for so many years, they yielded, as Tannahill records, an unusually valuable commodity:

> But whatever the truth about the flavor of Roman food, it was a fitting irony that the barbarians who materialized outside the gates of the city at the beginning of the fifth century A.D. should have demanded as tribute not only land, subsidies, and military titles for their chiefs—but three thousand pounds of pepper.

In a sad and ironic way, one could say that the Romans drank and spiced their empire out of existence.

THE DARK AND MIDDLE AGES

From the sixth to the tenth centuries, the barbarian hordes consolidated their power over western Europe. It was not a happy time. The feudal system fostered incessant quarreling and warring. For the majority, life was too often violent and short.

Through it all, the Church of Rome patiently and steadfastly husbanded its resources through its monastic orders and the metropolitan churches. Often these institutions served as the only havens amid the rushing tides of political and social chaos. The art and science of growing grapes and making wine were but two of the innumerable social and economic contributions secured by the ecclesiastic bureaucracy.

Unfortunately, wines suffered along with the society. The clay container gave way to the sturdier product of a crude new technique of bending wooden staves between hoops, and the ancient art of aging wine in hermetic conditions was lost for the nonce. Many problems of contamination plagued the earliest wine merchants who used wood. Because wood is porous and difficult to clean even with modern techniques using steam, wines made and stored in barrels were subject to a wide variety of bacterial contaminants. By contemporary standards, the wines were probably undrinkable.

Winemakers simply fell back upon ancient Greek and Roman practices of spicing and flavoring the harsher vintages into palatability. The practice of doctoring wines became so prevalent that a name was given to wines altered in this way— piments, from the Latin for coloring. In *The English Medieval Feast* (1931), William Mead evaluated their quality:

> The wines consumed in such enormous quantities were by no means always of a sort that would appeal to modern taste. Not infrequently, they were crude and sharply acidic and required softening to render them palatable. Hence they were commonly mixed with honey and spices and then called piments.

Indulgence: A Way of Life

Despite the adulteration of wine, a great deal was regularly consumed. The tribes of eastern Europe and Scandinavia, progenitors of the feudal lords, were hard-fighting, hard-living, and hard-drinking stock. Perhaps the hardness of life, revealed in "The German Push to the East," was responsible. Schwarz's 1949 translation of a thirteenth century account reveals that the Prussians, for example, knew little of writing or artful works, but were given to great hospitality:

> (Their greatest virtue is hospitality.) They freely and willingly share food and drink. They think they have not treated their guests politely and well if they are not so full of drink that they vomit. . . . They do this until man and woman, host and friends, big and small are all drunk . . .

A similar heritage is sketched by Allen, in *A History of Wine* (1961), for southeastern Europe—the areas of Hungary, Yugoslavia, and Bulgaria: ". . . when Macedon was at the height of its glory and luxury, the Macedonians, who never knew how to drink moderately, regularly got so drunk on their pre-dinner wine that they were quite incapable of doing justice to their food . . ."

By the time the Dark Ages waned, feasting and roistering had become a way of life for the well-off in England and western Europe. Mead (1931) paints an almost unbelievable picture of excess in celebration of the installation of Archbishop Neville at York in 1464.

> A partial list of the food includes 300 quarters of wheat, 300 tuns [1 tun = 252 gal.] of ale, 100 tuns of wine, 1 pipe [large wine cask] of hippocras, 104 oxen, 6 wild bulls, 1,000 sheep, 304 calves, 304 "porkes," 400 swans, 2,000 geese, 1,000 capons, 2,000 pigs, 104 peacocks, besides 13,500 birds, large and small, of various kinds. In addition there were stags, bucks, and roes, five hundred and more, 1,500 hot pasties of venison, 608 pikes and breams, 12 porpoises and seals, besides 13,000 dishes of jelly, cold baked tarts, hot and cold custards, and "spices, sugared delicates and wafers plentie."

Mead continues with the information that brews were the beverage of the common people. In 1309, London's population of 20,400 was served by 354 taverns and 1,334 registered breweries.

The amount of food and drink consumed is not surprising in the context of the times. In the early twelfth century, William of Malmesbury described English eating habits of one hundred years earlier: "In fine, the English, at that time . . . were accustomed to eat till they became surfeited, and to drink till they were sick." That excessive consumption was common throughout the world is evident from a comment of Garcilosa de la Vega, son of an Incan princess and a conquistador, ". . . the Indians drank in the most incredible manner: indeed, drunkenness was certainly their most common vice."

THE GREAT COUNTERCULTURE

The rise of the Islamic culture can be viewed as the first massive counterbalance to the destructive force of alcohol abuse. There had always been checks and balances, but heretofore no effective, total prohibition. However, even now there is considerable debate as to whether the original intent was to abolish all alcohol. In *Narcotic Plants* (1979), Emboden theorizes that "Mahomet's strictures were not a general prohibition, but rather a measure to prevent excesses—especially among the Bedouin soldiers."

An eclectic culture that assimilated Hellenic, Persian, Jewish, and even Christian learning, the Arabs recognized the power of the sword as well as that of the pen. Algebra was largely their invention, and they were pioneers in chemistry (the very names of the two disciplines coming from the Arabic).

By 720, Islam had progressed as far as the Pyrénées which separate Spain from France. Once over those mountains, the Moors met a sterner folk in the Christianized Franks who were not to yield so easily. However, as Wells records, for the most part, "Western Europe was a shattered civilization without law, without administration, with roads destroyed and education disorganized but still with great numbers of people with civilized ideas and habits and traditions." The aggressiveness of the "infidel" caused Christians to identify common interests and concerns.

*T*o drink is a Christian diversion
Unknown to the Turk or the Persian.
William Congreve

More than anything else during this dire period, however, it was the Christianizing of the Vikings which returned Europe to self-confidence and independence. By 911, these Vikings—literally, "Inlet Men"—had settled Normandy in northern France; the Duchy was ceded to their leader in 918 on condition of his conversion to Christianity. Eventually, William, Duke of Normandy, was to conquer the English at the Battle of Hastings and be crowned king on Christmas Day, 1066. At this point, the wine trade between France and England was established. In effect, two great drinking cultures had merged. Both the Anglo-Saxons and the Normans were heavy imbibers. While little has been written about the Norman drinking of the times, Van Voorst suggests in *The Portable Medieval Reader* (1949) their general lack of moderation:

> Excess in drinking appears to have been looked upon with leniency; for, in the stories of Reginald of Durham, we read of a party drinking all night at the house of a priest; and in another he mentions a youth

passing the whole night drinking at a tavern with his monastic teacher.

The reader will recall these as the forebears of the Normans of today who suffer one of the world's highest death rates from alcohol abuse.

A wide spectrum of pagan peoples had assumed Christianity at the time of the Treaty of Wedmore (878), and, as Wells reports, they were not so very different from one another.

> There were very small racial and social differences between Angle, Saxon, Jute, Dane or Norman . . . The issue between Christianity and paganism vanished presently from the struggle. By the Treaty of Wedmore the Danes agreed to be baptized if they were assured their conquests; and the descendants of Rolf in Normandy were not merely Christianized, but they learned to speak French from the more civilized people about them, forgetting their own Norse tongue.

All of these people accepted the banner of Christianity, and the stage was set for the great Crusades against the infidel. Another bond of note was that these converts came from cultures with long-standing traditions of heavy drinking.

Wine is one thing, drunkenness is another.

Robert Burton

AQUA VITAE

If there is a momentous development in the long history of alcohol, it must be the commercial application of the ancient science of distillation. Remarkably, it occurred very late in organized societies.

In the eighth century A.D. the Arabian alchemist Geber (Jābir ibn-Ḥayyān) authored a learned treatise called *Liber Investigationes Magisteri*. He found that

> Distillation is the raising of aqueous vapour in any vessel in which it is placed. There are various modes of distillation. Sometimes it is performed by means of fire, sometimes without it. By means of fire, the vapour either ascends into a vessel, or descends, such as when oil is extracted from vegetables, to preserve them fresh, since everything distilled possesses greater purity and is less liable to putrescency.

This writing confirms a well-developed science of distillation by the Middle Ages.

Alcohol *from the Arabs*

The most commonly accepted theory attributes the word *alcohol* to the Arabic. We know that *kohl* was a popular cosmetic eye shadow produced from distilling powdered antimony. *Al kohl*, or "like kohl," became alcohol. The association of the two terms is reinforced by a slang name the Moors coined for the Spanish cows with black eye markings—*alcoholados!*

Whatever the origin of the word "alcohol," experimental distillations of the substance occurred throughout Europe from 1100 to 1300. Before 1150 *weingeist*, or "wine spirit," appeared in Germany. Within another hundred years, the German priest Albertus Magnus wrote of *aqua ardens*. Normans may have distilled their apple cider in the twelfth century. Armagnac brandy appears in records of 1411. From a very early but unrecorded date, the Alsatians produced fruit spirits. In contrast, coffee and tea are not recorded in Europe until late in the Renaissance.

At the end of the thirteenth century, at the University of Montpellier, in southern France, there emerged an enthusiastic supporter of distillation. Arnald de Vilanova was a respected, learned professor. He not only praised his spirit, but created a name that was to endure, *aqua vitae* (quoted by Forbes [1948]):

Limpid and well flavored red or white wine is to be digested twenty days in a closed vessel, by heat, and then to be distilled in a sand bath with a very gentle fire. The true *water of life* will come over in precious drops, which being rectified by three or four successive distillations will afford the wonderful quintessence of wine. We call it aqua vitae, and this is remarkably suitable since it is really a water of immortality. It prolongs life, clears away ill-humours, revives the heart and maintains youth.

This kind praise from the world of science buttressed the broad-mindedness of the society. The newly developed use of wine essence, or ardent spirits, as medicine was to pervade western culture for five hundred years.

For Whatever Ails You

A good example of the extent of medical dalliance with ardent spirits is found in the work (1519) of a very prominent surgeon, Hieronymus Braunschweig.

Aqua vitae is commonly called the mistress of all medicines. It eases the diseases coming of cold. It comforts the heart. It heals all old and new sores on the head. It causes a good color in a person. It heals alopecia (baldness) and causes the hair well to grow, and kills lice and fleas. It cures lethargy. Cotton wet in the same and a little wrung out again and so put in the ears at night going to bed, and a little drunk thereof, is a good against all deafness. It eases the pain in the teeth, and causes sweet breath. It heals the canker in the mouth, in the teeth, in the lips, and in the tongue, when it is a long time held in the mouth. It causes the heavy tongue to become light and well-speaking. It heals the short breath. It causes good digestion and appetite for to eat, and takes away all belching. It draws the winds out of the body. It eases that yellow jaundice, the dropsy, the gout, the pain in the breasts when they be swollen and heals all diseases in the bladder, and breaks the stone. It withdraws venom that has been taken in meat or in drink, when a little treacle is put thereto. It heals the fevers tertian and quartan. It heals the bites of a mad dog, and all stinking wounds, when they be washed therewith. It gives also young courage in a person, and causes him to have a good memory and remembrance. It purifies the five wits of melancholy and of all uncleanness.

But even with all of these accolades quoted by Hallgarten (1979), Dr. Braunschweig did advise moderation: "It is to be drunk by reason and measure. That is, to understand, five or six drops in the morning, fasting with a spoonful of wine."

In 1506, as Cooper (1979) reveals, King James IV of England gave the medical guild called the Surgeon Barbers a monopoly on the manufacture of aqua vitae. The spirit was described in guild literature thus.

Beying moderatelie taken, it sloweth age, it strengethen youth, it helpeth digestion, it abandoneth meloncholie. It lighteneth the mynde. It keepeth and preserveth the head from whyrling, the eyes from dozeling, the tonge from lispying, the mouth from snoffying, the teeth from chatterying, the throte from ratlying, the stomach from wamblying, the harte from swellying, the hands from shiverying, the veynes from crumplying . . . trulie it is a soveraign liquor.

Such praises of the newly found ardent spirits were, undoubtedly, reinforced by the view, in existence since the dawn of time, that wine is medicinal. Lucia, in *A History of Wine as Therapy* (1971), traces this deeply held belief through eighteen centuries from Sumer to Babylonia, India, China, and Egypt. Medical writings and the lore of western civilization suggest "the therapeutic use of wine must have long antedated the oldest inscriptions that depict winemaking, found on the tomb of Ptah-Hotep, who lived at Memphis in Northern Egypt about 4000 B.C."

This new *aqua vitae* was simply a highly refined wine, the already treasured medical substance. Unfortunately, the science of the day was unable to discern that in such purity, alcohol had lost most of the beneficial or therapeutic elements that were present in the natural brews and wines.

From the banks of the Tigris to the River Thames, potable liquor had come a mighty distance. From a simple, naturally fermented staple in the diet to a distilled spirit credited with the property of immortality, liquor had risen to unwarranted heights. Perhaps if the recommended dosage of several drops taken in wine as advised by Braunschweig had been followed, spirits could well have remained in the medicine chest. But the combination of cultural traditions of heavy drinking and the promotion of distilled liquors as medicine combined to a fearful end. And, the common man was to suffer miserably for the next four hundred years.

*D*rink for a penny,
Dead drunk for a twopence.
Clean straw for nothing.
***from Hogarth's engraving,* Gin Lane**

SPIRITS FOR THE MASSES

Wine had been produced in southeast France near the present town of Bordeaux since the time of the Phoenicians. This fine product and another precious commodity, salt, were shipped to northern Europe by Dutch merchants during the Middle Ages. Some time around 1581, the enterprising sailors began to replace the wines with the local spirits produced at the river town of Cognac. In logical fashion, they dubbed the product *brandwijn* or burnt wine which was soon shortened to *brandy*. It became a favorite not only in Holland but also in England and the cold Scandinavian countries. This is the first distillate known to be traded among nations.

*T*here's but one Reason I can think,
Why people ever cease to drink,
Sobriety the Cause is not
Nor fear of being deam'd a Sot
But if Liquor can't be got.
                    American Doggerel

Around 1650 at the University of Leiden, Holland, an innovation occurred, significant because it made spirits affordable to many. Professor Franz de le Boë, known as Dr. Sylvius, loosed a tide that was to flood the English-speaking world for centuries. His objective was to develop a new diuretic by combining the juniper berry and aqua vitae. But his decision to use neutral, or nearly pure grain spirits as the base was the real advance because corn, wheat, and other grains were abundant and relatively inexpensive. Other contemporary liqueurs featured the more precious alcohols derived from fruits. Waters and elixirs made by costly methods appeared throughout Europe during the latter half of the sixteenth century. All the tantalizing herbs and spices common since ancient times were utilized, but Dr. Sylvius provided the key to mass distribution of distilled alcohol by his choice of a cheap, ubiquitous source material.

The new drink was immediately popular with the Dutch and travelers from other lands. Very little time passed before thirsty British soldiers carried the good news home. Sylvius had called the concoction *genevre* from the French for juniper. The English shortened it to gin, and a tradition of heavy drinking was established.

In 1689, William of Orange gained the British throne. One of his first acts was to place heavy duties on French wines and liquors in order to harm the traditional enemies of Holland. Responding to his influence, Parliament passed its "Act Encouraging Distillation of Brandy and Spirits from Corn." Citizens of the British Isles went on a binge that had never been equalled. Within twenty years, consumption of gin jumped from about half a million gallons to over 18 million gallons. Public drunkenness and social disorder reigned supreme. Since every Englishman had the right to produce and sell gin, it was available everywhere for a pittance.

In 1736, in hopes of arresting the disintegration of the society, Parliament passed a "Gin Act," which limited gin pro-

The utter degradation, caused in part by King William's encouragement of widespread gin production in the early 1700s, was depicted in Hogarth's famous Gin Lane.

duction. The new law was rendered useless by the creation of dozens of new drinks with catchy names like Old Tom, Ladies Delight, Crank, Mexico Sky Blue, and Cuckolds Comfort. Gin Palaces sported dozens of competitive products.

Throughout the 1700s, ardent spirits of all sorts became available to the common man. Rum from the colonies, Madeira, and luscious sweet wines from the Mediterranean vied with sugary sweet elixirs from Holland and France. Everywhere there was wide choice of beverage alcohols and a common acceptance of them as aids to health and relaxation. The same tide was inundating America.

EARLY AMERICANS' LOVE AFFAIR WITH SPIRITS

Clearly the colonists brought with them the traditions of their homelands, among which was a great appreciation for alcohol in various forms. One pilgrim's diary records the landing at Plymouth: "We could not now take time for further search or consideration; our victuals being much spent, especially our beere." The man who was to become the first governor of Massachusetts carried forty tons of beer to be well provisioned in his new country.

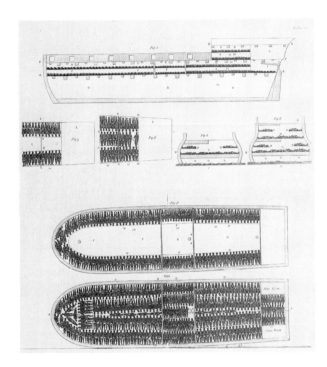

The deck plans for the frigate Brook, *built in 1781, shows the architect's careful placement of five hundred humans on the lower decks. Ships such as this were used in the triangle trade.*

Although a fledgling commercial brewery was operating from a log cabin in Boston as early as 1639, the basic responsibility for brewing resided in the cook in every kitchen as it had in the old world. Brewing was as much a part of everyday life as were canning and preserving other foods. By 1620 according to John Hull Brown, there was considerable inventiveness whenever there was a scarcity of local grains.

> The richer sort generally brew their small beer with malt . . . the poorer sort brew their beer with molasses or bran; with Indian corn malted with drying in a stove; with persimmons dried in a cake and boiled; with potatoes with green stalks of Indian corn cut small and bruised with pompoms; with Jerusalem artichokes which some people plant purposefully for that use, but that is least esteemed. (1966)

In 1631, heavy drinking was apparently so widespread a practice that the Virginia General Assembly singled out clergymen in a resolution stating, "Mynisters shall not give themselves to excesse drinkage or riott." An account of a typical funeral of the time indicates consumption of "22 gallons of cider, 5 of brandy and 24 of beere."

In 1670, the first commercial rum was distilled in Massachusetts from West Indian molasses. Down the coast in New Netherland, the Dutch Governor General set up a commercial still to produce both brandy and gin, the favorites of his coun-

trymen. The same still was used to produce rum when the British assumed control of New York.

The infamous but enormously profitable triangle trade soon developed out of Boston Harbor, along with Newport and Providence, Rhode Island. Fresh rum from Boston bought slaves on the African coast. This human cargo was traded by the ship owners' representatives for new molasses in the Caribbean. Then, the Boston distilleries happily used the molasses to produce more rum. Because it provided an inexpensive means of obtaining molasses for rum, the triangle trade continued until 1808 when Congress abolished the lucrative but regrettable slave trade.

In *Drinking in America* (1982), Lender and Martin trace the progressive dependence upon hard liquor and the general acceptance of its ravages.

> The sticking point was hard liquor and, more specifically, the realization that its use was becoming so prevalent that (at least to some observers) society was losing the ability to control drinking excesses. As the eighteenth century advanced, it became increasingly clear that the social norms that previously had controlled individual behavior with remarkable success were loosening. . . . One surveying party in North Carolina reported finding rum everywhere in 1728—people even cooked bacon in it. Visitors to the western areas of Virginia, New York, Pennsylvania, South Carolina, and some of the more remote parts of New England found intoxication quite common. The sight of down-and-outers sleeping off their whiskey became an accepted part of life.

By the middle of the eighteenth century, heavy drinking was as much an established part of recreation in the colonies as it had long been on the continent. A letter of Dr. John Brickell from 1737 illustrates the point.

> For I have frequently seen them come to town and there remain drinking Rum, Punch and other Liquors for Eight to Ten Days successively and after they have committed this Excess, will not drink any Spiritous Liquor till such time as they take the next Frolick as they call it, which is generally in two or three months . . . But, amongst the better sort, or those of good Economy, it is quite otherwise, who seldom frequent Taverns, having plenty of Wine, Rum and other Liquors at their own homes.

Home Distilling Common

One of the most prized possessions one could inherit at the time was a spirit still. One benefactor willed to his sons "a still, worm and tubb." But there was a codicil. The sons had to promise "that they shall still all their mother's liquor during her lifetime." In 1758, after being defeated twice in political elections, young George Washington won office by spreading 160 gallons

With cries of "Liberty and No Excise," Pennsylvania farmers applied the humiliating tar and feathers to the tax collector of Allegheny County in their brief and ludicrous Whiskey Rebellion.

of liquor among 400 voters! Obviously, liquor was very important to colonial life.

A point of conflict with the British, as serious as the tea tax, occurred when Parliament passed the Molasses Act in 1733. It allowed purchases of precious molasses from only the Crown-controlled islands and at a much higher cost than if purchased from the French or Spanish West Indies. The result was rampant, illegal molasses and rum running. However, the bothersome restrictions had the effect of encouraging distillation from other domestic sources such as corn and fruit.

Another major foreign factor in the spirits history of America occurred as a result of periodic famines in Ireland as well as restrictive mercantile laws that drove Scots first to Ireland and then to America. The sturdy, solemn immigrants included experienced Scotch-Irish distillers from Ulster with knowledge of the construction of stills. These fiercely independent people eventually became the backbone of the Revolution, in part from displeasure at having already been twice displaced by English laws. A new industry emerged at the end of the century in the hills of western Pennsylvania with whiskey made from the native rye. Whiskey soon became the standard for trade and barter on the frontier.

Liquor One of the First Taxes

After the war for independence, the struggling new government desperately needed sources of revenue. It took but a short while for Alexander Hamilton to convince the new President, himself a distiller, that liquor, along with other luxuries like snuff and sugar loaf, was a good item to tax. The first American president as a commercial distiller who in 1789 "netted $1,032 from the sale of distilled spirits, an amount [according to Getz, 1978] equivalent to $125,000 in 1978 dollars. . . ." recognized the potential of spirits taxes. His grist

mill and still at Mount Vernon had been operating since 1771; at one time he had as many as five stills in operation.

So, in 1791 a tax was imposed. The challenge to the struggling farmer was immense. By 1790, over 2,500 distilleries operated in the thirteen states and country folk who did not often see hard cash swapped whiskey and other staples to provide for most of their needs. Therefore, they rebelled.

The Whiskey Rebellion raised a storm, but it was quickly disposed of by a resolute President Washington. Following the tarring and feathering of a tax collector or two by an angry citizenry, the Chief Executive dispatched Lighthorse Harry Lee to Pennsylvania with some 13,000 troops, an army nearly as large as that which had captured Cornwallis. The protestors dispersed, and federal control over liquor was established, at least in principle.

Many disgruntled farmers simply pushed farther west hoping to avoid the revenue agents. Others took the Cumberland Trail to Kentucky. In circumstances quite as fortuitous as those of the Greek introduction of vinifera grapes to Italy, the Scotch-Irish distillers came upon a grain new to them—corn, which had been cultivated in Massachusetts as early as 1620 and in Kentucky by 1774. It was not used for distilling until molasses became scarce. The happy farmers derived tremendous advantages from this wondrous grain. First, it could be utilized as food both for humans and for livestock, and it produced considerably more tons per acre than rye. It was also a superb mash source. Kentucky bourbon was born.

The idea of liquor as medicine had persisted. Samuel Stern published *The American Herbal: Or Materia Medica* as late as 1801, providing dozens of recipes for punches and balms, each guaranteed to cure a particular ailment. Everything from rum to cedar bark wine found its way into this popular folk medicine book. Given the harshness of existence, it is readily understandable why the populace believed in the curative powers of spirits that warmed and delighted.

The choice of liquors depended largely upon the economics of the times, particularly in periods of scarce grain sup-

Statistics on the Cargo of One U.S.S. Constitution Voyage

- She carried 475 officers and men, plus 48,600 gallons of fresh water, 74,000 common shot, 79,400 gallons of rum.
- Reaching Jamaica on October 6th, she laded 826 lbs. of flour, 68,300 gallons of rum.
- Three weeks later in the Azores, she laded 550 lbs. of beef, 64,300 gallons of Portuguese wine.

- At the Firth of Clyde, Scotland, she took aboard 40,000 gallons of whisky.
- When she docked at Boston on 20 February 1780, there was aboard no food, powder, rum or whisky, only 48,000 gallons of stagnant water.

Source: Adapted from Peter F. and Frances D. Robotti, *Key to Gracious Living, Wines and Spirits* (Englewood Cliffs, N.J.: Prentice-Hall, Inc., 1972.), 3–4.

Though mechanization developed huge stills for commercial trade, the farm still was a common sight. These relaxed farmers are tending a peach brandy still in Delaware about 1870.

ply. During and after the Revolutionary War, all grain was in dangerously short supply. As Getz (1978) points out even with this dearth, General Washington considered it an absolute necessity that one gill, a half a pint, of whiskey be provisioned daily for each soldier in the armed forces.

> It is necessary, there should always be sufficient quantities of spirits with the army, to furnish moderate supplies to the troops. In many instances such as when they are marching, in hot or cold weather, in camp or in fatigue or in working parties, it is so essential that it is not to be dispensed with.

As grain became scarce, fruit brandies and rum were the common substitutes. Gin was also produced from common spirits and the juniper berry.

By the turn of the century, technical innovations began to occur in the distilling industry. Steam engines provided direct and controllable levels of heat, eliminating many scorched mash tubs and a much higher production from the musts. Copper condensing columns became more numerous around the country as well as stills of immensely greater capacity. Between 1800 and 1804, production more than tripled from one to three and a half gallons of spirits from a single bushel of corn. That was progress!

Temperance Born of Excess

In 1800, whiskey was available for 75¢ per gallon while fine peach brandy was pegged at $1.15 per gallon. Just twenty-five years later, abundant supplies of whiskey could be purchased for as little as 25¢ per gallon, practically the cheapest potable beverage on the market. During this period, largely from necessity, the aging of large stocks of whiskey became common. The concept of *old* being synonymous with *better* became accepted. In most cases, the unanticipated aging process did indeed develop superior, more mellow products. It wasn't long before *aged* varieties could bring three to four times the market price.

The worldwide impulse to temper the excesses of the times grew steadily. Drinking to excess was as common in America as in England. It should be noted that punch bowls held copious amounts, and that they were passed from person to person until drained. Flip mugs held as much as a quart.

The most outrageous, yet accurate example of officially recorded excess must be in the logs of the U.S.S. Constitution which sailed from Boston Harbor on 23 August 1779. The account of the amount of spiritous liquors disposed of on that one voyage is startling. One hopes there was some black marketeering along the way, since the sum total of all the gallons divided by the 475 men and officers aboard comes to 3 gallons per man per day.

There is no intent to shock, or to demean the American heritage in presenting these figures. They are historically correct and the circumstances within society that prompted excess provided a logical basis for the long overdue Temperance Movement. American Prohibition must be understood in the context of the degradation of a reeling, stuporous, groggy society. Sad to relate, when temperance had already been accomplished and America nearly dried out, the extremists had their day, and wrote one of the saddest chapters in American social history—Prohibition.

Prohibition 4

The Eighteenth Amendment was as much a sociological battle between urban and rural America as it was a measure to abolish alcohol. It attempted to control the relentless shift of power to the feared urban east and to keep political power vested in the largely rural Congress. Andrew Sinclair confirms this in *Prohibition: Era of Excess* (1964):

> In fact, national prohibition was a measure passed by village America against urban America. This conclusion is affirmed by the fact that San Francisco, St. Louis, St. Paul, Chicago, Cincinnati, Cleveland, Detroit, and Boston all rejected prohibitory laws during the period when the Eighteenth Amendment was being considered by Congress and the states.

The ultimate irony of this maneuver is that it was the farm belt, the bastian of the drys, which was devastated by the "noble experiment"—Whiskey is made from corn!

The result of this lamentable period of history was the well-meaning imposition of the will of a few to prevent satisfying the thirst of the many. Prohibition not only failed as a civil act, it probably spawned more serious social problems than those it sought to eliminate. It funded one of the world's great crime networks.

*A*bstinence is a wonderful thing if it is practiced in moderation.

Anonymous

*P*rohibition is better than no whiskey at all.

Will Rogers

*P*rohibition is an awful flop,
  We like it.
It can't stop what it's meant to stop,
  We like it!
It's left a trail of graft and slime,
It don't prohibit worth a dime,
It's filled our land with vice and crime,
Nevertheless—We're for it!

Franklin P. Adams

CULTURAL BACKGROUND

Prohibition can only be understood in terms of the very real evil it sought to correct. Between the end of the War of Independence and the grain gluts of the 1830s, much of the American culture had been disrupted. It was ceasing to be an agrarian society; industry sought new technologies and required growing numbers of steady, reliable workers. Cash, rather than farm commodities, had become the medium of exchange. These tumultuous changes occurred over decades, gradually challenging old, accepted ways of doing things like getting drunk on any pretense nearly every day.

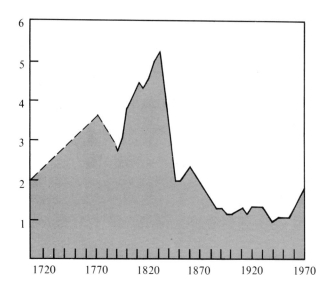

Figure 4.1 *Annual consumption of distilled spirits (rum, whiskey, gin brandy etc.) per capita in U.S. gallons.*

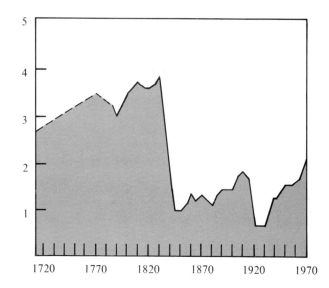

Figure 4.2 *Annual consumption of alcohol contained in all alcoholic beverages per capita in U.S. gallons.*

About halfway through the nineteenth century, the vast coalition of forces working against intemperance succeeded. Total consumption plummeted. In general, American people became temperate. Had wiser heads prevailed, whether committed to temperance for social or religious reasons, the drys could have consolidated their gains and enjoyed the new luxuries available as a result of the Industrial Revolution. But such are not the ways of history, so succeed they did in corking the bottle, after consumption had dramatically decreased (see figs. 4.1 and 4.2).

Such a precipitous drop in the total annual consumption could have come about only as a result of a massive social revolution. Indeed, one had occurred, which we now call the Industrial Revolution. To understand the magnitude of the change and how it came into being, one must go back and set the stage, so to speak, with a review of some little known facts about American history.

Our first president was a distiller; the Bureau of Alcohol, Tobacco and Firearms is currently in possession of Washington's still from Mount Vernon. A carpenter Washington hired at Mount Vernon, one Thomas Green, was promised the following: "four dollars at Christmas, with which he may be drunk for four days and nights; two dollars at Whitsuntide to be drunk for two days; a dram in the morning and a drink of grog at dinner at noon." A fellow Founding Father, John Hancock, once threw a party at which he provided 200 guests with 136 punch bowls and 300 bottles of wine and brandy after the meal.

In an article in the *Journal of Studies on Alcohol,* Rorabaugh (1976) provides insight concerning what lay behind this nonchalance:

Between 1790 and 1830 Americans seem to have indulged in a veritable alcoholic binge. Several

elements contributed to this phenomenon. At that time, Americans retained a belief that liquor was healthful, nutritious, stimulating and relaxing. This predisposition to drink meshed with a rising abundance of cheap whiskey as settlers planted fertile grain lands in the Midwest. Amid a grain glut, the price of whiskey fell to 25¢ a gallon, less than wine, beer, coffee, tea or milk. Then too, the preference for strong drink reflected the need to wash down poorly cooked, greasy, salty and sometimes rancid food. Americans, however, also drank to enjoy the effect. Intoxication met certain psychological and social needs prevalent in a period of economic turmoil and social dislocation.

EARLY ATTEMPTS AT REGULATION

The recently independent country, that is, the United States, had yet to develop the kind of consensus upon which organized societies rest. Throughout that turbulent century of organized temperance advocacy, the haves generally attempted to impose controls on the have-nots. In *The Alcoholic Republic* (1979), Rorabaugh explains the attempts of the former:

Members of society's upper classes, having failed in their efforts to reduce the number of licensed taverns, then sought to impose stricter laws for their regulation. Measures were enacted to discourage Sunday sales; to require all taverns to provide lodging for travellers; to revoke licenses if gaming were permitted on the premises; to prohibit sales to seamen; and to stop a slave from buying liquor without his

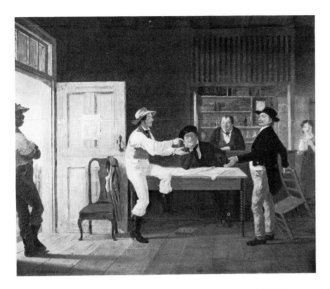

The primary setting for politics and affairs of state for the colonial politician was the local tavern, as seen in this 1844 painting by James Clonney.

American bars in the nineteenth century were great levelers; rich and poor, young and old met on common ground.

master's consent. These provisions, judging from their frequent modifications and reenactments, failed to stop the erosion of upper class authority.

Organized temperance societies simply provided an appropriate vehicle for all of the many forces that sought to keep the growing economic machine running smoothly. Timberlake develops this theme in *Prohibition and the Progressive Movement* (1963). For once, the end did seem to justify the means. The great liberal social ideas upon which American political theory rested could now be fulfilled by a wise government. The legislature could achieve where the pulpit failed.

If Progressivism desired to curb the power of an industrial and financial plutocracy, Prohibition aimed to remove the corrupting influence of one branch of the plutocracy—the liquor industry. . . . Prohibition did not command universal support, however, for its appeal lay largely with the old stock middle class sections of the American community . . . it was able to overcome the opposition of the urban masses and to impose its own standards of sobriety on the nation by law.

What began in most western nations as rightful indignation at alcohol abuse evolved into progressive, evangelical, Calvinistic theocracy, as Timberlake suggests. "Evangelical Protestantism sought to overcome the corruption of the world in a dynamic manner not only by converting men to a belief in Christ, but also by Christianizing the social order through the power and force of law."

Rorabaugh presents a convincing argument that the essential strength of an anti-liquor movement lay in the awakening aspirations of a new American nation.

Societies are vigorous and healthy when their institutions and ideologies reinforce one another. When a culture undergoes rapid, disruptive change, its social structure is altered, some of its institutions are weakened, its ideology loses vitality, and stress develops. How a society responds to these conditions determines its future. . . . The turning from alcohol to abstinence in the late 1820s, therefore, signified the vitality of American society. (1979)

The new consensus was, however, far from apparent in the conceptual stages of the Temperance Movement. Wide religious disagreement was evident. In *Ardent Spirits* (1973)

Kobler points to a dichotomy between strict and liberal Protestantism: "Puritanism, often confused with Calvinism, was largely an Anglo-American doctrine grafted upon the latter. European Calvinists attached no evil to social diversions like dancing and moderate drinking." American Episcopalians and Jews stood apart from religious tub-thumping anti-liquor advocates. German Lutherans, home brewers for centuries, were perplexed by the rigid cant. And Catholics, of course, saw in the movement another evidence of prejudice and hostility, feeling obviously excluded, as Kobler suggests, because of "Catholics as a class having shown scant interest in organized temperance, let alone prohibition. . . ."

The Influence of Benjamin Rush

During these troubled times, a towering figure and an apostle of continence garbed in medical robes, Dr. Benjamin Rush became the spokesman of unimpeachable scientific integrity for the view that distilled spirits were evil in any and all forms. The former physician general of the Army, Rush was instrumental in founding of Dickinson College and the Philadelphia College of Physicians and Surgeons, and had been a signer of the Declaration of Independence. Although he lectured and wrote constantly, his *immediate* impact upon drinking in the society was next to nil since the temperance movement had yet to take shape. However, he did make a significant contribution to the anti-liquor forces by motivating others and by being, so to speak, an authoritative reference. Sinclair documents this in *Era of Excess* (1964):

> In 1784, Dr. Rush published his famous pamphlet *An Inquiry into the Effects of Spirituous Liquors on the Human Body and Mind.* . . . His writings were the basis of the temperance sermons of the great preacher Lyman Beecher. . . . Beecher appealed to God's law as well as to medical knowledge . . .

In defense of his fine mind and original intent, one must point out that Dr. Rush spoke out against hard liquor, not brews and wines as is easily seen in these excerpts from Part II of the *Inquiry:*

> But it may be said, if we reject spirits from being part of our drinks, what liquors shall we substitute in their room? I answer in the first place,
> 1. SIMPLE WATER. . . .
> 2. CYDER. This excellent liquor contains a small quantity of spirit, but so diluted, and blunted by being combined with a large quantity of sugar matter, and water, as to be perfectly wholesome. . . .
> 3. MALT LIQUORS. The grain from which these liquors are obtained, is not liable, like the apple, to be affected by frost, and therefore they can be procured, at all times, and at a moderate price. They contain a good deal of nourishment. . . .

> 4. WINES. These fermented liquors are composed of the same ingredients as cyder, and are both cordial and nourishing. . . .

Rush represented a complete break with several hundred years of medical admiration for ardent (distilled) spirits. However, he was a perceptive student of the medical sciences and as such recognized the merits of the lighter beverages. But, as is always the case, zealots chose from his serious work only what served their partisan purposes. Before long, temperance had come to mean complete abolition of alcohol of any form.

What Rush and Beecher sparked was widespread indignation at the overwhelming nature and number of alcohol-induced problems. Society was nearly out of hand. It is difficult today to comprehend the universality of the intemperance. Rorabaugh, however, gives us a vivid sense of the place of alcohol in people's lives.

> Alcohol was pervasive in American society. It crossed regional, sexual, racial, and class lines. Americans drank at home and abroad, alone and together, at work and at play, in fun and in earnest. They drank from the crack of dawn to the crack of dawn. . . . Americans drank before meals, with meals, and after meals. . . . They drank in their youth and, if they lived long enough, in their old age. They drank at formal events, such as weddings, ministerial ordinations, and wakes, and on no occasion . . . [simply] when the mood called. (1979)

Temperance and the Big T

While perhaps a bit more aggressive in drinking too much than people in the old countries, Americans were far from unique in this period of excess. In *The Waterdrinkers* (1968) Longmate traces the anti-liquor movement from its origin through the lands of British influence, those societies so long smitten with ale and gin. Temperance societies, loosely coordinated, formed in England, Ireland, Scotland, and Canada, as well as in the United States where Longmate focuses on the early groups:

> The modern Temperance movement began in the United States about 1770 . . . the first formal pledge to abstain from drink was taken by those attending a meeting at Moreau, New York State in 1808, though signatories were still allowed to drink wine at public dinners or beer or cider at any time . . . the first pledge against all forms of intoxicating drink were probably taken at Boston in 1826 and at Hector, New York State in 1827 where members who had taken the "total pledge" were marked with the letter *T.*

The appellation *teetotaler* came probably not from the Hector enclave, but from a similar gathering in 1833 in Preston, England. A poor laborer by the name of Dickie Turner

This satire on drinking, painted in the 1800s, bears an eerie resemblance to the medieval feast and the gentleman's club of the 1700s, confirming the long-standing tendency to overconsume.

The conversion of Dickie Turner.

invaded a temperance pledge meeting half in his cups, only to be converted on the spot. His stirring speech of rejection of the wayward life included a local slang word meaning total support. According to reports cited by Longmate (1968), he shouted, "I'll have now't to do wi' this moderation, bothcration pledge. I'll reet down and out *tee-tee-total* for ever and ever."

THE MOVEMENT INTENSIFIES

Whatever the origin of the word, demanding that everyone be a teetotaler became the emotional shibboleth for the extremists, the fanatical fringe that eventually won a total political victory in America. The hard-shelled organizer mobilized the movement, through meetings, groups, peer pressure, pamphleteering, sermonizing, education, marches, rallies, and picnics. Harrison characterizes the mindless extremism of the movement in *Drink and the Victorians* (1971):

> Teetotalism gave the anti-spirits movement that precision of aim so necessary to reforming movements. Teetotalers used the same argument against anti-spirits societies which tolerated beer-drinking, as the anti-spirits societies themselves used against moderate spirit drinkers. The temperance movement was thus being launched on its path towards extremism—so that defects in the movement were remedied by attempts to close loopholes rather than by rethinking fundamentals, and the movement's original aim, the prevention of drunkenness, was subordinated to the pursuit of consistence.

Eventually, with the support of women who began to express their concerns and to organize for the first time, the anti-alcohol juggernaut gained respectability and even greater power.

The movement formed a giant tapestry, stretching over seas and continents, utilizing religious, social, and educational agencies to achieve its stated purpose—total abolition of alcoholic beverages.

During the 1850s, thirteen states succumbed, enacting some form of dry laws. Everywhere liquor forces were on the defensive, and the stage was set for the dramatic figures who could achieve final victory. Many, many bit players passed through the scenery, but it was Frances Willard who emerged as the *femme extraordinaire.*

In 1879 when she was elected president, the Women's Christian Temperance Union became her vehicle. It was the first effective, national research and propaganda unit, operating through hundreds of closely monitored local societies. She pledged to organize every town in the nation with over 10,000 in population—and succeeded. In achieving this momentous goal, she created the first feminist-dominated national movement.

One of Willard's most avid followers wrote a startling new page of anti-liquor history. In 1890, Carry Nation, a frustrated woman, joined the local Kansas WCTU. By her own admission, she could not manage her own life which was dominated by hatred for sex, freemasonry, tobacco, and alcohol. She made her indelible mark on 6 June 1900 when she drove her buggy to neighboring Kiowa, Kansas, and literally destroyed the inside of a local tavern by wildly hurling brickbats around to the dismay of the patrons. The hatchet came later. Kobler (1973) describes her driving out of town standing upright in her buggy, shouting "Peace on earth, good will to men."

If Carry was the flamboyant Barnum in this societal circus, Wayne B. Wheeler was the organizing Bailey. When his Anti-Saloon League was at its peak, 69,000 churches were among its supporters. Churches tendered contributions of over $2 million annually to the cause. By 1902, every school in the nation offered a course in Temperance, which was tantamount

Frances Willard, the first great American feminist, founded the Woman's Christian Temperance Union to further female suffrage as well as to promote prohibition.

Carry Nation kneels with her Bible after one of her thirty arrests for destroying taverns. Her fines were paid from lecture fees and the sale of souvenir hatchets.

to teaching total prohibition. All of this enormous, relentless social pressure caused twenty-six states to vote some form of prohibition by 1917, seventeen by referendum and nine by legislation.

Industry Unresponsive to Movement

It is a palpable historical fact that the brew and spirits industries did precious little to stem this growing tide. While there were some intelligent counter-arguments raised, particularly by those ethnic groups for whom wine or beer was an inseparable part of their regular meals, most of their efforts fell on deaf ears as the extreme position became the acceptable "Christian" position.

Kobler (1973) paints a grim picture of the "tied house" saloon in which the owner was inextricably indebted to the liquor supplier and he also reveals the intransigence of this group as a whole:

> Approximately three-fourths of the country's saloons were owned or controlled by the liquor wholesalers, who could have imposed decent behavior upon the consignee by threatening to cut off his supplies. They might thus have disarmed the antisaloonists, but greed blinded them to their danger. They might have forestalled prohibition indefinitely. Instead, they hastened its advance. During a convention of Columbus, Ohio, liquor dealers, in 1874, the question of serving minors was raised, whereupon a delegate argued: "Men who drink liquor, like others, will die, and if there is no new appetite created, our counters

will be empty as well as our coffers. . . . The open field for the creation of appetite is among the boys . . . and I make the suggestion, gentlemen, that nickels expended in treats to the boys now will return in dollars to your tills after the appetite has been formed."

In a manner of speaking, the liquor merchants brought the house of cards down upon themselves. And so the law came to pass. Both Houses of Congress passed the 18th Amendment in 1917, but it was not until January 1919 that the necessary two-thirds of the states ratified the Amendment. One year later—16 January 1920—Prohibition became the law of the land.

The evening before that fateful day, there was a jubilant nightlong victory celebration in the Washington, D.C. Congressional Church. Brave speeches thundered through the night from such luminaries in the long battle as William Jennings Bryan, "Thou Shalt Not Bury the Democratic Party in a Drunken Grave;" Bishop James Cannon, Jr. of the Methodist Church Temperance Commission; Senator Morris Sheppard who introduced the 18th Amendment; Andrew Joseph Volstead of Yellow Medicine County, Kansas—the very dry midwestern author of the Act; and the stalwart Josephus Daniels, Secretary of the Navy.

The Effects of Prohibition

With the birth of Prohibition, thirteen years, ten months, and eighteen days of wanton civil disobedience in the land of promise were unleashed. We gained some new catchwords from this

The scene here in 1925 Seattle can be considered typical of the enormous creative energy expended on supplying and fooling the public. Agent F. A. Hazeltine proudly surveys a 350 gallon still in a garage before destroying the still and its contents.

The scandalous practices of unscrupulous bar operators in many cities allowed children to purchase intoxicating beverages. Such practices fed the flames of Prohibition. Working class drunkenness was also rampant, resulting in the support for Prohibition by some early labor leaders.

period: *scofflaw,* one who scoffs at the law, and *The Real McCoy,* real whiskey from the "rum-running" vessels of a flamboyant but eminently dependable Irishman. The single attribute of this legendary Gael was his honesty. He never "cut" his Irish or Scotch whiskies with distilled water. From Boston to Miami, "the Real McCoy" assured the buyer of the genuineness of the product.

During this teeming, unsettling time, bribes and payoffs of local, state, and federal officials were common. In its naïve incompetence, the federal government devised at least seventy-five formulas for denaturing alcohol so it could be used only for commercial applications ranging from antifreeze and liniment to varnish and canned heat. Either the prescribed denaturing was avoided because of discreet payoffs or the product was, with the connivance of the inspectors, afterwards cleansed for human consumption. Either way, the law was generally ignored.

During this period from 1920 to 1933, federal enforcement agents arrested 517,000 liquor purveyors; seized 1,600,000 illegal stills, 9 million gallons of spirits, and one billion gallons of beer, wine, and cider, as well as confiscating 45,000 autos, and 1,300 boats used to transport liquor. And these were only the ones they caught!

What was bonanza to some became economic ruin to others. The farming industry lost a million jobs and over $20

million in investment capital in the first five years. However, corn syrup boomed from 150 million to over 900 million gallons annually because it was a major ingredient in bathtub gin. Physicians sympathetically prescribed 11 million bottles of therapeutic spirits annually. In the one year of 1929, 158,000 pounds of hops were sold as kitchen spice. Al Capone's income from beer sales alone came to $100 million during the prohibition years.

The Federal treasury suffered as well, losing over $500 million in taxes on the booze bought and sold by previously law-abiding citizens. Fifteen thousand Americans were crippled or killed by tainted liquor. The poor, as always, drank the dregs. Rich Americans continued to purchase their favorite imported Scotch and gin, smuggled in from Canada.

THE END OF AN ERA

Eventually, the same type of indignation that impelled the original temperance forces worked on the people of rational goodwill in our nation. Very prominent industrial and social leaders of the stature of the DuPonts and Elihu Root began to organize the political movement for liquor reform. A curious irony emerged when women took the prominent role in the return to sanity. Pauline Sabine was, at the time, sitting on the National Republican Committee as its first female member. In May of 1929, she helped form the Woman's Organization for National Prohibition Reform, a group that became known as the Sabine Women and eventually grew to over one million in strength. Having had a profound education in techniques of

Highlights

- Prohibition was as much a battle for control of political life between the urban and rural forces in America as it was a temperance movement.
- Prohibition in America and elsewhere failed. It helped foment the Great Depression in America and the collapse of the western economies.
- The control of the distribution of illegal liquor during the prohibition years provided a firm economic foundation for the crime network now known as the Mafia.

- The greatest irony about prohibition lies in its failure to reduce consumption below the temperate levels achieved as early as 1860. Then and now, Americans consume around two gallons of distilled spirits per year.
- The greatest accomplishment of the prohibition years was the emergence of the American woman as an effective national political entity.

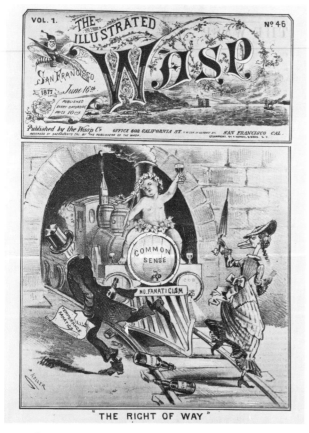

Unfortunately the "common sense" way espoused by the Illustrated Wasp *in 1877 was little observed. The cherubic Bacchus with his moderate amount of wine could have saved the country a great deal of needless suffering.*

national organization by observing those who fought *for* prohibition, women secured their right to vote with the 19th Amendment. From these two successes, women went on to champion repeal of Prohibition, a remarkably enlightened progression.

Both Franklin Roosevelt and Herbert Hoover, with some ambivalence, supported repeal during the 1932 campaign. The electorate chose the former to ink the death of Prohibition into the history books on 5 December 1933. The fight did not end then, however, and perhaps it never will. This hopscotching through the history of alcoholic consumption has been intended as a lesson in prudence. The argument will recur in each era because of the devilish forces of excess and because of those who seek to exorcise the spirit by radical surgery. That each individual has to come to terms with alcoholic spirits by learning moderation, the true temperance, is clear from Morris Chafetz's comments (1976) on the need to stress a rational, educated approach:

> And how preoccupied we are. We spend a good deal of time talking about drinking, thinking about it, worrying about it, looking forward to it. Look at the advertisements for alcohol. The message usually seems to be that you work your tail off all day long so that you can get to that beer or that drink. Alcohol is portrayed not as a small pleasure but as one of life's great rewards. This preoccupation itself can be called a problem with drinking. I don't think you have to drink to be an alcoholic. I think Carry Nation was an alcoholic—a nondrinking alcoholic. She couldn't take care of her daughter, couldn't live with her husband because she was so obsessed with the Demon Rum. Didn't she have an alcoholic problem?

Let us conclude this lesson with Dr. Chafetz's gentle wisdom—wisdom which can, indeed, make us truly a nation of temperate drinkers—like the Italians or the Jews.

There are, indeed, risks in taking alcohol, and my years of study in the field have made me acutely aware of them. But anything that affects human beings has a potential for harm. In excess, even oxygen and water, those essentials of life, can kill. Life itself is a risk, and I suspect the only sure way to be completely safe is to be dead. . . . You must make your own decision about the risk taking. You may decide not to drink at all. But if you choose to drink and you have made the decision armed with facts and free of guilt, you can . . . take more good than harm from alcohol.

Suggested Readings

Brown, John Hull. *Early American Beverages*. Rutland, Vt.: Charles E. Tuttle Co. Inc., 1966.
> A compendium of early drinking recipes and the taverns which served them.

Greeley, Andrew; McCready, William C.; and Thiesen, Gary. *Ethnic Drinking Subcultures*. New York: Praeger Publishers, 1979.
> Results of a survey on ethnic drinking.

Harrison, Brian. *Drink and the Victorians: The Temperance Question in England*, 1815–1872. London: Faber and Faber Ltd., 1971.
> Temperance in England from 1815 to 1872.

Kobler, John. *Ardent Spirits, The Rise and Fall of Prohibition*. Greenwich, Conn.: Fawcett Books, 1973.
> A journalistic approach to the dry years.

Lender, Mark Edward, and Martin, James Kirby. *Drinking in America: A History*. New York: The Free Press, 1982.
> A reasoned treatise on the continuity and ambiguity of Americans and their drinking proclivities.

Longmate, Norman. *The Waterdrinkers, A History of Temperance*. London: Hamish Hamilton, Ltd., 1968.
> One hundred years of temperance activity in England.

Mead, William Edward. *The English Medieval Feast*. Boston: Houghton Mifflin Co., 1931.
> A raucous recounting of excess in the Dark Ages.

Ross, James Bruce, and McLaughlin, Mary Martin, eds. *The Portable Medieval Reader*. New York: The Viking Press, 1949.
> The mood of the times at the birth of distillation of liquors.

Seltman, Charles. *Wine in the Ancient World*. Boston: Routledge and Kegan Paul, 1957.
> A captivating study of Greek and Roman drinking.

Sinclair, Andrew. *Era of Excess: A Social History of the Prohibition Movement*. New York: Harper & Row Publishers, Inc., 1964.
> A scholarly and reasoned treatment of the dry years and who caused them.

Tannahill, Reay. *Food in History*. New York: Stein and Day Publishers, 1973.
> The flavor of everyday life in eating and drinking habits.

Timberlake, James H. *Prohibition and the Progressive Movement, 1900–1920*. Cambridge: Harvard University Press, 1963.
> An engaging treatise on the political aspects of prohibition.

Ford's Chronology of Alcohol in History

It is an important and well-established fact that historians generally ignore drug use and misuse. This historical omission originates deep in the past, probably arising from some unconscious tendency to look the other way when it comes to acknowledging mankind's use of mind-altering substances, alcohol predominant among them.

Drug abuse is not new or unique. In *Narcotic Plants*, Emboden quotes historian Will Durant's observation in *Life in Ancient Greece:* "No civilization has found life tolerable without . . . the things that provide at least some brief escape from reality. . . ." In *The Facts About Drug Abuse*, the authors flatly state, ". . . Americans tend to overlook the capacity for misuse of licit drugs and overestimate the misuse of illicit drugs. As a consequence, we pursue widely divergent courses, depending upon the legal status of a particular psychoactive substance."

To provide an accurate historical perspective for the discussion of alcohol that follows, here are pertinent details of our heritage with the emphasis on those little known facts that relate to alcoholic consumption. There are some real surprises about the times and types of drug use!

Prehistory and Ancient Times (to A.D. 500)

1 billion years ago	Beginnings of life
200 million years ago	Honey and grapes ferment naturally as seas recede and seed-bearing plants develop
2 million years ago	Homo erectus

Alcohol is seldom mentioned in history books, but it has affected, and been affected by, many of the events that are.
from Alcohol The Delightful Poison

We are a drug culture: from the first cup of coffee and the cigarette in the morning, through the martini before dinner, into the wines and aperitifs, and finally the tranquilizer that, despite warnings to the contrary, is popped before bedtime.
from Narcotic Plants

40,000 years ago	All modern racial types have developed
17,000 to 14,000 years ago	Some indications that wild cereals (wheat and barley) were being exploited from Sinai to Syria; pounders and mortars in existence.
15,000 years ago	Grindstones first appear (Australia)
by 12,000 years ago	Oldest known ceramic vessels (Japan)

by 10,000 years ago

Good evidence that peoples in southwest Asia began process of domesticating animals and plants; mortars, pounders, edge-ground stone tools

9000 to 8000 B.C.

Fully agricultural communities established in Syria and Palestine; sheep domesticated in Iraq; floodwater farming in Jericho; emmer wheat, two-row barley, lentils and field peas cultivated; sheep, pigs and cows domesticated in Iraq; agriculture established in Oceania, probably sugarcane, yams, bananas and pandanus; East Asia—cultivation of rice and millet; rye in Syria

7000 to 6000 B.C.

Rice, barley, buckwheat, squash, maize and millet in Japan; widespread use of pottery; beans, agave, aloe and chili peppers in Mexico; use of grinding stones; agriculture in the Sudan, Aegean, Balkans and in Anatolia all three available wheat species—emmer, durum, einkorn—and some of the first examples of domesticated six-row barley; beans, squash, cotton and gourds in the Andes where grinding stones date from about 7500 B.C.; Amerindian farming included a variety of plants, among them maguey cactus which required roasting in pits for up to five days; economy in Mesopotamia based on simple irrigation technology and growing trade in luxury goods

6000 to 5000 B.C.

Trading among Greece, Italy, southern France, North Africa, Spain, Corsica and Sardinia; religious institutions seem to have had economic functions

(collection and distribution of surplus agricultural and manufactured goods); some of the first evidence of central storage facilities in the area where Iraq, Syria and Turkey meet; wild and domesticated rice in India; finger millet in Ethiopia; rice in the southern part of China, also plowshares, grinding stones; in the north millet; use of hoes, spades and narrow necked bottles; Chinese script in the process of formation; in the central eastern lowlands wild and domesticated rice, gourds, fruits, nuts and evidence of what was perhaps a threshing floor; rye in Romania

4000 to 3000 B.C.

Bronze Age in Thailand; economy based on rice; Sumerian writing includes about 1,500 pictographic signs; mass-produced pottery suggests use of true potter's wheel and molds; ration measure suggests central economic authority; lists of, or receipts for, dairy products, wheat and barley, bread, beer, clothing, sheep and cattle; ration list shows a day's bread and beer for 50 individuals (perhaps as wages); Sumerians could choose from among 16 varieties of brews; the Papyrus of Ani refers to *hek* as a common intoxicant; sorghum, bulrush millet and six other wild grasses evidenced by pottery decoration as well as by seeds in Ethiopia; plow known in northwest Europe; first year of the Jewish calendar (3760 B.C.); pre-Harappan and Indus civilizations, the western edge of Pakistan and Delhi had plow-based agricultural system, *Eleusine coracana* (perhaps derived from *Eleusine africana*), granaries, drainage systems; at eastern sites there were at least nine crops—rice, barley (2 varieties), wheat (3 varieties), cotton, sesame, date palm, peas, watermelon and brassica; religious beliefs; Indus script of 400 as yet undeciphered signs

3000 to 1000 B.C.

Hops were utilized to flavor brews; in Eastern Mediterranean olive and grape were brought widely into civilization; agriculture clearly the basis of subsistence in the Andes; Greeks and Egyptians dominate western culture; grape culture spreads into Italy, southern France and Spain through trade; wines made from a wide variety of sugar sources; Mongols make *kumiss*

from fermented mare's milk, *kephir* from milk of the camel and *airin* from that of the yak; Europeans make *pior* (barley beer), Polynesians *kavi* (fruit wine), Indians *arrak* (palm toddy), South Americans *pulque* (maguey cactus beer) and Incas *chicha;* squash, grapes, other berries and nuts in American Midwest; period of the Great Flood and it is written that Noah landed the ark at Mount Ararat, one of the highest in the Caucasus Mountains, and that he cultivated plants and made wines (2800 B.C.); Egyptians change from their 360 day calendar based on the sun and moon to their 365 day calendar (2772 B.C.); first libraries in Egypt; Hsai dynasty in China introduces the tithe system with annual distribution of fields; first legal system—Code of Hammurabi, Babylonian king of the First Dynasty; nearly 300 laws covering crime, laws of inheritance, permissible fees and guidelines for medical practice, and control and distribution of alcohol, among other regulations; in the Amazon basin, large open-mouthed urns probably used as brewing vats for sweet manioc beer *(chicha);* smaller bowls used for serving the gruel-like drink; in Andean South America, use of drugs in a religious context; Moses leads Israelites from Egypt to Canaan; Phoenicians become the predominant trading power in the Mediterranean; regulations concerning sale of beer in Egypt; prohibition decreed in China

1000 to 700 B.C.	Resettlement of Assyria takes place through control of cultivable lands and promotion of agricultural prosperity (plows supplied and grain reserves accumulated); first verified date of poppies grown in Egypt; Chaldeans use water-filled cube for measuring time, weight and length; Greeks settle along coast of Spain and in southern Italy; Celts move into England; in India medicine is divorced from the priesthood; Rome is founded; second king of Rome adds two months to the calendar to total 12
700 to 500 B.C.	Greek worship of Apollo and Dionysus gains acceptance; the poem "Works and Days" by Hesiod mentions cultivation of wheat, barley and grapes; Rome is declared a republic and is later invaded by the Etruscans; tragedy by Thespis based on a hymn to Dionysus; Solon's laws promulgated in Athens; many Old Testament books written down for the first time; a Greek anatomist discovers the connection between the sensing organs and the brain; grapes taken to Marseilles, later to Burgundy, Bordeaux, and Germany
500 to 300 B.C.	Etruscan political power and civilization decline; three Roman senators sent to Athens to study Solon's laws; Hippocrates, the "father of medicine," recommends wine; Plato is born (427); viticulture important in Italy and Gaul; Gauls sack Rome and settle in northern Italy; Alexandria is the center of Greek learning (Ptolemy begins the museum and library); Aristotle writes of distilling sea water to purify it for consumption; distillation of oils and herbs quite common
300 to 200 B.C.	Successful conquests by Romans; king of Sparta put to death in 241 for attempting agrarian reform; flowering of Iberian culture under Greek and Carthaginian influence; Romans' first contact with Greek medicine through prisoners of war; Egyptians introduce leap year into their calendar; building of the Great Wall of China; invention of ox-driven water wheel for irrigation; Cato the Elder: *De agricultura;* 20 million *amphorae* arrive in Rome from Spain alone each year

200 to 100 B.C.

Beginning of Roman domination of the world; Romans use slaves in agriculture and industry:

> Diodorus records that Celtic slaves were bought for wine, a luxury commodity of which a surplus was produced in Italy and which played an important role in competition within the Celtic aristocracy. Archaeological finds of *amphorae* of first-century BC date are made throughout the area of central Gaul . . .
>
> (Sherratt, ed. 1980)

In Iran cults of Dionysus and Heracles flourish for several centuries; c. 147 huge statue of Heracles reclining, bowl in hand, beneath an arbor of vines

100 to 1 B.C.

Germanic tribe invades Gaul; Roman victories and settlements in Jerusalem, Spain, Britain, Africa, etc.; Caesar assassinated in 44; nature healing practiced by a Greek physician in Rome; first cherry trees imported from Asia Minor to Rome; death of Herod in 4; probable date of Christ's birth 4 B.C.; heavy consumption of wine by Romans

A.D. 1 to 200

Roman invasion of Britain and founding of London (43); destruction of Jerusalem (70); persecution of Christians begins; Rome reaches height of its power (117); Huns invade Afghanistan; Goths invade Asia Minor and Balkan Peninsula; after period of dynastic rulers, both China and India enter periods of division; plague weakens Roman Empire (164–180); Galen extracts juice from plants for medicinal purposes (c. 190); Franks invade Spain; Picts and Scots attack Britain; Huns invade Europe and Russia

A.D. 200 to 500

Roman legions begin to leave Britain; books begin to replace scrolls (c. 360); Visigoths invade Italy and conquer the Vandals in Spain; Angles, Jutes and Saxons drive Picts and Scots from southern England; Vandals seize north Africa from the Romans and sack Rome; Mayan civilization flowering in Mexico; c. 365 Basil of Caesarea founds monastic institutions; Patrick goes as missionary to Ireland (432); alchemists search for the elixir of life

Medieval Times (A.D. **500 to 1500**)

500 to 700

Benedict of Nursia begins western monasticism (529); Columba establishes a monastery on Iona, off the coast of Scotland and converts the Picts (he is also thought to have distilled the first Scotch whisky); Mohammed is born (570); during the Dark Ages, culture—including viticulture—preserved by monastic orders; Caliph Umar destroys library in Alexandria (641)

700 to 1000

Jābir ibn-Ḥayyān (Geber), an Arab chemist, writes of *al kohl* in *Liber Investigationes Magisteri*. He covers the process of raising aqueous vapors—distillation—to obtain a common eye cosmetic called kohl which was made from antimony; the Chinese distill spirits from rice wine; hops in beer wort used for the first time in Bavaria (750); Arab goatherd discovers coffee (850); in Arab-dominated Spain vineyards are protected and wines abound despite religious prohibitions; Vikings discover America and name it Vinland because of the profusion of wild grape vines; heroes in the Anglo-Saxon epic *Beowulf* drink ale, beer, wine and mead (c. 1000)

1000 to 1300

The oldest brewery currently in operation founded at Freising in Bavaria (1040); William, Duke of Normandy, conquers England at the Battle of Hastings (1066) and initiates aggressive wine trade with the French; the First Crusade initiated to free the Holy Land from the Moslems (1095); Crusades continue though a futile effort to defeat Moslems in the Holy Land (final defeat 1291); Lisbon Cathedral built (1147); white spirits from sweet fruit are distilled (commonly as *alcool blanc*); Henry II of England invades Ireland and finds native spirit called *usquebaugh*

1300 to 1500

Renaissance begins travel, exploration, and development in the arts, commerce, and western culture; alcohol commonly being used for medical purposes; Genghis Khan captures Peking (1214); Thomas Aquinis is born (c. 1225); apothecaries in Italy commonly produce spirits spiced and sweetened—the earliest liqueurs; Marco Polo in China (1271–1295); Arnald of Vilanova, Professor of Medicine at Montpellier, popularizes a panacea he calls *aqua vitae*—the water of life (c. 1290); for the next 400 years, it is a part of medical pharmacopoeia: "It prolongs life, clears away ill-humours, revives the heart and maintains youth." Bubonic plague begins in India (1332); the Black Death spreads over Europe (1347–1351) and common prescriptions include cordials and aqua vitae; religious ceremonies, feasts, and celebrations are popular drinking occasions, giving rise to names such as Bride-Ale for the bride, Lamb-Ale for the lambing, and Harvest-Ale; wine trade develops between Portugal and England because of English-French conflicts; Chaucer dies (1400); first licensing of French distilleries in Alsace and Armagnac (1411); island of Madeira settled by the Portuguese and developed for agriculture, including grape growing (1420); Michel Savonarale adds attar of roses to aqua vitae, creating Rosolio at Dominican monastery in Florence (1450); Germans produce grain spirits called *schnapsteufel*—the devil's drink— precurser of modern schnapps;

Leonardo da Vinci born (1452); Johann Gensfleisch, who assumed his mother's family name (Gutenberg), invents the printing press in Mainz, Germany (1453), opening the way for modern communication; Christopher Columbus leaves on first voyage to the New World and discovers Indians using tobacco for medicinal and religious purposes (1492); on his second trip (1493), Columbus takes sugar-cane from the Canary Islands and plants it in St. Croix, Virgin Islands; the widespread planting of cane eventually supports the rum trade, the first major alcoholic spirit of the Western hemisphere; monk who accompanied him is first to describe the tobacco plant; first record of tax imposed by government on Scotch whisky (1494); treaty in which Spain and Portugal agree to divide the New World between them (1494); on his third voyage, Columbus discovers natives in what is now South America making *chicha* beer by the process of masticating corn until the saliva enzymes change starch to fermentable sugars (1498)

Early Modern Times (A.D. **1500 to 1700**)

1500
to 1550

Inca citizens had labor obligations to the state which increased production of cloth and maize (and beer brewed from it) to be able to fulfill its obligations of hospitality and gifts in exchange for that labor; Scotland makes peace with England, opening whisky trade (1503); Augsburg merchant imports spices from East Indies to Europe (1506); first New World sugar mill is established in the West Indies (1508); recipe for Benedictine Liqueur is developed in 1510 but remains in private hands until 1884; first attempt to restrict practice of medicine to licensed and qualified doctors; Reformation begins when Martin Luther protests the sale of indulgences (1517); coffee in Europe for the first time; Cortes finds fermented agave beer among Aztecs and soon distills the first tequila (1519); chocolate brought to Spain from Mexico (1520); hops from Artois introduced into England and Amaretto liqueur developed in Saronno, Italy (1525); German surgeon Hieronymus Braunschweig praises use of spirits in medical practice in *Das Buch zu Destillieren;* Catherine of Medici moves to France to marry Henry II (1533) and brings Rosolio, made from roses, aniseed, fennel, dill and coriander, creating a courtly fashion of drinking liqueurs; distillation forbidden within city limits of Bordeaux because of danger of fire from vapor in the air; Spanish mining silver in Mexico

1550
to 1650

Eau-de-vie-de-cidre (or applejack) produced in Normandy (1553) and later named Calvados after town which took the name of a Spanish galleon visiting the area; first governmentally licensed brewery in the Americas in Mexico City (1554); an Aztec dictionary is published (1555); first beer produced for sale in glass bottle in Germany; John Hawkins, on his first trip to the New World, begins slave trade between Africa, West Indies and Spain (1562) and introduces sweet potatoes and tobacco into England on his return; Shakespeare is born (1564); first German cane-sugar refinery

(1573); Lucas Bols creates a commercial liqueur distillery in Amsterdam (1575); recurring outbreaks of plague throughout Europe during the entire period; Jerez wine commonly distilled to fortify and preserve sherry (1580); Dutch ships carry first "burnt wine" or brandy from Cognac, France, to England and Lowlands (1585); severe corn shortage in England (1586); Carthusian monks are given secret Chartreuse recipe by a soldier of Henry IV of France (1605); Virginia Company formed, 120 colonists go to Virginia and early grape experiments begin (1606); hop cultivation begins in America; colonists begin growing wheat in Jamestown (1618); beginning of Thirty Years' War (1618); first Negro slaves in North America arrive in Virginia (1619); pilgrims land at Plymouth Rock to replenish victuals and "beere" (1620); Governor John Winthrop makes first prohibition move at Boston in attempt to outlaw all liquor (1630); first public brewery in New Amsterdam owned by Peter Minuit (1632); apple seeds imported from England; strong liquor, games, and dancing not allowed at New England inns and taverns (1633); Kirsch and cherry brandy are popular medications during outbreak of cholera in Alsace (1634); a Massachusetts ordinance sets the maximum price for an ale quart not above a penny; the Massachusetts Bay Colony awards the first commercial brewing license in New England to Captain Robert Sedgewick (1634); Massachusetts ordinances regulate the operation of ordinaries (taverns); quinine increasingly used for medicinal purposes; first commercial distillery in the Colonies operated by William Kieft on Staten Island makes spirits from corn and rye (1640); Augier Cognac firm founded (1643) in France—oldest yet in continuous existence; Governor Winthrop reports on the arrival of 800 butts of sack on four ships (1646)

1650 to 1750

Dr. Sylvius at the University of Leiden, Holland, distills neutral aqua vitae and adds juniper berries in search of a diuretic; for western civilization this product of distillation, gin, leads to a flood of grain spirits; grape vines planted in South Africa and brandy follows within four years (1655); rum is first commercially produced in Massachusetts from West Indian molasses (1657); infamous Triangle Trade begins (rum from Massachusetts purchases slaves in New Guinea who are traded in the Indies for molasses which is brought back to Boston to make more rum); British acquire the Kieft Distillery when the Dutch surrender New Amsterdam; they rename it New York and change the spirit to rum (1664); Maryland votes to go dry (1668); William Penn makes beer commercially in Philadelphia (1665); yeast first viewed under a microscope by Dutch scientist Van Leeuwenhoek (1680); he is first to describe microscopic organism that could only have been bacterium (1683); Dom Pérignon creates champagne at the Abbey d'Hautvillers outside Épernay, France (c. 1690); De Kuyper firm founded in Amsterdam and first Curaçao made from West Indian oranges (1695); one New England orchard produces 500 hogsheads of cider annually by 1671; first "state" excise tax on liquor—Pennsylvania (1684); William Laird first makes

applejack spirit in New Jersey (1698); Methuen Treaty—England places low tax on Portuguese wines and imposes high tax on French wines (1703); Rocher Freres firm founded (1705), oldest existing liqueur distiller in France; Cassis is distilled from black currant berries and is treasured for vitamin C (1712); tea introduced into colonies but favorite nonalcoholic beverage is chocolate (1714); rum is popular in New England and beer in Middle Colonies; Martell Cognac firm founded (1715); five million gallons of legal gin produced in England (1720), longlasting aftereffect of William of Orange's "Act Encouraging Distilling of Brandy and Spirits from Corn"; within another twenty years this total had risen to 20 million gallons; Scotch and Irish farmer/distillers immigrate to Colonies because of crop failures, famines, religious persecution and taxation over a period of years; over 2 million gallons of West Indian rum imported to New England (1728); Parliament passes Molasses Act raising tariffs on molasses from non-British territories (1733); Parliament restricts the sale to English consumers of gin to minimum of two gallons and raises taxes in a futile attempt to make gin too expensive for the poor (1736); first mention of "malt spirits" in England is in George Smith's *The Complete Book of Distilling* (1738); Booth's Gin firm founded in London (1740); drunkenness prevalent in the Colonies (as early as 1735 sale of spirits was prohibited in the entire colony of Georgia); rum becomes staple on British Navy ships to avoid scurvy; America's first medical pamphlet (1745) describes treatment for lead poisoning caused by drinking rum that was distilled in lead pipes; British conquer Scots at Battle of Culloden opening the Highlands and leading to the export of malt whisky (1746); Giacomo Justerini emigrated from Italy to London and started liqueur firm (1749), making Aqua Mirobilis—firm still there selling J & B Scotch whisky

Late Modern Times (A.D. 1750–1900)

1750 to 1850   Colonists' consumption of legal (tax-paid) spirits reckoned at 8 gallons per person per year—four times modern rate (1750); Marie Brizard founds distillery in Bordeaux and makes anisette (1755); Industrial Revolution replete with cotton gins, steam-driven engines, and factory industries; when tobacco prices drop sharply in England, many Colonists begin planting corn and wheat instead; entire Harvard University class suspended for excessive drinking (1760); George Washington orders copper still from England to make and sell spirits; Parliament passes the Sugar Act adding taxes to colonial textiles (1764); wine cultivation in California by the Franciscans (1769); John Woodhouse first produces fortified wine, Marsala, later to become popular (1773); Vintage Port first made in Portugal; Declaration of Independence, written by Thomas Jefferson in Indian Queen tavern in Philadelphia, adopted by Continental Congress (1776); the cork first used as common stopper allowing wine to bottle age (1781); state liquor tax opposed in Worcester, Massachusetts, because liquor believed necessary for the morale of farm workers (1782); Dr. Benjamin Rush publishes treatise on harmful effects of alcohol (1784); the Reverend Elijah Craig supposedly creates bourbon from grain whiskey and limestone waters

(1789); life expectancy tables show that Americans live longer than Europeans; several thousand *legal* distilleries in Pennsylvania—whiskey 25 cents a gallon (1790); first federal excise tax of 20 cents to 30 cents per gallon imposed on spirits (1791); at a party given by John Hancock 200 guests are supplied by 136 punch bowls and 300 bottles of wine, plus sherry and brandy for dessert; over 2,500 legal distilleries in the United States with thousands of unlicensed secret operations (1792); President Washington sends troops to western Pennsylvania to quell Whiskey Rebellion of farmer/distillers (1794); over the next 20 years Scotch and Irish farmers push west in hopes of escaping taxes and many settle in the hills of Kentucky and distill grain spirits; after British suppression of Irish rebellion, the United Kingdom is established (1800); U.S. excise taxes on spirits are repealed (1802); importation of African slaves is prohibited (1808); the first Temperance Society organizes in Moreau, New York; 2,000 registered distilleries in Kentucky produce 2 million gallons of whiskey (1810); Peter Smirnoff opens distillery in Moscow (1818); construction of the Erie Canal (1817–1825); the Reverend Lyman Beecher forms the National Temperance Society; first United States railroad operates over short distances (1826); McCormick reaper patented (1834); Supreme Court decides that the several states can regulate their own liquor trade; first successful continuous still built in Ireland (1836); blending of full Scotch and Irish malt whiskeys with grain spirits from continuous stills becomes common practice, creating vast export potential for both spirits by the end of the century; many German brewers immigrate to America in the 1840s; Captain Sutter produces grape brandy for the California gold miners (1843); Irish immigration triples in 1847 because of potato famine in Ireland; Adolph and Edouard Cointreau establish a liqueur production firm in France (1849); gin completely devoid of sugar is produced and designated London Dry Gin; thirteen states have some form of prohibition

1850
to 1900

Madeira wines at the height of their popularity in the United States (1852); Bordeaux wines classified (1855); Pasteur proves fermentation caused by living organisms (1857) and invents pasteurization—at first for wine (1861); the Civil War (1861–1865); first federal income tax enacted (1861); the phylloxera plant louse begins to destroy the traditional European vineyards (1863); with European wines and brandies in short supply, whiskeys become popular; New York City has 750 saloons and 200,000 inhabitants (1865); Rock and Rye liqueur created in the United States from fresh fruit, sugars and whiskey (1872); Women's Christian Temperance Union founded (1874); first pasteurization of beer for shipping stability (1876); Charles Hires begins making and selling root beer (1877); eighty percent of Italian population is involved in wine production and sales (1880); in Britain sale of beer to children under 13 is forbidden (1886); Anti-Saloon League founded in Oberlin, Ohio (1893); commercial production of pasteurized milk begins (1895); Bottled in Bond Act allows delaying payment of federal excise taxes until spirits are fully aged (1897)

Contemporary Times (1900 to the Present)

1900

Two of five Americans live in urban areas and the world's alcoholic beverages are now developed in the sense that every known source of sugar has been used to make alcohol; Carry Nation becomes a symbol for the temperance movement by flinging bricks about in a Kansas saloon

1906

Drambuie Liqueur, made with Scotch whisky, is first sold (recipe in existence since at least 1746)

1909

British Commission finally defines Scotch as grain whisky ending a 50 year controversy about blending malt and grain spirits; Cognac brandy-growing areas defined by law though already established by tradition

1914–1918

The First World War; four hundred labels of Irish whiskey are available for sale in the United States (1916); U.S. purchase of the Virgin Islands ratified and Congress sends the Eighteenth Amendment to the states for ratification (1917)

1920

On January 16th prohibition becomes the law of the land

1925 to
1929

Over 60,000 churches are affiliated with the Anti-Saloon League; a police commission in New York City estimates the existence of 32,000 speakeasies, more than double the number of pre-prohibition taverns

1933

Twenty-first Amendment formally ends 13 years, 10 months and 18 days of prohibition on December 5th

1934 to
1950

Two dollar per proof gallon excise tax applied to all spirits; first beer sold in cans in the United States with over 700 commercial brewers (1935); spirits tax raised to $4 per gallon (1941); America declares war on the Axis Powers (1941); proof gallon tax raised to $6 (1942); $9 per proof gallon becomes tax rate on distilled spirits (1944); with the Moscow Mule cocktail (vodka and ginger beer), an era of light, mixing spirits comes into fashion in United States (1948)

1950 to
1983

Distilled spirit tax raised to $10.50 per proof gallon (1951); organization of Irish Distillers Ltd. to distribute all spirits made in Southern Ireland (1966); American distillers allowed to produce light whiskeys to compete with Canadian whiskies (1972); American consumption of processed sugars exceeds one hundred pounds per person annually; Gallup Poll estimates that 71 percent of American adults consume some form of alcoholic beverage (1976); Tequila sales rise to over four million cases annually (1978); eighty-six Kentucky distilleries produce 160 million gallons of spirits (1979); Vodka sales exceed 40 million cases (1980)

PART TWO

FERMENTED
BEVERAGES

Wine: A Common Heritage

*A*s the waters receded, Noah's ark settled on Mount Ararat in the Caucasus range, near the present-day borders of eastern Turkey, Armenia, and northern Iran. In Gen. 9:20–21 it is reported that "Noah began to be a husbandman, and he planted a vineyard; and he drank of the wine and was drunken. . . ." While earlier reality may be lost in antiquity, this is very early credible evidence that fruit was produced systematically. Since grape juice ferments naturally in temperate climates, it's a pretty good bet that Noah and his confreres grew the fruit as much for alcohol as for fresh food.

Several hundred miles to the south of Mount Ararat, western civilization was born where the Tigris and Euphrates rivers meet at the Persian Gulf. In this pastoral, mineral rich area, one of the early plants cultivated was the *vitis vinifera* grape vine, the ancestor of all great wines consumed today. *Vitis vinifera*—the vine that grows wine.

GRAPE GROWING: AN EARLY EXPORT

The early grape-growing and wine-making systems developed in Sumer were propagated to the neighboring Phoenicia, Egypt, on to Greece, and finally to that magnificent boot of Italy. Wine was commonly written about by 2100 B.C. Around 750 B.C., Greeks from Chalcis founded a colony in northwest Italy where the soil proved ideal for grape growing. Eventually, the Romans organized western civilization around the wine grape. By the time of Julius Caesar, about 100 years before Christ's birth, every country along the vast Mediterranean made and exchanged wines in commerce.

*W*ine is the child of sun, earth, the collaboration of art, patience, time and care, the triple communion. Firstly, with soil into which it sinks its roots, and from which it receives soul and body. Secondly, communion with ourselves. It educates our taste, training us to turn our attention inwards, frees the mind and illuminates the intelligence. Lastly, wine is a symbol and the means of a social communion. Around the table, all guests are at the same level when the cup is raised.

Paul Claudel

*N*othing more excellent or valuable than wine was ever granted by the gods to man.
Plato

It is easy to understand why the earliest cultures consumed grape wine. It was a natural gift of the Creator and a vital source of nutrients and an aid to relaxation at a time when precious little of either was to be had. Similarly, mead or honey wine was probably stumbled upon when some thirsty ancient drank what he thought was water from an abandoned beehive. A hive filled with rainwater is an efficient fermenting container for the residual honey.

The great river below Bingen-on-Rhine still carries barges filled with wine products past picturesque castles and steeply terraced vineyards.

Brewing required a little more ingenuity, but it surely was also accomplished at a very, very early date. The husks of grain contain enzymes which, under the influence of heat and water, convert the grain starches to maltose sugar. Hence the fermentation of starchy grains to brews after a germination period or even after it has been processed into maltose rich breads.

Ferments Necessary for Survival

The inclusion of natural ferments other than alcohol in man's diet was gradual but widespread. In a brief but comprehensive *Fact Book on Fermented Foods and Beverages* (1973), Beatrice Hunter details the problems that led to the discovery and development of these natural preservatives.

> In early times, man was plagued by famine. Any means he could find to conserve food when it was bountiful was a vital element of survival. . . . he learned to dry and smoke meat and fish. . . . he had no concept of why foods spoiled. . . . he discovered that meat, fish, and plant foods, when fermented, could be kept for long periods of time. Sometime during that period, man also learned that salt was sometimes a necessary agent for successful

fermentation of foods, although he had no concept of the fact that salt inhibited the development of toxin-producing microorganisms.

To this day, many peoples who exist without the benefit of refrigeration depend upon the fermentation of fish and the ubiquitous legume to be assured of enough protein for survival. The first food to be fermented was fish, an absolute essential in the Oriental diet. While the fermentation of alcohols did not play nearly so necessary a role in survival, in many primitive societies wines and brews offered what little respite there was from a grim and gritty life.

In the modern world, the grape is cultivated more extensively than any other fruit. Wine from fruit, however, lags considerably behind beer from grain in total consumption, almost in the ratio of one to three.

Wine: A Legacy of the Monks

When the mighty Roman Empire finally succumbed to the Goths around A.D. 475 and the prevailing culture collapsed into the Dark Ages, wine making and many other civilizing activities became functions of the Church. The bacchanalian rites (associated with Bacchus) that had dominated Athens, Phrygia, and Thrace had blurred and blended with time into the most

Peter Mirassou and a helper transport barrels of wine to be transferred to railroad cars, about 1913.

sacred ritual, the Holy Mass. The cathedrals in large centers of population and the monasteries of the great church communities provided for civil and judicial services as well as preserving and developing techniques of husbandry of grain and grape, as suggested by Seward in *Monks and Wine* (1979),

> The extent of monasticism's contribution to wine-growing and distilling is rarely appreciated. Monks largely saved viticulture when the Barbarian invasions destroyed the Roman Empire, and throughout the Dark Ages they alone had the security and resources to improve the quality of their vines slowly and patiently. For nearly 1,300 years almost all the biggest and the best vineyards were owned and operated by religious houses. It was the abbey of Romanee-Saint-Vivant which supplied Louis XIV's burgundy, while the largest vineyard in Burgundy, Clos de Vougeot, belonged to the Cistercians, whose fourteenth-century wall still encloses the vines. In Germany monks created hock and moselle; on the Rhine Johannisberg was the work of Benedictines and the Steinberg at Hattenheim of Cistercians.

Seward also acknowledges the vital organizational role that monks accepted in a shattered society when roads and regional commerce had been abandoned. "They provided the age's social and cultural services; dispersing charity, keeping the only hospitals and schools. . . . they had a pastoral function, providing christenings, marriages and consecrated burial ground as well as Mass and confession."

By the fifteenth century, distilled spirits and sweet liqueurs gradually emerged, first as medicines and inevitably as social drinks. Medicinal use of alcohol is recorded as early as 3500 B.C., but the original discovery of medical applications probably dates back thousands of years earlier. In early times all forms of alcohol were considered therapeutic. The father of medicine, Hippocrates, observed that "wine being a diuretic

and laxative is in many ways beneficent in acute diseases." (In Seward [1979].) It must always be kept in mind that through all the centuries of the formation of western thought, alcohol was deemed vital to *health*.

In both literature and history the nineteenth century is often called the Golden Age of Wine. In 1800, nearly 80 percent of the Italian nation was employed in some segment of the wine industry. France produced wines of incredible finesse, perhaps not matched today by our post-phylloxera vintages. Yet in those halcyon days, the technology was rough and primitive at best. Fully one quarter of all wine musts spoiled during initial fermentation. Despite thousands of years of practice in making wine, man knew little about bacteriological spoilage, and the handling, storage, and shipping practices fell far short of the skills developed in ancient Rome.

In the second half of the tumultuous nineteenth century, the Industrial Revolution affected viticulture and wine making as well as mechanized enterprises. Pasteur's probings resulted in an explanation of fermentation from which the science of biochemistry grew. At the same time industrial engineers produced the mechanical tools, crushers, pumps, filters, and, bless the day, corked bottles which restored the hermetic aging practices of Greece and Rome.

W ine cheers the sad, revives the old, inspires the young, makes weariness forget his toil, and fear her danger, opens a new world, when this, the present, palls.
> ***Lord Byron***

GRAPE SPECIES

The signal accomplishment of Bacchus was inspiring industrious Romans to select the most promising strains from among the thousands of wild grape vines. Patient cultivation brought out the qualities which we revere today in individually distinctive grape varietals that were perfectly mated to disparate climates and soils.

Among the profusion of berries, the vinifera grape is uncompromising in its many needs—a temperate climate, abundant sunshine but not searing heat, at least six months of 50° weather for maturation, and, for the very best wines, cool evenings. Although this variety of berry will survive in marginal conditions, all of the above are necessary to produce the truly great wines of the world.

With some variations, viticulture areas girdle the earth like a giant belt between the parameters of thirty degrees to fifty degrees north latitude, and thirty degrees to forty degrees

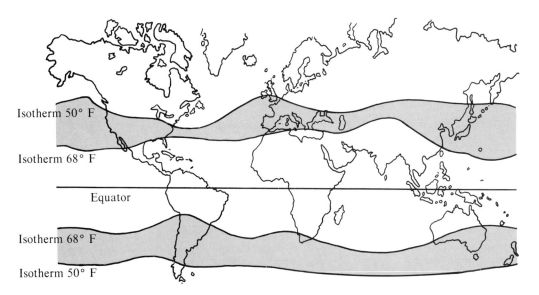

Figure 6.1 *The natural weather zones compatible with the development of vitis vinifera.*

south latitude. Within this belt lies the great basin of the Mediterranean where it all began, the incomparably beautiful Mendoza in the central part of the Argentine, southern Russia, Australia, and sunny California (see fig. 6.1).

Grapes belong to a vast botanical family called *vitaceae*. The genus *vitis* contains many species, but among these it is the *vinifera* that dominates wine making. The grapes were profuse throughout Europe before the ice-age floes which pushed the vines southward to the Mediterranean basin. Probably all known grape types that will survive in colder regions have been put to the test of fermentation and have been measured against the vinifera. Most have been found wanting in flavor intensity and complexity. However, it is patently unfair to measure these promising and often experimental wines against the best and noblest vintages from Europe and California. A fairer measure would be to blind taste the fine wines of the American east and other areas against the lesser wines from the other traditional growing areas. There is no reason to apologize for the very fine wines which are produced in the many states which lie outside of the natural vinifera habitats.

But, it is a fact that since early Colonial times, the search has gone forward to develop the style and grace of European wines from grapevines which can withstand the short growing seasons and the heavy winter weather. In his authoritative text, *Grapes Into Wine* (1981), Philip Wagner tells of the breakthrough in this quest occasioned by Ephraim Bull in 1843 when he developed the hardy, heavy-bearing Concord:

> Persons with some background in botany had long
> since come to realize that the cultivated native grapes

were in fact accidental hybrids . . . What did matter was that the possibility of creating entirely new sorts of grapes by the hand of man was dramatically advertised and instantly seized upon. The grape is so malleable genetically that the possibilities are endless. Hybridizing the grape is indeed a little bit like playing God and in the mid-nineteenth century it became a lifelong vocation for some and a sort of gentleman's hobby for many more.

Wagner also points out the considerable resistance of some commercial interests in France to the development of hybrids. Often it was the independent researcher who led the way to the development of crosses between the traditional vinifera and the native American vines.

As many as 100 wineries produce commercial wines today from dozens of hybrid grapes to the obvious satisfaction of their many thousands of customers. In addition to these newer producers, many of the Eastern wineries continue to make red wines from the traditional grapes such as Concords and Muscadines and white wines from Catawba, Delaware, Dutchess, Elvira and Noah.

The new hybrids often carry the names of their hybridizers, and others have gained common names in commercial use. Many have romantic French connotations such as Baco Noir, Ravat Noir, Chancellor, Marechal Foch, Verdelet and Rayon d'Or. This tendency to French appellations comes naturally, since the French have been most active in hybridizing research and now produce hundreds of thousands of gallons of

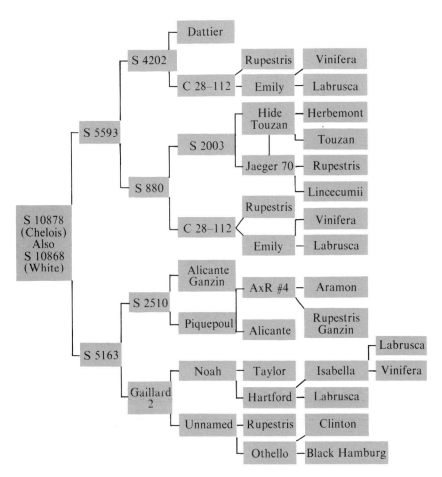

Figure 6.2 *The enormous complexity of hybridizing is shown in this family tree prepared by Dr. John McGrew who says even this reconstruction must be taken with a grain or two of salt. However, it does demonstrate the crossings of labrusca and the resulting hybrids with vinifera.*

common wine from their new hybrids. The point of importance is that wine grape growers have constantly extended the horizons of an art and science that had originated quite accidentally in nature as precious pollen of many varieties of grapes spread indiscriminantly on the breezes of fortune. Over thousands of years of natural evolution, the best of the vinifera developed. We will see what research and determination can do to catch up with Mother Nature.

THE HYBRIDS

While there is always some chance hybridization through airborne pollination of grape plants from field to field, variety to variety, deliberate hybridization is an incredibly slow and complicated undertaking. The traditional method is to pollinate the flowers of one variety with microspores from another so that the seeds bear the characteristics of both parents. Only about 25 percent of the plants from these seeds are put to vineyards to fruit. Cuttings from rootings of the successful plants are propagated and crossed again and again, in the search for an elusive new wine.

Since hundreds of thousands of acres had been destroyed by the phylloxera, the French imported literally millions of cuttings from the United States, including all three native families—the riparia, rupestris, and the labrusca—for rootstock resistant to the phylloxera. Also included were the Isabella, Clinton, Othello, and Noah—all American hybrids. By 1929, there were a half-million acres of hybrids in France, and the total rose to over one million acres in 1958 but has since declined steadily to the present 600,000 acres.

Wine grape cultivation in the Midwest and East of the United States includes at least twenty-three French hybrids, twenty-two native American varieties, and at least twelve viniferas. Grape experimentation is moving so fast that exact counts are impossible. About one-third of the wineries outside the West Coast produce hybrid wines with most concentrated in southern Ohio, Indiana, and the remaining midwestern states.

Some crossing of vinifera in California has produced commercial varieties such as the Ruby Cabernet from a cross of Carignane and Cabernet Sauvignon and the popular Emerald Riesling from a cross of White Riesling and Muscadelle. However, the majority of commercial hybrids are French in origin.

The new boom in boutique wineries reaches across the nation as represented by the charming wineries of the Lawlor family in McGregor, Iowa, and La Crosse, Wisconsin. The Christina label is named for enologist daughter Chris, who produces a range of varieties made from native grapes from Missouri hybrids from Lake Erie, as well as fruit varieties, including cranberry apple.

Today, France has over 600,000 acres of hybrids, nearly double the entire California grape plantings of vinifera wine varieties. In the eastern United States, there are nearly as many hybrids in cultivation as native American grape stocks. France developed the hybrids partially due to the high cost of grafting on phylloxera-free rootstocks after the plague. The hybrids also proved resistant to some traditional diseases such as black rot.

More than sixty wineries in the United States today offer hybrid wines for sale, primarily in the newer planting areas of the East such as Ohio, Texas, Missouri, Indiana, and Michigan. The older wine grape growing areas on the eastern seaboard remain heavily planted in Concord and other American varieties and in experimental plantings of vinifera.

VITICULTURE REGIONS

Wine making was the first, and still remains a primary, source of alcohol. Wine and food are symbiotic in culture. There is no other alcohol (and few foods) receiving so much adulation from such people as the weekly wine columnist to the literally hundreds of writers of both learned and frivolous books on the subject.

I prefer to think of American wine enterprise in terms of three distinct viticultural zones. Such a division provides both perspective and appreciation for the adventurous and really challenging experiments that have been undertaken in this far-flung enterprise. Areas must be judged according to their own merits and widely differing potentials.

The first and, by far, most important viticultural zone is California which dominates American wine making. A second viticultural area is the sliver of land on the West Coast running

from Monterrey, Mexico—bypassing California—to the Okanagan Valley in Eastern British Columbia. Most growers in these areas use vinifera for wine grapes, but the cultivation and wine-making techniques are sufficiently distinct from those of California for the two to be considered different zones. In addition, many British Columbia growers are converting from hybrid and native grapes to the European grape. The third area on my personal viticultural map involves the other states of the Union and Canadian provinces east of the Rockies—from Texas to New York and from Florida to Ontario. Before considering grape growing and wine making in general, it will be profitable to look briefly at the development of procedures in these three areas.

Wines of the East

The largest geographic area includes forty-seven states and small pockets of Eastern Canada. Wine grape growing is experiencing a widespread resurgence all over this vast nation. Only a few states today are without winery licenses. While New York, with over 100,000 tons annually, and both Pennsylvania and Michigan, above 30,000 tons, dominate production east of the Rockies, steady increases in production will occur in dozens of states with hospitable climates for wine grape production. In the West, Washington is the only state other than California that matures over 100,000 tons of wine grapes annually. In the East, native American grapes and hybrids dominate the plantings. However, in each state and province from Texas to Ontario, one can find Chenin Blanc, Johannisberg Riesling, or perhaps Ruby Cabernet along with the Concords, the Seyval Blanc, Aurore, Baco Noir, and other hybrids.

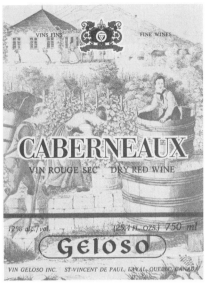

One of the more enterprising wineries in Canada is Vin Geloso, Inc. A native of Italy, Mr. Geloso returns each year at harvest to select personally grapes to be shipped to Quebec to become wines of the most imaginative appellations such as Entre Deux Poissons— *Between Two Fish and Beausoleil—Good Sunshine. They call these vintages Quebetalian!*

As early as A.D. 1000, Leif Ericson reported a profusion of grapes on the islands of the Atlantic and the shores of North America, probably in the area we know as Nova Scotia. For centuries Norse literature referred to these lands as Vinland. Similarly, in a report to his superiors in 1636, the Jesuit explorer Pere Le Jeune commented, "In some places there are many wild vines loaded with grapes; some have made wine of them; through curiosity I tasted it and it seemed very good." Historical notes point to many thousands of efforts by pioneers from all nations to establish wine industries in the new countries similar to those in the old. Both the trying and the failing are heavily documented in the early period. The native grapes simply produced good fruit but lesser wines.

Lord Delaware decreed in 1619 that every householder in his colony would henceforth maintain ten vines specifically for the production of wines. In 1623, another decree mandated that all plantations cultivate two acres of mulberry trees and grape vines, the fruits of which were to be vinted. However, by

Healthy vinifera in the fan arrangement in Ontario, Canada. The vines are developed in several shoots that separate at the ground level so that they can be laid down and covered in winter.

1624, the Southern plantations had all but abandoned efforts to grow the imported vinifera grape species which had succumbed to nematodes, to the then unidentified phylloxera, or to the various native fungi that ravaged the delicate vinifera plantings brought from Europe. Sporadic attempts to grow vinifera along the eastern seaboard ended in abysmal failure; while the native grapes produced good fruit, the wines were for home use, unsatisfactory for commerce.

The beginnings of the modern era of east coast wine making were the experiments of Ephraim Bull which eventually led to the species named for the town in which he did his work. To this day, the Concord dominates plantings in the East. Some seventy years before Bull's pioneering work, the vinifera Mission grape had entered California through the efforts of the Franciscan Fathers in their famous Missions. While the vinifera was finding a new home in the West, literally thousands of crossings, both planned and accidental, were providing eastern growers the opportunity to produce a more satisfactory drinking wine.

The final great surge in a patient and ongoing search occurred in the last years of the nineteenth century. By that time, French vignerons were using phylloxera-resistant native American rootstock to grow the traditional vinifera grapes in all vineyards. French growers also began to cross American grapes with the vinifera hoping to produce a higher yield with some traditional wine taste characteristics. Thus began a new era for hybrids.

Vinifera in the East

The new era in vinifera cultivation in the East began after the Second World War. The first quarter of this century had seen the adaptation of the hybrids from France which were sturdy enough to withstand the winters and were thought to have some of the desirable varietal characteristics of the vinifera.

Pioneers in this era were Philip Wagner of Richmond, Maryland; Grayton H. Taylor of the Taylor Wine Company

and Charles Fournier of Gold Seal, both in upper New York state; and Aldhemar de Chaunac of Brights Winery in Ontario. By 1951, Brights had in cultivation ten acres of Chardonnay. About this time a volatile and determined emigrant winemaker from Russia, Dr. Konstantin Frank, was hired by Gold Seal for the sole purpose of developing the vinifera and its wines. His persistence led to the development of more than sixty varieties of vinifera on nearly as many different American rootstocks and the production of many commercial vinifera wines by the 1960s.

Generally the plantings in the colder climates of the Northeast are situated in relatively frost-free areas such as the fringes of the Finger Lakes, microclimates along the Hudson River, the Atlantic Coast and the southern shores of Lakes Erie and Ontario. Further south, where frost is not of consequence, plantings can occur away from the warming water. Also in the South there are considerable plantings of the native rotundifolia which has produced consistently fine wines since the sixteenth century. Today major wineries operate in Arkansas, Georgia, Michigan, New York, Missouri, New Jersey, and Ohio.

The debate continues concerning the unusual flavors of native American grape wine, flavors which have traditionally been thought to be imparted by a chemical in the skins called methyl anthranilate; now, however, there is even some controversy about the chemical. The flavor, a reputed "foxiness," is musklike and, like all flavors, is far from constant. Cattell and Miller comment on the difficulty of knowing how the term "foxiness" is being used:

> For example, looking at five well known labrusca
> varieties, modern researchers point out that Catawba
> and Delaware are almost never foxy, whereas Niagara
> is always foxy; Concord is seldom foxy, whereas Ives is
> often foxy. Among the muscadines, the Scuppernongs
> are frequently foxy. Unfortunately, "foxy" has come
> to be a much misused term that is sometimes
> erroneously used to cover not only all of the native
> American grapes, but the French hybrids of the East
> as well. (1980)

Many American native grapes are harvested early and cold pressed to reduce the foxiness. Four factors can moderate the labrusca anthranilate residual flavor: heat, sweetness, oxidation, and age. Heavy concentrations of sugar modify the foxiness, and, for this reason alone, the native grapes have been developed predominantly as sweet wines. The new fermenting technique of carbonic maceration offers new hope for elimination of these off flavors since the pesky anthranilate flavor seems to dissipate under the pressure involved in this style of fermentation.

Winterkill

The most severe problem with vinifera grape vines grown outside of the warm climates is winterkill. Vines can often withstand one freezing and thawing, depending upon the amount of moisture that solidifies into ice within the vine roots and trunks. However, this stress can be intolerable when the cycle of freezing and thawing is repeated several times during the winter. Winds can also be damaging when they dry out the dormant vines above ground. Since the days above 50° F available in such areas as Ontario and upstate New York are often at the minimums needed to mature the fruit, the early ripening varieties fare better (see table 6.1).

While vine stress and disease most certainly are not limited to areas outside California, these marginal vinifera growing areas suffer substantially more wood, and subsequent fruit, damage. Hybrids also suffer from winter injury more than American varieties. The choice of planting areas is critical in that the correct ambient air temperature and appropriate soil drainage are both essential to healthy vinifera. Poorly drained clay soils located in predominantly wind-exposed areas will, during dormancy, invite dehydration above the ground and excessive moisture-freeze damage below. Those areas of the East that lack adequate and lasting snow cover of more than six inches invite severe root cracking as the temperatures rise and fall through winter. Another problem in all fruit production is the tendency to overcrop. The orchardist anxious to meet the growing demand for precious vinifera fruit fails to prune adequately, creating fatigue and winter damage in the wood. In the coldest areas, the vinifera must be severely pruned and broadly trellised to expose the leaves to the maximum amount of sun in adjustment to the shorter growing seasons.

However, these problems are not insoluble. Chinese grape specialists recently reported that a vinifera called *Vitis Amuensis* is thriving on the Siberian border where winters plunge to 58 below. The Russians have for years propagated vinifera in areas with severe winters by careful pruning, winter soil covering of plants, and chemical and irrigation treatment, as well as careful breeding.

While the experimentation goes forward with native vines, hybrids and new vinifera strains outside California, it is well to regard the comments of pioneer hybridizer Philip Wagner in the March 1979 issue of *Wines and Vines.*

> I found that the 13 most popular hybrids in France occupy 487,000 acres . . . my figures for all the true wine grapes in California is 289,000 acres . . .
> Putting aside quality comparisons, this means that the French drink at least as much Baco Noir as they do Cabernet—more, as a matter of fact, since a high proportion of the wines containing Cabernet is not drunk at home but exported.

The West Coast Excluding California

While certainly not a viticultural zone in the strict sense of the term, because of the myriad growing microclimates, there is a continuity in viticulture and wine making along the range of mountains that form the West Coast. Of course, Mexico provided access for the Spanish friars who boldly thrust Mother Church and vinifera plantings to northern California. Today Mexico has about one-third as much wine grape acreage as

TABLE 6.1 Vinifera and Hybrid Plantings in the Eastern United States

	Whites	**Reds**
Hybrids	Seyval Blanc	Foch
	Chancellor	Aurore
	De Chaunac	
Viniferas	Chardonnay	Aligote
	Gewürztraminer	Cabernet Sauvignon
	Johannisberg Riesling	Gamay Beaujolais
	Pinot Gris	Merlot
	Sémillon	Pinot Noir

(A)

(B)

Successful vineyards are not strangers to snowpacks. Here are the terraced vines under heavy drifts in the High Penedes of Torres Vineyards in Spain (A) and the Wollersheim vineyard in Wisconsin (B). December days above 50°F can cause a calamity by activating the sap during a normally dormant period. A six-inch snow cover protects the root structure from hard freezing.

Pinot Noir snuggling up to the mountains of western Oregon? A Pinot Noir directly on its own roots, without aid of pesticide, herbicide or fertilizer? Yes, a Pinot Noir that was awarded third place in the Olympiad in Paris in 1979, a scant few points behind the famous Chambolle-Musigny. David Lett's Eyrie Vineyards is representative of the potential of many microclimates around the nation, particularly on the western coast.

Innovative technical advances abound in the new vineyards in the Pacific northwest as pictured in these shots of the magnificent Chateau Ste. Michelle Winery and of bilateral cordon in the vineyards. There are 725 vines per acre with steel stakes at every other vine supporting a three-wire, T-type trellis. The overhead center point circular sprinkling system utilized in other eastern Washington agriculture delivers the thirty inches of irrigation water plus applications of nitrogen and sulfur.

California, and a steadily increasing consumption similar to that of the United States. In the northernmost tip of grape growing country, the Okanagan in British Columbia, the vinifera promise lies some years ahead, but native grapes and hybrids abound. In between, but particularly in Washington and Oregon and now in Idaho, there exists a thriving, experimental and immensely confident vinifera industry.

Washington State's annual production of Concord grapes for juice now nears 200,000 tons, with higher yields per acre than the Eastern states. Small growing pockets in Oregon and northern Idaho, not to mention the Yakima Valley and its environs in eastern Washington, produce classic reds and whites of substantial finesse when compared to the wines of other growing areas.

The desertlike expanses in the central portion of Washington State offer both sun and soil as well as ample water as accessible as the water tap. With only ten inches of rainfall per year, the area is watered by a highly sophisticated irrigation system that utilizes the huge Columbia River. In a 1981 paper published in the American Chemical Society Symposium Series, enologist Joel Klein predicted cultivation of up to 20,000 acres of vinifera by the end of the century and 200,000 acres in future years. That's about half of the current California wine grape plantings.

The technical problems are preparation of vines for winter hardiness and the production of grapes with unusually high levels of both sugar and acid. Every decade or so the winters mimic the severity of the East Coast winters, which places great stress on new vines. It may be surprising, but there are nearly two hours more of sunshine per day than in California which contributes to the high sugars and acids. However, highly sophisticated researchers from Washington State University and a stream of California consultants are meeting these challenges both in the field and in the winery.

Oregon and Idaho also have substantial areas hospitable to the vinifera and between them offer a minimum of 50,000 to 75,000 acres for future supplies of fine vinifera wines. The white varieties—Johannisberg Riesling, Gewürztraminer, and Chardonnay—fare extremely well, as do Sémillon and Chenin Blanc. The Pinot Noir seems to thrive particularly in Oregon and credible Cabernet Sauvignon vintages have been produced by a number of Northwest vintners. Another signal advantage is the absence of the phylloxera from the Northwest, permitting direct plantings from cuttings and earlier commercial crops than possible from grafted vineyards in California.

Vinifera in California

While much can be expected in future years from the mushrooming wine industry across the nation, for many years it will continue to be dominated by California, its vinifera grapes, and its 540 wineries. Nearly 86 percent of all American wines consumed in the States originate in California with another 5 percent from New York and the remainder from various states. While practices vary because of such stark contrasts as growing vinifera in the scorching Vinho Verdes in Portugal and growing it in the relative cool of the upper Rhine, what follows in the remainder of this section are descriptions of the viticulture and enology of California as generally typical of this species.

In addition to its preference for warmer climes, other features distinguish the vinifera. It is deciduous; that is, the foliage falls annually. The vine is hermaphroditic, self-pollinating, and is normally propagated by cuttings. This fact alone has facilitated its journey to hundreds of hospitable growing areas girdling the globe.

The vinifera possesses a very low tolerance to some pests, diseases, and climatic disturbances, as all the pioneer viticulturists discovered in America. Despite this sensitivity, it thrives in soils suitable for few other growing things. It disdains the attention required of many other fruits, often developing best under a little stress, with little water and fairly intense heat. The vine taproot will often extend as deep as thirty feet in search of moisture and the mineral rich treasures of that strata—including boron, zinc, cobalt, copper, iodine, manganese, molybdenum, and nickel—which creates the complexity of its fruit and wines.

Chalk, limestone, slate, and gravelly loam are desirable hosts, preferably on deep slopes which provide a natural drain for excess moisture. Wet feet are a detriment to the vine. It is for this reason that one sees so many hillside vineyards. Gravel soils, in addition to facilitating deep root development, reflect

Rugged pioneer in a pioneering time, Pierre Mirassou, flanked by his two brothers-in-law about 1880, foresaw a great wine future for California.

the sun during the day and retain some precious heat during cold nights. Yet those cold nights are essential and are the reason all great vineyards lie on the banks of river systems or near the cooling ocean breezes. In the scorching interior plains and valleys, grape skins dry out, losing their resilience. The vital acids that develop fruit tartness tend to respire from the porous skins and both the fruit and resulting wines are fat and flabby. The large tonnage producers of common wines of the world are found in the steaming heat of the Midi of southern France, in northern Africa, and in the vast San Joaquin Valley in California.

Rabbits love to eat the tender shoots of young vines, and deer feed happily on the mature plants. Starlings, linnets, and other birds hit the vineyards, with the uncanny timing of nature, about the same time as the harvesters, and with a good deal more mobility. Probably 10 percent of the crop is lost to these feathered friends. Birds can devastate a vineyard in minutes. Anxious growers utilize netting and noise guns, and silently curse their fate. Before cultivation a new area is studied over several years and a record made of the temperatures each day during the growing season, about 180 days. Since a minimum of 50°F is required to move the plant to life, every degree above that minimum is recorded as a unit of heat. If, in a particular region, the average temperature is recorded as 70°F during the season, it is said to have 20 units. Multiply the units

(A)

(B)

The towering spires of church buildings are found in vineyards throughout the world. Pictured here are the Spanish style Christian Brothers Novitiate in the Mayacama Mountains above Napa, California (A) and the majestic Serbian monastery at Oplenac, Yugoslavia (B).

TABLE 6.2 Heat Summation Regions of California

Region	Location	Days
I	Santa Rosa, Napa	Less than 2,500
II	Mid Napa Valley, Sonoma Valley	2,501 to 3,000
III	North Napa Valley, Livermore	3,001 to 3,500
IV	Lodi, Ukiah	3,501 to 4,000
V	San Joaquin Valley	4,001 and above

TABLE 6.3 Soil Temperatures of California (At depths of 50 cm)

Type	Temperature
Frigid	Less than 47°F (no grapes can grow)
Mesic	47–59°F (marginal grape growing)
Thermic	59–72°F (80% of grape growing)
Hyperthermic	72°F (bulk and dessert table grapes)

TABLE 6.4 World Wine Production (Hectolitres)

Country	1981	1980
Italy	84.0	84.3
France	69.6	84.1
Spain	42.4	48.2
U.S.S.R.	31.0	29.4
Argentina	21.6	23.3
U.S.	18.4	16.5
Portugal	10.5	11.5
Romania	6.5	8.9
W. Germany	4.9	8.7
Yugoslavia	8.0	6.7
WORLD TOTAL	344.6	370.6

Source: Adapted from UNFAO. *Wine, Current Situation 1981–82* (April, 1982), 2.

times the 180 day season, and the result is a total of 3,600 *degree days* for the growing area. To put that into perspective, a minimum of 1,700 degree days is required to grow grapes and the maximum range is 5,200 degree days. California has the full range of degree days (see tables 6.2 and 6.3).

Even within famous wine growing regions, the degree day summations vary considerably. For example, in the relative cool of the Carneros region and the lower Napa Valley, along the Rhine river in Germany, and in the chilly Champagne district in northern France, some of the world's finest wines are produced at 2,500 degree days or less. In contrast, the 4,000 degree days near Fresno produce the dessert, brandy, and inexpensive bulk wine grapes like those of southern Spain, Algeria, and the Midi in France.

There are but 24,000 acres of grapes in the Napa Valley, and the Champagne area in France is limited to a mere 54,000 acres. Contrast these gem-like regions to 400,000 plus acres of grapes in the San Joaquin Valley in California, or the vast Languedoc of hot southern France, composed of a million plus grape acres, yielding nearly 5 percent of total world production.

Grape plantings worldwide are estimated at approximately 24 million acres from which some 60 million tons are harvested. This produces about 8 billion gallons of wine each year.

Half of the entire world production originates in Italy, France, and Spain (see table 6.4). Nearly all farmers, of whatever type, in these countries reserve some space for the wine grape, either for home consumption or for commerce.

Frank Leslie's 1884 wood-block print, A California Vineyard, *shows the role of the Chinese in early California grape harvesting.*

WORLD WINE PRODUCTION

Half of the world's production of wine grapes occurs in the European Economic Community nations, posing special challenges for internal commerce in those tightly grouped nations. Russia, on the other hand, has shown dramatic gains in wine consumption because of increased acreage in recent years as the government encourages production and consumption of lighter beverage alcohols. Much of the lower class wines from these heavy yields are being converted to brandy and other commercial alcohol products. The nearly 100 million gallons imported by the United States seems destined to increase if European overproduction continues. Only in the aperitif and dessert categories are American imports of European wines slowing.

Since most of the traditional wine-imbibing nations are at the saturation level for consumption, with France, Italy, and Spain now dropping way below their traditional 30 gallons per capita, the natural target for this abundance of liquid sunshine is the affluent American market with consumption barely over 2 gallons per person. The industry in the States is fledgling at best and hesitant of massive expansion in an era of super-inflated real estate.

In both Italy and France, the greatest wine-consuming nations, there has been a gradual decline in per capita consumption since 1970, the first year of the Common Market. Italy has dropped from 111 liters per person to 90 in one recent year alone! France fell from a massive 141 liters per person in 1956 to 96 liters in 1980. In contrast, the non-producing countries and those with modest internal wine productions seem to

TABLE 6.5 Imports of Table Wine to the United States

Country	1960 (%)	1981 (%)	1981 (Gal.)
Italy	35.1	59.6	59,859,900
France	37.2	12.5	15,053,600
Germany	16.4	12.8	13,034,000
Portugal	2.1	6.2	5,366,400
Spain	2.8	5.3	3,979,800
Greece	1.6	1.2	570,700

Source: IMPACT (15 April 1982), 9.
Note: All shipments 1981: 100,828,000 gallons

TABLE 6.6 Top Markets for United States Wine Export (Thousands of Gallons)

Rank	Country	First Half 1981	First Half 1982
1	Canada	2,678	2,634
2	United Kingdom	506	536
3	Japan	167	163
4	Bahamas	135	112
5	W. Germany	211	108
6	Panama	37	92
7	Colombia	172	91
8	N. Antilles	127	87
9	Venezuela	47	86
10	L.W. & W.W. Islands	81	83
	Other Countries	1,001	757
	Total—All Countries	5,161	4,750

Source: IMPACT (15 October 1982), 10.

be escalating in consumption as are the United States, Canada, Britain, Germany and, particularly, the Soviet Union because of official policy pushing wine in preference to vodka.

In the United States, the predictions are all upward. United States wine consumption jumped from 200 to over 500 million gallons over the past decade. Another doubling is anticipated by some forecasters before the end of the 1980s.

The trend over the past ten years, revealed by figures given in Marvin Shanken's trade journal, *IMPACT,* has been a growing preference for table wines which leapt from 32 percent of the market in 1960 to over 74 percent in 1979, and should leap to a projected 91 percent in 1990. A scant twenty years ago dessert wines held 54 percent of the American wine market. There seems to be an increased awareness of wine as a beverage of moderation, the beverage that is itself a food— the choice of a new generation of consumers raised with wine in their diets.

This trend toward table wine is vital in the American market which is catching up with the international market where nine out of ten bottles of wine consumed are table wines, the food wines with less than 14 percent alcohol (see table 6.5). The association of wine with food and gracious dining has been the primary goal of the wine industry since the Second World War.

American producers strenuously object to the foreign duties placed on their wines. Aside from American military bases abroad, Canada is the largest importer of American wine (see table 6.6). Severe import taxes are inhibiting, particularly in some European countries. By contrast, American imports of foreign produced wines are increasing at a very definite pace.

Italy rose to the top of the scale with a healthy 60 percent market share of all wines entering our nation largely due to a phenomenon called Lambrusco, a medium sweet, slightly fizzy wine from the Po Valley in the north of Italy. Very simply, it matched with the taste preferences of millions of soda-swilling Americans. Along with the Lambrusco, Rosato and Bianco have come the Soave, the Valpolicella, the Frascati, and a host of other table wines from that productive wine country.

The sugar content of Lambrusco types and many other imports, such as the popular German wines, may well be the key to the import wine boom, although many a connoisseur and wine buff would deny it. The intensely sweet Annie Greensprings, Boone's Farms, and Cold Ducks were the earlier favorites of the generation now well into drier table varieties. Italy ships well over 20 million cases of Lambrusco annually, a share of the market many a California vintner would cherish.

LARGE COMPANIES DOMINATE AMERICAN MARKETS

In many countries such as France, wine grape production involves hundreds of thousands of individual farmers and winemakers. Small cooperatives receive the harvested grapes and often ferment them in the local villages. Negociants or wine brokers assemble the unfinished wines for aging, labeling, and marketing. By contrast American wine making and marketing are concentrated in the hands of relatively few enterprisers, as is true of most American commerce. In effect, the big are very big, but the medium producers are quite substantial by European standards. There is also a new and significant increase in small wineries that produce fewer than 10,000 cases annually.

The ten largest American producers in 1981 sold 334 million of the roughly 510 million gallons of California wines. The two giants, Gallo and United Vintners (owned by Heublein), accounted for 34 percent of the total wines produced in California, with Gallo producing an awesome 26 percent. Aside from these titans, corporate America is well represented in the vineyards and the marketplace (see table 6.7). Seagram's owns Paul Masson, Gold Seal and an import company. National

TABLE 6.7 Leading Wineries and Grape Buyers

Retail Sales[a]		Total Crush		Grapes Purchased	
Gallo		Gallo		Gallo	
United Vintners		United Vintners		United Vintners	
Almadén	75%	Guild	50%	Early California	50%
Guild		Early California		Almadén	
Paul Masson		Almadén			
				Bronco	
Christian Bros.		Bronco		Christian Bros.	
Franzia/Taylor	10%	Christian Bros.	20%	Franzia/Taylor	20%
C. Mondavi (Krug)		Franzia/Taylor		LaMont	
Sebastiani		LaMont		Paul Masson	
		Paul Masson		Vie Del	
Beringer		Vie Del			
Bronco	5%			Calif. Growers	
Gibson		Calif. Growers	5%	Delicato	5%
Giumarra		Delicato		Giumarra	
R. Mondavi		Giumarra			
				Beringer	
		Delano		Brookside	
		East Side	5%	C. Mondavi	5%
		Gibson		R. Mondavi	
		C. Mondavi (Krug)		San Martin	
		Sebastiani		Sebastiani	
		Woodbridge		Sonoma	
TOTALS	90%		80%		80%

Source: Harold Rogers, "Leading Wineries and Grape Buyers," *Western Fruit Grower Magazine.*
Note: Because of the difficulty of ranking wineries below the top four or five, names are in alphabetical order in the size group listings.
Percentages are rounded to nearest multiple of five.
[a]Retail sales are estimated domestic sales of brand-label wines.

Distillers have owned Almadén for a number of years. The new kid on the block is Coca-Cola with ownership of the Wine Spectrum which created Taylor's California Cellars after purchasing Taylors of New York along with Monterey and Sterling in California. Now even the august Budweiser brewing giant has entered the fray as a bulk wine distributer in cooperation with Labatts of Canada which owns Lamont, one of the great bulk winemakers in California. Confusing? It shouldn't be. It's as American as apple pie!

A Good Investment for Foreign Capital

Attesting to the future of the fine growing areas of California, a number of major foreign investments have occurred in recent years. Moët-Hennessy, the great French champagne and cognac producers, have invested heavily in Domaine Chandon in the heart of the Napa Valley. The huge German conglomerate Peter Eckes has purchased the Franciscan Winery. An Austrian, Barbara de Brye, owns Hanzell Vineyards in Sonoma. Cambiaso is in the hands of Thai businessmen. Another French Champagne producer, Piper-Heidsieck, has joined with its importer, Renfield, in a joint venture with Sonoma Vineyards. And on it goes, attesting to the certainty of a glorious future for California wines.

A presage of things to come is the cooperative enterprise of the Baron Philippe de Rothschild of the famous Chateau Mouton-Rothschild and the Mondavis of Robert Mondavi Winery. Their Napamedoc Cabernet Sauvignon, now in the barrel, will be released in 1983. It has already brought $83,000 a barrel at a charity auction, suggesting strong interest in the Napa Valley and the excellence of its wines.

AN AMERICAN BROTHERHOOD

Since the late Middle Ages, there have been societies patterned on monastic orders which supported the growth and extension of the wine culture of their regions. In France alone, there are sixty-four such ensembles, from the *Compagnie des Mousquetaires d'Armagnac* (Company of Musketeers of Armagnac) and the ribald *Les Étonneurs Rabelaisiens* (The Rabelaisian Barrel Fillers) to the august and prestigious Burgundian *Confrères de Tastevin* (Brother Winetasters) which counts more than one thousand members resident in the United States.

Through the tireless efforts of Grand Commander Norman E. Gates, the purely American *Knights of the Vine* now proudly claims chapters in nearly twenty cities. During his business career in northern Africa and in France, Gates belonged to no fewer than eighteen brotherhoods. Returning to the United States, he decided the time was ripe to bring together those with this special reverent, intense love of wine. Enophiles from Georgia to Minnesota are now able to share their love of the vine with kindred souls in a happy and judiciously ceremonial manner. *Per Vitem! Ad Vitam!*—Through the Vine! Toward Life!

OTHER WINE LOVERS UNITED

Wine creates brotherhood in many other ways, almost beyond the credulity. Organizations, clubs, societies, guilds, and simple neighborhood tasting groups command the attention of both the exalted and the mundane among us. This phenomenal interest is unique among foods and attests to the lasting powers of the grape that have inspired so many for so many centuries.

The leading and most prestigious of the consumer groups in this country is *Les Amis du Vin*—the Friends of Wine. Centered in Silver Spring, Maryland, and still directed by its founder, Ron Ronte, *Les Amis* sponsors thousands of tastings for clubs around the nation, conducts tours of wine-growing regions and reports six times a year on the fields of wine, brews and spirits in its magazine, *The Friends of Wine*.

Few other consumer products could inspire the creation of a professional organization such as the Society of Wine Educators which now numbers nearly one thousand teachers, retailers, writers and winemakers. Founded in the summer of 1977 with the help of the Wine Institute, the Society conducts annual conventions that amount to massive educational seminars on all aspects of wine grape growing and wine making.

A dozen or more professional and technical organizations, ranging from the Wine Institute and the American Society of Enologists in California to the American Wine Society and Wine East near the other coast, combine to expand the professional horizons of the bourgeoning American wine enterprise. Add to these the fraternity of wine journalists now writing for the majority of the metropolitan dailies and major magazines and you have a truly gigantic movement directed at the enhancement of a single liquid food.

The incredible interest in wine now brings up to three hundred wine educators together each year in convention for the Society of Wine Educators. The conviviality of the courtly order of the Knights of the Vine is portrayed as Grand Commander Norman E. Gates welcomes Jerry Banchero as Master Commander of the Seattle Assemblage.

Highlights

- Both wines and brews emerged at the birthplace of western civilization around the Tigris and Euphrates rivers.
- The grape culture is limited to two temperate bands which girdle the globe in the northern and southern hemispheres.
- The great wine grape family is known as the *vinifera*, the vine that makes wine.

- Over half of the world's wine production occurs in Italy, France, and Spain.
- United States wine consumption, while still low, is increasing rapidly.

Finally, recognizing the growing interest in all areas of the wine culture and its rich heritage, Fromm and Sichel, Inc., worldwide distributor for The Christian Brothers, have established the first American Wine Museum in San Francisco.

WINE AS FOOD

A problem of wine merchandising not commonly recognized is the *unavailability* of wine in many of the major food markets of the nation. States such as New York and Pennsylvania operate under legal strictures concerning the sale of wine in food stores, the one favoring special liquor retailers and the other a state store system. Seventeen states have some restrictions on the sale of wine in grocery stores. Since wine when readily available is purchased over 70 percent of the time by females—the major food shoppers—one conjectures that there will be a considerable increase in total consumption of wine if and when major states change laws regarding distribution.

Other states that have changed from state stores exclusively to allowing retailers to sell wine show clear evidence of that increase. In 1970, the last year of state-store-only sales, Maine retailed 185,000 gallons of wine. Nine years later that total had skyrocketed 944 percent to an astonishing 1,931,000 gallons. Similarly, Idaho consumption rose from 180,000 gallons to 1,487,000 gallons when wine was placed in retail stores.

Despite the really quite shallow penetration of the total consuming market to date, the growth pattern for wine has been healthy, solid, and in the direction appropriate to moderate drinking. The forecasters see a billion gallons in sales by 1990, more than double the current per capita intake. That is, indeed, a fertile vineyard.

A visit to the Wine Museum of San Francisco is a must for scholar and novice alike. The exhibits include sculpture, artifacts, paintings, prints and the noted Franz W. Sichel glass collection. Books in seven languages tell the history and the glories of the wine culture. This interior view of the museum shows a fifteenth century lindenwood sculpture of St. Genevieve, patroness of French wine growers.

Growing Wine Grapes

Seat-of-the-pants grape growing and wine making has grudgingly given way to science. The devastation of the world's vineyards in the latter half of the last century encouraged new approaches to the ancient practices. As a result, the operation of a vineyard is now a highly sophisticated undertaking.

Here is a brief sketch of what happens from the plowing to the harvesting. In new vineyards, it is now common to allow land to lie fallow for at least one season after it is cleared of other vegetation. It is during this full cycle that the viticulturist takes his measurements of sun, soil, ambient air temperature, wind, and the like. The plot is rip plowed to three feet deep so that methyl bromide may be administered and is then covered with a protective tarpaulin. This procedure rids the soil of fungus and other latent diseases which could attack the new vines.

PLANTING

While there are ideal areas for cultivation of each type of vinifera grape, the most popular varietals are increasingly planted throughout all viticulture areas in California. Despite this obvious market response, there was a listing of grapes and their most suitable planting climates in a recent issue of the *Monterey Vineyard Winemaker Notes* (see table 7.1).

Before it is planted, the field is fenced at a cost of about four dollars per square foot to ward off the ravenous deer. In most modern operations, an irrigation sprinkler system of plastic tubing is implanted in the ground every third row, six to eight vines apart, adding a tidy $2,500 in costs per acre. This

TABLE 7.1 Plantings in California Climates

Climate	Location	Grapes
Coldest	Upper Monterey, Sonoma, Maria, Santa Cruz	Pinot Noir, Pinot Blanc, Johannisberg Riesling, Gewürztraminer, Grey Riesling
Medium cool	Monterey, Napa Carneros, Sonoma, Santa Barbara	Pinot Blanc, Chardonnay, Sylvaner, Grenache, Grey Riesling, Johannisberg Riesling, Petite Sirah (and sometimes Zinfandel)
Medium warm	Upper Napa Valley, San Luis Obispo	Sémillon, Sauvignon Blanc, Chenin Blanc, Zinfandel, Cabernet Sauvignon, Petite Sirah, Grenache, Napa Gamay, Mondeuse, French Colombard (and sometimes Chardonnay)
Hot	Central Valley: Modesto, Fresno, Lodi, Bakersfield	French Colombard, Ruby Cabernet, Barbera, Carignane, Palomino, Tinta Madera, Grenache

Source: Monterey Vineyard Winemaker Notes, 2.

*T*hese lodes and pockets of earth, more precious than the precious ores, that yield inimitable fragrance and soft fire; those virtuous bonanzas, where soil has submitted under sun and stars to something finer, and the wine is bottled poetry . . .

**Robert Louis Stevenson
(On wine of the Napa Valley)**

A tractor trenching for underground irrigation pipe that will feed underground sprinklers used largely for frost protection. Another system, drip irrigation, employs small drip emitters close to the ground, avoiding evaporation from overhead spraying.

system not only distributes water and occasional herbicides, it is also a vital tool for warding off frost in the spring. The sprinklers are turned on when the temperature drops to 32° F so the water will form icicles which release heat as they freeze, thereby keeping the canes and buds in warm cocoons.

NURTURING

Generally, the practice today is to plant with distances of roughly 8 to 12 feet between rows and plants. The sprinklers are positioned every third row, about eight vines apart. This practice accommodates about 400 to 430 vines per acre. The clearance allows easy access for most modern equipment including automatic harvesters. Sprinkler systems can also be used to cool the vines in intensely hot regions. Older vineyards in the European mode are noticeably more tightly packed with vines, most of which are head trained and spur pruned on short erect trunks, the spurs projecting like thorns around a crown. These low-set vines, reminiscent of dwarfed trees, require much hand labor and are now being eliminated as the vines exhaust themselves over time.

In recent years, vineyardists have shown great interest in drip irrigation which directs a constant, moderate flow of water, as often as needed, to the ground near the trunks of the vines. Obviously, this technique conserves precious water supplies and can be utilized to stimulate growth at particular periods during maturation.

The basic vineyard practices described here vary from country to country because of tradition and the many variables in climate, topography, and soils. The trellises in cathedrallike towering rows in the Portuguese Vinho Verde both protect the fruit from the blazing sun and provide cool tunnels for maximum fruit maturity. Ladders up to 30 feet high are used to harvest the highly acidic fruit. In direct contrast, several hundred miles to the north, Bordeaux vineyard workers must stoop to reach the tightly packed and tangled canes and fruit of the Cabernet Sauvignon.

Modern practice favors two types of trellised vines, one utilizing spurs, and the other utilizing canes. Spurs are simply short wooded arms or branches which are retained each year at pruning with sufficient buds for next year's crop. The heavy-bearing varieties are often spur pruned, for example, Carignane, French Colombard, and Chenin Blanc.

Spur pruning develops the fruiting buds from the first two nodes. In cane pruning the fruiting buds are located farther out on the cane and usually the first few buds are sterile and unproductive. Cane pruning utilizes two to four larger canes or branches which are chosen each year in the winter pruning and which usually contain six to fifteen buds. For cane pruning, the vines are cultivated to a higher, more easily reached level and the canes spread over trellis wires. The goal is to obtain more sunlight on the leaves and fruit which means larger crops. For ideal development, the growing leaves and fruit should receive about 4,000 foot candles of sunlight, with 10,000 the absolute maximum. This system works best with shy bearing varietals such as Cabernet Sauvignon or Chardonnay. However, the blessing often disguises a potential problem, overcropping. In one test, scientists achieved 20 tons per acre, four times the ideal, through stretched canes.

The newest method of pruning combines the best features of the cane and spur techniques. It is called bilateral cordon, and it requires two thick cane arms which form a giant "T." Individual thick wood spurs emerge from each arm. Both advantages are thus obtained, the strength of the wood and the means to trellis the emerging canes for greater sun exposure. It takes more time to establish the cordon, but it becomes a long-term timesaver in pruning. All the cordon methods seem

Terms

ampelography Detailed descriptions of grape varieties and their climatology.

berry Individual grape which varies widely in size according to variety and growing conditions.

berry set The period during which pollinated flowers develop into fruit berries.

bloom The wax-like coating on matured grapes which protects the fruit from the sun and collects airborne yeast cells.

botrytis cinerea Fungus that attacks ripening grapes extracting moisture without breaking skins; desirable in late harvest grapes of the *auslese* style.

bud The round organ found on canes, containing shoots and flower clusters for next year's development.

cane A one-year shoot of wood of from 12 to 15 nodes retained at pruning for the following year's growth.

cane pruning The method of retaining canes for fruiting units usually of lighter bearing varieties to spread the canes for more fruit.

clone Vine produced vegetatively from a selected mother vine.

cluster Grape bunch weighing from 1/6 to 2/3 of a pound at harvest.

cordon training The method which divides the trunk into two permanent branches extending along a trellis wire and uses spur pruning.

crop control Management of total fruit production by pruning and cluster thinning.

degree days The heat summation of average degrees above 50° F over the growing period.

field budding Attaching a vinifera shoot to a rootstock growing in the field.

head training The method in which the trunk of the vine is divided into short T-like arms bearing the spurs or canes.

native rootstock Varieties of grape vines such as vitis rupestris and vitis riparia on which European vinifera are grafted for wine fruit production.

Phylloxera vastatrix Native American plant louse which infected the world's vinifera vineyards in the nineteenth century; native American vines, largely resistant to the louse, are now utilized worldwide as rootstock for vinifera's production.

scion The fruit variety grafted or budded onto a rootstock.

spur A short one-year growth containing one or two nodes.

spur pruning The method of retaining spurs for fruiting units, usually of heavy bearing varieties.

(A)

The sweep of California vineyards is illustrated in these one-mile-long rows in the Paul Masson Pinnacles Vineyard in Salinas Valley (A). In contrast, Almadén's early plantings in northern

(B)

California in 1852 display the tightly packed European-Style rows of the time (B).

(A)

(B)

Over thousands of years, grape-growing practices have been adapted to the diverse climates in Europe. Here are vines in the searing heat of Sicily, where the leaves protect the fruit from the sun (A) and in the wild cultivation of the Trentino (B).

Figure 7.1 *Hundreds of years ago the Romans discovered that the secret of fine wine lies in severe pruning of the grape crop. The traditional head-pruning techniques are spur growth (A) and the extension of canes over trellises (B). The newest method, called bilateral cordon pruning (C), interweaves the lateral growth around permanent trellis wires.*

(A)

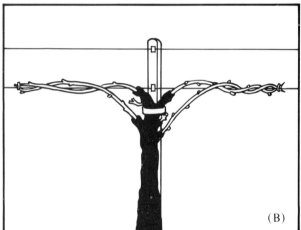

(B)

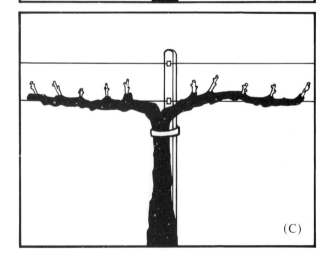

(C)

Pictured is the devastating phylloxera and her eggs magnified 125 times. Both root and leaf varieties of the aphid exist, with the leaf type able to migrate by wings in late August to new plants. Biological enemies and insecticides control the leaf type, and resistant root stock controls the root gall phylloxera.

to give better control at first production, an essential element for wine quality (see fig. 7.1). All these technical features illustrate how exacting is the job of growing good wine grapes. Obviously, little is left to chance. Almost universally today, the vinifera cuttings are grafted either in the nursery or in the field on native American rootstock.

INFESTATION

In Greek, *phyllo* means "leaf" and *xera* means "dry" (hence xerox is dry copying). Combine the root words, and you have the devastating plant aphid called *phylloxera vastatrix,* native to America, which was inadvertently carried around the globe in viticulture experiments in the nineteenth century.

The scourge spread from vineyard to vineyard, from country to country, undaunted by all attempted cures. Vineyards were flooded, sulfurized, replanted, and prayed over, but all were to be devastated again by the louse. Finally a scientist isolated and identified the aphid as the culprit and found its predilection for growing galls on the root structure from which it secreted enzymes that literally severed the supply of sap to the upper structure. It caused the leaves to brown and dry out, thus inhibiting photosynthesis and growth. Researchers noticed, however, that the transplanted American vines appeared resistant to the pest and deduced that the species had grown resistant over many years of exposure. From that time on, selected American rootstocks became the plumbing systems for

(A)

(B)

(C)

Several steps in field grafting of American rootstock are shown. First, the vitis rupestris *is stripped of its foliage, and a* vinifera *bud is inserted and taped about twelve inches from the ground (A). A protective "bunnyfoiler" milk carton surrounds the graft as the* vinifera *shows its first leaves (B). Very often the bud will fail to take, and the plant returns to its natural leaf structure, requiring another graft the following year (C). These grafted vines will yield fruit for twenty-five years or more.*

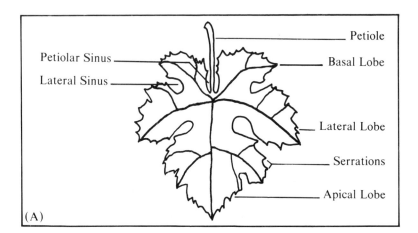

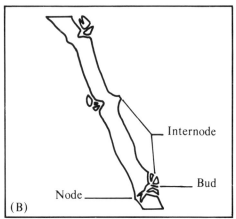

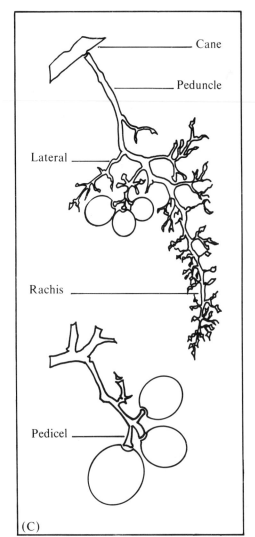

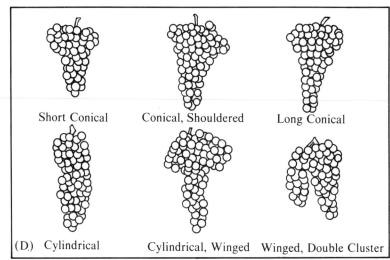

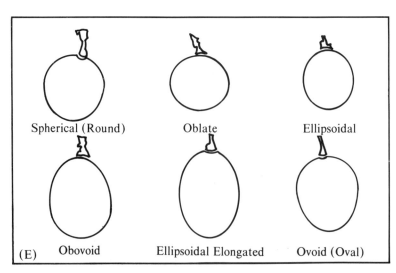

Figure 7.2 *Typical vinifera grape leaf with five lobes* (A); *main features of the cane* (B); *structure of the grape cluster and its attachment to the cane* (C); *common grape cluster shapes* (D); *grape berry shapes* (E).

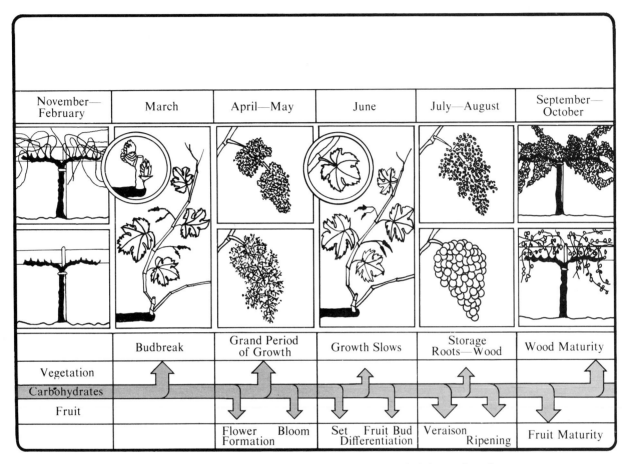

November—February	March	April—May	June	July—August	September—October
	Budbreak	Grand Period of Growth	Growth Slows	Storage Roots—Wood	Wood Maturity

Vegetation
Carbohydrates
Fruit

| | | Flower Bloom Formation | Set Fruit Bud Differentiation | Veraison Ripening | Fruit Maturity |

Figure 7.3 *From budbreak in March to harvest in September, frantic growth occurs in both fruit and wood.*

the world's great vinifera vines. Only a few isolated growing areas today, such as Washington and Oregon, are without infestation and so plant directly from varietal cuttings. Phylloxera-free areas outside the United States include Chile, most of Australia and small pockets in Champagne and the Douro.

Another unique and creative, if not scientific, tool for preventing animal damage is the common waxed milk carton. While fencing can keep out deer, rabbits ignore fences. But milk cartons keep the rascals away from the tender young grafts. The cartons look a little ludicrous; nevertheless, their use accomplishes the purpose admirably.

YIELDS

At the fourth leafing of the vine, sufficient fruit matures to send commercial pickers into the field. In that year, perhaps 1½ tons per acre will be harvested. By the seventh leaf, the plants will be producing up to 6 tons per acre and can be expected to produce for at least thirty years. The tons per acre vary widely, depending upon the type of grapes, the growing area, the conditions that prevail and the cultivation practices.

In 1979, California wine grape growers were paid on the average of $299 per ton for white grapes and $169 per ton for the dark skin varieties. In that same year, the average yield was 5.73 tons per acre compared to 6.96 tons the previous harvest. The smaller the wine grape harvest per acre, the higher the price it will bring since the fruit will almost always be of better quality. Lesser varieties yield as high as 8 tons per acre, although some California hybrids yield up to 10 tons per acre. In years of great demand, the most desirable grapes, such as Chardonnay and Cabernet Sauvignon, command much more than $1,000 per ton. In 1982 Pinot and Chardonnay grapes from vineyards in Champagne brought $2,760 per ton. Consider what can be generated in dollars from a single acre of premium grapes.

Red wine grapes—6 tons @ 175 gallons per ton = 1050 gallons = 420 cases = 5,040 bottles @ $3.00 each.
White wine grapes—4 tons @ 150 gallons per ton = 600 gallons = 240 cases = 2,680 bottles @ $3.00 each.

The growing pattern varies considerably in different geographic areas and microclimates. The grapes are planted to allow for a progressive utilization of crushing and fermenting equipment over the harvesting season. Fortunately, nature also cooperates in that each variety of grape has a slightly different maturation period. The catch is that when the fruit in a field reaches that ideal balance of sugar and acidity, immediate harvesting is necessary to avoid a deterioration of one of the vital qualities. While there are variations even between vineyards as close as a mile apart, here is a typical grape-growing cycle.

January to March—pruning and cultivation to assure maximum quality.

March—the selected canes begin the budding process, and new vines are grafted.

April—during a period of seventy-five days leaves develop and flowers augur new berries.

May—the berries are set for new bunches; ten to twenty days.

June—clusters continue early growth as cells develop; forty to forty-five days.

July and August—cell expansion and engorgement with fruit sugars occurs as does variety pigmentation.

September and October—harvest and fermentation; forty-five to fifty days.

November and December—vineyards become dormant, storing energy for the winter and the development of new canes in the spring; 170 to 190 days.

The Demand for White Wines

Of course, not all plantings are to the wine grape varieties. Of the approximately 645,000 acres in California grapes, 330,000 are in wine varietals. Another 250,000 produce raisin types, and there remain 65,000 which mature as table fruit.

One of the current problems that primarily time, and also possible substantial replanting or field grafting, can solve is the predilection of the new American consumers for white wines. Generally, white wines are made from white grape varieties, although light reds and sometimes completely white vintages can be coaxed from dark-skinned types by rapid separation of juice from skins in advance of fermentation. Worldwide, the scale tips to reds. In anticipation of a market for dark-skinned grapes, the Sunshine state widely missed the mark in recent plantings because it planted red and not white grapes. For this reason, many traditional deep reds such as Cabernet Sauvignon and Pinot Noir are now produced in rosé or even white wine versions. California's major plantings of current grapes show a tremendous increase in white wine varieties during the past ten years. (see table 7.2).

A considerable number of grape growers have turned in recent years to T-budding to convert mature but young (less

TABLE 7.2 Wine Grape Acreage

Varieties	1981	1971
Red Wine		
Zinfandel	28,368	21,424
Cabernet Sauvignon	22,496	7,616
Pinot noir	8,993	3,446
Petite Sirah	8,503	5,604
Gamay/Gamay Beaujolais	8,136	3,673
Merlot	2,264	426
TOTAL	78,760	42,189
White Wine		
French Colombard	56,639	18,660
Chenin blanc	37,567	8,689
Chardonnay	19,766	3,057
White Riesling	11,118	1,856
Sauvignon blanc	9,558	1,594
Gewürztraminer	4,709	732
TOTAL	139,357	34,588
TOTAL POPULAR VARIETIES	218,117	76,777

Source: The Wine Institute. 15 July 1982 release.

than 10 years old) vineyards from dark-skinned to white varieties. The advantage over pulling the vines and beginning the lengthy process again is obvious. The conversion can be made for about $1,500 per acre. Full production can be achieved in as little as three years since the new shoots arise from fully healthy vine stock with over a 90 percent success rate. The procedure is named for the inverted T-shaped cut very high on the vine near the trellis wires. Two buds are inserted, grafting wax applied, and the graft is covered with wide plastic tape designed to protect the cambium tissue. This procedure can be expected to convert thousands of California red vines to the more popular white varieties. Table 7.3 summarizes the viticultural characteristics of both red and white varieties.

Like France's Midi, which produces most of the large wine grape crop, the vast San Joaquin Valley produces the largest amount of the California crush. This 400 mile stretch from Lodi to Bakersfield accounts for an impressive 90 percent of the total harvest of grapes. The Thompson Seedless alone exceeds 700,000 tons, nearly 60 percent of the total, but many fine varietals, particularly the heavy-bearing French Colombard and Chenin Blanc are producing very acceptable wines in the hot Central Valley. Centrifuged and vinified between 55° and 60°F, these wines are used in the jug white wines by major producers.

Several hundred varieties of vitis vinifera are grown in California, but thirteen types provide 87.4 percent of the total crush for wines. Since the demand is so heavy for white wines, growers and winemakers compete for a smaller supply of white grapes, for 459,069 of a total of 1,380,393 tons. The serious impact that consumers' increasing preference for white wine has had on the industry can be seen in the statistics released by the Wine Institute (see table 7.2).

TABLE 7.3 Wine Grape Varieties in the North Coast Counties of California

Varieties for White Wines	Leafing	Vine Growth	Pruning Method	Harvest Period	Avg. Cluster Weight, Lb.	Productivity Tons/Acre
Chardonnay	V. early	V. vigorous	Cane	Early	1/8–1/4	2–5
Chenin blanc	V. early	V. vigorous	Spur	Mid-season	1/3	5–8
Flora	Early	Moderate	Spur	Early-mid	1/5–1/3	4–6
French Colombard	Mid	V. vigorous	Spur	Mid-season	1/3	6–9
Gewürztraminer	Early	Moderate	Cane	Early	1/5–1/6	2–4
Grey Riesling	Early	V. vigorous	Spur	Early	1/5–1/3	5–7
Pinot blanc	Early-mid	Moderate	Spur	Mid-season	1/6–1/4	3–5
Muscat Canelli	Early-mid	Moderate	Spur	Mid-season	1/3–1/2	2–4
Sauvignon blanc	Early-mid	V. vigorous	Cane	Early-mid	1/6–1/5	4–6
Sémillon	Late-mid	Moderate	Spur	Early-mid	1/3	5–8
Sylvaner	Late-mid	Moderate	Spur	Mid-season	1/5–1/4	3–5
White Riesling	Early-mid	Moderate	Cane	Mid-season	1/5–1/6	4–6
Varieties for Red Wines						
Cabernet Sauvignon	V. late	V. vigorous	Cane	Late	1/8–1/5	3–5
Carignane	Late	Vigorous	Spur	Late	1/3–1/2	5–8
Gamay	Late-mid	Moderate	Spur	Late	1/2–1/3	5–7
Merlot	Late	Vigorous	Cane	Late-mid	1/7–1/5	3–6
Petite Sirah	Late	Moderate	Spur	Mid	1/3–1/2	4–7
Pinot noir	V. early	Moderate	Cane	Early	1/10–1/8	2–4
Zinfandel	Late-mid	Moderate	Spur	Mid	1/2–2/3	4–7

Source: Division of Agricultural Sciences. University of California, *Wine and Grape Varieties in the North Coast Counties of California* by A. N. Kasimatis, Bruce E. Bearden, and Keith Bowers (Richmond, Calif.: Agricultural Sciences Publications, 1977), 6–9.

The birds and the bees are an anathema to the vineyardist. The robin or the pesky linnet ravages the bunches of grapes; the birds are followed by the busy bees. As well as being reduced in quantity, these bruised bunches enter the fermenter as oxidized, off-flavor material.

According to current federal law, those wines which mention the grape variety, such as Cabernet Sauvignon, on the label are classified as varietals, and must have a minimum of 75 percent of the named grape in the wine. The competition for the very limited crush from the best white varietals will increase, as will the prices demanded by growers and vintners. Inevitably, this will lead to greater emphasis upon the generic wines identified only as burgundy, rosé, chablis, and rhine, or simply as table wines, with no identification of grapes used.

Aside from the boom and the bust nature of all agricultural enterprises and the fickleness of the public as to color preference, a number of natural calamities periodically confront the wine grape grower. The most dreaded is spring frost which, at 22° F or below, can decimate or even totally ruin the crop. To increase protection against this, the traditional smudge pots and propeller-driven blowers are giving way to sprinkling systems, mentioned earlier, which in warm weather provide irrigation by delivering 50 gallons of water per minute per acre. Bees and migratory birds (200 species including starlings, linnets, and robins), mineral deficiencies of the soil, sleet and rain, leafhoppers, mildew, and adventurous mammals all take their proportionate tolls.

As one can see, viticulture is a complex, expensive, and technically demanding form of agriculture. Those who choose wine grape growing as a livelihood and succeed are a canny, up-to-date, scientifically oriented lot who know the meaning of risk as well as success.

THE HARVEST

There exists a wondrous clock that sets into motion all the growing things of the earth. Even so, vinifera mature in an evenly spaced sequence that allows the winemaker to have his tanks available as each species is harvested and ready for fermentation. In late August to mid-September, the Chardonnay, Gewürztraminer, and Pinot Noir reach maturity. From mid-September to mid-October, about the middle of the season, the harvest is the rich and full-bearing whites, including the Sauvignon Blanc, Semillon, Sylvaner, Chenin Blanc, the heavy-bearing French Colombard, as well as the reds such as Zinfandel, Merlot, and Petite Sirah. Finally, from the middle of October on, the heavy Carignane, Gamay, and the prized Cabernet Sauvignon come to bear. In the picking season grape farmers dread the intense, violent, scorching hot days which can tamper with this finely tuned clock and bring nearly all varieties to maturity at once.

No matter the country or terrain, wine harvesting is a wild, frenzied affair mostly accomplished by skillful human hands. The knife which was developed so many centuries ago in Rome still severs from the vine most of the fruit headed for the vintner. A skilled picker can harvest the astounding amount of 2,000 pounds of grapes in a single day.

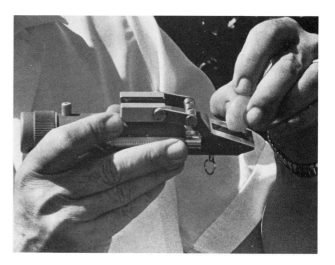

The hand refractometer provides an accurate eye measurement of sugar content, allowing field judgment of readiness for harvesting.

Advancements in Harvesting

However, in contrast to the hand picker, a mechanical picker can harvest 100 tons of grapes per day. Not surprisingly, in these days of mechanization and soaring labor costs, mechanical picking is increasing. Handpicked grapes cost about $60 per ton to harvest compared to $40 for harvesting by machine. But because of the narrow spaces between the rows in many of the older vineyards, and quality control problems inherent in the equipment, the increase in machine harvesting has been very slow to date. Today only a small proportion of California's annual crush destined to become premium wine is harvested by machine. But many of the technical problems will yield to improved equipment. An example is the pulsator picker which vibrates the base of the vine unlike earlier models which quite literally whacked the fruit from the vine; unfortunately, they sometimes whacked bird nests, trellis staples, and other sundries into the harvest.

The most recent advance in harvesting is field crushing. This technique is utilized with both hand harvesting and mechanical picking. Since the most serious problem at this time is oxidation of the juice from broken skins, the fruit is crushed and destemmed immediately at harvest and is placed in tanks with a cover of CO_2 or SO_2. When these tanks are discharged into the fermenter at the winery, the grapes are literally but seconds from the vine in terms of exposure to the air. No matter how much care is exercised when using the traditional open air gondola, the weight of the grapes themselves inevitably crushes and breaks skins of the lower layers. The time lapse from handpicking baskets to gondola and finally to the winery some miles away may be several hours. Field crushing eliminates a vexing, age-old problem of browned juice.

(A)

(C)

(B)

(D)

Traditional harvesting the world over, as shown here in northern Italy (A) and (B), in Bordeaux (C), and in California (D), consists of picking into small hand-carried baskets that are *then emptied into gondolas that transport the grapes to the distant wineries in quantities of several tons.*

LATE HARVESTING

The botrytis is a cryptogamic fungus that develops on selected bunches of grapes at various times, but is most desired in the late harvesting season. There is a myth about the discovery of the effect this mold has in developing wines of incredible finesse and richness. As the often-told tale goes the Bishop of Trier in Germany was absent from his estates in 1716 when harvest time approached. Fearing a reprimand, no one else dared give the word to pick the grapes. Those harvested on his late return had a great infestation of fungus spores, but the wine, though less in quantity, was ethereal. Whatever the accuracy of the story, late harvesting is now practiced wherever possible. However, not all late harvested grapes are botrytised; in fact, few in California can claim this desired mold growth.

The fluffy grey fungus called *botrytis cinerea* develops on the skin, reducing the tissue without actually breaking the skin. It extracts the fluids, metabolizing more organic acids than sugars so that the berries eventually shrivel, concentrating the sugars and other solids. Some of the usually dominant tartaric acids are converted to glycerol and gluconic acid, the two elements which combine to create a velvety, buttery flavor and taste in the wines, quite unlike anything else in the world.

The Germans continue the tradition of late harvesting by producing various versions of sweet vintages under the following designations: *Spätlese,* late harvested; *Auslese,* selected bunches; *Beerenauslese,* late harvested, individual berries; and *Trockenbeerenauslese,* a tongue twister that means picking only berries that have appropriately shrunk and are late harvested (*Trocken* means dry). Finally, there is a specialty called *Eiswein* from berries that have actually been frozen before harvest, originally the result of waiting overlong for the botrytis to do its work.

Some American vintners have been successful in capturing grapes affected by botrytis in the vineyards at the precise time in the maturing of the grapes to produce something very much akin to the late-harvested grapes of Europe. While the botrytis spores are present throughout the grapes' life cycle, they are often dispersed by the breezes before they become active on the skins. Some wineries such as Grand Crú and Beringer have gone to great lengths to cultivate the growth both in the vineyards and in the winery laboratories. It is no easy task in California to replicate the favorable conditions that give rise to these exquisite wines in Northern Europe.

However, the desire to have a little sweetness in wines—either from late harvest fungus or simply from retention of natural grape sugars, is a very, very old desire indeed. The Greeks not only worked to retain natural sugar, they added more sugar, as well as dozens of other flavoring agents. It is a common practice throughout the wine-making world to add a reduced form of grape juice, a syrup if you like, to a completely dry wine to obtain harmony and balance as well as commercial consistency. In California this sweetner is called concentrate; in Germany it is *süssreserve*. The effect is identical. The level of sweetness in the rosé or liebfraumilch can be kept constant to the joy of the consumer.

The competition for traditional grape hand-harvesting is the relatively new family of twelve-foot-high, tractor-driven mechanical harvesters that harvest as much as an acre per hour and convey the fresh fruit to waiting gondolas.

The latest mechanical innovation in grape harvesting was borrowed from other fruit handling. The Up-Right harvester has a pivotal pulsator, a channel that literally takes hold of the base of each vine while the picking rods point up under the fruit and canes, gently separating the one from the other. All of the mechanical units have the advantages of speed, relative thoroughness, and the ability to work during the night when the fruit and vineyards are cool, as well as much lower labor costs. However, relatively flat land is required, as is a large capital investment for seasonal equipment.

Another interesting method of concentrating sweetness was developed in Southern Europe—in Italy, Spain and the Jura Mountains in France—and consists of sequestering grapes on mats or screens until they lose much of their water content and are nearly raisined. Around December or January, the grapes are placed in barrels, and a long fermentation is set in motion, often lasting up to six months. The resulting wines are as luscious as the grapes themselves, but, because they travel poorly, they are destined for local markets exclusively.

LIGHT WINES

The latest variation in merchandising offers wines with fewer calories, comparable to *light* soda pop and *light* beers. Since the primary calorie constituent in table wines is the alcohol, light wines contain lower alcohol levels, often in the 8 to 9 percent range in contrast to the normal 12 percent by volume.

This reduction is achieved by any of several methods. One employs a large infusion of grape juice into the fermenting must, after which the wines are centrifuged, cleansed of yeast and, one hopes, freed from further fermentation. A second and more certain procedure involves picking the grapes at lower sugar levels, say 19 percent sugar, so that the must will yield a maximum of 9 percent alcohol. While this technique is more reliable in terms of the desired alcohol levels, there may be some imbalance in the wine because of the young fruit. As with the *Vinho Verdes* of Portugal, early harvested grapes will inevitably contain a higher acidity because of the young fruit. In our age of calorie counters this imbalance may well be forgiven. A third method utilizes heat in a centrifuge process to evaporate some of the alcohol from a completed fermentation. Taylor California Cellars recently won a court case for their right to advertise such wines as less caloric, in keeping with the trend in many other foodstuffs to appeal to the calorie conscious.

VINTAGE 1978

Chateau Ste. Michelle

Washington State

ICE WINE
WHITE RIESLING

Produced and Bottled by Ste. Michelle Vineyards, Woodinville, Wa.
Alcohol 8.4% by Volume. Sugar at harvest 37% by weight.
Residual sugar in the wine 17% by weight.

The unique conditions for the famous German Eiswein presented themselves in Chateau Ste. Michelle's small Grandview, Washington winery on 8 November 1978. The fruit was botrytised, or noble-rot-infected, when the hard freeze hit. Harvested at high sugar and high acid, the yield was one-third of normal Riesling must. Slow-fermented for nearly two months, the wine was bottled at 17.9 reducing sugar and .99 acidity, yielding an incredibly balanced, complex and luscious wine.

(A)

(B)

(C)

(D)

Grand Crú Vineyards of Glen Ellen, California, recently demonstrated a unique approach to late harvesting by inducing botrytis on specially harvested Gewürztraminer grapes. The mold was inoculated in Roux bottles (A), selected grapes were spread on a tray (B), then the mold was sprayed on the grapes (C), and allowed to develop. Crushing and fermentation yielded 7.1 percent alcohol and a rich 32 percent residual sugar, as well as a deserved gold medal at the Los Angeles County Fair (D).

INCREASED CONSUMPTION EXPECTED

At a 1980 meeting of beer and wine wholesalers, Louis R. Gomberg, lawyer, statistician, and dean of the California wine consultants, provided a perceptive commentary on American wine consumption.

> Let me draw two statistical pictures . . . Worldwide, beer consumption now runs about 20 billion gallons a year. This figures out at about 5 gallons per capita. Wine consumption worldwide is about 8 billion gallons or around 2 gallons per capita . . . In the U.S. total beer consumption last year was approximately 5 billion gallons for a per capita level of around 24 gallons. Wine consumption was some 430 million gallons for a per capita level a shade under 2 gallons. Beer outranked wine, 12 to 1.

Gomberg projects wine consumption ultimately at 10 gallons per capita as it is in West Germany and other European countries apart from the major wine producers. He points to the over 100 million adults in this country who acknowledge use of alcoholic drinks, of whom only a mere 5 percent drink wine regularly with meals. One adult in twenty uses wine frequently. The remaining nineteen provide a tremendous market potential. Gomberg predicts an 850 million gallon United States market by 1990, a tremendous increase over 1980.

The stately Liebfrauenkirke in Worms, Rheinhessen, lent its name to the most popular, medium sweet German wines, vastly popular in the United States, as Liebfraumilch. These soft wines have helped to popularize white wines. Similar wines from the Moselle are called Moselblumchen, or little flower of the Moselle. Another from the Zell is Zellerschwartze Katz.

Fermentation

The alcohols we consume all derive from fermentation. This procedure is but one of the common, catalytic functions in the endless cycle of growth, decay and regeneration which supports human life on this planet. Alcohol fermentation consists of a breakdown of plant and fruit sugars by enzymes which are released in fermentation by yeast cells. We think of it generally in terms of beverage alcohols, but there are literally hundreds of other industrial and medical applications of controlled molds and ferments producing such common chemicals as riboflavin, penicillin, streptomycin and monosodium glutamate. Up to 20 percent of all prescription drugs result from fermentation (see table 8.1).

THE THERAPEUTIC VALUE OF FERMENTATION

Very early in the development of organized societies, it became vital to assure a continuing source of food beyond harvest times. The earliest attempts at preservation utilized smoke and salt, two procedures in use even today. Smoked meats were less palatable, but avoided putrefaction. Similarly, salted meats and fish resisted spoilage.

Like natural sugars in fruits, vegetable sugars yield to bacterial ferments, particularly lactic acid. Many reach a level of acid concentration, as do cucumbers in pickling, which renders bacteria inoperative and preserves the food. This same bacteria, lactic acid, sours milk for yogurt and cheese and is a secondary fermenter in wines.

*G*reat fleas have little fleas,
Upon their backs to bite 'em,
And little fleas have lesser fleas,
And, so on, ad infinitum.

Doggerel

*W*ine is light, held together by water!
Galileo

TABLE 8.1 Products of Fermentation, Listed by Source

Yeast	Bacteria	Molds
Alcohol	Acetic acid	Amylase
Baker's yeast	Glutinate	Citric
Riboflavin	Protease	Steroid
Invertase		Finoric
		Penicillin

While ancient societies had no understanding of what caused illness, observations over centuries created the old wives' tales, attributing therapeutic properties to wines and other fermented foods. Beatrice Hunter, in *Fact/Book on Yogurt, Kefir*

Harvesting wagons, a giant press and treading in California are all depicted in The Vintage, *from* Harper's Weekly *in 1878.*

and Other Milk Cultures (1973), explains the value of fermented milk cultures to human pathology.

> Contrary to the information dispensed by the U.S. Department of Agriculture Yearbook, yogurt and other milk products *do* have unique health values not present in sweet milk. Of primary importance, fermented milk products, in developing millions of powerful lactic acid bacteria, hinder the growth of, or kill outright, some dangerous pathogenic organisms responsible for illness or death in humans and animals.

Milk is quite as rich as wine, containing generous amounts of minerals, fats, proteins, sugars, and, like wine, consists mostly of water which makes easier the dispersal of fermenting agents. Hunter cites specific examples of how yogurt inhibits or even kills such dread pathogens as salmonella and diphtheria, claiming that in experiments "The acid medium of the yogurt was the deciding factor, since all of the pathogens were able to survive when yogurt was neutralized with caustic soda."

While the ubiquitous soybean is nearly indigestible in its harvested form, lactic acid fermentation produces from it a protein-rich curd which the Chinese call tofu. This mild product can be fermented a second time with rice, fish, or other foods to produce sofu. The Japanese have fermented tofu, which they call miso, for thousands of years, as well as katsuobushi, a fish. In addition to valuable proteins and nutrients which these products yielded, they also provided spice, seasoning, and character in the otherwise bland diets of early man.

But there are bad as well as beneficial ferments. Putrefaction of food is itself a ferment, and when butyric ferments break down sugars, starches, and acids, they usually spoil the host products. Ammoniac ferments break down nitrogenous materials, creating salts of ammonia which can be utilized by plant life to aid in future growth.

Common to these disparate ferments is the need for nourishment and moisture. The essential fluids and other elements, such as amino acids, vitamins, and purines, occur naturally in fruits, grains, and vegetables. While fruits and grain musts were fermented regularly through the centuries, it was not until the middle of the nineteenth century that the chemical mystery was solved by Louis Pasteur's work on yeast and bacteria. Indeed, the disciplines of biochemistry and microbiology that dominate modern understanding of life processes grew from Pasteur's incisive work.

Terms

acetobacter A bacteria which oxidizes and decomposes alcohol in wine, creating vinegar; kept inactive by SO_2 and by protection against exposure to atmosphere.

acidity Degree of tartness due to natural fruit acids such as tartaric, succinic, malic and citric; total acidity usually recorded as tartaric, the dominant acid.

aldehyde Volatile compounds created during the oxidation of alcohols; a step between alcohol and acid; creates particular aromas and flavors in wine.

anaerobic Without the presence of air; wine fermentation takes place anaerobically below the surface of the juice.

apiculate yeast Wild yeast that collect on the skins of grapes; most die above 4% alcohol; eliminated at crushing in most American wineries.

auslese German term for selection; in progressive degrees of late harvesting, the *Auslese, Beerenauslese,* and *Trockenbeerenauslese* concentrate the sugar and through Botrytis mold produce luscious, sweet wines.

botrytis cinerea Also known as *Pourriture Noble* in French, and *Edelfäule* in German; the "noble mold" grows following warm weather and high humidity; it shrinks the skins, concentrating the sugar and extracts; responsible for wines known as Sauternes, Ausleses, and as *Tokay Aszu* in Hungary and *muffa nobile* in Italy.

brix Named for the chemist who devised the scale, indicates sugar content in must or wine as measured by hydrometer or refractometer.

chaptalization The process of adding cane or beet sugar to musts lacking sufficient amounts for alcohol stability; a common practice in Europe but forbidden in California.

enology The science of wine making.

enzyme Organic matter released by yeast cells; it catalyzes or breaks down sugar molecules into alcohol and CO_2.

ester Volatile compounds formed by combinations of alcohols and acids that provide distinctive odors and bouquet.

ethyl alcohol Also called ethanol; the potable alcohol created by fermentation of sugars.

fermentation Biochemical breakdown of fruit and plant sugars by yeast.

fusel oils Higher alcohols that occur in fermentation in minute quantities such as amyl and butyl; provide tastes and bouquet; constitute less than one tenth of one percent of wine.

glucose and fructose Main fruit sugars, with the same chemical formula as other minor sugars in grapes, including galactose, mannose, and milibiose, and non-fermentable pentose sugars which include arabinose, ribose and xylose.

invertase Enzyme which converts sucrose to equal parts of fructose and glucose permitting fermentation to occur.

lees Residue settled out of the fermenting tanks and the aging barrels.

malo-lactic fermentation A secondary fermentation induced by the lactic bacteria which changes malic acid to lactic acid, releasing CO_2; desirable in red wines (but not generally in whites) to preserve high acid level.

must Grape juice before fermentation.

pH Literally the concentration of hydrogen ions in solution; a practical measurement of acidity; high pH corresponds with low acidity on a scale of 0 to 7; green grapes have very low pH and flabby, overripe grapes without acids have high pH; desirable pH levels are between 3 and 4.

phenols Compounds found in skins, stalks, and seeds of grapes; in heavy concentration in red wines fermented on skins; some preservative and antiseptic functions.

saccharomyces cerevisiae: var. ellipsoideus Particular strain of yeast cultivated in America for wine and beer ferments; desired for its high tolerance to alcohol, rapid growth, and ease of removal.

spätlese German term for late harvesting of grapes; generally sweeter and softer wine.

stuck fermentation Stoppage of fermentation due to heat, cold, or death of yeast cells.

sulfur dioxide Stabilizing element used in wines and on vines since ancient times; inhibits bacteria and yeast activity and lessens browning in both the musts and the wines, in excess produces burnt match smell; denoted as SO_2.

tannin One of the phenolics found in skins and seeds; of particular importance to the preservation and life of red wines; the source of bitterness and astringency; mellows with time.

volatile acidity The level of acetic acid or ethyl acetate in wine which creates the vinegary smell and can actually destroy the wine.

yeast Airborne plant organisms that operate on various plant forms, reducing them by molds and fermentations.

ALCOHOL FERMENTATION

For the student of beverage alcohol, the ferments of interest are the *première* ferments, those caused by minute, airborne plant cells called yeast (fig. 8.1) which are so tiny it would take 10,000 cells to measure one inch. Millions of these microscopic cells appear as if by magic and adhere to the skins of grapes at harvest times. Most other ferments operate in the presence of air, but the particular yeasts in alcohol production are anaerobic, or at least they operate ideally in total immersion in the fluid, apart from the atmosphere. To produce the same amount of alcohol while exposed to the atmosphere, they would require twelve times the nutrients. In this sense, the Good Lord made the grape with its nearly 90 percent water structure a perfect natural fermenter.

A curiosity of this wildly complex biological operation is that both participants—the fermenter and the fermentee—are members of the plant kingdom. One is the berry, a spermatophyte, and the other is a yeast, a thallophyte, which have some kind of mystic symbiosis!

The word yeast derives from the Greek *zestos,* meaning "boiled," and the Sanskrit *yâs(y)ati,* meaning "it seethes." Fermentation comes from the Latin root *fervēre* meaning "to boil." And that is exactly what the winemakers have watched through the centuries, seething and boiling.

Grape fermentation probably predated other fruit fermentations largely because of the rich composition of the grape in terms of nutrients and because of its watery base. Most other fruit ferments, such as those of apples or berries, require the addition of some nutritive elements and water. Many old fruit fermentations call for the addition of raisins or dehydrated grapes.

Wine, one of the noblest cordials in nature.

John Wesley

Many wineries around the world still employ the wild yeast that comes naturally with the fruit. Termed apiculate yeast, these strains often have low tolerance for the alcohol which they produce and consequently die at 5° to 6° proof alcohol concentrations. Others, particularly the *saccharomyces cerevisiae var. ellipsoideus* yeasts, continue their work until full decomposition of the sugars is completed. One of the by-products of Pasteur's magnificent work was the isolation of this particularly effective yeast. In California wineries, as in many of the world's breweries, this particular yeast is cultured and used exclusively in the fermentation process, the wild yeast being eliminated at the time of crushing by administration of

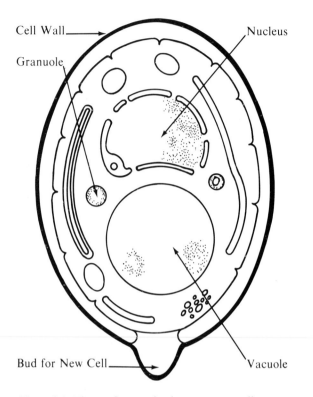

Figure 8.1 *The wondrous and industrious yeast cell.*

sulfur dioxide, SO_2. The saccharomyces have the admirable qualities of high toleration of alcohol, rapid growth in must, and ease of cleanup after the job is done.

Louis Pasteur was hired by the wine industry in France in 1856 primarily to discover why so many wines were lost to spoilage. From the beginning of the nineteenth century, considerable research had already developed intriguing notions about the functions of yeast, but the puzzle was yet to be solved. Pasteur found that the life of the yeast coincided with the span of the fermentation. He prevented post fermentation spoilage by the application of heat to the wine, what we now call pasteurization. Ironically, today this term is more often associated with milk than with wine.

In his definitive book *The Yeasts* (1920) Alexandre Guilliermond describes the still puzzling cycle of these essential ferments.

> The yeasts hibernate in the soil. . . . Transportation through the air seems to play an important role. . . . Hansen states that yeasts are always found in the atmosphere. . . . Their numbers seem to be increased during June to August and especially at the beginning of September. During the other seasons one may not find them as readily.

A mother yeast cell will spawn two dozen offspring before expiring. Guilliermond explains this growth process.

> Practically all of the yeasts divide by budding; it is the characteristic method for multiplication. The bud appears as a little prominence separated from the wall of the mother cell by a very narrow collar. Little by little it increases in size. When it has acquired a certain size, always smaller than the mother cell, it separates, the daughter cell increases in size and soon equals that of the mother cell after which it, in turn, buds.

It is not difficult to imagine the astonishment and wonder that the chemist Pasteur must have felt as this age-old mystery was solved before his inquiring eyes. All of the beverage alcohols of mankind, from time immemorial, have been dependent upon the work of a microscopic, single floating plant cell—awesome!

THE PROCESS

Yeast cells secrete biological material called enzymes which are composed of numerous amino acid chains, essential proteinaceous matter for all living organisms. The principal wine-making enzyme termed *zymase* triggers at least twelve different enzymatic actions involving another half-dozen enzymes. The center of attraction for all of this frenetic activity is the carbohydrate known to us as sugar. In grapes, there are about equal amounts of glucose and fructose, which are two of the three forms of $C_6H_{12}O_6$. The chemical description of fermentation derives from a French chemist, Gay-Lussac, who in 1810 set forth the formulae of the process.

What happens in fermentation is relatively simple even though the chemistry is quite complex. In the process of dividing, each molecule of sugar splits into four new molecules, two each of alcohol and carbon dioxide. The approximately 180 grams in a molecule of glucose are divided thereby into approximately 92 grams of ethyl alcohol and 88 grams of the carbon dioxide gas. Here is that chemical formulation as set forth by Amerine and Singleton in *Wine* (1968):

$$1 \text{ glucose } (C_6 H_{12} O_6) \longrightarrow 2 \text{ ethanol } (CH_3 CH_2 OH) + 2 CO_2$$

In addition to this tidy work, each molecule of sugar also releases 56 kilocalories of raw energy. In the biological process, the yeasts utilize about 40 percent or 22 kilocalories, leaving the remaining 60 percent to escape the fermenting vessel in the form of heat. Billions of yeast cells operate in an average fermentation.

A similar fermentation takes place naturally in human digestion. Gastric enzymes, rennin and pepsin, ferment many of the starches we consume, while their acidity neutralizes harmful bacteria in the stomach. Muscle glycolysis also employs a similar process whereby sugars stored in the muscles are broken down to release energy. Therefore, it is possible to be a teetotaler in terms of *ingestion,* but not in terms of *digestion!*

In spite of the complexity of the transformation, both the must and the wine remain essentially fruit juice, a nourishing food. Many of the components of wine, of which scientists have isolated about 350, remain fundamentally unchanged: acids, some sugars, cellulose, oils, and so on. But other components are created by the chemistry of fermentation. Surprisingly, the extracts, the residual solids, amount to less than 3 percent of the wine weight (see table 8.2).

"Hexoses" are equivalent to the 6 molecule sugars, fructose and glucose. The higher alcohols are synonymous with fusel oils, and the tartaric acid figure represents the concentration of all wine acids. The components arising during the fermentation are the alcohols, esters, tannins, and acetaldehyde.

The most important of all these constituents to the harmony is, of course, the ethyl alcohol which acts as the wine preservative, just as lactic acid does for pickles. Alcohol additionally provides both odor and taste as well as the sedative and tranquilizing effects. At 13 percent and above, alcohol provides distinctive odor or aroma. Dry wine extract, the combination of all the elements other than water, constitutes as little as 2 percent of the total fluid, but a powerful 2 percent. The acids provide the characteristic fruitiness and contribute to the sheen or brightness of the wine. These major chemicals have a definite impact on wines (see table 8.3).

A minor component produced in fermentation is glycerine which adds to the body as well as adding a hardly detectable but unique sweetness. The pigmentation and tannins in the grape skins and seeds fall under the broad heading of phenolic compounds. Of these, the tannins are the most vital since they protect the wines from spoiling in addition to providing the astringency for which red wines are noted. In the oxidative process during aging, these tannins assume some carbon dioxide. Both pigments and tannins brown with age and provide many of the precipitates or residue at the bottom of the bottle.

The volatile constituents of wine are often detected in their excess rather than in their harmony. The higher alcohols, esters, and aldehydes, as well as the principal volatile acid, acetic acid or vinegar, lend the unique qualities of complexity in smell and taste. Without them, wine would be water and alcohol and no more inviting than straight vodka and water. It is always the harmony of these diverse elements that produce the superlative wines.

Acid Balance

Aside from sweetness, the most prominent elements in a wine are the natural fruit acids. Acid balance is essential to the overall harmony of fermented grapes. The way these fruit acids are

TABLE 8.2 Chemical Constituents of Table Wines

Components	Unit	Range	Red, Avg	Rosé, Avg	Dry White, Avg	Sweet White, Avg	Champagne, Avg
Carbon dioxide	%	0.01–0.05*					1.5
Chloride†	ppm	10–80	35	40	33	30	30
Sulfate	ppm	70–1000	680	600	700	700	600
Sulfur dioxide	ppm	0–590	109	120	142	171	88
Calcium	ppm	29–99	62	70	63	61	67
Copper	ppm	0–9	0.2	0.1	0.2	0.2	0.3
Iron	ppm	0–20	6.0	3.0	4.7	3.8	7.5
Potassium	ppm	180–1620	794	673	780	698	740
Sodium‡	ppm	10–200	85	160	113	97	68
Methyl alcohol	ppm	20–230					
Ethyl alcohol	% (vol)	10.2–14.2	12.2	12.2	11.9	12.4	12.5
Higher alcohols	ppm	140–417	298	249	254	218	246
Glycerol	%	0.4–1.5	0.9	0.8	0.7	0.9	0.7
Acetaldehyde	ppm	5–292	46	80	91	128	83
pH		2.84–4.07	3.68	3.45	3.52	3.50	3.20
Acetic acid	ppm	220–1490	470	290	290	430	500
Citric acid	ppm	T–500					
Lactic acid	%	0.1–0.5	0.2		0.2		
Succinic acid	ppm	500–2000					
Tartaric acid	%	0.4–1.1	0.6	0.6	0.6	0.6	0.7
Hexoses§	%	0.02–4.80	0.21	1.12	0.29	4.07	1.50
Pentoses	%	0.08–0.20					
Total esters	ppm	60–557	280	260	244	288	191
Volatile esters	ppm	19–192	79	73	68	80	34
Tannins	%	0.01–0.36	0.18	0.05	0.03	0.03	0.04
Amino acids	ppm	100–2000					
Choline	ppm	17–41					
Mesoinositol	ppm	220–730					
Thiamine	μg/l	0–240	10	10	20		
Riboflavin	μg/l	60–220	130	130	90		
Pantothenic acid	μg/l	70–450	370	290	370		
Pyridoxine	μg/l	220–820	470	370	260		
Nicotinic acid	μg/l		960	410	570		
Cyanocobalamin	mμg/l	9–25	12	10	3		
Folic acid	μg/l		15	21	18		
Biotin	μg/l	0.6–4.6					
Total solids‖	%	1.7–8.3	2.9	2.6	2.4	5.7	3.3

Source: Reproduced with permission from Leake, C. D. and Silverman, M.: ALCOHOLIC BEVERAGES IN CLINICAL MEDICINE. Copyright © 1966 by Year Book Medical Publishers, Inc., Chicago, 24.

*Range values of 0.01–0.05% apply only to normal still (nonsparkling) wines.

†Higher values have been reported from wines produced in European coastal areas.

‡Values indicated here apply to most wines; Higher values, up to 815 ppm, have been found in some American and European wines treated with ion-exchange resins.

§Usually the hexoses occur as glucose and fructose in a 1:1 ratio. In certain products, such as so-called kosher wines, the beverages are artificially sweetened, and the sugar content may be as high as 15% or more.

‖Customarily the total solids of wines are described as "total extract."

Dr. A. Dinsmoor Webb is shown operating a gas chromatograph at the University of California at Davis. This gas chamber permits identification of minute components of wines.

TABLE 8.3 Major Wine Chemistry and Its Effects

Major Chemical Components	Visual and Tasting Effects
Sugars Glucose, fructose sucrose, lactose, pentose methylpentose, maltose and others in trace amounts	Sweetness, viscosity, flavors
Alcohols Ethanol, methanol and higher alcohols such as isoamyl, isobuytl, n-hexyl	Aroma, flavor, body and microbiological stability
Aldehydes Acetaldehyde, acetoin, L. diacetyl, hydroxymethyl, furfural	Aroma, flavor, complexity
Acids Tartaric, malic, succinic, citric, acetic, inorganic acids, tannic, ethyl acetate	Tartness, flavors, stability, aroma
Hydrogen ions (pH)	Flavor, color, stability
Polyphenols Anthocyanins, flavonols, vanillin, pigments	Astringency, flavor, color, microbiological stability
Vitamins B-complex, pantothenic acid, nictinic acid, Vitamin P	Complexity, nutrition
Esters Combinations of acids and alcohols	Aroma, bouquet, flavor
Minerals Potassium, sodium, iron, copper, magnesium, trace amounts of others	Complexity, bouquet

TABLE 8.4 Scale of pH

Number	Range
0	Equals total acidity
2.3	Is equivalent to lemon juice
2.5	Makes wine tart and acidulous
3.1	Is close to vinegar in tartness
3.2–3.3	Is ideal for most white wines for microbiological stability
3.4–3.6	Is sufficient in red wines that have tannic microbiological stability
3.95	Has so little acid the wine is flat
7	Is neutral with no acidity

measured by grape growers and winemakers can be confusing to the novice consumer. Very often there are two statements in the literature or on the label concerning acidity—one gives the total acidity as a percent of the volume and the other states the pH of the fluid. It is important to understand these quite distinct measurements.

First, the *total acidity* includes both the *fixed* and the *volatile* acids that can be measured in the must or the finished wine. Now, an easy way to distinguish between fixed and volatile acids is to remember that the volatile portion is acetic acid which, in the presence of air, can transform the wine to vinegar by reducing out the alcohol. Volatile acidity is always present in minute proportions and, if plentiful, gives off the vinegary odors.

By contrast, the *fixed acids* are those that provide the style and character of the wine—tartaric, malic, succinic, citric—and they are usually expressed in terms of a percent of *tartaric,* the dominant acid. Now, the sum of the volatile and fixed acids equals the total acidity—usually totaling from .6 to .9 percent. That's fairly straightforward.

When it comes to understanding what pH means, the layman is often reduced to mumbles. Here's an easy way to place the pH factor into logical perspective. Since chemically it is a measurement of the hydrogen ions in the wine, it really gives you a rough intensity level of active acidity. The pH tells us of the acids that actually impinge upon our tongues and palates and create definable tartness.

The pH scale actually includes total acidity at one end—the one at the number 0. At the far end of the scale, the number 14 measures no acidity but rather total alkalinity. It follows then that the number 7 registers neutrality between acidity and alkalinity. Memorize table 8.4, and you will easily master pH in wine.

Cherry wood casks over 300 years old are shown in the sherry bodega of Los Apostoles.

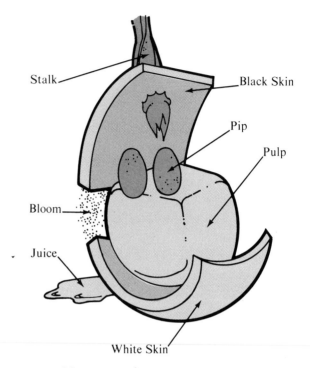

Stalk

Black Skin

Pip

Pulp

Bloom

Juice

White Skin

Figure 8.2 *Anatomy of a grape.*

Obviously, the lower the number, the higher the fixed acidity, which is what we taste. As was stated in the previous section, the amount of sugar in solution affects the intensity of the acid taste, as do the coldness or warmth of the wine and the presence of carbon dioxide in sparkling wines, the presence of tannin in red wines, or any flavoring agents.

To sum up: In the total acidity, stated as a percent of volume, the lower the number the lower the amount of acidity. A wine of .5 percent would be quite flat to the taste. A wine of .9 percent would be quite tart. In the pH measurement the opposite is true. The lower the number, the more acidic the wine.

W ine is, indeed, a living thing, brash in its youth, full-blossoming in its maturity, but subject, if not used, in time, to senility, decay, and death.
Brother Timothy Deiner, F.S.C.

In certain growing areas such as Germany, Washington State, and some of the eastern states, the grapes mature at above the ideal 1 percent of total acidity. Three methods are employed to reduce the acid content to acceptable levels. Amelioration, which amounts to watering the musts, is permitted although loss of fruitiness in the wine often occurs as a result. Biological reduction occurs with the bacterial conversion of malic to lactic acid and, finally, certain chemical salts and syn-

thetic polymer resins can precipitate the acids to crystals for ease of removal. Unless care is taken, off flavors can occur in the latter process.

Within the grape itself, the acidity is highest near the seeds and lowest at the skins. As a consequence, the higher acidities occur in the second and third pressings of the musts as compared to the ideal balance in the original free run juice, that which falls freely before pressing. The many variations between grapes from different vineyards and different picking conditions, as well as the wide spectrum of total acidities in finished and aging wines, almost mandates the blending process. Nearly every wine in the world is blended to attain a balance in taste qualities. The balance in acidity maintains the bright color in red wines and the pleasurable fruitiness in the whites and inhibits bacteriological spoilage in both.

The critical effect of acidity in wine can be perceived by sipping from two glasses of water into one of which you have placed a small amount of lemon juice. You will discover the pleasant, refreshing, and inviting finish of the one with the acid; because of their lack of acidity, flat wines seldom satisfy. Ideal total acidity in white versions is considered to be .8 percent as compared to .6 percent in red wines. In the United States wine is measured in terms of tartaric acid although many other types are present.

The sugar that sacrifices itself to the fermentation function is the other crucial element in grape juice. Sugars in must are measured according to a scale invented by a man named Brix, or perhaps by his predecessor, Balling. The measurement of 20 Brix or Balling simply means that the fluid has 20 grams of sugar for every 100 grams of solution at 20°C. These are the solids available for fermentation, and they dictate the alcohol production. Together with the acid concentration, they decide the price paid for grapes. As with pH, there is an appropriate range (see table 8.5).

The Brix and acid levels are measured from a sampling taken in the field to determine when to harvest, and are measured again when the gondola arrives at the fermenter, at times during the fermentation, and finally during the cleaning and aging periods. Usually the winemaker will have predetermined the degree of sweetness or Brix desired in the finished wine. About 2.3 degrees of heat is generated during the conversion of each percent of Brix, so that many of the fermenting tanks are now equipped with polyurethane cooling jackets to slow the process.

During fermentation, both color and phenolic compounds emerge as a result of contact with skins and seeds. Red wines are kept in contact with the skins for specific periods, often up to three or four days. White wines can be made from red or dark-skinned grapes, but the process of separating the pulp and juice without color transfer is tricky. Nevertheless,

TABLE 8.5 Limits for Sugar, Acid, and pH Levels in Wine

	Minimum	Maximum	Ideal
Brix (sugar)	18%	24%	22%
Total acid	.6%	1%	.7–.9%
pH	3	3.8	3.5

the majority of French champagnes utilize Pinot Noir, a deep-colored red grape. Very short contact with the skins during fermentation, often as little as a half a day, produces the rosé or pink wines. The phenolic compounds in red grape skins is almost double that found in white or light skin grapes, although the seeds of both have heavy concentrations. White wines are predominantly fermented off their skins, regardless of the skin color, so that they have relatively slight concentrations of phenolics. Some white musts are left on the skins for very short periods of time to obtain a slight tannic effect in the wine.

The theoretical yield of alcohol is 51.1 percent of the Brix or sugar content. For all practical purposes, the range is 48 to 50 percent. Hence a fermentation with 21.5 Brix should produce alcohol content of about 11 percent (see table 8.6). The 12 percent designation on most American labels allows a half percentage either way because it is virtually impossible to hit the mark with every batch.

TABLE 8.6 Brix (Residual Sugar), Acidity, and Percent of Alcohol in Various Wines and Spirits

Brand Name	Type	Alcohol (%)	Brix	Acid (%)
Alexis Lichine '70	P. Chardonnay	13.2	0.5	0.68
Alianca '70	Rosé	12.0	0.5	0.80
Almadén Cream	Sherry	19.5	7.0	0.45
Bon Dieu des Vignes '70	Graves	12.0	0.5	0.69
Christian Bros. Meloso Cream	Sherry	19.5	7.0	0.45
Christian Bros. Château La Salle	Dessert	12.0	9.5	0.72
Cockburns Sp. Reserve	Port	20.0	5.0	0.42
Danish Kijaka	Blackberry	20.0	15.0	0.56
Duff Gordon Santa Maria Cream	Sherry	20.0	8.0	0.45
Galliano	Liqueur	45.7	21.5	0.09
Gallway's Irish Coffee	Liqueur	40.0	25.5	0.08
Harvey's Bristol Cream	Sherry	20.0	10.5	0.465
Hiram Walker Blackberry	Brandy	40.0	14.0	0.075
Hiram Walker Cherry	Brandy	40.0	15.0	0.12
Hiram Walker Peach	Brandy	40.0	16.0	0.075
Manischewitz Cream	Concord	12.5	9.5	0.585
Mateus	Rosé	12.0	0.0	0.75
Meirs No. 44 Cream	Sherry	18.0	11.0	0.48
Mouton Cadet '70	Bordeaux	11.5	0.5	0.62
Mouton Cadet '67	Bordeaux	11.5	0.0	0.60
Prinzessin Moselblumchen '68	Moselle	10.5	1.5	0.57
Sandeman	Sherry	19.0	8.5	0.44
Taylor Tawny	Port	18.0	8.0	0.46

Source: Vintage (June, 1974), 18.

A handful of men can supervise the seventy-tank crushing and fermenting facility of the Christian Brothers at St. Helena from a central control tower and can direct the flow of newly crushed juice through crushers, presses, fermenting tanks and, finally, to aging-tank farms. The thirty-five jacketed tanks provide a cool atmosphere for fermentation of white and rosé wines. The regular stainless steel tanks contain red wines fermenting at ambient air temperatures. The farther from the control core, the larger the fermentation tanks; expansion in future years will utilize this same control tower.

In fermentation, the must, in effect, protects itself from the air-activated acetobacter by expelling a blanket of CO_2 over the top of the fermenting tank. From the time the wine leaves that tank, it is protected from exposure to air both to prevent oxidation and to foil the ever-present acetobacter vinegar maker. While this medley of sugar conversion merrily proceeds, aldehydes and esters form compounds of alcohols and acids and volatiles create the distinctive odors and tastes.

Secondary Fermentation

Finally, there often occurs a natural secondary ferment called malo-lactic fermentation which is little known outside of the winery. Winemakers of old noticed that it generally happened in the spring, about the time of bud break, almost as if the wine attempted to react again to the warming sun. It was recognized as a natural phenomenon as early as 1864, but was not fully understood until 1900. Now it is utilized, or avoided, according to the preference and needs of individual wineries.

One advantage of this fermentation is microbiological stability. In malo-lactic fermented wines, the winemaker is assured of clarity and color stability after bottling as well as considerably extended shelf life for the wine. The fermentation is caused by a single-celled bacteria which reduces the malic acid in wine to lactic acid, lessening the overall acidity and releasing CO_2, causing gassiness in the process. The accumulation of multiplying cells can produce turbidity or cloudiness in the bottle, so normally the process is either encouraged or inhibited long before bottling.

Highlights

- There are hundreds of fermented products being made today, including foods, and industrial and commercial products.
- The grape ferment probably predated all others since the grape is so rich in minerals and with its large water content provides the natural medium for fermentation.
- Louis Pasteur explained the mysteries of yeast fermentation and bacterial spoilage in the 1850s.

- About 48 percent of the grape sugars are converted into alcohol, mainly ethanol.
- The two critical elements in wine fermenting are the Brix or percent of sugar and the acid level in the harvested grapes.
- A secondary bacterial fermentation, called malo-lactic, transforms the malic acid to lactic acid and is desirable in reds and to be avoided in whites.

The famous aging cellars of the Christian Brothers, typical of the late nineteenth century winery buildings, were designed virtually as above-ground caves with thick walls that help retain the coolness necessary for proper aging.

Malo-lactic fermentation is desirable in red wine production where the taste goal is astringency rather than acidity, and where longer life is desired. In whites grown in cooler climates, malic acid dominates so that it is desirable to bring the acid level down. In California, where the acid levels are often on the low side, malo-lactic fermentation is shunned in favor of centrifuging the new wines, keeping them cool, and rendering them sterile by infusion of greater concentrations of SO_2.

The problem with SO_2 lies in noticeable amounts of objectionable sulfur on the tongue or in the nose. Malo-lactic fermentation also produces an acid called diacetyl which is responsible for the buttery flavor and finish in many red wines. In excess, diacetyl yields a sour milk or sauerkraut odor because it originates from the same type of ferment as these two other foods.

Finally, a winery produces many commercial by-products such as tartaric acid, tannins, vinegar, and oils that may be utilized in everything from sodas and babyfoods to photographic processing. In sum, the wine grape, so abundant and productive, provides for man in many a wondrous way. It is the only food that continues developing and enriching itself once bottled—truly a living symphony!

Residual Sugar in Wine

One final comment should be made about residual sugar. Since Americans and many Europeans appreciate the taste of sugar, wines with recognizable sugar levels dominate some markets. Wine snobs decry these sweeter wine blends while themselves consuming copious quantities of trendy sweet liqueurs and sugar-laden desserts. It is one of the ironies of the current wine renaissance that wines with sugar are deemed of somewhat lesser elegance. Of course, this is nonsense. It all depends upon the style of wine that is being consumed.

Many traditional wine cultures around the world treasure all styles of wine—the ascetic dry wine, the bright and elegant medium dry rosé and the full, rich dessert variety.

Still *Wines*

9

While operating procedures vary from country to country, still wines are those produced without carbonation or herbal compounding. It is possible in production to enhance as well as to ruin good fruit. Practitioners argue, aside from the romance of it all, whether wine making is an art. Without a doubt, it is at least a sophisticated craft involving great skill, perception, and judgment at each step in the process. In this respect, it is distinguished from other beverage alcohols which are produced more mechanically. Amateurs do not make great wines, even by accident!

Financial controversy about grape prices is avoided by grower and winemaker through an independent sampler employed by the state of California. Before the gondola packed with grapes tips them into the hopper, this inspector takes samples of the grapes from each side of the gondola, including grapes from the upper and lower levels. He utilizes a hand refractometer which bends light through the solution revealing on a scale the amount of sugars. This sampling reveals the true sugar/acid ratio of the batch at hand, and the results are accumulated for the produce of an entire vineyard in order to establish grape prices.

It is at this point that sulfur dioxide is administered to render inactive the wild yeast accumulated on the fruit skins. In all but a few areas of the world, cultivated yeasts are developed in the laboratory to assure more rapid, more exact, and much more controllable fermentations. While the practice of using sulfur probably originated with the Greeks, its widespread acceptance certainly dates from the late Middle Ages

I often wonder what the Vintners buy
One-half so precious as the stuff they sell.
Omar Khayyám

when wood replaced the smoother amphorae for storage and transportation. Lamb and Mittelberger (*In Celebration of Wine and Life,* 1980) write that

> it wasn't until the sixteenth century, when the Middle Ages had receded into the pages of history, that enologists adapted a known technique—the burning of sulphur—to the sterilization of their vats and casks; sulphur was useful, too, as an agent in arresting fermentation, and as a preservative during the aging process in wines.

From this point in the process, red-skinned grapes are treated in a manner differently from the whites. They are allowed to ferment with their skins and seeds. This process introduces phenolic compounds, primarily pigments and tannins, that eventually impart the bitter tastes and astringency. As much as .4 percent by weight in these musts originates as tannins.

Terms

amphora Greek, Egyptian, and Roman jars for shipping and storing wine, usually lined with pitch.

apéritif French for appetizer; therefore, a wine designed to whet the appetite before the meal, such as vermouth.

appellation controlée French system for controlling growth and production of top wines; wines so designated are, in effect, guaranteed.

aroma Odor of wine generally attributed to original grapes.

auslese Late harvested grapes touched with botrytis mold.

beerenauslese Literally "berry selection," refers to wine from handpicked botrytis molded grapes.

blending Simply mixing or marrying two batches of wine, an almost universal technique because few batches are perfectly balanced.

bouquet The odor from wine attributed to the aging process and not the original grapes.

breathing Term for the controversial yet persistent theorizing about the bouquet of wines developing by standing after the removal of the cork.

cask Large container, usually made from oak, for aging or shipping wine.

cellar Underground storage room for aging wines, originally chosen for cool atmosphere.

centrifuge Mechanical device to whirl wine solids away from the wine.

chai French ground-level wine warehouse.

château bottled French for estate bottled.

claret English term from Middle Ages for red wine from the Bordeaux area of France; now also a blend or generic red wine.

cork Bark of oak tree used as airtight stopper.

corky A term to describe wine ruined by diseased cork.

cru French for "growth"; also a classification, such as *grand cru,* to designate better vineyards and vintages.

cuvée A batch or a blend of wines.

decanting Pouring wine from the bottle to another container usually to draw off without sediment.

deposit Sediment precipitated in bottle aging.

dry The absence of sugar; medium dry, the presence of up to 2% sugar; medium sweet, the presence of 3–5% sugar; sweet, the presence of 5% or more sugar; the sugar is that retained from the fruit.

edelfäule German for the late harvest botrytis mold on grapes.

eiswein Very rare wine produced from ripe grapes that have been partially frozen on the vine before picking.

enology The science of wine making.

estate bottled Wine grown, vinified, and bottled on the property adjacent to the winery.

filtering The procedure used to strain out suspended solids created in fermentation or aging.

fining The procedure used to clear wines of solids by adding materials that combine with the sediment and settle to the bottom of the holding tank.

foxy A term used to describe the intense aroma of wines made from native American grapes—the Concord smell.

frizzante Italian for medium bubbly wine.

fruity A term to describe wine, particularly those young and remarkably acidic, like the fruit from which it was made.

generic Originally the regional European wines like Burgundy or Bordeaux; now usually designates a blend of wines without specific varietal concentrations; the generics today are Burgundy, Chablis, Rosé, Sauterne, Rhine, and Claret.

goût French for "taste"; hence *goût de bois* is woody taste and *goût de terroir* is racy taste or peculiar flavor.

hectare French land measurement containing 2.47 acres.

hectolitre One hundred litres or 26.4 gallons, the common metric measurement.

hock English word for Rhine-type wines.

hydrometer Floating instrument used to measure the density or amount of solid matter in fluid; hence sugar in must or wine.

keller German for "cellar."

lees The sediment left in the bottom of a fermenter or wine cask.

Limousin A forest in France producing particularly valuable oak for aging casks.

maderization The process of oxidation in wines which produces dark colors; is often associated with a woody taste.

may wine Light, usually white, wine which is treated with woodruff.

mis en bouteilles French for "put in this bottle"; usually followed by *au château,* meaning the wine was grown and bottled there.

musty A negative term meaning an unpleasant moldy smell in wine.

négociant A French wine shipper.

nose Both the natural aroma grape smells and the bouquet odors which derive from aging—all the smells in wine.

ordinaire French for everyday table wine.

organoleptic Examining wine, or any other food, involving all the senses.

pasteurization The process of heating wine to 150° F to kill yeasts and bacteria, used only to stabilize inexpensive vintages.

press A series of mechanical devices to separate juice from pomace, all the way from free run to hydraulic presses.

pourriture noble The French for "noble rot" or desirable botrytis cinerea on overripe grapes.

racking Drawing wine off its lees into a clean cask.

red wine Literally any coloration from the skins in the wine; hence, classically, both red and rosé wines.

rosé wine A light red produced by limited skin contact time in fermentation.

sack Wines mostly from the Mediterranean and mostly sweet and fortified.

sec The French word for "dry."

sediment The deposits of solid materials thrown off or precipitated during aging.

spätlese German for late harvesting; generally sweet and soft wine.

tirage First bottling of wine, syrup and yeast in French champagne; means "to draw off."

trockenbeerenauslese Trocken means "dry" in German so these are the latest of the late-picked berries that are nearly devoid of water from noble rot.

ullage Amount of wine lost by breathing through the walls of the casks while aging; the empty space in cask which results from the breathing of wine through pores of the barrels during aging.

varietal A wine with the particular grape name on the label, guarantees a predominance of that particular grape in the bottle.

viniculture Wine grape cultivation.

vintage The annual grape harvest; hence a vintaged wine derives from the grapes grown in the year named; it is not necessarily a guarantee of quality, only of age.

viticulture Grape cultivation.

wine The beverage produced by fermentation of natural sugars in fruits and certain flowers and vegetables.

woody The smell of wood derived from long aging in casks, which can be attractive or unpleasant.

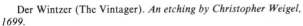

Der Wintzer (The Vintager). An etching by Christopher Weigel, 1699.

A state inspector uses a core sampler to extract grapes for sugar-acid measurement.

Pumping-over, the old method of extracting various levels of pigmentation from dark-skinned grapes, involves the recirculation of juice from the bottom of the tanks back through the cap of skins and seeds on the surface of the fermenter.

An auger, the screw device in the hopper, pushes the bunches forward into the crusher-stemmer where the grapes are crushed and separated from their stems. Modern crushers, which can handle up to 60 tons of grapes per hour, generally utilize paddles to break the skins as the product eases forward, enabling the fluid to escape through progressively smaller holes in the rotating housing. Eventually, the crushed grapes slip through the last of the holes, leaving the stems, leaves, and other MOG (material other than grapes) to be ejected at the end.

The wine press is truly the most important single piece of equipment in the modern winery. Ideally, only the *free run juice* that separates naturally from the skins and seeds and contains the smallest amount of solids is used. As much as 75 percent of the juice falls free in this manner, but the remaining portion must also be salvaged. These second and third portions require pressure squeezings and are called *press runs*. Filtered, centrifuged, and fermented separately, the press runs produce lower quality, often highly tannic and acidic wines which are used for blending purposes. The final hydraulic pressings can produce so many off flavors that this wine is reserved for distilling into brandy.

But the first press, centrifuged, and cold-fermented wines emerge with a fresher, fruitier finish since the musts ferment at a slower, more steady rate. The solid materials normally in the must at quantities of 10 percent or more are reduced to less than 1 percent before fermentation begins. Wines of pronounced varietal character are not diminished in style or character after centrifuging and fermentation. Second and third pressings with their greater concentrations of solids can be centrifuged to very acceptable wines.

(A)

In ancient times, both heavy weights and the manually operated basket screw press provided the immense pressure needed to extract the maximum in juice (A). A worker is shown using such a press today in the region of Trentino Italy (B).

(B)

FERMENTATION

A great deal of effort is put into the culturing of particular strains of saccharomyces yeast. Each winery cultures its own and introduces it into the fermenter at about 1 gallon for every 100 gallons of wine must. After this occurs, nature takes its pleasant course. The greatest fear of the winemaker is a stuck fermentation, a term describing the situation when the temperature in the fermenter becomes too high and the yeasts are killed. Fermentation of these dormant half-wines can sometimes be restarted through cooling and aeration, but poor quality inevitably ensues. Consequently, a great deal of attention is directed to the temperature and the progress of the yeasts in the fermenters to ensure that the heat created by fermentation is controlled. Most fermentations are concluded in a matter of days or weeks, but the widespread use of cooling jackets has led to especially slow fermentations of up to several months. Wines made in this manner retain a maximum fruitiness since the normal heat of fermentation is drastically reduced.

There follows a period of racking and fining which may take up to several months. These steps are designed to clean up the fresh young wines, freeing them of spent yeast cells and other extraneous solids suspended in the process of fermentation. In the traditional method of racking, the wine rests in a holding tank which, because of gravity, permits the natural descent of all remaining lees to the bottom of the tank. Fining consists of introducing substances to hurry the settling process and to eliminate other solids that do not naturally release from the fluid. The American consumer prefers bright and shiny drinks so that this process is especially important in wines intended for the United States market. Fining agents today include gelatin casein, at about 1 ounce per 100 gallons, and a clay mineral called bentonite, at 4 pounds per 100 gallons. As these powders sift gently down through the tank, proteinaceous materials coagulate, eliminating turbidity from the finished wines.

The enormous strength and imperturability of wine is proved in the filtering process. The best new filtering equipment combines a vacuum tank and diatomaceous earth. Whether through this mud pack of ancient earth or through fine filter pads, the wine emerges clean and healthy, ready for a period of tank aging before bottling. Malo-lactic fermentation may be induced or avoided. Acidity may be lowered through chemicals, such as calcium carbonate, which combine with tartaric acid to precipitate crystals. Acidity is often lacking in hot climate harvest areas, like Spain, where the new wines are "plastered" with gypsum or calcium sulfate to raise acid levels.

The adaptation of the centrifuge to wine making opened new vistas for light, clear wines by reducing the natural solids.

Fermenting tanks with jacketed cooling exteriors at the Torres Winery in Spain.

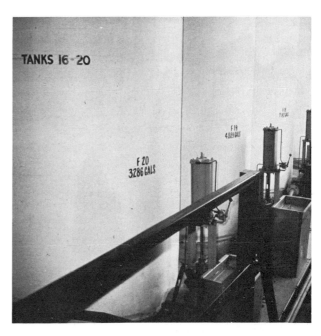

Similar fermenting tanks at The Christian Brothers in the Napa Valley.

The innovative new technique of macération carbonique *is shown in these pictures from Montevina Wines in Plymouth, California. The grapes are dumped whole into special 5,000 gallon fermenting tanks. White zinfandel juice is pumped into the tank carrying the yeast cells in order to fill all the air space and to initiate extra-* berry fermentation. Intra-berry fermentation also proceeds through osmosis. When the free juice reaches dryness, the whole mass is pressed, and some fermentation continues from the intra-berry must.

(A)

(B)

The cooper's tools (A); the measurement of a barrel end (B); and the endless task of repairing the valuable barrels (C). The design and construction of barrels has changed little from earliest times.

(C)

Once filtered, the product is finally ready to be aged. Since wine is a living food product, changing and adapting to its environment for years, the techniques employed in winery aging are varied, complex, and of the utmost importance. Thirty types of wood are in use for cooperage throughout the world, with oak universally judged the best. European oak, particularly *Quercus robur* possesses substantially more tannin and other extracts than other oak types and is, therefore, the most preferred. A European barrel today can cost a California wine-maker over $300. *Quercus alba,* available on the eastern coast of the United States, is most common among American woods. American cooperage ranges from $60 to $100 per barrel.

Fifty to fifty-five gallon barrels have the most desirable impact on the wine. Thirty-one pieces of wood constitute one

of these barrels which can have a life of up to 100 separate wines. Such a small barrel provides 3.75 inches of wood exposure to each gallon and can execute its aging in half as much time as a 500 gallon container.

What occurs in the container is not fully understood, but it is certain that the barrel staves somehow impart an extract to the wine. Up to 10 percent of dry oak is tannin, similar to tannin in grape skins. Another phenol called vanillin is present in oak in sufficient amounts to affect the wine. Very often, wines will be introduced at early aging to younger barrels where the extract impact is greatest and then will be moved to older casks for longer periods of resting. Finally, the wines that show unusual promise are moved again into smaller casks for finishing.

4 695 6500
mission 695 6544

(A)

(B)

(C)

Just as children in the same family develop at different rates, wines develop at quite distinct paces, even though vinted and barreled from the same vineyards on the same days. This fact necessitates a wide variety in styles of cooperage as well as constant monitoring and tasting of the developing wines. Brother Timothy is shown recording a monthly check of cabernet in a several thousand gallon cask (A). The cooper at Robert Mondavi Winery finishes construction of a new French oak barrel (B). The phenomenal Almadén Cienega warehouse contains 37,299 fifty-gallon oak barrels with an elevated carriage to facilitate the topping off of the ullage (C).

SMALL OAK IN CALIFORNIA

Since table wine production enjoyed but muted interest in the period after the Second World War, it was not until the 1960s that the advantages and uniqueness of small cooperage became widely recognized in the California wine industry. Pioneers such as Andre Tchelistcheff at Beaulieu Vineyards and Brother Timothy at the Christian Brothers had long used the smaller casks for preferential lots, but the majority of the table wines emerged from large cooperage to the bottling rooms.

After 1960, debate about, and experimentation with, cooperage occurred often at heated levels. A distinct "oaky" flavoring (the overtones from the small cooperage), which became common in wines produced in the sixties and seventies, had as many detractors as enthusiasts. The work of Professor Vernon Singleton at the University of California at Davis isolated substantial differences in wine character imparted from American and European oak. Wines housed in American oak contained higher levels of odoriferous vanillin and oak lactone so that a pungent nose was characteristic of the wines. In contrast, the European oak produced nearly double the tannin and phenols in the wines so that these were notable for both body and astringency. This research suggests that the more typically assertive Cabernets from Bordeaux, for example, or any other uniqueness typical to a certain winery's product is as much derived from the wood as from the soils and grapes.

Obviously, the small barrel has greater impact on the contents since more wine touches the wood. Consequently, the barrel more rapidly dissipates its extractives, with an effective life of about seven years. With the cost of European cooperage of this size exceeding $300, there is considerable experimentation going on with air-drying of the staves and fire coopering to see if American oak can more closely approximate the impact of the precious imports.

History provides abundant ironies, none more accidental than the discoveries of the attributes of oak both to the distiller and the vintner. While oak was preferred as the carrier for wines, spirits, and other foodstuffs in the Middle Ages, it was treasured not because of what it *did* but because of what it *did not* do. It *did not* impart off tastes of pine or eucalyptus, and its minute pores also assured little leakage. It was only when William of Orange cut off the prodigious flow of cognac to England that the effect of the barrels became apparent. By the time the stocks backed up in the barrels were tapped, the brandy had gained subtle nuances of smell and taste whereas formerly it had been harshly congeneric. The new technique of aging all spirits in oak extended throughout the western culture.

Similarly, the vintners began to observe significant changes when wines were stored in oak, particularly the highly tannic red wines that were allowed slightly more time in wood before bottling. Then, as now, topping off or filling the ullage space was done to prevent wine spoilage. Topping off is the procedure of adding the same type of wine to the barrels to

(A)

(B)

The large redwood casks in California are used extensively for fining and cleaning up jobs (A), *while stainless steel is used for settling tanks* (B).

(A)

(B)

Where wine barrels abound, creativity follows as seen in these attractive examples of barrel carving. Note that aside from the artistry, the barrels contain aging wines under the careful eye of the cellar master (A). Shown here are the famous Nierstein German casks (B).

compensate for evaporation. Topping off practices vary widely in wineries throughout the world. In California many winemakers fill the barrels each month throughout the aging period.

Whereas huge reds may remain in wood up to four years and can be matured in the bottle for another hundred, whites and rosés can be sold within two years after vintage with no wood aging. However, some noble varietals, Chardonnay, for example, can be kept in oak for three to six months.

Redwood tanks and those composed of stainless steel and glass are generally used today for wines of optimal fresh and fruity finish. Redwood is generally neutral in terms of complexing the wines and therefore is ideal as a container for racking and for the secondary malo-lactic fermentations. This transformation of malic to lactic acid softens the wine and stabilizes it against some bacteria. It is generally avoided in white wines through centrifuging and applications of SO_2.

The aging, or the complexing effect, in wines has been a wonder since the earliest recorded history of wine making. Greeks regularly aged wines up to fifty years in amphorae, jars lined with pitch and sealed tight. Egyptians adopted this custom, concentrating the fluids over the years to the point that the addition of nine parts of water was required before consumption. Many of the transformations of the five primary acids into aldehydes and esters are now demonstrable chemical facts. However, why they occur in barreled and bottled wine but not in any other bottled food does remain a mystery.

A variety of techniques have been developed over the years to shorten or even bypass the time required for aging. When you consider that millions of gallons of wines rest for three to five years, and consider the expense that such long periods of aging incur, you can well imagine why winemakers are interested in discovering new procedures for aging. Fast aging methods have included heat treatments, ultrasonic cobalt radiation, and infusing wood chips (100 pounds per 1000 gallons) with the same general properties as the wood staves. None have been successful.

THE CORK STOPPER

Simultaneous development of bottle shape and of the cork stopper resulted in the modern day corked and sealed wines, which imitate the hermetically sealed ancient amphorae. This opened the door to the modern golden age in wine making. Patient adaptation of the wine bottle gradually led in the eighteenth century to the elongated, cylindrical bottle appropriate for binning. As H. Warner Allen reports in *A History of Wine* (1961):

> Bottles were no enduring home for wine as long as they were compelled by their shape always to stand upright. . . . As Henry Purefoy evidently discovered, the cork in the upright bottle was not in contact with

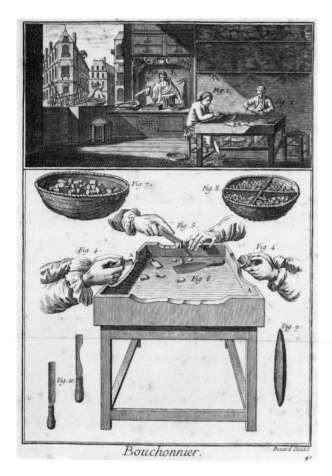

The line engraving, Le Bouchonnier, *shows the painstaking carving of early corks.*

Brother Timothy is pictured with selections of his famous corkscrew collection on display at the St. Helena Wine and Champagne Cellars. Included are over 1,300 devices from twenty-six countries.

the wine and soon dried and shrank. Below it was an air bubble, which provided vinegar and other hostile microorganisms, filtering through . . . with an ideal breeding ground.

Because of their buoyancy, corks were utilized in fishing and other enterprises by the Greeks and Romans, but not until around 1700 were they married to the bottle. In 1771, another advancement was made when the port bottle assumed its now familiar shape. Only four years later man recorded his first great vintage port—bottle aging had arrived.

Braudel traces the significance of the cork seal to the redevelopment of fine wines again in western civilization as a gradual process.

> And clarifying, bottling and the regular use of corks were still unknown in the sixteenth-century and possibly even in the seventeenth. By the eighteenth-century, the whole system was in working order, and collecting old empty bottles for wine merchants was one of the lucrative activities of London thieves.

CORKPULLERS

The famous British wine writer, Hugh Johnson, has described the application of cork as

> the most important event in the history of wine. . . . However well our ancestors may have been able to make their wine . . . it could never have reached anything like the point of soft, sweet perfection which a claret or burgundy can, if it is given the chance, today.

Since that day, literally thousands of devices have been invented to remove the cork. Knives, hooks, levers, screws, gears, and even rack and pinion gears have been employed. One device in Brother Timothy's famous corkscrew collection has an astounding 175 moving parts!

In 1946, the California Wine Institute commissioned a study under the direction of Paul Fredericksen to evaluate different types of corkscrews. The results of his fine work were published as *Corkscrews That Work,* which reports that the

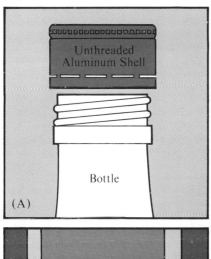

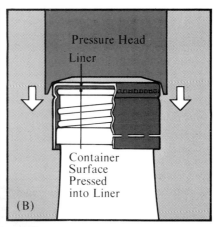

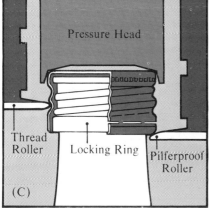

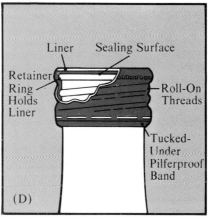

Figure 9.1 *The diagrams of the Alcoa RO (roll-on) demonstrate the sealing factors including the pilferproof band that must be broken to release the cap. A metal film in the top liner prevents oxygen entering the bottle.*

"hollow wire helix" type, commonly called the "waiter's corkscrew" provides the minimum cork breakage and the maximum pull with the least effort. The hollow center of the turning worm allows the cork to remain generally intact, and its length is sufficient to penetrate the bottom of the cork, gaining some purchase for the subsequent leveraged lift.

But many non-screw openers can also be found. Certainly the most ingenious ever developed are the tongs which literally remove the neck of the heavily encrusted vintage port bottles. Tongs are heated red hot and closed over the neck, below the heavily laden cork. The immediate application of a cool towel neatly cracks the glass, eliminating the whole upper portion along with the sediment-covered cork. A similarly novel adaptation of an ancient technique is found in what is now commonly called the AH SO remover. In previous centuries, this two-pronged device was known as the Butler's Friend since it permitted one to filch wine from numerous bottles and then to replace the cork intact. The AH SO remover consists of two prongs which are inserted alongside the cork which is then removed with a gentle turning movement.

Because of the innumerable types of corkscrews invented over the years—some strange, some austere—it is not surprising that dealers in these arcane antiquities formed an association in London on 1 October 1974, with the august title of the International Correspondence of Corkscrew Addicts. At this historic assemblage, Brother Timothy of the Christian Brothers was elected the first *Right of the Correspondence* because, in their collective wisdom, Americans would rather be Right than President. Though other Rights have since replaced him, the group appropriately named this corkscrew-collecting Brother a perpetual *Just Right*. Fifty members from seven countries now comprise this most singular wine-oriented group.

Selections from the vast cork-puller collection of Brother Timothy, now numbering over 1,500 types from thirty-one countries, may be seen both at the Christian Brothers Wine Museum near Ghirardelli Square in San Francisco and at the winery in St. Helena. From elaborate Elizabethan creations to the ultra fundamental, teflon-coated AH SO of today, they provide ample illustration of humans' conviction that wine is something special, something apart from other beverages.

TO CORK OR NOT TO CORK

A small debate is ongoing over the comparative benefits of cork closing and the seal attained by pilferproof screw caps. Some contend that chemical adaptation known as wine aging can be achieved just as completely under a variety of non-cork closures that includes aluminum, plastic, and pilferproof screw caps (see fig. 9.1). Research indicates that oxygen exchange continues through these closures at about the rate of .01 cubic centimeters per month during the aging cycle. Yet wine lore today holds the cork in mystical reverence as the only stopper that can maintain the wine's true potential. And since the majority of purchasing consumers swear by cork, one can consider the argument to be practically, if not scientifically, irrelevant.

With over 600 firms engaged in the trade, Portugal currently supplies about half of the world's production of cork stoppers, about 200 million kilograms annually. The source oak tree, *Quercus suber* thrives only in the Mediterranean climates—Portugal, Spain, France, Italy, and North Africa—as Thomas Jefferson woefully discovered when he tried and failed to cultivate it in Virginia. Up to thirty years of growth is required before the bark can be stripped in nine year cycles. Only the very best grade is suitable for wine bottles, and the cost runs between $50 and $60 per thousand corks.

Following grading, the cork is cut into strips which are fed to a punching machine that cuts out the appropriate sizes of corks. The length rises according to the intended length of aging, ranging from 38 mm. for common wines to 44 mm. for fine wines. Wines destined for long aging periods require the longest closures. The cork planchets are allowed to season for about one year before shipping. The cork cell walls are extraordinarily resilient, showing great flexibility under pressure and a tendency to return to natural size. The final step before insertion is application of a film of silicone and paraffin which assures both adhesion to the bottle and ease of removal.

With a heavy demand for such a very limited supply, the move to alternative closures seems inevitable. Composition and plastic closures have been used for some time, particularly with the sparkling wine varieties. It is a fairly safe bet that major and prestigious wine companies on the continent and in the United States will soon begin campaigns designed to convince the consumer that the essential in aging is limited exposure to the atmosphere—no matter the color or character of the stopper that accomplishes it.

PASTEURIZATION

A great deal of controversy rages over the use of the time-honored technique of pasteurization in order to obtain microbiological stability. Even Galen, the Roman physician and winemaker, used a crude heat exchange technique. Allen (1961) reports that Galen's "father had discovered that by heating his wine in a bad year he could prevent it from going bad—a definite anticipation of pasteurization." The controversy arises over using heat with premium quality wines intended to continue chemical growth once bottled. As a practical matter, the technique is limited to lower price wines as well as those of the dessert and fruit variety not designed for bottle aging. The premium quality wines are carefully filtered in sterile conditions to remove unwanted yeasts and bacteria. The technique of pasteurizing is simple enough. The wine is passed through a heat exchanger at 180°–185°F for about a minute, and the task is done.

Over a dozen California wineries, including such giants as Almadén and United Vintners, now merchandise the bag-in-the-box for bulk wines. From about sixty thousand units in 1975, this unique market probably expanded to over five million units in 1981. Ranging from one gallon to twenty liters in capacity the plastic/cardboard containers offer the attraction of light weight and easy use without exposure to the atmosphere.

BLENDING AND BOTTLING

Two other important procedures in wine making are blending and bottling. From the barrel, wines are blended, filtered again, and bottled. With the exception of a handful of small wineries, or with particularly splendid batches of varietals, all wines in the world are blends. Even the vintage-dated selections contain subtle blends of complementary batches within the wine-making year. For example, the great appellation wines of Bordeaux are predominantly blends of Cabernet Sauvignon, Merlot, and Cabernet Franc. Blending arises from the most obvious need to balance the wines in terms of color, acidity, complexity, bouquet, and so on. It is at this final stage of wine making, sometimes years remote from the vineyard, that the whole procedure approaches art.

Blending practices vary widely from winery to winery because of the relative differences in aging stocks and, more fundamentally, because of the point of view of the winemakers. Brother Timothy of the Christian Brothers, a foremost proponent of selective blending, and other blenders at major firms have long held that judicious merging of the parts creates a more harmonious whole. It goes without saying that there must be sufficient supplies of like wines in the winery to accomplish that harmony.

The blender works intuitively just like any good chef, although his choices involve tonnages rather than ounces. He blends minute proportions of the available stocks in hundreds of combinations in order to achieve the desired product. He may daily taste, organoleptically, over one hundred samples of blends. The winemaker seeks the defects, the off odors, the wanting hues, the imbalances in sugar, acid, and tannin. These nuances are incredibly subtle and can be detected only with the hushed concentration of a mystical rite.

Therefore the blender must intellectually isolate the fundamental qualities—aroma and bouquet, acidity, sweetness or lack of it, tannin, alcohol itself as a separate entity, body or viscosity, the oaky perfume of the barrel, oxidative evidences, and the complexity which results from the marriage of all of the above. Within these parameters, the blender utilizes judgment and memory. He judges how each new combination measures up to the memory of the idea of a perfect blend, or at least to the memory of the previous blend assembled in that laboratory some six months earlier.

Sweetness is a vital factor, particularly in the sensitive American market which favors sugared drinks. Indeed, high sugar content can help preserve the wines. However, it is not to sugar alone that the blender looks because alcohol itself and glycerine-prone wines of cool growing climates yield their own sensations of sweetness.

The natural tannins in the wine from skin exposure during fermentation and from extraction in the aging barrels are a regressive factor. Constantly under chemical attack, the tannins and phenolic compounds continually mollify in the wine and, therefore, must be most carefully adjudicated by the blender so that the color remains appropriate and the desired astringency does not fade. In contrast, the acids maintain a continuity and strength during the aging process. This points to the need for a strong acid base in any long-lived wine.

The alcohol level cited on the label can vary up to two degrees in table wines, usually between 11 and 12 percent, and this has a major impact on both tactile response and on the body of the merging wines. That body or mouth feel is perhaps the most mysterious of all the sensations, but also the most easily recognized since we silently tally every single fluid we ingest for its body, ranging from the ponderousness of syrup to the airy lightness of water. The blender must adjust the body of each combination to satisfy his current customers' idea of that particular variety of wine.

If all of this seems terribly complicated, that's because it is. Blending requires the training necessary for any art. In order to appreciate the complexity of blending, one needs to understand the attitude expressed by one of the world's most respected master blenders, Brother Timothy: "Wine, like the human being, is born, passes through adolescence, matures, grows old and, if not drunk in time, becomes senile and dies."

Philip F. Jackisch in the American Wine Society's manual called *Wine Blending* commented on what has been overlooked about the blending process versus the single year vintage:

The many types of filters prove the flavor stability of wines. The American preference for clean, clear drinking products demands heavy filtration. Shown here is a common plate and frame filter. Many types of pads are employed between the radiatorlike plates, and the wine is pumped through at about twenty-six pounds per square inch.

Some 20 years ago Singleton and Ough at the University of California at Davis, showed that mixing two commercially acceptable wines of similar quality never gave a blend that was poorer in sensory scoring than was the poorer of the pair . . . it may be true that the popularity of unblended vintaged varietal wines in the U.S. has reduced the average wine quality below what it could be with careful blending.

After a period of settling, the blended wines are rough filtered, chilled in tanks in cold rooms at about 28°–30° F, and then sterile filtered prior to bottling. These steps all help to clarify the wine and to eliminate the floating solids which can leave sediment in the bottle. The predominant solids, called potassium bitartrates, are potassium from the soils and tartaric acids of the grapes which combine during fermentation. While they are harmless and possess neither taste nor aroma, their presence often offends the consumer and, therefore, they are anathema to the winemaker. A variety of pad filters are used in filtering with the most popular being a muddy cake of several inches of diatomaceous earth. Cold rooms have tanks of up to ten thousand gallons in which most of the potassium bitartrates are crystallized and literally strained out before the final filtration.

Wine-tasting Procedures

10

One of the major difficulties faced by the American wine merchant is the concept of the *connoisseur*. Somehow there has developed the totally erroneous myth that only certain gifted and meticulously trained *savants* can distinguish the merits of the bottle. Sheer nonsense! Admittedly, either through special and prolonged training or with extraordinary natural talents, some charmed souls can and do perceive subtleties in fruit acid, identify tannin, sort out floral beauties, and recognize distinctive varietal nuances far more rapidly and certainly than others. However, the recognition of their superior talents has never inhibited my judgments, for those personal reflections upon tasting are as uniquely correct as any other judgment made about what I do and do not like in food.

Therefore, wine tasting should always be a joyous and confident affair, full of anticipation and searching, rewarded by that hint of recognition and jarred by a memory full of previous associations. Make no mistake, wine may well be the most complex and satisfying of foods, but it is still taken to measure by sight, smell, taste, and aftertaste. In these simple dimensions we are all truly unique experts!

For those bent on gleaning the full range of the tasting experience, several excellent texts are recommended: *Wines, Their Sensory Evaluation* by Amerine and Roessler, *How to Test and Improve Your Wine Judging Ability* by Irving H. Marcus, and *Wine Tasting* by Michael Broadbent. These and other scholarly publications provide excellent points of reference and common catchwords around which a wine tasting can be corralled into acceptable vocabulary. However, the infinite difficulty in communicating taste perceptions can be summed

All wines are by their very nature full of reminiscence, the golden tears and the red blood of summers that are gone.

Richard Le Gallienne

Man, as a social animal, requires something which he can sip as he sits and talks, and which pleases his palate, whilst it gives some ailment to the stomach, and stimulates the flow of general thoughts in the brain—civilized man must drink; but it should be wine.

Dr. Robert Druitt

up by the semanticist Adrienne Lehrer who directed a seven-month weekly wine tasting group bent on standardizing the language.

There is no evidence to suggest that a stable set of norms was ever established . . . What the experiment shows is that in a friendly, casual, social setting, the requirements for precise communication are rather low, even if people are motivated to use language carefully and thoughtfully.

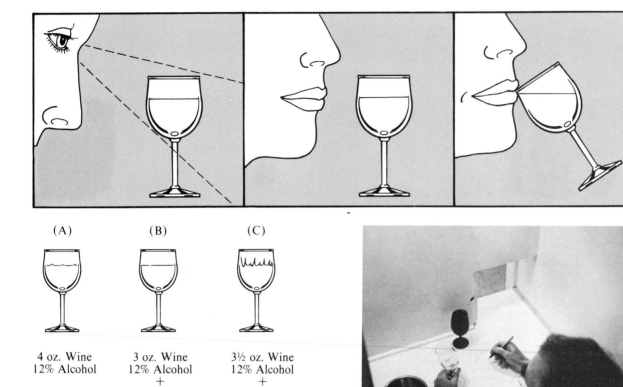

(A) (B) (C)

4 oz. Wine
12% Alcohol

3 oz. Wine
12% Alcohol
+
1 oz. of Water

3½ oz. Wine
12% Alcohol
+
½ oz. of Brandy

Figure 10.1 *Looking is nearly as important as smelling and tasting. The legs or molecular chains, clinging to the sides of the glass increase with alcohol and sugar content and are signs of long bottle age. A great deal can be discerned by color and consistency before the glass is first brought to the nose. A sharp, full whiff then reveals the aroma and bouquet.*

The tasting booths at the University of California, Davis campus are designed to eliminate all distractions from the wine being rated.

The above being accepted, I suggest the set of descriptive words from Broadbent as being sufficiently precise for the amateur and expert alike. I suggest that you utilize these standards and words to record your reactions in all of the wine and spirit tastings which follow. Each tasting selection has been chosen for its typicality and general availability in most markets.

Basic Descriptive Words in the Order of Tasting

Red Wines

| **Appearance** | *depth:* very light (VL)[a], light (L), medium-light (ML), medium-full (MF), full (F) or deep, very full (VF) or deep, opaque
colour/hue: purple, purple-rimmed, ruby, red, tile-red, brown-tinged, red-brown, mahogany
clarity: bright, lacking brightness, bitty, hazy, cloudy; light or heavy sediment | **Nose or bouquet** | *condition:* clean, unclean (sulphury, oxidized, etc.)
fruit: fruity, lacking fruit, varietal, named variety
development: dumb, immature, undeveloped, well-developed, forthcoming, very mature
quality: poor, ordinary, good, fine, great, magnificent |

Palate *apparent dryness:* (noticeably) dry; slightly or unusually sweet (for a red wine); tannic
body: very light (VL), light (L), medium-light (ML), medium (M), full-bodied (F), heavy
tannin: mellow, noticeably drying, marked
acid: supple, soft, refreshing, marked, over-acid, tart
fruit, flavour: fruity, lacking fruit; vinous; very flavoury, lacking flavour. Describe flavour—use analogies when appropriate
development: well-developed, very mature, mature, beginning to mature, undeveloped, green
overall balance: well-balanced, unbalanced
length and finish: long flavour, short; lingering, fine aftertaste

White Wines

Slight difference of emphasis, particularly regarding colour and sweetness:

Appearance *depth:* colourless, very pale, medium, deep
colour/hue: green-tinged, yellow-green, yellow, straw, yellow-gold, gold, amber, deep gold, brown
clarity: star-bright, bright . . . dull, cloudy

Nose or bouquet more or less as for red wines

Palate *dry/sweet:* bone dry, dry, medium-dry, medium-sweet, sweet, very sweet
body, acidity, fruit, development, balance, finish—more or less as for red wines. Tannin is not normally a factor in white wines.

Words Used in the Description of Wine, by Category

Words in Common Use

acid/acidity	finish	soft
aroma	fruity	sweet
balance/	grapey	tannin, tannic
well-balanced	hard	tough
bouquet	harsh	vinegary
clean	poor	watery
dry/	refreshing	
medium-dry etc.		

Words Which Need Qualifying

aftertaste	flat	ordinary
big	full	penetrating
bland	heavy	peppery
body	light	positive
bright	little	rich
character	long	round
coarse	mature/maturity	sour
dull	meaty	strong
fat	medium-	weak
fine	neutral	youthful

Words to Use with Care

astringent	flinty	robust
baked	forthcoming	rough
bite	green	sharp
bitter	hot	smoky
corked	iron	stalky
dumb	maderised	tang/tangy
earthy	mouldy	tart
extract	nutty	varietal
feminine	oxidized	vinous, vinosity
flabby	piquant	woody
	pungent	zesty/zestful

Additional Qualitative Descriptions

aromatic	mellow	silky
breed, well-bred	metallic	smooth
complex	musty	spicy
distinguished	noble	subtle
elegant	perfumed	supple
finesse	powerful	unripe
flowery	raw	velvety
fragrant	ripe	well-developed
insipid	scented	yeasty
luscious	sensuous	

Terms

acetic Vinegary smell; sharp, over-tart on the palate. A vinegary condition resulting from the action of acetobacter, harmful ferments that attack wine left open in bottle, or fermented at too high a temperature, or carelessly bottled. Ullaged wine, whether in cask or bottle, will usually be suspect. The latter is usually due to poor, wormy or dried-out corks, which let air in and wine out (weepers), the remaining wine often becoming acetic and undrinkable.

acid, acidity On the nose: mouth-watering, refreshing (tartaric), sometimes like raw cooking apples (malic); detectable on the tongue, giving wine essential crispness and zing. 'Volatile' acids are more pronounced on the nose, 'fixed' acids (tartaric, succinic and citric) less so. Esters of both acids make an important contribution to the overall bouquet of wine. There are several types and degrees of acidity commonly found in wine, some beneficial and some detrimental. The right sort of natural acidity is an essential component part of a sound wine; it acts as a preservative, produces bouquet and provides the essential bite and finish. It also stimulates the gastric juices—one of the oft-forgotten main purposes of any table wine. Lack of acidity can be detected by a general flabbiness, lack of vitality and a weak watery finish; excess acidity by a sharp tart effect on the tongue. Youthful acidity tends to mellow with age. Some wines, such as Vinho Verde, champagne, and wines from the Saar and Ruwer, have a deliberately and refreshingly-high acid content. Fruity acidity is perhaps the most desired characteristic of German wines. (*See also* tartaric, malic and sorbic.)

aftertaste 'The internal bouquet' that sometimes remains in the throat and back nasal passages after a wine has been drunk. Unpleasant if the wine is strong-flavoured and in poor condition; at its best, however, the hallmark of a great wine and usually part of what is more poetically referred to as a 'lingering farewell'.

alcohol In *pure* form the higher alcohols, amyl and butyl, have unpleasant, throat-catching odour, phenethyl has an intense rose-like smell and ethanol a burning sensation. However, diluted, as in wine, alcohol is scarcely detectable on the nose, though it can be assessed by its 'weight' in the mouth, by a sort of burning taste and, cumulatively, by its well-known effects on the head of the imbiber. Although table wines may vary only three degrees (3% by volume), from light Moselles around 11° to Rhône and Sauternes in the 13° and 14° bracket, the effect on the weight, character and strength of the wine is most marked.

almonds, bitter The smell of almond kernels or bitter almonds emanates from a badly fined wine, possibly 'blue' fined. Probably drinkable but not sound.

apples A fresh, raw smell, indicative of an immature young wine (*see* malic acid).

aroma That part of the smell of wine derived from the grape, whether distinctly varietal or merely vinous (oenologists also use the word in respect of odours resulting from fermentation) as opposed to bouquet (q.v.) derived from development of the wine itself in bottle.

aromatic Fragrant, a richness of aroma and taste, spicy overtones, particularly from aromatic grape varieties, such as muscat.

asbestos Odour imparted by new filter pads or old, dirty, overused pads in bottling. Wine has flat alkaline taste.

astringent A dry, mouth-puckering effect caused by a high tannin content (often accompanied by a high degree of acidity). Might well soften and mellow as the wine matures. Not bitter.

austere Somewhat tough and severe; simple, un-complex, possibly undeveloped.

baked A 'hot' rather earthy smell produced by burnt and shrivelled grapes due to excessive sunshine and lack of rainfall. A characteristic of red wine produced in hot vintages in the Rhône Valley and in naturally-hot wine-producing areas such as southern California, Australia and South Africa.

balance The combination and relationship of component parts. (*See* well-balanced.)

banana Overtone on the bouquet of wines made from frost-bitten grapes; also a specific smell of old wine in poor condition.

beery An undesirable smell caused by secondary fermentation in bottle. The wine may be drinkable, just, but will be basically unsound, poor on finish.

beetroot, boiled Reminiscent of, and recognition symbol for, the *pinot* grape aroma.

big A wine full of flavour and high in alcohol, tannin, acidity and extract.

bite Inferring a substantial degree of acidity (plus tannin). A good factor in a young wine. Generally mellows with age.

bitter, bitterness Detected on the palate, on the back of the tongue and finish. Mainly unpleasant. A taste, not a tactile, sensation, though it can be a desirable quality in certain wines (usually an acquired taste) and vermouths. Bitterness is derived from either chemical salts or vegetable extracts. A certain bitterness can be imparted by colouring matter, though the depositing of this during maturation will normally reduce its pristine harshness. Polyphenols extracted from wooden casks, particularly when dirty and contaminated, will also, when oxidised, impart a bitter taste to wine. More rarely an unpleasant bitterness due to *amertume*, a bacteriological disease.

bitters Substances added to wine (for example, in the making of vermouth) that have a bitter taste and stimulate the appetite and digestion. They can be of vegetable origin, like gentian, or aromatic, containing volatile oil, like orange peel. Quinine has a similar effect, plus additional properties such as a remote action on the nervous system.

blackcurrants The nearest fruit-smell to the *cabernet-sauvignon* grape. Detectable in some degree wherever the grape is used but particularly marked on wines from Pauillac, and to a slightly lesser extent Margaux. Perhaps the first major clue to Bordeaux wine in a blind tasting.

bland Not complimentary: mild, easy, characterless; not unpleasing.

body The weight of wine in the mouth due to its alcoholic content, extract, and to its other physical components. These factors stem from the quality of the vintage and geographical origin, and in turn affect the style and quality of the wine. Wines from hotter climates tend to have more body than those from the north (compare the Rhône with the Moselle, for example).

bottle-age Extremely hard to describe but easily recognizable on the bouquet to an experienced taster and a vital factor in the judgment of a wine's age/maturity and development in bottle. On white dessert wines a mellow, honeyed quality; on reds a breaking down of raw edges to reveal forthcoming softness and mellowness.

bottle-sickness Temporary oxidation after bottling, which wears off.

bouquet In the broadest and often-used sense, the pleasant and characteristic smell of wine. In the narrower sense, the odour created by the wine's own development: by the esters and aldehydes formed by the slow oxidation of fruit acids and alcohol. (*See also* aroma.)

breed A distinctive and distinguished quality stemming from the combination of fine site, soil, *cépage* and the skill of the *vigneron*.

buttery Self-descriptive smell and taste (not texture).

caramel A slightly burnt, toffee-like flavour which can have a literal origin in the case of certain spirits but can only be reminiscent in the case of wine. A characteristic flavour of madeira and marsala, for example.

carbon dioxide Responsible for the sparkle of champagne and sparkling wines and the tingle of *spritzig* or slightly effervescent table wines.

cedarwood Characteristic scent of many fine clarets.

character A wine of any quality which has unmistakable and distinctive features.

characteristic Having the style and character of the grape, district, vintage, etc. Often sweepingly used to avoid a detailed description.

clean Absence of foreign and unpleasant odours.

cloying A sweet and heavy wine which palls; lacking the acidity to make it crisp and interesting.

coarse Rough texture; lacking breed and possibly indifferently made. Do not confuse coarseness with the rough rawness of a fine but completely immature wine.

common Lacking breed, but none-the-less sound and drinkable.

complex Many-faceted smell and taste. The hallmark of a developing fine wine.

cooked A heavy, sometimes sweet but not unpleasant smell from the use of sugar, concentrated must or high temperature during vinification.

corked An 'off', oxidised and thoroughly obnoxious smell. A very over-used and misunderstood expression; the *sommelier's* nightmare.

corky Having a distinct smell of cork, arising from a poor, soft or disintegrating cork, or one infected by weevil. A poor cork can, of course, let air in, in which

case the wine may oxidise completely and become 'corked'. Indeed, the two expressions are frequently interchanged due to lack of agreement over definition.

creaming A light, slightly frothy *mousse*. Half-sparkling.

crisp A desirable feature in white wines; firm, refreshing, positive acidity.

deep An adjective that needs qualification: deep coloured; deep bouquet, depth of flavour—opposite to superficial, indicating underlying richness, layers of flavour.

delicate Charm and balance in a light wine of some quality.

depth Richness, subtlety—seemingly 'layers' of flavour, all interlocked.

developed In relation to wine is a maturity stage: undeveloped, well-developed (mature, balanced, rounded), over-developed (over-mature, cracking-up).

distinguished Marked and exceptional character and breed.

dry Not sweet; absence of residual sugar; fully fermented out.

dull Appearance not bright; nose and palate lacking interest, zest.

dumb Undeveloped, but with inherent promise of quality. Often the sign of an 'adolescent' stage.

dusty An evocative cellar-like smell; possibly high tannic content.

earthy Characteristic overtone derived from certain soils.

eggs, bad (hydrogen sulphide) Disagreeable, but harmless. Probably due to bad cellar-treatment.

elegant Stylish balance and refined quality.

extract Soluble solids (strictly speaking excluding sugar) which add to a wine's body and substance.

fat Fullish body, high in glycerol and extract. If sweet, verging on unctuous.

feminine Subjective and abstract term indicating a style of wine which is attractive, not heavy or severe, with charm—whatever delightful qualities all but a misogynist might conjure up!

filter-pads *See* asbestos.

fine An all-embracing expression of superior quality. Perhaps the most overworked adjective in the vinous vocabulary.

finesse Grace, delicacy, breed, distinction.

finish The end-taste. A wine cannot be considered well-balanced without a good finish, by which is understood a firm, crisp and distinctive end. The opposite, a short or poor finish, will be watery, the flavour not sustained and tailing off inconclusively. The correct degree of the right sort of acidity is a decisive factor.

firm Implies a sound constitution and balance, positive in the mouth, as opposed to flabby.

flabby Feeble, lacking crisp acidity, probably without finish. Either a poor wine or one that is cracking up.

flat Dull, insipid, lacking acidity. Or merely a sparkling wine which has lost its sparkle.

flinty An evocative overtone. Certain white wine grapes grown on certain soils have a hint of gun-flint in the bouquet and flavour, e.g. Pouilly blanc fumé.

flowery Fragrant, flower-like. Certain Moselles in 'full bloom', for example.

forceful Marked character, probably well-endowed with tannin and acidity; assertive.

foxy The curious and distinctive earthy tang, flavour and finish of wine made from native American vine species. It does not imply an animal smell but relates to the wild or 'fox' grapes.

fragrant Attractively and naturally scented.

fresh Retaining natural youthful charm, vitality (and acidity).

fruity Attractive, fleshy quality derived from good ripe grapes; but not necessarily a grapey aroma.

full (bodied) High in alcoholic content and extract. Filling the mouth. A table wine with an alcoholic content probably over 13° G.L. (i.e. per cent alcohol by volume). In the context of fortified wines a heavy sherry, port or madeira at the top end of the alcohol and sugar scale.

garlic, wild A faint reminiscent whiff denoting the presence of sorbic acid.

gentle Mild, pleasant, unassertive.

geraniums Not a complimentary flower simile: a geranium-like odour caused by the presence of an obscure micro-organism derived principally from esters formed during fermentation.

goaty A reference to a rich ripe animal-like flavour. For example, ripe fat Pfalz wines made from the *traminer* grape.

graceful Abstract: elegant, unassertive, stylish.

grapey A rich *muscatelle*-like aroma produced by certain grape varieties, including *muscatelle* itself and crossings like *scheurebe* and *müller-thurgau*.

great Almost as over-worked as fine. Should be confined to wines of the highest quality which, in practice, means top growths of good years: having depth, richness, character, style, complexity, fragrance, length and aftertaste.

green Unripe, raw and young. Youthful mouth-watering acidity produced by immature grapes, or the unsettled acidity of an immature wine.

grip A firm and emphatic combination of physical characteristics. A satisfactory and desirable quality in port, for example. The opposite to flabbiness and spinelessness.

hard Severity due to the over-prominence of tannin and, to a lesser extent, acidity. Usually the product of a hot vintage or over-prolonged contact with skins and pips during fermentation. Time usually mellows.

harsh Self-descriptive. Due to excess tannin and/or ethyl-acetate associated with acetic acid.

heady High in alcohol. Tipsy-making.

hearty Robust, zestful, warm, alcoholic; generally in respect of red wine.

heavy More than just full-bodied; over-endowed with alcohol and extracts. Watch out for the context in which it is used. For example, a strapping Rhône wine will appear too heavy for a light summer luncheon but would be the right weight to accompany a steak and kidney pie in mid-winter. 'Heavy' is also an official definition: a fortified wine subject to the higher rates of duty.

hedonistic A simple subjective, personal rating, e.g. pleasant to the individual taster.

high-toned Nose of assertive volatile character.

hollow A wine with a foretaste and some finish but without sustaining middle-flavour. A failing rather than a fault.

honest A somewhat condescending term for a decent, well-made but fairly ordinary wine.

honeyed Characteristic fragrance of certain fine mature wines such as Sauternes and *Beerenauslesen:* indicative of bottle-age.

implicitly sweet Apparent sweetness from other sources than sugar, e.g. glycerol, alcohol.

inky 'Red ink': an unpleasant, tinny, metallic taste due to the presence of tannate of iron produced by the action of tannin on iron—a nail in a cask will have this effect. Tannate of iron happens to be the chief constituent of ink.

insipid Flat, somewhat tasteless. Lacking firmness, character.

iron A faintly metallic, earthy-iron taste derived from the soil. Noticeable in some St.-Emilions and in these circumstances entirely natural, adding recognisable character.

legs The English term for globules which fall down the sides of the glass after the wine is swirled. Also known as 'tears'. Generally indicative of a rich wine.

lemon Lemon-like overtones. For example, noticeable on some fine but immature white Hermitage wines.

light A low degree of alcohol (under 12° G.L.). Lack of body. A desirable characteristic of certain styles of wine like young Beaujolais and Mosel-Saar-Ruwer wines. Rather confusingly, 'light' is an official term for a natural, unfortified, table wine.

limpid Clear (appearance).

limpidity Colour appears to have extra sheen, outstanding brightness.

little Scarcely any bouquet or aroma. Either a wine of no quality or character, or Dumb (q.v.).

lively Fairly explicit. Usually in reference to a fresh, youthful wine; or an old wine with fresh and youthful characteristics.

long Lingering flavour; a sign of quality.

luscious Soft, sweet, fat, fruity and ripe. All these qualities in balance.

maderised The heavy flat smell of an overmature, somewhat oxidised white wine (sometimes accompanied by brown-tinged colour and flat taste). *See also* oxidised.

malic acid Although without smell, its presence due to unripe 'green' grapes has mouth-watering, cooking-apple nose; mouth puckering. A 'malolactic' fermentation in cask converts the raw malic acid into softer and more amenable lactic acid.

manly Or masculine: positive, possibly assertive, even aggressive; a big wine, 'muscular'.

meaty Heavy, rich almost 'chewable' quality.

medium (body) Neither light nor heavy in alcohol and extract—probably between 12° and 13° G.L., depending on the style of wine.

medium-dry Containing some residual sugar but dry enough to be drunk before or during a meal.

medium-sweet Considerable natural sugar, but not really a dessert-wine. Many German wines come into this category and are better drunk without food.

mellow Soft, limpid, mature. No rough edges. A characteristic which is normally associated with maturity and age.

metallic Tinny—not a pleasant quality (*see also* Inky). Usually due to some metallic contamination during wine making, storage in cask, or bottling. If distinctly unpleasant and associated with a deepening of colour (of white wine) and a tawny deposit, due to copper contamination.

mouldy An undesirable flavour imparted by rotten grapes or stale, unclean, casks, etc.

mousey Smell and taste, flat yet acetic. Sign of bacteriological disease, *tourne,* usually affecting only wine in cask.

mushroomy Specific smell of some very old wines.

musky A difficult term: spicy/dusty.

must Unfermented grape juice.

musty Due to poor casks or a cork fault. If the latter, allow the wine to stand after pouring and the smell may wear off after only a few minutes.

neutral Without positive flavour or marked physical characteristics. A common feature of very many blended wines, from quite respectable commercial burgundy to litre-bottled carafe wine.

noble Indicates stature and breed; a wine of towering elegance.

nuance Having components reminiscent of specific smells, e.g. of almonds, of struck flint.

nutty A crisp rounded flavour associated with full-bodied dry white wines like Corton-Charlemagne, or good quality amontillados. Fine old tawny port has a distinct smell of cobnuts.

oak An important factor, particularly in relation to fine wines. Oak casks impart an 'oaky' taste and smell, desirable in moderation, undesirable if over-apparent.

off-taste Unclean, tainted or diseased wine; though not necessarily undrinkable.

old Can be a factual statement or imply a state of bouquet and taste adversely affected by over-maturity. Lacking freshness.

olfactory To do with the sense of smell and its perception.

ordinary In wine terms is mildly derogatory: a wine of no pretensions or with no merit.

organoleptic The testing, by use of the senses, in an analytical context, of wine and food.

oxidised Flat stale off-taste due to exposure to air.

peach-like Self-descriptive. Characteristic of the bouquet of certain German wines, notably ripe Moselles from the Ruwer district.

peardrops An undesirable overtone sometimes noticeable on poorly made white wines of lesser vintages. Wine probably unstable and in dubious condition, but may be quite drinkable.

penetrating Powerful, with almost a physical effect on the nostrils. Almost certainly high in alcohol and volatile esters.

peppery A sort of raw harshness, rather hard to define, due to immature and unsettled component parts which have not had time to marry. Noticeable on young ruby and vintage port and many full young red wines. Probably higher alcohols.

perfume An agreeable scented quality of bouquet.

piquant Fresh and mouthwatering acidity. A desirable and customary feature of wines from the Moselle, Saar and Ruwer and from other districts, like Sancerre. Less desirable but quite attractive in other youthful red and white table wines with a little more than their fair share of acidity.

poor Not 'off' or bad, but of no merit, character or quality.

positive Marked and noticeable, as opposed to little or dumb (q.v.).

powerful Self-explanatory, but more appropriately used in the context of a big red wine rather than a light white wine, a Rhine wine with a full, flowery bouquet.

pricked An unpleasant sharpness due to excess volatile acidity. A pricked wine will not be pleasant to drink and will be beyond treatment. It may *just* be drinkable and will not have reached the final vinegary stage.

prickly Indicates on nose, but particularly on the palate, a sharp-edged, raw, possibly almost effervescent quality. Only tolerable in certain circumstances: raw, young Vinho Verde and such like.

puckering, mouth- A tactile sensation induced by high tannin content.

pungent Powerful, assertive, heavily-scented or spicy, very often indicating a high degree of volatile acidity as in old madeira.

quality Three senses: quality wine, like fine (q.v.) wine can be a vague and general term, often abused. In the E.E.C. 'quality' wines are legally defined, with statutory minimum criteria. In the abstract sense, a wine exhibits quality by virtue of its correctness, refinement and clarity of colour; its pure varietal aroma with harmonious overtones of bouquet; with all its component parts well-balanced, with rich and complex flavour, long finish and fragrant aftertaste.

refreshing Pleasant, thirst-quenching acidity.

resinous Literally imparted by the addition of resin, mainly to Greek table wines. A very old practice but something of an acquired taste.

rich Self-explanatory. Should not automatically imply sweetness, rather a full ensemble of fruit, flavour, alcohol and extract.

ripe Wine in full bloom, having reached its maturity plateau. A mellowness prior to its decline. Ripe grapes give a wine a natural sweetness and richness.

robust Full-bodied, tough yet rounded. A good strapping mouthful of wine. Could apply equally to a 13.5° Châteauneuf-du-Pape or Taylor '48.

rough A coarse, edgy sort of wine, usually of ordinary quality.

round A feature of a well-balanced, usually mature, wine. No raw immature edges.

rubbery Probably presence of mercaptan, a disagreeable 'accident' of complex chemical background, not infrequently seen on old white wines due to the breakdown of sulphur.

rugged Big, masculine, high in alcohol, probably tannic.

salty One of the so-called four primary tastes, but perhaps the least applicable to wine. A self-descriptive tang characteristic of good fresh manzanilla.

sap The little-used equivalent of a somewhat enigmatic French term implying the quality of inherent life that will develop a fine young wine.

savoury Rich, spicy; mouth-smacking flavouriness.

scented Positive, grapey-flowery, high-toned aroma.

sensuous Rich, smooth, opulent flavour and texture.

severe Hard, unyielding and probably immature.

sharp A degree of acidity between piquant and pricked. Implies a stage beyond that of being attractively refreshing. It could, however, become mollified with bottle-age.

sick Diseased, out of condition.

silky A firm yet distinctly soft texture on the palate. A characteristic of most really fine dessert wines, also of good quality Pomerols.

simple Better than ordinary. Straightforward, un-complex.

smoky A subtle overtone characteristic of some grapes in certain white wine districts, e.g. good *pinot-chardonnay*. *See also* flinty.

smooth Soft, easy texture. No rough edges.

soft Self-descriptive. Mellow; no rough edges; tannin and acidity fully married and absorbed.

solid Full-bodied, four-square, packed with alcohol, tannin and acidity. Undeveloped.

sorbic acid Not a natural grape acid but one sometimes added as a preservative. Its presence can be detected by a faint garlic-like odour.

sound The first thing a wine should be: appearance clear and bright; wholesome, clean bouquet and flavour. No faults.

sour A term to be used with care. To the English, sour has an off-taste, over-acid connotation. Others use the word as a synonym for acid.

sparkling A wine containing an induced degree of effervescence—the basis and whole point of a certain class of wine, such as champagne, the sparkle being obtained by the controlled release of carbon dioxide when the bottle is opened.

spicy A rich, herb-like aroma and flavour bestowed by certain grape varieties such as *gewürztraminer*.

stalky Reminiscent of the smell of damp twigs; a damp *chai*-like smell. This stalky or stemmy aroma is detectable in young wines and can arise from overprolonged contact with grape stalks during wine making.

stimulus That which provokes a sensory response.

strange Untypical, having a 'foreign' smell or taste.

strong Powerful, alcoholic.

sturdy Fairly tough, substantial.

suave Soft, supple and harmonious.

subtle Veiled richness, unobvious complexity.

sugared/sugary Several connotations: a sweet smell and blandness of a *chaptalised* wine; high sucrose content of a rich dessert wine.

sulphury Sulphur, in its various forms, not only has a very pronounced volcanic smell but its presence can be detected physically by a prickly sensation in the nostrils and the back of the throat, like a whiff from a sulphur match or coke oven. It is commonly used as an antiseptic, for cleaning casks (by burning sulphur sticks) and bottles (using a mild SO_2 solution) and if carelessly used or over-used its undesirable odour will be retained. The bouquet of many young wines is masked by a whiff of sulphur which is quite harmless and often wears off a short while after the wine has been poured out.

superficial Without depth or follow-through.

supple Easy to taste and sense, hard to define. A combination of sap, vigour and amenable texture.

sweet A wine with a high sugar content, natural or contrived. The essential characteristic of any dessert wine. There are two types of sweetness; that which is merely sweet and the other which is from the richness of fine, well-ripened grapes. The former kind will always remain sweet (e.g. Pedro Ximenez sherry), the latter will dry out as it ages. Fine Rhine wines and Sauternes can be recognized by the smell emanating from *pourriture noble* but even dry wines can have a 'sweet', honeyed or grapey sweetness on the nose. The principal sweetening elements are fructose, sucrose, glucose; also, but less sweet, glycerin and alcohol.

syrupy Usually used in connection with an excessively rich, ripe Sauternes, *Trockenbeerenauslese* or perhaps sweet sherry.

tactile That which provokes a response which can be physically felt (touched), e.g. sulphur, effervescence, velvety, creamy, burning (alcohol).

tang, tangy Rich, high-toned, zestful bouquet and end-taste of an old madeira, old sherry, tokay.

tannin An essential preservative derived from grape skins during fermentation. Part of the maturation process consists of the breaking down of the tannin content; it is precipitated over a period by the action of proteins and becomes, with colouring matter, part of the deposit or crust left in the bottle. The presence of tannin dries the roof of the mouth, grips the teeth and sometimes has a 'dusty cellar' smell. It is a particularly noticeable physical component of young red wine (Bordeaux in particular) which has a practical purpose: to 'cut' fatty foods and clean the palate. Tannin is less of a factor in white wines as grape skins—the main source—are removed prior to fermentation.

tart Sharp and tongue-curling due to over-acidity, often with a touch too much tannin. This condition can be due to premature harvesting of grapes or a late bad harvest. The wine could recover and soften; it may, on the other hand, disintegrate. More pronounced than piquant (q.v.).

tartaric acid One of the good and essential acids in wine. Its chief virtue is the effervescent *spritzig*—cooling and refreshing—quality it provides (most marked in a good Vinho Verde, for example). Tartaric acid in the form of free acidity or acid tartrate of potassium is widely distributed in the vegetable kingdom but its chief source is the grape. Its presence gives wine its healthy, refreshing tang and contributes greatly to its quality and crisp finish. Occasionally it can be seen, as light white flakes, precipitated in white wine and sherry which have been subjected to an unusually low temperature.

taut Somewhat severe, probably immature, firm, unyielding.

thin Deficient in good natural properties; watery, lacking body.

threshold Level at which a given smell or taste can be perceived. Thresholds vary from person to person, from substance to substance. It is possible with practice to lower (improve) olfactory and gustatory thresholds.

tough A full-bodied wine of overpowering immaturity (not necessarily young) with an excess of tannin. May well turn out in time to be a great wine.

twiggy Like stalky and stemmy, a 'reminiscent' smell; mildly derogatory and usually relating to somewhat coarse young wines. A fine mature claret would never be described as twiggy. A raw young bourgeois one could.

unbalanced Component parts ill-matched: over-tannic, over-acid, lacking fruit, etc.

unripe Two senses: immature, raw; 'green'; malic acidity of wine made from grapes not fully ripened.

vanilla Purely descriptive in one sense, though it can be detected in a more literal sense in the bouquet of some brandies; a tannic-like compound derived from oak giving certain cask-aged wines a distinctive aroma.

velvety Another textural connotation, related to silky and smooth, but implying more opulence.

vigorous Lively, healthy, positive flavour associated with youthful development.

vinegar The smell of ethylacetate, one of the simple esters, indicative of bacteriological infection. The wine will be unfit to drink, acetic, and beyond redemption.

vinosity Having firm, well-constituted, vinous character.

vinous A pleasant-enough and positive winey smell or taste. '

volatile acidity This is present to a greater or lesser extent in all wine, but excess volatile acidity is undesirable and usually indicates the first step in acetic deterioration (*see* vinegar, above).

watery Lacking fruit, extract, low in alcohol and acidity.

weak Low in alcohol, feeble fruit and character.

well-balanced A satisfactory blend of physical components: fruit, acid, tannin, alcohol, etc., and, to a lesser extent, of the intangible elements: breed, character, finesse.

withered Usually in reference to an old, dried-out wine, losing fruit and 'flesh' with age.

wood Distinct and desirable odour derived from aging in wooden casks (*see also* vanilla).

woody An undesirable taste imparted by wine kept too, long in cask.

yeasty Descriptive smell of ferments, live or dead. If detected in bottled wine, a sure indication of impending or recent secondary fermentation.

young, youthful A positive attractive feature: fresh, with youthful acidity; immature.

Source: Michael Broadbent, *Wine Tasting*, 6th ed. (Christie Wine Publications, 1979), 91–100.

[a]I use abbreviations in my own notes. The possible confusion between initials is avoided by tasting, and using words, in a regular order and under appropriate headings. Under 'palate', D, MF indicates 'dry, medium-full bodied'. Other abbreviations I use: fl. (flavour), bal. (balance), Y (young/youthful), V/A (volatile acidity), B/A (bottle-age), mat. (mature), ex (excellent), t & a (tannin & acidity), and so forth.

Irving H. Marcus provides guidelines for testing.

Preparing the Wines for Component Testing

Preparing wines for component tests calls for overloading them with varying amounts of a particular component. (My term, "overloading", evolves from the belief that the base wine was component-balanced by the winemaker.)

To achieve this end, a solution is first prepared according to formula, after which measured amounts of the solution are added to the wine.

Assuming that 2 oz. (a quarter cup) of wine will be used per glass per judge (the recommended amount), simple arithmetic will provide you with the amount of component-overloaded blend or blends you will need for each test. These can be prepared a day or so beforehand (with the exception of the tannin blends, which should be readied just before tasting) and the wines can be kept refrigerated until needed. The red wines should be removed from the refrigerator in time for them to reach room temperature before being offered for tasting. Empty wine bottles (fifths or tenths) with screw caps can be used as storage vessels.

The blending pattern to be followed with each of the components is described below, first for the 4-Step Lineup tests and then for the Paired Comparison tests.

Preparing Blends for the 4-Step Tests

The preparation of the blends discussed in this section involves, in each case, the making up of an intermediate solution of component and wine, then using this solution to produce the required three blends (the fourth step being that of the base wine alone).

Sweetness. Use cane sugar, not powdered sugar. An added glass or other container is needed in making the sugared blends in order to pour the sweetened wine from one vessel to another until the sugar is completely dissolved.

To make the solution, dissolve a teaspoon of sugar per 3 oz. of wine required (allow a minimum of 1 oz. of solution per judge). Use this *solution* to prepare the blends in the following proportions:

> *Light sweet* 1 teaspoon for every 2 oz. wine.
> *Medium sweet* 2 teaspoons for every 2 oz. wine.
> *Very sweet* 1 tablespoon for every 2 oz. wine.

These blends may be prepared ahead of time and kept in clearly marked containers.

Total Acid. Dissolve ¼ teaspoon Citric Acid into 5 oz. of the base wine. Use this *solution* to make three wine blends in the following proportions:

> *Light acid* 1 teaspoon per 2 oz. wine.
> *Medium acid* 2 teaspoons per 2 oz. wine.
> *High acid* 1 tablespoon per 2 oz. wine.

These blends may be prepared ahead of time and kept in clearly marked containers.

Volatile Acid. Blend 1 tablespoon of distilled vinegar of 5% acidity (check the label) into 5 oz. wine. You will need 3 oz. of this solution per judge. Use this *solution* to make three blends in the following proportions:

> *Light acetic* 1 teaspoon per 2 oz. wine.
> *Medium acetic* 2 teaspoons per 2 oz. wine.
> *High acetic* 4 teaspoons per 2 oz. wine.

These blends may be prepared ahead of time and kept in clearly marked containers.

The vinegar may be red if red wine is being used for the tests. However, white distilled vinegar serves the same purpose with red wine and is of course essential with white wine tests. It is not necessary (but is better) to use a wine vinegar.

Tannin. Dissolve ¼ teaspoon of Tannic Acid into 9 oz. of wine, allowing 2 oz. of this solution for each judge. Use this *solution* to make three wine blends in the following proportions:

> *Light tannin* 1 teaspoon per 3 oz. wine.
> *Medium tannin* 2 teaspoons per 3 oz. wine.
> *High tannin* 4 teaspoons per 3 oz. wine.

Do NOT prepare these tannic acid solutions ahead of time. Tannin acid tends to hydrolyze to gallic acid with the passage of time and gallic acid can be toxic. As an added safety measure, the judges should be warned not to swallow these samples but to spit them out.

Even though you will be preparing these tannin blends just before the tests are to take place, mark each container clearly for identification.

Preparing Blends for Paired Component Testing

In contrast to the need for readying multi-blends for the four-step tests above, it is necessary here merely to prepare blends for single-step comparisons per component. Since the judge is required only to decide which of two glasses offered him at a time contains the wine that is stronger in a particular component, the extent to which a wine should be overloaded for this single step test is subject to a certain leeway. This involves your assessment of the experience of the judge or judges. While newcomers to wine judging can sometimes do as well as experienced tasters in simple component tests, in general the greater the wine knowledge of the judges the smaller should be the component differences among the wines offered them. I therefore feel some differentiation should be made on the basis of wine experience.

Following this concept and using the same preparatory patterns presented for the 4-step tests, the overloading of a wine for the paired tests should be made according to this guide:

Beginner Match the blending pattern for the most overloaded wine in the 4-step preparations *(Very Sweet, High Acid, High Tannin, High Acetic)*.
More experienced Match the pattern for the *Medium* blends in the 4-step preparations.
Connoisseur Match the blending pattern for the *Light* blends in the 4-step preparations.

With the exception of the tannin augmentation, the blends can be prepared a day beforehand and kept refrigerated until needed.

In contrast to the sequence in which the blending instructions have been presented, it is better to begin the actual judgings with the 2-step tests before undertaking the presentation of the 4-step tests.

Source: Irving H. Marcus, *How to Test and Improve Your Wine Judging Ability* (Berkeley, Calif.: Wine Publications, 1974), 59–62.

Finally, it is recommended that you pay close attention to the task at hand, allowing all your senses to concentrate on the individuality of the ounce or two in the glass. This focus involves all the awareness at once, organoleptically. Study the sheen, the color intensity, comparing it to past sightings of similar wines. Hold the glass above a white surface for the best view. Take a strong, swift smell allowing the olfactory nerves to compare this new sensation to the thousands of other smells. Taste slowly, sloshing the fluid around the mouth so that the thousands of individual taste buds can react as the fluid gently warms to body temperature. Swallow slowly, allowing the commingling of taste and feel to release new vapors which rise through the cranium once again prodding the olfactory judgments. Sound forbidding? Why?—when we do this nearly every time we drink, artlessly, without conscious observation. Slow down the effortless, natural process, and you master the trick of comparative wine tasting!

LEVELS OF EVALUATION

While everyone can theoretically taste as equals, obviously there exists various levels of perception and sophistication in tasting. Dr. Richard R. Nelson, Technical Director of Andres Wines, Ltd. of Canada, has devised a chart identifying three distinct levels in wine appreciation (see table 10.1). In a pamphlet titled *Pleasure, Enjoyment and Quality* published by the American Wine Society, Dr. Nelson describes the mechanisms as hedonics for the novice, as cognition for the amateur and as judgment for the wine expert. Most serious wine drinkers fall somewhere between the latter two, progressively acquiring the arcane knowledge of variables which provide distinction in the glass.

Dr. Nelson asserts that

Quality can only be measured by people with a memory of sensory stimuli of which it is comprised and with the education that permits its judgment . . . Quality is an intellectual phenomenon that occurs between the wine and the taster . . . Experts

TABLE 10.1 Levels of Evaluation

	Novice *(1st level)*	**Amateur** *(2nd level)*	**Expert** *(3rd level)*
Determination Mechanism Governing Factor	Pleasure Hedonics Physiology	Enjoyment Cognition Experience	Quality Judgment Education

Source: Reprinted with permission of the American Wine Society. Complete copies of "Sensory Identification of Wine Constituents" can be obtained by sending $2.50 to AWS, 4218 Rosewold, Royal Oak, MI 48073.

recognize Quality as through deductive response to definitive sensory stimuli and through inductive judgment of psycho-physical and psychological perceptions.

That being said, and agreed to, one who is on the journey from simple hedonism to a clearer perception of the infinite variables in wine tasting should have confidence in personal judgments rather than the mandates of self-appointed wine experts. Each of us can advance to the second level of classification and, with patience and persistence, perhaps attain that exalted third level. Whatever level we achieve, it's a barrel of fun trying! Table 10.2 shows a rating form that may be used to record your evaluations.

SUGGESTED TABLE WINE TASTING

The list in table 10.3 and the tasting lists in subsequent chapters have been selected for availabilities and arranged in a proper order of tasting, featuring the light to heavy, dry to sweet, and light to dark. Look for the perceptible gradations in odors and flavors between each wine, brew, and spirit as you work through the tasting rosters. It is advisable to expectorate the samples in this large wine tasting to avoid confusion by the end of the session.

TABLE 10.2 Wine-tasting Rating Form

WINE TYPE: _____

APPEARANCE

	POSITIVE CHARACTERISTICS		NEGATIVE CHARACTERISTICS	
	Bright, clear, clean, full-bodied, good viscosity, color typical for type.		Cloudy, hazy, dull, sediment, color slightly off, crystalline deposits, body too thin.	

		WINE #1	WINE #2	WINE #3	WINE #4
TOTAL 1	TOTAL APPEARANCE (Maximum 4 points)	_____	_____	_____	_____

AROMA AND BOUQUET

	POSITIVE CHARACTERISTICS		NEGATIVE CHARACTERISTICS	
	Distinct varietal characteristic, fresh, fragrant, fruity, spicy, clean, complex, pleasant, aromatic.		Distinctly off, moldy, green, woody, metallic, oxidized, sulphuric, rotten eggs, vinegary.	

		WINE #1	WINE #2	WINE #3	WINE #4
TOTAL 2	TOTAL AROMA & BOUQUET (Maximum 4 points)	_____	_____	_____	_____

TASTE AND FINISH

	POSITIVE CHARACTERISTICS		NEGATIVE CHARACTERISTICS	
	Smoothly balanced, rounded, full-bodied, definite flavor, lasting finish, elegant, crisp, pleasant, sound, no faults, well made wine.		Flabby, insipid, cloying, lacking, hollow, stemmy, harsh, bitter, empty, thin, rough, hot burning, oxidized, vinegary, flat, sharp, obscure flavor.	

		WINE #1	WINE #2	WINE #3	WINE #4
TOTAL 3	TOTAL TASTE & FINISH (Maximum 12 points)	_____	_____	_____	_____

		WINE #1	WINE #2	WINE #3	WINE #4
GRAND TOTAL 1,2 and 3	TOTAL WINE POINTS: (Maximum 20 points)	_____	_____	_____	_____

RATINGS:　GREAT 18–20　FINE 15–17　GOOD 12–14
　　　　　　FAIR 9–11　　POOR Below 9

Source: The Christian Brothers.

TABLE 10.3 Table Wine Tasting

Wine	General Style	Suggested Brand
Muscadet	Very dry, acidic, sharp, light in body	Marquis de Goulaine
Chardonnay	Complex, full-bodied, with a touch of oak	Sonoma Vineyards, The Christian Brothers, Paul Masson
Fumé Blanc	Dry, smoky, herbaceous	Robert Mondavi
Orvieto	Light in body, crisp and pleasingly tart	Antinori
Chablis	Medium to full body, assertive mouth feel and good acidity	Wente Bros.
Grey Riesling	Light, almost dry, soft	Wente Bros.
Chenin Blanc	Medium body, light, sweet finish	Charles Krug, Beringer
Johannisberg Riesling	Medium dry, tart, light	Monterey Vineyards, Ste. Michelle, Callaway
Liebfraumilch	Light body, medium sweet, pleasant acidity	Blue Nun
Sauvignon Blanc	Medium sweet, full body	Mirassou
Rosé d'Anjou or Tavel Rosé	Crisply dry, very light body	B & G
Rosé	Medium body, mellow, and sweet	Mateus, Lancer's
Burgundy	Very dry, full body, rich	Inglenook Vintages, The Christian Brothers, Louis Martini
Zinfandel or Gamay Beaujolais	Medium body, softer finish	Robert Mondavi, The Christian Brothers
Cabernet Sauvignon	Medium body, dry and aromatic	B. V., Inglenook, Louis Jodat, Robert Mondavi
Pinot Noir	Full-bodied, tannic, subtle elegance	B. V., Louis Martini, The Christian Brothers

The consultant for the suggested wine tastings is Tom Stockley, wine columnist for the Seattle Times *and author of* Winery Tours in Oregon, Washington, Idaho and British Columbia *and* Great Wine Buys.

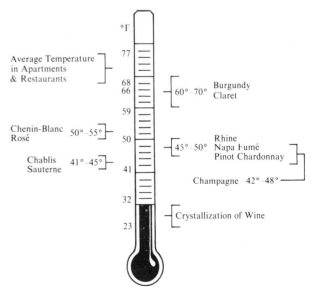

Figure 10.2 *The ideal serving temperatures of wine.*

151

Sparkling Wines

11

Wines with marked carbonation are a relatively new phenomenon. Today a clear distinction is made between naturally effervescent wines and those artificially carbonated. The federal government mandates the distinction by imposing a tax of $3.40 per gallon on the secondary fermentation type, compared to only $2.40 per gallon on those carbonated with CO_2. Despite the heavier tax, the predominant production in the United States is in the twice-fermented type called sparkling wine. There are various kinds of wines in this category. Champagne, for one, is not synonymous with sparkling; instead it refers only to *white* wines which have been fermented twice with up to four atmospheres of carbonation. Red wines made with similar production methods are generally called Sparkling Burgundy. Cold Duck is a red variety containing a pronounced sugar level. Finally, Champagne Rosé or Pink Champagne refers to the light red sparkling wine.

Development of this universally pleasing wine type is generally attributed to the perceptive cellar master of the Benedictine Abbey at Hautvillers, near Rheims, France. Although Dom Pérignon's eyesight was failing, his palate was intact, as was his passion for experimentation. Andre Simon, in *A History of the Champagne Trade in England,* reports that a good deal of work was being done at this time with sugar and molasses to make wines "brisk." It is generally accepted that the Benedictine wine master was the first to utilize a cork stopper for his brisk wines instead of flaxen tow dipped in oil. In *Beverages, Past and Present,* Emerson paints the picture of an imaginative innovator: "The theory has been advanced by some writers . . . that the discovery of champagne was purely accidental, but the facts do not sustain the idea, for the old monk was not given to loose methods." Somewhere between 1660 and

The bubble winked at me and said
You'll miss me brother when you're dead.
Oliver Herford

You can have too much champagne to
drink, but you can never have enough.
Elmer Rice

Champagne with foaming whirls,
As white as Cleopatra's melted pearls.
Lord Byron

1680, the monk perfected his beverage as Simon tells it: "Champagne was practically unknown in England when Charles II returned from France in 1660. It became fashionable at his Court, and the fame spread rapidly, first among the nobility, and later among the monied class."

How stable this champagne was, and what level of quality it achieved is left to conjecture, but Allen does report in *A History of Wine* that "the quicker it was drunk the better, for it would only grow muddier and muddier with the sediment due to the fermentation in bottle and soon lose its fizz in the bottles standing upright." Reams have been written in praise of this most romantic of all the vinous kingdom. Whether accidental or designed, the charm of the bubbly is as unmatched in repute as it is simple in the production process.

Terms

atmosphere Fifteen pounds of pressure at sea level; sparkling wines may contain up to six atmospheres.

blanc de blanc White champagne produced from white grapes, usually from Chardonnay; most French champagne is produced from the red Pinot Noir grape.

brut The white champagne with the least sugar; nearly all sparkling wines have a minimum of one percent sugar.

champagne rosé Pink sparkling wine, dry or medium sweet.

cold duck A unique red sparkling wine of the United States, quite sweet and heavy.

crackling Somewhat less carbonation in the bottle, like French *cremant*.

dégorgement French for the removal from the bottle of the sediment created in the second fermentation.

dosage The sugar which is added to champagne before bottling.

doux The sweetest French champagne, comparable to Cold Duck in the United States.

extra dry Refers to the champagne with slightly more sugar than Brut, or about 1.5% by volume. The term is confusing since it means being drier than *sec* which in France has about three percent sugar.

liqueur d'expédition The dosage of sugar added at the time of bottling to create French champagnes with different levels of sweetness; Brut has about .5% to 1% sugar; Extra Dry, from 1.5% to 3%; Sec, from 3% to 5%; Doux, from 5% to 10%.

liqueur de tirage The extra sugar added to the bottle to create the secondary fermentation in the bottle.

méthode champenoise The technique of producing the secondary fermentation in individual bottles and aging the sparkling wine for a certain period on the yeast lees which gather in the bottle neck.

mousseux The word that designates French sparkling wines produced other than in the Champagne region.

pétillant A medium sparkling or crackling wine.

pupitres The special racks for storage of sparkling wines during the secondary fermentation in which bottles are turned to settle the lees.

remuage Called riddling in the United States, this is the process of turning the secondary fermentation bottles in their racks to settle the lees on the cork.

schaumwein Schaum means froth in German; thus, a common term for sparkling wines.

sekt German for sparkling wine.

sparkling burgundy Red wine fermented again to produce extra bubbly, dry or medium sweet, wine.

sparkling wine Wine of high natural carbonation resulting from secondary fermentation; up to 6 atmospheres or about 90 pounds per square inch on the bottle surface.

spumante Italian for sparkling wine, either bottle or bulk-fermented.

THE FUTURE OF SPARKLING WINES

Without doubt, the appeal of sparkling wines has become universal, with major consumptions in such diverse economies as the Soviet Union, Chile, Germany, the United States, and the primary wine countries. Italy has fifty firms producing sparkling wines with the DOC appellation, mostly low alcohol muscat types, and Germany has ninety-three cellars producing nearly 230 million bottles of *sekt* each year. In addition, the Germans import another fifty-four million bottles of sparkling wine.

On both the high and low ends in terms of quality and production methods, the demand is constant and growing. One plant in Moscow alone, with over 200 employees, produces 6,200,000 bottles annually, using a bulk fermentation system.

In contrast, some traditional bottle fermenting companies, such as Korbel in California, produce about half that number of bottles annually. Schramsberg in the Napa Valley rests the wine on the yeast in the bottle for a minimum of three years and produces a scant 250,000 bottles annually.

Each method of production has its aficionados and detractors on both the wine-making and the consuming side of the fence. Because of labor and time constraints, the bulk processes are gaining ascendency, and the cost savings in these bottles can be expected to convert many new wine customers to the bubbly in the years to come. The single factor that could produce a meteoric rise in domestic consumption would be the removal of the $3.40 per gallon champagne tax which was imposed years ago to help pay for the Second World War.

Champagnes were born in this church-and-cloisters complex, the Abbey d'Hautvillers, constructed in the seventh century. Its severe, simple architecture suggests the clean, sharp perception of fine champagne.

At the Abbey d'Hautvillers in the seventeenth century, the nearly blind cellar master Dom Pérignon perfected the techniques of producing sparkling wines.

One of the pioneer California champagne makers produced a 1912 Œil de Perdrix and a 1914 Extra Dry. The Masson champagne cellars were devastated by the San Francisco earthquake. On display at the winery is the original champagne equipment.

THE CHAMPAGNE CONTROVERSY

Consumption of sparkling wines enjoyed a startling increase in the early 1970s with the immense popularity of Cold Duck. Since that period, the American producers have seen a steady, if not spectacular market. California has twenty-nine firms in the business; New York, ten; and others are scattered around the wine-producing states. Gallo merchandises Andre Champagne at over four million cases a year. United Vintners, under the Lejon and Jacque Bonet labels, sells more than a million cases.

The wines produced for several centuries in that northernmost area of vinifera growth in France must have been clean, sharp, and tart, as they are today. The Champagne area was planted to cultured vines by the Romans in the fourth century B.C. The region had been a crossroads for kings and conquerors for centuries. Throughout calamitous times, the giant dank caves of Champagne continued an uninterrupted production of superlative wines. Hence, it is appropriate to begin the study of champagne with that method first developed by Pérignon, perfected throughout 300 years of practice, the method in which the secondary fermentation occurs in the very bottle purchased by the consumer.

Since the Versailles Treaty following World War I, the French have testily claimed, under international concordats, that there is but one *champagne,* the wine originating from the region of the same name. They insist that any other use of the term is fraudulent. Germany and Italy adopted, at the French request, such other descriptive terms as *sekt* and *spumante* to describe sparkling wines. But the United States and Russia have consistently held that champagne is and should be understood universally as a generic term and that much market confusion results when this is ignored.

> "*D*iscovered" is not the proper term, since sparkling wine was known in its native province and even in England before that time, but it is nevertheless to Dom Pérignon that much of its early fame is due.
>
> ***Andre Simon***

MÉTHODE CHAMPENOISE

The process of champagne production begins with the selection of only ripe, sound grapes which may originate from any number of vineyards. Unlike other French growing regions, Champagne's products do not receive the Chateau identification. The dark-skinned Pinot Noir grape dominates over the less utilized and more expensive Chardonnay grapes.

Nowhere on earth is greater care exercised in the selection and sorting of grapes than in Champagne. Only the perfectly ripe, hand-sorted fruit shorn of extraneous material is set apart for the cuvées.

Ultramodern champagne fermenting rooms are shown at the Moët & Chandon winery.

Four separate pressings are made for French wines: the *tête de cuvée, première taille, deuxième taille,* and *rebeche.* Generally, the first two pressings of must are used in champagne; the remainder is vinified and sold locally as still wine. The first pressings are better balanced. Extreme care is exercised to obtain the least amount of color transfer since these are mostly red-skinned grapes. The yeasts absorb some of the loose color pigments during fermentation. The cellarmasters in the giant firms review these musts before fermentation, and, where needed, add sugar in a process called *chaptalization* assuring sufficient alcohol production. Fermentation was formerly carried out in large oak casks, resin-lined, for up to twenty days, but now much stainless steel is used.

(A)

(B)

At Napa's Domaine Chandon, riddling or shaking the secondary fermentation lees to the neck of the bottles is ancient and time-consuming (A). Two riddlers at work in an Italian wine cellar (B).

In recent years, bottle-fermenting companies in Europe and the United States have developed a number of devices to accomplish the riddling without handwork, including giant holding pens which shift the bottles around, working the lees down into the neck of the bottles. Shown are riddling racks at Korbel in California.

The fermented wines lie quietly until mid-winter when they are racked several times, reevaluated, and blended. In early April the wines are pumped into the bottles which house the wine until consumption. Judgment at this preliminary stage is accomplished by the *chef du cave,* the most important figure in champagne making. He tastes, blends, and retastes, again and again, until he reaches what he considers an appropriate blend. The blend is called the *cuvée;* to this is added a *liqueur de tirage* of cane or beet sugar at about 3 percent of the bottle volume or 24 grams of sugar per liter. The sugar is consumed by new yeast creating the secondary fermentation in the bottle. Either enough yeast cells remain to attack the new sugar or special strains may be added. The bottles are capped, and Dom Pérignon's magic then occurs.

During this secondary fermentation, the bottles are slanted in special hinged trays called *pupitres.* A trained craftsman turns the bottles and shakes them in a process known as *remuage,* designed to clarify the wine and to settle the sediment to the neck of the bottle. A trained cellarmaster can turn or riddle up to 32,000 bottles a day. Ideally, the carbonation should reach 6 atmospheres or 90 pounds per square inch during this period and about 1 percent of new alcohol is produced. Some are marked for shipment after two months, but others will progress to the aging cellars in the neck down position, which allows the wine to age directly in contact with the spent yeast and the lees. The unique character and yeasty aroma of French champagne develops through this unusual aging technique.

The caves at Moët & Chandon extend an incredible eighteen miles beneath the peaceful countryside. The aging wines rest on the

yeast in these bottles until the day of dégorgement *when the lees are extracted and the* liqueur d'expédition *is added.*

Some California bottle-fermenting firms and some in Spain and France are experimenting with mechanical devices to achieve this laborious riddling. About half of the French Taittinger is now riddled by 120 machines, taking ten days compared to the normal six weeks. Korbel has a device that will hold forty cases, gradually tilting them by means of an inflated air bag. Although both the manual and the mechanical processes are costly, they are vital for the yeast-to-wine exposure.

At the completion of the bottle-aging time, it is necessary to remove the collected sediment cleanly, without disturbing the wine. The inventive French developed the perfect solution to this problem by immersing the neck of the bottle in a solution of brine which freezes the already impacted lees. The cap is loosened, and the frozen sediment, which looks like a popsicle, flies out. Many firms now employ machines for disgorgement. At this point, any lost wine is replaced together with a new *dosage* of sugar called the *liqueur d'expédition.* By this time, each individual bottle has been handled 120 times! Remember this when you notice the phrase which only *méthode champenoise* wines can carry: "fermented in this bottle."

TABLE 11.1 Champagne Classifications

	Style	Sugar Level *(%)*
Brut	Driest	Up to 1.5
Extra Dry	Dry to medium dry	1.5–3
Sec or Dry	Medium sweet	3–5
Demi-Sec	Sweet	5–7
Doux	Very sweet	7+

Originally, all champagne contained sugar at a level which we now would consider very sweet. But over the years, the market demanded less and less sweetener. Champagnes are classified according to the sugar level (see table 11.1). Both French and American producers conform to the classifications.

The French occasionally do produce vintage champagne, but only in exceptional years. This is because the harvest generally produces quite acidic and unbalanced wines which necessitate liberal blending to achieve quality standards. *Blanc de Blanc,* a white champagne, is made completely from

white-skinned grapes. White wine champagnes are much lighter than the others, lacking the assertive Pinot Noir character, and are also considerably more expensive to produce.

In sum, the French champagne business is steeped in lore and tradition. And why not, when it produces such enormous profits for thousands of growers, producers, and merchants? A single acre in the Champagne area would be valued today at over $100,000. There are about 25,000 of these grape acres in the region with an incredible 15,000 owners. It seems that everyone is involved in the business, and certainly everyone who is involved carefully husbands the resource and reputation of Champagne. Within the last decade, the pressures of supply and demand have been so great in this delimited area that 5,000 new hectares have been authorized for cultivation, and the ability of the major houses to answer the market's need has still been restricted. While modernization has permitted fermentation in closed vats as well as mechanical riddling, most of the Champagne makers follow the traditional methods of production.

French sparkling wines produced outside the Champagne region are called *vin mousseux,* or frothy wines. Nearly all French wine districts produce a local sparkling wine, but two vineyards dominate the mousseux field, both near the Loire River. Those produced as Vouvray are the most closely controlled in that the alcohol level must be at least 9.5 percent and the base wine must be the famous Chenin Blanc grape. Sparkling Saumur, which need contain only 40 percent Chenin Blanc, is a heavier, often sweeter sparkling wine. Both are produced in the méthode champenoise and both are also produced in a slightly effervescent style called *pétillant.*

A huge Vaslin press is uncrated and put to use in Sonoma Vineyards. In a joint venture with the two-hundred-year-old Piper-Heidsieck French Champagne firm and Renfield Importers, the Sonoma winery is producing méthode champenoise *sparkling wines. The objective is 100,000 cases by 1985. The hand-fed Vaslin, widely used in the Champagne area, gently presses the grapes, avoiding color exchange.*

(A)

(B)

(C)

(D)

Housing the aging bottles of sparkling wines over the centuries has occurred in both magnificent and mundane settings. Always searching for coolness and stability in temperature, vintners dug deeper and deeper into the earth, forming cathedrallike caves. The entrance to Taittinger's caves has ornate carved doors (A). A typical French champagne cave with the bottles now resting fully on the necks to settle the lees (B). Sheer rock walls with rows of pupitres at Taittinger (C). A cellar master in Italy's Trentino district inspects a very old library of bottles of sparkling wine (D).

OTHER CHAMPAGNE PRODUCTION

The popularity of sparkling wines has never diminished throughout the centuries. Consequently, nearly every producing area has enjoyed success in its effervescent productions. Naturally, the traditional bottle fermentations remain quite popular in many regions because of their distinctive yeasty tones. The first recorded commercial bottle fermentation in Spain occurred in 1872 at the Codorniu winery which had been in existence since 1551. Currently the winery produces upwards of 100 million bottles of sparkling wine per year in their ten miles of underground cellars. Since it reaches American markets at considerably lower prices than French champagne, Spanish *espumoso* bottled as *bruto* and *seco* can be expected to rise sharply in popularity. Other widely distributed labels are Freixenet, Castellblanch, and Bodegas Bilbainas.

Asti Spumante was the first champagne produced in northern Italy, in the 1850s near the town of Asti by a local vermouth producer, Carlo Gancia. The local muscat grape used in the bottle-fermenting process never produced a satisfying dry competitor to the French versions but, with the advent of the bulk champagne process in the beginning of this century, it did develop into a vastly popular dessert or sipping wine.

California winemakers, including the pioneering Haraszthy at Buena Vista, early discovered the fine sparkling wines to be made from the California version of the vinifera grape. French méthode champenoise, cuvée and production methods were adapted to the local grapes and the equipment imported from the old country. By 1905, Paul Masson had produced the famous Œil de Perdrix, the slightly pink "Eye of the Partridge" and by 1908 was producing over 800,000 bottles per year using the méthode champenoise. As early as 1896, a transplanted Czech named Francis Korbel experimented with the classic champagne production and the Korbel firm has been continuously producing fine vintages since 1907. Another pioneer of the time in both white and red bottle-fermented wines was Italian Swiss Colony.

Eastern American sparkling wines did not develop until the middle of the twentieth century, but now they are commonly produced by nearly three dozen wineries in over ten states attesting to the universality of the appreciation of the bubbly. However, the vast expansion in sparkling wine production came about because of the inventive enterprise of a Frenchman named Eugene Charmat.

The Charmat Process

Appropriately, it was a Frenchman who, in 1910, conceived the technique which is now used for the vast majority of the sparkling wine enjoyed worldwide. Known in France as the *méthode charmat*, it is simplicity itself. Following the selection of the cuvée, the most critical step because the base quality is determined at this time, the wines are placed in specially constructed tanks of approximately 500 gallons which are capable of sustaining up to 250 pounds of pressure per square inch. Upon

The charmat tanks at Christian Brothers contain up to two thousand gallons of refermenting wine which is clarified and bottled away from the yeast and lees of secondary fermentation, yielding crisp, clean sparkling wines.

inoculation with a carefully measured dosage of sugar and yeast, the secondary fermentation occurs in this large, controlled tank in the same manner that it does in the millions of individual bottles in the traditional method.

After several weeks of fermentation, the newly effervescent wine is usually transferred to a second tank for settling, cold stabilization, and filtration. It is then bottled cold and under pressure. The entire system is then freed for another fermentation cycle which takes about two months. It is easy to grasp the enormous savings in labor and processing with the charmat method over the traditional bottle fermentation and aging.

The closed cuvée bulk system produces more sparkling wines than any of its competitors, and it is bound to grow apace simply because of its efficiency and its ability to deliver very sound sparkling wines. What the system cannot produce is the time period of resting on the yeasty lees which is characteristic of the traditional method. However, if good wines are utilized in the cuvée, it is logical that excellent, clean champagne will emerge in the marketplace.

The Germans use closed cuvée for the majority of their sekt, and the Soviet Union has advanced the technology of this system to become the largest producers of bulk "champanska" on earth at above 150 million bottles per year. Their unique technique filters the cuvée through several tanks in stages to increase the yeast contact to more closely parallel the champenoise-finished wine. In 1980, the Soviet goal was 230 million bottles which would have required a massive amount of hand riddling. The future of bulk champagne is secure, as is the resurgence of the classic champenoise!

In passing, particular credit should be given the Germans among all the producers of sparkling wines worldwide. The Germans produce several levels of the product: *schaumwein*, the common; *sekt*, a minimum of nine months aged; *prädikat sekt* which must contain a minimum of 60 percent German wine in the cuvée; and *Deutscher sekt*, which must be

(A)

(B)

These pictures demonstrate the costly but manifestly efficient transfer system in which the secondary fermentation occurs in bottles which are then separated from the wine, washed and used again for final bottling. The complexity of the transfer equipment is shown at Taylor Cellars (A). The champagne cuvée fills the

bottles automatically for secondary fermentation. Finally, the machine through propulsion of nitrogen, an inert gas, disgorges the lees (B). These bottle labels may state that the champagne was bottle-fermented *as opposed to the* fermented in this bottle *of the traditional* méthode champenoise.

all German wine. Both the American and German governments mandate a level of 3.5 atmospheres CO_2 pressure. Also like the Americans, the Germans label as "effervescent" anything above 19.2 pounds per square inch; thus, there is great ambiguity and no certainty of pressure levels at the time of consumption. Both mandatory levels are imposed arbitrarily for tax purposes, and the buyer should be aware that the longer the bottle sits on the shelf, the greater the chance of gas escaping. Finally, one can detect a larger average bubble in the closed cuvée productions than the méthode champenoise because secondary fermentation and aging in a small bottle produces a slightly finer bubble.

The Transfer Method

A technique which utilizes both of the above methods is called the transfer process. Developed in Germany in the 1930s, this procedure uses a bank of champagne bottles for the actual fermentation period. However, these bottles are connected by piping to large settling tanks similar to the charmat tanks in which the newly fermented wines are settled and polished. While the settling occurs, the original bottles are washed and readied to receive the new sparkling wines that are now cleansed and inoculated with the appropriate sweetening dosage. Sparkling wines produced in this transfer process can be identified by the words "Bottle Fermented" in contrast to the traditional "Fermented in this Bottle."

To some vintners, the best of both worlds is achieved through the transfer method because speed and economy are wedded with some extended exposure to the yeast. However, the initial investment limits it to the larger producers, those who sell in the hundreds of thousands of cases. Gancia in Italy and Almadén, Paul Masson, and Weibel in California utilize elaborate transfer lines.

Transfer system vintners claim a great consistency in the marketed bottle since the wines are all merged in the clarifying

and fining tanks, and since there is more uniform CO_2 pressure than in the méthode champenoise in which each bottle must be exposed to the atmosphere before corking. These are the same arguments as those advanced for the much simpler and less expensive charmat procedure!

PÉTILLANT AND CARBONATED WINES

Two more categories of sparkling wines are produced here and abroad, although little is written, or even known, about them. Pétillant wines are recognized by the European community as semi-sparkling wines produced naturally with the malo-lactic secondary ferment. Carbonated wines, quite simply, are those charged with CO_2 in the manner of a soda pop. In Europe, these are known as aerated wines.

Both of these categories require lesser wines for the cuvée, and the bottles are correspondingly less expensive in the marketplace. Often these wines are born of surplus supplies, but with sufficient carbonation, surprisingly good products can be made from indifferent wines.

The most famous and successful of the pétillant category must be the ubiquitous lambrusco types. No other single vinted product has commanded as much of a share of the American market as these slightly fizzy, usually medium sweet blends from the north of Italy. They are responsible for the resurgence and even domination of Italian producers in American markets. While many a pundit awaits their demise in the Cold Duck fashion, they have apparently struck a firm chord in America. Popular in Italy for a hundred years in drier versions, the majority of the lambrusco types popular in America are of mundane but satisfying quality.

One example of a carbonated wine is Baby Duck, an invention of the Canadian wine industry which can be found currently in some American and British markets. Reputed to be the biggest selling single type in Canada, it slakes the enormous thirst of the soda consumer.

Bright's Pussycat from the Canadian side of the Niagara Falls proves that meeting the demand spells success. Over sixty million bottles of this light, low-alcohol, medium-sweet sparkling wine have been produced from the native labrusca, Concord and Niagara, ideally suited for such a wine. It, Cold Duck and Baby Duck have been enormously successful for Canadian wineries.

The battle rages between the French and their supporters, who believe that anything less than bottle fermentation is an abomination, and the charmat and transfer producers who quite proudly produce equally fine wines in their speedy and efficient machines. Amerine and Singleton sum it up in *Wine* (1968):

> The bottle-fermented sparkling wine is usually clarified by expensive and tedious hand processing, whereas in the bulk process the methods of production and filtration are less costly. The bulk processor usually achieves high quality in his sparkling wines by emphasizing fruity-grapey qualities. The bottle-fermented sparkling wines may be produced so as to emphasize age-derived flavors by allowing time for yeast autolysis and aging reactions.

In the end, you puts down your penny, and you takes your choice!

TABLE 11.2 Sparkling Wine Tasting

Wine	General Style	Suggested Brand
Pétillant Wines		
La Salle Rosé	Medium sweet, full-bodied	The Christian Brothers
Crackling Rosé	Light body, medium carbonation, refreshing	Paul Masson
Sparkling Wines		
Nature style (bone dry)	Bone dry, medium body, high acid	Blanc de Noir Korbel Sehrtrocken Hans Kornel Schramsberg
Brut Champagne	Medium to full body, sharp, flowery nose, piquancy with tight, tiny bubbles	Moët Chandon The Christian Brothers Codorniu Freixenet
Extra Dry Champagne	Touch of sweetness, full body, mellow	Paul Masson
Asti Spumanti or Sparkling Moscato	Medium body, lively true muscatel aroma and taste	Bolla Angelo Papagni
Sparkling Vouvray	Medium full, medium sweet	Frederic Wildman

SUGGESTED SPARKLING WINE TASTING

Pétillant wines contain less carbon dioxide than champagne but are still notably effervescent. Tasters should be aware that the chill of the fluid and the action of the carbon dioxide gas combine to confuse the taste sensations. Many people with high sugar thresholds have difficulty recognizing sugar in Brut Champagne, although it normally is found at the 1 percent level. Similarly, the often higher acid levels are softened in impact.

Other Traditional Ferments

Of all the abundant fruits in nature, the grape remains uniquely suited for the conversion to beverage alcohol because it is mineral rich, water laden, and balanced in glucose and acid. However, since the natural habitats of grapes and many other fruits are severely limited, it is quite natural that man would put other available harvests to the same purpose. Yet it takes much ingenuity and persistence to ferment many other sugar sources since few ferment as easily as the grape.

MEAD: AN EARLY FERMENT

Although anthropologists argue the point, honey wine probably placed second to the grape as an early source of alcohol. Once exposed to water, the nectar of bees ferments as rapidly and cleanly as the grape from the action of the same airborne yeasts. It is a reasonable guess that ancient man stumbled upon this alcohol source by finding a rain-filled abandoned beehive, rather like an oversize grape.

Every language in the western world, and most in the eastern, have a word to describe honey wine. It is *madhu* in Sanskrit, *metu* in Old High German, *methy* in Greek, and *sura* in India where honey was often combined with grain ferments. One of the holy books of India, the Rig-Veda, which warns, "sura is poison in a leathern bottle . . ." suggests our own period of Prohibition was no new phenomenon. Many of these ancient drinks also contained hallucinogenic herbs.

*I*n the wide-striding Vishnu's highest footsteps there is a Spring of Mead.

from the Rig-Veda

*I*f barley be wanting to make into malt,
We must be content and think it no fault,
For we can make liquor to sweeten our lips,
Of pumpkins, and parsnips, and walnut-chips.

Massachusetts Colony citizen, 1630

In *Making Mead* (1978), Acton and Duncan provide some captivating historical insights:

It is likely that mead was made even before the wheel was invented. Cave paintings of primitive stone-age men depict the collection of honey from bee colonies, and any addition of water to this would automatically produce a mixture which could be fermented by wild yeasts.

The pastoral scene, replete with babe in arms, shows the importance of early apple fermentations in Cider Mill, *an oil painting by William Tolman Carlton.*

The authors trace the well-documented history of honey as sweetener to the western world before the sugar cane or sugar beet arrived on the scene.

Honey was for thousands of years the principal sweetening agent known to mankind; honey and mead were the givers of life, wisdom, courage and strength right from the earliest history, through Hindu times, on through Aristotle and Virgil until they found powerful echoes in the Bible. Even our own Celtic ancestors made mead and a form of metheglin by mixing honey with the juice of the hazel tree which was to them a magic tree.

Other interesting tidbits of mead's survival through the best and worst of times includes comments on the "Elizabethan times, when drinking standards reached their lowest ebb." A form of mead became a component in the *piments* used to stretch and make palatable mixtures of fruit juices, wines, and spices. Among these blends were the following: *hippocras,* named for the father of medicine, which combined grape juice and honey plus medicinal herbs—shades of early patent medicines; *metheglin,* from the Welsh word for "medicine," which had both a profusion and heavy concentration of kitchen herbs as well as an occasional fortification with distilled spirits; *cyser,* a staple in Britain, a mixture of apple cider and mead; and a gaggle of others including *bishop, negus, caudle, boswell,* and *lamb's wool.*

A perceptive anthropologist and student of the impact of alcohol on people, John M. Cooper, summarizes the history of this subject in "Alcohol Beverages of the World," *Medical Missionary Magazine* (December 1943):

> Fermented (non-distilled) alcoholic beverages have a very much longer period. They do not go back to the very beginnings of our race, but their origins can be traced back beyond dated history to at least the late neolithic times . . . fermented alcoholic beverages were very widely used among primitive peoples, but were far from being universal . . . In a very general way it may be said that fermented alcoholic beverages were found among peoples whose staple food supply came from grain agriculture.

Edwin Loeb, in "Primitive Intoxicants" in the *Quarterly Journal of Studies on Alcohol* (December 1943), also pointed to a lack of universality by showing that the Indonesian, the aborigine of New Guinea, the North American Indian, the Polynesian, and the Micronesian did not have alcohol in their diets. Donald Horton, in the same journal (September 1943), cited an example of how important alcohol had become to some still existing primitive peoples: "Excessive drinking is learned in childhood as a matter of custom, even infants at the breast being given distilled liquor. Excessive drinking is the only important past-time in Chamula."

However, Cooper (1943) warns that while drinking was nearly universal among the primitive peoples who harvested grain and had ready sources of fermentable sugars, the patterns of drinking varied widely. "Climate is not a major determinant . . . Nor are the facts explained on the basis of race. Actually some Caucasoids and some Mongoloids are light drinkers and some are heavy drinkers." Cooper demonstrates that the product consumed is directly related to the indigenous source materials.

THE UNIQUE ROLE OF MEAD

Among all of these potential ferments, none has the history or the unique properties of that flowery nectar, honey. Fermented honey appeared at least 20,000 years ago. The methods employed for preservation and fermentation in this dim past probably differed little from those employed today by many remote African tribes. To make mead, honey is squeezed from the comb and combined with other fruits and water. Within three days, the alcohol product is ready to be consumed, having been flavored and nurtured in its fermenting by the other fruits or saps.

However, the unique contribution to human welfare has already been made by the industrious bee long before the alcohol production. The nectar gathered by the bee is largely composed of sucrose and water. In the process of making the honey, the bees contribute to its preservation for man. First, they reduce the moisture to below 19 or 18.5 percent which raises the osmotic pressure to the degree that destructive microorganisms cannot grow. In addition, the bees add two es-

sential enzymes to their product. The first, invertase, converts the 12 carbon sucrose to glucose and fructose, just as it does when barley is malted for brewing. This process also adds to the osmotic pressure which protects the honey from spoilage in the atmosphere. Another enzyme called glucose oxidase reduces a portion of the glucose to the chief acid in honey called gluconic acid. This lower pH, or increase in acid, makes the mixture additionally hostile to bacterial growth. Because of these two wondrous chemical components, honey may be stored for years with little deterioration.

*H*ere in this hive we're all alive,
Good liquor makes us funny.
If you are dry, step in an try
The flavor of our honey.
Frankford Tavern Sign (early 19th century)

Other Common Ferments

In addition to mead there was a wide range of non-grape wines people prepared in antiquity which even today are cultivated in our society and in widely dispersed cultures of the world. Too often this segment of ferments is dismissed as inconsequential, which is very wide of the historical mark.

In *Food in Antiquity* (1959) the Brothwells report on non-grape ferments as natural gifts of God which were accepted with delight by the ancients but which are now mostly ignored because of the convenience and abundance of grape wine. In the desert, the Israelites regaled in *manna* from heaven, the secretions of small insects on the twigs of the tamarisk that had to be gathered early in the morning before the ants got to them. They tell of the sap and palm oil, the sweet juice of the papyrus in Egypt, and the natural sugarcane of India. They claim "the use made by recent aboriginal groups of such exudations from the eucalyptus of Australia and the species of pine in America suggest that early man might have tapped sugary sap from a number of trees, which were later neglected as civilization (and also bee-keeping) advanced."

In *The Structures of Everyday Life,* Braudel tells of the development of cider as a source of alcohol in the regions beyond possible grape cultivation.

> A few words about cider. It originated in Biscay where the cider apple trees came from; they appeared in Cotentin, the Caen region and the Pays d'Auge towards the eleventh or twelfth century . . . it competed with beer and met with some success, since beer was made from grain and drinking it sometimes meant going without bread.

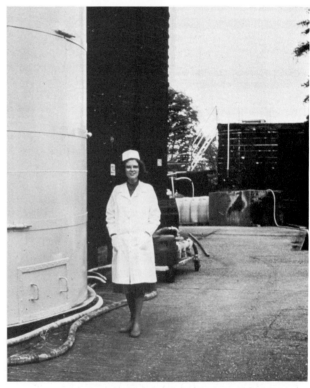

In 1946 Merrydown was a cottage industry in Sussex with an annual production of 400 gallons. Now it fills about 18,000 bottles of cider daily. Eight thousand tons of fine apples are used by the plant each year. A six-to-eight-week fermentation occurs in 40,000 gallon oak vats before nine months of aging and a final blending of the ciders. Shown are the original apple press and outdoor aging tanks.

Our own history as a nation is replete with evidence of determination to secure a constant supply of intoxicants. The eastern seaboard states often lacked the proper conditions for vinifera grapes and barley beer. For example, Johnny Appleseed is seldom given full credit for the uses that were served by the apple, although H. B. Weiss (1954) does note his work in *The History of Applejack.*

> Everyone drank hard cider, in all places—at funerals, church raisings, weddings, meetings, and upon every occasion. Many babies, before they walked, were given mulled cider at night. Men and women were said to drink a quart of hard cider before breakfast . . . Sometimes it was fortified with rum and the entire apple crop went into the manufacture of cider.

The step from cider to applejack or apple brandy was simplicity itself in the early days, requiring no still and no complicated equipment. The cider was left on the back stoop on a chilly night, and nature conveniently froze the water, leaving concentrated brandy. Weiss reports that "in *Americana Ebriatus* by Hewson L. Peeke, Dr. Peters is quoted as saying that cider was a common table drink which the inhabitants of Connecticut purified by frost, separating the watery part from the spirit which was placed in vessels and colored by Indian corn."

It is certain that once intrigued by mead and grape wine, man spent a great deal of effort and time in attempting to produce similar products from readily available sources of sugar. Since dates and their palm trees are native to many warm climes, and since they have flourished since 50,000 B.C., date wine with its sugary sap, called palm toddy or *gur,* has been a common ferment found from India to the Philippines. One early record of date and palm wines is depiction of them on walls in the pyramids, with date wine apparently in more abundant use. In the South Pacific this drink is called *vin de nipa,* or wine of the Nipa palm, a low, densely leaved, stumpy tree. But this is only one way in which man cleverly uses the palm tree which has been used for over 300 purposes, from feed to charcoal.

One tree found in the Near East, the Mahua, develops as much as 300 pounds of flowers which, when dried, contain up to 20 percent sugar which is fermented. Crude beers or plant wines from the tapioca root and the maguey cactus were common in what is now Central and South America. The seemingly innumerable permutations of the word *arrack,* or *raki,* suggest the many variations of rice and palm wine distilled into potent spirits throughout eastern Europe and Asia for centuries.

The ingenious Asian nomads were responsible not only for the invention of dried or powdered milk, but also for a ferment from mare's milk. Defatted powdered milk was easily transported on long nomadic treks. Less easily transported but certainly more appreciated was *koumis,* a wine made from milk that was churned and fermented in a leather bag. The product is still popular in parts of Russia today, as are a camel-milk version called *kephir* and one from the yak called *airon.*

*I*t's a bad 'arvest that don't wet the gleaner's whistle.

Mr. Jorrocks

FERMENTATION TECHNIQUES

In general, fermentation techniques for fruit and sap wines parallel the grape productions. The significant difference is the need for additional nutrients and often sugars to support the yeast development. Citric or other acids may be added if the mash is lower than 0.5 percent acid. The primary additives are sugars—cane, sucrose, glucose, invert, syrup, or molasses—which are now allowed commercially up to a maximum of 25 Brix and also up to 14 percent of the solids after fermentation. Sixteen states license fruit and berry wineries in the United States.

The fruit is generally pressed, often heated, and then fermented on the skins to gain additional character in the wine. Most berries and fruits are immediately susceptible to oxidative browning, so rather high levels of sulfur are usually applied. Water may also be added, up to 35 percent of the total volume. The true berry flavors generally hold well, even when distilled into berry brandies.

Popular types include honey, dandelion, mint, rhubarb, apple, pear, blackberry, and cherry, with most wines ranging between 8 and 20 percent in alcohol. In addition, in Europe and Russia where the source materials abound, wines are produced annually from mountain ash berries, bilberries, black currants, gooseberries, strawberries, elderberries and sloe berries—the one that is also used to produce a flavored gin. Because of the great advantage to production, many types of fresh berries are frozen in 55 gallon drums providing fresh, fermentable fruit year round. The thawing process actually assists in the fruit breakdown and release of pigments and flavors.

Mead ferments generally require citric or other acids to bring down the pH as well as tannin to create the desired astringency associated with fruit wines. Other additives may include ammonium phosphate for yeast nutrition, Vitamin B_1, and Epsom salts.

Old and Fascinating Ferments

Among unusual recipes for beverage alcohol, none is quite so exotic as the following Oriental Mutton Wine given in Tannahill (1973), said to produce 9 percent alcohol: "40 catties

Highlights

- Other fruits and plants that could be fermented grew naturally around the fringes of the grape culture.
- Cider and pear wine, called perry, are probably the most produced of other fruit wines, as are palm and date ferments in the tropics.

- Most non-grape wines require the addition of sugar and nutrients for complete fermentation.

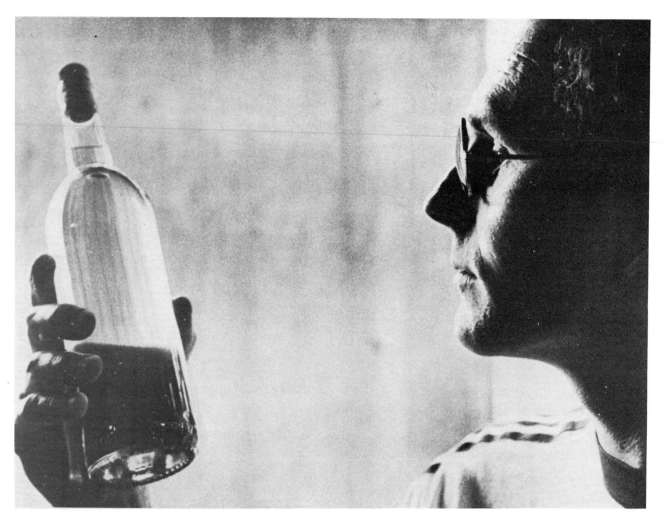

Unlike many berry fruit winemakers who produce traditionally sweet versions, Paul Thomas of Seattle represents a small band of artisans who make completely dry, well-balanced berry wines designed for consumption with the finest meals. Often Thomas will pay at least twice as much for berries as one would for grapes.

[1⅓ lbs.] cow's milk, 1¼ pints of skim milk, sound and curdled, 8 oz. brown sugar, 4 oz. honey, 4 oz. fruit of dimocarpus, 1 catty of raisins, mixed drugs, and a sheep 4 yrs old of a castrated male."

Tannahill suggests the extent of medical applications of various and, to us, strange wine, herb, and food concoctions.

When, in the nineteenth century, interested Europeans began to inquire into the *Pen Ts'ao*—the Chinese pharmacopoeia—they discovered many "wines" which certainly had their origin in wild rather than settled lands. Among those listed were deer wine, tiger bone wine, tortoise wine, snake wine, dog wine, and mutton wine. (The latter four were, respectively, good for bronchitis, palsy, lassitude, and strengthening the stomach, kidneys and testicles.) Among the ingredients for a number of these "medicinal" drinks was *kumiss*, loosely translated by the Victorians as "cow's milk whiskey." (1973)

There is irony in the newly touted medical applications of many of the herbs that were additives to these primitive tonics. A researcher in Texas recently found a chemical in almonds quite as effective as aspirin for headaches and other minor discomforts. Another researcher found a parallel between Mexican peyote and the ergot or mold rust used in Eleusinian ceremonies for several thousand years in Greece (Wasson, *The Road to Eleusis*).

The point is that much has been lost of these natural and contrived ferments which originated in the fecund human mind and the fullness of the chemical symphony that is nature. Surely it was not alcohol itself or the profusion of other elements that caused the ancients to praise the combination; it must have been that alcohol served as a convenient, sprightly medium.

TABLE 12.1 Fruit and Berry Wine Tasting

Type	General Style
Apple cider	Light, fragrant, often dry
Rhubarb	Light, fruity, and spicy
Plum	Aromatic, light body
Concord grape	Medium body, tart flavor
Raspberry	Medium body, fruity
Blackberry	Full body, mellow, and medium sweet
Loganberry	Very sweet and full
Mead	Very full and sweet

A Nontraditional Ferment

A new product now circulating in western states is called *non-alcoholic* wine. Originating in Australia under the Castella label, the line includes a Fruity White, Roselle, Sparkling Spumante, and Sparkling Roselle. These non-wines are promoted specifically as alternatives to soft drinks, which they indeed are, at considerably increased prices.

FRUIT AND BERRY WINE TASTING

Brands in this style of wine generally enjoy limited distribution, being consumed largely in the vicinity of the winery. Consequently, here suggested are the most frequently produced types. Acquisition of others indigenous to the tasting location is urged. As a consequence of the emerging wine revolution, fruit wines are enjoying their own renaissance, with many winemakers demonstrating consummate skills in producing most satisfying wines with true fruit flavors.

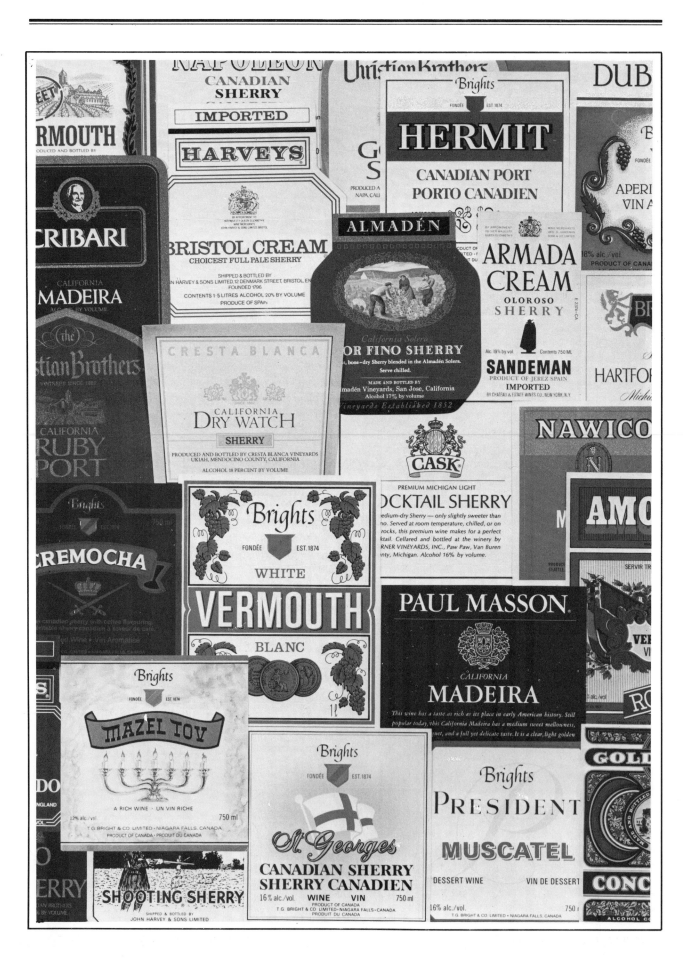

Dessert and Aperitif Wines

13

Man is a tinkerer, in the winery as well as in the kitchen. Like the fruit and berry wines, the dessert wines, or fortified wines as we know them today, were the result of many years of patient experimentation.

EARLY SWEET WINES

The first object to be tinkered with in the dessert category had to be honey wine—mead. Beatrice Hunter in *Fact/Book on Fermented Foods and Beverages* (1973) recounts how widespread was its popularity.

> Both the ancient Greeks and Romans made mead, and knew it under the Latin name, *hydromel. Mulsum* was a form of mead with wine added. In Scythia, it was called *medos;* in Greece, *methu;* in India, *madhu;* in Ireland, *mid;* in Germany, *meth;* in the Slavic countries, *medu;* in Lithuania, *medus;* in the Teutonic [Celtic] areas, *metheglin;* and in England, *mead. . . .* The Nordic races valued mead highly, and it was the drink of heroes. The Nibelungen heroes drank *meth* out of golden goblets and ox horns. The high halls of Valhalla flowed with mead . . .

The key point in this passage, aside from the fact of the universality of the beverage, is found in the words "with wine added." They indicate that the popular mead became a flavoring agent used to make undrinkable wines palatable. Honey flavored dozens of edibles, and centuries were to pass before sugar canes or beets migrated to the continent for sweetening tasks. Mead on the tongue retains all of the luscious mellowness of the original handicraft of the bee.

Give me Sacke, Old Sacke, Boys!
To Make the Muses Merry,
The Life of Mirth and
the joy of the Earth,
Is a cup of good old Sherry!

Pasquil

If I had a thousand sons, the first humane principle I would teach them should be to forswear thin potations, and to addict themselves to sack.

Falstaff

Aperitifs of Ancient Origins

The principal additive in contemporary dessert wines is brandy, and distillation was not utilized until well into the thirteenth century. However, the development of aperitif, or before-dinner, wines dates at least to Roman times, as Allen (1961) reports in *Wine.*

> The aperitif craze according to Pliny, who frowned upon it, started in Rome in the reign of Tiberius, some forty years before he wrote his *Natural History* in A.D. 70. At that time, he tells us, the fashion came in of

The sherry triangle in Andalusia produced wines of style before the birth of Christ and through the following centuries.

drinking on an empty stomach and taking wine regularly before meals. He stigmatizes it as an outlandish innovation recommended by doctors who were always trying to advertise themselves by running some newfangled idea.

When the Moors were finally evicted from their continental base in southern Spain, the trade in luscious, sugar-rich wines was reestablished. By Chaucer's time, the fourteenth century, Spanish wines were enjoyed in London. Allen conjectures that Falstaff would have rebelled at thin, insubstantial wines for his sack; Allen then draws a comparison between sack and sherry.

> Early in the sixteenth century the wines exported from Jerez to England received the name Sack, a name which was later extended to cover wines exported from other wine regions, the Canaries, Malaga and so on. Unlike Sherry it had no geographical significance. Such wines were too heavy and sweet to be drunk in their home where climate and custom called for a young beverage wine.

The British and other residents of northern climates had an apparently insatiable appetite for the heavy, sweet wines that the folks in the Mediterranean held in little esteem. Braudel tells of the growth in this export wine:

> Englishmen very early on established the great reputation of Malmsey, liqueur wines from Candia and the Greek Islands. Later they launched port, malaga, maderia, sherry and marsala, all famous wines with a high alcohol content. The Dutch created the popularity of all types of spirits from the seventeenth-century onwards . . . The southern people looked jeeringly upon these drinkers who in their opinions, did not know how to drink and emptied their glasses in one gulp.

These early sweet wines that were heavily traded and enormously popular in England and other northern countries were not fortified because brandy had not developed as a social spirit. Distilled wine's first use was medicinal, as a potent drug administered by physicians. In his 1893 tome entitled *A Philosophical and Statistical History of the Inventions and Customs of Ancient and Modern Nations in the Manufacture and Use of Inebriating Liquors,* Samuel Morewood indicates this.

> The first spirit of which there is any account in Europe, was made from the grape, and sold as a medicine both in Italy and Spain, under the Arabic term *alcohol*. The Genoese, in the thirteenth century, dealt largely in it, and are said to have acquired considerable sums in the sale of this article, likewise named *aqua vitae*. In 1270, a Florentine physician recommended *spirit of wine* as possessing great virtues and effecting valuable medicinal purposes.

THE SPANISH WERE FIRST

It is, of course, sheer conjecture to fix a date when some inventive Spanish winemaker thought to add a bit of brandy to his solera. As will be explained, the solera system was of great

Terms

amontillado Dry nutty sherry wine from Spain.

amoroso Medium dry sherry wine from Spain.

angelica Pure fermented grape juice mixed with brandy.

aperitif A wine often fortified and aromatized with special herbs to stimulate the appetite before eating.

arenas Sandy soils in the Andalusia in Spain.

arrope Concentrated juice used to flavor and color sherries.

baking A technical process designed to create the caramelized taste as flor yeast gives; controlled heating in warehouses.

barros Clay soils in the Andalusia.

bodega Ground level Spanish aging cellars.

butt Standard sherry cask containing 132 gallons.

cocktail sherry Dry version of domestic sherry often with a percentage of flor sherry to create the fino nuttiness.

cotto Italian cooked juice used to flavor and color marsala.

cream sherry Sweet version of domestic sherries from 9 to 14% sugar.

criadera The initial level, or nursery casks, of Spanish aging of sherry wine.

crust The sediment hardened over the years in Vintage Ports.

dessert wine Normally a wine that is fortified, rich in sugar and served at dessert or on social occasions.

dry sherry Similar to cocktail sherry, but more on the dry and nutty side.

estufa Heated warehouse used to bake Madeira wines.

fino The driest, most delicate of the Spanish sherries.

flor Variety of yeast indigenous to Spain that grows on top of aging wine, creating nutty flavors.

fortified wines Those with increased alcoholic strength imparted by the addition of grape brandy.

hippocras Sweetened, flavored wine of medieval times.

kosher wine Pure unmixed wines approved by a rabbi for sacramental purposes; mostly dessert concord types.

lagar Pressing or stomping trough formerly used in Spain and Portugal.

licoroso Sweet fortified wine.

lodges Port warehouses in Vila Nova de Gaia across from Oporto, Portugal.

madeira Baked dessert wine from the Isle of Madeira.

manzanilla A wine similar to fino, but produced near the seacoast, so not a true sherry.

marsala Sicilian wine, sometimes dry but mostly sweet.

mistelle Grape must with no fermentation because of the immediate fortification by brandy, used for sweetening vermouth and aperitif wines; called Angelica in California.

moscato muscat Ubiquitous family of grapes grown in warm climates and used for dessert wines, for example, Muscatel in California.

oloroso Full-bodied, deeply colored, very sweet sherries.

palma Chalk marking on sherry barrel which denotes developing fino sherry.

palomino The primary grape of the Spanish sherries.

pedro ximinez The secondary wine of the Jerez used for the sweetening of sherries.

pipe A large cask containing 138 gallons used to carry port down to the lodges; a Madeira pipe is about 110 gallons, a sherry pipe 132.

plastering The system of adding *yeso* or gypsum to Spanish wine must to raise the acid levels.

port of the vintage Rare identification of the vintage year; not to be confused with bottle-aged Vintage Port.

puttonyo A basket used to pick overripe grapes in Hungary; the measure of these rich grapes added to a wine which indicates its level of sweetness.

rancio A term used to describe special pale aged Spanish wines.

ruby port Deep, full-bodied red dessert wines, aged 3–5 years in wood.

sack Any one of the sweet wines produced in the Middle Ages in the hot climate of the Mediterranean.

solera The Spanish system of blending wines by moving them through a succession of barrels from year to year and drawing the final product from the lowest level.

tawny port Wine of special paleness or tawny color developed through long aging of Ruby Port up to 20 years.

tokaji aszu Hungarian wine from the Furmint grape sweetened with puttonyos of moldy grapes; one of the world's longest lived wines.

tokay In California, a sweet dessert wine made for blending port, sherry, and often angelica.

venencia A cylindrical silver cup on an extended whalebone handle which allows tasting of sherries through the flor growth.

vermouth From Old English *wermōd* (man-courage, pride); aromatized special aperitif and dessert wine.

vin doux French for sweet wine.

vinho generoso Portuguese for fortified wine.

vintage port Bottle-aged port.

wormwood *Artemisia absinthium,* a herbaceous plant the flowers of which are used to flavor vermouth and many liqueurs.

These three engravings demonstrate the persistence of the wine trade from the Middle Ages' vineyards and harvesting to the eighteenth-century cathedrallike bodegas when Sherry was already a highly refined type of wine making.

antiquity in Spain, as was the flor yeast that reduced the alcohol level within select barrels. But the brandy soon contributed to Spain's economy, as Allen suggests. "Already in the sixteenth century the city of Jerez counted in its revenue *la renta del aguardiente,* the excise duty levied on the brandy used to fortify export wines."

There are scattered historical references to white fruit liquors or *alcool blanc* throughout northern Europe in the twelfth century. The first licensed brandy distillery in France is recorded in the year 1411 in the Armagnac region. Apple brandy originated in the eleventh century in northern France where it exists today undiminished in popularity and is known as Calvados. Because development of commercial ardent spirits encompassed a span of nearly 300 years, a great deal of experimentation must have taken place in the family kitchen. The housewife who made both beer and wine as a matter of course, and sweetened or spiced each as common practice, could hardly have resisted the temptation to distill a little bit of each, once the technique was explained to her. This theory is bolstered by the knowledge that Henry II found widespread local production of *usquebaugh* in Ireland as early as 1172. Moonshining, then or now, is not all that difficult.

Commercial Distillations Fortify Wines

This book, however, is concerned with each potable alcohol in terms of its commercial application. Sherry and port, the two giants of the dessert wine field, were developed commercially in the sixteenth and eighteenth centuries, respectively.

A very satisfactory definition of fortified wines appears in Alexis Lichine's *Encyclopedia of Wines and Spirits:* "Wine to which brandy has been added sometimes to stop fermentation, and to increase alcoholic content. Some examples are Port, Sherry, Malaga, and Madeira. In America the term [fortified] is illegal and such wines are usually called dessert wines." (1969)

The reader may wonder why the term "fortified" persists if, indeed, it is illegal according to domestic authority. Quite simply, it is an internationally accepted term and an accurate reflection of what has been done to the wines. The noted authority, L. W. Marrison (1970), explains the popularity of fortified wines in *Wines and Spirits:* "However, there is a considerable demand for stronger wines than these [still wines]—stronger than yeasts can live in. Some wines are therefore raised in alcoholic strength to about 18 or 20 percent, or even more. Such are sherry, port, madeira, etc., the fortified wines . . ."

To comprehend the original increase and the current decline in the consumption of American dessert wines, one must review briefly how ardent spirits were introduced into widespread social consumption.

Andalusian Magic

In *Moonshine* (1971), Esther Kellner reports the generally accepted theory about the advent of distillation.

> The discovery of distillation has been linked with the name of Rhazes, the greatest physician of the Islamic world. . . . One of the interesting traditions found on the long road from the hot, dry sands of Mesopotamia to the cool, lush hills of Kentucky is that the Arabs taught distilling to the Moors of northern Africa, who carried it to Spain about A.D. 1150. From there it spread into Europe and across the British Isles, reaching a high degree of perfection in Ireland before it was brought to America.

But from our point of view, the spirit entered the dessert wine field in the incredibly beautiful, arid, and dusty triangle of southern Spain known as Andalusia. It is also historically certain that this area was very early important in production, as Morewood indicates:

> Mariana tells us, that the vine was among the first objects of the early husbandry of the Spaniards . . . If, according to this writer, Tubal, the son of Japheth, were the first man that peopled Spain, after the flood, no doubt the art of winemaking, as practised by Noah, was made familiar to the Spaniards.

The Moors, while conquering the land, did not neglect the production of the native grapes. By 961, they had promulgated agricultural practices, including grape growing, which were religiously followed throughout all the glorious days of Spanish dominion throughout the new world. While the Moors prohibited the making of wine from the grapes, the native population would never have given up this ancient birthright. It should be recalled that by the second century A.D., as many as twenty million amphorae of wine were shipped annually from the Andalusia to Rome.

Marrison (1970) describes the really substantial contributions of the Moors to Spanish agronomy.

> It was the Moors who encouraged viniculture so greatly in Andalusia, which was, in the eighth to the eleventh centuries, the greatest centre of civilization in the world. Cordoba, their capital, had half a million

inhabitants; now it has less than 100,000. The *Calendar of Cordoba,* promulgated in 961, embodied their directions to winemakers as well as to other agriculturalists. It was their advice which guided the viniculture of the Americas, which was everywhere founded by the Spanish Jesuit missionaries.

Marrison emphasizes the growing demand through the Dark Ages for potent spirits. The technique of aging wines in sealed containers to produce delicate, ethereal aromas and tastes was lost in a brutish culture. What was sought was the effect rather than the style. Alcohol was the objective.

Piments Dominate Dark Ages

In this atmosphere, there arose a new wine technician, the *pigmentarius,* whose sole task became making the wines palatable. His products, known as *piments,* dominated nearly 800 years of vinous consumption. For example, a popular English recipe for a piment in the thirteenth century called for "gynger, synamon, and graines, sugour, and tournesol [sunflower]; and for comyn pepull, gynger, cannel, long peper and claryffyed hony."

While wine writers have uniformly denounced these early punches, man has nevertheless consistently sought exotica in his food and drink. At the zenith of Roman power and glory, Galen the Physician provided a *theriac* or tonic for his beloved ruler Emperor Marcus Aurelius, which was reputed to cure everything from lumbago to flatulence. Like the medicines from Sumerian and Egyptian times, the theriac was steeped in aged wine and was mixed with wondrous potions: duck's blood, the bile of bulls and bears, poppy juice, incense, juniper berries, mushrooms, aniseed, gentian, licorice, turnip; also carrot seed, orrisroot, ginger, hemlock, fennel, pepper, turpentine, raisins, and garlic tops. Lucia, in *A History of Wine as Therapy* (1971), documents the importance of these piments in early pharmacopoeia.

> As late as the eighteenth century, on the authority of the ancients, kings and commoners still believed fanatically in the power of the theriacs to alleviate all disorders of body and mind, to subdue the most diverse miseries, to restore perfect vigor, and to confer everlasting youth. The story of these panaceas is a poignant chapter in the history of wine in medicine.

In defense of the medicinal practitioners of the times, the great healer Galen found in wine the most delicate of medicines and the highest of virtues. Upon the passing of his friend, Marcus, Galen records his solemn visit to the deceased ruler's wine cellar:

> So, in execution of my duty, I deciphered the vintage marks on the amphorae of every Falernian wine and submitted to my palate every wine over twenty-five years. I kept on until I found a wine without a trace of bitterness. An ancient wine which has not lost its sweetness is the best of all.

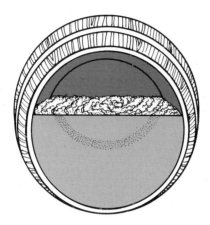

Figure 13.1 *The flor yeast actually forms a greyish, thick mold on the surface of the aging wine, constantly working its chemical wonders.*

THE GREAT SHERRY WINES

The sack wines of Shakespearean repute were considerably more formidable than the light and airy Fino or Amontillado known and loved today. H. Warner Allen, in *A History of Wines* (1961) advanced the theory that "sack" comes from the Spanish verb *sacar* which means "to take out." The export product seems to have been better appreciated in colder climates. In fact, export tax records of the time included wines from Málaga, the Canaries, Cypress, and other Mediterranean points. All were called sack. Eventually, sherris sack, the wine which originates from the town of Jerez, became distinguished for its unusual quality. What was unique and clever about sherris sack was the barrels of the solera system in which it was produced. Allen reports on its earliest use.

> There is no record of the date when the Solera system was first developed, but it is certainly of great antiquity. What the Germans sought to do by the construction of gigantic Tuns, the Jerez growers accomplished by storing their wines in a series of butts of reasonable size. From the final tier of butts with the oldest wine they drew the wine needed for consumption. . . .

It was not just the system of intermingling and aging wines that was innovative, but also the adaptation of an indigenous yeast in the process. This unique film-yeast creates a growth on the surface of the wine which is found naturally only in Spain and a small region of France. This protective scum forms in swirls reminiscent of flowers, hence the *flor* appellation. Early winemakers must have taken pleasurable note that the wines beneath the surface were not easily spoiled like the others exposed to the atmosphere. Allen (1961) describes the action thus:

> The *flower* greedily absorbs all the oxygen within reach, before it can penetrate to the wine below the surface and promptly attacks and devours any other invading alien microbes. . . . If Nature had endowed the general run of wines with the gift of attracting a similar shield, fine vintage wines might have survived the replacement of the amphora by the cask, maturing in wood to a good old age, though they would have lacked the subtleties of bouquet and flavour belonging to a natural wine bottled up in an air-tight receptacle.

Xeres—Scherish—Jerez

Dominated by a variety of cultures over its 2,300 years, the city after which sherry was named has had a tumultuous history. The Phoenicians and Greeks dominated the land for nearly 1,000 years, planting their grapes and leaving behind the city's first known appellation, Xeres. For a brief period, the Romans claimed the land and used the word *Ceret* for the city. Eventually, the Moors brought their libraries, culture, and agriculture and dominated the land for the better part of 800 years under the name Scherish. Finally, in 1264, the Christian King Alfonso X drove out the Moors, claiming the city and giving it its present name of Jerez de la Frontera.

The Andalusian winemakers had two advantages over their competitors. First, they had developed the solera system of blending wines which merged strong and weak wines to a profitable end; second, they had available to them a natural blanket which protected those aging wines from spoilage. For its sustenance, the flor yeast (see fig. 13.1) oxidized some portion of the wine alcohol, leaving the end product slightly weaker.

Sometime between the eleventh and sixteenth centuries, the practice of fortifying the wine before shipment became common. There is no known record of the first use of *eau-de-vie*, nor of how rapidly the practice spread. What we do know is that the Jerez shippers introduced this technique which was to become of enormous importance in the commerce of the English empire.

Sherry Wine Making

The small pocket of land which produces sherry wine lies at the southernmost tip of Spain, bordered by both the Mediterranean Sea and the Atlantic Ocean. It is a romantic land, one of flamenco dancers, gallant equestrians, and bullfighters.

Throughout the years, three distinct growing areas have developed within the sherry zone. The most desirable fruit is grown to the north of Jerez in the *albariza,* a soil composed of chalk, magnesia, and clay. To the south lies the *barros* earth of red, iron-rich clay. Finally, running to the ocean is the *are-*

As essential artisans in the vast and flourishing sherry trade, the coopers are a privileged class in Andalusia. For over two hundred years the butts have been coopered with American oak. Cut in staves in the United States, the wood is air dried and fired in the shaping, with one worker dousing the wood to avoid charring.

A critical stage in sherry production—the critical choice lies with the young wine itself. Placed in huge anadas, *the wine must either develop the flor film or be relegated the following year to oloroso stock.*

nas which means "sand" in Spanish. This latter area produces about twice as many tons of grapes per acre as the other lands and so is given over to the lesser sherry-blending wines.

The Palomino grape dominates production, up to 90 percent of the total, but the sugar-rich blending wines come largely from the heavier Pedro Ximinez grape. An unusual viticultural practice of pruning to a single large cane on each vine has been developed over the centuries.

The traditional practices have given away to modern wine-making techniques. In past years, the newly harvested fruit was spread over mats to age in the hot Andalusian sun for a day or so. The grapes were then placed in the lagares in which the juice would be expressed by groups of singing stompers. These effective but dated procedures have given way to pneumatic presses and other modern winery equipment designed to obtain the maximum juice from the tough-skinned, white sherry grapes.

Fermentation begins immediately and follows a violent, surging pattern in which the cultured yeasts develop alcohol from sugar-rich musts. There are actually two stages in the fermentation process and both take place in the large whitewashed warehouses called bodegas which resemble massive churches. The first stage is a rather violent spurt of activity taking up to a week, and the secondary fermentation begins almost immediately and progresses well into the winter, often until late December at which time the wines are first racked and then classified.

The Unique Aging Classifications

Much has been written, but little has been understood, about this age-old process of classifying the wines destined for the elegant finos and the rich olorosos. The technique of segregat-

ing the barrels is simple enough. Chalk marks on the barrel ends signify the current status of the wines inside. These marks are known as *rayas* and *palmas*.

The need to classify results from a unique mold called *flor* which develops naturally in this geographic area and almost nowhere else on the face of the earth. Unlike most other yeasts, flor grows on top of the aging wine in the presence of atmosphere, gently reducing a portion of the alcohol while complexing the chemistry of the aging wine. The name *flor*, Spanish for "flower," derives from the grayish sworls of mold that develop on the top of the working wines. Since this first aging stage takes about six months and occurs in barrels with *open* bungs, the flor has ample time to grow and also to protect the otherwise air-exposed wines from becoming vinegar because of airborne acetic acid.

It is this very desirable condition that necessitates the rigorous classification system for sherries. The first grading simply separates those barrels in which the flor has begun to develop. The wines which have shown promise as finos are racked and fortified slightly with brandy to about 15% alcohol, a level at which the flor can continue to grow. The *rayas* chalk marks, from one to four, indicate best to worst in terms of potential. Those that do not give evidence of good flor growth are fortified up to 18% alcohol to stem further flor growth, and these wines will become the olorosos. The taste testing of these developing wines is accomplished by plunging a device called a venencia cup through the surface mold to extract a small sample of the wine. This is accomplished with great skill and flourish by cellarmen to the astonishment of visitors as the wine is poured from on high into waiting wine glasses without a drop spilling.

In a few weeks, a second classification takes place during which the *palmas*, resembling the victory sign, are placed on

A sherry cellar master prepares a mixture of egg whites and thyme, the perfect fining agents to cleanse the young wines of fermentation solids.

The young wines with flor growth are racked and transferred to soleras, stacks of barrels three high. No more than one-third of each barrel may be withdrawn, and that amount must graduate down each year from the top, to the middle and, finally, to the bottom row. These butts serve up to fifty years constantly intermingling new wines with the old.

The poet Shelley referred to these rich aging cellars as Cathedrals of Wine. A Spanish cooper is shown at his trade in front of a barrel already designated as oloroso. American white oak is used because of its low porosity and mild tannin.

barrels of lightness and finesse that will become the best of the finos. A palma with a crossing line becomes a *palma cortado* to signify a stout fino, in the Amontillado style. The butts age in the sun in courtyards for the second period of flor growth and classification, often up to a year and a half, before entering the final stage of sherry aging in the famous soleras. Those retaining rayas at this stage are destined to become lesser, blending wines.

This constant attention to the uniqueness of each barrel and the further complexing of young and old wines in the solera make sherry one of the most technically demanding of all wines. The marriage of these wines of such a wide spectrum of taste and flavor is a triumph of the blender's art. The mixture is both vertical and horizontal from a technical standpoint. That is, new is mixed with new, old is mixed with old, new is mixed with old, and the old and the new vintages become one through blending. In addition, these blends follow an age-old pattern in the soleras, portions from the bottom being taken for bottling and replaced by portions from the barrels above.

The alcohol and sweetness levels are adjusted by the blending done just before bottling. A high alcohol concentration is mandatory in those sherries which are to be shipped worldwide since flor cells remaining in the finished wines would happily reconstruct their gray superstructures once the bottles had been opened and the contents exposed to air. Many of the lesser solera sherries are deliberately sweetened by the raisined Pedro Ximinez and are given appropriate deep color by boiled must called *vino de color* and, perhaps, additional brandy for shipping stability. The best casks are reserved for delicately dry finos in their pristine innocence.

TABLE 13.1 Chemical Constituents of Dessert and Cocktail Wines

Components	Unit	Range	Muscatel, Avg	Port, Avg	Dry Sherry, Avg	Medium Sherry, Avg	Sweet Sherry, Avg	Dry Vermouth, Avg	Sweet Vermouth, Avg
Chloride	ppm	10–50	20	30		40			
Sulfate	ppm	400–1200	700	600		800			
Sulfur dioxide	ppm	0–160	105	100	107	93	94		
Calcium	ppm	32–72	49	57		60			
Copper	ppm	T–1.1	0.4	0.5	0.4	0.4	0.5		
Iron	ppm	1.0–5.5	2.0	3.5	1.9	2.5	3.4		
Potassium	ppm	109–1420	775	939	713	757	815	*	*
Sodium†	ppm	15–405	139	94	73	78	85	‡	‡
Ethyl alcohol	% (vol)	16.4–21.7	19.7	19.8	20.0	19.9	19.8	17.7	17.1
Higher alcohols	ppm	156–900	356	384	292	401		388	369
Glycerol	%	0.02–1.67	0.57	0.53	0.96	1.02		0.21	0.59
2,3-Butylene glycol	ppm	65–1050							
Acetaldehyde	ppm	15–217	99	68	79	55			
Hydroxymethyl furfural§	ppm	0–1149							
pH		3.14–4.48	3.79	3.84	3.71	3.68	3.79		
Acetic acid	ppm	150–540	300	330	410	400	330		
Citric acid	ppm	0–1030							
Succinic acid	ppm	190–1420							
Tartaric acid	%	0.29–0.89	0.38	0.43	0.42	0.40	0.41	0.50	0.45
Hexoses	%	0.88–15.1	11.6	11.7	2.0	3.1	10.7	4.7	15.4
Total esters	ppm	93–730	248	305	335	419			
Volatile esters	ppm	17–201							
Tannins	%	0.01–0.16	0.05	0.10	0.02	0.03	0.05	0.04	0.06
Amino acids	ppm	18–70							
Thiamine	µg/l		130	130		50			
Riboflavin	µg/l		240	240		110			
Pantothenic acid	µg/l		240	240		120			
Pyridoxine	µg/l		640	640		190			
Nicotinic acid	µg/l		2050	2050		880			
Folic acid	µg/l		29	29		9			
Cyanocobalamin	mµg/l			25					
Total solids	%		13.5	12.6	4.7		10.7	3.8	8.8

Source: Reproduced with permission from Leake, C. D. and Silverman, M.: ALCOHOLIC BEVERAGES IN CLINICAL MEDICINE. Copyright © 1966 by Year Book Medical Publishers, Inc., Chicago, 44–45.

*Potassium values for all vermouths range from 624 to 1201 ppm.

†Higher values have been found occasionally in dessert wines treated with ion-exchange resins.

‡Sodium values for all vermouths range from 110 to 115 ppm.

§Hydroxymethyl furfural results from application of heat to sugars. It has been reported in concentrations up to 66 ppm in pasteurized grape juice.

Centuries of practice have made nearly perfect this progenitor of all fortified dessert wines. It is easy to be confused by the profusion of Spanish sherry names. They are broadly categorized by sugar and alcohol content into two different types. The dry *finos* are the first category, with pronounced nutty flavors developed by intense flor yeast growth. The finos fall into three subgroups. *Fino* is light, very pale, but elegant and sharp on the palate. *Manzanilla* is also light, dry, and nutty, but possessed of special aroma due to its birth near the sea in Sanlúcar de Barrameda. *Amontillado,* the third fino, develops because of longer barrel aging to a fuller body and darker color.

The second type of Spanish sherries, called *olorosos,* also possesses the characteristic nutty overtone, but most are rich in sugar, usually 7 percent or more, and are often higher in alcohol (see table 13.1). The categories of oloroso are *Amo-* *roso,* the driest of the lot; *Oloroso,* with pronounced sweetness; *Cream,* full in body and also sweet; and *Brown,* appropriately deep and sugary.

American Sherries

As the California wine industry matured, it was natural that producers develop methods of creating the popular European dessert varieties. Because of the unique functioning of the flor yeast, and its natural habitation only in southern Spain, alternative methods came into being to create the fine, nutty, or baked character in domestic sherry wine.

The primary alternative, used almost universally today in both California and the American east, is through heating which creates a gentle caramel flavor. Some American sherry achieves this desired tone through long periods of aging in small oak barrels, and other batches are infused with special flor cultures, in an attempt to create the same kind of flor development as in Spain. However, these methods are time consuming and costly, while the baking technique is inexpensive and the end result quite satisfactory. Other dessert-type wines made in California such as Madeira and Malaga, also result from the baking method.

Grapes used for sherry in California include the Thompson Seedless, Palomino, Flame Tokay, Mission, Grenache, and other low-color white varieties. First, the wine is fermented quite dry and is called *shermat*. A small amount of sugar is desirable during baking for the creation of special flavors. The baking period, however, does not transpire quickly as in an oven, but is rather like a gentle, sustained period in a hot climate. The shermat is fortified up to 15 percent alcohol by volume and placed in tanks in rooms with temperatures up to 140°F, for periods of up to 120 days. An oxidation or breakdown of the wine chemistry occurs, similar to that which is induced by the Spanish flor yeast, yielding aldehydes which produce the characteristic nutty flavors.

The final step before bottling is the adjustment of the sugar and alcohol levels, and the process is again similar to that used in Spain to sweeten wines. The California vintners usually utilize sweet Angelica wine, adjusting the volume to as high as 10 percent for the cream sherry varieties, approximately 3 percent for the golden sherries, and as low as 1 percent for the cocktail and dry varieties.

At least twenty-five Eastern wineries also produce sherry wines by similar processing. Some utilize a submerged flor technique developed in Canada, and others allow several months of settling in the baking tanks because of the unique high acid properties of the Concord, Duchess, and Niagara grapes.

Credit should be given to American ingenuity in mastering the production techniques (borrowing from the Spaniards and the Madeirans and other Mediterranean vintners) to develop a wide variety of fine sherry-type wines, often the equal of the wines of that unique flowery mold of southern Spain.

PORT

While the birthdate of fortified sherry is lost to history, the addition of spirits to Portuguese wine is well documented and clearly the result of a political decision! While Portuguese wines had been traded with England and the northern countries for centuries, the English preferred the already sensuous vintages of their beloved claret from the Bordeaux area of France. William, the Dutch-born king of England, sought to destroy the French wine market by imposing severe trade duties, while lowering those on Portuguese goods.

In 1703, the Treaty of Methuen gave preferential duty rights to wine from Portugal in exchange for a similar privilege for English woolens, and the clothing merchants had the best of the bargain for a number of years. In fact, Portuguese wines

Though most ports are blended after several years at rest, the special vintages are bottled for long aging. Here is a special rack of ports that time has literally enveloped and encrusted.

of that time were nearly undrinkable. Harsh, acidic, and often mixed with everything from elderberries to honey, the wines were disdained by the refined Britons. Improvement in quality took nearly a half century, and it consisted of a fortifying technique similar to that used for several hundred years in neighboring Spain. Allen explains in *A History of Wine* (1961):

> A handbook of 1720 points timidly to the eventual solution of the problem. If the Douro wines were to be palatable, their fermentation must be checked, before they had lost every trace of sugar. . . . It must be remembered that all experiments had to be conducted in the dark with trial and error as the only guides, since the principles of fermentation were a complete mystery . . .

The breakthrough intimated here was the use of spirits as an additive *during the fermentation process*. Until this time, their sole purpose the making of a beverage wine which could take the place of the French natural wines and it was by the purest accident that there issued from them Port as we know it today, a wine to be drunk after . . . a meal.

By 1756, the Oporto Wine Company was created by Royal Charter with the express purpose of enforcing standards for both grape growing and wine making that would enhance the trade. Allen also reports on the development over that century of the glass container which was shifting constantly toward the 1770 shouldered bottle which could be binned and racked allowing for the collection of sediment in the neck. "No one yet realized the importance of a big, well-fitted cork, since the vintner did not understand that the invasion of hostile microbes from without was a far greater danger than changes of atmosphere in the surrounding air . . ."

Little by little, it all came together during that century of desperate experimentation, and the traditional link between the English and the Portuguese in making and merchandising fine ports was established for all time to come.

No nation is drunken where wine is cheap . . .

Thomas Jefferson

(A)

(B)

The Douro River, shown at Pinkao in the heart of the Douro Valley, has been the artery for the delivery of its precious cargo since the Middle Ages (A). The wine terraces, which have literally been hand constructed, also require hand labor to tend the vineyards. Workers wear long grass capes to keep off the rain while they prune the canes in January (B).

The Breathtaking Douro

It would be difficult to imagine more spectacular and downright difficult terrain to work with than the reaches of the Douro River which extend sixty miles from Oporto to the Spanish borders. The vineyards are literally carved at times into cliffs as high as 2,000 feet from the river level in soils that accommodate ideally the deep-rooted vines. The weather is likewise dramatic, ranging from days above 125° F in summer to nearly freezing in winter.

Through the centuries before the phylloxera plague, the vines were of mixed parentage, grown and harvested indiscriminately. Today, over a dozen varieties dominate, including the Touriga, similar to a Cabernet, the Bastardo, and the Mourisco, as well as the Tinta types which yield deep color. Harvest time is a period of great celebration and merrymaking, although the traditional stomping of the grapes in lagares has generally given way to mechanical pressing. Before mechanization, it has been clear that the treading and stomping would extract maximum color essential to long life and character in port.

The grapes are brought to huge estates called *quintas* where the original fermentation is terminated by the addition of brandy when the alcohol level is 6 to 8 percent. The sugar-rich wine is then racked into the traditional pipes for shipment

brandy had been utilized to stabilize sherry wine only *after aging*. The trick, of course, lies in the observation that the fermentation process terminated completely at certain alcohol concentrations. We now know that neither bacteria nor yeast can survive above 14 percent alcohol, but the eighteenth century Portuguese winemaker knew only that he could sell more if his wine retained some sugar. Allen further documents the accidental discovery of port.

The cautious 1720 recipe of a small dose of brandy for the fermenting wine, three gallons to the pipe, was a step in the right direction, but the expedient aroused an outcry and all the troubles of the Douro wine in this country were for many years ascribed to it. It must be remembered that such experiments had as

This scene has altered little through the centuries. The 140 gallon pipes are laded at the upper Douro ports and lazily drift down the spectacular river gorge in the Rabelo boats.

down to Oporto on one of the world's most graceful vessels, the *barcos rabelos,* most of which have nowadays been sadly replaced by the railroad.

Across the river from the city of Oporto lies a small town called Vila Nova de Gaia, the location of the many lodges and aging cellars where the ports are matured and blended, and from which they are shipped. Generally, then, port is a blended wine not unlike sherry but with some important differences. Some ports, those that develop into Tawny port, may be aged up to twenty years before blending and finishing. The younger ports retain more natural coloration and are termed Ruby port.

A specialty in port is Vintage Port, which is not blended between years and can be kept in the wood no more than two years before bottling and further aging in glass up to another ten or twenty years. When a wine comes in rich and full-bodied, the vintner simply declares a *vintage* and segregates that batch of wine. The first Vintage Port occurred one year after the founding of the United States. Vintage Ports always identify the shipper and the date of bottling on the label and are generally sensuous, mellow delights. Until the Second World War, all those fine vintages were bottled in Britain, but now they are commonly shipped bottled from Portugal. The popularity of port continues in the colder countries such as Britain, northern France, and the Netherlands.

American Port

As in Portugal, American winemakers utilize a number of familiar red-skinned grapes in order to obtain deep color extraction for their fine ports. Zinfandel, Mission, and Grenache are popular, as are Tinta Madeira, Touriga, Ruby Cabernet, Souzão, and Rubired or Royalty. A number of techniques are employed, including heat treatments and constant punching of the fermenting cap of skins, to effect that critical color transfer. As the skin cells die and disintegrate, the pigments more rapidly release.

Some batches are fermented nearly dry for blending purposes, but most are terminated early as in Portugal by racking the fermenting fluid and adding very high proof brandy. A characteristic of domestic port is smoothness, owing in part to the nearly neutral spirit used.

Inexpensive ports are routinely pasteurized in California and are in the marketplace within months of harvesting. Premium level ports receive years of aging in oak in a manner similar to the solera system in Portugal and are marketed in both the Ruby and Tawny versions. A limited amount of white port is produced in California from white-skinned grapes, but it has the tendency to oxidize and darken and, therefore, must be consumed relatively young.

In sum, while the share of the market held by dessert wines is dramatically decreasing in the United States, part of the cause is the enormous growth in table wines. While the whole category is declining, there is evidence that finer ports and sherries are again becoming part of a gracious lifestyle.

MADEIRA

Located 500 miles southeast of Portugal, and only 40 miles away from the African coast, the forty-mile-long island of Madeira has a history as bizarre as any seafaring saga. Used as a

All port wine rests in these low-ceilinged lodges like these in the small town of Vila Nova de Gaia, across from Oporto.

wine colony for the seafaring Portuguese for nearly 300 years, it produced mostly young red wines for Portugal and Spain. There are also records of brandy distillation as early as 1704, about the time that the British Ambassador Methuen was developing the preferential wine trade with the mother country.

But before this time (and after that of the Phoenicians and other early Mediterranean travelers who knew the island group as the Enchanted Islands) the island had been seldom used because it was totally covered by impenetrable forests. The intrepid Portuguese, however, eventually solved that problem by sending Captain João Zarco to claim the property in 1418. He intentionally set the whole island afire and waited for several years until the fires banked down. After they did, the enriched soil soon became the lushest known on earth.

Its history is replete with both ups and downs of dramatic proportions. The most fortuitous was the 1633 ordinance

passed by Charles II of England which prohibited exports to the colonies from any non-British ports with the exception of Madeira and the Azores. Since the island was strategically located for ships to take on water before crossing the Atlantic, enterprising merchants also loaded the holds with Madeira wine barrels creating ballast and a several hundred-year-old tradition of Madeira drinking in America.

The First Estufa

While fortification with brandy lay several hundred years ahead, the swaying, sloshing trip over the Atlantic, often in hot, steamy shipholds, created unique aging in these stout wines. The idea of the *estufa,* or heating shed, gradually emerged from this happenstance. Allen tells of an inventive Mr. Tavey who made his own mechanical aging device. "He suspended from a beam of a steam engine in a temperature of from 90° to 100° a quarter cask of Madeira, where it oscillated for three or four months, as it acquired all the softness and character of wine that had been shipped to and from the East Indies."

In 1852, oidium mildew ravaged the island vineyards, and in 1872, phylloxera nearly wiped the hillsides clean. Indeed, Madeira has historically run the gamut of boom to bust.

Fruit and sugarcane were originally the primary agriculture on Madeira, but that soon gave way to unique and pleasing wine grapes. Its summer is mild, and its winter practically nonexistent, so the grapevine finds there a beneficent natural habitat. Wines produced on Madeira now range from quite dry aperitifs to very rich dessert types.

Madeira's wine-processing techniques are as unusual and unique as the island is picturesque. In past years, sledges and toboggan-like baskets were used to move the harvest down the steep terrain. The vines are trained on six-foot-high trellises (not unlike those of ancient Egypt) which protect the fruit from the ravages of the tropical sun. The primary grape used is the Verdelho, with lesser plantings of the Sercial, the Bual, and the Malvasia or as it is called in Madeira, the Malmsey. Only the ripest of grapes are harvested for wine making, necessitating four or five separate passes through the vineyards over several weeks. Frequently the grapes are field pressed into a *mosto* which is carried in 12 gallon goatskins down the steep slopes by runners to the main town of Funchal.

> . . . and every one o' em sure lived up to its name. They tasted, one and all, just like plain Rainwaters.
>
> ***Eighty-year-old man in a letter to Ray Brady, quoted in a* Vintage *article***

A period of two weeks is involved in the fermentation, and the resulting wine is termed *vinho claro* to which a small amount of brandy is added as in sherry making. The vinho claro is placed in barrels in the estufa for the baking period that simulates the long ocean trips of old. To assure against a rapid caramelization of the wines, these estufa have unique government heat seals which break to warn the winemaker when the temperature inside exceeds 130 degrees F. However, in these gentle sweat boxes, Madeira wines gain their characteristic nutty, caramel tastes.

Following this mandatory estufa period, the wines are further aged in wood casks for up to two years. Another fortification with brandy follows the aging creating a wine now titled *vinho generoso*, which is ready for bottling and the market. The baking and aging, as well as the high brandy content of Madeira, give these flavorful dessert specialties particularly long age potential. Madeiras are said to be capable of retaining essential flavors for a century or more!

The vast majority of Madeiras are sold as blends, but some wine is sold under the name of each of the four principal grapes. The most delicate and driest of the group comes as Sercial, an excellent aperitif wine that can easily substitute for a fino sherry. Verdelho is often bottled quite dry, but it can also be consumed before the meal. *Bual,* dark brown and fuller in body, is also fuller in sugar content. *Malmsey,* from the Malvasia grape, is rich and luscious like its Malvasia counterpart produced throughout the Mediterranean. Finally, *Rainwater,* originally a trade name developed by William Habersham in Savannah, Georgia, in 1817—blended to be paler and lighter than the others—is now an authentic product of the island. It ranges from dry to sweet.

COMMANDERIE, MALAGA, AND MARSALA

Commanderie has a proud history of production extending over 1,000 years, the oldest named wine in continuous use in the world. Its authoritative name came in 1191 from a segment of the Christian Crusaders who settled on Cyprus after the final loss of Jerusalem to the infidels. These Christian Knights Templar were both warriors of the church and dedicated winemakers, and they spread the fame and fortune of this unique, sweet wine.

Commanderie is produced from the red Mavron and white Xynisteri grapes. Throughout the centuries, the wine was both fermented and aged in pitch-lined jars which were buried to escape the prevailing heat. Modern methods of production now prevail, but Commanderie remains true to its history, being a huge, commanding, and sweet dessert wine.

A second popular traditional dessert wine comes from the small area at the southeast corner of the Andalusia in Spain called Málaga. No longer a major factor in international trade, Málaga is produced in the manner of neighboring sherry from Pedro Ximenez, Muscatel, and other hot climate varieties. A procedure not unique in Spain is the addition to the fermentation of boiled-down grape juice, called *color,* and the newly harvested grapes are also allowed nearly to raisin in the sun before fermentation commences. Aging occurs in barrels in a system very similar to the sherry solera, so the aged wine is always a blended, enriched product.

Marsala burst on the scene much later than these other traditional Mediterranean delights. It was the brainchild of a very canny Englishman on the Italian island of Sicily. John Woodhouse in 1773 shipped 60 pipes or barrels of local wines to England, and to stabilize them for the trip, he added to each a few gallons of brandy. The venture was successful. However, since his intent was to capture some of the considerable dessert wine trade, he kept experimenting with the age-old methods of sweetening and flavoring the abundant but somewhat flat local grape wines.

Within twenty years, he established the first of the *baglios,* the enchanting fortress-like stone wineries that now dominate the scene. What really placed Woodhouse in the chips

Cypriot wines with the king of the Mediterranean—Commanderie St. John. Surprisingly, Commanderie retains the low alcohol content it had at its founding during the Crusades. This is the oldest continuously labeled wine in existence.

Sicily's famous Marsala wines are aged in small casks for up to five years, developing their dry, nutlike character.

was an order placed in 1800 by Admiral Lord Nelson to provision his ships and the subsequent praise that the Admiral heaped upon the wines.

Three grapes comprise the total vintage, with Grillo and Cataratto dominating, and about 15 percent of the harvest in the Inzolia. As in the Douro, the grapes are harvested and fermented together producing a rather strong, slightly bitter, straw yellow base wine. From this base, four major Marsala types are produced. *Vergine* is solera aged for a minimum of five years and is typically dry. *Superior* indicates a minimum aging of two years in both dry and slightly sweet versions. *Fine* Marsala is generally light bodied, aged for four months, and is often used as the base for flavored Marsalas. Finally, the *Speciale* are richly flavored wines including banana, mocha, cherry, almond, and egg.

Over half of the production today falls in the *Speciale* category, and these wines do not garner the Denominazione di Origine Controlatta appellation. However, the great contribution of Woodhouse to the dessert field, perfected over ensuing years, was the technique of boiling down the must to create a *mosto cotto* akin to syrup which is added back to the base wine along with the *sifone* or brandy spirits. In this sense, the inventive Woodhouse produced the ultimate adulteration utilizing the experience of the ancient Roman, the pigmentarius of the Middle Ages, the fortifying skills of the Spaniard, and the perspicacity of the British merchant.

OTHER AMERICAN DESSERT WINES

The foregoing pages have outlined the classic dessert wines of the Mediterranean basin. Long before humans developed the proclivity for austere, sugar-free vintages, these rich and warming drinks were favored throughout western civilization. It is an unfortunate accident of history that the cheapest sources of beverage alcohol in the United States were considered to be inexpensive port, sherry, tokay, and muscatel. Just a few decades ago, dessert wines dominated the total American wine trade, with a large percentage of this volume directed to the unfortunate consumer who contributed a new word to the lexicon—the wino. As a matter of fact, the wino merely represents the least financially independent of all the sad victims of the disease of alcoholism.

Fortunately, there seems to be emerging a trend to single out the better of the lot in domestic dessert wines, with an upswing in the production and sales among quality firms such as The Christian Brothers, Paul Masson, Quady, J. W. Morris Port Works, Almadén, and Inglenook. Dessert wines can provide the most appropriate accent to a full meal. However, it is a chancy and delicate balance, one that needs nurturing to the end that the new American wine culture incorporates these incomparable social graces.

Another casualty of the poor image of dessert wines is Tokay, all but extinct now in California production. Unlike the famous Hungarian late-harvested and crushed Tokaji Aszu, American Tokay generally is a blend of Ruby port and sherry,

and often also Angelica. It is a unique, filling, and warm after-dinner treat, quite unlike any of its counterparts.

In summary, the remarkable technical competence of California winemakers shows true to form in the dessert-making field. All American dessert wines are distinctive and different in style from their European equivalents. The hallmark of these domestic desserts is smoothness, particularly because of the lighter, purer fortifying material. It is to be hoped that the new surge in wine consumption in the United States will encompass the American as well as the traditional import dessert varieties. Many, such as the famous Tokaji Aszu from Hungary, can now be found in the larger import markets. Each of the European countries produces unique dessert wines by means of endless variations of the techniques discussed in these pages.

APPETIZER AND SPECIAL FLAVORED WINES

Appetizer and flavored wines are nearly as ancient as fermentation itself. In fact, only the vast growth in popularity of drier table wines has relegated them to a minor category. Flavorings were all too necessary in former years to make palatable the often crude and bacteria-laden wines.

Most of the spirit concoctions of early America also involved liberal use of sugar, spice, and everything nice. Today, the principal appetizer or before-the-meal wines are sherry and vermouth, and mostly the dry or cocktail sherries at that. The dominant additive in vermouth is the flowers of the wormwood (see fig. 13.2), a shrub found throughout Europe.

But this is by no means the only additive. Some others often used are allspice, anise, bitters, orange peels, cinnamon, cloves, coriander, quinine bark, rose leaves, hyssop, marjoram, cascarilla, cinchona, horehound, hops, lemon, rhubarb, saffron, valerian, elder flowers, yarrow, and zeodary. Traditionally, the recipes for vermouth are closely guarded secrets. Nearly always, these wines have been considered to have unique medicinal properties because of the herbs. The herbs are infused or steeped in prepared wines which are fortified and then further aged after removal from the herb tanks.

The commercial production of aromatized wines called vermouth dates from the mid-1700s near Turin, Italy. By 1800, Louis Noilly was producing it in Lyons, France. It is now produced throughout the world and generally in two distinct styles, the dry French and the sweet Italian.

The herbs are infused in the alcohol, often under heat for more thorough transfer of essential oils and flavors. The sweetened wine is added to this alcohol herb mixture, and time is allowed for a complete marrying of the products. The vermouth is then pasteurized and refrigerated for several weeks to precipitate tartrates and other solids as with table wines.

The French dry vermouths generally utilize a combination of 80 percent Hérault, a very dry wine, and 20 percent *mistelle,* which is produced by brandy fortification of fresh grape juice. The wines are infused with, or rest on, the herbs

Figure 13.2 While vermouth dates from relatively recent times as a commercial wine, its principal botanical, the shrub artemisia absinthium, *has been in both the pharmacopoeia and the kitchen since the dawn of history.*

The House of Cinzano has been making vermouth from carefully guarded herbal mixtures since 1757. These quaint pot stills and alambicco *pots are used to produce the brandy and to steep the spices and herbs into extract.*

for at least a month, then drawn from the tanks, chilled to precipitate tartrates, and bottled for aging of up to three years.

The sweeter Italian varieties require significantly higher concentrations of herbs, up to 1½ ounces per gallon, and are often produced from more distinctive but still inexpensive wines such as muscatel. There is generally a higher sugar level in these wines, frequently up to 15 percent by volume in the Italian types. American vermouth is generally produced at higher alcohol levels than those from the Continent, up to 20 percent by volume.

Some traditional flavored wines remain unsweetened and unfortified. Examples include the popular German white May wine, which is steeped in woodruff, and the white wine of the Greeks, Retsina, which is flavored with resin. Other European flavored wines that can be readily found in American markets include bitter Byrrh, St. Raphael, Dubonnet, and Lillet. Quinine bark is the dominant flavoring element of the first three which are made from red wines. Lillet is sold both Red and Blonde.

Highlights

- The appreciation of sugar-rich, aromatic wines on the Continent came about as a result of centuries of adulteration of distasteful wines.
- Fortification of wines with alcohol grew from the efforts of sherry makers to replace alcohol reduced by flor yeast.
- Portugal systematized fortification by doing it during the fermentation process to retain residual sugar.

- Heat aging as in the madeira *estufas* had a mellowing effect now common in dessert wine making.
- Dessert wines range from very dry and light—such as *fino* and *Sercial*—to richly sweet *port* and *cream sherry*.
- Vermouth and other aperitifs stimulate gastric juices, provoking the appetite.

Through its Mont La Salle division, the Christian Brothers Winery continues its traditional role of providing a full line of both dry and dessert wines for religious use.

TABLE 13.2 Dessert and Aperitif Wine Tasting

Wine	General Style	Suggested Brands
Fino sherry	Sharp, nutty aroma, pale color, very dry, light bodied, austere, assertive flor character	Duff Gordon Hartley Gibson
Amontillado Montilla	Light flor overtone in nose and palate, dry, medium amber, some richness	Albero Don Tomás
Cocktail sherry	Floral nose, nutty, warming flavors, medium body	Christian Brothers Dry Oloroso
Cream sherry	Rich, full-bodied delight with warm, nutty flavors and lasting finish	Harvey's Bristol Taylor's New York
Sercial madeira	Light body, dry with baked caramel tone, crisp finish	Madeira Paul Masson
Marsala	Sharp aroma, medium body, bitter finish	Superiore Dry
Sweet vermouth	Huge vegetative nose, pronounced sweetness, long bittersweet finish	Cinzano Paul Masson
Port	Full oaky nose, warming, buttery impact, sweet and lasting finish	Morris Portworks Christian Brothers Ficklin Vineyards

Finally, in the special natural wine category, are the "pop" wines such as Annie Greensprings, Boone's Farm, and the old standby, Thunderbird. In this category, under California laws, vintners may add approved substances to grape or other fruit wines which were not part of the original fruit. Hence, for example, apple alcohol and natural strawberry flavoring can be utilized to make sweet, frothy, low alcohol thirst quenchers. The flavors must be natural, nonsynthetic. Although they are the bane of the true wine lover, they are as traditional as vermouth and other flavored Greek and Roman wines. Further, they are as American as the Wine Flip and the festive punch bowl.

As with sparkling wines, production of vermouth remains small but steady, and special natural wines apparently passed their zenith in the early and mid-1970s. However, with the several thousand year history of light flavored wine and the imagination of California blenders, one must not overlook the potential of some new fad wine for a generation raised on Kool-Aid and soda!

> *B*ending his foal unto the vine, and his ass's colt unto the choice vine, he washes his garments in wine, and his clothes in the blood of grapes.
>
> ***Genesis 49:11***

KOSHER AND SACRAMENTAL WINES

Essentially, kosher and sacramental wine may be produced from any vintage that meets the criteria for purity and nonadulteration. It is even produced from pure frozen concentrates, allowing freshness year round.

The dominance of the sweetish Concord wines in the United States for both kosher and sacramental wines leads to the mistaken belief that all ritual wines must be sweet. Around the globe, both dry and lightly sweet versions are vinted from Cabernet and other fine varietals as well as the traditional American Concords. What has been required for kosher wines from the days of Melchizedek (the priest-king of ancient Salem) is the certification by a rabbi that the wines have been produced according to accepted standards.

Many denominations—Episcopalian, Lutheran, Eastern Orthodox and Roman Catholic—use wine in religious services. The present use of bread and wine in the sacrifice of the Roman Mass extends from the twelfth century and originated in the profound rituals of antiquity. In the fifteenth century, the wine for Mass was specified as grape wine, confirming already established practice.

SUGGESTED DESSERT AND APERITIF WINE TASTING

The spectrum of delightful and intriguing tastes in the dessert and aperitif category exceeds the still wines in the sense that each production is unique. Compared to the naturally fermented table and sparkling wines, dessert varieties are deliberately fashioned by their makers for some striking individuality. You are urged to spend the time and money to assemble an original tasting list as diverse as those suggested below. Your life will be enlivened forevermore by these or other charming wines used in cooking, at the table, and on social occasions. As the "wino" image wanes, Americans are sure to discover dessert wines, a minor but secure category in all wine-oriented cultures.

Suggested Readings

Acton, Bryan, and Duncan, Peter. *Making Mead.* Andover, England: "Amateur Winemaker," 1978.
Modern mead making in England.

Allen, H. Warner. *A History of Wine.* London: Faber and Faber Ltd., 1961.
A recounting of the growth of the wine culture in western civilization.

Amerine, Maynard A., and Roessler, Edward B. *Wines: Their Sensory Evaluation.* San Francisco: W. H. Freeman & Co., Pubs., 1976.
The essential text for serious wine drinkers.

Amerine, Maynard A., and Singleton, Vernon L. *Wine: An Introduction for Americans.* Berkeley: University of California Press, 1968.
A textbook for laypeople.

Broadbent, Michael. *Wine Tasting.* 6th ed. London: Christie Wine Publications, 1979.
An excellent exploration of the tasting process with the smells and tastes of most wines identified.

Brothwell, Donald, and Brothwell, Patricia. *Food in Antiquity.* London: Thames & Hudson, Ltd., 1969.
Excellent review of the sources of food and drink in early cultures.

Cooper, John M. "Alcohol Beverages of the World." *Medical Missionary Magazine* 17(1943), 150–153.
Thoughtful article on the universality of ancient intoxicants.

Emerson, Edward. *Beverages Past and Present.* 2 vols. New York: G. P. Putnam's Sons, 1908.
Vivacious and anecdotal review of wines and spirits.

Guilliermond, Alexandre. *The Yeasts.* Translated and revised by Fred Wilbur Tanner. New York: John Wiley & Sons, Inc., 1920.
The primary textbook on yeast cultures.

Hunter, Beatrice Trum. *Fact/Book on Fermented Foods and Beverages, An Old Tradition.* New Canaan, Conn.: Keats Publishing, Inc., 1973.
All the answers about basic food ferments, from wines to soybean curds.

Hunter, Beatrice Trum. *Fact/Book on Yogurt, Kefir and Other Milk Cultures.* New Canaan, Conn.: Keats Publishing, Inc., 1973.
Everything about milk and cheese cultures and ferments.

Kellner, Esther. *Moonshine: Its History and Folklore.* New York: Weathervane Books, 1971.
An irreverent but delightful picture of backyard booze.

Lichine, Alexis. *Encyclopedia of Wines and Spirits.* New York: Alfred A. Knopf, Inc., 1969.
A comprehensive source book for every wine and spirit shelf.

Marcus, Irving H. *How to Test and Improve Your Wine Judging Ability.* 2d ed. Berkeley, Calif.: Wine Publications, 1974.
An easy-to-read, thoroughly professional treatise on wine tasting.

Marrison, L. W. *Wines and Spirits.* Great Britain: Penguin Books, 1970.
Basic paperback covering all the major countries.

Morewood, Samuel. *A Philosophical and Statistical History of the Inventions and Customs of Ancient and Modern Nations in the Manufacture and Use of Inebriating Liquors.* Dublin: Wilborn, Curry, Jan, and Co., 1838.
Absolutely priceless survey of how it used to be as seen through the eyes of a nineteenth century writer.

Seward, Desmond. *Monks and Wine.* New York: Crown Publishers, Inc., 1979.
Witty and charming review of the contributions of monks to viticulture.

Wagner, Philip M. *Grapes Into Wine.* New York: Alfred A. Knopf, Inc., 1981.
An essential book for those who wish to understand the dynamism and vitality of Eastern wine making by one of the pioneers in the hybrid grape field.

Weiss, H. B. *The History of Applejack.* Trenton, N. J.: New Jersey Agricultural Society, 1954.
A history of cider and cider brandy in early America.

Brews 14

It is important in reviewing the field of alcoholic beverages to comprehend the nearly elemental role which brews have taken in nearly all societies, in nearly all times.

ANCIENT BREWS

In *The Great American Beer Book* (1980), James Robertson sets the ancient stage:

> By 4000, the Babylonians had made sixteen different types of beer from barley, wheat, and honey. Bittering agents (to add character to the taste and a degree of shelf life) have been used in beer making since 3000. For almost three thousand years beer was important to daily life and religion in ancient Egypt. It was in common use in China about 2300 B.C., and the ancient Incas had used a corn-based beer for centuries before that continent was discovered [by Europeans].

An example of brews associated with religious fervor can be found in the actions of Ramses III, king of Egypt from 1198–1167 B.C. His royal sacrifices to the gods involved pouring on the altar 30,000 gallons annually, the equivalent of 320,000 glasses per month!

Early societies used beer as a staple food as well as a major source to replace lost body fluids. For example, the common Egyptian subsisted on beer, the bread from which the brew had been made, and a few odd vegetables. Soldiers along the ancient Nile were compensated partially with rations of beer.

*H*ere's to the girl that I love—
I wish that she were nigh.
If drinking beer would bring her here,
I'd drink the damn place dry!

Old Toast

*A*s he brews, so shall he drink.

Ben Jonson

A Babylonian tablet from 6000 B.C. portrays the preparation for a religious ceremony in which beer was used. An Assyrian tablet dated circa 2000 B.C. indicates that Noah carried beer aboard the Ark and another depicts over 100 medicines with beer as the base. Beer was easily within the reach of the Egyptian and Sumerian since it was fermented from underbaked, coarse breads that contained generous amounts of maltose. A day or so of fermentation was all that was required to turn the water in which these bread chunks soaked into palatable although rough brews which could be extracted from the amphorae by long straws. Eventually, the brews were strained and refined with spices, dates, and herbs.

The sacred books of India provide hundreds of references to brewing and to the consumption of another ferment known as *soma* which was made from the juice of asclepias or

195

Terms

adjunct Any one of a number of grains or other additives blended with barley malt in brewing.

ale A light brew of pronounced hop character traditionally top fermented; also an English festival at which ale is the main beverage.

barley The primary grain used to produce beer, grown nearly everywhere in the temperate zones.

barrel The primary unit of measurement for the sale of beer, a cask containing 31 gallons.

beer Since the sixteenth century, the term is used to distinguish the hopped variety of brews from the unhopped, which was then termed ale; today the word beer encompasses all brews.

bitter Very heavy, highly hopped draft beer.

black and tan Stout and mild draft beers mixed in the glass.

black velvet Stout and champagne mixed in the glass.

bottle Glass container introduced in the nineteenth century which revolutionized the packaging and sale of beer.

brewer's grains The residue of the mash tun after sparging; normally sold as cattle feed.

brewmaster The chief brewer responsible for the character and style of the brew.

bung hole Hole for filling beer barrels.

can A primary container for beer made of steel or aluminum and of various sizes.

carbonation The process of adding or infusing CO_2 immediately before bottling; there are 2.2 to 2.4 volumes of CO_2 already in beer following the fermentation process.

chitting The appearance of rootlets or growth in the malting stage.

cooper The craftsman who makes and repairs wooden casks.

copper The brewing kettle in which hops and wort are boiled.

dextrin A soluble starch carbohydrate formed in brewing; a great portion of the body of beer.

dextrose One form of sugar created in malting.

draft (br. draught) The type of beer dispensed directly from barrels.

enzymes Organic matter from the grain which converts starch to sugars.

ester A compound created from acids in fermentation providing distinctive bouquet.

extract The total amount of materials for fermentation from the grains and adjuncts.

fermentation The conversion by yeasts of sugars to alcohol and carbon dioxide.

finings Materials used to clarify beers.

fusel oil Higher alcohols and their esters with distinctly distasteful flavor and smell.

germination The initial process of growth in any seed.

glucose $C_6H_{12}O_6$, a sugar developed from fruits or starches.

green malt Germinated malt not yet dried or kilned.

grits Coarsely ground hulled grain, usually corn, used as beer adjunct.

head The foam on beer.

hogshead A fifty (or more) gallon cask.

hop-jack The vessel which receives the wort after brewing and strains out the hops.

hops A perennial plant providing the female cone used in brewing.

hydrometer An instrument used for measuring specific gravity or extract content in brewing.

isinglass A pure form of gelatin often used in fining brews.

jacob's ladder A conveyor used to transport beer casks to the loading dock.

kiln A large structure usually with a conical roof used as a stove in drying green malts.

lager The popular beer on the Continent and in the United States distinguished as light and less hoppy; *lagern,* from German, is "to cellar or store."

lauter tub The straining tank in which the wort is separated from the brewer's grains.

liquor The term used universally in brewing to indicate water.

lupulin The yellow resinous powder on the strobiles of hops used to flavor and preserve beers.

malting Steeping, germinating, and kilning or drying grains which initiates the change of grain starch to sugar called maltose.

malt tower The top level of a brewery where the malt and cereal adjuncts begin their journey down successive floors in the beer-making process.

mash The porridge-like mixture of barley malt and adjuncts which is mixed with hot water (liquor) to create the wort.

mash tun The large vessel in which the enzymes break down the starches and proteins in advance of brewing and fermentation.

near beer Dealcoholized beer, hence a cereal beverage.

oast The kiln in which the new hops are spread to dry.

original gravity The extract of wort before fermentation.

pasteurization The process by which beer passes through a heat exchanger raising the product to as high as 160° F to destroy bacteria and microorganisms.

pepsin A proteolytic enzyme involved in digestion.

peptonize To digest or dissolve through fermentation.

pH The degree of alkalinity or acidity; the scale is divided into 14 values with the number 7.0 being a neutral point; the lower the number, the higher the acidity, and the higher the number, the greater the alkalinity.

phenol Part of the carbolic acid chain, a compound found in nature, particularly in wood stocks, which creates bitterness in taste; is used as a preservative in wines and beers.

plato Technical term in brewing (like Brix and Balling in wine making) meaning the percent of fermentable solids in the mash.

polishing The final steps of filtering and fining in beer finishing, designed to clear the product to its final sheen and brilliance.

porter A draught beer popular for several centuries in the British Empire, equivalent to a mixing of light beer and heavy ale.

precipitate To separate out solid particles in a beer, usually through chilling.

priming The addition of cane sugar or other sweet solutions to ales and stouts just before bottling, making them not unlike sparkling wines in having greater sweetness and more CO_2.

protease Protolytic enzyme in brewing which breaks down proteins.

protein Compounds created of complex amino acids constituting all living cells, animal and vegetable.

racking Drawing off finished beer, from stored beer, into casks or bottles for distribution.

roasted malt Dark malt used for coloring beers.

ruh The storage of beer after fermentation.

shine The luster or brilliance of the beer.

sparging The spraying of hot water over the mash tun to facilitate the release of the extract.

steam beer A very highly carbonated beer of top fermentation, originated in California.

steeping The process by which the barley grain is soaked in huge cisterns to begin the germination process.

stout Beer made from fully roasted, full flavor malts; generally a sweeter and more hoppy type of ale.

tied house An arrangement illegal in the United States whereby the tavern purchases all its products from one brewery.

tun Originally a British term for a 252–gallon cask, now used as a name for various sizes of brewing tanks.

vat Another name for a tun or large vessel.

viscosity The resistance to flowing or pouring; used to measure the body of alcohol beverages.

weiss Beer from wheat malt, which is pale and tart.

wort The fluid from the mash tun containing the malt and adjunct extracts and hot liquor which will be fermented into beer.

yard of ale The tall glass shaped like a horn and approximately three feet high, once popular in British taverns.

yeast The unicellular plant organism common in nature which ferments sugars into alcohol and CO_2.

zymase A group of enzymes which promotes the fermentation of sugars.

Labels on Kirin brews from Japan picture the mythological Chinese animal that foretold the birth of Confucius.

other creeping plants. The references are vague but stress the sacred and mysterious aspects of inebriation, an attitude not dissimiliar to that of the less sophisticated American and Mexican Indians with their long history of the use of hallucinogens. Michael Weiner in *The Taster's Guide to Beer* (1977) provides this information:

> The worship of the gods was a service of intoxication, for the priests and for the people. . . . *Soma* was drunk to excess by both priests and people. . . . As to the nature of the beverage *soma,* Samuelson . . . quoted above, says: "The drink *(soma)* is believed to have been prepared from the juice of a creeper (asclepias). . . ." Another intoxicating beverage was *sura,* the drink of the common people, much more intoxicating than *soma,* and made from an Indian grass *(panicum),* water, honey, curds, melted butter and barley.

The controversy over the source of *soma* is outlined in *Narcotic Plants* (1979) by William Emboden, who cites the pharmacologist Quazilbash's assertion that the "plant had to be soaked in milk, crushed, filtered, mixed with honey, and the brew allowed to ferment." Whatever the source materials, it is abundantly clear that brews could be made synergistically to produce an ethereally satisfactory intoxication through the admixture of alcohol and plant drugs, a practice which even today has a good deal of currency.

As a charming bit of mythology, the Goddess Isis, the female principle of life and goddess of fertility, was credited by the Egyptians for the gift of brewing. Many of the priestesses in that ancient land retained the office of brewer. Some conjecture that Isis must have created this largess as long as thirty thousand years ago, although written records do not extend that far back.

There are records, however, that show that by 2300 B.C., the Chinese brewed *kiu* from rice. The Incas treasured their *chicha* and *sora* made from maize. On his third voyage, Columbus wrote of the Indian women who chewed kernels of corn to introduce the enzymes from the mouth necessary to convert the starch to sugar for fermentation. The Spanish explorers of Mexico and South America discovered similar common brews made from the agave plant. The Aztecs had as many as 400 gods devoted to *pulque* beer made from *aguamiel,* the sap of that ubiquitous plant. Somewhere along the line it became known as the "milk of the green cow" since it was consumed while still frothing from fermentation. Today Mexicans consume over a million liters a day of this bountiful harvest in over 1,100 *pulquerias.*

*H*eaven above does not equal one half of
me,
Have I been drinking soma?
In my glory I have passed beyond earth
and sky,
Have I been drinking soma?
I will pick up the earth and place it here
and there,
Have I been drinking soma?

from the Rig-Veda

All over the world, various types of brews were made in every ancient society. The Greeks called their beers *zythose,* close to the Egyptian *zythum.* The early Romans had *cerea* and *cervisia,* the root word for the most popular yeast used today, *cerevisiae.* Africans for centuries had their *bousa* and later *bousza* (the probable origin of our word *booze*) which was made from millet, and they had another brew called *wheda* made from maize.

In *Moonshine* (1971), Esther Kellner records the commonness of beer in Mesopotamia and Egypt.

Mesopotamian housewives made beer along with their bread, sometimes for their families, sometimes to sell. Barley bread, barley beer, and onions constituted the food of the poor. . . . Mesopotamia had meeting-and-eating places not unlike small taverns. . . . Barley beer was brewed, consumed and relished in Egypt in much the same way. During his ten years of study at the temple school, a medical student had for his daily fare three loaves of bread and two jugs of beer. The ration for a laborer was the same, plus a bunch of onions. Schoolboys drank two jugs of beer per day.

In *Food in Antiquity* (1969), the Brothwells report much the same about classical societies.

Indeed, Plutarch states that before the advent of viticulture mead was the drink offered to the gods and that foreign peoples lacking the vine, still drank mead. Pliny and Columella also state that mead and beer were drunk prior to wine in Italy, and Pliny adds with disgust that beer was imbibed "neat," not with water as was the practice with wine. Nevertheless . . . when the early agriculturists began to produce cereal and fruit (including the grape) in quantity, mead did not stand up to much competition.

The Roman historian Tacitus wrote in the first century A.D. of a "German drink prepared from wheat or barley by fermentation to a certain resemblance to wine." And his countryman, Pliny records the universal presence of alcohol beverages: "The western nations have their intoxicating liquor, made of steeped grain. Thus drunkenness is a stranger in no part of the world . . ."

Nor did the practice of adulteration we have so graphically traced in wines escape the fertile imagination of the brewers. A man of enormous creativity and patience, Robert Harley included a recipe for *mum* in his *Harleian Miscellany* in 1682, and his recipe was passed on by Edward Emerson (1908) in *Beverages Past and Present.*

To make vessel of sixty-three gallons, the water must be boiled to the consumption of a third part. Let it then be brewed, according to art, with seven bushels of wheat-malt, one bushel of oat-malt, and one bushel of ground beans; and when it is tunned, let not the hogshead be too full at first; when it begins to work, put to it of the inner rind of the fir three pounds, of the tops of fir and birch, each one pound; of *carduus benedictus* dried, three handfuls; flowers of *rosa solis,* two handfuls; or burnet, betony, marjoram, awens, penny-royal, flowers of elder, wild-thyme of each one handful and half; seeds of cardamum bruised, three ounces; bayberries bruised one ounce; put the seeds into the vessel: when the liquor hath wrought awhile with the herbs, and after they are added, let the liquor work over the vessel as little as may be, fill it up at last, and when it is stopped, put into the hogshead ten new-laid eggs not cracked or broken; stop all close and drink it at two years old; if carried by water it is better.

I'll bet it is!

THE MIDDLE YEARS

While beers were flavored in order to preserve them, a turning point came with the introduction of the perennial hop plant for that purpose. There is a record of a hop garden in cultivation as early as A.D. 768. And in the year 1079, Abbess Hildegard of Rupertsburg published *Physica Socia* with this recommendation: "If one intends to make beer from oats, it is prepared with hops, but is boiled with *grug* (herbs most likely) and mostly with ash leaves." (In Emboden [1979].)

In medieval Europe, beer, which was both taxed and tithed, was a staple of barter. By 1376, over 1,000 brewmasters lived in Hamburg. Early in the seventeenth century, Einbeck, from lower Saxony, became one of the first brews in international trade and for centuries set the quality standards. It was high in alcohol and well hopped. By 1614, Munich brewers organized to raise their quality standards to match those of Einbeck, the name of which has since been corrupted over the years to designating a type of beer called *bock*.

The Elector of Bavaria in 1516 issued a momentous edict which has persisted to this day; it was designed to protect the purity of the brewing process. Originally intended to create more tax revenue to support costly military adventures, the *Rheinheitsgebot* restricted brewing ingredients to barley, water, yeast, and hops. Behind the edict was the theory, which proved correct, that better brews would generate more sales and greater income for the state. Bavarian breweries to this day comply with the *Rheinheitsgebot* by law as do breweries in much of Germany and, by practice, in all of Norway and Switzerland.

By the end of the sixteenth century, British brews had gained a prominence which remains today. Edward Emerson (1908) documents the British appetite: "In fact, it may be said in all truth that the old English people never assembled at any function without ale being on the premises or near at hand." Though hops had been introduced into that island culture as early as 1500, they were generally used to flavor only what was known as *lager* beer, the German style of bottom-fermented brew. For many centuries, Britons clung to the practice of producing ale only from pure barley malt in its unadulterated form.

In fact, Braudel writes that hops were actually forbidden in England until as late as 1556, and he includes a ditty from Trevelyan's *History of England* that sets the scene.

> Hops, Reformation, bays and beer
> Came into England all in one year.

Heineken, with its famous de Haarberg *(haystack), in 1620.*

Like their wineries (and later their distilleries), monastery breweries were important scientific and economic centers during the cultural abyss of the Dark Ages.

Eventually, however, the merging of tastes in the consumer led to the creation of a new style. It was common by 1730 for the customer to ask for *alf 'n alf*, a glass containing half ale and small lager beer. An enterprising brewmaster named Ralph Harwood from the east side of High Street made a new brew containing both. At first called *entire butts*, it gradually became known as *Porter* in honor of the local porters who preferred the blend.

Beer is inextricably intertwined with both the sacred and the profane in western civilization, having been husbanded through the bleak Dark Ages by the monasteries, as was wine. Michael Weiner points to the particularly strong religious advocacy of beer in *The Taster's Guide to Beer*.

> Three saints are listed as patrons of brewing, and they are very distinguished members of Christian hagiology indeed: St. Augustine of Hippo, author of the *Confessions* and the most influential of the early Christian philosophers; St. Nicholas of Myra, better known to us as Santa Claus; and the Evangelist, St. Luke, "The Beloved Physician." But there are a myriad of other saints involved with brewing: St. Thomas à Beckct, the later martyred Archbishop of Canterbury, when he went to France in 1158 to seek the hand of a French princess for Prince Henry of England, brought with him as gifts several barrels of English ale.

I'll no more be a nun, nun, nun,
I'll no more be a nun!
But I'll be a wife,
And lead a merry life,
And brew good ale by the tun, tun, tun.
Anonymous

All of the great events and festivities of the Middle Ages carried the name "ale," since it was the socializing drink. Surviving is the bride-ale, or bridal feast; funerals were grave-ales, and there were give-ales, for charities, clerk-ales, and even cuckoo-ales. The responsibility for brewing in the early and later Middle Ages fell to the baker-housewife. Edward Emerson (1908) comments on the transition of brewing from being a housewife's chore to being an occupation worthy of the dignity of the male chauvinist.

> In the very early days of beer making, and especially in Germany, the duty was left to the women, as it was considered degrading for a man to have anything to do with beer except to drink it, in large quantities; but when it became of monetary value then the dignity, as well as the woman, was pushed aside with the result that it was generally conceded that the old idea of dignity was entirely wrong.

America's oldest existing brewery is D. G. Yuengling and Son Brewery founded in 1829 in Pottsville, Pennsylvania where it still brews a full line, including Old German Brand and Porter.

In seventeenth century Europe, beer was the common beverage at every meal. Other popular drinks were introduced as a result of colonization, including coffee, tea, and chocolate. Big cities supported big breweries. In 1592, Pope Clement VIII approved coffee for human consumption and attributed to it mystical powers.

Weiner (1954) paints a vivid picture of the enormous quantities of brew consumed in England in her pre-colonial times. "Individual consumption was substantial, in part, no doubt because of the shortage of drinkable water. Ladies-in-waiting at the court of Henry VIII were allowed a gallon of beer (160 ounces) for breakfast alone."

AMERICA, THE BREWER

American colonists brought with them strong predilections for brew consumption. While the flowering of the industry came in the early nineteenth century with the massive German immigration, barley was planted as early as 1605 in Virginia. In *Brewed in America*, Stanley Baron (1962) demonstrates how dearly the sailors and pilgrims alike appreciated the stuff when he quotes the famous letter of a passenger explaining why they were put ashore at Cape Cod, considerably north of their intended destination: ". . . we could not now take time for further search or consideration, our victuals being much spent, especially our beere." Baron explains that the unwary pilgrims were hastened ashore by the sailors and made to drink the local waters to conserve the remaining brew for the trip home; Baron gives several additional examples of ale use in the Colonies.

John Winthrop, the first governor of Massachusetts, brought 10,000 gallons of beer with him in 1629, along with a strong belief in government control of its consumption. By 1634, taverns were both licensed and severely restricted, as in this ordinance: "It is ordered that no person that keeps an ordinairie (tavern) shall take above 6d. a meal of a person and not above 1d. for an ale quart of beer." In Virginia John Smith wrote in 1629: "For drink, some malt the Indian corne, others barley, of which they make good Ale, both strong and small, and such plentee thereof; few of the upper Planters drinke any water; but the better sort are well furnished with Sacke, Aqua vitae and good English ale."

Well through the last two centuries, this class tradition was sustained in America. Wines belonged to the privileged, while beer and ale quenched the poor people's thirst. By 1640, virtually every household was also a brewery. Since barley did not fare well as a crop and corn was abundant, early brewers reverted to the Egyptian procedures for brewing as described by John Winthrop.

> The English have found a way to make very good
> Beere of this Graine which they do either out of bread
> . . . way of making Beere of bread . . . break it or
> cutt it into great lumps, as big as a man's Fist or
> bigger . . . and proceed every way about brewing it,
> as is used in Brewing Beere of Mault, adding hopps to
> it as to make Beer . . .

Fortunately, hops for flavoring grew wild in the new land. This fermenting of bread was preferable to the laborious natural malting practice with corn. It consisted of planting a shallow patch of corn and allowing it to grow for about ten days during which time the starch in the kernels naturally changed to maltose sugar.

Since the early years in western civilization, there has existed a thinly veiled prejudice of the wine consumer against the "boorish" beer drinker. The Roman Governor of Gaul expressed this patrician contempt in an early epigram.

> Whence art thou, thou false Bacchus, fierce and hot?
> By the true Bacchus, I do know thee not!
> It smells of nectar—thy brain burning smell
> Is not of flowers of heav'n, but weeds of hell.
> The lack-vine Celts, impoverish'd, breech'd, and rude,
> From prickly barley spikes they beverage brew'd;
> When I should style thee to approve thee right,
> Not the rich blood of Bacchus, bounding bright,
> But the thin ichor of old Ceres' veins
> Express'd by flames from hungry barley grains,
> Child-born of Vulcan's fire to burn up human brains.

Despite vestiges of this lingering prejudice, "Vulcan's fire" has done well in the Americas. John Alden of Mayflower fame was a cooper and his decision to ride out the starvation years of 1620–1621 was important to the economy of the colony.

Baron in *Brewed in America* (1962) reports on the assumed kinship that brewing had with health. "The availability of beer was considered to be essential to the maintenance of good health. The governor, Sir Francis Wyatt, wrote to England sometime between 1623 and 1624 that there had been great sickness in the colony because of 'want of beere, poultry, mutton,' etc. . . ."

In the 1630s, the Dutch settlers brewed everywhere. Their governor, William Kieft, established a brewery and many control ordinances. Baron reports that as many as one quarter

The famous Chicago Architectural Firm of Aug. Maritzen designed and built brewing buildings reminiscent of the august Rhine Universities, as stolid as the men for whom they were built.

of the homes in New Amsterdam sold tobacco and beer. Similar benevolence about beer can be seen in the following quote from *Brewing in Canada*. "In detailing the diet of a farm laborer in the little colony of New France, the Provincial of the Jesuits in Quebec mentions that in addition to their allowance of flour, lard, oil and vinegar, codfish, peas and so on, 'They are given a chopine of cider a day or a quart of beer.'" By 1668, another official, Jean Talon, established a brewery to combat the tendency to strong drink.

Strong drink, largely in the form of rum, began to dominate in the later years of the seventeenth century in competition with beer, wine, and cider. With the widespread cultivation of apples, cider became the usual choice from among the many fruit ferments.

Nearly every major figure in our early history was associated in one way or another with brewing. Samuel Adams, Thomas Jefferson, George Washington, James Madison, Patrick Henry, Benjamin Franklin—brewers all. The sporadic English duties on molasses, sugar, and spirits and wines from abroad caused a spurt in both home and commercial brewing.

A family gathering in a nineteenth century New York beer garden depicts the role of brews in the lives of European immigrants.

Toward the end of the 18th century, local jurisdictions encouraged domestic production both for economic reasons and as an early defense against the growing ravages of ardent spirits in the young nation. Baron (1962) reports a Massachusetts law which encouraged brewing "as an important means of preserving the health of the citizens of this commonwealth, and preventing the pernicious effects of spiritous liquors." The battle began which would ensue for another 120 years between those who saw virtue and continence in the traditional wines and brews and those who saw degradation in all alcohol but particularly in the rums and new grain spirits from the western lands of Pennsylvania and Kentucky.

The German Invasion

While, in one sense, brewing was as common as baking in the Americas, the industry did not fully develop until the Germans arrived. Up until this time, brews in America were made in the British way; they were rather murky, lightly carbonated, top-fermented ales and porters. A Philadelphia brewer named John Wagner is said to have brought the bottom-fermenting lager technique to America from his native Bavaria. Baron (1962) writes of the German contribution.

> The German engulfment of the American brewing industry, which began here in the 1840s had a curious analogy in England at least three centuries before, when the brewing of hopped beer in contrast to the traditional unhopped English Ale was practically controlled by German and Dutch brewers. The experience in England was, however, an isolated phenomenon not based, as it was in America, on large scale immigration.

The sturdy, skilled and self-confident Germans who fled religious persecution at home made possible the establishment of a bona fide, domestic, commercial brewing enterprise not unlike that established in the spirits trade by the enterprising Scotch-Irish a few years earlier. But it was not technique alone

that the Germans brought to America. More important were the strains of yeast they imported for the mashes because they created the lighter, highly carbonated lager. In addition, the German brewmaster's long experience in aging the brew in chilly caves and cellars brought about a full term secondary fermentation further carbonating the product.

Because breweries in America, as in Europe, were among the primary industrial enterprises, the new type of beer brought about a minor industrial explosion in the new lands. In 1850, 421 commercial breweries were in operation in America. The number of firms more than doubled to over 1200 in the next decade just before the Civil War.

In 1857, Eberhard Anheuser acquired a brewery in St. Louis. Henry Weinhard established his in Portland. Schlitz, Pabst, and the other pioneers founded today's giant firms. Americans had taken to the light, clean, fragrant lager beer that needed no rum or honey as flavorings.

August Krug, the forefather of the pioneer California vintner, began what was to become the Schlitz Brewery in the basement of his Milwaukee restaurant in 1849. His bookkeeper, Joseph Schlitz, eventually assumed the company in 1856, giving his name to the new enterprise which fostered many innovations including the introduction of the pure European yeast strains, the brown bottle to protect the product from harmful light rays, and, eventually, the popular "pull-top" can.

What these pioneer American brewers shared, in addition to a common language, was industry and an openness to technological change which became the guiding spirit of American brewing as the century came to a close. Technology and hard work became the handmaidens of the brewing industry.

Technology and Consolidation

The manifold benefits of the ongoing industrial revolution brought immense power to this new industry headed by determined, resolute Germanic brewers. So strong was their domination of the industry that the early proceedings of the United States Brewers Association were transcribed in German. The critical impact during this time came from science and technology.

The first occurred when Louis Pasteur focused on brews rather than wines as explained in *The Pabst Brewing Company* (1948) by Thomas C. Cochran.

> In the 1870s, Pasteur turned his attention to beer as the best medium for the continuation of his experiments, and thus he developed the theoretical basis for modern fermenting practice . . . These researches led directly to Pasteur's *Études sur la Bière* in 1876, his theory of infectious diseases . . . and his discussion of virus and vaccines, published in 1880.

Along with this contribution to brewing, Pasteur's discoveries fostered the medical science of microbiology. During this period hand labor gave way in brewing as it did in other

industrial enterprises. Pneumatic powering, artificial refrigeration, the crown bottle cap, the automatic glass machinery—these and many other advances contributed to the efficiency of the brewing process.

At the same time, the labor movement gradually gained strength which contributed to the consolidation of the breweries, a trend continuing to this day. Another factor which tended to make the strong stronger and drive the smaller companies out of competition was the influx of British beer syndicates around 1890. The large British firms began to buy into the St. Louis and Chicago markets bringing with them the traditional British system of "tied-houses," literally, taverns that owed their allegiances to a single brewer in exchange for monetary benefits. In meeting but eventually beating this challenge, the American brewing industry dropped from a total of 1,972 brewing firms in 1870 to 1,313 by 1916 and to an incredible low of 40 in 1980. Consolidation led to strength, the hallmarks of the American economy. Two breweries, Anheuser-Busch and Miller Brewing Company, now command over half the domestic market.

While the buildings on the outside may not be very different today, the work accomplished inside depended heavily upon hand labor at the turn of the century, as seen in these pictures of Seattle's Rainier Brewery. The rustic structures of 1878 became substantial brick edifices in 1900.

A bottle-molding machine in action.

Prohibition

A word is in order concerning the brewing industry's contribution to the culmination of the several hundred year war of the prohibitionists. In a biting and quite logical commentary written in 1931 called *The Old Time Saloon,* George Ade places a considerable share of the blame for Prohibition on brewers themselves who were sanctimoniously pushing the True Temperance beverage while ignoring the mayhem that their fight with the British wrought on society.

> Both sides began to fondle the retailer and offer him tempting inducements. The average saloon served one make of beer and no other kind. . . . Then the syndicate and the native beer barons began to open their own places and furnish them and look around for

dependable partners to officiate behind the bars. . . . Hundreds of men without capital or much business experience were set up in business by the breweries.

As Ade describes them, saloons around the turn of the century were hardly the convivial meeting houses of previous eras. Little children brought pails in to be filled for their elders, and high school children bellied up to the bars. Little wonder, as Ade reports, that the Rockefellers and Kresges, anxious for steady work forces, fed the coffers and participated in the political power plays of the Anti-Saloon League:

> . . . scandals . . . surrounded the retail liquor business and . . . so worked upon the public sentiment that when the Anti-Saloon League began a major attack along the whole front it attained all of the objectives and scored a bloodless victory and sat on top

The world famous Anheuser-Busch Clydesdale team.

A Schlitz wagon from around the turn of the century.

of the world, because those most familiar with the old-time saloon were not prepared to come forward with any adequate defense or any convincing alibis.

Eschewing any kind of united front with the distilling industry or with modern forces in the society, many of these brewers were soon reduced to making ice cream, sausages, spaghetti, and soft drinks in their large brewing plants.

Baron (1962) sums it up. "What cannot be denied . . . is that the Anti-Saloon League was tougher, more ruthless and realistic than the forces arrayed against it . . . The breweries were also surprisingly maladroit in their public relations." The tenacity of purpose, penchant for hard work, and solid Christian ethic prevalent within the community of brewers simply prevented their understanding or acknowledging the growing indignation in the society that had yet to spend itself completely and that would in time lead to the sad episode of prohibition.

MODERN CONSUMPTION OF BREWS

It should not be surprising to find that the West Germans are the greatest beer drinkers in the world today, at about 150 liters annually. That's nearly 40 gallons per head per year! In addition to that, they also consume about 12 gallons of wine per capita per year (see table 14.1).

Despite the growing impact of American wine consumption in the seventies, beer has enjoyed a fabulous decade (see table 14.2). The total barrels sold rose over 40 percent in the period, and Anheuser-Busch forecasts an astonishing 185 million barrels before the end of the eighties, paralleling, even exceeding, the growth in wine consumption over the same span. The marked feature in this growth has been the emergence of

TABLE 14.1 Leading Countries in Per Capita Beer Consumption

Rank	Country	Gallons
1	West Germany	38.8
2	Czechoslovakia	37.0
3	East Germany	36.3
4	Australia	35.4
5	Belgium	32.8
6	Luxembourg	32.5
7	Denmark	32.3
8	New Zealand	32.2
9	Ireland	30.7
10	England	29.5
11	Austria	27.7
12	United States	24.6
13	Netherlands	23.6
14	Hungary	23.0
15	Canada	22.5
16	Switzerland	18.6
17	Venezuela	16.5
18	Bulgaria	16.1
19	Finland	15.1
20	Spain	14.8

Source: IMPACT (1 November 1982), 10.

the premium and super-premium labels. Premium beers exceed other industry growth by 5 percent. Another spectacular increase occurred in the low calorie "light" types. While only 20¢ per six-pack separates the price of regular and premium beers, people are definitely buying up! United States breweries produced over 168 million barrels in 1980.

While the import beer category is still a minor segment of the market, much smaller than import wines—4.4 million barrels in 1980—there is consistent growth in the category and

TABLE 14.2 Exploding Growth of Beer
10 Year Sales Performance
(In Millions of Barrels [Each 31 Gallons])

Year	Package	Draft	Domestic Total	Domestic % Gain	Imported Total	Imported % Gain	All Beers Total	All Beers % Gain
1979	148.7	19.4	168.1	3.3	4.4	29.4	172.5	3.8
1978	144.6	18.1	162.7	3.7	3.4	36.0	166.1	4.2
1977	138.7	18.2	156.9	4.4	2.5	8.6	159.4	4.5
1976	132.1	18.2	150.3	1.1	2.3	43.7	152.6	1.6
1975	130.2	18.4	148.6	2.2	1.6	23.0	150.2	2.4
1974	127.2	18.2	145.4	5.1	1.3	18.1	146.7	5.2
1973	120.3	18.1	138.4	5.0	1.1	22.2	139.5	5.1
1972	114.2	17.6	131.8	3.5	.9	0	132.7	3.5
1971	110.1	17.3	127.3	4.5	.9	12.5	128.2	4.6
1970	104.6	17.2	121.8	4.8	.8	14.2	122.6	4.9

Source: *The Beverage Analyst* (June 1980), 18.

TABLE 14.3 Beer Import Market by Country
(Millions of Gallons)

Country	1960	1965	1970	1975	1980	1981	Average Annual Compound Growth Rate[a] 1960–1970	1970–1975	1975–1980	Percent Change[b] 1980–1981
Netherlands	2.6	3.7	7.4	19.8	55.5	65.2	11.1%	21.6%	22.9%	17.5
Canada	3.6	4.1	4.2	12.8	47.5	51.9	1.4	25.2	30.1	9.2
Germany	4.2	7.1	9.5	8.5	14.8	18.2	8.5	−2.2	11.6	23.2
Mexico	0.2	0.5	0.9	3.4	10.2	10.9	13.5	31.5	24.5	5.9
United Kingdom	0.2	0.3	1.0	2.1	3.1	3.3	19.2	15.2	8.1	5.5
Ireland	0.3	0.4	0.6	0.6	2.0	2.2	8.1	—	25.9	10.0
Australia	*	*	*	1.3	2.0	1.9	9.9	+	10.2	−9.2
France	*	*	0.1	*	1.0	1.6	12.7	−10.0	+	62.3
Japan	0.1	0.2	0.3	0.6	1.2	1.6	10.2	12.0	15.5	27.0
Philippines	0.1	0.5	0.6	0.6	0.7	1.2	17.1	0.6	0.8	74.1
China	—	—	—	*	0.4	0.8	—	—	79.6	87.6
Denmark	0.8	1.2	1.2	0.6	0.8	0.6	4.8	−12.7	5.1	−23.4
Norway	0.1	1.5	1.2	0.8	0.5	0.5	24.4	−7.9	−9.8	−4.8
Other	0.1	0.2	0.4	0.8	1.8	2.2	12.1	14.0	17.7	20.9
TOTAL	12.4	19.8	27.6	52.0	141.6	161.8	8.3%	13.5%	22.1%	14.3

Source: *IMPACT* (1 April 1982), 6.

[a]Based on unrounded data.

[b]Addition of columns may not agree because of rounding.

*Less than 50,000 gallons.

evidence of growth in prestige markets (see table 14.3). Finally, the consolidation of minor brands by major companies capable of heavy mechanization and advertising continues apace. In a manner familiar to many modern industries, the prestigious and powerful dominate the market.

Although the theory cannot be proven, historical speculation suggests that brewing came before baking of leavened breads. Michael Jackson in *The World Guide to Beer* (1977) finds the argument plausible in that the discovery of light, high-rising bread could have occurred in many a primitive kitchen where beer was the goal. As every housewife knows, it is ru-dimentary fermentation and release of carbon dioxide within the warm dough that makes the bread rise.

The idea that beer may have pre-dated bread is not unreasonable. It is difficult to make acceptable bread with barley, because the gluten content of the grain is low, and the loaves do not hold together very well. . . . Beer can be brewed, though less easily, with wheat, but the grain makes excellent bread. Thus the brewer and the baker have been able to pursue their crafts in a perfectly complementary way.

This Kirin ad from 1908 portrays a distinctly male clientele, and a portly one at that.

This charming depiction of an Egyptian bakery, ca. 2000 B.C., shows the brewers and the bakers working in parallel lines.

It is abundantly evident from these few brief historical references and consumption figures that brews were, and still are, universal. However, it was to the Germanic tribes and their successors that brews became the primary beverage. In terms of per capita consumption, the northern Europeans still prevail. Today, the United States consumes nearly five billion gallons of beer annually or an average of 24 gallons per capita. This considerable ingestion ranks our nation only twelfth, far behind West Germany, with nearly 40 gallons per capita, and the following countries in approximate order of imbibing—Czechoslovakia, East Germany, Australia, Belgium, Luxembourg, Denmark, New Zealand, Ireland, Britain, and Austria.

When it is noted that the United States consumption of both wines and ardent spirits hovers around the 2 gallon per capita figure, the truly dominant role of beer emerges. Since malting is the first step in the preparation of most liquors and liqueurs, the importance of this ancient art cannot be overstated.

*H*ere's to a long life and a merry one,
A quick death and an easy one,
A pretty girl and a true one,
A cold beer—and another one.
Anonymous

SOURCE MATERIALS

The nearly universal source material for brewing today is barley malt because of its ease of transportation from areas where it grows abundantly. In most cases, it is supplemented with other less expensive grains, such as rice, corn, wheat, oats, and rye. Actually, barley will mature nearly everywhere in the temperate zone where the palm tree and the grape will not survive. It withstands severe winters and often provides more than one cropping.

Its ancient predecessor was called *hordium spontaneum*. This spontaneous grass may well have been the first grain cultivated by man and remains today one of his most useful cultivars. In *Brewing* (1943), Hind speculates that "barley was the predominant cereal of the ancient world; the basis of barter and exchange in Chaldea 3,000 to 5,000 years before Christ." And from the Brothwells' *Food in Antiquity* (1969) we learn that "barley and wheat are the cereals that occur most persistently in Mesopotamia and Egyptian archeological sites, and they appear to have been introduced into Europe together." Rye and oats seem to have been treated as secondary grains. Only in the Orient did another grain dominate early brewing; rice provided the plant starch for Oriental alcohol beverages.

The ubiquitous sources of brewing starch—barley, wheat, corn and rice—symbolize this enormous, international enterprise.

Here is barley ready to be harvested.

Today world production of barley exceeds 2½ billion bushels annually. As the largest brewing nation, the United States emerges also as the largest grower, although half of the domestic crop of over 400 million bushels ends up in the animal feed box. In addition to the brew kettle, malted barley finds its way into most other distilled liquors and into a host of foods as a flavoring.

In brewing, both the two-row and the six-row varieties of the grain are used with approximately 25 percent of the production from the American two-row type. The rows are determined by the number of flowers that form the barleycorns after fertilization. The dominance of the six-row is natural since it thrives as a dry land crop with heavy plantings in the Midwest and the Dakotas. The two-row variety is more heavily cultivated in the less arid lands of Washington, Oregon, Idaho, Montana, and Colorado. Europeans still favor the two-row varieties. Both are relatively low in nitrogen, allowing maximum release and conversion of the sugars. The two-row, while richer in starch content, is lower in enzyme concentrations. No matter which variety is used, barley malts provide the essential head, flavor, and body in brews.

While there is some controversy about the use of other cereals and adjuncts in the production of American brews, it is only natural that producers in corn (see fig. 14.1) and cereal-rich America have turned to these lighter, less flavorful sources, particularly as consumers, over the past half century, began to favor lighter, more subtle tastes and flavors. Economy results from practicality and, so long as less expensive grains meet the popular tastes, it is probable that American brewers will continue to utilize these other grains for their popular beers while using more traditional and malty mashes for their super-premium offerings which compete directly with the growing flood of imported beers.

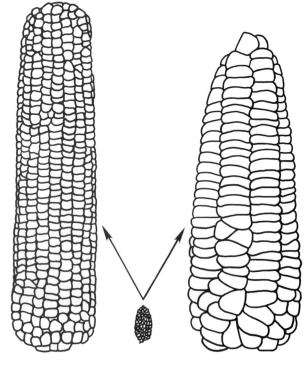

Figure 14.1 Just how far the industrial and agricultural revolutions have taken us can be visualized by comparing the modern cornbelt dent ear (left) *and the Peruvian flour corn ear* (right) *with the minuscule primitive maize ear from about 5500* B.C. *found in the Bat Cave* (center).

One of the largest members of CAMRA adhering to the ancient pure ale production methods is Samuel Smith's of Tadcaster, England.

One group in Britain called CAMRA, the Campaign for Real Ale, is comprised of 150 branches with over 30,000 enthusiasts who are promoting a return to naturally produced beers like the German Rheinhcitsgebot. However, they are fighting an uphill battle because even in the land of Ale nine out of ten pints are made with modern production methods. There are, however, such brews as the popularly imported Samuel Smith Old Pale Ale which fulfill the desires of CAMRA.

Cereal Adjuncts

A variety of cereal adjuncts or ancillary sources of sugar for fermentation are employed in modern brewing, often constituting up to 40 percent of total material. Not only do these additives cost less, they also tend to produce lighter, paler, and snappier beers more in keeping with popular tastes. Prior to purchase by the brewery, a number of the grains are processed into flakes not unlike popular breakfast cereals. Others come in the natural state and must be boiled to gelatinize the starch in advance of brewing.

While some of these other cereals also contain malting enzymes, the early development of barley for brewing came about because of the high concentration of the amylase enzymes needed for the conversion of their own and the adjunct

starches to sugar as well as the protease enzymes to reduce protein concentrations. Besides rice, oats, and wheat, a number of corn forms are used including grits, refined grits, and meal. Similarly, brewing syrups were introduced toward the end of the last century because they are directly fermentable and can provide desirable taste characteristics.

Hops

One of the grandest and most fortuitous marriages in nature has to be that of the brew and the hops. *Humulus lupulus* was known to ancient civilization but attained its enduring destiny in central Europe in the middle of the thirteenth century. In fact, its addition to common brews of that period created the distinction between continental beer and English ales.

Hops were cultivated and perhaps even used in wines and brews from very early times, as Jackson (1977) reports:

Hops were known to the early civilizations, and Pliny's study of natural history mentions them as a garden plant. He knew the hop as a plant whose young shoots were eaten in spring—like asparagus—and this custom is still sometimes observed in areas where it is grown. Apparently the hop grew wild among willows "like a wolf among sheep," and thus the Romans

One of the world's oldest techniques for producing top-fermenting, clear pale ale finds new application around the world in the manner of the experimental boutique wineries. Here are three examples. Brewing at Belhaven originated with English monks in the fifteenth century, yet even today the brewery uses pure barley malt, hops, yeast and syrup. The hops are added to the casks which are sent to the taverns. In faraway Australia, Cooper claims to follow the Queen's College procedures dating from 1340 with no filtration but natural carbonation occurring in the bottle. Finally, in

1976, Jack McAuliffe chose to relocate the old Albion Brewery, begun in San Francisco in 1875, a bit to the north in the Sonoma wine country. This land was originally named New Albion, or New England, by Sir Francis Drake, and his famous Golden Hinde appears on McAuliffe's label. Also of pure mult without additives, New Albion Ale uses top-fermenting yeast and eschews filtration or pasteurization, allowing the carbonization to occur naturally in the aging bottle. The new brews and ales are things to behold, and to quaff!

called it *Lupus salictarius*. This was the origin of its botanical name, *Humulus lupulus*. The ancients may have used hops in beer. Records of the Jews' captivity in Babylon refers to a *sicera* (strong drink) *ex lupulis confectam* ("made from hops"). This drink [presumably] prevented leprosy.

Wherever it began, the practice of hopping European beers eventually gained foothold in Britain, and by the sixteenth century, the hop plant was accepted as the essential flavoring and stabilizing agent, no matter what the brewing method. Hind explains hops' particular advantages in *Brewing*. "No substance is known to meet the need of a preservative so well as certain constituents of the resins of hops, which insure the soundness and stability of beer, without danger to health or detriment to the yeast."

Hops are a perennial plant, emerging each year from root stumps in a manner not unlike that of grape shoots. The shoots climb wires or strings attached to 12–20 foot high trellises. Mechanically harvested today, the cones are separated from the leaves and stems and are sent to a kiln called an *oasthouse*. There they are spread 18 to 24 inches deep and covered with cloth. It takes about six hours for the blowing heat to dry out the cones which are transferred to another house for cooling. The finished product is sent directly to the brewery or to a processing plant to be made into pellets.

It is the cone-shaped flower of the female hop which contains the natural tannins, resins, and essential oils, particularly the bitter alpha acid called *humulon* and the beta resin called

lupulon. These constituents provide the unique chemistry of brews, including the desired bitterness and antiseptic preservation.

The Water

Water is the major ingredient in beer, as it is in wine, the difference being that it must be *added* during the production of beer. Therefore, breweries through the centuries have been located near sources of pure water. For example, the famous Czechoslovakian Pilsen brewery was established in 1842 near artesian wells which contain water almost devoid of calcium. Contemporary brewers who do not have access to such waters chemically treat polluted waters to remove impurities and undesirable minerals. Many major brewers claim that local waters impart uniqueness to their brews, but this is a vanishing tradition as major breweries begin to decentralize their production facilities.

Yeasts

Nothing in the entire process is more closely guarded and cultivated than brewer's yeast. According to Jackson (1977), the earliest fermentations occurred naturally because of airborne yeasts.

The earliest brewers merely permitted this fermentation to happen naturally, and hoped that this

Skilled artisans tie the cords on the tall trellises based on seven-foot squares, while workers below bury the cord ends and other workers follow behind them planting shoots from last year's crop. As in the grape industry, Washington hop planters do not trust seeds. Growing as much as a foot a day during the summer, the mature hops follow the sun in a clockwise pattern around the

cords. If started the wrong way, the plant unfurls and begins over the right way. Harvested by tractors with huge gondolas, the plants are cut both top and bottom, and delivered to a stationary picker that shears the cones away from the gangly stems for drying in the kiln.

extremely unpredictable process would produce a drinkable brew. There is, though, evidence from early pictograms that they knew an outside agent was at work in the fermenting vessels, and that this substance could be recovered from the dregs of the brew. At least one archaeologist has claimed that some primitive form of yeast selection was being carried out in 1440 B.C. Since the Jews noted that they had time to bake only unleavened bread before they fled from Egypt, it follows that they knew how to leaven it.

The Dutch scientist Anton van Leeuwenhoek first isolated a single yeast cell and observed it through a microscope

in 1680, but 200 years transpired before the complete explanation came with Pasteur's research in the years 1857 to 1860. Emil Hansen of Carlsberg Brewery demonstrated conclusively that there are many strains of *saccharomyces;* the one he identified and cultured was named *Carlbergensis,* in honor of the brewery where he did his work. That strain is still used for bottom fermentations, while top fermenting is most often induced by the familiar wine yeast, *cerevisiae.*

Traditions die excruciatingly slowly, however, and the scientists did not quickly impress the proud and experienced brewers as Hind (1943) notes in *Brewing:* "the application of scientific instruments in breweries came comparatively late and it was not until 1760 that the breweries began to appreciate the value of the thermometer." As in wine fermentations, the yeast cake or froth produces endless strings of billions of fungus cells which secrete the familiar enzymes necessary to catalyze the biochemical conversion of sugar to ethanol and carbon dioxide.

MALTING

To understand brewing requires an understanding of malting. The first step in the brewing process involves the conversion of starches to fermentable sugars. This is begun by steeping the carefully sorted rock-hard barley kernels in large tanks of heated water. When the grains absorb enough to be 45 percent water, germination is induced (see fig. 14.2). The endosperms multiply, releasing the previously encased amylase enzymes, including diastase, protease, and maltase, which convert the starches and proteins. Within a week, shoots and rootlets appear, fed by the new sugars called maltose.

The trick is to terminate the growth at the precise moment when the maximum starch conversion has been achieved, before the rootlets consume much of the new sugar solids. This termination occurs under intense heat in a kiln or oven. Usually, 140° F is applied as a minimum, and the heat rises to as high as 230° F for browned or burned malts. Naturally, the moisture drops, with a goal of no more than 4.5 percent water in finished malts. Moisture levels above this induce mold during storage.

*A*nd malt does more than Milton can,
To justify God's ways to man.
A. E. Housman

The malts destined for the light lagers will be malted at the lowest temperatures, and those designed to create the rich, burnt tastes of ales and stouts are exposed to the highest temperatures in the kiln. Sulfur is now used during drying to reduce the nitrosamine concentrations to safe levels. Because of the heavy investment in equipment and the technical skills involved, a separate malting industry has grown up in the United States. Few brewers prepare their own malts, preferring to purchase finished malts tailored to their special needs.

MASHING

There are two separate heatings in brewing, neither of which involve fermentation. That comes later. First, the sacks of malted barley that have been screened for cleanliness are dumped into huge grinders which produce a fine barley grist ready for mashing. At the same time, measured amounts of

Acrospire—
The Beginning of
Another Barley Plant

Barley Starch Changes to
Maltose Sugar Inside Seed

Rootlets
or Chits

Figure 14.2 *Germinated barley, now called green malt.*

grain adjuncts are prepared, and pure, clean water is heated to 170° F in the tun. With variations for particular brews, the grains and adjuncts are introduced into the nearly boiling water. In the intense heat, the malting process begins again, and the solids dissolve into a thick, creamy porridge.

The important enzymes in this process are the amylases (which convert the starches) and the proteases (which break down the proteins for clarity in the beer). The proteins dissolve into amino acids and peptides which constitute an important portion of the nutrients the working yeast needs for growth during the fermentation period. This whole mashing period is precisely controlled and totally automatic. The right periods of time for the conversion of each type of grain in the mash are predetermined as are the ideal temperatures for each step in the process.

When the conversion of sugars to fluid is accomplished, the brewer empties the mash tun through a serrated bottom or through a mash filter into a lautering tub. In German, the word *lauter* means "to make clear," and that is precisely what the product becomes at this time. The first surge of warm, sugary fluid, now called wort, flows easily from the tub. Successive washings or spargings with hot water release the maximum in wort from the now-spent grains. Brewers use the word *Plato*, as vintners use the word *Brix*, to signify the level of fermentable solids which have developed in the wort. While these steps are mostly automated today, every effort is made to produce the maximum of fermentable sugars.

There is a great deal of effort expended to recapture spent grains, called stillage, for cattle feed, a worldwide practice from time immemorial. Indeed, one of the tricks that revenue agents used during Prohibition in order to locate illegal stills was to

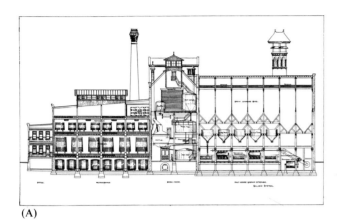

(A)

(B)

This is a compact, turn-of-the-century brewery in Buffalo. It used the Saladin malting system, a series of chambers with vented floors in which the barley was both steeped and dried. The malted grain was then ground, mashed and brewed in the other wings of

the same building (A). Today brewers purchase commercial malts developed to their specifications. In the modern Saladin malting chamber, shown at the Kirin Brewery, the stirring device advances on tracks (B).

look further wherever they observed well-fed cattle and hogs. For example, a subsidiary of the Schlitz Brewing Company, Murphy Products, markets over 20 million dollars' worth of stillage annually. Each barrel of beer produces 40 pounds of wet grain in a Schlitz process that eliminates the traditional drying for feed.

Another major brewer, Olympia from Washington State, is embarking on an imaginative program to eliminate a waste product and to meet the growing demand for petroleum substitutes. Following the dictates of a city directive to reduce its sewage discharge by 1982, the company constructed a still that will utilize alcohol produced from spent grains and other by-products with the goal of producing up to 700,000 gallons of gasohol-quality ethanol. The 190° proof ethanol will be denatured and sent to service stations.

In the lautering process, the goal of the brewer is to release about 14 percent sugar or 14 Plato. The Plato measurement represents the number of grams of sugar per 100 grams of wort. The first portion of the wort from the mash tun will contain as much as 20 Plato. The brewer then sparges or washes down the lauter tub with hot water to rinse out the remaining wort. This portion can contain as little as 2 Plato or 2 percent maltose sugar. These portions blend to an average of 14 Plato. The sugar to alcohol conversion rate in fermentation is about one-third. Thus, 14 Plato yields about 4 percent alcohol.

A certain amount of confusion remains about beer strength because of the various methods of identification on the container. In many states alcohol content is given, if at all, in terms of weight. In others, the measurement is by volume. The British, who measure strength by volume at 20° C, are not required to indicate the alcohol content on the container. Confused? So are most others except, of course, the brewers. This confusion provides one more argument for the adoption of the Gay-Lussac system of measuring all alcoholic beverages on a scale of 1 to 100, with each figure representing the exact percent by volume.

Find the twenty-six steeds aiding in the barley harvest in nineteenth-century eastern Washington.

BREWING

The second step in brewing seems to be the most misunderstood. In German, the word *brauen* means "to boil," and brewing thus refers to the procedure by which hops are literally boiled into wort to extract materials which provide long term stability and resistance to spoilage. In the 20,000 gallon copper brew kettle, the hops and wort boil from one to nearly three hours, depending upon the desired level of hopping. In addition to releasing the flavor of the hops, boiling the wort clarifies it of proteinaceous matter and readies it for fermentation. Many breweries today utilize compacted hop pellets because of ease of storage and handling while others still prefer the natural cones. Either way, the resin transfer creates the familiar bitterness in beer.

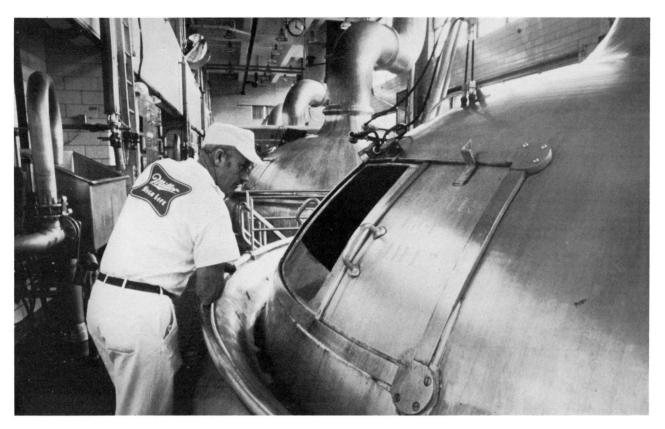

Hops being added to the boiling brew kettle.

In Kulmbach, Germany, an ancient amphora containing brewed material was unearthed, the earliest evidence of European brewing. Kulmbach remains an important brewing center where EKU Kulminator is made. Kulminator is said to be the world's strongest beer, reaching up to 14 percent in alcohol. Produced under the Rheinheitsgebot strictures, the brewing process is extended to develop the high alcohols shown by "In excess of 9.5% by weight" on the label.

International breweries such as Kirin maintain vast fermenting rooms.

An answer to the expensively housed fermenting tanks is seen in the UNI-TANKS developed in the late 1960s at Rainier Brewing Company in Seattle. This unique tank contains the fermenting, aging and carbonation steps, eliminating all of the costly transfers required in the conventional systems. A new tank farm under construction in Seattle is pictured in the open air behind the brewery buildings. Thirty breweries around the world now use UNI-TANKS.

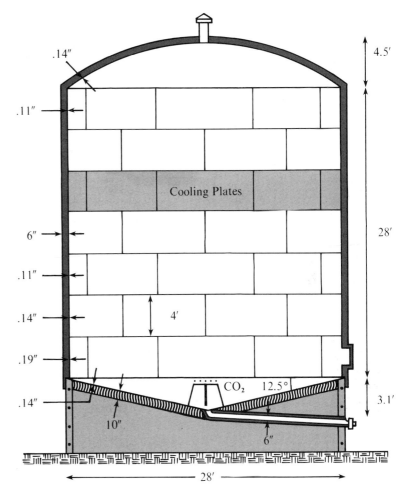

The boiling process also kills any bacteria in the wort and eliminates any further activity of the starch-converting enzymes. In sum, the boiling of the wort accomplishes a number of goals advantageous to the brewer: clarifying the beer of unwanted materials, imparting taste and character from the hops, and sterilizing the beer.

The clarified wort is separated from the hop material through an extractor called a hop-jack which has a slotted false base on which the hops settle. The extractor also removes other proteins known as trub which are precipitated during the boiling. The hot wort passes by a plate with cooling fluid to accomplish the rapid heat exchange necessary to cool the wort to fermentation temperature.

FERMENTATION

All of this highly technical and complicated preparation leads to the critical step of fermentation, the natural process set in motion by the Creator. Even here human ingenuity has added control and style, for there are two quite distinct classes of yeast and methods of fermenting beer. The breakthrough came by accident, then was developed by practice, when brewers began to observe more stable brews being produced by suspended or bottom fermentations and in cooler conditions. Jackson (1977) describes this turning point.

> It was eventually observed that, if beer could be kept at low temperatures, it did not go sour. This was possible where there were caves, and especially if natural ice was plentiful. It was also noticed that, if the casks of beer were stored in caves packed with ice, the yeast gradually settled to the bottom of the brew. The beer was therefore much clearer, and did not have to be "skimmed" before sale. This technique of *bottom fermentation* seems to have been first mentioned in 1420, in the minutes of the Munich town council. . . . The foothills of the Bavarian Alps were an ideal location for bottom-fermentation brewing.

With the introduction of artificial refrigeration before the turn of this century, the universal popularity of lager beer was assured. These lighter Bavarian, Bohemian, and Viennese brews became an accepted standard for the world.

However, now, as then, there are two distinct fermentation methods. The top-fermenting or surface yeasts create the tangy ales, and the bottom fermentations produce the lighter types. The traditional open fermenter produces a rich harvest of yeast which is regularly skimmed off like a fluffy cloud and sold as a by-product. The closed fermenter has the twin advantages of superior cleanliness and more rapid alcohol conversion. The distinction, however, is now blurring somewhat because ales are regularly produced in modern closed fermenters with suspended yeasts.

Once cooled, the wort is introduced into the fermenter as are the yeasts. Fermentation takes place for periods of up to two weeks. The Plato, or original gravity of the wort, de-

TABLE 14.4 Conversion Chart

	By Weight	By Volume	By Proof
Lager	3.5–3.8	4.375	8.75
Malt	4.5–4.8	5.625	11.25

termines the alcoholic strength of the beer. The German Erste Kulmbacher firm produces a whopper of a beer at 14 percent alcohol, which is above the average alcohol of table wine. This is accomplished by lengthening the fermentation process through the gradual addition of fermentable sugars. Normally, brews in the United States are marketed between 3 and 5 percent with the majority at the lower ranges. Some very rare strong beers go to 10 percent, but most malt liquors hover around the 5 percent mark. Also to meet the popular tastes of the day, the extremely popular beers are produced very light on the hops with plenty of cereal adjuncts to moderate the impact on the palate.

Since beer is the only alcoholic beverage merchandised in this country in which the alcohol can be cited by weight, confusion results. If you want to know for certain the *proof*, it is possible to convert alcohol by weight to proof (see table 14.4). This is accomplished by dividing the weight by .8 and multiplying that answer by 2.

LAGERING

The term lagering comes from the German *lagern* which means "to cellar" or "to store." Thus lagering is a period of resting similar to aging of wine. The lagering of beer enables carbon dioxide in the brew to bind with the fluid in a manner similar to that of wine made by *méthode champenoise*. In addition, the undesirable solids are literally precipitated, again not unlike the three weeks of cold filtering in the wine cellars in advance of bottling. A number of vital objectives of conditioning and finishing are achieved during this resting period in addition to the flavor enhancement of the beer.

Some breweries also induce a secondary fermentation during this two- to six-week lagering period. Called kräusening, it involves the introduction of new, partially fermented wort which induces a secondary fermentation similar to that in sparkling wine. As with the wines, these kräusened beers maintain more tightly bound, smaller carbon gas bubbles.

Light and Clean Is Best

Much as with wine, the demand in today's market is decidedly for clean, bright, and effervescent brews. Filtering, largely by the milipore filters, is, therefore, critical to continued customer acceptance despite the influx of heavier, malty brews from around the globe. In unique circumstances, particularly in Britain, beers are kegged in the natural state—unfiltered, unfined, unpasteurized, and without sulfur dioxide. These are the

Lager cellars are usually huge refrigerated rooms with gleaming stainless steel aging tanks. At Budweiser, a worker is shown in the unique step of feeding beechwood chips into the tanks which kräusen *the aging beer.*

rare and flavorful brews that CAMRA seeks as the standard, but they are the exception and not the rule anywhere.

The predominant number of beers are fined, filtered, pasteurized, lightly carbonated at bottling, and sent on their way to the market with a reasonable shelf life. About fifteen minutes are required for the leisurely trip the bottles and cans make through the pasteurizer which reaches about 140° F at the center, a sufficient temperature to kill the microorganisms capable of growing in the beer.

In American brewing, the exception to this heat exchange lies in the draft and kegged beer for on-premise consumption. While some are flashed momentarily with steam, most keg beers reach the market fresh and unpasteurized, a delight to the discerning customer. About 11 percent of the total production in the United States is draft.

Polishing

During the polishing step, a number of stabilizing additives may be introduced. Gum arabic and peptones help maintain the beads. Alginates are employed as foam stabilizers. Proteases dissolve particles, preventing haze (or cloudiness). Anti-oxidants such as ascorbic acid and sodium bisulfate provide longer shelf life. Caramel or invert sugar and pigmentations balance the color and sheen. Acetic acid, grapefruit oil, juniper, licorice, and a number of acids create desirable taste complexity. While some brewers use no additives, it is fair to say that these and other chemicals are acceptable and part of modern food-processing (see table 14.5). While the purist may be aghast, the vitality in the marketplace affirms the support of the consumer—the ultimate judge.

TABLE 14.5 Chemical Constituents of Beers

Component	Unit	Range	Lager, Avg	Malt Liquor, Avg	Ale, Avg	Bock, Avg	Stout, Avg	Danish, Avg	Dutch, Avg	German, Avg
Carbon dioxide	%	0.45–0.55	0.51	0.50	0.51	0.49	0.50	0.50	0.52	0.49
Fluoride	ppm	0.1–0.9	0.5		0.1					
Hydrogen sulfide	ppm	T–0.10	0.01	0.02	0.03			0.02	0.01	0.02
Phosphate	ppm	50–350	150							
Sulfur dioxide	ppm	1–20	4.9	5.4	5.0		6.0	4.8	4.0	5.0
Calcium	ppm	20–70	40		64	60				
Copper	ppm	T–0.40	0.16	0.18	0.15			0.10	0.07	0.17
Iron	ppm	T–0.64	0.10	0.13	0.16			0.07	0.13	0.19
Magnesium	ppm	50–300	200			52				
Potassium	ppm	130–1040	400			420				427
Sodium	ppm	68–550	70							
Methyl alcohol	ppm	0								
Ethyl alcohol	%(vol)	2.9–7.5	4.84	6.41	4.73	5.73	6.97	5.10	4.75	5.61
Ethyl alcohol	%(wt)	2.3–6.0	3.87	5.14	3.79	4.59	5.60	4.08	3.80	4.49
Higher alcohols	ppm	42–76	60							
Diacetyl	ppm	0.03–1.00	0.12	0.20	0.16			0.10	0.08	0.09
Acetaldehyde	ppm	2.3–19.5	9.1							
pH		3.90–4.70	4.34	4.41	4.42	4.32	4.00	4.32	4.35	4.52
Lactic acid	%	0.08–0.50	0.13	0.15	0.11	0.21	0.48	0.14	0.15	0.17
Total carbohydrate	%	2.1–8.3	5.0		4.15	3.42				
Hexoses	%		1.25	1.26	1.52	1.92	1.13	1.22	1.12	1.35
Total esters	ppm	23–55	40							
Tannins	ppm	100–385	211	199	192			185	270	295
Isohumulones	ppm	6–40	22	11	20			25	27	30
Protein	ppm	630–6160	3160	3700	3350	5700	5200	2650	2850	3930
Amino acids	ppm		210							
Ammonia	ppm	5–40								
Thiamine	µg/l	20–60	50							42
Riboflavin	µg/l	300–1200	500			250				249
Pantothenic acid	µg/l	400–900	500			550				
Pyridoxine	µg/l	400–900	600			592	770			470
Nicotinic acid	µg/l	5000–20,000	10,000			6340				8500
Biotin	µg/l	0–15	5							
Total solids	%	2.79–6.10	4.53	3.87	4.80	6.04	4.98	4.09	4.06	4.59

Source: Reproduced with permission from Leake, C. D. and Silverman, M.: ALCOHOLIC BEVERAGES IN CLINICAL MEDICINE. Copyright © 1966 by Year Book Medical Publishers, Inc., Chicago, 19.

TABLE 14.6 Sales of Leading United States Brewers (Thousands of Barrels)

Brewer	1960	1965	1970	1975	1980	1981	Average Annual Compound Growth Rate[a] 1960–1970	1970–1975	1975–1980	Percent Change 1980–1981
Anheuser-Busch	8,500	11,841	22,202	35,200	50,160	54,500	10.1%	9.7%	7.3%	8.6
Miller	2,377	3,667	5,150	12,862	37,300	40,300	8.0	20.1	23.8	8.0
Jos. Schiltz	5,694	8,607	15,129	23,279	14,954	14,305	10.3	9.0	−8.5	−4.3
G. Heileman	646	1,011	3,000	4,535	13,270	13,965	16.6	8.6	24.0	5.2
Pabst	4,738	8,219	10,517	15,669	15,091	13,465	8.3	8.3	−0.8	−10.8
Adolph Coors	1,907	3,560	7,277	11,950	13,779	13,261	14.3	10.4	2.9	−3.8
Stroh	2,075	2,402	3,276	5,133	6,161	6,194	4.6	9.4	3.7	0.4
Olympia	1,497	2,461	3,379	5,577	6,091	5,708	8.5	10.5	1.8	−6.3
Genesee	805	1,310	1,475	2,200	3,600	3,625	6.2	8.3	10.3	0.7
Falstaff	7,083	7,940	6,636	7,480	3,901	3,596	−0.6	2.4	−12.2	−7.8
C. Schmidt	1,802	2,361	3,040	3,330	3,625	3,300	5.4	1.8	1.7	−9.0
F&M Schaefer[b]	3,202	4,600	5,749	5,881	3,572	2,939	6.0	0.4	−9.5	−17.7
TOTAL	40,326	57,979	86,830	133,096	171,504	175,158	8.0	8.9	5.2	2.1
Total/Domestic	87,900	100,400	121,900	148,600	173,300	176,700	3.3%	4.0%	3.1%	2.0%

Source: IMPACT (1 April 1982), 3.
Note: Includes tax-free withdrawals.

[a]Based on unrounded data.
[b]Purchased by Stroh in 1981.

In contrast to other ferments, beer pasteurization is absolutely essential to the shelf life of high volume beers which are transported around the world from major brewing centers. Hundreds of bottles and cans are processed by huge machines such as those at the Oranjeboom brewery.

Packaging

The growing consolidation of the production of beer by fewer and fewer companies results largely from the efficiency of production and bottling equipment. For example, major firms can bottle 1,200 units a minute compared to 200 or 300 in the small plant. This efficiency can be translated into more funds for advertising and promotion, a vital element in the highly competitive metropolitan markets (see table 14.6).

The breakthrough of monumental importance in packaging came in 1935 with the introduction of metal cans. About a quarter of today's production is canned, although the environmentalist moves from state to state, hoping to abolish through relentless pressure, the often carelessly discarded container. It can be safely predicted that the fight against the can will continue for decades to come. Where beer is sold in the local market exclusively, as in many portions of the United Kingdom, there is widespread use of the standard 10-ounce glass bottle.

Oddly enough, while impervious to light, the cans are more vulnerable to the environment because they have a much higher heat conductivity level than glass. One test concluded that the aluminum can receives as much as 250 times the heat from the air as glass, but that fact would hardly be accepted by the two-fisted tavern patron for whom there is no earthly respite to match that cold can of beer.

TYPES OF BREWS

Throughout the world, there are thousands of distinct brews from hundreds of fermentable starches. Various types of brews, both domestic and imported, are generally available in major metropolitan areas (see table 14.7). One beer of immense historic importance is pulque, produced throughout Mexico for

TABLE 14.7 Types of Brews

Brew	Description
Lager	Most popular beer in the U.S. Light amber, effervescent, usually low in alcohol, averaging 136 calories. 3 to 4 percent alcohol.
Light lager	Even lighter through elimination of dextrine in order to lower calories, low alcohol, high barley malt for taste, 85 to 95 calories on the average.
Pilsner lager	Brewed in the manner of famous Bohemian lager noted for pronounced but pleasant hop character.
Bock	Utilizes darker roasted malts and much sweeter finish—deep in color and large in body.
Malt liquor	Nomenclature for higher alcohol in the U.S.; usually above 5 percent, often more malty and bitter taste.
Ale	Formerly top-fermented brew with aromatic finish, fuller body, and pronounced hop bitterness. Higher alcohol.
Porter	British ale with somewhat heavier body, slightly sweet finish, and more malty character. 5 percent alcohol or more.
Stout	Very dark ale also produced in England— very sweet and very strong on the hops.
Near beer	Beer with no more than .5 percent alcohol, light and cereal-like.
Steam beer	Sharp, hoppy beer from pure barley malt, bottom-fermented with high CO_2 from second fermentation in bottle at very high temperatures with steam added at 50 lbs. per square inch.
Weiss beer	Pure wheat malt, top-fermented like ale with pronounced CO_2 from bottle fermentation.
Sake	Rice beer, high in alcohol, light in body, and usually tart like a wine.

Highlights

- Brews were made long before recorded history and were a staple in the diet of many early peoples.
- Early brews, like early wines, were often heavily flavored.
- Barley is the main grain used in brewing although many others are also used, such as corn, rice, millet, oats, and wheat.

- Malting is the critical process by which enzymes change the grain starches to sugars which can ferment.
- Hops are universally used as a preservative and flavoring agent in brewing.
- The trend in recent years to light, lagered brews is contrasted to a new preference for more flavorful types.

Like huge milking machines, keg fillers still require human hands—in this case to hammer in the bung. At Budweiser, the filler operates at about 360 kegs per hour.

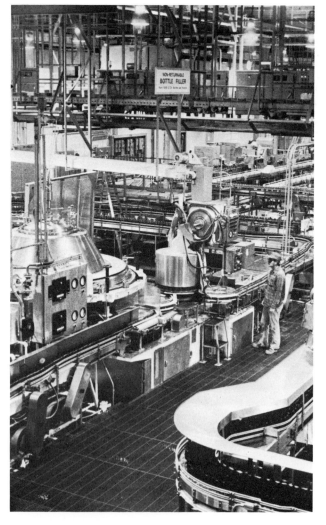

Bottle and can fillers are dazzling in terms of speed and efficiency.

The Abbey of Orval, founded in 1070, is the site of the famous thrice-brewed Trappist beer from Orval Monastery Brewery in southeast Belgium. The name Orval derives from an ancient tale in which a fish supposedly returned a lost wedding band to a princess. In gratitude she caused the monastery to be built and to be called the Golden Valley. Trappist monks still rise at 4:00 A.M. each day to tend the brewery. A full-bodied, well-aged heavy ale, Orval remains unfiltered, tasting of the yeast that made it.

hundreds of years. The sugar source, a native cactus, produces an acidic, milky beer, the favorite of the common man. Commercial beers are now competing with this traditional favorite.

Any listing but scratches the surface and is even inadequate to cover the diversity of styles within the categories, particularly in the older, heavy-brewing regions of Europe. For example, within the literally hundreds of brewing traditions in Germany alone, there can be said to be three major brewing styles. Munich beer has always been appreciated for its soft, malty brews. In contrast, the Pilsen has the image of a lighter, peppery, hop-accented brew. Finally, the Dortmund style is considered to be something of a compromise between the Munich and Pilsen.

Michael Jackson, in *The World Guide to Beer* (1977), appropriately sums up the magnificent diversity of brews: "There was once a famous advertising slogan which proclaimed, quite simply: 'Beer is best.' It didn't say which."

Brew-tasting Procedures 15

*T*he tasting of brews requires the same deliberate process set forth previously for wines. The beers should be allowed to come nearly to room temperature to reveal the maximum in tastes. Equipment must be scrupulously clean because brews are extremely sensitive to contamination. One of the primary factors in judgment lies in the head or foam produced on pouring. The better brews maintain a frothy foam from three to five minutes, the best up to eight or ten minutes. Pour directly to the bottom of the glass to provoke the release of carbon dioxide and flavor constituents.

Many of the wine-tasting procedures also apply. Look for clarity as a positive factor, although many beers made with dark malts and those not pasteurized will naturally be somewhat hazy or cloudy. Learn to distinguish between the pale gold of light American lagers and the increasing brownness that extends almost to murkiness in the bock. These hues enhance enjoyment when properly appreciated.

The aromas in beers yield some of the same complexities found in wines, although many exist on subtle, sub-threshold levels. The pronounced maltiness and hoppiness which are altogether desirable characteristics combine to overpower the esters, such as the fruit esters (melons, pears, apricots, or apples) that emerge so insistently in white wines. However, the esters can be recognized with sufficient concentration. They contribute subliminally to the overall flavor, but can be immensely satisfying when perceived independently. Obviously, off smells foretell some taste corruption ahead. The pungent barley malt can also yield many aromas from a light, toasty aroma to a distinctively burnt finish. Use the same short, sharp intakes in the nostrils and patient evaluation for maximum success. For someone used to rapid beer quaffing, this slow and deliberate procedure seems unnatural but can be immensely rewarding. James Robertson describes some of the dominant flavors in brews and explains their chemical sources (see table 15.1).

TABLE 15.1 Flavor Constituents of Beer

Primary Flavor Constituents (intensity above 2.0 Flavor Units)
Ethanol
Hop bitter compounds (e.g., isohumulones)
Carbon dioxide
Specialty beer components
    Hop aroma compounds (e.g., humuladienone)
    Caramel-flavored compounds
    Esters and alcohols (high gravity beers)
    Short-chain acids
Defects
    2–trans-nonenal (oxidized, stale)
    Diacetyl 2–2, 3–pentanedione (fermentation)
    Hydrogen sulfide, dimethyl sulfide, etc. (fermentation)
    Acetic acid (fermentation)
    3–methylbutyl–2 enylthiol (light struck hops)
    Other (microbial infection)

Secondary Flavor Constituents (intensity 0.5–2.0 Flavor Units)
Volatile
    Banana esters (e.g., isoamyl acetate)
    Apple esters (e.g., ethyl hexanoate)
    Fusel oils (e.g., isoamyl alcohol)
    Aliphatic acids
    Ethyl acetate
    Butyric and isovaleric acids
    Phenylacetic acid
Nonvolatile
    Polyphenols
    Various acids, sugars, and hop compounds

Tertiary Flavor Constituents (0.1–0.5 Flavor Units)
2–phenethyl acetate
Isovaleraldehyde
Acetoin
Methional
Valerolactone

Other (less than 0.1 Flavor Units)
All remaining

Source: James D. Robertson, *The Connoisseur's Guide to Beer.* (Aurora, Ill.: Caroline House Publishers, Inc., 1982).

Robertson describes the common odors and flavors of beer in this way:

Pleasant herbal odors—aromatic hops which may give sensations of clover, verbena, sage, parsley, orange, orange peel.

Vinousness (winelike quality)—presence of esters, an organic compound formed by the reaction of an acid and an alcohol. While it is considered an advantage in an ale, it is not attractive in a pilsner.

Leather, Paper, Cardboard, Woodiness—oxidation, exposure of the brew to oxygen.

Soapiness—Octanoic acid (or Caprylic acid), a fatty acid which may take on primary animal tones or a rancid character.

Cheese—Isovaleric acid resulting from the oxidation of isopentyl alcohol (isopentyl alcohol is also called isoamyl alcohol or simply amyl alcohol).

Banana—Isoamyl acetate, an acetic ester of amyl alcohol from fusel oil, called also amyl acetate, banana oil, or pear oil.

Milk—lactic acid, resulting from bacterial fermentation of starch, molasses or sugar.

Green apple—acetylaldehyde or dehydrogenated alcohol, reactive organic compound intermediate in the state of oxidation. Undergoes self-esterification when heated.

Medicinal—Phenolic, soluble acidic compound derived from actions of a phenol with an aldehyde.

Corn—Dimethyl sulfide, a compound containing two methyl groups in the molecule.

Butterscotch, butter—Diacetyl (or biacetyl), a diketone with a buttery flavor; it is the flavor in butter, a contributing flavor in coffee and tobacco, and is used to synthetically flavor margarine.

Rubber boot, skunk—presence of mercaptan, a compound analogous to alcohols and phenols but that contains sulfur in place of oxygen.

Nail polish remover—Acetone (or dimethyl ketone). In beer it is probably caused by bacterial fermentation of corn mash.

Rancid butter—Butyric acid resulting from oxidation of normal butyl alcohol or butyl aldehyde or by fermentation of molasses. May also be caused by the action of anerobic bacteria on lactic acid.

Wet basement—Butyric fermentation or oxidation.

In the mouth, a greater chewiness or body is found than in wines. The hops, the malt, the profusion of carbon dioxide gas, and the persistent astringency from the hops make beers quite flavorful. While sweetness comes through very often, acid is rarely detected because of the intensity of the other elements. However, as with wine, acidity is essential for the sharp fruitiness, and its absence results in flat, insipid beer. The alcohol in most domestic and import brews remains a minor factor—most are in the 3.5 to 4 percent alcohol range in which

the normal hotness or sweetness of alcohol is subliminated. Some malt liquors or ales contain 5 percent alcohol or more, yielding definite alcohol overtones and mouth feel. Many brews are stabilized with sulfur dioxide, as well as with citric and

TABLE 15.2 Brew Tasting

Brew	General Style	Suggested Brand
Bottom-Fermented Lagers		
Lagers	Light body, bright, clear, golden color, some malt in nose and slight hop flavor	Rainier Budweiser Kirin Carta Blanca
Light lagers	Light body, medium carbonation, touch of maltiness, pale gold, slight head	Rainier Light Miller Lite
Export	Clean, malty nose, light but full flavor, golden sauterne color, very dry, more alcohol than lager or pilsner	Cold Spring Export Lolland-Falsters Danish Export
Pilsner	Rich, clean, fresh flavor, greenish golden hue, highly hopped flavor	Diekirch Pilsner Pilsner Urquell Pinkus Pils
Top-Fermented Ales		
Pale ale	A burnt molasses nose and caramel in palate, strong tang of hops, golden in color with hint of copper, full-bodied, full assertive flavor	Samuel Smith Pale Ale Bass Whitbread
Brown ale	Full round body, dry/sweet palate with hint of honey, pleasant balance of hops, slight reddish hue in color	Vaux Double Maxim New Castle Brown Ale
Copper ale	Winey quality with citrus undertones, complex flavor, highly acidic yet full-bodied	Rodenbach Belgium Beer
Bottom-Fermented Dark Beer		
Bavarian smoked beer (specialty)	Dark amber color, unequivocally hickory smoke taste, full, heavy body, long finish	Kaiserdom Rauchbier
Top-Fermented Dark Beer		
Stout	Roasty malt nose, dark brown in color, creamy head, rich, thick hearty body, should have a hint of molasses in taste if brewed correctly	Guinness Stout Koff Imperial Stout
Specialty		
Sake	Light body, intense nose reminiscent of grain, mellow and fruity	Chiyoda (Suntory)

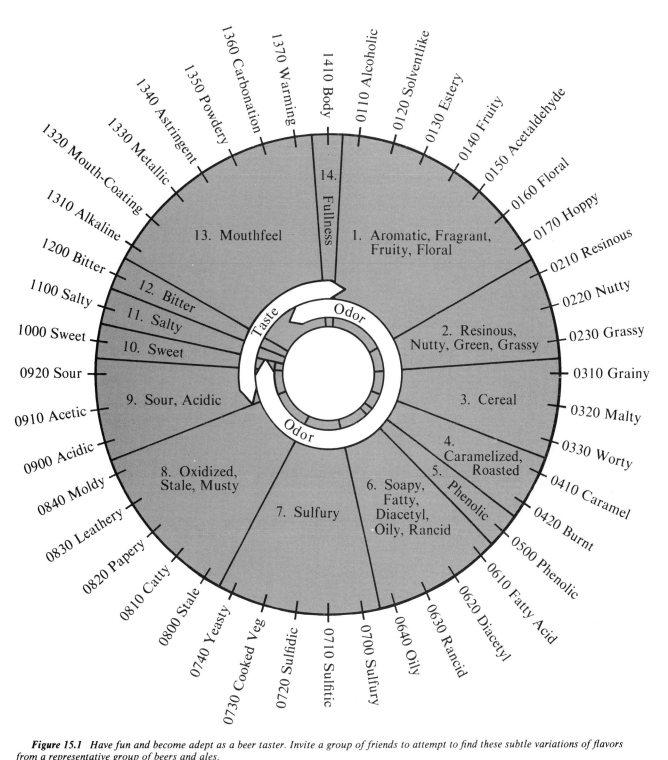

Figure 15.1 *Have fun and become adept as a beer taster. Invite a group of friends to attempt to find these subtle variations of flavors from a representative group of beers and ales.*

Charles Finkel who is the owner of Merchant du Vin, a national firm that imports fine brews, acted as consultant and adviser on the selection and descriptions for our brew tasting.

tannic acid, for microbiological stability, but the most sensitive of palates would be required to recognize the sulfur burnt-match smell and taste.

Michael Jackson, in *The World Guide to Beer* (1977), provides some colorful adjectives to this tasting process. He believes that the head should be *rocky,* that is, the froth should have high and uneven peaks that maintain themselves for a long period. The head should form a *lacework* on the inside of the glass as you consume the brew. Aside from the aroma, one should find *distinctive character,* the ultimate balance between the sweet fullness of the malt and the snappy accent of the hops.

Finally, that most distinctive of all brews, sake, should be tasted in a singular manner. While most sake is now consumed chilled in the fashion of an American white wine for which it is often mistaken, the traditional way of serving it is best. The small serving bottle is called a *tokkuri,* and the delicate cups into which it is poured are *sakazuki.* Best served mulled to about 100°F, slightly above body temperature, sake is generally served with small morsels of food. A great tradition surrounds this service. Sake cups are always filled to the brim, and the exchange of cups between persons is a symbol of great affection.

NATURAL FERMENTATIONS

This section concludes coverage of natural fermentations and their compoundings. Almost from the beginning of time, humans have expended enormous energy and exhibited both perspicacity and ingenuity to the end of assuring a continuing supply of various alcohols. Nothing on the horizon precludes continuing efforts toward that worthy goal. It is fitting to close this portion with a tribute from Dr. Lucia's *Wine and Your Well Being* (1971) with my emendation that his sentiments encompass not only wines, but brews and all the other concoctions and toddies created by the fecund human mind.

> With time, it is likely that other salutary attributes of wine will be made known. Nevertheless, the character of wine has not altered throughout the ages. Wine was born, not invented. The grape, with the bloom of yeast on its skin, contains all that is necessary to render the final vinous product perfect, even without the intervention of man. Strange to say, the miracle of fermentation is only partly understood even today, and the wine that emerges from it resists our complete analysis. Like any old friend, it continues to surprise us in new and unexpected ways.

Suggested Readings

Ade, George. *The Old Time Saloon: Not Wet—Not Dry, Just History*. New York: R. Long and R. R. Smith, Inc., 1931.
   The story of saloons in pre-Prohibition days.

Baron, Stanley. *Brewed in America: A History of Beer and Ale in the United States*. Boston: Little, Brown & Co., 1962.
   Our own love affair with brews.

Cochran, Thomas C. *The Pabst Brewing Co.: The History of an American Business*. New York: New York University Press, 1948.
   Interesting survey of one of the pioneer firms.

Hardman, Michael. *Beer Naturally*. London: Bergstrom and Boyle Books, Ltd., 1976.
   The stunning photographs by Thea Bergstrom make this book a must; a brief text outlines the complete beer story.

Hind, H. Lloyd. *Brewing Science and Practice*. New York: John Wiley & Sons, Inc., 1943.
   The basic textbook.

Jackson, Michael, ed. *The World Guide to Beer*. Englewood Cliffs, N.J.: Prentice-Hall, Inc., 1977.
   A beautifully illustrated, easily read coverage of brewing nations, one by one.

Robertson, James D. *The Connoisseur's Guide to Beer*. Aurora, Ill.: Caroline House Publishers, Inc., 1982.
   A splendid guide book through all the breweries of the world.
——. *The Great American Beer Book*. New York: Warner Books, Inc., 1980.

Vogel, Edward H., Jr.; Schwaiger, Frank H.; Leonhardt, Henry G.; and Merten, J. Adolf. *The Practical Brewer: A Manual for the Brewing Industry*. 2d ed. USA: Master Brewers Association of America, 1977.
   Technical information.

Weiner, Michael A. *The Taster's Guide to Beer: Brews and Breweries of the World*. London: Collier Macmillan Publishers, 1977.
   A compendium of historical and topical information about the major breweries of the world.

PART THREE

DISTILLED
BEVERAGES

The Distilling Process 16

The emergence of ardent spirits can be understood only in the context of several historical movements. The first was the opening up of the entire world to travel and conquest, which began during the High Renaissance, and of its resources to the relatively small populations of the times. In the era of exploration and acquisition Europeans amassed not only land but also an unbelievable wealth of foodstuffs. The second historical movement was the Industrial Revolution, the harnessing of mechanical energy to exceed the natural power of man and beast. These dynamic and still little understood periods in human history are discussed in *Consuming Passions: The Anthropology of Eating* (1980) by Farb and Armelagos:

> The fact is often ignored that the Industrial Revolution could not have taken place without the Agricultural Revolution that preceded it, and that was based on an increase in production due both to new crops from the Americas and to new methods of farming. Yields of foods were increased substantially by such simple techniques as the rotation of crops. . . . The selective breeding of cattle also greatly increased the yields of meat and milk. In such ways, what had been an inefficient system of agriculture was eventually replaced by large-scale mechanized farming that took on the character of modern industry.

Such innovations set the scene for many new experiences for the human animal—leisure and wealth to indulge the most arcane of spiritual and carnal appetites as well as trade routes leading to products that could satisfy both. Tannahill, in *Food*

> *T*he true water of life will come over in precious drops, which being rectified by three or four distillations will afford the wonderful quintessence of wine. We call it *aqua vitae*.
>
> ### Arnald de Vilanova
>
> *T*he popular mythology of alcohol is a vast and vehement book. It is also a book of massive durability. Almost every vision of alcohol that the human imagination has summoned up during some six thousand years of fascinated scrutiny may still be found among its pages.
>
> ### Berton Roueché

and History (1973), lists some of the significant imports which the Industrial Revolution made possible.

> The New World produced none of the traditional spices that had helped to stimulate the voyages of discovery. But it was to contribute to the diet of the Old World several new foodstuffs which were to be of the greatest importance in the centuries to come . . .

Terms

aguardiente Spanish for spirits.

akvavit, aquavit Scandinavian terms for light white spirits.

alcohol Ethyl alcohol created in fermentation.

aldehyde Flavor congener created in fermentation and distillation.

alembic A distilling pot.

bottled in bond Label guarantee of claim about proof and age (e.g., one hundred proof bourbon straight whiskey of at least four years aging).

bubble cap Device in patent still which allows the spirit vapors to rise through the plates.

congeners Generic term for the impurities such as esters, aldehydes, and fusel oils.

diastase Enzyme in malting barley which converts the starch to sugars.

esters Organic compounds that impart odors to spirits.

feints The same as tails—the congeners coming over after the middle liquors.

fusel oil The higher alcohols created in distillation, often found in the tails.

heads That portion of congeners which emerges first from the still; also called foreshots.

hydrometer Floating device to measure specific gravity of fluid—marked in alcohol units.

malting The germination of grain for spirit production, conversion of grain starches to sugars.

mash Moist grain in which the starches have been converted to maltose for fermentation.

middle liquors The portion separated from the heads and tails, from a second run through a still, the desired spirit.

oxidation The chemical process by which spirits decompose, essential in the aging process.

patent still Also called Coffey or Continuous Still, consisting of at least two columns with separating plates designed for continuous distilling.

plate The separating platform used in the patent stills on which the various congeners and liquors return to fluids.

pot still Also called alembic or *alambic*—the basic device for single batch distillation.

potable spirit Spirit fit for human consumption.

proof spirit In America a spirit of 100° proof contains 50% water and 50% ethyl alcohol; a spirit at 80° proof contains 40% alcohol, etc. Proof is always double the actual alcohol content.

schnapps German and Dutch term for spirits.

Basic distilling equipment, including hydrometer, depth gauges, casks and carboy, has changed little through the years.

The cooper's art has changed not at all since this engraving from the Industrial Revolution era, titled Tonnelier, by Patte in 1762.

To Europe came maize or Indian corn, to become a staple food in northern Spain, Portugal and Italy, and, later, in the Balkans. Potatoes, which, though an agent of disaster in Ireland, were to be a useful source of vitamin C to many other peoples. Chocolate, peanuts, vanilla, the tomato, the pineapple, "French beans," lima beans, the scarlet runner, red peppers, green peppers, tapioca and the turkey—all widened the horizons of the European cuisine.

The logical consequence of these slowly emerging riches was refinement and sophistication in eating as well as the ca-

pacity to support a growing population. And that is precisely what happened, as Farb and Armelagos (1980) indicate:

One phenomenon of modernization has been an increasingly rapid increase in population. In 1750 the total population of the world was probably about 750 million; by 1830 it had increased to a billion; by 1930 it was two billion, and by 1975 four billion. In other words, the human species needed millions of years to reach a population of a billion, but thereafter the second billion was added in only a hundred years, the third in thirty years, and the fourth in a mere fifteen years.

These authors distinguish between population growth as a result of medical advances and as a result of better nutrition, and they argue that the latter was the real key. The growth, and the seemingly endless supply of grains that supported it, provided the necessary ingredients for the development of distilled spirits which merely satisfied one more appetite, one not completely quenched by natural ferments.

Braudel (1981) traces the ups and downs of the availability of grain in three centuries. During the best of times, grain provided both food and drink.

> The triumph of bread arose because grain—and also alcohol made from grain, as a Polish historian has pointed out, thus vindicating the propensity of peasants in his country to drink and not only eat their grain—was the least expensive foodstuff in relation to its calorific content. In about 1750, it cost eleven times less than meat, sixty-five times less than fresh sea fish, nine times less than freshwater fish, six times less than eggs, three times less than butter and oil.

W̲e must recall that Nature's laws
Are generally sound.
And everywhere, for some good cause,
Some alcohol is found.
There's alcohol in land and tree,
It must be Nature's plan
That there should be, in fair degree,
Some alcohol in man.

Alan Herbert

DISTILLED SPIRITS IN HISTORY

The Saracen Umar ibn-al-Khaṭṭāb, the second Moslem caliph, conquered Egypt in A.D. 641. In a fit of gargantuan folly, he burned to the ground the magnificent Alexandrian library established about 300 B.C. by Ptolemy I. His reasoning? The Koran contained the sum of wisdom necessary for a venerable life! In those horrendous flames expired the collected wisdom of science and art, from east and west, including the origins of systems designed to separate substances through heat—distillation.

But although this extreme act destroyed forever the historical records of distillation and many other sciences, inferences about them can be drawn from bits and pieces found in other documents. An article in *Chemistry* (March 1968), dates the earliest known distilling vessel to the year 3500 B.C. The device is described as a simple double-rimmed pot, the outer ridge designed to collect heated vapors and oils. Historians generally agree that such stills were employed very early both for food preparation and for cosmetics. Morewood in his 1838 study traced the logical progression of distilling equipment as the Arab world gained ascendency:

> The trade of the East, which had long continued in the hands of the Egyptians, was in 640 transferred to the Saracens by the Caliph Omar [*sic*]. It is therefore more natural to infer that the Saracens had received through the Egyptians, a knowledge of the still from the inhabitants of India.

Throughout the early centuries of the Christian era, numerous references mention the process of distilling, but strangely, none connect that function with the history of wines and brews. Even earlier, Aristotle related the procedures for distilling sweet water from the salty sea. In fact, the word *distill* derives from the Latin *destillare* which means "to drip." In sum, there is no credible evidence that the best of minds had any intent to refine alcoholic beverages the way herbs, minerals, and oils were being distilled. This monumental discovery of the distillation of alcohol cannot be determined with certainty, but it probably occurred many years after Pliny at the end of the woeful Dark Ages.

It is not surprising that the discovery is credited to the Arab world. Aside from the capricious Caliph Umar, the Arabs nurtured and developed science in an aggressive and effective manner. Samuel Morewood (1838) offers proof of their collective intelligence: "In Spain, the Caliphs had formed a library of 600,000 volumes . . . Cordova, the capital of the Spanish Caliphs . . . gave birth to more than 300 writers and above seventy public libraries. . . ."

In science, art, and agriculture, the Arabs continued to mature during the dark years unlike Europeans whose societies were in disarray. Consolidating the knowledge of Greece, Rome, and Egypt, the Arabs broached new frontiers in both science and practice. In *Wine and Spirits* (1970), Marrison agrees with the consensus that distillation came into widespread practice for cosmetic and culinary ends since the Arabs in the time of Mohammed were prohibited from consuming alcohol in any form.

> At some unknown early date the Arabs had used distillation for extracting perfumes and had built a flourishing trade in these commodities, which were almost necessities for those who could afford them, in those unsanitary days. . . . By the twelfth century Salernus was writing about distillation, and a hundred years later Albertus Magnus gave a description of the process.

Pre-Arab References

That distilling flourished before the Arab surge in science and conquest is not in doubt. Greeks and Romans utilized heat to produce balsams, vegetable oils, sulfuric acid, gums, and resins. Three common techniques were employed: *distillatio per*

(A)

(B)

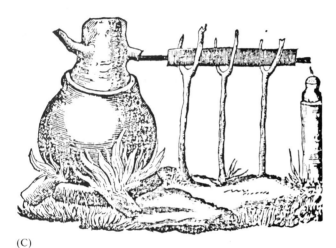

(C)

(D)

Simple distillation contrivances were pictured in 1838 by Samuel Morewood in his elaborate treatise on spirits. An operating still discovered ten years ago in Laos (A) bears striking functional resemblance to the Columbo still shown in Morewood (B). The Laotian still employed fireplace stones of hardened clay, a gourd

for the alembic or expansion chamber, bamboo piping (sealed with leaves) to the cooling pot and a teak cooling basin. The other two sketches from Morewood show stills used in the Georgian Islands (C) with ti-root beer and in Ceylon (D) with a rice mixture.

ascens, *distillatio per decensum,* and *distillatio per filtrum.* The scientists steamed, dripped, and filtered out the elements they prized as we do today. In *A Short History of the Art of Distillation* (1948), Forbes writes of the acquisitions of the Arab world:

> Pharmacy and other branches of medicine could flourish and the Arabian knowledge of commodities was much larger than that of older generations. In their hands the distillation of water, vinegar, rose oil and other perfumes and essential oils grew to become a true industry.

The chemistry of distillation is first found in a rambling work entitled *Liber Investigationis Magisteri* written by the Arab Geber (Jābir ibn-Ḥayyān) sometime before 1050. The first use of the term *alembic* is attributed to another Arab by the name of Al-Razi, and the Greek root for *alembic* means "earthen jar or vessel."

A liquor vessel found with the Laotian still, with a leaf stopper, unchanged in style over hundreds of years.

For a couple of hundred years, alchemist monks and physicians experimented with Geber's new distillate, leading to what was probably the first systematic application of the technique in the Medical School in the southern Italian town of Salerno, long a center for the chemical sciences. It was in Salerno about 1100 that ardent spirits became part of the medical pharmacopoeia. Braudel affirms Salerno as the probable site of the initial development of western distilling, citing it as the center of medical research. Soon after, or perhaps at about the same time, the Spanish winemakers discovered alcohol's wondrous capacity for stabilizing Andalusian wines. H.B. Weiss in *The History of Applejack* (1954) confirms the Salerno connection:

> In the twelfth century a recipe for making alcohol, used by Salernitan [*sic*] apothecaries, said, "On mixing a pure and very strong wine with three parts of salt and heating it in the vessels destined for that purpose, there is obtained an inflammable water which burns without consuming the material on which it is placed."

A highly refined spirit would be required for such flaming.

In the early thirteenth century, Albertus Magnus wrote about the most important method of alchemy in *De Secretus Mulierum,* there describing recipes for aqua ardens: "When wine is sublimed like rose-waters, a light inflammable liquid is obtained." This links the process with the quite common herbal distillation. Forbes (1948) places these interrelated discoveries in perspective in *Short History of the Art of Distillation.* "The discovery of mineral acids and somewhat earlier (eleventh or twelfth century) that of *alcohol* may be said to mark the beginning of a new stage in history, the transition of the old and the new chemistry."

Widespread Experimentation

Another pioneer of distilling, Raymond Lull (1235?–1315), actually believed that the ancients knew of the properties of heated wine but kept them secret. Whatever the merit of such conjecture, once the secret was out, the techniques for the production of palatable essences, at least for laboratory purposes, developed quite rapidly. Lull was a romantic character who studied and taught Arabic and was, therefore, familiar with the works of Geber and other scholars. Lull also invented the shorthand of using letters to refer to chemical properties. His contemporary, Arnald de Vilanova, is credited with naming *aqua vitae,* after separating it from the hundreds of essences then commonly distilled, ranging from water to rose oil. As far away as China, a treatise written in A.D. 1120, *Pei-Shan Chin Ching,* covered the techniques of distillation. This suggests that the application of distillation to wine, while incredibly late in coming to alcoholic beverages, was a very old technique in the science laboratory and in the production of commercial oils and essences.

DISTILLATION.

In 1887 Julius Bien produced this hand-colored lithograph depicting the history of distilling.

What Lull, Arnald, and their contemporaries really contributed were the techniques of *rectification* which, by reduction of the water carried over to less than 35 percent, produced much purer spirits, those capable of flaming. Forbes (1948) records the quick surge in the development of distillation techniques.

> On the other hand, many products came to be distilled on an industrial scale as they profited from the growth of the mining and metallurgical industry in the early sixteenth century, which was in turn stimulated by rising capitalism. Hence many technological handbooks were published in which the manufacture of mercury mineral acids, sulphurs and similar compounds by distillation on a large scale were described.

In the three hundred years from the early Italian and Spanish alchemic labs to the birth of the industrial sciences, very little occurred in the technology of distillation of liquors. The production of hard liquors had a secondary role simply because it was not yet of commercial significance. Spirits were largely medicinal and a curiosity. Alcohol was derived from grain and fruit. Wines and beers were the potable alcohols. Forbes distinguishes between rural and urban practices thus: "Home brewing remained quite common in the villages, but in

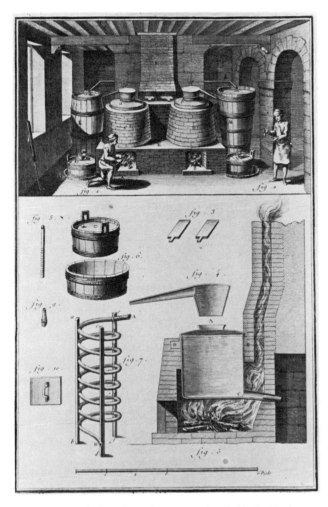

Equipment for brandy production was detailed in Defehrt's 1762 engraving, Distillateur.

Italians Introduce Old Flavors

Little wonder that the Italians with their leadership in distilling both essential oils and alcoholic spirits were the first to combine these techniques to make rudimentary liqueurs. For well over 1500 years, Italy was the consuming culture, the spice trader of the world. In the early 15th century, Bernhard of Treviso was utilizing quicklime in distilling high proof spirits. It was a simple step for experienced blenders to temper strong spirits with good herbal flavors. In fact, it was the marriage of Henry II, King of France, to Catherine of Medici which brought sweet liqueur making to France, a nation which has since generated millions of gallons of cordials and untold more millions in francs as a result of the fortuitous marriage.

Undoubtedly the application of aqua ardens, or distilled spirits, to medical practices prompted the use of the product in the home as well as encouraging commercial production. After all, once observed in action, a crude still was no more difficult for a thirteenth century peasant to construct than it is for the contemporary moonshiner. Surely the apothecary soon had generous competition from amateur producers. Forbes records that "it is still possible that the Black Death (1348 and later years) favored the spread of the use of strong alcohol drinks which were then often prescribed as medicine for this terrible scourge."

With widespread production and use, abuse was inevitable. Forbes cites a 1496 Nuremberg ordinance that decrees: "from now on Sundays or other official holidays no spirit shall be kept in the houses, shops, or market, even in the streets of this town for the purpose of sale or paid consumption." Perhaps this is the earliest Blue Law! At about this time, there existed a public record of taxes paid on malt for Scotch whisky. Also, Genoese sailors were transporting a spirit made of wine from southern France to England. The first Englishman to use the word *still* was said to have been Thomas Gile, a surgeon to Henry VIII in the early 1500s. At the conclusion of the fourteenth century, hard spirits were found everywhere on the Continent. In 1360, Frankfurt laws attempted to control the then common *schnapsteufel* or brandy devil. From time to time, church authorities condemned spirits consumption as sinful and, even worse, as a waste of precious commodities.

A Slow Growth

Peter Hallgarten reports in *Spirits and Liqueurs* (1979) that the smarter distillers soon discovered that the bad wine vintages could indeed be put to good new purpose.

> In 1559, when Peter Morwyng published his *Treasure of Evonymous,* wine was no longer distilled solely by apothecaries and for medicinal purposes; there were already a certain number of "distillers", in London, who distilled spirits of a kind from the unsound wines and wine-lees which vintners and coopers were only

the town brewing became an industry side by side with the earliest industries in the West, soap and sugar . . . In the fourteenth century Annesfort had no less than 350, Haarlem 50 breweries." Yet during the same period, the mechanics were in place for large-scale alcohol production, as Forbes also points out:

> The production of essential oils, perfumes and the extract of herbs and flowers for medical use was originally more or less concentrated in the monasteries . . . As early as the fourteenth century a county like Burgundy had large plantations growing lavender, borage, salvia, violets, roses, lilies, etc. which either were used dried or distilled with water or alcohol. In Dijon no less than eleven stills were in use for this purpose.

The Transitional Years: A Mini-Chronology in the Development of Aqua Ardens *(Some dates approximate)*

Sixteenth Century

1493	Columbus takes sugarcane to the Virgin Islands
1500	Capitalism emerging as High Renaissance begins
1503	Peace between England and Scotland opens Scotch trade
1504	Hops to England and lager beer developed
1517	Reformation begun as a result of Luther's protest
1519	Braunschweig publishes book on miracle medicine spirits
1519	Cortes distills Aztec beer from agave
1526	Ullsted invents test for proof by burning spirits on cloth
1533	Catherine de Medici brings liqueurs to France
1533	Applejack produced in Normandy under the name of *eau-de-vie-de-cidre*
1542	Heavy taxes on drinks in Bavaria
1551	First licensing of alehouses and taverns in England and Wales
1560	French brandy trade to England is well established
1562	The word *still* first appears in English book
1568	Dean of St. Paul's Cathedral invents bottles for beer
1575	Distilling is common in northern Europe; Bols opens Scheidam, Holland distillery
1580	Wine brandy is distilled regularly in Jerez, Spain
1585	Dutch ships carry burnt wine (brandy) from Cognac to Holland & Scandinavia

Seventeenth Century

1618	Thirty Years' War commences in Europe
1620	Corn spirits are common in Germany
1632	Apple seeds are imported to colonies from England
1633	Dr. Sylvius invents medicine called *genever*—gin
1634	Cherry liqueur and cherry brandy used to fight cholera epidemic in Alsace
1640	Kieft establishes Dutch still for spirits in America
1650	Tea is first drunk in England
1651	Rum is a common distillate in the West Indies
1657	Rum is first produced commercially in Massachusetts
1659	Brandy is produced in South Africa
1675	Delaware forbids corn and grains in distilling
1689	When William and Mary ascend the English throne, local gin is promoted and French brandy discouraged
1690	500,000 gallons of gin are consumed in England
1692	Gin replaces beer as a ration on Dutch ships

Eighteenth Century

1700	Four of five men are engaged in farming
1703	Methuen Treaty lowers taxes on Portuguese wines and raises duties on French—port trade is begun
1714	Two million gallons of gin are consumed in England
1718	Hydrometer is invented to measure amount of alcohol in solution
1729	Five million gallons of gin are consumed in England
1732	Eleven million gallons of gin are consumed in England
1733	Molasses Act is passed to force colonies to buy British product
1734	Over thirteen million gallons of gin are consumed in England
1735	Iron and steel industries are developed
1740	Booth's Gin firm is established in London
1742	Nineteen million gallons of gin are consumed in England
1750	Consumption of spirits in the United States is estimated at eight gallons per capita
1764	Spinning Jenny is invented
1769	Wine grapes travel to California with the Franciscans
1772	Thirty-two distilleries operate in Scheidam, Holland
1781	Cork first used as a wine bottle stopper
1789	Elijah Craig makes the first bourbon
1791	United States establishes the first federal tax on whiskey
1794	There is an exodus west by Scotch and Irish farmers with their stills to escape tax men

Nineteenth Century

1800	Thirty years of experimentation begins with column stills
1808	The Union Temperance Society is formed in Moreau, New York
1814	First practical steam locomotive built
1824	Gay-Lussac establishes alcohol scale *(alcoolomètre)* for measurement
1833	Payen separates diatase, the first enzyme to be prepared in concentrated form, from malt extract
1836	Coffey invents the first workable continuous still

1837	Scotch is first blended with neutral grain spirits	1857	Pasteur isolates yeast fermentation and bacteria in wines
1843	Captain Sutter makes brandy for Forty-Niners in California	1870	Brand names for gin and whiskey appear in England and the Americas
1848	French revolution weds science and economy and promotes both	1874	Women's Christian Temperance Union is formed
1850	Dry gin is first produced in London—made without heavy sugar level	1900	Two of five Americans live in cities
		1900	All liquors of the world have been discovered and commercialized

too pleased to sell to them at very low rates. Morwyng claimed that spirit distilled from either good or bad wine was equally good, since whatever was bad in unsound wine could not be its spirit, its soul, but merely its grosser body. . . .

A combination of factors inhibited widespread use of spirits. Through the end of the Middle Ages, and well into the Industrial Revolution, the vast majority of people lived from hand to mouth. The new spirits were difficult to produce, relatively expensive, and undoubtedly fiery to the taste.

The universality in spirit consumption had to await the liberation of man from the land, and the development of personal wealth. In *Consuming Passions* (1980), Farb and Armelagos set the stage.

> The modern cultural adaptation . . . emerged first in Britain, then in Western Europe and North America . . . spreading rapidly around the globe—and even penetrating into the lands of remote pastoralists, horticulturists and hunter gatherers. Often regarded as synonymous with the Industrial Revolution. . . .

Agriculture Makes Progress Possible

The authors place great stress on the agricultural revolution which preceded the industrial growth and really made it possible. The release of laborers from the land was essential to any industrial progress. Populations in the past had grown only when the food supply could support them. Consider these revealing figures. In 1750, the world population was about 750,000,000. Within one hundred years of the agricultural revolution, the one billion mark was passed. The next century that billion doubled, and today we tax our globe's capacity to produce food for an incredible 4 billion people.

The agricultural revolution made available more and better grains such as barley, oats, wheat and rye for the growing urban populations. Eventually, these grains of life were produced in surplus quantities and could be more easily diverted to distilled spirits for man's pleasure rather than all being necessary to his survival.

In contrast to the slow development of distilled spirits, brews and fruit wines were available for the asking, at least during an abundant harvest. In *Beverages Past and Present* (1908), Emerson explains another reason why it took time for alcohol to become favored. It just didn't taste very good to wine drinkers!

> The growth of alcohol as a beverage was extremely slow and except in one period during the latter part of the fifteenth century there was never much preference shown it, for owing to the potency very few indeed could drink it without a liberal dilution. Alcohol therefore was too ardent for the general class of drinkers and in order to obtain something stronger than wine, and yet considerably milder than pure spirit, they soon decided upon *aguardiente de uva* or brandy.

Eventually, experimentation led to refinements in processing which reached their zenith in the adaptation of columnar distilling in 1832 by Aeneas Coffey in Ireland. But from a practical viewpoint, the movement toward perfection began with various designs to cool or condense the spirits, then went further with the concept of continuous addition of distilling material attempted as early as 1575, and finally matured with the techniques for rectifying and blending. These techniques, commonplace today, required the imaginative and assiduous application of the developing technology before the public found these new spirits to their liking.

No Matter the Terms

A number of words were applied to the distillates in early years, but alcohol emerged as the universal name. Those authorities who attribute it to the Arabic do so because antimony, a common eye shadow, was produced by a distillation process. The new distillate was *al-koh'l* (like antimony). That the Moors called a distiller an *alcoholador* and cows with black rings around their eyes *alcoholados* buttresses the theory of the origin of the word.

The common term *aqua vitae* surely came from Arnald, and Forbes reminds us that Arnald's pupil, Lull, had no doubt

. . . I have no objection to a man's drinking wine, if he can do it in moderation. I found myself apt to go to excess in it, and therefore, after having been for some time without it, on account of illness, I thought it better not to return to it. Every man is to judge for himself according to the effects which he experiences.

Samuel Johnson

that the newly found element was an "emanation of divinity . . . destined to revive the energies of modern decrepitude." Of course, water of life was adopted in France as *eau-de-vie,* in Ireland as *usquebaugh,* in Scotland as *uisce beatha,* and in Germany as *weingeist,* or wine spirit, as well as *aqua ardens,* or ardent waters. Other references to the fluid, which figured importantly in medicine for centuries, were Latin terms—*aqua vini, spiritus vini,* and *vinum ardens.*

Another series of terms which figured importantly in early distillation, ones which are still used today, derive from the Arabic for sweet juice. Variations of *'araq* (arrack, arraki, arack, and raki) describe homemade spirits from palm sap, rice, dates, and berries throughout the European and African continents. As early as 1108, there are references in Hungary to raki made from plums, known today as slivovitz.

What is unknown are the dates or methods of adaptation from the alchemists' laboratories to the homes of the common man in such widely separated places as the steppes of Russia, the bogs of Ireland, and the plum orchards of the Balkans. But it must have been rapid and nearly universal as these diverse societies shared in common a prodigious thirst for alcohol in any form.

Whatever its appellation, once discovered and refined, spiritous alcohol developed a nearly essential relationship to the well-being of humans which can predictably be projected to the end of human existence. Berton Roueché, a thoughtful and perceptive commentator, discusses human needs in *Alcohol: The Neutral Spirit* (1960).

The basic needs of the human race, its members have long agreed, are food, clothing, and shelter. To that fundamental trinity most modern authorities would add, as equally compelling, security and love. There are, however, many other needs whose satisfaction, though somewhat less essential, can seldom be comfortably denied. One of these, and perhaps the most insistent, is an occasional release from the intolerable clutch of reality. All men . . . have sought . . . some reliable means of briefly loosening its grip.

The most conspicuous result of their search, if not the most effective, is a colorless liquid called ethyl hydroxide, or, more popularly, alcohol. It is also the oldest, the most widely esteemed, and the most abysmally misunderstood.

Endemic Heavy Drinking

Social upheaval inevitably takes its toll in human misery, and the agricultural and industrial convulsions were no exception. There occurred massive dislocation of people. Thousands of rural people sought employment and new lives in urban centers, many lacking skills for employment and survival. With overconsumption of alcohol already a given, new depths of dissipation were sounded.

In 1637, Englishman John Taylor touted his countrymen's love of ale:

. . . and in conclusion, it is such a nourisher of Mankinde, that if my mouth were as bigge as Bishopsgate, my Pen as long as a Maypole, and my Inke a flowing spring, or a standing fishpond, yet I could not with Mouth, Pen or Inke speak or write the true worth of Ale.

An Irish ditty of the time also speaks volumes.

There never a day have I for drink,
But Saturday, Sunday, Monday.
Tuesday, Wednesday, Thursday, Friday.
Och! The dickens a day I have for drink,
But Saturday, Sunday, Monday.
    Whoop, hurrah,
Tuesday, Wednesday,
Thursday, Friday.

Farb and Armelagos (1980) comment on this predilection of the Irish:

A long history of uncertain food supply and occasional severe famine has also contributed to heavy drinking in Ireland . . . Alcohol, in these circumstances, provided the social and psychological satisfaction, as well as the caloric energy, that people elsewhere obtain from food.

As alluded to in earlier chapters, the western European peoples drank heavily, and still do. To avoid the appearance of prejudice toward the Irish and the English, consider this sixteenth century poem by one Chin P'Ing Mei from China, which confirms that overconsumption was also common in the inscrutable East!

Make merry over wine.
Three cups, and already
The walls of sadness are overthrown.
Also, no sooner are we sober
Than sadness walls us in again.

Figure 16.1 *An early American pinewood still depicted by Morewood had an elaborate system of cooling chambers.*

Not drunk is he who from the floor,
Can rise alone, and still drink more.
But drunk is he who prostrate lies,
Without the power to drink or rise.
                                    T. L. Peacock

'Tis not the drinking that is to be blamed,
but the excess.
                                    John Selden

Early American Spirits

The discovery and colonization of the Americas coincided with the universal usage of spirits in the mother countries. It was inevitable that the developed thirsts of the pioneers would support indigenous spirit making. In *The Life and Times of the Late Demon Rum* (1965), J. C. Furnas dates the arrival of spirits in the United States: "Spirits probably came to the colonies with the first English and Dutch settlers. Dutchmen of that day seldom went far without their 'genever' (gin) that was a major contribution to civilization—and to human misery." In his book on what was probably the very first popular American drink, Furnas recounts the real distaste and even fear of plain water that the colonists brought with them from across the seas.

> Water—flavorless, colorless, proverbially weak—was suspected of diluting physical vigor and settling cold on the stomach, whereas it stood to reason that 'jolly good ale and old' warmed and strengthened . . . when stuck with water as the only drink available, the self respecting colonist mixed in molasses, vinegar, or sassafras to mask the implied disgrace to his purse and insult to his palate.

The first commercial distillery in the colonies was erected by the Dutchman William Kieft, governor of New Amsterdam in the year 1640. For the following twenty years, the still's yield was gin and brandywine, favorites of the Dutch. As early as 1650, the British in New England established trade in rum, fish, and lumber in exchange for West Indian molasses. Eventually, after the English took over New York, the first still was put to rum production also.

Many a fortune was born of the shrewd bartering in New England rum and African slaves. This commerce in several kinds of human misery presaged some of the clashes that led to independence by the colonies and continued until the turn of the nineteenth century.

Most of the molasses used in the making of New England rum originated in the French and British Caribbean Islands. An incensed British Parliament passed the Molasses Act in 1733 to raise duties on molasses from competitors. As usual, regressive taxation led to progressive smuggling. In *Alcohol, The Delightful Poison* (1975), Alice Fleming reports that "in a single year, 1763, some fifteen thousand hogsheads of molasses were imported into Massachusetts, but taxes were paid on only a thousand."

A Spirited Heritage

American spirit consumption can only be understood in the context of what went before. It is folly to run from the fact that our forebears were prodigious drinkers, just like their contemporaries in Europe.

William Rorabaugh (1979) suggests that early Americans' bland diet may be, in part, responsible for their overindulgence.

> The taste for strong drink was no doubt enhanced by the monotony of the American diet, which was dominated by corn. In the winter Americans ate dried, parched corn kernels; in the summer, roasted green ears; in the autumn, freshly boiled golden ripe ears dripping with melted butter. But it was corn pummeled into hominy or ground into meal that was ever present at all seasons. It appeared on the table three times a day as fried johnny cakes or corn bread. . . . Corn was also fed to the hogs, and the hog meat was eaten in the form of salt pork, smoked ham, and lard. Each day, it was calculated, the typical adult American ate a pound of bread, most often made with corn meal, and a pound of meat, usually salt pork. . . . This proportion of meat in the diet was probably the highest in the world.

Through western history, governments have restricted the use of precious food grains, frequently banning distillation.

Highlights

- The original concept of spirits as "water of life" was universal.
- Distillation of substances other than alcohol existed before Christ's birth.
- Wine and brew distillates emerged in the eleventh century and spread slowly throughout the world.

- Early spirits were utilized as medicines.
- Heavy drinking was endemic in colonial American society.

This is a typical, simple copper pot still that was used in the nineteenth century. This unit is on display in the Oude Meester Brandy Museum, Stellenbosch, South Africa.

A nineteenth-century copper pot still of considerable capacity, with the cooling worm intact, is shown at the Oude Meester Brandy Museum, Stellenbosch, South Africa.

As early as 1230 in Nuremberg, Germany, there is such an ordinance recorded. During the famine of 1433, the Common Council of Augsburg outlawed distillation of anything but oats, then in good supply. Delaware Colony passed a similar mandate against corn distillation in 1675. Already a commercial distiller in 1771, General George Washington wrote to the convening Continental Congress suggesting the creation of Public Distilleries to allay the shortage of liquor in the army that resulted from the British blockades. The tensions between the food larder and the liquor cabinet have existed since the discovery of distillation.

However, in the forty years following the Revolutionary War, there was a literal glut of grain. Corn, hogs, and cider dominated the American diet for the same reasons that rice dominated the Chinese diet and dates the Mediterranean diet.

They were there for the taking, thus inexpensive. Rorabaugh records the abundance of inexpensive distilled and fermented beverages compared to expensive imported teas, coffee, and spirits. He links spirits and heavy food in a veritable syndrome of overeating and overdrinking common to this day:

> . . . the speedy ingestion of salt pork and fried corn cakes tended to produce headaches, nausea, and upset stomachs. Indigestion was very common and was widely blamed on seasonal fevers, bad water, or overexertion. Dyspepsia, like other illnesses, was commonly treated by drinking whiskey.

Hard liquor was, and is, very much a part of the American diet.

THE DISTILLING PROCESS

Distillation is quite a simple chemical process which these next few pages outline. In its most basic form, alcohol distillation consists of separating the ethyl alcohol formed in fermentation from its base materials by means of heat.

There are two types of basic stills, the containers within which alcohol is vaporized. The adaptations and variations of the basic mechanism are mind boggling. The first type, the pot still, operates with a single batch of beer or wine at a time. The second type, the patent still, is actually a mechanical refinement of the pot still within which the alcohol can be vaporized on a continuing basis and with infinitely greater control. The process, then, involves vaporizing alcohol through the application of heat and reducing that vapor, by cooling, to fluid again.

The Basic Pot Still

There is no better illustration of the workings of a pot still than the one employed by the Kentucky moonshiner. The process begins in a mash barrel which is usually a 55-gallon oak barrel filled with pure water, cracked corn, cane sugar, and perhaps molasses for flavoring. Baker's yeast will induce the fermentation which requires several days. This single mash batch will provide for two separate runs through the pot still. Ideally, the mash will produce about 7 to 7.5 percent alcohol, about double the strength of popular beers.

A simple pot is constructed of copper of sufficient size to accommodate about 25 gallons of wash or mash with an additional 10 gallon headspace. The pot will have a porthole for the introduction of the mash as well as a temperature gauge near the top of the head. The simplest stills use a wood-burning oven below the pot. When the temperature in the pot reaches 173°F, alcohol vapors begin to rise through the head into the cap.

Pure ethanol boils at 172.9°F (78.3°C). However, experience indicates that other constituents always rise with the alcohol from the wine or brew mash. Since water and alcohol are miscible, that is, capable of being mixed, they comfortably share the same space without bonding. Consequently, the alcohol vapors easily rise from the surface of the watery mash. The word *azeotrope* describes the bonding of two or more substances in distilling. This occurs in alcohol distilling when the ethanol content rises above 97.2 percent. Consequently, there is never any truly pure (or anhydrous) alcohol in a conventional still. As a rule, the alcohol content of a first run through a still will be *doubled* or *tripled;* that is, it will be sent back through the still at least one more time. Hence, if the mash contains 10 percent alcohol, the first run through the still will yield 20 to 30 percent alcohol or 40° to 60° proof. This is called the singlings or first run. Higher proofs are achieved by doublings or additional runs through the still.

How It All Works

The cap's function is to deflect into the mash a portion of the congeners, freeing the steaming vapors for their passage through a series of tubes and chambers, each designed to remove increasing amounts of the offensive congeners. An optional device called the *slag box* enables the searing steam to expand rapidly in a relatively confined space. In that instant of expansion, more fusel oils coagulate and descend to the floor of the slag box from which they are eliminated periodically by a release valve. More copper tubing conveys the surging and now relatively clean steam to another 50-gallon oak barrel named the *thumper.* As a rule, the thumper contains a new batch of fermenting mash which itself acts as a fine filter. The vapor is released into the barrel at the bottom and rises gently through the roiling mass creating a rhythmic, harmonic noise, hence the "thumper."

The final device for the modern moonshiner is the *flake box or condenser,* generally another 55-gallon barrel. Now you understand why the alcohol agents of the federal government are so interested in the destination of used cooperage. About 10 feet of copper tubing carries the now cooling steam through a chamber of circulating cold water. It is in this final step that the vapors return to a fluid state.

Fractioning: The Important Step

A great deal of human ingenuity has been channeled into the mechanics of separation and condensation. The ultimate palatability of the spirit depends upon the fractioning of diverse congeners present in the vapors. Frustration with the limitations of the process eventually led to the discovery that different levels of purity occur at precise but different stages of cooling. If the middle liquor could be removed at its most pristine level, containing only desirable traces of the fusel oils and aldehydes, it would emerge from the still nearly palatable. From this experimentation grew the idea of a tower or a column of segmented sections, or fractioning chambers, each capable of trapping fluids at increasingly cooler temperatures. Over the years adaptations in the tower led inevitably to the continuous still, in which both selectivity and speed could be assured.

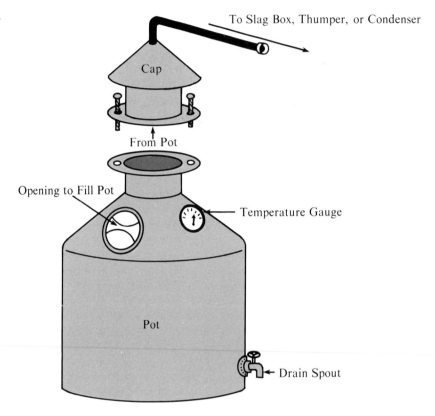

Figure 16.2 *All of the essential distilling mechanics were realized in the moonshine apparatus—from the temperature-controlled pot, through an expansion cap, a slag box to relieve the heavy congeners, a purifying trip through new mash and a continuous cooling chamber.*

To Slag Box, Thumper, or Condenser

Cap

From Pot

Opening to Fill Pot

Temperature Gauge

Pot

Drain Spout

Even with advancing technology, the basic pot still remains an important device in liquor production. Many spirits, as will be seen in subsequent pages, must by law be produced in modified versions of the basic pot still described in this section. Pot stills are ideal for the production of spirits of great character and style, such as cognac and single malt Scotch. Indeed, the distinctiveness of these distillates would be lost in the fractioning chambers of the patent still.

Some modern pot stills contain up to 4,000 gallons of wash and are capable of producing up to 1,000 gallons of spirits from a single twelve-hour run. The primary advantage of the pot still both in the Middle Ages and today lies in the capacity of the distiller to make immediate and continuing sensory evaluations of the emerging spirit. The operator merely draws a sample and, in addition to technical tests, evaluates by smell and taste. Approximately one-half of the run will be diverted into a spirit safe as a desirable first run product, with the portions preceding and following—the heads and the tails—likely to be mixed into the next wash to extract the maximum in alcohol. These middle liquors in most operations are run back through the system emerging at a relatively high and acceptable proof at about a quarter of the original wash volume.

A final advantage is the simplicity and portability of the total pot still operation. While a great deal of dexterity and skill may be exercised in choosing the grains, in keeping the

TABLE 16.1 Illicit Liquor Production by Federally Seized Stills 1978 vs. 1979

	1978	1979
Federally-seized stills	361	40
Est. no. days operated	40	40
Daily capacity (P.G.)	9,370[a]	1,509[a]
Produced, seized stills (P.G.)	374,800	60,360
Fed. excise tax rate	$10.50	$10.50
Revenue loss U.S. Treasury	$3,935,400	$633,780

Source: Dan Hecht, ed., *The Liquor Handbook* (New York: Gavin-Gobson Associates, Inc., 1980).
[a]Estimated by *The Liquor Handbook.*

wash from scorching, in maintaining the right temperature to produce clean spirits, and in diverting the heart from the congeners in the heads and tails, it is not necessary that the operator possess an engineering or a mechanical degree. Rather, this is a technique that can be passed from father to son and carried out as a logical part of the harvest on a rural farm, as was done by the Scotch-Irish who sought freedom in the Americas.

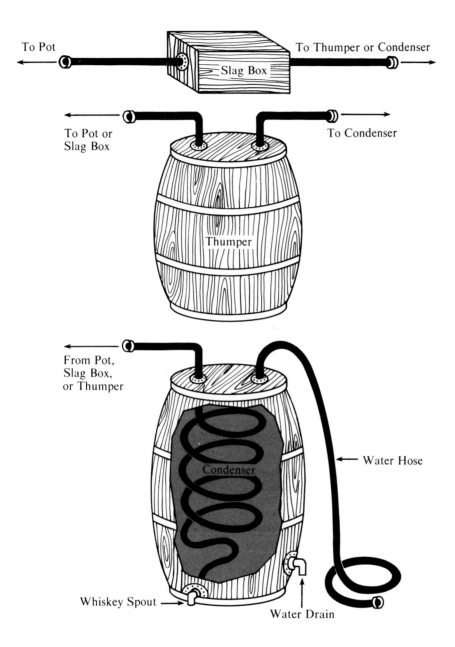

Highlights

- The pot still permits immediate sensory evaluation of the emerging spirits.
- Simple pot stills are generally small and easily transported units, capable of wood firing and stream cooling.
- Generally, two runs are required with pot spirits, the second (or doubling) is done apart from the heads and tails of the first run.

- The pot still is slow and cumbersome compared to the patent still's speed and ease of separating spirits at various proof levels.
- Illicit whiskey production from pot stills has been all but stamped out in recent years, more by economics than by federal agents.

*T*he still is gone, the still is gone,
I could hear it in the splash
When you emptied out the mash,
When you broke those jugs to smash,
The still is gone, what will we do?
**(Song about Big Six Henderson,
Federal Revenuer)**

*E*at not to dullness. Drink not to elevation.
Benjamin Franklin

The Continuous Still

It is recorded in many books that Aeneas Coffey discovered a new kind of continuous still in 1830, making possible an entirely new method of spirit production. While it is true that the Irish exciseman (liquor tax collector) did, indeed, patent a magnificent double column device in 1832, that mechanical wonder was but the final adaptation of dozens of chambered columns developed during the previous eighty years, largely in Europe.

What Coffey and Stein sought in Ireland was also pursued by Derosne and Cellier in France—a continuous application of the alcohol wash. In many countries, taxes were based on the *size* of the still and not its product in volume, thus encouraging larger and more rapid distillations. In pot distilling, speed is equivalent to poor quality. More important to experimenters' motivation, the pot still was simply too small and too slow to meet the demands of the growing spirit market.

First, there was the explosion in gin consumption during the 1700s which pushed to the limit pot stills producing nearly neutral spirits combined with juniper and other flavorings. By 1772, there were twenty-two distilleries in the small town of Scheidam, Holland, all working to full capacity.

Edward Adam had furthered the development of the theory of rectification. His research was conducted at the University of Montpellier where Arnald christened aqua vitae some 500 years earlier. The hydrometer and the Gay-Lussac *alcoolomètre*, or alcohol level scale, aided the distiller in accurately determining alcohol concentrations. The French Revolution progressively wedded the economy to science and technology.

Some of the stills in Ireland preceding Coffey's breakthrough were huge, up to a 20,000–gallon capacity. They met the excise regulations in that they allowed the government to measure and tax the size of the still according to the quantity of the alcoholic wash which was fed on a continuous basis through the base of the conical still releasing spirits up into a number of chambers. However, the product was of such low proof and poor quality that up to three runs were necessary.

But Coffey's 1832 patent still, a modification of his earlier work, was the real breakthrough; it added a second chamber or tower so that the first wood and copper *analyzer* tower on the left acted as the separating unit. The *new wash* dripped down through its twelve chambers, meeting steam from below which stripped the alcohol. The second or *rectifying* tower on the right received the steamy alcohol spirits which condensed as they rose up through fifteen copper plates. In this unit, the upper five plates contained the desired finished spirit. The unit was ingenious because the new wash wending its way down through the copper tubing in the second column provided part of the cooling and condensing function while the transferred heat provided a preheating of the new wash.

Altogether, Coffey's work was a remarkable coalescence of technology. The initial operation of Coffey stills constituted single batches after which the system was flushed with water. It was not long before the French and the English simply kept the system in continuous operation all day long. Morewood (1838) describes its impact on the industry.

The Coffey still was an immediate success. Dingler reports that in 1836 there were already stills treating no less than 13,600 L[iters] of wash per hour with 6.5–7% of alcohol and in the days of Payen hourly

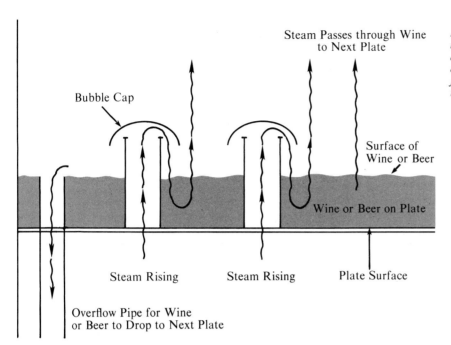

Figure 16.3 In the operation of a bubble cap in a continuous still, steam passes through the distilling material (wine or beer), stripping alcohol as it rises toward the second, or rectifying, column. Bubble caps deflect steam through the wine on each plate.

Steam Passes through Wine to Next Plate

Bubble Cap

Surface of Wine or Beer

Wine or Beer on Plate

Steam Rising

Steam Rising

Plate Surface

Overflow Pipe for Wine or Beer to Drop to Next Plate

(A)

(B)

Mechanical complexity is seen in the control panel of the Christian Brothers brandy still (A) and the four-story extension of the columns (B).

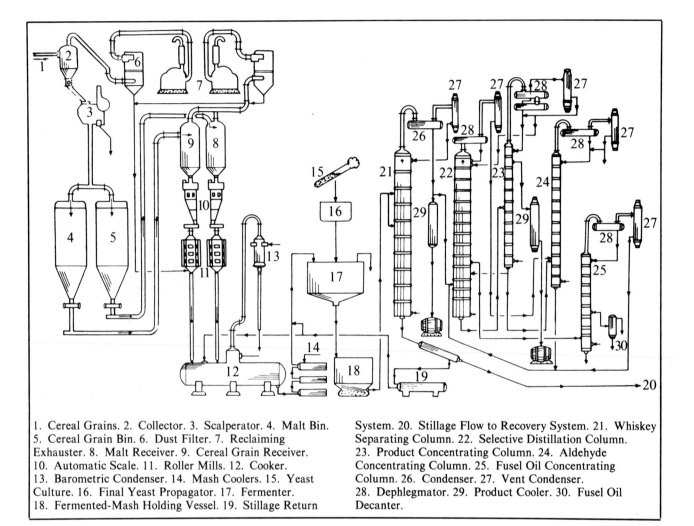

1. Cereal Grains. 2. Collector. 3. Scalperator. 4. Malt Bin. 5. Cereal Grain Bin. 6. Dust Filter. 7. Reclaiming Exhauster. 8. Malt Receiver. 9. Cereal Grain Receiver. 10. Automatic Scale. 11. Roller Mills. 12. Cooker. 13. Barometric Condenser. 14. Mash Coolers. 15. Yeast Culture. 16. Final Yeast Propagator. 17. Fermenter. 18. Fermented-Mash Holding Vessel. 19. Stillage Return System. 20. Stillage Flow to Recovery System. 21. Whiskey Separating Column. 22. Selective Distillation Column. 23. Product Concentrating Column. 24. Aldehyde Concentrating Column. 25. Fusel Oil Concentrating Column. 26. Condenser. 27. Vent Condenser. 28. Dephlegmator. 29. Product Cooler. 30. Fusel Oil Decanter.

Figure 16.4 The basic two-column Coffey still has been adapted into a bewildering sequence of stripping and condensing columns designed to purify the spirits to a precise degree for each type of distilled spirit. (Reprinted, by permission, from K. Peterson and A. R. Johnson *The Encyclopedia of Food Technology.* AVI Publishing Co., P.O. Box 831, Westport, Conn. 06880.)

capacities of 20,000 L. were no exceptions. They easily gave the 80 proof alcohol in one operation and therefore worked very cheaply as compared with the Continental stills. Soon they were used all over England.

It is easy to comprehend why nearly all of the spirits of the world are now produced in adaptations of the Coffey still. As the trend toward lighter and lighter distillates became a fact in the twentieth century, the independent moonshiner was rendered obsolete. He failed the ultimate market tests of quality and price.

As is so often the case with technological expansion during these past two hundred years, other complementary developments emerged at about the time that Coffey provided the means to mass produce. Saville invented the steam regulator in 1857. In *Irish Whiskey* (1973), McGuire singles out two other tools that replaced art and instinct with the certainty of science.

The invention of the saccharometer and its perfection over the eighteenth and nineteenth centuries changed guesswork into precise knowledge . . . The other, and probably the more important invention was the hydrometer which was improved and developed during the eighteenth century. The Sikes hydrometer emerged and is still used . . . With all doubts on the strength of a spiritous beverage being removed it left flavour as the deciding factor in successful marketing.

Present-day patent stills are sophisticated adaptations of the Coffey still. The diagram of a bourbon still demonstrates increasing complexity but strict adherence to Coffey's basic plan.

Rectifying—the Decision Level

The great versatility of the patent still occurs in the second of the two columns, the rectifier. Should the distiller desire a

Highlights

- The patent or Coffey still permits a continuing flow of wash twenty-four hours per day, greatly reducing the cost of operation.
- The fractioning chambers permit access to the spirit at various proofs, permitting the economy of a single run through the still.
- The patent still is a very complicated machine, requiring skilled operators and heavy investment.

- The invention of the unit came at a time of great demand for neutral spirits for gin making and for spirits to replace the phylloxera-scourged brandy.
- The patent still is ideal for the production of clean, high proof, neutral spirits and the higher proof distillates popular today.

heavily congeneric bourbon, the product may be removed at 120° proof or less, containing 60 percent alcohol and a great deal of congeneric residue. In contrast, if the distiller seeks neutral spirits for vodka, he will extract the liquor from a much higher plate in the column where the proof exceeds 190° proof, or over 95 percent alcohol—a neutral spirit lacking any congeneric character.

Since the heat source is back at the foot of the other column, the highest plates in the second column are the coolest in the whole system. Consequently, the volatile elements that vaporize first, the aldehydes, are the last to condense again. These heads often are diverted to another small recitifying column yielding more alcohol, and aldehydes which are discarded.

The next few plates contain the desired spirits called middle liquors in the pot still runs. For neutral spirits and American brandy, these plates accumulate these fluids scant inches below the aldehydes, which requires a delicate balance of heat through the system.

Finally, the lower plates capture the heavier congeneric concentrations called tails which have the highest boiling points, up to 220° F, and which, therefore, condense first as the temperature drops. Included are the higher alcohols and many esters. Up to 25 gallons of these congeners are discarded hourly. The ability to extract these heads and tails at various concentrations provides the operator with a tremendous advantage over the pot still. The speed of operation and the great volumes of production dictate the use of the patent still for all but a few select spirits. A big patent still can produce up to 400 gallons of distillate per hour, ten times the spirits produced by a pot still.

Stillage

The residue that falls to the base of the first column contains about 8 percent solid matter. This stillage comprises another profitable enterprise for the distiller and a valuable source of protein in agriculture. Collected and dried, the solid products

A distillery laboratory.

not only contain residual starches and proteins, they have also been enriched by the yeast residues. Additionally, some mashing procedures employ a percentage of this stillage to control the pH and the speed of original mash fermentations, which is termed *sour mashing*. Annual market stillage constitutes an additional 500,000 tons for American distillers.

A Primer in Proofs

Perhaps nothing else in the wine and spirits field causes more confusion than the word *proof*. While there is talk now of standardization, it will probably be a long time coming.

The first hydrometer was invented by John Clarke around 1725, although over sixty years passed before the English Parliament adopted this standard to measure alcohol content. Bartholomew Sikes (often spelled Sykes), a British exciseman of some ingenuity, developed this simple method of measuring alcohol in immersion.

Figure 16.5 *A comparison of British and American proof systems with the sensible French measurement by volume.*

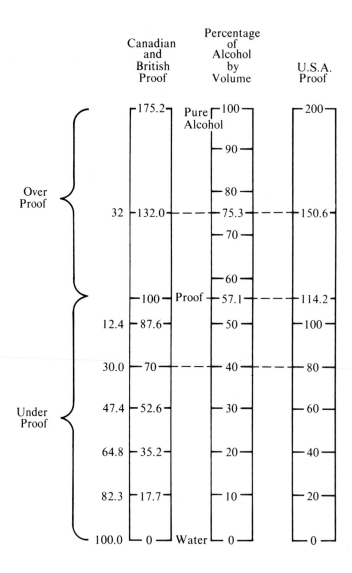

Note: 1. Start with percentage of alcohol by volume.
2. To convert to Canadian proof multiply it by 1.75.
3. To convert to U.S.A. proof multiply it by 2.

There are three major methods of determining alcohol level, and very grave confusion is created in the public about the word *proof*. While it was not difficult to measure by crude techniques whether the alcoholic content was sufficient for the buyers' purposes, the tax man had a much more difficult task in imposing charges on the *exact* alcohol concentration.

It is worth a few minutes of diversion from this text to study two of the three systems. First, the American system is simple enough on one level. The proof of the spirit is said to be exactly twice the alcohol content in the container by volume. The French, or Gay-Lussac, system is easier yet. It is the *exact* amount of alcohol by volume, the same system now used to

determine alcohol in wines. While these two measurements may be readily understood, Mr. Sikes has science on his side.

His hydrometer is calibrated to float at the proof point when the vessel contains 57.1 percent alcohol. This strange chemical oddity occurs because alcohol weighs 12/13ths as much as the same amount of water—to put it another way, the alcohol molecules are able to insinuate themselves between the larger water molecules. Sikes decided everything above this level would be overproof, and everything below underproof. Consequently, American 100° proof is Sikes' 87.5° underproof.

Confused? So are most of your friends, and this dilemma will have to await some form of international agree-

TABLE 16.2 Average Caloric Content of Distilled Spirits (Whiskey, Brandy, Gin, Vodka, Rum)

	Alcohol			Total Cal/ 100 cc	Total Cal/oz	"Typical Serving," oz	Total Cal/ Serving
Proof	% Vol	Gm %	Cal %				
151	75.5	59.9	419.3	419.3	125.8	1.5	189
110	55.0	43.6	305.2	305.2	91.6	1.5	137
100	50.0	39.7	277.9	277.9	83.4	1.5	125
90	45.0	35.7	249.9	249.9	75.0	1.5	112
86	43.0	34.1	238.7	238.7	71.6	1.5	107
80	40.0	31.7	221.9	221.9	66.6	1.5	100

Source: Reproduced with permission from Leake, C. D. and Silverman, M.: ALCOHOLIC BEVERAGES IN CLINICAL MEDICINE. Copyright © 1966 by Year Book Medical Publishers, Inc., Chicago.
Note: The caloric content of distilled spirits may be calculated entirely on the basis of alcohol content. For most of them, the total solids yield less than 2 calories per serving.

TABLE 16.3 Variant Proof Measurements—The Proof of Things

Beverage	How Measured	Range of Alcohol	Average Serving	Approx. Amt. of Alcohol
Rum	Proof	80–151° Proof	1 oz. @ 151° Proof	3/4 oz.
Bourbon	Proof	80–100° Proof	1 oz. @ 100° Proof	1/2 oz.
Brandy	Proof	80° Proof	1 oz. @ 80° Proof	4/10 oz.
Liqueur	Proof	54–100° Proof	1 oz. @ 60° Proof	3/10 oz.
Beer	Weight	3.5–4%	11 oz. can	4/10 oz.
Dessert Wine	Volume	18–20%	3 ozs.	6/10 oz.
Table Wine	Volume	12–14%	5 ozs.	6/10 oz.

Source: Gene Ford, *The ABC'S of Wine, Brew and Spirits* (Seattle: Murray Publishing Co., 1980), 117.

ment; until then, the consumer must rely upon memory to calculate the not insignificant difference. To wit, consumption of shots from a British bottle stating 100° proof is tantamount to drinking 114.2° American proof.

Without question, the Gay-Lussac, or French version for proof, remains the simplest and most logical. At level 100°, the fluid is 100 percent alcohol. At the bottom end, at level 1, the fluid contains 1 percent alcohol. This is the system we now use in calculating the percentage of alcohol in wine and no one gets confused. Perhaps in the spirit of conversion to the metric system, this confusing jargon will give way to the French method. It is possible to determine calorie variations according to the proof of the spirits consumed (see table 16.2).

In the United States we measure different alcoholic beverages differently. Table 16.3 shows a comparison of those measurements.

THE UNITED STATES SPIRIT MARKET

Before proceeding into discussions of separate spirits, one might find it helpful to know our current preferences in distilled spirits (see table 16.4). In general, the white goods have remained steady or gone up. The brown goods are down.

TABLE 16.4 Distilled Spirits in United States Trade (Share of Market by Percent)

Spirit Type	1960	1975	1981
Whiskey			
Bourbon	29	17	14.4
Blends	31	13	7.8
Scotch	9	13	10.3
Canadian	5	11	11.9
Irish			0.2
TOTAL	74	54	44.6
Whites			
Gin	9	10	9.3
Vodka	8	20	21.3
Rum	2	4	7.1
Tequila		1	1.7
TOTAL	19	35	39.4
Specialty			
Brandy	3	3	4.3
Cordials			10.0
Mixed Cocktails			1.8
TOTAL	7	11	16.1

Source: IMPACT (1 October 1982), 1.

Healthy gallonage increases have occurred in the white spirits and the specialty spirit class, particularly in cordials and cocktails. In these figures there is evidence of more selective purchasing reflecting growing affluence and life-styles that permit association of luxury goods and liquors in the United States.

IMPORTED SPIRITS

The United Kingdom, Canada, and Mexico dominate the import spirits market. The purchases of spirits from the British Empire have nearly tripled over the past decade. The slight drop for the United Kingdom in 1979 reflects the softening Scotch sales. Also, as a bet for the future, Italy, which is emerging with a strong wine market in the United States, will undoubtedly create new demands for their many spirits and liqueurs (see table 16.5).

A comparison of per capita alcohol consumption among countries shows the United States toward the bottom of the top twenty (see table 16.6). However, the increasing consumption of wine by Americans is expected to move our standing higher in the years to come.

TABLE 16.5 Imports of Distilled Spirits by Country of Origin (Millions of Gallons)

Country	1960	1976	1980
United Kingdom	21.9	59.2	53.3
Canada	12.6	48.0	53.0
Mexico	0.2	9.0	11.3
France	1.6	4.3	6.1
Italy	0.3	1.6	2.7
Jamaica	0.2	0.8	1.5
All Others	0.5	1.5	4.3

Source: IMPACT (1 October 1982).

TABLE 16.6 Top Countries in Alcohol Consumption

Rank	Country	Gallons Per Capita
1	Luxembourg[a]	49.4
2	West Germany	47.3
3	Czechoslovakia	43.6
4	East Germany	41.9
5	Australia	41.0
6	Belgium	39.8
7	Austria	38.0
8	Denmark	37.6
9	New Zealand	37.3
10	France	36.7
11	Hungary	35.2
12	Ireland	33.0
13	Switzerland	32.8
14	Spain	32.6
15	United Kingdom	32.6
16	Portugal	30.7
17	United States	28.8
18	The Netherlands	28.7
19	Canada	27.0
20	Italy	25.5

Source: IMPACT (1 December 1982), 8.
Note: Based on total population.
[a]The real per capita consumption in Luxembourg is considerably lower but is inflated by large volume border trafficking.

Cognac and Brandies

The first, certainly the most majestic, and undoubtedly the most praised spirit throughout the world is that elixir, that subtle distilled essence of the grape and its wine—brandy. It is logical to assume that it became the first common distillate because the process of distillation was developed in southern wine regions, namely Italy and Spain. In *Brandies and Liqueurs of the World* (1976), Hannum and Blumberg suggest a span of at least 150 years for that development:

> The first mention of the distillation of wine in the Armagnac region is contained in a legal document dated 1411 and conserved today in the offices of the French *departement* of Haute-Garonne. In the early 1500s wine was being distilled into *eau-de-vie*. . . . By 1559 the lawmakers of Bordeaux thought it necessary to forbid distillation within the city for fear that a disastrous fire would occur. From its secret, alchemical origins, distillation of brandy or *eau-de-vie* had progressed until by the mid-seventeenth century it was being sold from pushcarts on the streets of Paris.

Similar patterns of development no doubt occurred all over the Mediterranean basin and even in the beer-brewing Germanic and Slavic regions. The same expansive urge that sent the daring Phoenicians out on the broad and stormy Atlantic with the original vine cuttings invited centuries of Italian, Flemish, and Norse traders to work the coasts of France, England, Scandinavia, and even remote Russia. This is the region that produced French kings and queens as well as incessant wars between Protestants and Catholics. There is abundant evidence that the first international trade in distilled spirits developed from the city of Cognac in the early sixteenth century.

Cyril Ray records in *Cognac* (1974) the various products which initiated the international trade market.

> The Romans also brought to the coasts of the region their Mediterranean methods of salt extraction: by the end of the tenth century, if not earlier, the production and sale of salt, corn and wine had brought prosperity. . . . By the twelfth century, these basic commodities of civilized living were being regularly exchanged, in impressive amounts, for the salt cod and salt herring, the furs and the timber, of the north, the trade being carried on largely in Flemish and Hanseatic bottoms, which called in at English ports, coming and going. . . . This trade with England increased when Henry II succeeded to the English throne in 1154, already the husband of Eleanor of Aquitaine. . . . the greatest wine growing region of France . . .

It was inevitable that this new and potent type of alcohol would become an important new commodity traveling the sea lanes of Europe. The prosaic Dutch dubbed the new product *brandewijn* or "burnt wine" and happily entered it into a trade that endured for six-hundred years, particularly to cold and clammy Britain and within chilly Holland where its warming powers were particularly prized.

Brandies fall into three general levels on the basis of taste and character rather than geography. In this tiering, cognac rests at the base, being the most pungent and aromatic of the trio. American brandy sits at the top as the lightest, and the other brandies of the world fall somewhere in between in terms of style. Naturally, production methods dictate these differences.

C laret is the liquor for boys; port for men, but he who aspires to be a hero must drink brandy.

Samuel Johnson

COGNAC

Cognac is that brandy produced within the *departements* of Charente and Charente–Maritime in southern France. About 150,000 acres are included in the six subdivisions of this region. The town of Cognac became the first great brandy exporter and remains to this day the leader in the field.

The river Charente for which the *departement* is named meanders through the pleasant countryside, touching on the rural towns of Jarnac and Cognac on its journey to Rochefort and the Atlantic. This is pastoral, cattle grazing and grape-growing country, far removed from the breathtaking, romantic castles of the Loire Valley to the north.

The earliest cognac firm that has remained in continuous operation is Augier, founded in 1643. Others, and their founding dates, are Martell in 1715, Hennessy in 1765, Rémy Martin in 1724, and Hine in 1775. The longevity of the world-recognized labels reveals the stability of the area as well as the strict adherence to standards of quality established by law in 1909 and revised in 1936, but established by practice easily some 300 years earlier.

In the 1936 standards, the boundaries of the subdistricts, the soils, and the types of grapes to be cultured were carefully circumscribed. The Grande Champagne produces the most subtle spirits from very chalky soils. Surrounding it in a semi-circle is an area called Petite Champagne. Together, these two areas supply 20 percent of the cognac grapes. The brandies of Petite Champagne mature more quickly than those of the Grande, and together they provide the blends known as *Fine Champagne*.

Most of the wines for cognac distillation derive from the other four areas—Borderies, Fins Bois, Bons Bois, and Bois

The Brandy Distiller, *an eighteenth-century etching.*

Ordinaires. The Fin Bois area alone produces nearly 40 percent of the cognac vintages. Within the six areas, there are approximately 30,000 individual grape growers. There are 4,000 stills registered to individuals, as well as twenty-five cooperative distillers and 200 professional distillers.

The professional distillers produce over 60 percent of the annual spirits production, with another 9 percent handled by the cooperatives, and the very considerable remaining 27 percent produced by the *bouilleur de cru*, the independent growers. After distillation, the huge companies take over in the same manner as they do in the French wine districts. The big shippers market 94 percent of all cognac, with 5 percent sold through the cooperatives and a tiny 1 percent by the independents.

Source Grapes

In pre-phylloxera days, the Folle-Blanche grape dominated the cognac plantings. Since this variety did not take well to grafting on louse-resistant American rootstock, the plantings gradually gravitated to the Saint-Émilion grape, which accounts now for about 90 percent of the vintage, along with some scattering of Colombard. Unlike other French *appellation controlée* districts, there are no restrictions here on the size of the crops or the vine prunings, since the best distilling wine is devoid of marked flavor and is generally quite harsh and acidic. In fact, the high yields produce the desirable low alcohol wines in the 7 to 9 percent range. The Saint-Émilion has another attribute in that it matures late in the season allowing the neighboring Bordeaux pickers to work both harvests!

Fermentation and Distillation

In advance of fermentation, the wines are pressed so that the free run juice may be fermented away from the pips and skins.

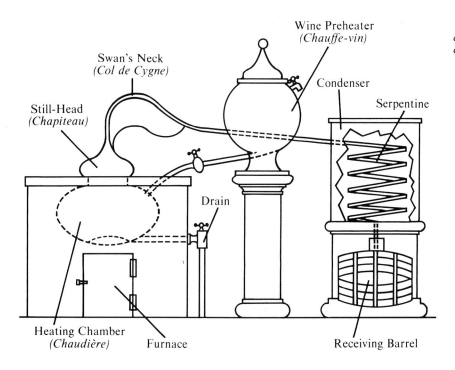

Swan's Neck
(Col de Cygne)

Still-Head
(Chapiteau)

Wine Preheater
(Chauffe-vin)

Condenser

Serpentine

Drain

Heating Chamber
(Chaudière)

Furnace

Receiving Barrel

Figure 17.1 *The incredible finesse in cognac originates in these finely engineered and tuned steam kettles.*

While the independent farmers produced their "Cape Smoke" in small copper pots, producers of commercial brandies in South Africa have always employed sophisticated cognac-type pot stills such as this unit from 1818 on display at the Brandy Museum at Stellenbosch. Modern units employ the same technique in distilling all South Africa's pot still brandy.

While flat and harsh wines are the objective, the intrusion of tannin and phenols from skins and seeds would create intolerable congener levels in the stills. A horizontal press extrudes the free run, and the lees then undergo a gentle hydraulic pressing. The two lots are joined and sent immediately to the fermenters. Within two weeks, the greenish, sharp, low alcohol wine is delivered, heavy with sediment, to the stills.

While literally thousands of people are involved in the production of cognac, the process is nevertheless extremely closely controlled. Distillation may take place between September 1st and May 31st, with the bulk being done immediately after fermentation. The particular type of still used, the *alambic charentais*, has been employed for over 300 years. Both the cutaway diagram and the photograph depict the typical still with a pre-heater or *chauffee-vin;* whether or not to use this piece of equipment is practically the only option in the process.

The wine enters the system by passing through the preheater which is a huge onion-shaped device on a pedestal. The fresh distillate passes through the bulb on its way to the condenser and exchanges heat with the new wine. The partially heated wine enters the *chaudière* next, where it is heated directly by wood or gas flames. At about 170° F, the alcoholic vapor rises through the still head or *chapiteau* and out through the graceful swan's neck. Passing through the pre-heater, the vapors condense in the water-cooled, serpentine condenser. The product drops directly into the waiting barrel as a milky distillate often between 50° and 60° proof, a very strong alcoholic distillate. This first run is called the *première chauffe* and comprises about one-third of the volume of the original wine. Three first runs or *brouillis* are necessary to fill the thirty-hectoliter pot for a second run; the charge of brouillis put in is limited to twenty-five hectoliters.

Terms

aguardiente Spanish for spirits, usually brandy.

alambic armagnacais The pot still (and its variants with single columns) used in Armagnac.

alambic charentais The basic cognac pot still.

bagaceria Portuguese pomace brandy.

basquaise Oval, flat bottle traditionally used for Armagnac.

bonne chauffe The second distillation from which the *coeur,* or heart, is taken.

bouilleurs de cru Grape growers who make and sell their brandy independently.

bouilleurs de profession Professional distillers.

brandewijn Literally "burnt wine" in Dutch—brandy.

brouillis First run from the alambic pot still.

caramel Burnt sugar, tasteless and odorless, used to balance color components in spirits.

chais Low, ground-level warehouses for aging brandy.

chapiteau The pear or olive-shaped top or head of the boiler pot.

chaudière The alambic boiler pot.

chauffe First cognac distillation.

chauffe-vin A wine preheater used by some distillers, generally placed between the boiler and condenser.

col de cygne The unique swan's neck piping to the condenser.

compte d'age The symbol used to designate the age of cognacs beginning the August after distillation.

crus The six major grape-growing regions around the town of Cognac, such as Champagne and Bois Ordinaires.

égrappé Marc produced by removing stems from the pomace.

GL The Gay-Lussac symbol for alcoholic concentration.

grappa Brandy produced from the lees of fermentation, including skins, pulp, and seeds.

la part des anges The barrel ullage in Cognac chais, or warehouses, that evaporates continually.

le coeur The heart of the run, or the middle liquor.

limousin oak Thick, sturdy oak from a forest near Cognac which yields the most desirable cooperage for cognac.

marc French brandy made from the fermentation lees; also called eau-de-vie de marc.

négociants Brokers who buy, blend, age, and market spirits.

paradis Particular warehouse for storing the oldest of cognacs of up to 100 years of age.

pineau de charentes Unique blend of sweet fresh grape juice and brandy produced under appellation since 1935.

pomace The same as marc; the pulp, skins, and seeds from fermentation used to produce brandies.

produit de queue The tails or feints coming over last in distilling.

produit de tête The heads or aldehydes which vaporize first.

serpentin The serpentine condenser coil.

testa and coda In Italian, the heads and tails.

troncais oak Light, slender oak from central France.

uralt German brandy aged at least one year.

Cognac is always twice distilled with the heads and tails from the first run added back to another first batch for redistillation. The second distillation of the brouillis is the critical run. About ten hours later, the *bonne chauffe* (good heating) emerges with the distiller carefully monitoring the run to save only the precious *coeur* or heart of the run, consisting of 40 to 50 gallons, taken at about 140° proof. Again the *secondes,* the heads and tails, are diverted back for another first distillation. Nothing is wasted.

Aging

Immediately off the still, cognac is a distinctly unpleasant and noxious spirit. Like many other great discoveries in history which were accidental, the unique marriage of Limousin oak and the distillate came about because of the unexpected and discouraging import duties placed on the product by the hostile British King William of Orange. The producers stored the products in wood, hoping for better days.

Luckily, the wide-grained oak cooperage from the neighboring Limousin forests worked wonders, mellowing the harsh congeners, creating a thing of beauty. Only the lower trunk portions of these eighty-year-old trees are used for the desired concentrations of tannin and vanillin. In recent years, because of inevitable shortages, cooperage has been made from the taller and less intense *Troncais* oak from central France.

The split staves age in the open air for three years before the *tonnelleries* or barrels are constructed. Today, machine-made casks or *barriques* are often used for initial periods of aging. Sometimes cognacs are cut to 100° proof with distilled water before aging in musty warehouses called *chais* but, for the most part, they are aged at full strength. New spirits normally spend about a year in the most pungent new oak before

The famous brandy-aging warehouses called chais, *contain rare Hennessy cognac.*

A brandy maker at Asbach "noses" out his blend.

> Bacchus' blessings are a treasure,
> Drinking is the soldier's pleasure;
> Rich the treasure, sweet the pleasure,
> Sweet is pleasure after pain.
> ### John Dryden

they are transferred to older cooperage. In spirit aging, oxidation is the desired effect, so the ullage or evaporation is encouraged. The escaping water and alcohol form what the French call *la part des anges,* "for the angels," the equivalent of twelve million bottles of brandy escape each year into the atmosphere above the town. The chemical complexing in aging produces a light coloration of the originally white spirit. The tannin content as well as the acidity increases, and the cognacs of great age, up to forty years, acquire a slightly sweet finish. These special cognacs designed for great age are transferred to glass carboys and are placed in special storages named *les paradis.* Many producers, such as Hennessy and Martell, maintain blending *paradis* of a half century of age.

Maturing, Blending, and Marketing

While literally thousands grow, ferment, and distill cognac, the aging, blending, and marketing functions devolve on a very few old firms. Three—Hennessy, Martell, and Courvoisier—market nearly 50 percent of all annual sales.

All cognacs are blends, and the *maître de chais* constantly samples and assesses all aging cognacs to check their readiness for blending and bottling. The first blending may occur in the first year, long before bottling time. Other cognacs that indicate great promise and development are set aside unblended for later use.

The Hennessy Paradis *bottle graces its contents.*

Cognac Classifications

When the final blend is readied for the market, it is given one of three broad classifications.

- 3 Star—Over 80 percent of all cognac is marketed in this three-to-five-year range. Generally, these cognacs have a woody, slightly sweet finish.
- V.S.O.P.—These specialties average seven to ten years of aging, developing a remarkable smoothness and oaky complexity.
- Napoleon—Now little used, this older category represents a small fraction of total sales. Proprietary names, such as *Cordon Bleu* at Martell and *Bras d'Or* at Hennessy, signify that they are fifteen to twenty years old, very smooth, vanillan, aromatic cognacs.

Additives used in rectification, aside from distilled water, are limited to wood chips, cane sugar up to 2 percent by volume, and small quantities of caramel to balance the color. The older blends never employ chips or sweetening; instead, they develop finish solely from the aging barrels. The letters are not controlled by law but generally imply the following: E, especial; F, fine; V, very; O, old; S, superior; P, pale; X, extra. Hence V.S.O.P. may be read as Very Superior Old Pale, although the spirit in the bottle may not necessarily correspond to the words. In addition, there are other names such as *Extra, Extra Vieille,* and *Grande Reserve* which are usually, but, unfortunately, not always, reserved for the finer *paradis* blends.

While these letter designations can be confusing, the letter "X" predated brandy as a symbol of quality, as Emerson (1908) indicates.

> That the letter *X* was most commonly written so as to represent a cross, long before the Christian era, seems remarkably strange when we are brought by consequences to the full conviction that the cross of Christ was the true symbol of perfection. . . . The application of the letter *X* to whiskey, ale, or beer was, and continues to be, a distinguishing mark of its strength and purity . . .

The current Hennessy *paradis* blend on the market retails at more than $125 per bottle, demonstrating the unique role that finer cognac plays in the spirit trade.

Glass of brandy and water! That is the current but not appropriate name; ask for a glass of liquid fire and distilled damnation.
Dr. Robert Hall, c. 1780

ARMAGNAC

In the romantic land of Dumas where d'Artagnan led his Musketeers, the home of the fiery *Gasconois,* there lives another fiery French spirit—armagnac. Second only to cognac in reputation and distribution, this brandy is the first historically recorded, being licensed in 1411. It is likely that the isolated location, eighty miles to the south of Cognac, far from the shipping ports, explains its smaller trade and fame. Armagnac production is about 10 percent that of Cognac.

Armagnac was divided by the 1909 law into three distinct regions. As in Cognac, the regions consist of charming, quiet farmlands and pleasant rolling hills with no major metropolitan centers. Much of the fighting throughout the Hundred Years debacle took place in the region, and as a result, many fortifications erected then remain today. The Ténarèze constitutes the central zone; its chalky soils make fiery, light-bodied brandies necessary to balance all armagnac blends. Haut-Armagnac girdles Ténarèze to the east and south producing from limestone soils the smallest in both volume and quality for the vintage. Finally, Bas-Armagnac to the west, is the largest region and cultivates over 25,000 acres of brandy vineyards with soils of sand, clay, and slate. The city of Eauze in Bas-Armagnac is its marketing center.

While as many as twelve grapes are authorized for cultivation, the Folle Blanche, Saint-Émilion, Blanquette, Colombard, and a new hybrid named Baco 22A dominate. The latter is a cross between the Folle Blanche and an American native grape named Noah which produces well in Bas-Armagnac. Cooperatives control the production of the 100,000 acres in vines in the area which is about half as large as in the pre-phylloxera era. One-third of the crop goes to brandy production. The same objective of low alcohol and high acid is achieved in these vintages. Fermentation proceeds away from the skins as in cognac resulting in a wine seldom above 10 percent alcohol.

Distillation

The basic *alambic armagnacais* combines the principles of the pot and column stills. Formerly, itinerant *bouilliers de cru* traveled the countryside with mobile stills. Most armagnac is now distilled by merchants and the cooperatives in the winter months. The still utilizes a short rectifying column atop the *chaudière* in which the wine is allowed to splash down through the plates, releasing the rising vaporized spirits. Since there is but a single run through the still, these columns have gradually increased in height, lowering the impurities and raising the proof. Armagnac may be taken from the still at a maximum of 144° proof.

Aging and Rectifying

Armagnac follows cognac aging practices, utilizing the fine quality oak from nearby Monlezun forests. The black oak staves are dried for several years before being coopered into 400–liter casks. The fresh spirits spend one year in new wood, heavy with tannin, and are then transferred to more mature barrels. The assertive oak mellows the fiery armagnac within three years, although some may be marketed legally at about two years.

The 3 Star armagnacs generally have a minimum of three years in wood, and those labeled V.O. or V.S.O.P. have from four to ten years. The traditional *basquaise* oval bottles have given way to conventional styles in recent years. The cooperatives market under a number of brand names including *Marquis de Caussade* and *Haut Baron*. Major independent firms include Janneau and H. A. Sempe. Very little is shipped to the United States; most armagnac is exported to Scandinavia and West Germany.

Highlights

- Cognac is a very stylized French spirit controlled by government standards from berry to bottle.
- Because of the type of stills used, both cognac and armagnac rank high in congeneric content.

- Huge marketing firms sell the majority of French brandies.
- The youngest and sweetest of French brandy is sold as 3 Star with various other gradings for those of greater age, dryness, and complexity.

(A)

(B)

(C)

The classic alambic armagnacais *supports a short rectifying column above the* chaudière *(A). Cognac-type pot stills which also* have been legal in Armagnac since 1972 (B). The portable small-column still was a common sight until recent years (C).

261

*T*he gods who are most interested in the human race preside over the tavern. The tavern will compare favorably with the church. The church is the place where prayers and sermons are delivered, but the tavern is where they are to take effect, and if the former are good, the latter cannot be bad . . .

Henry David Thoreau

AMERICAN BRANDY

In the latter half of the nineteenth century, the wine business flourished in a newly found paradise of ideal soils and abundant sun in California. In a wave of immigration not unlike that of the German beer makers earlier in the century, German, French, and Italian winemakers dotted the landscape from the traditional southern California Mission lands to the farther reaches of the North Bay. The great wine names of this day— Krug, Martini, Inglenook, Beaulieu, and the Christian Brothers—settled in for secure vinous futures.

Of course, brandy accompanies wine grape growing. The earliest brandy makers were the Franciscans in their proud and magnificent missions. *America's Brandyland*, a pamphlet produced by the Brandy Advisory Board of California, recounts the story of Mission San Fernando which produced the impressive total of 200 barrels of brandy in 1830. As early as 1819, there is a notation of brandy being purchased for the handsome sum of $80 a barrel. It was Louis Vignes, one of the first to grow grapes in the Los Angeles region, who sired the early brandy according to the *Brandyland* pamphlet (1977).

> Vignes could be considered the father of California brandy; he believed in aging his brandy for years in oak casks to add to its smoothness. One visitor observed that Vignes' brandy, "when six, eight, or ten years old became of fine amber color, and was then a rich, oily liquor, very palatable."

The enterprising Captain Sutter erected a brandy still at his camp to serve the needs of the thirsty Gold Rushers. By 1860 a dozen producers were scattered around the state, but it took the increased demand in Europe (staggering under the vast phylloxera plague) and the Southern Pacific Railroad to create in the sunny San Joaquin Valley both America's fruit and vegetable basket and America's Brandyland.

At the turn of the century, the unique merits of California brandy became apparent worldwide. The State Board of Viticultural Commissioners earned a gold medal in the 1899 Exposition in Paris for a brandy that was produced from the same grape used in cognac, the French Folle Blanche. But the fame of the American spirit was short-lived because of the double impact of the return to production of famed French brandies following grafting of vines onto American rootstock and of Prohibition in 1919, which curtailed the growth of the American industry. Following repeal, the bulk of the American-made brandies served as high proof fortifying spirits to meet the demand of dessert winemakers. It was not until the end of the Second World War that brandy making came of age in California.

In 1938, a state government program attempted to establish a steady supply of brandy grapes with 10,000 growers and 250 wineries participating. The war brought the San Joaquin potential to the attention of the great liquor companies, and such venerables as Schenley, National Distillers, and Seagrams began to produce brandy. The Seagrams organization acquired the Paul Masson Winery and also became the marketing arm for The Christian Brothers' wines and brandy. At war's end, The Christian Brothers expanded their Reedley facility in the middle of the San Joaquin valley, pioneering in technology with the aim of producing unique, light, and flavorful brandies quite distinct from their European counterparts.

The *Brandyland* pamphlet tells of the perceptive work of Alfred Fromm and Franz Sichel in cooperation with Brother Timothy of The Christian Brothers and Otto Meyer of Paul Masson in a quest for a truly distinctive spirit, that would not be an imitation of the heavy-bodied, congenerically complex Cognac.

> These men worked out what they considered to be six essential characteristics of the blend: bouquet, body, lightness, dryness, smoothness, and flavor. The brandy must have an aroma and flavor characteristic of the grape. It must not be dominated by oak or by artificial flavors. It should first of all display an inherent fruity or grapey quality. And it should be light and soft to the taste, largely the result of patient aging. (1977)

Shades of Louis Vignes!

California Brandy Grapes

That magnificent stretch of real estate called the San Joaquin Valley, which separates the huge mountain chains in California, is a veritable agricultural paradise. Prominent among the fruits, nuts, and vegetables grown there are the grapes that develop copious doses of sugar in the blazing sun, those destined for dessert wines and brandies.

Throughout the years, over 125 varieties of grapes have been cultivated in this fabulous area. The Thompson Seedless is by far the heaviest crop of any grape in the nation. It is a familiar table grape, one which is also ideal as a raisin. Over 350,000 tons of the Thompson, some $25 million worth in value, ends up as brandy. The Thompson Seedless possesses some of the same qualities sought in French brandy grapes: low alcohol, neutrality and high acidity. Other grapes used in minor

Brandy grapes arrive from San Joaquin Valley vineyards.

The tremendous girth of the columns in a modern still dwarf the technician on the second level.

Perelli-Minetti Winery operates this two-column unit, making high-proof spirit for blending in the taller column and beverage brandy in the shorter. Valves permit the interconnection of the two columns into a single unit.

These are the large pot stills employed by the Christian Brothers in their unique blend of pot and patent brandies.

amounts in California brandy are the original Mission grape, the Tokay, the Grenache, and the Malaga. Many of these grapes produce up to 10 tons per acre in the valley's intense warmth.

Distilling in California

Stark contrasts between French and American brandies occur at production level. After the Second World War, the continuous still technology was highly sophisticated, following nearly a century of bourbon and other high proof spirit making in the east. Consequently, the continuous still became the ideal production tool. Only minuscule amounts of pot still brandy spirits find their way into American bottles.

Some Pot Still Spirit

The largest producer of American brandy does utilize a percentage of pot spirit. The Christian Brothers operate both copper pot and patent stills at Reedley. However, as shown in the photograph, these pot stills are quite different from French *alambics*. The American penchant for building the better mousetrap is apparent in these huge pot stills which accommodate 4,000 gallons of wine in each batch and produce about 1,000 gallons of spirit from each run.

The complete run requires fourteen hours, with the first four hours producing the heads. The middle liquors take another four hours, yielding finished spirits of the character of the *bonne chauffe* in cognac. The remaining time distills out the tails. This single run produces a relatively clean but heavy spirit of approximately fifty to seventy-five parts per million in aldehydes which is ideal for blending purposes. The size of the pot, 4,000 gallons, compared to the approximately 340 gallon limitation in cognac, provides for both volume and speed.

The brandy maker must be vigilant about the minutest change in the spirit flow that is recorded on monitors.

While the objectives are identical, the methods differ between the centuries-old cognac warehouses and those of California. Shown here are the brandy-filled barrels stacked five high on pallets in hangar-type buildings. The brandies rest from three to five years in a cooperage.

Only at the end of the long aging period, when the barrels are emptied, is the $10.50 excise tax imposed.

The 500-liter barrels of Madero XXXXX aging brandy of Mexico are destined for blending of pot and column still products before bottling. Madero also produced some 100 percent pot-still brandy similar to cognac.

Continuous Stills

California brandy stills are both large and complex. The Perelli-Minetti towers soar to over sixty feet, while those of The Christian Brothers top off at a more conventional height of thirty-five feet.

The Christian Brothers operate two patent stills in tandem, each capable of operating twenty-four hours per day for the five to six month annual distilling period. The first of these stills was constructed in 1947, the second in 1958. Over the years, The Christian Brothers have benefited from the cooperative involvement of their worldwide distributor, Fromm and Sichel, a subsidiary of the world's largest spirit producer, Joseph E. Seagram and Sons. Utilizing the years of experience of Seagrams, the company has pioneered in the development of automatic controls and other technologies in brandy making.

The finished wine called distilling material, or DM, is cut or diluted with water to the 7 percent alcohol level. This DM enters near the top of the separating column at the impressive rate of 7,000 gallons per hour. Aldehydes and fusel oils are systematically eliminated in the rectifying column and

as many as fifty samples are analyzed daily to assure a constant flow of even, clear spirit. Any brandy emerging at less than the desired standard is simply diverted back through the process as is residual material resulting from the processing of the heads and tails. The Christian Brothers take the final spirit from the still at 169° proof, nearly 30° proof degrees above the final run in a cognac still. That which is taken above 170° proof is termed neutral brandy which may be employed as high proof fortifying material for dessert wines.

This imposing machine is kept in balance very much like a tempestuous teapot since changes in temperature, pressure, and concentrations can each alter the emerging product. The evidence of all this skill and technology lies in the impressive capacity of about 400 barrels of top quality distillate daily.

Aging and Rectifying

Off the still, American brandy is no less fiery and in need of tempering than cognac. The vast majority of the spirits age in American white oak, which has considerably less chemical transfer than the French barrels. Most are previously used whiskey barrels. The brandy is cut with demineralized water to between 115° and 130° proof to be aged for a minimum of two years. The Christian Brothers average four years of age in their blends, stacking the 55-gallon barrels six pallets high to age in huge, ambient-air warehouses in the valley.

During the period in the barrel, ullage accounts for about 5 percent of the volume, evaporation raising the proof a percent or two. The barrels are emptied, and the spirit is cut with demineralized water to the selling level of 80° proof at which time the $10.50 per proof gallon federal excise tax is imposed. In keeping with the original objective to produce light, slightly sweet brandy, up to 2 percent invert sugar may be added as well as the ubiquitous and tasteless caramel which assures uniformity in color.

Highlights

- The vast bulk of American brandy is produced in giant continuous stills.
- American brandies are characterized by their light body and hint of sweetness compared to the heavy aromatic cognacs and other continental brandies.
- All are blends but some, such as The Christian Brothers X. O., contain high proportions of pot still spirits.
- American brandy is one of the few dark-colored spirits currently increasing in sales.

Also at this stage, the brandy maker at The Christian Brothers exercises that consummate skill of the blender, adding just the right amount of aged pot still spirits, perhaps as much as 10 percent of the total volume, to produce the unique balance, smoothness, and character. The new blend marries in the 30,000 gallon stainless steel tanks for up to six months before entering the bottling line which handles up to 200 units per minute.

From the mechanical pruning and harvesting of the grapes to the high-speed bottling lines, American brandy makers adopt the latest in mechanical sophistication while clinging stubbornly to the traditional art and skill of the master blenders, truly a triumph of old and new in producing one of the world's lightest spirits yet full of character.

MARKETING

While there are over a dozen American brandy makers and up to two hundred brandy labels in America, several large firms dominate the market as in Europe. However, California brandies totaled over 5.5 million cases in 1979, nearly 80 percent of all grape brandy consumed in the United States. The Christian Brothers produce almost 40 percent of the annual sales, followed by Paul Masson, Schenley with a number of brands including Coronet and J. Bonet, and the winemaker E. J. Gallo, a relative newcomer in large production with their brandy called E & J.

As with all spirits, there are regions of popularity in which brandy holds an unusual percentage of the market (see table 17.1). Generally speaking, these are the northern states, perhaps because of the frigid weather or the native populations which have traditionally favored this spirit.

Import Brandies

While the American producers hold the dominant position in this market, roughly three of four bottles consumed, import brandies continue with aggressive marketing to hold firm to slightly up. The United States remains the number one importer of cognac worldwide.

TABLE 17.1 Top Ten Markets
for Brandy
1980 vs. 1981
(750 ML Per 100 Persons)

State	1980	1981
Wisconsin	382.4	358.2
Minnesota	198.4	193.2
District of Columbia	165.7	189.4
Nevada	176.5	161.1
North Dakota	93.0	98.3
California	77.9	80.7
Montana	63.5	62.0
Alaska	52.2	60.3
New Hampshire	60.3	57.7
Maryland	37.6	46.8
National average	40.0	40.8

Source: Dan Hecht, ed., *The Liquor Handbook* (New York: Gavin-Gobson Associates, Inc., 1982), 277.

OTHER FRENCH BRANDIES

Since the Middle Ages in practice, and since Napoleon as a legal right, the French grape grower could produce wine spirits for home consumption without permit. Over time, brandy making grew to be a village event, participated in by many growers using portable equipment—no hiding in glens like the Irish and the Scots. Marrison in *Wines and Spirits* (1970) gives a vivid description of the production of the brandy developed from the lees of wine fermentation, containing the pips, skins, seeds, and other solid matter.

The solid mass of skins, stems, and pips, called *gennes* in Burgundy, has been hard packed into casks or a vat and covered with a mortar of clay to keep out *Acetobacter*. He has occasionally inspected it and filled up the cracks which formed as autumn turned to winter and the *gennes* dried. Then it is dug out and water added, the whole mixed up into a slurry and slowly fermented.

The brandy distilled from the hard-packed, smelly mass grew to be called *marc*. Marc is produced in France in widely dispersed areas such as Aquitaine, Burgundy, Languedoc, and Auvergne. Marrison points out the inherent danger of the passing over of more than trace quantities of methyl alcohol derived from the pips and skin concentrations. Without careful selecting out of the considerable heads and tails, marc could well become *eau-de-mort* instead of the water of life!

Similar brandies produced in the other wine nations include *bagaceria* in Portugal, *tresterbrantwein* in Germany, dopbrandy in South Africa and, of course, *grappa* in Italy. The vast majority of these rough and heady *lees* brandies remain in local consumption, although in northern France there is some commercial *marc de bourgogne* from both red and white grape residue. However, marc remains for the hardy!

Other nations producing brandy on a commercial level, some in international trade, include Italy, Spain, South Africa, Greece, Portugal, Germany, Peru, and Australia.

*I*f ever I marry a wife,
I'll marry a landlord's daughter,
For then I may sit in the bar,
And drink cold brandy and water.
Charles Lamb

ITALIAN BRANDY AND GRAPPA

It will not be surprising to learn that Italy produces vast amounts of distilled wine spirits. Perhaps the largest brandy maker of the world is Distillerie Stock, a company widely known for its vermouths and liqueurs. Hannum and Blumberg (1976) record its market: "Today, from its headquarters in Trieste, brandy and liqueurs are shipped to over one hundred different countries, and new plants have been established in the United States, Australia, South Africa, and South America." Stock is by far the best selling Italian brandy label among an incredibly diverse 2,000 Italian brand names. Other international trade names include Riunite and Buton.

The word *grappa* derives from the Gothic for grape bunch, an appropriate name since the whole bulk is involved. Originally, grappa was sold at very high proofs, but most today is produced below 80° proof and is consumed cold and neat, in the manner of Danish *akvavit* or French Calvados.

In large distilleries grappa is produced in the same manner as conventional brandies, but with special attention to the dephlegmator (condenser) designed to eliminate the heavy portions of methyl alcohol. The heads and tails are discarded and, for the most part, a short nine-month aging period precedes bottling and sale as *giovane,* meaning "as clear as water." Some is barreled in oak, some in ash or mulberry, with various periods of aging: *vecchia* is aged up to two years; *stravecchia,*

very old, up to four years. The thirty or so commercial grappas on the Italian market today have killed the Italian moonshine industry by assuring both quality and price.

Since a 1948 agreement with France, no Italian brandy producer uses the word cognac in labeling.

SPAIN

It all began in Spain, with the Moors. Naturally, the center of brandy production grew around the sherry industry in Jerez. And it still remains there. Over 50 percent of the production of one of its famous sherry makers, Domecq, is brandy. Huge amounts of both high proof and commercial brandies are made all over the huge wine-growing land of Jerez, about 13 million cases annually. But because of the influence of the sherry wines, as well as the cooperage in which many of the spirits are aged, the tendency of Spanish brandies is to be heavy in body and sweet in finish. Hannum and Blumberg (1976) describe the Spanish product: "The brandies . . . tend to be quite sweet, with heavy doses of woodiness and rather pronounced sherry-like aromas and flavors, the latter often arising from the use of sherry as a flavor additive or from aging the brandy in barrels previously used for sherry."

These Spanish brandies come from huge continuous stills for the most part, but some producers, such as Torres in the north, utilize pot stills patterned after those in Cognac.

*O*ur water is not *aqua di vite* (water of vines), but *aqua de vita* (water of life) because it gives life to men.
Giovanni di Rupe

SOUTH AFRICA

For over three hundred years, both wines and brandies have been supplied to the British Empire from the hundred-mile strip of land north and east of Capetown. An incredible 50 percent of the grape crush passes to the brandy stills which are of both the pot and the continuous types. Brandy ranks number one in domestic spirit consumption, and great quantities are shipped to Commonwealth countries.

By law each blend must contain a minimum of 25 percent of the pungent pot still product assuring a style and assertiveness to South African brandy. Tax credits favor long aging for the brandies. They are finished with a touch of sugar and caramel as are most of the wine spirits of the world. Export brands carry some of the same designations as the cognacs such as 5 Star and V.S.O.P. The largest exporter is the K. W. V. Co-operative, with other leading labels, such as Bertrams and Castle, found in many markets.

This picturesque vineyard nestled in the mountains of South Africa typifies the three hundred-year-old wine and brandy vineyards. Over seventy-four hundred farmers produce about the same amount of wine as does Portugal.

Highlights

- In major wine nations, much local strong brandy is distilled from the pomace left from wine making.
- Greek, Spanish, and other Mediterranean brandies tend to be on the sweet side and are often flavored with fruits and herbs during rectification.
- Italy produces fine brandies and equally fine *grappa* or pomace spirits all over the country.
- South African brandy is a favorite throughout the Commonwealth countries.

GREECE

While they were not the inventors of distilling, the Greeks did become early brandy producers. One of their brandies still conjures goodwill throughout the world, as Hannum and Blumberg (1976) report:

> The largest-selling Greek brandy based beverage is *Metaxa*, which is exported to over one hundred countries around the world. The base spirit of Metaxa is grape brandy, although sufficient sweetening and flavoring elements are added so that it is marketed in the United States as a "Greek specialty liqueur" . . .

Cambas, the major exporter of Metaxa, also offers a medium sweet conventional brandy. Other Greek brandy-based bottlings include the resinous Mastika and the anisette-flavored Ouzo. The proclivity for very sweet drinks along the Mediterranean is deeply rooted in history and tradition.

GERMANY

Germany is unusual in the brandy spectrum. It imports from Mediterranean countries nearly all the base wine for production despite its own rather considerable grape growing. In practical terms, German grapes are too economically precious and unsuited in style for spirit making. The national spirit of Germany is schnapps, corn or barley liquor. Despite this fact, about a quarter of the spirits consumed are brandies, and the nation represents a good brandy import market. One firm recognized worldwide is Asbach which imports only French wines for its cognac-style pot stills and uses only Limousin oak for aging. Their Asbach Uralt is a cognaclike, light, extremely aromatic delight.

OTHER BRANDIES OF NOTE

Portugal has produced *aguardiente* and *bagaceria,* pomace brandy, since they inherited the process from Spain to mellow their port wines, but little is found on the open market. Turkey, Cyprus, Israel, the Balkans—nearly every nation which raises grapes—also distills some sort of brandy, mostly for local consumption.

A fair amount of the spirit is found in South America, with the most famous being Pisco from Peru, Chile, Argentina and Bolivia. Named for the Incas who apparently were the first to produce it, Pisco utilizes a strain of muscat grapes grown in the Ica Valley of Peru and in other areas. Its fame developed at the time of the Gold Rush in California when it was shipped in quantity in amphoralike jars lined with beeswax. The fortyniners tamed it with citrus juice and called it Pisco Sour, a drink still popular in Baghdad by the Bay.

Australia, with its considerable wine industry, produces a number of local brandies, the most famous being from the Seppelt Wineries. Even the Chinese produce a light American-style brandy with the inviting name of Sunflower. All of these national brandies amount to a scant percentage of international commerce, but they do demonstrate the accessibility and popularity of the grape spirit.

Spirit-tasting Procedures

*L*ike the fermented beverages, each of the spirit sections also has a suggested tasting. While the acquisition of all of the suggested types of alcohols may come to a tidy sum, there is merit in sensing each new beverage at the time it is covered in the text. The tasting involves but a few ounces of each, so you will accumulate a considerable and diverse liquor cabinet by the end of the book. Since spirits generally have a long shelf life, these choice liquors and liqueurs can delight your guests and provide exquisite accent to fine cooking for many months to come.

Use the rating form printed in the wine-tasting chapter for all of the spirit tastings. The labels suggested here are those in general commerce around the United States, but many substitutions can be made if these particular selections are not available in your market. Ask your friendly spirit merchant for substitutes. The purpose is to achieve as great a diversity in styles as possible in the first tasting, letting your imagination, interest, and pocketbook determine future tastings.

SPIRIT TASTING IN GENERAL

Obviously, tasting and testing of high proof beverages must be done with greater care than that necessary with the light alcohol wines. The following suggestions are designed to provide an interesting, fruitful experience before the spirit obscures the awareness sought.

The ideal procedure involves two sets of glasses for each spirit in the tasting. The first set should contain about an ounce or so of the spirit directly from the bottle. The second should contain the same amount of spirit cut in half by the addition of distilled water. The host should be certain that this dilution process is done with precision.

As in wine tastings, there should be available simple, unsalted or unspiced breads and cheeses to cleanse the palate between tastings. There should be plastic buckets available for tasters who wish to expectorate the samples instead of swallowing. For the initial tasting, I recommend that a small portion of each liquor be swallowed to measure the aftertaste and the peculiar warming effects from many strong liquors.

The glasses should be placed so as to have easy access back and forth between the sets to confirm the nuances between selections as the tasting proceeds.

In the Nose

Ninety-nine percent of the judgment of spirits in the distillery occurs in the nosing of the samples. By now you recognize the primal role of the trigeminal nerves in determining desirability of, or repugnance toward things we eat. Since spirits often tend to be more intensely aromatic than wines, be sure to take clean, powerful sniffs separated by several minutes to allow the essential character to impress the mind. Impressions such as the obvious smokiness in Scotch, the grainy, woodlike pungency of straight whiskey, the fruity and herbaceous overtones in cordials, and the nearly floral composition of the lightest spirits should be apparent in the nosing. A blindfolded child with little or no exposure to ardent spirits can distinguish the light and heavy spirits by the nose alone. Take particular care to mark and commit to memory these aromatic values.

The world of spirits encompasses nearly every flavoring known to humans—some dominant, others subtle—often masking the true flavors of the informing alcohol.

On the Palate

Naturally, the heavy concentrations of ethanol in 80° to 100° or more proof spirits tend to obscure many nuances of the four tastes—sweet, sour, bitter and salt—just as the malt hops and carbon dioxide do in brews. Further, the vast majority of drinkers today take their liquors with water, soda, or juice mixers. Therefore, the true tastes of the spirits are seldom, if ever, engaged. For the purposes of this experimental tasting, the second glass containing spirit cut with distilled water will yield all of the native flavors because the spirits are quite miscible in the new element. After all of the tasting, you may wish to return to the first set of glasses and taste each of the samples at full strength. You will easily discover that the first sample at full proof will overpower the values of all that follow.

The most important element in spirit tasting is the "nose."

Obviously, the full-bodied, harsher spirits will dominate the palate and provide easy recognition. Some more patient deliberation will be required to liberate the taste elements in the lighter spirits. While you are limited to the four tastes, the congeneric concentrations and variations provide a veritable symphony from smooth and mellow to harsh and hot. Your judgment will be required here as in wine tasting even though some of the types may be personally repugnant. Look for balance and style according to the standards for that particular spirit.

In the Throat

Generally, there is a more distinctive and lasting *finish* with spirits than with many wines. The bigger spirits such as Jamaican rum or single malt Scotch warm all the way to the tummy. Words such as intense, fiery, and crisp are often used to describe the aftertaste of the big spirits, just as smooth and mellow equate with the milder types.

Again, generally speaking, many of the descriptive phrases and words set forth in the wine-tasting section can serve as the basis for communication about spirits.

SUGGESTED COGNAC AND BRANDY TASTING

TABLE 18.1 Cognac and Brandy Tasting

Spirit	General Style	Suggested Brand
California brandy	Light body, aromatic with a hint of sweetness, warm finish	The Christian Brothers, Paul Masson, Korbel
California special brandy	Medium to heavy body, pungent, dry and assertive finish	The Christian Brothers X.O.
German brandy	Medium body, assertive nose, sharp flavor with a sense of sweetness	Asbach Uralt
Spanish brandy	Medium to heavy body, sharp nose, definite sweetness and oily finish	Torres
Cognac	Powerful nose, big body leading to warming, smooth finish, pleasant buttery or oily finish, hint of sweetness	Hennessy V.S.
Cognac	Highly aromatic nose, dry and full body, warm and polished finish	Courvoisier V.S.O.P.
Armagnac	Powerful nose, steely and hot mouth feel, strong finish	Any available
South African brandy	Big, smooth and mellow finish	Oude Meester, K. W. V.
Greek brandy	Assertive nose, strongly sweet mouth feel, hot and warming, huge body and hot finish	Mextaxa 3 Star

White Fruit Spirits

19

The French term *alcool blanc* means white spirits, but the name is something of a misnomer. Virtually all spirits are white when taken from the still so that the term theoretically includes everything. Second, the nomenclature can be too restrictive when it is interpreted to mean fruit brandies only, since many of the mélange of native spirits—for example, those under the broad umbrella of the various spellings of arack or raki—derive from combinations of fruit sap and grain. However, for the most part, alcool blanc are brandies produced from fruits other than grapes.

As a class, these spirits have certain production limitations that will keep them ever in a minor role in the spirit market. The foremost problem is that few fruits contain the rich vitamin and mineral content of grapes. To compensate for this, most recipes call for the addition of raisins or other additives to sustain the fermenting yeast. Few other fruits contain the high percentage of fructose and glucose as grapes so that molasses or cane sugar must also be added to the must of non-grape brandies in order to create sufficient alcohols. While the natural fruit flavors generally transfer quite well in the fermentation process, those distinctive flavors and aromas often tend to bleach or wash out in the searing heat of a still. But despite these difficulties, popular fruit brandies do constitute a significant part of total production.

SOURCE FRUITS

Throughout the centuries, the most desirable fruits were cultivated through a process of natural selection. Naturally, then,

white spirit making became centered in the most prolific fruit-producing areas. The most popular of the surviving white fruit spirits and their sources appear in table 19.1.

FERMENTATION

Without question, only the best fruits are selected from the croppings because the slightest imperfection or blemish will carry over into the spirits. Consequently, white fruit spirits are extremely expensive to produce. The solid fruits such as apples and pears must be pressed, mashed, and thoroughly sauced in advance of fermentation to make all the fructose available to the yeasts. Berry types, rich in fructose, are simply broken or separated lightly and allowed to ferment as they come from the fields.

TABLE 19.1 White Fruit Spirits and Their Sources

Spirit	Source
Apricot	Apricot
Baie d'alise	Rowanberries
Baie d' houx	Holly berries
Baie de sureau	Elderberries
Bourgeons de sapin	Pine buds
Cassis	Black currant
Coing	Quince
Enzian	Gentian root
Fleurs d'acacia	Acacia flowers
Fraise	Strawberries
Framboise	Raspberries
Genévrier	Juniper berries
Groseille	Red currants
Kirsch	Cherries
Mirabelle	Mirabelle yellow plums
Mûre	Mulberries
Mûre de ronce	Blackberries
Myrtille	Bilberries
Nèfle	Medlars
Pêche	Peaches
Poire Williams	Williams pears
Pomme	Apples
Prunelle	Sloe berry (blackthorn)
Quetsche	Alsatian blue plums
Reine-Claude	Greengage plums
Slivovitz	Sliva plums
Sorbier	Rowanberries

The fruit mash cannot be diluted for fear of flavor loss. Surprisingly, where grapes are rarely fermented longer than a month, some other berries and fruits are fermented as long as a year. Cherries, as well as black currants and prunes with up to 18 percent sugar, will produce up to 10 percent alcohol. Raspberries contain up to 6 percent sugar, but many other fruits have such small concentration of sugars that the ethanol is inevitably light. Apples, some plums, and some peaches have the ideal .5 percent to .8 percent acidity, but some berries achieve over 2 percent acidity, much too tart for proper wine balance. Nearly always, the pits, skins, and pips remain in the fermenting must, if for no other reason than that they are too difficult to remove. Some few types employ broken or cracked pits, such as almond that releases bitter almond overtones caused by a chemical called amygdalin.

Some idea of the cost of the raw materials can be gained when you consider that twenty-two pounds of mirabelle plums equal a single liter of spirit, or that a full fifty pounds of Williams pears reduce to a single bottle, or that a bottle of framboise requires up to thirty pounds of first rate raspberries.

Finally, some fruits with low sugar for fermentation work better when an infusion or maceration process precedes distillation. The fruit is infused in alcohol already distilled from other fruit. The mash is allowed to settle as vermouth does, during which time the desired essences leach out into the alcohol. The alcoholized mash is then distilled directly, usually in pot stills.

DISTILLATION AND AGING

For the most part, fruit brandies are double distilled in cognac-styled pot stills. Generally, the fruit enters the pot unfiltered from the fermenters. The first run is taken at 30 percent alcohol, or 60° proof, though sometimes at less in order to preserve the fruitiness. The final run may be no higher than 120° proof.

Fruit essences see little if any aging. The drier and more assertive types, such as slivovitz, may be wood aged. Others are ready for the bottle and immediate consumption directly from the still. If aging seems desirable, the vessel will be glass or paraffin-coated wood to inhibit any chemical exchange from the container. This precaution is taken because the spirits, unlike grape brandy, need little mellowing and mollifying for palatability. The steps of filtering, racking, centrifuging, and wood aging are not used in this delicately balanced system.

RAKI, ARRACK, ARAK, ETC.

The range of spirits produced in the Near and Far East, as well as in India and down through the African continent, is bewildering. In Lebanon and Syria, arak made from grapes could as well be called brandy. In Turkey and the Balkans, raki has been produced over the centuries from potatoes, plums, rice, molasses, grape wine, and combinations thereof. There is a Mahua tree in India which has flowers so rich in sugar that wine and spirits can be produced from them. Of course, both palms and dates, as well as the sap running in their veins, produce raki. For most, a trip to the country of origin is necessary for tasting.

THE MOST FAMOUS: CALVADOS

Normandy, the famous region of northwestern France, was named for the Viking Norsemen who conquered it in the ninth century. Since grapes could not mature well in the climate, the resourceful invaders turned for drink to the abundant apple trees that had been planted there in the eighth century by Charlemagne. In *The World Guide to Spirits, Aperitifs and Cocktails*, Tony Lord recounts the progression from the drink to the name:

> When the Norsemen took this land they found parts were covered with wild apple trees. They and the native Bretons fermented the juice of these apples to make a rough cider. Some 600 years later, in 1553, a document records that Gilles de Gouberville successfully distilled the rough cider into an apple brandy. Five years later, the Spanish galleon *El Calvador . . .* was driven on to the Normandy coast in a storm. A town near the site of the shipwreck took the name Calvados . . .

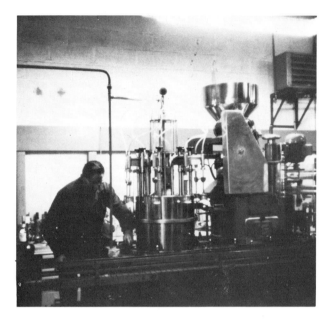

A modern Calvados laboratory.

In the heart of the Calvados region of Pays d'Auge, ancient pot stills with the characteristic swan neck are used for the entire output.

Moreover, the Normans, that I may speak of them also, were at that time, and are even now, proudly apparelled [sic], delicate in their food, but not excessive. They are a race inured to war, and can hardly live without it.

William of Malmesbury

Production

In the manner of the cognac region's grape growers, apple growers deliver the annual crop to cooperatives for processing. The largest portion of the crop is devoted to cider consumed in the region with about 20 percent ending in the brandy stills. Aside from the d'Auge region where the traditional cognac *alambic* is in use, the predominant equipment is the column still. Two runs are required in the d'Auge *alambic,* the first as low as 40° proof to retain the fruit, and the second at a top of 142° proof, slightly above the cognac level. The young spirits designed for quick consumption may be treated with wood chips and be slightly sweetened, but the best is stored in Limousin oak casks capable of holding 10,000 liters and is marketed quite dry, at about 90° proof.

The calvados in international trade comes in *Vieux* or *Reserve*, indicating a minimum of three years in wood. V.O., or *Vieille Reserve*, must be at least four years old, while the names *V.S.O.P. Extra, Napolean*, and *Hors d'Age* all indicate aging periods of five or more years. One might note the imitation of their cognac neighbors to the south.

Tony Lord (1979) reports that

calvados is a vital part of the Norman way of life. They will have *un 'tit Calva* as a pick-me-up in the morning, and halfway through their evening meal a larger glass, usually swallowed in one gulp, which they have nicknamed the *trou Normand* (Norman holemaker) to settle their stomachs. Finally, they will have another glass after dinner with their coffee.

Huge stationary cider presses and stone mashing wheels were common sights on American colonial farms.

The second Robert Laird, early marketing genius for Laird's Applejack, is shown at the company plant. The firm is operated now by the eighth generation of Lairds.

I William McDermott lives here,
I sells good porter, ale, and beer.
I've made my sign a little wider,
To let you know I sell good cider.
Early Tavern Sign

APPLEJACK

Applejack, or cider brandy, was also extremely popular in colonial America. This was partly because of the availability of apple trees which were propagated in the new lands as early as 1632. While apples were, and are, a delicious fruit, their huge crops and the ease of fermenting dictated that cider would be the preferred form of consumption. In *Early American Beverages* (1966), John Hull Brown reports that "cider soon became perhaps the most popular drink for the people. It could be made locally and in great quantities. There has been recorded one orchard which produced sufficient apples to make five hundred hogsheads of cider in 1671." Brown also records a wide range of brews and spirits common in those times: "rum, egg nog, apple and peach brandy, whiskey, molasses beer, spruce beer, persimmon beer, mead, many varieties of cordials." However, it was the two white spirits that retained some character of their fruit base—apples in the north and peaches in the south—that dominated the scene.

The company that practically owns the American market today was founded in 1780. Laird and Company, now in its eighth generation of family managers, proudly states on its label: "Applejack today is one of the purest of spirit beverages.

Only tree ripened apples are used. No cultures, yeast, starters, sugar or blending agents are ever used."

The earliest applejack was separated from its watery base in a most fundamental manner. On a cold evening, the cider remained on the stoop. By morning, the water froze, leaving a nearly 120° proof alcohol, dubbed *hedgehog quills*, *essence of lockjaw*, or *Jersey Lightning*. Applejack as prepared today according to the purity standards of Laird contains a blend of 35 percent straight cider brandy and 65 percent neutral grain spirits. The brandy is aged up to four years in wood before the blending which allows a pleasant apple aroma in a nice sipping spirit.

FLAVORED BRANDIES

A clear distinction should be made between spirits produced directly from various fruit bases and those called "flavored brandies." The latter popular beverages are compounded products, usually consisting of a brandy or neutral spirit base into which flavorings are introduced. While pleasant, inexpensive, and often quite sweet, they fall short of the real thing.

Fruit-flavored brandies with American labels must be made from a base of grape brandy bottled at no less than 70° proof. In contrast to a true liqueur, it need contain no minimum sugar level. Consequently, many of these flavored varieties are decidedly less sweet than similarly flavored cordials. Blackberry and apricot have been favorites over the years, and ginger has gained acceptance in recent years.

SUGGESTED WHITE FRUIT SPIRITS TASTING

Throughout the world, industrious farmers and merchants produce enchanting light, fruit-based spirits from locally grown

Highlights

- *Alcool blanc* is an inclusive term covering all white fruit spirits other than grape brandy.
- Most fruit brandies are consumed in the areas of production.

- Apple brandy is the world's most often shipped and consumed white brandy.
- Only pure, fresh top grade fruit is used in the production of white fruit brandies.

fruit. Unfortunately, because of the difficulty in capturing and maintaining these delicate essences, the spirits do not travel well. With the abundance of grain and grape spirits in international trade, most white fruit spirits remain local oddities. Also confusing to the novice is the variation in names from one country to the next. For example, *kirsch* in Alsace refers to tart cherry brandy while the same product is called *Kirschwasser* in the nearby Black Forest of Germany. Raspberries in Alsace become *framboise,* while the same fruit in Germany produces *Himbeergeist.* (Incidentally, the Germans add *Wasser* to those fruit mashes that are directly distilled and *Geist* to those macerated in alcohol.) These fruit brandies are often confused with fruit-based liqueurs which generally come much sweeter and with a combination of herbs and fruits. For this tasting, make a special effort to locate only pure fruit spirits.

TABLE 19.2 White Fruit Spirits Tasting

Spirit	General Style	Suggested Brand
Applejack (American)	Piercing nose, medium body, and definite apple flavorings	Laird's
Apple Brandy (French)	Attractive fruity nose, complex flavoring, smooth woody character	Calvados
Cherry (French or German)	Light floral nose, sharp but pleasing mouth feel, true cherry flavors	Kirsch or Kirschwasser
Plum (Yugoslavian)	Oaky nose, bitter and sharp taste, yet true fruit flavors, long finish	Slivovitz
Peach Flavored (American)	Nice floral nose, smooth and easy taste, medium dry, nice peach character	De Kuyper National Distillers
Blackberry Flavored (American)	Huge nose, thick body and strong fruit flavoring, strong finish	Arrow Heublein
Apple Liqueur	Highly aromatic, medium sweet	Berentzen, Appel, Schenley

Irish Whiskey

20

*D*espite the uncertainty of much of the history of distilled spirits, few authorities dispute the claim of the Irish to be the first to produce in quantity a distillate from grain. Many writers cite the references of Henry II to the local *usquebaugh* liquor he found on his conquering trek in 1170. This was close to the time of the earliest experiments in Salerno, Italy, and certainly before those recorded in Spain. The famous St. Patrick and a succession of fellow monks from the continent had brought brewing, as well as Christianity, to the island as early as the sixth century. One priest on Patrick's household staff was a brewer. Since nearly all education resided in these roving Churchmen, the techniques of distilling could well have traveled across the channel with the monks before the time of Henry II.

The noted historian of Irish distilling, E. B. McGuire, explains in *Irish Whiskey* (1973) that commercial distilling did not become a common practice until after the fifteenth century.

> A few scraps of information about spirit drinking appear a century later [than 1170] . . . but even in 1450 the wording of a statute that "Irish wine, ale, and other liqure" was to be sold by the King's measure properly sealed . . . indicates that the spirits were no more than "other liquor." There is other evidence that distilling was not commonly practised before the fifteenth century. Vessels, including an ancient worm . . . appeared to have been used as stills. None of them suggest a date earlier than 1400 judging from the materials, solder used and their condition, but they lend support to a probability that distilling operations were purely domestic.

*N*ever a philtre found with such power to charm and bewilder, as this we are quaffing.

Thomas Moore

*G*od invented whiskey to keep the Irish from ruling the world.

Doggerel

In *Beverages Past and Present* (1908), Emerson points out that the vaunted *usquebaugh* was in reality a cordial-like compound when he cites the following recipe from a 1602 book entitled *Delights for Ladies:*

> To every gallon of good *aqua composita* put two ounces of chosen licorice, bruised and cut into small pieces, but first cleanse from all his [*sic*] filth, and two ounces of annis seeds that are cleane and bruised. Let them macerate five or six days in a wooden vessel . . . those groundes which remaine, you may redistill, and make more *aqua composita* of them, and of that *aqua composita* you may make more *usquebath*.

Other additives, such as heather honey, herbs, and saffron, were also mentioned. We are not dealing simply with semantics here, but with a recognition that the techniques of pimentation (adulteration of bad wines) so common on the continent would

281

Terms

blends Before the 20th century, blends referred only to mixtures of pot distillates; now the term refers to mixtures of pot spirits and grain spirits from continuous stills.

brugh-fer Pronounced broo-fer, early Gaelic for brewer.

courmi Early Gaelic for ale.

dextrine Gum-like carbohydrate formed by heating starch.

exciseman Since 1651 the British tax officer.

gauger The exciseman who measured the wash or the still and at times the spirits themselves for tax-collecting purposes.

low wines The liquors from the first pot distillation.

poteen Or potheen—literally, a small pot—the spirits produced by illicit distillers in Ireland.

usquebaugh Used interchangeably with aqua vitae, means "water of life" in Gaelic; found very early in literature; pronounced "us-gay-baha," hence believed to be the base for the word "whiskey."

certainly have been introduced in fair measure by monks at such an outpost of the Church. In addition, this recipe suggests the commonness of home distillation, as well as the inevitability of the scorched, undrinkable nature of the initial *aqua composita*. In *The World Guide to Spirits, Aperitifs and Cocktails,* Tony Lord reports that "many households ran their own still—making a new batch of whiskey was part of family life. In 1633 a chronicler wrote that the 'Irish eat raw meat which boyleth in their stomachs with aqua vitae which they swill in after such a surfeite, by quarts and pottles.'"

In fact, consumption of distilled spirits became such a universal problem that restrictive legislation was enacted in Ireland as early as 1556. It was curious legislation, however, and not effective in curtailing merchandising. This was because while innkeepers were required to purchase licenses to distill, a freeman, the nobility of the time, was allowed a home still. Laws like this were rarely taken seriously so that the Irish Parliament finally passed the first major systematized excise tax on liquor in 1661, about which McGuire editorializes in *Irish Whiskey* (1973):

> Perhaps no country has suffered more from the excessive height to which duties on spirits have been carried than Ireland. If heavy taxes, enforced by severe fiscal regulations, could make a people sober and industrious, then the Irish would be the most of any upon the face of the earth.

Unfortunately, the legislation resulted not in control, but the opposite—two hundred years of bloodshed, lying, cheating, and systematic disobedience. Fraud was so widespread in the industry that companies, to protect themselves, destroyed their records of distillations. This leaves us now with few if any records outlining those early four hundred years of commercial distillation in Ireland.

Figure 20.1 *In medieval Europe, taxing authorities employed gaugers who literally checked the level of the fill of the stills and the finished barreled spirits to impose their levies. (From a fifteenth century woodcut.)*

The most inane of these capricious laws was the 1779 tax which penalized smaller stills and thus encouraged enormous machines which spewed out horrendously bad spirits. The incredible obtuseness of those responsible for the legislation decimated the distilling industry and drove many a legitimate operator into an illicit trade. They simply moved out into the country and defied the government gauger. It was during this period—1780 to 1823 at which time the still size law was repealed—that the Irish moonshiner had his day. Legitimate distillers in Ireland in 1780 numbered 1228. Ten years later, the number had dwindled to 246. But those that did survive, and most were in big cities near export markets, became the giants of the business within the next century.

The great myths about *poteen* developed during these forty-odd years as well as the skills that eventually crossed the Atlantic and led to the bourbon industry in America. Esther Kellner in *Moonshine* (1971) traces the history of many of the craftsmen who became very adept with small, readily portable stills. One of the most charming of the tales concerns a particularly active *elfin* being named Willy Rau who became the patron saint of the poteen maker. "The first few drops of every new batch of whiskey were thrown upon the cottage thatch as an offering to Red Willy, who in return would lead the gaugers astray, perhaps even lose them entirely in an unfamiliar bog."

The many technical improvements of the first half of the nineteenth century led finally to sanity and order in taxation and control. Even so, up to the turn of the twentieth century, the Irish distiller preferred to produce ethereal blends of his beloved pot whiskey, haughtily ignoring the growth of a new competitive force in their fellow Irishmen and in the London grain distillers who were gradually converting the British palate to softer and softer blends of grain spirits with the Irish and Scotch malts. The enormous popularity of true Irish whiskey faded by 1900 both in the United States and in the British Empire.

SOURCE MATERIALS

Throughout the centuries, the source grains in Irish distilling have included native barley, rye, maize, wheat, and even oatmeal. After the 1785 tax was imposed on the mash volume, oats were used less frequently since they tend to swell and thus increase the mash volume. Also, wheat and other rough grains were avoided because they tended to coagulate and stick in the ever and ever larger distilling apparatus.

While many different types of grain are made into spirits worldwide, barley dominates wherever it is available. The natural and abundantly available enzymes in barley make it the preferred grain, so much so that it constitutes at least 10 percent of any grain mash. Barley has a higher concentration of diastase than other grains, this enzyme being the white soluble substance which converts starch to sugar. The conversion occurs when the grain is treated with hot water, at which time it is called *dextrin*, an opaque jelly ready for conversion. Fifty grams of diastase enzymes will convert 100 kilograms of dextrin to maltose.

Giant grist mills prepare the fine barley malts for mashing.

*I*t keepeth the reason from stifling, the stomach from wambling and the heart from swelling, the bellie from wirtching [sic], the guts from mumbling, the hands from shivering and the sinews from shrinking, the veines from crumpling, the bones from aking and the marrow from sacking. And trulie it is a sovereigne liquor if it be orderly taken.

Ralph Holinshed

Today, barley grown in Ireland forms the largest segment, up to 40 percent, of total Irish whiskey grains. A distinguishing and unique procedure in Irish malting comes from mixing *unmalted* barley at levels up to 50 percent with the conventionally malted barley grain in the mashing tanks. This procedure necessitates a much higher maltose conversion in the mashing process and contributes both to the body and the flavor of the spirits. While burning peat was the heat source for drying the malt for many a poteen maker, there is no flavoring today of the barley malt by resinous smoke as there is in Scotch malting.

Irish whiskey progresses through three separate still operations in banks of copper stills such as these at Midleton.

Spirit safes are paired in Irish whiskey making.

FERMENTATION AND DISTILLATION

An extended fermentation period occurs, up to eighty hours in closed fermenters, to produce the low alcohol distillers' wash. Because of the influence of the nineteenth century tax laws which favored larger equipment, the Irish continue to employ the largest pot stills in the world. Some of their kettles can hold up to 33,000 gallons of wash. Originally, triple distilling was necessary to tame the wild bulk, and this unique practice survives today. The original mash of more than 30,000 gallons will reduce to about 3,000 gallons of very clean, high proof spirits after the third run. Generally, Irish whiskey is taken off the still at 172° proof, several degrees above American brandy, which attests to its finesse and delicacy. Therefore, the uniqueness of Irish whiskey originates with those three trips through successive, connected pot stills and its resultant high proof.

With the advent of the continuous still, the Irish pot distiller clung tenaciously to his conventional, unsullied pot distillates, even to the point of commercial disaster. Ironically, Aeneas Coffey was himself an Irish tax collector and it was he who gave to the rest of the distilling world the system that was to reduce the cost of spirit making on an order of ten to one, while still achieving high volume, high speed, and exact control

Here's to Irish, as whiskey with a heart,
That's smooth as a Leprechaun's touch.
Yet as soft in its taste as a mother's embrace,
And a gentleman's saying as much.

Irish Toast

of congenerics. Consequently, the future was in the lighter blends. The Irish whiskey that Queen Elizabeth quaffed and that Samuel Johnson praised was threatened by the massive output of the Coffey machine. Today very little pot still Irish whiskey can be found; the vast majority of Irish whiskeys are blends of pot spirits and grain spirits from column stills.

The young whiskeys are matured in oak barrels, or used sherry and bourbon whiskey casks, for periods of up to twelve to fifteen years. By law, all Irish must see at least three years in the barrel. The blender of Irish whiskey must make the same intuitive and educated decisions about the blends to be married for bottling as any other blender/artist of the spirit field.

Idyllic setting for the most famous of all—Old Bushmills.

A symbol of international prestige, bottles from Old Bushmills, the world's oldest licensed distillery which began production in 1608.

MARKETING

Following the disastrous eclipse of the popularity of Irish whiskey at the end of the nineteenth century, and after successive world wars in this century, Irish is currently making a concerted and successful penetration of the whiskey markets of the world. This resurgence was made possible by a marketing merger of the three major Irish whiskey producers. Irish grain distillers had been quick to recognize the benefits of coordinated marketing; as early as 1877, the patent still grain distillers formed Distillers Company, Ltd. to promote their blends, but not until 1966 did the fortunes of the Irish turn the corner when Cork Distillers, John Jameson & Son, and John Power formed Irish Distillers, Ltd. Included were some of the most popular labels including Paddy and Tullamore Dew. Northern Ireland's Bushmills, licensed in 1608 and thus the oldest licensed distillery in existence, joined the other three in 1972. And now all Irish whiskey, a total of sixteen labels, originates from this amalgamation.

Recently, Irish Distillers announced a $60 million expansion plan aimed at increasing output up to 50 percent within five years. The United States market is the main target of this sales effort, with labels in distribution under the direction of some of this nation's giants in sales (see table 20.1). Among these are Old Bushmills imported by Jos. Garneau, Tullamore Dew by Heublein, Jameson by Calverts, and both Paddy and Murphy's by Austin Nichols & Company.

Highlights

- All Irish pot whiskey is triple distilled, and only native grains are used.
- Most Irish is sold as blends of pot distillates and grain distillates from continuous stills.

- No peat smoke is employed in the malting process.
- Irish mash often contains up to 50 percent unmalted barley.
- Irish whiskey must be aged a minimum of three years.

TABLE 20.1 Top Ten Markets for Irish Whiskey 1980 vs. 1981 (In cases)[a]

State	1980	1981
California	71,247	70,311
New York	32,192	34,676
Massachusetts	11,051	13,792
Washington	13,115	12,914
New Jersey	11,158	11,767
Illinois	12,061	11,226
Pennsylvania	8,926	10,620
Texas	9,327	9,977
Florida	9,372	9,158
Maryland	7,231	8,559
TOTAL	185,680	193,000
U.S. total	276,145	287,351
Percentage U.S. total	67.2%	67.2%

Source: Dan Hecht, ed., *The Liquor Handbook* (New York: Gavin-Gobson Associates, Inc., 1982), 229.

[a]Estimated.

TABLE 20.2 Irish Whiskey Tasting

Spirit	General Style	Suggested Brand
Whiskey	Intriguing flowery nose, light body, smooth and complex, lingering finish	Old Bushmills Three Star
Crested ten	Nice nose, sherry, oaky flavor, mellow and smooth	Jameson
Pot whiskey (15 years old)	Assertive nose, strong and malty flavors, pungent and warming, long finish	Jameson
Liqueur	Herby nose, light body with bitter, almond-like tone, smooth	Irish Mist Tullamore
Liqueur	Strong aroma of chocolate which continues in smooth taste, full body, creamy	Bailey's Irish Cream

SUGGESTED IRISH WHISKEY TASTING

Unfortunately, Irish whiskeys are not as easy to find around the nation as is Scotch, and many of you may be hard pressed to find sufficient labels for a complete tasting. Look hard, particularly for the older, pot-still types.

Scotch Whisky

The tendrils entwining Scotland and Ireland are many and diverse—language, Christianity, fierce independence of character—but none so widely encompassing as a visceral involvement with the making and consuming of grain spirits. The Scots derive from a Gaelic tribe that had earlier migrated to the western Isles, some say from the very Antrim that boasts the proud Old Bushmills, the world's oldest licensed distillery. In *Whiskies of Scotland* (1979), Derek Cooper speculates that the Scottish nation

> derived its Christianity from an Irishman too: a remarkable saint called Columba who stepped ashore on the island of Iona in the year 563. And there's good reason to believe that the knowledge that barley could be metamorphosed into *uisce beatha,* the water of life, came over the sea from Ireland as well.

Whatever the long lost truth of the matter, it can be stated as fact that the liquid spirit of this craggy and wind-blown land is as individualistic as the rugged people who make it. Their fundamental character can be seen in an old Scottish tradition, that of bringing, when you visit, a piece of coal, a piece of bread, and a bottle of Scotch—for what is of more importance to life than warmth, food, and good drink.

SCOTCH WATER OF LIFE

Cooper (1979) cites the earliest written record of Scotch that appears on the Scottish Exchequer Rolls from 1494 which records "eight bols of malt to Friar John Cor wherewith to make

*P*haeron had a son,
Who married Noah's daughter.
And nearly spoiled the flood,
By drinking up the water;
Which he would have done—
I at least believe it
Had the mixture been
Only half Glenlivet.

Anonymous

aqua vitae." In 1505, the Surgeon Barbers were empowered with the sole right to sell spirits. The first excise taxes were imposed in 1644. However, as early as 1557, Bessie Campbell was enjoined by the Magistrates from selling spirits except on market days. There is mention of the famous Ferintosh distillery at Culloden in 1699. So the general availability of *uisce beatha* (the Scottish spelling of *usquebaugh*) was evident. In 1738, George Smith's *Complete Book of Distilling* identified the product as malt spirit, and in 1755, Johnson's dictionary mentions *usquebaugh* as "an Irish compound distilled spirit, drawn from aromatics; the Highland sort, by corruption they call whisky." Actually, in Gaelic, water is *iske* or *isque*. No matter, the Scots in the Highlands brewed the precious drink early as *uisce beatha* and later as *whisky.*

Terms

barrel Scotch distillers use butts of 110 gallons and hogsheads from 55 to 65 gallons.

draff The remains from the mash tun or about twenty-five percent of the malt and cereals which goes to cattle feed.

feints Impure congeneric wastes which come over last from the second run.

fillings The new scotch whisky from the stills.

foreshots The first part which emerges first from the still in the each run, full of congeners. Together with the feints, they are returned to another wash for redistillation.

gill The shot measure in which Scotch is sold, equalling about 5 fluid ounces.

grain spirit Alcohol distilled from grain and generally wood aged.

kiln The building with the pagoda in which the green malt is dried partially over peat reek or smoke.

low wine First run product to be redistilled.

malts Unblended pot-still Scotch from one distillery.

overproof A spirit of more than 100 proof sikes.

peat reek The oily, acrid smoke from burning dried peat, used to dry and to flavor green malt for Scotch.

pot ale Residue stillage from the first distillation used for cattle feed, also called Burnt Ale.

rectification The purification of distilled spirits.

rummager Rotating arms with chains that keep the product from sticking in the wash still.

single whisky The spirit from a single distillery; grain or malt types.

spent lees The stillage or residual material after the second distillation.

spirit safe The glass box in which hydrometer and thermometer measure spirit as it flows from still; it is always locked to prevent spirit pilferage.

spirits still The third still used for the final run.

steeps Tanks in which barley is malted.

underback The worts receiver.

vatting The blending of two or more single malt whiskies.

wash The fermented fluid ready for the pot or patent still.

washback The fermenter in Scotch making; it often has up to a 10,000–gallon capacity.

wash still The first still for the first distillation of alcoholic wash.

wort The liquid containing the converted sugars which is ready for fermentation.

In addition another episode of history recounted by Cooper (1979) tells of the ingrained Scottish bibulous characteristic.

> Although the Danes had a horrifying reputation for imbibing akvavit, the Highlanders seldom lagged behind. In 1588 Frederik II of Denmark drank himself to death. . . . after a carousing state visit from King Christian the Londoners delightedly renamed the Magpie and Stump tavern, near the Old Bailey, the King of Denmark. But when Christian's sister Anne, who married King James VI of Scotland, introduced to London a Danish courtier who had outdrunk every nobleman in Europe, he was finally seen under the table after a three day boozing bout by Sir Robert Lawrie, a Scot, "unmatched at the bottle, unconquered in war."

The citizenry being not only heavy drinkers, but also fiercely independent, it was not until the Act of Union in 1707 that their Parliament got around to taxing what they deemed the birthright of all, pot spirits. From as early as 1505, only the Surgeon Barbers could *sell* Scotch, but everyone *made* it. When the Act of Union was passed, the Scot simply moved out into the glen, hidden from daily commerce, and there continued his untaxed production. In 1715, the English gained powers of taxation and, being more experienced at collecting monies, sent a military expedition into the Highlands to establish a tax-collecting network. However, it was not until the Battle of Culloden in 1746, and the defeat of the Stuart Pretender, Bonnie Prince Charles, that the inevitable London governmental hegemony was established. The Gaelic language was prohibited, and merger of the two nations became a fact.

Although it would be many years before the production of spirits became a fully controlled function, figuratively speaking, the road to the Highlands was opened at Culloden. In fact, for several hundred years the "smugglers," or illicit whisky merchants, were quite prominent businessmen of their day. Cooper records that

> smuggling became as much a part of agricultural life as ploughing and haymaking. Around Glenlivet and Tomintoul alone, blessed with abundant burns and peat there for the cutting, 200 illicit stills were operating. Barley was turned into whisky, which was then exchanged for money to pay the rent and buy the seed for more barley.

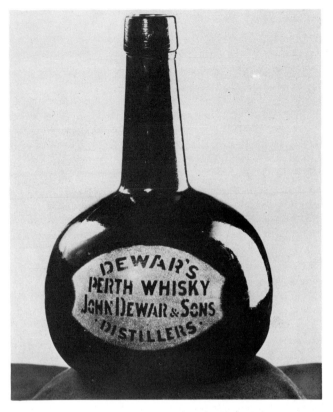

John Dewar & Sons were the first to bottle their Scotch for sale.

*T*hee Ferintosh! Oh Sadly lost
Scotland laments frae coast to coast!
Now colic grips and barkin' hoast
May kill us a',
For loyal Forbes' chartered boast
Is Taen awa'!
**Late 17th Century Ditty about the
Loss of the Ferintosh Distillery**

brandy shortage in 1880 enabled these prosperous and experienced grain whisky blenders to become international figures. They were innovators who acknowledged the enormous capacity for speed and production of the Coffey still and tempered its product with the aromatics for gin and with pot-still Scotch to meet a demand formerly filled by Continental brandies. The stubborn Scottish single maltsters resisted the adulteration of their distinctive spirits and unwittingly gave both power and purse to the London merchant who happily dealt in all spirits. By 1880, the Distillers Company, Ltd. had merged the diverse interests of this group of merchants and offered stocks for sale as one of the first public liquor corporations. The great war between the maltsters and the blenders was nearly over when, by 1900, these blending giants were producing thirty millions of gallons of spirits annually.

One final romantic note of that tumultuous century involves George Smith who in 1824 became the first licensed Highland malt whisky maker. His mentor, the Lord of Aberlour, provided Smith with a pair of hair-trigger pistols to protect himself from hostile home distillers and smugglers. Smith's malt, The Glenlivet, was the first licensed and remains to this day one of the best single malt Scotch whiskies. Smith, by the way, never fired the arms. An odd dozen or so other Speyside producers hyphenate their names to the famous Glenlivet, each with considerable merit, but the government has protected this heritage since 1880, permitting only the original to be labeled *The Glenlivet*.

PRODUCTION OF SCOTCH

On 28 July 1908, the Royal Commission in Great Britain finally resolved the fifty-year-old legal argument about what constitutes Scotch by defining it as blends of grain spirits from continuous stills with single malt pot-still spirits. This definition assured the commercial security of the grain spirit blenders.

Source Materials

For centuries, oats have reigned as the foremost crop in Scotland, although native barley fields have also been long cultivated below the Firth of Tay. Both for ease in handling and

As in neighboring Ireland, the governmental attempts to collect tribute simply institutionalized moonshining on a grand scale. In the early nineteenth century, illicit stills were confiscated at a clip of 14,000 annually.

THE VOICE OF REASON

The Scottish Duke of Gordon finally and reasonably proposed to the British Parliament laws of taxation which would make the production of licensed whisky profitable. The Commission of 1823 consequently recommended passage of an act which changed the nature of spirit making in both Ireland and Scotland. This law also spurred the growth of legal commerce of the fine malt spirits to that great market to the south, Great Britain, a trade which had long been neglected. For example, only 5 of the 114 distilleries in the Highlands sent their product to London in the year 1821. In 1860, with a stroke of genius, a broker by the name of Andrew Usher blended some pungent malt whiskies with now quite abundant grain products from Coffey stills. Though many a fight would lie ahead between those in favor of blending and those opposed to the idea, a new force in the spirit market was born.

Between the time of that fortuitous merging and the year 1900, the great trade names of Scotch were born. Walker, already around in 1820, was joined in 1884 by Buchanan, in 1850 by Dewar, and in 1877 by Mackie. The phylloxera-induced

It all begins with fine barley.

Water tanks in the foreground and malt kilns behind symbolize the essentials in Scotch whisky.

*I*nspiring bold John Barleycorn,
What dangers thou cans't make us scorn!
Wi' tippeny, we fear nae evil,
Wi' usquebae, we'll face the devil!
                              Robert Burns

for the abundance of the diastase enzyme for sugar conversion, barley has always predominated in the production of brews and spirits. In the early years, only native grains were employed in Scotch spirit production. However, in this century, most of the grains for Scotch have been imported since the native variety of barley remains too high in nitrogen. Imported barley from as far away as America and Australia provides richer starch content, as well as the low moisture desired in advance of malting. Scotch, then, has broken with the tradition of making spirits primarily from native crops.

While this reduces the importance of the *grain* in distinguishing Scotch, two other native elements have not been duplicated in attempts by distillers across the globe to imitate the Scots. The first of these is Highland water, unmatched for purity and clarity. The clean, bubbly burns or springs attracted the "smugglers" who did not, however, immediately recognize the uniqueness the waters imparted to their spirits. The other indigenous element is the result of centuries of compression of heather, fern, and grasses to make a compact fuel which is called *peat*.

The benevolence of past eons emerges in these peat cakes.

292

Giant malting floors are required for the rapid conversion of starch to maltose.

A distillery worker checks the specific gravity of a completed wort at the Johnnie Walker Cardow plant.

*T*here's something yet I have forgotten,
Which yet prefer to roast or sodden.
Wine and wastles, I dare say
And that is routh of usequebay.

Cleland

When harvested, peat is 90 percent water, but it dries cleanly and slowly, so that it has long been used as a source of natural heat. The early distillers utilized the available peat energy to heat home and factory as well as to dry the green malt, using screens to allow the heat and smoke to filter through the grain. On the way to the kiln chimney, the smoke implants a character, a smokiness and individuality that distinguishes Scotch from all other alcoholic beverages. The smoke or *peat reek* is surely the most native of source materials.

Malting, Mashing, and Fermenting

As in nearly every other major spirit production, Scotch malting, which takes about twelve days, is accomplished today in professional malting houses rather than in distilleries. The delightful aromas, the huge warehouses with their drying rooms, the quaint kilns with their pagoda roofs—all belong to a bygone era. Many of the maltsters now use the saladin boxes or drums for mechanical advantage, but the germination process is identical. However, these malting houses do still use peat ovens for part of the drying cycle to impart the smoky character, while utilizing gas for the rest of the drying process.

These wood fermenting tanks, called washbacks, are at King William distillery.

Giant pot stills dominate the stilling process, but it is the consummate skill of the stillman at the spirit safe that perfects the product.

One other distinction is maintained. Single malt Scotches are distilled from a mash of barley, and only barley. While many grains are utilized for blending grain whiskies, single malt Scotch is exclusively a barley-based spirit.

The grist consisting of cleaned and ground malt is introduced into thousand gallon mash tuns in which four separate washings will occur, with water up to 160° F. The remaining conversion of starch to maltose takes place over a fifteen hour period, usually resulting in about 12 percent fermentable materials. This new sweet wort is cooled to about 70° F and pumped into 10,000 gallon washbacks in which fermentation occurs. A relatively short fermentation of about forty hours takes place which produces a wash with alcohol in the 5–7.5 percent concentrations.

The Stills

Malt whisky emerges from traditional onion-shaped pot stills. About a week passes from mashing to the second and final run through the still. Of course, this double distilling is as old as Highland Scotch. In ancient times it was called *tarruing dubaith.* In fact, progressively there were third distillations called *treatarruing* and even a spirit of four runs with the euphonious name of *uisge bea' a ba' ol.* So the idea of using the same kind of equipment to rectify or to purify by degrees is deeply entrenched in Scotch distilling.

While these still machines have grown to substantial size throughout the centuries, the shape and construction varies little from the pioneer equipment. The first of the two stills is called the wash still, a container of considerable size which often holds from eight to ten thousand gallons. Most have a rummager, or a series of chains on long arms, to move the heavy wash and keep it from sticking. The first run emerges at a very low 35° to 40° proof, milky white with congeners. This product, termed low wines, is introduced into the second or spirit still, which is generally about half the size of the first.

The barrel line of matured Scotch whiskies.

The stillman exercises careful judgment in cutting the middle liquors from the foreshots and tails during this second run. Depending upon the objective for that particular distillate, the congeners can be light or heavy within a very narrow range of cutting. He visually monitors the spirit through the excise safe, or spirit safe. At the precise moment that the foreshot congener level is sufficiently low, the stillman diverts the pipe to the spirit receiver. After the middle spirits have been obtained, he again diverts the pipe so the remaining spirits fall into a feints' receiver, joining the foreshots. This residue is then directed back to a new batch of wash so that there is continual reworking of the feints which, of course, always contain some alcohol. The stillage is called *pot ale,* and it is processed for cattle feed as in other spirit making.

TABLE 21.1 Cooperage for Scotch Whisky Aging

Container	Gallonage
Butt	110
Hogshead	55–65
American Barrel	38–42
Quarter	25–35
Octave	10–15

Single malt Scotch whiskies are ready for blending at Johnnie Walker.

Maturing Scotch Malts and Grain Whiskies

As with most other distillates, the congenerics must be mellowed by wood aging to achieve palatability. Indeed, the really broad range of types of Scotch require great finesse in both maturing and blending. These final two steps in the spirit chain are of absolute importance for Scotch. The malts mature at differing rates, depending upon the climate of the area. For example, in the moist Lowland islands, the barrels lose alcoholic strength, but not volume. Consequently, as with aging wine, the spirits are checked weekly, and the progress of these hundreds of thousands of butts, hogsheads, and barrels is registered in computers, the data available at a moment's notice to the master blenders. By law all whisky must be aged a minimum of three years, although most rests in casks for much longer periods. Naturally the single malts often require extended periods in wood, up to twelve years or more (see table 21.1).

The aging spirits are reduced in potency with distilled water to about 110° proof and closely secured by the exciseman and the distiller in bonded warehouses. It was the Immature Spirits Act of 1915, partially a conservation measure, that mandated the minimum of three years in cask before whiskies could be marketed. Originally, the primary source of wood barrels was the beloved sherry casks that came from Jerez brimming with the flavor residuals of fino, oloroso, and amontillado. Today many of the casks are once-used American bourbon barrels which cannot be employed again for that spirit.

THE GEOGRAPHY OF SCOTCH MALTS

While a great deal of romance and historical chance influenced this vast and scattered enterprise, there is sufficient individuality in the regional malts to guard and nurture them carefully. The divisions are blurring somewhat today, primarily because of the constant shifting between companies and between divisions within companies of stocks of malts for blending. But one must recognize that the genius and artistry of the master blenders maintain the true style and character of each blend through uncanny management of the huge quantities of barreled spirit.

Many Scotch patent stills are constructed like the original Coffey design with a rectangular configuration. They include insulation to conserve the heat.

The most prized malts are those from the Highlands, from the original smugglers' sites. These lie north of a boundary which roughly bisects the nation on a line from Greenock to Dundee, in the northern two-thirds of the country. About 150 distilleries operate today in these yet peaceful glens which provide the most robust and aromatic, though often the lightest in body, of malt distillates.

Like wine, Scotch passes through a fine filtration machine.

The second division involves Lowland Malts which are few in number today, with only eleven distilleries in operation. Only two of these have labeled products. Historically, these were the least distinctive whiskies, and they gradually gave way to grain spirits production. Cambeltown Malts from the southernmost reaches of the Scottish islands have also fallen on sad times. A single distillery, Springbank, bottles under its own name. Cambeltown malts are known for their robust character and flavor intensity. Finally, the *Islay Malts* (pronounced eyeler), in the historical island setting to which the Irish tribes immigrated, provide quick maturing, peaty whiskies that are treasured by the blender for their verve and excitement.

Whiskies are tapped for blending.

GRAIN SPIRITS

The revolution occasioned by Mr. Coffey's still has not yet run its course, but few of the world's distillers are more adept at producing fine blending grain spirits from the continuous process than the British. In 1875, the Distillers Company, Ltd. was formed in recognition of the capacity of the new stills to supply vast markets. In 1885, a counter group in Edinburgh, called the North British Distillery, was formed to produce Scotch grain spirits, but the die had been cast in the south. The two brandy-short decades at the end of the nineteenth century enriched these giant merchants. Today, to supply the vast market now well entrenched throughout the world, the grain distillers produce two million gallons each week. The magnitude of these operations is described by Cooper:

> In the sidings the railway vans specially constructed for carrying bulk wheat and maize are run over a hopper and the grain is dropped through chutes before being raised by elevators to the top of the granaries. The complex uses 20 tons of maize and seven tons of malt every two hours and the storage capacity is vast—when working to full capacity the distillery gets through 3000 tons of grain a month.

The final arbiter for the Scotch blend is a person and an idea of perfection.

Skilled blenders mix the single malts and grain spirits according to the blenders' "nosed" formulas.

John Dewar & Sons' charming crock bottles from early years.

The malted barley and unmalted cereal grains are mashed into a porridge-like mass completely free from the peat reek of the malt whiskies. Everything is on a larger scale. The washbacks will reach 40,000 gallons in size. The patent stills, similar in size to those for American brandy, will utilize up to 8,000 gallons of wash per hour. The clean, nearly neutral grain spirits taken from these massive stills must undergo wood maturation up to three years.

Each of these hundreds of thousands of casks are monitored as regularly as errant children; some are impetuous, others sedate, all unpredictable. Cooper reports of a D.C.L. subsidiary, Scottish Grain Distillers, that the equivalent of 33,000 bottles evaporate daily, and the warehouseman checks 1,000 casks of malt whisky and 2,000 of grain each day.

Once the critical decisions have been made, the blending and marrying of the diverse spirits is a relatively simple procedure. There is a filtering before bottling, and rectifying with some caramel to produce the desired evenness in light straw tones.

THE HUMAN TOUCH: BLENDING

What makes Cutty Sark and Glenlivet so distinctive and different is the resolute adherence to the nuances of blending. In a sense, this is the taming of the wildest and the enlivening of the blandest. It is obvious that these many spirits will mature to quite different tasting and smelling entities. Through their many years of experience, Scotch blenders can anticipate the style and character of the whiskies that will emerge years ahead—the stocks with which they will work. And the demand subtly changes from year to year. Cooper quotes one blender on this subject: "Today we're using between 30 and 40 whiskies in a blend as opposed to 10 or so pre-war." But, of course, the demands of the public have become proportionately more refined and the demand for consistency all the greater. As a result, the above blender "uses Speyside to give it this lovely phenol character, Islay to give it strength, Lowland to give it volume, grain to give it background and not kill the fusel oil and so on."

MARKETING

Because the grain distillers of London gained control of the Scotch whisky industry, the product was aggressively exported, first to meet the phylloxera-plagued cognac trade and later as an abundantly available spirit in international trade. Only about 20 percent is drunk in tiny Scotland. Vast amounts of Scotch have traditionally been shipped around the world in bulk without benefit of brand labeling. For example, six million gallons of Scotch were shipped to Japan in 1977, most of which were blended into fine labels like Suntory in direct competition with labeled Scotch. This practice continues today, although now there is much more concern about the adulteration of the bulk sales with inferior distillates.

Low grade and low price Scotch, known to be blends of local grain spirits with purchased Scotch, is found in the European markets. Some nine million gallons are shipped annually from Scotland in bulk, mainly to Japan, Brazil, and Argentina. In fact, Scotch whisky comprises up to two percent of all British exports and is a key element in their balance of payments.

Yet it is the United States which dominates with up to 30 percent of all Scotch exports. While there has been some lull in recent years occasioned by the general shift of the market to white goods, Scotch has an enduring and profitable share of the American spirit trade (see table 21.2). Other prime markets are Australia, Belgium, Canada, France, Italy, Japan, Spain, Venezuela, and West Germany.

One can easily comprehend the sales objectives of the new Irish whiskey promotion by noting the tremendous gallonage of Scotch shipped to American shores since the Second World War. A battle of titanic proportions between Scotch and Irish will ensue as the overall portion of that import market held by brown spirits recedes, or perhaps even if it enlarges again in years to come.

Despite the fact that there are some two thousand brand names of Scotch, only about 100 are sold in Scotland, and the majority of annual sales resides in a very few firms as is the case with other major spirits. The top ten share about 70 percent of the total Scotch market, and, in most cases, these giants are assuming larger shares of the pie every year.

TABLE 21.2 Top Ten Markets for Scotch Whisky 1980 vs. 1981 (750 ML Per 100 Persons)

State	1980	1981
District of Columbia	575.2	530.9
New York	379.3	344.6
New Hampshire	261.0	249.7
New Jersey	230.4	235.0
Nevada	258.9	219.5
Florida	212.0	208.2
Connecticut	140.7	147.4
Alaska	130.7	144.7
Maryland	135.6	138.2
California	150.1	137.2
National average	122.6	117.7

Source: Dan Hecht, ed., *The Liquor Handbook* (New York: Gavin-Gobson Associates, Inc., 1982), 208.

TABLE 21.3 Top Scotch Labels in the United States (Sales Rounded Out)

Brand	Importer	1981 Cases
Dewar's	Schenley Imports	2,400,000
J & B	Paddington Corp.	2,175,000
Cutty Sark	Buckingham Corp.	1,775,000
Johnnie Walker Red	Somerset	1,575,000
Chivas Regal	Seagrams	1,025,000

Source: Montana Beverage News (December 1982), 17.

The bottled blends, such as J & B, Cutty Sark, Dewar's, and Johnnie Walker, are the most prestigious (see table 21.3). Sold in both 86° proof and 86.8° proof bottlings, they are heavily advertised. The next largest share of the American market comes in bulk containers for bottling and labeling in this country and, though generally lower in price, amounts to 40 percent of the total. The smallest segment of the Scotch market both in this country and worldwide lies with the single malt Scotches. These single malts from single distilleries and occasionally blends called *vatted malts* contain no grain spirits. A small amount of Scotch is directed to liqueur specialties such as Drambuie and Lochan Ora. This third in our study of the great spirits became the leader in world sales as a consequence of the shift to spirits of grain which is in abundant, year-round supply and because of the development of still technology which led to speed and economy while providing for close control of taste and flavor.

Highlights

- Scotch may be either a single malt or a blend of single malts and grain spirits.
- Most Scotch sold is blended and a considerable portion of the total production is sold in bulk for blending with local spirits throughout the world.
- A single malt Scotch is the product of pot stills at a single named distillery.

- The most distinctive element in Scotch is the peat reek or smoke that penetrates the malt in the drying process.
- All malt Scotch whiskies must be pot distilled and go through the still twice.

SUGGESTED SCOTCH WHISKY TASTING

Because of the wide variety of labels and styles of Scotch, it is advisable to ask your local spirit merchant to assure you of the various levels in your tasting. You will be both surprised and gratified at the diversity and the nuances in aroma and taste. Here are some labels that are generally available, in order of tasting.

TABLE 21.4 Scotch Whisky Tasting

Spirit	General Style	Suggested Brand
American Bulk (Bottled)	Faint pleasing nose, light body, weak but malty taste, fast finish	Any available
Scotch	Attractive bouquet, medium body, peaty, malt character, light finish	Dewar's Schenley
Scotch	Soft nose, dry and mellow, complex flavor, light finish	Chivas Regal Seagrams
Scotch	Assertive nose, medium body with smoky tone and light finish	J & B International Distillers
Single malt (12 years old)	Soft nose, medium to heavy body, intense flavors, particularly peaty, gentle finish	The Glenlivet Seagrams
Single malt (10 years old)	Big nose, intensely peaty, big body, rich and mellow, long finish	Laphroaig Barton Brands
Scotch liqueur	Spicy, herby nose, medium body, fairly dry for liqueur, light texture and smooth	Drambuie

Liqueurs and Bitters

*L*iqueurs, or cordials as they are commonly known in the United States, are sweetened concoctions having some type of alcoholic spirits as the base. However, the history of the type is far from prosaic, encompassing everything from the alchemist's magic to the witch's brew!

The word liqueur derives from the Latin *liquēre*, which means "to be liquid." At its simplest, the cordial results from dissolving something pleasant in something that perhaps is not. Hannum and Blumberg speculate on the invention in *Brandies and Liqueurs of the World* (1976):

> . . . it remains unknown whether the first spices and fruits were added to alcohol for reasons of health or merely to render palatable what was probably a harsh, fiery, and often poorly distilled spirit. Many of the early experiments were more concerned with finding a universal solvent or transmuting base metals into gold than with creating an enjoyable alcoholic beverage.

Whatever the original motivation, spirits throughout the last 900 years have been infused with everything from saffron to sassafras, all with reasonable success. Liqueurs, as commercial spirits, entered reasonably late and almost surely as an offshoot of the experiments with aqua vitae in the hundreds of monasteries spread across western Europe.

Desmond Seward, in *Monks in Wine* (1979), records the historical importance of monasteries in the development of liqueurs.

> The religious orders have played a considerable part in the development of distilling. . . . In their early days spirits were regarded as essentially medicinal. . . . monks were best equipped for such an uncommercial

C andy
Is Dandy.
But, Liquor
Is quicker.

Ogden Nash

enterprise . . . from about 1650 a remarkable number of monasteries developed their own liqueurs.

By the 15th century, Michel Savonarale reported in *De Aqua Vitae* of Franciscan monks who were making liqueurs from all of the common fruits, herbs, roots and seeds.

As time passed on, so did the secrets of the elixirs, as Hannum and Blumberg (1976) document.

> At first the processes of distillation remained secret except to the initiated few. As distillation became better understood and as spices, herbs, and sugar from New World colonies arrived in Europe, the bitter medicines of the Middle Ages were transformed into intriguing new alcoholic drinks. No longer could the secrets of the alchemists remain hidden.

It will not be surprising, then, to learn that the first recorded migration of a rosolio liqueur from Italy was as part of the baggage of Catherine of Medici when she went to France to marry Henry II. Later on, the Sun King, Louis XIV, popularized many cordials during his long reign from 1643 to 1715.

Terms

certified food color Product derived from distillation of coal tar, used for food coloring.

cordial The American term which is interchangeable with liqueur—from the Latin *cordis* or "heart."

distillation In liqueurs, the process of distilling a spirit menstrum or redistilling after maceration.

liqueur A cordial or product produced by combining a spirit base with extracts or flavorings and containing a minimum of 2½% (by weight) of sucrose or dextrose.

maceration Similar to tea steeping, a process in which the raw materials are placed in a container with spirits menstrum to soak out flavors and colors.

neutral spirits Distilled spirits taken above 190 proof that are devoid of flavor and used as a spirit base for a liqueur.

percolation A process in liqueur production similar to brewing coffee. The raw materials are placed in a basket and spirits menstrum is pumped over the basket so that it percolates through and extracts the flavors.

spirits base Any spirit used as the base liquor or the spirits menstrum in cordial production—vodka, brandy, scotch, etc.

spirits menstrum A mixture of a spirits base with water used to soak out the flavors of extracts or as the base for distillation or redistillation of cordial materials.

sugar syrup Also known as simple syrup, or sugar mixed with water at about 7 pounds per gallon.

The magnificent Monastery, La Grande Chartreuse, was once the proud motherhouse to 226 monasteries throughout Europe. Today Carthusian monks operate the distillery for Chartreuse liqueurs at Voiron.

Recipe
AQUA CELESTIS
John French 17th Cent.

Take of Cinnamon	And	Germander
Ginger		Ground pine
Cloves		Mace
Zedoary		White Frankincense
Nutmeg		Tormentill
Galangall		Hermodactyle
Long Pepper		Pitch of Dwarf Elder
Citron-pill		Juniper Berries
Spicknard		Bay Berries
Lignum-aloes		seeds and flowers of Motherwort
Cububs		seeds of Smallage
Cardamums		Fennel
Calamus aromaticus		Anise
Rosemary		leaves of Sorrel
Marjoram		Sage
Mints		Fel-wort
Penny-royal		flowers of Elder
Stechados		Roses
Rue		Leaves of Scabious
the lesser Moonwort		Egrimonie
Centory		Fumitary
Sow-thistle		Eye-bright
Pimpernell		Mayden hair
Endive		Red Saunders
Aloes of each two ounces		Pure Amber
Rhubarb, of each two Drams		dryed Figges
Raisins of the sun		Dates, stoned
Sweet-Almonds		Graines of Pine, each an ounce

Of the best Aqua vitae to the quantity of them all, of the best hard sugar, a pound, of white honey half a pound, the adde

the roote of Gentaine	flowers of Rosemary
Pepperwort	root of Briony
Sowbread	Wormwood, all half an ounce

Now before these are distilled, quench gold being made red hot, oftentimes in the foresaid water, put therein oriental Pearls beaten small an ounce, and then distill it after twenty foure hours infusion. This is a very Cordiall water, good against faintings and infection.

Source: Hurst Hannum and Robert S. Blumberg, *Brandies and Liqueurs of the World* (Garden City, N.Y.: Doubleday & Co., Inc., 1976), 146–48.

The original Lucas Bols distillery for liqueurs, established in 1575.

Many learned treatises of the times claimed these soft delights had therapeutic and curative powers for illnesses ranging from madness to measles. One quote from a 1556 book by Konrad von Gesner titled *The Newe Jewell of Health* establishes liqueurs as possibly "restoring members of the body." Powerful medicine!

Each new substance or drug was first used as a medicine and then became a luxury of the wealthy. Braudel (1981) explains this relationship.

> Sugar, for example, was a luxury before the sixteenth century; pepper was still a luxury in the closing years of the seventeenth; so were alcohol and the first 'aperitifs' at the time of Catherine de Medici. . . . Similarly, medicinal sugar vied with honey in general prescriptions in Byzantium. It appears in the pharmacopeae of the Salerno school in the tenth century.

By 1575, an enterprising Dutchman, Lucas Bols, set up shop in a little shed and with a small kettle produced dozens of delightful waters. The fact that his company prospers to this day may be the result of his personal philosophy about his productions: "Do not mutilate nature. Guide her to perfection."

While the Italians may have started it all and still produce many world famous liqueurs, the business now belongs largely to the French and the Dutch. Emerson, in *Beverages Past and Present* (1908), reinforces the importance of quality of base materials and production and suggests that they made the difference: "While these liqueurs have had a very important part in making France famous as a country of beverages, it must not be forgotten that if the country did not furnish the fine wines and brandies, the manufacture of the cordials would be almost impossible . . ."

The earliest cordials were almost universally made from common herbal concoctions simply because they were in the medicine chest; the therapeutic impact of herbs was already known. By the 19th century when fruits began to be used in liqueurs, they had changed from being considered medicine to being social beverages. The first fruit cordials, generally known as *ratafia,* were mild macerations of soft fruits such as strawberries or gooseberries in local brandy. In fact, toasting in *ratafia* became a kind of ceremonial ritual of state in France, a fitting conclusion to every important diplomatic treaty.

After the Napoleonic Wars, the liqueur industry experienced another surge. In the late nineteenth century, converging economic and social factors—industrial growth, prosperity, newly established trade routes, the introduction of exotic cuisine, the explosive increase in the numbers of people on the earth, and in general the "belle epoque"—together created the necessity for the enormous productive capacity of our now familiar continuous still. Great and passionate appetites could be sated inexpensively through mass production of the base spirits and the availability of limitless herbs, seeds, and fruits.

Unusual concoctions with racy names proliferated. For example, popular types were Rose Without Thorns, Venus Oil, Harem's Delight, Illicit Love, Parfait Amour (still available today), Maiden's Cream, and the like, most often touted as aphrodisiacs.

Oddly, America has produced little in the way of native liqueurs, being satisfied instead to mass produce the least complicated bulk cordials, such as crème de menthe, sloe gin, and coffee liqueur. Rock candy and bourbon, popular as a nostrum as early as 1872, eventually became Rock and Rye. The most famous of domestic cordials is Southern Comfort, a blend of freshly peeled peaches, peach kernels, citrus extracts, and good old native bourbon. Several cordials, such as Wild Turkey, have been introduced with fanfare in recent years, but the market still belongs to proprietary brands from Europe.

THE GREEN MUSE

Certainly the most famous liqueur, one which is now banned in most of the world, is absinthe. *Artemisia Absinthium* is that often used flavoring plant, wormwood, from which is extracted a bitter oil used to make absinthe. Invented by a French doctor as a medicine to fight malaria in 1792, absinthe in production was a light, yellow-green liqueur containing sixteen herbs including anise, chamomile, coriander, mélisse, and veronica. It became the craze in Paris in the last half of the nineteenth century; marketed at a very substantial 138° proof, the alcohol potency alone was sufficient to stupefy. But it was the cumulative narcotic effect of the wormwood that eventually led to its formal banning both in France and the United States in 1915. However, the taste was so established that it spawned a host of imitations of the essential licorice taste, including *Pernod* and *Pastis* in France and *anis* and *anisette* elsewhere.

A captain bold of Halifax, who
lived in country quarters,
Jilted a maid who hanged herself
next Monday in her garters.
His guilty conscience smited him,
he pined and wilted daily:
He took to drinking ratafia
and thought upon Miss Bailey.

Anonymous

The tragedy of absinthe was aptly described by Emerson, who wrote in 1908, "The drinking of absinthe in France has become about universal; no class or condition is exempt from the habit . . . and, sad to say, too often in excess."

SOURCE MATERIALS

This section could be swiftly completed by stating that everything your garden grows can be utilized in liqueurs, or at least all plants of reasonable palatibility. In addition to extracts or flavoring agents, two other materials are essential—a base spirit and some sugar.

Most countries that produce cordials quite naturally utilize the local spirits; brandy is used in France and Italy, gin in Holland, and so on. However, in recent years, high proof neutral spirits have become dominant. Some say over 90 percent of the base for liqueurs is neutral spirits because they are both free of cogeners and inexpensive, two excellent recommendations.

The sugar can be from molasses, honey, cane or beet sugar, or some source of natural fructose and glucose. From the minimum of 2½ percent of total volume, the sugar level often goes up to 40 percent. Those liqueurs with the heaviest volumes of sugar are known as the *crèmes*. Synthetic flavorings are prohibited in most areas of production, although the liqueurs are often tinted with food coloring or natural agents, such as yellow from saffron, green from leaves, brown from tea or cocoa, and red from cherries. Only the finest quality of extracts with the purest oils and essences is used.

Herbs

As we have seen, the early medical use of this type of liqueur involved dozens of herbs known to have specific effects on man. In contrast to a woody plant, a growing herb lacks persistent woody parts and is generally cultivated for food or medicinal purposes. Many of the earliest herb liqueurs are still sold today, and this class of liqueurs is by far the most sophisticated. For

The essential oils, essences and fragrances that create the uniqueness in liqueurs are derived from combinations of percolation, maceration and distillation techniques. Here are the Chartreuse maceration tanks and stills common to the industry.

At Marie Brizard, two distinct methods are utilized to macerate the desirable flavoring agents from herbs. The hot method, shown here, is used primarily for seeds, plants, roots and herbs which require greater intensity to release the flavors.

this reason, herbal liqueurs are the most expensive and difficult to duplicate. The two most famous in this category are both over several hundred years old, yet neither has been successfully matched. *Chartreuse,* born in a Carthusian monastery near Paris in 1605, now contains up to 130 herbs and plants on a brandy base from a very carefully guarded secret formula. It is marketed in two versions, the more powerful green hue at 110° proof and the lighter yellow at 80° proof. The spicy, minty amalgam of the herbs and plants defies description, although it can be said that the yellow comes through much softer and perhaps a touch sweeter.

Bénédictine claims an earlier parentage, around 1510, in the fertile mind of Dom Bernardo Vincelli at the Benedictine Abbey of Fecamp, forty miles north of Le Havre. This precious cordial is said to contain dried plants, twenty-seven herbs, and brandy. A favorite of local fishermen, it was served fifty-fifty with the local brandy. In 1928, the company adopted this blending procedure in producing B & B, a blend of Bénédictine and five-year-old cognac which now accounts for nearly three quarters of their sales. Both Bénédictine and B & B are sold at 86° proof, and both are full in body with deep, rich mellow tastes quite in contrast to the light spiciness of most herbal liqueurs. At the Bénédictine distillery, there is a display of over 800 pretenders to the name, in other words, products inauthentically labeled Bénédictine. These frauds certainly attest to the popularity and uniqueness of the ancient recipe. Obviously, the motto of these monks has served them well— DOM—*Deo Optimo Maximo*——"To God, Most Good, Most Great."

The Harvey Wallbanger of the 1960s' craze brought *Galliano* to nearly every American market. As with the French herb liqueurs, Galliano and many of its Italian counterparts tend to be yellow in color and are also generally quite sweet in finish. Not quite a hundred years old, Galliano production involves several distinct distillations of source materials which provide a very sweet anise-vanillan finish which makes it an excellent cocktail ingredient. The vast success of Galliano spawned mini-booms for similar products from Italy, such as *Liquore Gaetano, Valentino,* and even an American imitator called *Neapolitan Liqueur.*

However, as a class, these herbal liqueurs remain too complex and individualistic to be copied to the satisfaction of their aficionados. Therefore, this group forms a roster of proprietary labels that develop broad consumer acceptance and profitability. The customer knows the product, and orders by name, not by class.

Seeds and Plants

The distinction between herbal liqueurs and those developed with seeds and plants is a very fine one. Both have throughout the centuries been deemed medicinal or at least therapeutic. The distinction comes from whether the seeds or nonmedicinal plants dominate in the product. The problem in classifying derives from the practice of blending dozens of similar seeds and plants to obtain the right balance of flavors. However, the most

Bright green anise seeds of the highest quality provide the pungent, delicate flavoring for Marie Brizard Anisette, along with twenty other aromatic herbs.

N ext crowne the bowl full
With gentle lamb's wool;
Adde sugar, nutmeg, and ginger,
With store of ale too;
And this you must doe
To make the Wassaile a swinger.
Herrick's Hesperides

widely produced seeds and plants have such dominant character that they are easily recognizable and really determine the popularity of the products. The most popular are anise, caraway, cumin, mint, and coffee, each so easy to reproduce that all major liquor houses sell them. There are few proprietary exclusives in this category.

For example, it could be said that the old firm of Marie Brizard, established in the Bordeaux area of France in 1755, produces the most famous *anisette* in the world. However, the aniseed grows worldwide and is a popular flavoring in many foods and drinks. Consequently, there are dozens, if not hundreds of anise-like liqueurs. Similarly, *kümmel* has world fame as a liqueur with both caraway and cumin, as well as a touch of anise. There are dozens of similar bottlings.

The dominant types in this class in terms of total consumption are mint and cacao which produce crème de menthe, green and white, crème de cacao, and the many coffee-flavored liqueurs. Finally, *amaretto* with its pronounced bitter almond-marzipan tone, is the newest seed cordial to excite the American market. The original brand, Amaretto di Saronno, now has dozens of imitators. It should be noted that the amaretto made from apricot pits does possess a treasury of good things including potassium, magnesium, iron, calcium, riboflavin, thiamin, and vitamins. In addition to the abundance of sugar in most of these seed–plant varieties, there are many other residual chemicals of value. Perhaps this is why the French have always called liqueurs *digestifs,* digestives or stomach settlers!

The essential ingredients in Grand Mariner are the bitter, tropical oranges that exude fine oils from their skins and grapes for cognac from the Grande and Petite Champagne districts.

TABLE 22.1 Imports of Cordials and Liqueurs
by Country of Origin
1978 vs. 1979
(Tax Gallons)

Country	1978	1979
Bottled		
Italy	1,192,194	1,117,296
France	1,193,848	1,144,850
United Kingdom	897,529	851,619
Denmark	9,904	13,246
Greece	252,081	201,778
Mexico	37,043	92,060
Jamaica	12,094	8,257
Other	320,624	469,426
TOTAL	3,915,317	3,898,532
Bulk		
Italy	849,345	952,771
France	174,249	185,118
United Kingdom	11,128	12,525
Denmark	24,595	24,931
Greece	–	118
Mexico	1,691,268	2,142,269
Jamaica	294,994	223,701
Other	408,936	542,008
TOTAL	3,454,515	4,083,441
Total		
Italy	2,041,539	2,070,067
France	1,368,097	1,329,968
United Kingdom	908,657	864,144
Denmark	34,499	38,177
Greece	252,081	201,896
Mexico	1,728,311	2,234,329
Jamaica	307,088	231,958
Other	729,560	1,011,434
TOTAL	7,369,832	7,981,973

Source: Dan Hecht, ed., *The Liquor Handbook* (New York: Gavin-Gobson Associates, Inc., 1980), 296.

Fruits and Peels

As mentioned earlier, fruit ratafia and liqueurs came into being directly as alcoholic drinks. These were created for taste, not for health. Some of the innovators already had ample experience in the production of fruit wines and fruit brandies, so it was a simple step to meet the new demand for rich, sweet cordials.

By the tenth century, the Oriental orange had migrated to Europe, preceding by a couple of hundred years the popular bitter East Indian orange. These and other popular citrus liqueurs derive their essential flavorings from the oils in the skins. Today *Cointreau* is marketed in over 200 countries and emanates from thirteen widely dispersed distilleries. Founded in 1849, the firm claims a full 25 percent of the international liqueur market. To understand this scope, one should know that *one* Cointreau plant uses 600 tons of orange peels annually.

Two of Cointreau's competitors travel under the following names: *Curaçao,* after the island from which the orange comes and *Triple Sec. Goldwasser,* a coriander-flavored variation of *Triple Sec,* is marketed containing small flecks of gold leaf in memory of the days of the alchemist.

The tart red cherries of southern Denmark provide the flavoring for the popular *Peter Heering Liqueur,* formerly known as *Cherry Heering. Crème de Cassis* from the small, blue-black currants of southern France is newly popular as an aperitif, and when mixed with white wine, is called *Kir.*

Many hundreds of lush fruit-flavored cordials are produced around the world from indigenous fruits largely for local consumption. With the major plant sources, it is difficult to personalize the end product to the level of distinctness possible with the major herbal liqueurs. Those that achieve international status do so because of superior marketing (see table 22.1).

The hot maceration process in extracting herbal flavors is often combined with distillation. Shown are the hot maceration tanks from which the flavored fluid is transferred to pot stills. The spirit is later filtered and mixed with more fruit, alcohol and sugar for the final blend.

This handsome row of small pot stills has been in operation making Bols liqueurs for over one hundred years.

While it has neither fruit nor peel, no catalogue would be complete without mention of the famous Scotch concoction called *Drambuie.* Its name a contraction of the Gaelic phrase *an dram buidheach*—"the drink that satisfies," Drambuie consists of malt whiskies aged up to twenty years, a bit of grain whisky, sugar syrup, essential oils and a generous amount of strongly flavored heather honey. This pungent honey was popular as a flavoring agent in the mead melomels and piments of the Middle Ages. The secret recipe for this delight was bestowed on a Captain MacKinnon by Bonnie Prince Charles in 1746.

A very merry, dancing, drinking, laughing, quaffing and unthinking time.
                                                        John Dryden

PRODUCTION METHODS

Three production techniques are involved, often in tandem, to produce liqueurs. The first of these is termed *percolation,* and it closely resembles the coffee-brewing process. The flavoring agents are placed in a tray or bag at the top of a tank, and the base liqueur or *spirits menstrum* is continually pumped over the tray. The essential oils or flavorings gradually leach into the tank below. At times, distinctive herbs are percolated separately and married back to the flavored alcohols from other percolators. At other times some or all of these individually flavored spirits are redistilled together. Obviously there are many variations in the percolation of fruit essences.

Another frequently used method for extracting the vital essences, especially in the production of fruit liqueurs, is called *maceration,* a procedure comparable to steeping tea. The process, also called *infusion,* sometimes requires six to eight months during which the fruits soak in a huge tank of spirits menstrum in the manner of vermouth steeping. The alcohol acts as a solvent, separating the desirable flavors from the skins. The same problem of retaining the light, delicate fruit flavors exists as in winemaking. After distillation, the essential oils oxidize easily and rapidly. The finished product is strained off the tank to be used as a flavoring or as a base spirit for redistillation. At times, heat is also used with the percolation and maceration steps.

The third and most important of the three techniques is *distillation,* accomplished either directly from the fruit mash or following percolation or maceration. When the distillation is done directly, it usually involves the stronger flavoring agents such as juniper, lavender, mint, fennel, and thyme which can withstand the heat in the still together with the brandy or other base liquors. Only a single run through the pot still is required since this step amounts to a redistillation, being the second run of the base liquor.

However, in the vast majority of liqueurs, maceration, percolation, or both, precede the distillation step. Generally, the flavored spirit is taken from the still at quite high proofs, up to 190° neutral spirit level. Years of experience at the major companies have led to just the right combination of these three procedures to assure continuity in final product.

MATURATION AND RECTIFICATION

While there is often a short period of aging in the macerating tanks or with some distilled flavored spirits, very little barrel or tank aging occurs with the finished product. In most cases, these are uniquely and sensitively balanced concoctions designed to be consumed before their essential oils and essences separate into clouds and hazes. In fact, some—such as anisette, kümmel, and curaçao—are cold stabilized (as are wines) in advance of bottling to reduce even further oils and chemicals that could precipitate on the shelf or in the refrigerator.

TABLE 22.2 Specific Gravities of Arrow Cordials

Cordials	Proof	Specific Gravity
Kirsch Liqueur	90°	0.9570–0.9630
Ouzo Liqueur	90°	0.9515–0.9550
Ginger Flavored Brandy	70°	1.0140–1.0180
Sloe Gin	60°	1.0289–1.0310
Apricot Flavored Brandy	70°	1.0370–1.0410
Peach Flavored Brandy	70°	1.0410–1.0460
Rock & Rye	60°	1.0490–1.0550
Blackberry Flavored Brandy	70°	1.0510–1.0550
Peppermint Schnapps	60°	1.0520–1.0580
Coffee Flavored Brandy	70°	1.0670–1.0730
Triple Sec	60°	1.0710–1.0770
Blue Curaçao	54°	1.0795–1.0828
Curaçao	54°	1.0824–1.0864
Amaretto	56°	1.0865–1.0935
White Crème de Menthe	60°	1.0790–1.0850
Green Crème de Menthe	60°	1.030–1.090
Crème de Banana	54°	1.1100–1.1160
Crème de Almond	54°	1.1230–1.1260
Dark Crème de Cacao	54°	1.1205–1.1250
White Crème de Cacao	54°	1.1315–1.1355
Choclair	54°	1.1300–1.1350
Crème de Strawberry	44°	1.1240–1.1310
Anisette	60°	1.1300–1.1340
Crème de Cassis	40°	1.1530–1.1570
Caramella	54°	1.1460–1.1510
Crème de Cafe	50°	1.1535–1.1585
Honeydew Melon	50°	1.0515–1.0555
Pina Colada Liqueur	50°	1.0960–1.1000
Cinnamon Schnapps	60°	1.0700–1.0740
Spearmint Schnapps	60°	1.0550–1.0590

Source: Courtesy Heublein Spirits and Wine Company.

Fruit blenders can identify the type, age, and character of fruit-flavored essences by nose alone as easily as the Scotch blender can pick the characteristics of aged malts for his blends. The blender assembles the portions of redistilled spirits, macerated spirits menstrums, water, sugar, and food colorings into a gigantic harmonious blend.

Because of the variation in these blends, particularly in the volume of sugar and the body of the fruit spirits, there is a wide range in the specific gravity of various liqueurs (see table 22.2). The bartender's awareness of this fact allows him to arrange the brightly colored layers of the Pousse-café cocktail. For a patriotic drink, try layering a red noyau, a white crème de menthe, and finally, on top, a blue curaçao.

BITTERS

This final class of early distillates was actually developed several hundred years after liqueurs, but it was, in a way, the reincarnation of the earliest herbals. Dr. Sigert's original Angostura Bitters was designed as a malaria fighter and later became a standard medicine for the Royal Navy, no doubt the precurser

And, so as adversaries do in law, strive mightily, but eat and drink as friends.

Shakespeare

"You know, Sir, drinking drives away care, and makes us forget whatever is disagreeable. Would you not allow a man to drink for that reason?" JOHNSON. "Yes, Sir, if he sat next *you.*"

James Boswell and Samuel Johnson (in Life of Johnson**)**

of the taste for gin and tonic. Today bitters generally serve the specific purposes of stimulating digestion or accenting other drinks, although some hangover recipes claim therapeutic powers.

Source Materials

The primary element in all bitters is, of course, bitter bark or root such as quinine from the cinchona tree, which grows in South America, India, Java, and Indonesia. Also known as Jesuit bark, it has been used for centuries to reduce fevers. In addition to the chief bittering agent, a host of seeds and barks are employed, as well as a base liquor as in any other liqueur making.

Production

The steeping or maceration procedure is the primary production method due to the numbers of herbs and plants involved. For example, *Angostura Bitters* is said to use 343 herbs and spices which are soaked in rum for flavor transfer. Angostura is sold at 90° proof in grocery stores without being affected by liquor controls. Today, nearly 100 recipes call for Angostura, including the Old Fashioned, the Singapore Sling, the Whiskey Sour, and the Champagne Cocktail.

Other famous brands vary in the degree of bitterness. *Peychaud's* from New Orleans, an ingredient of the famed Sazerac Cocktail, is a little more bitter. In contrast, *Campari* is so mild that the bottle is labeled an *Aperitivo*. The popular Negroni Cocktail contains about equal parts of dry gin, vermouth, and Campari. Similarly, *Amer Picon*, a mixture of oranges, gentian, and cinchona bark, works very well with soda as a pleasant aperitif.

309

Highlights

- Herb and plant liqueurs originated as medicines primarily in monasteries and apothecaries.

- Fruit liqueurs emerged as social beverages.

- Liqueur production involves three major techniques: percolation, maceration, and distillation, often in combination.

- Bitters were originally tonics or stomachics and now are largely cocktail accents.

- Bitters, because of the intensity of their bitterness, are generally not subject to liquor laws.

TABLE 22.3 Top Imported Cordials

Brand	Cases
Kahlúa	1,502,000
Amaretto di Saronno	850,000
Baileys Irish Cream	575,000
Grand Mariner	346,000
Drambuie	320,000
Bénédictine (B & B)	255,000
Tia Maria	210,000
Yukon Jack	185,000
Galliano	160,000
Midori	100,000

Source: Stateways (September/October 1981), 46

LIQUEUR MARKETING

As with all major spirits, the United States market is dominated by several major brands. As a category, liqueurs are gently rising in consumption with domination by the well-known labels (see table 22.3).

SUGGESTED LIQUEUR TASTING

Liqueurs abound like flowers in May. These few items should intrigue you to conduct a series of tastings, after asking the liquor merchant for copies of the many recipe books made available by the distributing companies.

Because of the enormous variety and plethora of names, a cordial dictionary is offered to provide an introduction to the general types and the best known liqueurs (see table 22.5).

TABLE 22.4 Liqueur Tasting

Liqueur Flavorings	General Style	Suggested Brand
Anise and brandy	Richly flavored, medium sweet, highly spicy, hot	Ouzo
Peach, bourbon, and citrus	Light nose, fresh peach and fruity flavor, light body and clean finish	Southern Comfort Brown-Forman
Mint and neutral spirits	Light nose, medium light body, and a little sweetness with a strong mint character	Arrow Heublein
Almond	Full nose, medium sweet, strong nutty flavor, long finish	Amaretto di Saronno Glenmore
Bitter orange	Inviting nose, dominating orange character, medium body, quite sweet	Triple Sec Schenley
Mint crème	Flowery nose, heavy body, very sweet, strong mint flavor	Crème de menthe De Kuyper National Distillers
Coffee	Light nose, full body, very rich coffee finish	Kahlúa Hiram Walker
Medium bitters	Sharp nose, medium body, bittersweet with orange tone, nearly mellow	Campari
Bourbon/herbs	Pleasant nose, full body, orange and herb tones to flavors, mellow	Wild Turkey Austin Nichols

TABLE 22.5 Cordial Dictionary

Liqueur	Spirit Base	Proofs	Herbs	Seeds	Fruits	Others
Advokaat (Advocaat) Holland's creamy, thick eggnog from yolks of new eggs and neutral spirits, low in alcohol and often flavored	Brandy	34°				X
Amaretto Unique, extremely popular apricot-almond cordial	Brandy and neutral spirits	54°	X	X		
Amaretto & Cognac Unique, proprietary blend of popular apricot and almond flavors; has probably been made since 1525	Vodka and Brandy	50°	X	X		
Amer Picon Oranges, herbs, and brandy combine in this pleasantly bitter French liqueur	Brandy	78°	X		X	
Anisette Mild, sweet licorice flavor from aniseed	Brandy or neutral spirits	60°	X	X		
Apricot Liqueur Very popular and made in many brands; usually brandy macerated with fresh apricots; sweeter and less potent than apricot brandy	Apricot brandy	80°			X	
B & B Liqueur D.O.M. Half Bénédictine and half brandy marry in this unique blend; less sweet than Bénédictine	Cognac	86°	X	X		
Bailey's Original Irish Cream Liqueur Irish cream, Irish whiskey, chocolate, and other natural flavorings	Irish whiskey	34°				X
Bénédictine D.O.M. Rich and sweet secret formula of over 20 herbs macerated, percolated, and distilled with brandy; invented by Benedictine monks around 1500 as a medicine	Cognac	86°	X	X		
Blackberry Liqueur Sweet, full bodied by maceration of ripe blackberries; pure blackberry brandy often added for flavor and finesse	Neutral spirits or brandy	50°			X	
Boggs Cranberry Liqueur An unusual, tart, domestic cordial	Neutral spirits	40°	X		X	
Caffe Lolita U.S. blend of various imported coffees	Neutral spirits	53°		X		
Campari Secret Italian recipe for this pungent, bittersweet red aperitif; popularly served with soda	Brandy	72°	X		X	
Chartreuse (green) Over 130 wild herbs, as well as various fruits, spices, and flowers are blended in this 900–year-old secret recipe of the French Carthusian monks	Brandy	110°	X	X	X	
Chartreuse (yellow) Sweeter, milder, and lower in alcohol than the original Green Chartreuse	Brandy	80°	X	X	X	
Chéri-Suisse Swiss chocolate and cherries for a beautiful pink cordial	Brandy	52° or 60°			X	X
Cherry Marnier Full flavored with hints of almonds and a deep cherry color	Cognac	46°		X	X	
Choclair Rich U.S. chocolate-coconut liqueur	Neutral spirits	54°			X	X
Coconut Liqueur Rich, full, with a snappy coconut taste	Neutral spirits	60°			X	
Cocoribe Liqueur Coconuts blended with Caribbean rum	Rum	60°			X	
Coffee Liqueur Sweeter and less potent than coffee-flavored brandy, but rich and aromatic	Neutral spirits	53°		X		
Cointreau White and fragrant, slightly tart orange-flavored liqueur; from the wild oranges of the Indies blended with Mediterranean sweet oranges	Cognac	80°			X	
Cordial Médoc Sweet, red, and mellow blend of herbs, crème de cacao, and curaçao	Brandy	80°	X	X	X	
Crème de Banane (Banana liqueur) Sweet, usually yellow, richly pleasing banana flavor by maceration of the fruit; made all over the world	Neutral spirits	56°			X	
Crème de Cacao (brown) Full-bodied, rich blend of cacao and vanilla beans	Neutral spirits	54°		X		

TABLE 22.5 Cordial Dictionary

Liqueur	Spirit Base	Proofs	Herbs	Seeds	Fruits	Others
Crème de Cacao (white) Milder than the brown yet still sweet and satisfying	Neutral spirits	54°		X		
Crème de Cassis Very sweet, intense black currant liqueur which uses both fruit and leaves; made by macerating in brandy; other flavors such as red currants and raspberries may be added	Cognac	40°	X		X	
Crème de Fraises The full flavor of fresh, ripe strawberries from maceration; often flavored with the fruit brandy	Strawberry brandy	50°			X	
Crème de Framboise Light in body, medium sweet from maceration with fresh raspberries and then compounding or distilling with spirits	Raspberry brandy				X	
Crème de Menthe Cool, pleasant, mostly peppermint refresher; the only difference between green and white is color	Neutral spirits	60°	X			
Crème de Noya (Crème de Noyau) Beautiful almond fragrance and flavor from extracts of peach and apricot kernels	Brandy	60°		X	X	
Curaçao (orange, blue, brown, white, etc.) Made from the bittersweet orange peels of the West Indies, fragrant and subtle; first steeped in water, then in the base spirit after which it undergoes distillation and rectification	Cognac	60°			X	
Cyner Fascinating and fun bittersweet liqueur made from artichokes	Brandy	33°	X			
Drambuie Honey and secret herbs in an aromatic and flavorful blend; mellow and sweet with definite Scotch taste	Scotch	80°	X			X
Élixir D'Anvers Made in Antwerp from herbs and seeds; bittersweet and soft	Neutral spirits		X	X		
Fior D'Alpe Sweet, slightly pungent, light yellow herbal blend flavored with flowers	Brandy	92°	X		X	
Forbidden Fruit Honey and citrus fruits, including the shaddock and orange, make this light and fragrant, bittersweet; reddish brown color; a unique American invention	Whiskey	64°			X	
Frangelico Brownish gold delight made from a blend of wild hazelnuts, berries, and herbs in a private formula	Brandy	56°	X	X	X	
Galliano Secret formula of over 80 spices, herbs, and fruits creates this soft, rich, pale amber Italian liqueur	Brandy	70°	X	X	X	
Ginger Liqueur Maceration of ginger roots, dry and spicy	Neutral spirits	60°		X		
Goldwasser (Danzig Goldwasser) Tiny goldflakes of 22–carat gold swim in this charming blend of orange peels, caraway seeds, and anise, but the gold is tasteless and harmless; also produced is Silberwasser with silver flakes	Brandy or Neutral Spirits	76°	X	X	X	X
Grand Marnier Distinctive and beautiful full orange flavor from the bitter curaçao orange peels using only Cognac as its spirit base.	Cognac	80°	X		X	
Green Tea Liqueur Japanese liqueur made from two teas; with subtle fragrance and light, medium dry taste	Neutral spirits		X			
Irish Coffee Liqueur A graceful blend of Irish whiskeys, fine coffees, herbs, and sugar	Irish whiskey		X	X		
Irish Mist Liqueur Irish whiskeys, honeys, clover, and herbs combine in this mellow, unique, amber-colored delight	Irish whiskey	80°	X			X
Kahlúa Smooth, rich, and very popular Mexican coffee liqueur; thick and creamy	Neutral spirits	53°		X		
Kümmel Gracious, usually sweet blend with the basic flavoring from caraway seeds as well as cumin, coriander, and anise; made all over northern Europe	Vodka or neutral spirits	70°	X	X		

TABLE 22.5 Cordial Dictionary

Liqueur	Spirit Base	Proofs	Herbs	Seeds	Fruits	Others
Lochan Ora Beautiful blend of Scotch whiskies, sweetened by native honey and flavored by a private selection of spices and herbs	Scotch whisky	70°	X			X
Mandarine Napoléon (Crème de Mandarine) Quite sweet Belgian delight with the flavor of ripe tangerines, medium sweetness, and lovely dark orange color; by maceration and distillation	Cognac	80°			X	
Maraschino Marasca sour cherries with crushed kernels flavor this aromatic, translucent liqueur from Yugoslavia or Italy; cherry brandy is often added for bouquet	Cherry brandy	54°			X	
Mastic (Masticha) From Greece, a distinctive resin (from the cashew tree) and licorice-flavored sweet, white cordial	Brandy	92°	X	X		
Midori Proprietary brandy from Japan with the refreshing, fun taste and aroma of honeydew melons	Neutral spirits	46°			X	
O'Darby Irish Cream Liqueur Subtle flavor of chocolate enlivens this distinctive rich Irish cream	Irish whiskey	34°		X		X
Ouzo Sweet, white, and delicious liqueur flavored by anise and other herbs	Brandy	90°	X	X		
Parfait Amour Liqueur Unique, very sweet, violet-colored liqueur with the taste of violets, rose petals, vanilla, citrus peels, and other flavors	Brandy		X	X	X	
Peach Liqueur Sweeter than peach-flavored brandy, and milder, but still delicious; usually maceration or percolation of ripe fruit in neutral spirits with some kernels	Peach brandy and neutral spirits	60°			X	
Pear William's Liqueur (Poire Williams) French Anjou pears flavor this pleasant and delicate cordial	Pear brandy	60°			X	
Peppermint Schnapps Light, slightly sweet, and thoroughly pleasing mint liqueur	Neutral spirits	60°	X			
Pernod Soft, sweet, and licorice flavor from a secret French recipe	Brandy and neutral spirits	86°	X	X		
Peter Heering Private Danish formula for a wonderful, sweet and smooth cherry liqueur; produced by the Heering family for over 160 years	Cherry brandy	49°			X	
Pimm's Cup No. 1 Bittersweet, lemon-flavored and amber-colored delight invented over 100 years ago in Pimm's Oyster Bar in London	Gin	67°	X		X	
Pineapple Liqueur (Crème d'Ananas) Pineapple fruit liqueur made in Hawaii and Holland; the rum base is often matured in oak	Rum				X	
Pistasha The proprietary Regnier label indicates pistachio nuts are used in this rich, green nutty liqueur	Cognac and neutral spirits	48°		X		
Praline Liqueur New Orleans offers this smooth, rich vanilla and pecan cordial	Neutral	40°		X		
Prunelle (Crème de Prunelle) Very sweet and full-bodied dark liqueur with a base of wild plums; made in France and Holland	Prune brandy and neutral spirits	60°		X	X	
Rock and Rye Rock candy and steeped fruits in a favorite American-invented cordial	Rye whiskey	54°			X	X
Sabra Chocolate and orange flavors in a bittersweet, deep brown, well-balanced Israeli liqueur from the desert Sabra cactus	Neutral spirits	52°		X	X	
Sambuca Anise and the flavor of the witch elderberry bush combine in this white, delicate Italian cordial	Brandy	84°	X	X		
Sloe Gin Deep rich red cordial from sloe berries steeped or macerated; often other fruit flavors are added, and wood aging is common	Neutral spirits and Gin	60°			X	

TABLE 22.5 Cordial Dictionary

Liqueur	Spirit Base	Proofs	Herbs	Seeds	Fruits	Others
Southern Comfort American blend of peaches, oranges, and herbs	Bourbon	100°	X		X	
Strega Fruits, spices, barks and over 70 herbs, with angelica the primary flavor, combine in this private, gold Italian liqueur	Brandy	80°	X	X	X	
Tia Maria Two hundred-year-old private formula for Jamaica's somewhat light and dry but richly aromatic coffee liqueur	Rum	63°		X		
Triple Sec Family of orange-based liqueurs from bitter oranges, including Cointreau and Grand Marnier	Neutral spirits	54–60°			X	
Tuaca Complex, semi-dry, golden Italian liqueur from five hundred-year-old formula of herbs, fruit, and other flavors	Brandy	70°	X	X	X	
Van Der Hum South African orange-based cordial mixed with essences of other fruits, seeds, and barks	Brandy	63°		X	X	
Vandermint Dutch mint chocolate, very sweet and candy-like		50°	X	X		
Wild Turkey Liqueur An amber color and undisclosed herbs and spices distinguish this liqueur	Bourbon	80°	X	X		
Yukon Jack Canadian Liqueur Smooth, somewhat dry, and well-balanced blend	Canadian Whiskies	100°				

Suggested Readings

Barleycorn, Michael. *Moonshiner's Manual*. Willits, Calif.: Oliver Press, 1975.
   Outrageous but thoroughly complete instructions on how to break the law by moonshining.

Bell, Donald A. *The Spirits of Hospitality: An Overview of the Origin, History and Service of Alcoholic Beverages*. East Lansing, Michigan: The Educational Institute of the American Hotel and Motel Association, 1976.
   Fine working review of the field for professionals.

Cooper, Derek. *Guide to the Whiskies of Scotland*. New York: Cornerstone Library, 1979.
   A fine, authoritative review of the Scotch whisky industry.

Fleming, Alice. *Alcohol, The Delightful Poison*. New York: Dell Pub. Co., Inc., 1975.
   An easy-to-read, thoughtful and brief history of humans and drink.

Forbes, Robert James. *Short History of the Art of Distillation: From the Beginnings up to the Death of Cellier Blumenthal*. Leiden, Holland: Brill, 1948.
   Scholarly presentation of distilling equipment from the ancients to the continuous still.

Ford, Gene. *The ABC'S of Wine, Brew and Spirits*. Seattle: Murray Publishing Co., 1980.
   Illustrated questions and answers on all things in beverage alcohols.

Furnas, J. C. *The Life and Times of the Late Demon Rum*. New York: G. P. Putnam's Sons, 1965.
   A history of that woeful period in America called Prohibition.

Hallgarten, Peter A. *Spirits and Liqueurs*. London: Faber and Faber Ltd., 1979.
   A penetrating look from the inside by an extraordinarily qualified and educated wine and liqueur merchant.

Hannum, Hurst; and Blumberg, Robert S. *Brandies and Liqueurs of the World*. Garden City, NY: Doubleday & Co., Inc., 1976.
   Well-researched and handsomely illustrated source book. A must for your spirit library.

McGuire, E. B. *Irish Whiskey.* Dublin: Gill and Macmillan, 1973.
Detailed historical survey of Irish whiskey production and the laws that have influenced its development.

Magee, Malachy. *1000 Years of Irish Whiskey.* Dublin: O'Brien Press, 1980.
From the Old Bushmills at Antrim to the Irish Distillers Group at Midleton—a complete history.

Murphy, Brian. *The World Book of Whiskey.* Chicago: Rand McNally & Co., 1979.
All you need to know, recounted in a book of easy language and beautiful illustrations about Scotch and other whiskeys of the world.

An Old American Custom: Some Facts About Beverage Alcohol in America. Pamphlet of Licensed Beverages Industries, Inc., 1972.
Delightful and accurate account of early American consumption.

Packowski, George W. *Distilled Beverage Spirits.* rpt. from *The Encyclopedia of Food Technology,* vol 2. Westport, Conn.: Avi Pub. Co., 1974.
The basics in an easy-to-read form.

Ray, Cyril. *Cognac.* New York: Stein and Day Publishers, 1974.
A warm and lighthearted but accurate picture of a warm and lighthearted spirit.

Ray, Cyril, ed. *The Compleat Imbiber: An Entertainment.* New York: Rinehart and Co., Inc., 1957.
An anthology of articles in praise of, and in jest about, drinking.

Robotti, Peter F. and Frances D. *Key to Gracious Living, Wine and Spirits.* Englewood Cliffs, N. J.: Prentice-Hall, Inc., 1972.
A loving review of wines and spirits and the foods with which they harmonize.

Gin

Until well into the nineteenth century, it was a rare occurrence, indeed, to be able to purchase an unflavored wine or liquor. An anonymous poem by a Londoner (c. 1712) demonstrates the abysmal ubiquity of flavoring agents by praising an innkeeper who "serves genuine claret, undisguised by art./ Quick to the taste, and cheerful to the heart."

DR. SYLVIUS AND THE JUNIPER

Dr. Sylvius, born Franz de le Boë, was a physician who lectured on anatomy and the chemical aspects of medicine at the University of Leiden. He experimented with medicines containing herbal extracts, including oil of juniper. The *Buch der Natur* by Megenberg, published in 1295, tells of this oil gained by descensory (drip) distillation.

> From the juniper tree an oil is made thus. Take two clean pots and put one on top of the other and the pot on the top should have a hole in the bottom. The upper pot shall be filled with the wood of the juniper tree, that is dry and it shall be closed well so that no smoke can escape and a great fire shall be lighted around it. If then the wood inside is heated the oil flows from the upper pot into the lower one, but there is very little of it. (In Forbes [1948].)

Apparently there was a great deal of oil of juniper in the sixteenth century, and its diuretic properties were well known. By 1550, juniper waters were prescribed for many illnesses. In about 1650, Sylvius created a blend of rough proportions of

That humble and much reviled liquid which is the most especially English of all spirits.

George Saintsbury

these waters and *aqua vitae* and named the nostrum *genever* from the French *genievre* or "juniper."

This product represented, in a manner of speaking, the democratization of hard liquor. Its production could continue using grain spirits year round and its materials were much less costly than those of cognac and other fruit brandies. Within a few years, the enterprising firm of Bols in Amsterdam was producing a commercial *genever*.

Also, before long, English soldiers carried the tasty delight home, calling it Dutch Courage or *gin,* short for *genever.* Around the port cities of Plymouth, Bristol, and Portsmouth, gin soon caught on as the "spirit of the masses" in contrast to the expensive port and brandy.

What really made gin what it is today was that misnamed period of history called the Glorious Revolution. The staunchly Protestant William and Mary, called to the British throne by Parliament after landing in England with a Dutch army, brought with them from Holland a passionate hatred for everything Catholic and French. One of their first acts involved the advocacy of domestically distilled corn brandy which, naturally enough, was blended with the oil of juniper.

Terms

botanicals Flavoring ingredients used in making gin—the primary one being the juniper berry. Others are coriander, angelica, orrisroot and cassia bark.

brandewijn The Dutch equivalent of London dry gin, produced with neutral grain spirits.

flavored gin Very old-style spirits made by steeping gin with various popular flavors including lemon, sloe berries, orange and the like.

genever Dutch word for gin, interchangeable with Scheidam gin, named for the production city.

gin English word corrupted from the Dutch *genever*.

jenever Spelling of gin in Belgium.

jonge genever Dutch for the younger of two major types of gin; less flavorful than Oude Genever.

London dry gin Gin produced by the English and Americans in which juniper, the flavoring agent, dominates.

mouterij Malt house in Holland.

moutwijn The base spirits for Holland gin, produced by three passes through pot stills.

moutwijn genever A Dutch gin twice redistilled over botanicals.

Old Tom gin British gin flavored with sugar syrup.

oude genever The second major classification of Dutch gin in which the malty flavors of the spirit are as prominent as the juniper tastes.

Pimm's Cup No. 1 Special sweet drinks using gin as base.

Plymouth gin Gin produced in town of Plymouth using Dartmouth river water for cutting.

wacholder German equivalent of gin ranging in style from light *wacholderkornbrant* to heavy *steinhäger*.

The next fifty years saw a pastiche of laws alternately promoting and discouraging production of gin. No matter what the government did after 1720, nothing could stanch the flood. In 1727, 5 million gallons of gin were drunk by about 6 million people. This rose to 20 million gallons by 1742. By 1750, huge segments of the population were on a perpetual gin jag, and governmental attempts to counteract it proved unsuccessful. For example, in 1729, the restrictive license-to-produce laws were met by drunken mob protests. Then, in 1736, lawmakers tried restricting minimum sales to two gallons, hoping to stem consumption by the poor who could not afford that much at once. New brands born during this period were My Lady's Eyewash and Royal Poverty. The miserable failure of a law was rescinded in 1742.

A NATION BEFOGGED BY GIN

In *Cheers,* (1940) Francesca White comments on the universality of gin consumption in eighteenth century England:

> The spirit was to be had everywhere. It was sold by apothecaries and barbers, by tobacconists and many merchants, who offered it to their clients over a business transaction. It was hawked in the streets and sold in the jails where William Smith, an early prison reformer, counted in 1776 "no less than 30 gin shops at one time in the King's Bench, and I have been credibly informed by very attentive observers that upwards of two hogshead or 120 gallons of gin which they call by various names, [such] as vinegar, gossip, crank, mexico, skyblue etc. were sold weekly. . . ."

At long last the Industrial Revolution came to the rescue of this society *in extremis*. As industrial and mercantile activities employed the populace, wanton drunkenness gradually abated. The magnificent gaslit Gin Palace in which the tantalizing gin specialties came from huge barrels, emerged as the forerunner of today's opulent restaurant or tavern. These establishments were social centers for the whole family—like early English inns, places where a commoner could have social status and recreation commensurate with his new financial status.

Marrison (1970) reports on the creative contents of those prominent gin barrels:

> In the eighteenth and early nineteenth centuries, the most surprising constituents were added to spirits to give them "kick" and taste. Oil of vitriol (sulphuric acid) and oil of turpentine were commonly, not exceptionally, added. Sabine in *The Complete Cellarman* of 1811 makes "British Gin" by taking "spirits (one in five); one pennyweight oil of vitriol; one pennyweight oil of juniper; one pennyweight oil of almonds; half pint spirits of wine, and 2 lb. lump of sugar. Dissolve the sugar in 6 quarts water and simmer half an hour, constantly skimming it and when cold, add the spirits of wine and oils and put it to your spirits."

It was during this period that London dry gin emerged from the morass by gaining popularity with the upper classes as part of their movement to better health. Already established was the awareness that sugar was inimical to long life. In a counter-movement all over the continent of Europe, flavored

The glazed stoneware bottle of a century ago has its attached wooden stopper embossed with its makers name, Lovatt and Lovatt, Ltd.

Drinking gin was a family affair!

Gin. A modern nickname for the liquor called *geneva* or *genevre,* because when beggars are drunk they are as great as kings.

Bailey's Dictionary (1720)

and somewhat drier gin-type spirits became popular. It was steinhäger and wacholder, in Germany, barovica in Slovakia, and klickowatch in the Balkans. Flavored gins follow from essences of local fruits as the night follows the day.

The final surge in the popularity of gin occurred with the cocktail revolution during American Prohibition, and gin engulfed the United States. For years the British armed forces had mixed their favorite gin with coolers, particularly those containing quinine to treat tropical fevers. However, in America, the 1920s and Prohibition provided the ideal circumstances for gin to become popular. First, gin was ridiculously simple to make, requiring only a bathtub, some essential oils including juniper, and some loathsome moonshine of the simplest, least palatable sort. In a few days of soaking—voila, gin!

The dry martini was created in the Knickerbocker Hotel in New York City, and contained London dry gin, dry vermouth, and orange bitters. Freezes, flips, and crushes abounded. In a recipe book of 1930 titled *Shake 'Em Up,* no fewer than 34 of the first 44 drinks used some combination of citrus juices. Most contained gin—gin and fruit juice, as American as apple pie!

SOURCE MATERIALS

Gin utilizes some grain or neutral spirits, oil of juniper, and a host of other aromatics but principally coriander. There are three very distinctive classes of gin available commercially: Hollands or Scheidam gin, the closest to the original; London dry gin, made in England; and London dry gin made in America.

The primary flavoring agent for all three is juniper, an evergreen shrub that grows wild all over the face of the earth. Thirteen varieties exist in the United States although distillers prefer the oil-rich blue-black berries that grow in Italy and Yugoslavia. Only the best of the fruit is used, with about five pounds able to supply the flavoring for 100 gallons of spirit base. Other familiar flavorings in gin include coriander, as already mentioned, angelica root, anise, caraway, fruit peels, cardamom and the like. Although the flavorings may be similar, the production methods differ substantially for each gin type.

HOLLANDS GIN PROCESSING

Hollands or Scheidam gin still retains a flavor intensity reminiscent of a single malt Scotch or an Irish whiskey. The Dutch utilize about equal parts of barley, corn, and rye in the mash

(A)

(B)

Gin stills are always variations of short pot stills with small fractioning columns as seen here at Heublein (A) and Beefeaters (B).

which produces an alcohol wash termed *moutwijn* or malt wine. In some rare cases, the botanicals are introduced directly into this wash before distillation in conventional pot stills. In other instances, the moutwijn passes through the still for a second distillation in advance of maceration with the botanicals. At any rate, both types are taken from the still at a low 100° to 110° proof, assuring a strong "whiskey" overtone to the juniper-laden spirit.

In the small town of Scheidam today there are over 100 gin producers, attesting to the vast popularity of their native spirits. The venerable Bols firm is the oldest and still the largest in the field. A wide variation in types of gin is appreciated in the Low Countries, but most exports are *jonge,* or young mild gin which is usually rectified by the introduction of light molasses spirits. Flavored jonge is also popular in local consumption. Even this mildest of Hollands would surprise the confirmed gin lover with its challenging aroma and brisk taste.

LONDON DRY GIN: BRITISH AND AMERICAN

There are very subtle taste distinctions between London dry gin produced in Britain and that made in the States. The processing is very similar. Gin made in London utilizes a formula of 75 percent corn, 15 percent barley, and 10 percent mixed grains. The critical difference is the lower proof of the spirit used. The range from 170° to 180° proof assures some measure of whiskey taste that can be perceived in the nose and on the tongue. In contrast, all American gin by definition must be made from *100 percent neutral spirits,* no matter the grain source.

The Gin Still

There are two types of distillation involved in dry gin, one being the traditional gin-head procedure in huge stills in which the botanicals are placed in a gin head in wire mesh so that the spirits rising during redistillation will strip the flavorings on their way through. This is the reverse of the percolation head in liqueur production. The still operator allows the foreshots and the feints to separate from the heart of the run which enters a gin receiver. The feints and foreshots are redistilled for their alcohol content in another run through the still.

The cold-mix system employed by many modern distilleries involves a maceration of the botanicals in the spirits base in advance of the flavor distillation. Most of this product is then pot distilled, separating out the heads and tails, and rendering a very light and aromatic spirit.

The control panel for the gin stills at Hiram Walker.

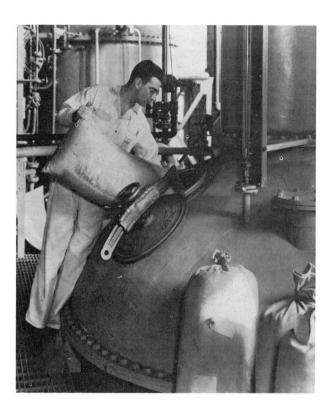

The botanicals are placed in the gin head according to formula.

A distinction, though subtle, can be found by tasting one after another, for example, a Tanqueray and a Schenley's or Seagram's American-made London dry gin; the distinction is a slightly higher juniper and coriander character in the American gin as contrasted to a softer taste and a hint of malt in the import.

The economic marvel in this production lies in the immediacy of sale; aging is not required. In fact, gin too long on the shelf can cloud because of oxidation of the essential oils. Once cut by distilled or demineralized water, gin is shipped to the market as one of the producer's most profitable hard liquors.

One other category of gin exists under United States law, and that is compounded gin. In essence, this is bathtub gin in which the flavoring agents are introduced into the spirits after distillation until sufficient oils have seeped into the spirits which are then bottled and sold. Very little of this inferior product is marketed today.

MARKETING

As with the other liquors studied, the sales in American and British gins are dominated by the huge, massively advertised brands. Very minuscule amounts of the traditional Hollands gin enter the American market each year, although they do enjoy vast popularity on the continent.

On the Beefeater bottling line, constant visual checks are performed to assure fill levels and product quality.

A small quantity of Bols moutwijn *is further wood aged and sold without infusion of juniper oils as* Corenwijn. *Here are the aging facilities for this specialty at Bols.*

The British and American producers continue to make considerable amounts of flavored gins, with the sloe berry variety the most popular. Most of these are slightly sweetened before bottling and are generally the product of long maceration of the fruit in high proof spirits. The flavors are intense. Old Tom gin is still produced in London by Boords, Tanqueray, and Gordon's. While contemporary Old Tom is slightly sweetened, it is far from its sugary predecessors of the last century.

The gin taste remains popular the world over, and many countries use a variety of spirits with the juniper as a flavoring agent. The German *wacholder* is similar to London dry gin because it is a corn spirit with juniper flavoring. The finest of these productions are called steinhägers, and they originate in the town of Steinhägen in Westphalia. Wacholder is characterized by a striking juniper effect obtained from a direct distillation of berries into the spirit.

The original Pimm's No. 1, a flavored cocktail produced from a recipe devised in an 1880s' fish house, uses gin as its base liquor. Dozens of cocktails are made with gin, a holdover from Prohibition days.

TABLE 23.1 Top Ten Markets for Gin 1980 vs. 1981 (750ML Per 100 Persons)

State	1980	1981
District of Columbia	263.8	278.9
New Hampshire	248.5	236.0
Delaware	187.7	209.0
Nevada	199.6	184.0
Maryland	153.4	152.5
Florida	168.8	151.1
Georgia	169.2	150.2
Connecticut	158.2	146.4
South Carolina	139.8	146.1
Vermont	149.5	139.9
National average	94.9	92.9

Source: Dan Hecht, ed., *The Liquor Handbook* (New York: Gavin-Gobson Associates, Inc., 1982), 237.

Highlights

- The primary flavoring agent in all gin is the oil of juniper but many other common botanicals are also used.
- Hollands or Scheidam gin uses spirits taken from the still at low proof, assuring malt whiskey tastes.
- London dry gin is characterized by a muted presence of malt character and generally light botanicals.

- American-style gin must employ 100 percent neutral spirits in the base and generally has a more pronounced juniper character.
- Flavored and compounded gins have a very small portion of the American market with the exception of a few favorites like sloe gin and Old Tom gin.

SUGGESTED GIN TASTING

In gin, there can be found three rather general tastes quite like those in brandy. The originating Dutch in Scheidam still employ a warm whiskey-like base. The British gin makers use considerably lower proof spirits than the Americans, creating a complexity easily discernable in comparison to the predominant juniper tone in gins produced in the United States.

TABLE 23.2 Gin Tasting

Spirit	General Style	Suggested Brand
London dry gin (United States)	Sharp aroma, intense flavoring, medium body, fast finish	Bar gin, generally bottled by local distributor
Extra dry gin (United States)	Pleasant aroma, sharp, clean taste, intensely juniper, deep color	Seagram's
London dry gin (London)	Bright nose, soft and complex flavoring, clean finish	Beefeaters, Kobrand
London dry gin (London)	Appealing bouquet, complex flavoring, hint of malt, easy finish	Gilbey's
Plymouth gin (Plymouth)	Soft nose, light body with very smooth mouth feel, lasting finish	Coates
Genever gin (Scheidam)	Whiskey nose, herbaceous and malty taste with juniper dominance, strong finish	Bols National Distillers
Liqueur	A sharp citrus flavor with gin flavors	Pimm's Cup No. 1

Rum

The history of rum involves the islands that arc from the tip of Florida to the Venezuelan coast, the Greater and Lesser Antilles. Conquering and pillaging peoples relentlessly swept into their safe harbors, decimated the native populations by engaging in the heinous slave trade that supported the early commerce in molasses and rum, and pirated both the lush trade routes between the continent and the colonies and the ships that dared to sail them.

Christopher Columbus, on his second voyage to these gloriously beautiful islands, planted the first sugarcane in the western hemisphere. Picked up at the Canary Islands off the northwest coast of Africa which was at that time a principal growing area for sugarcane, the shoots were set into the ground at Saint Croix and forevermore fixed the economy of the Islands Columbus had mistakenly named the Indies.

The lush, tropical climate provided ideal growing conditions for the sugarcane then so popular throughout Europe. The produce of these islands eventually replaced the honeybee as the supplier of food sweeteners. Oddly enough, no one had yet thought to ferment or distill the easily obtained product of cane. However, lacking fruits and grains, the early settlers soon made the transition. There are records of rum distillation on the Islands as early as 1526. The Arabs introduced sugarcane to Europe as early as A.D. 636. It had taken 900 years for the first cane sugar spirit to be produced.

In *Beverages Past and Present* (1908), Emerson reports that sugarcane plantations were common at the beginning of the sixteenth century and that, soon after, so was the commercial production of Barbados "water." He quotes from an

> Wits may laugh at our fondness for molasses, and we ought all to join in the laugh with good humor. I know not why we should blush to confess that molasses was an essential ingredient in American independence. Many great events have proceeded from much smaller causes.
>
> *John Adams*

Irish manuscript dated 1651: "The chief fuddling they make in the island is rum-bullion alias kill-devil and this is made from sugar-canes distilled, a hot, hellish, and terrible liquor."

While there remains controversy over the origin of the word *rum*, it is probably a corruption of the Latin for sugarcane, *saccharum officinarum*. Whatever the derivation, "*kill-devil*" soon became inextricably involved with seafaring and with the well-being of countries on both sides of the great ocean. British ships used rum as ballast for the long journeys home. The American colonies devoured vast amounts of molasses both as food and in distilled drink. Molasses was at the end of one leg in the infamous triangle trade along with rum and slaves that sent ships laden with rum to Africa for slaves who were taken to the Indies to work the fields to yield more molasses bound for Boston harbor.

Terms

anejo A blend of rums aged at least six years.

bagasse The sugar-rich core of the canes.

blackstrap molasses The dark, sugar-laden material separated from the cane sugar crystals—essentially a waste product in sugar production that becomes the primary source for rum fermentations.

centrifuge Huge vessels in which the sugarcane juice is swirled to extract the sugar.

clairin Inexpensive rum from a single run through a pot still—popular in Haiti.

dunder Material from a finished distillation used to sour a new mash, extending the fermentation time.

grog Early name for watered-down rum attributed to sailors serving under Admiral Vernon who wore grogram coat and trousers.

limings The scum formed on top of molasses when sugar is centrifuged—often added to fermentations of heavy rums as is dunder.

loggerhead Metal tool with a bulbous end heated and used to warm rum and beer drinks in colonial times.

London dock rum Rums matured in damp cellars in London.

madilla The middle run or heart of the liquor which is separated from the heads and tails.

saccharum officinarum Cane sugar from which rum derives.

ADOPTED BY HIS MAJESTY'S NAVY

Rum became the staple drink on the British flag vessels and nearly every other ship that plied the broad Atlantic. Aside from assuring a happy crew, the spirit, being rich in Vitamin C, helped to prevent scurvy. The word *grog* is said to have originated from a shortening of the word *grogram,* the rough cloth worn by Admiral Edward Vernon who was the first to order diluted rum be the official provision on his majesty's ships. The sailors derisively called Vernon "Old Grog" for the ration of one part rum to three parts water, and the name was soon applied to hundreds of grog shops that purveyed rum in the Islands.

For at least 150 years before the War of Independence, rum dominated the American spirit market, if for no other reason than that the slave trade provided inexpensive and copious supplies of fermentable molasses. After Congress outlawed slave trading by American vessels, the country gradually turned inward to the spreading rye fields of western Pennsylvania for its spirit source.

Although the colonists had been fermenting and distilling any and all sources of fructose and glucose, few of these sources were accessible year round, especially not at the incredibly low price of Indian molasses. Flips, grogs, shrubs, yards of flannel, loggerheads, spices, and toddies abounded as drinks from rum alone or with flavored wines and brews. Bimbo was rum, sugar, water, and nutmeg. Mimbo lacked only the nutmeg. By 1750, the colonists consumed up to 8 million gallons of rum. By 1790 molasses and rum accounted for one-fifth of American imports. Nearly every occasion of American colonial life, from the christening to the funeral, involved rum, just as British ceremonies always included ales.

The daily "tot of grog" kept the British navy afloat.

Tannahill in *Food in History* (1973) provides a rationale for this:

Alcohol in its various forms—the stronger the better—was the great sustainer of eighteenth-century America. It quenched the majestic thirst that resulted from too much salt meat and fish; it was a social ice-breaker in new communities; it even became a political tradition. When George Washington ran for the legislature in 1758, his agent doled out almost three Imperial or 3¾ American, gallons of beer, wine, cider or rum to every voter.

Harvesting the sugar-rich cane is a hot, humid affair involving a great deal of hand labor. The canes are separated, cut into manageable size and delivered to the mill on flatbed cars or trucks.

THE FOOLISH MOLASSES ACT

With established drinking habits in mind, one can easily comprehend the outrage of the people toward the British Parliament and their 1733 Molasses Act which became at least a secondary cause of the American Revolution. In their time-honored stupidity in taxing liquors, Parliament sought to restrict the source of all molasses to the British-owned islands which sold their molasses at higher prices than the French or Dutch did. Of course, the colonists virtually ignored the act, and rum running became the order of the day. With no effective way to police the shipping lanes, the British lost both the battle with, and the respect of, the colonists. The term *rum running* found new life over one hundred years later with diversion of spirits involving those same islands because of a strictly American folly called Prohibition.

Two final contributions to our language from grisly activities during this developmental period of rum are *buccaneer* and *barbecue*. The French word *boucanier* refers to the hunter of wild pigs and oxen both of which abounded on the islands from the time of early Spanish settlers. At this time the term referred to hunters turned pirates who, with semi-governmental approval, plundered the ships that sailed near the sparsely settled Spanish-controlled islands for almost 200 years. The second term fully incorporated into our language and practice is *barbecue*, probably from *barbacoa*, Spanish for the wooden lattices on which the native Carib Indians salted and smoked dried meat. The Caribs were not at all selective as to the source of that meat!

Some enchanting rum recipes from the past include the following:

Rum Shrub . . . Take 34 gallons of proof rum, 2 ounces essential oil of orange, & some of lemon dissolved in a quart of spirit and 300 lbs. refined sugar in 20 gals of water. Add dash of tartaric acid. Agitate. Add 20 gals water. Settle two weeks, rack and bottle.

Classic Rum Punch . . . "One of sour, two of sweet, three of strong and four of weak." Those [four] being lime, bottled syrup, rum and cold water.

Eighteenth Century Planter Punch . . . Into a marble basin place, 1,200 bottles of rum; 1,200 bottles of Malaga; 400 quarts of boiling water; 600 lbs of best sugar; 200 powdered nutmegs and the juice of 2,600 lemons. A boy in a mahogany boat floats around to serve the 600 guests.

For Ague . . . For seating in yer bed, to releave aches and paines, into ye heavy cream put a good measure of cyder and cane sugar. Whip until it peaks, stirring in as much rum as ye cream will hold. Put powdered nutmeg on top.

SOURCE MATERIAL AND PRODUCTION

The single source material for rum, aside from water, is the sugarcane. Therefore, the process of removing sugar crystals from the sugar-rich shoots is fundamental to the spirit. The shoots grow to as high as 15 feet and can be propagated directly from a cutting. These productive plants not only supply our beloved sweeteners, but are useful in dozens of other products from phonograph records to cosmetics and dyes.

To produce sugar, the center of the stalk or the *bagasse* is rolled under pressure to express the sugar juice which is heated to clarify it and to remove impurities. The resulting thick syrup is centrifuged up to 2,200 revolutions per minute which flings out the actual solid sugar crystals. The residual, dark mass, termed blackstrap molasses, still contains up to 5 percent sugar which is fermentable without further processing.

The beer or wash resulting from fermentation can be distilled by any or all of the now familiar methods of alcohol separation, which creates quite distinctive classes of rum. Indeed, the most popular types of this popular spirit are, not surprisingly, those that experience rapid, light fermentation and distillation in the largest of continuous stills. Pot stills are used to make the traditional pungent, powerfully aromatic rums evocative of kill-devil. Either way, rum retains high ester levels making it always one of the more pleasant aromatics in the spirit trade. While there has been massive consumer choice of the light and white, each island or other producing area has its own distinctive product. The following sections describe the most popular rums from light to heavy.

Salud, pesetas y amor, y tiempo para gozardo. Health, money, love and time to enjoy them.

Puerto Rican Toast

LIGHT RUMS

Light and medium rums dominate the market because of their easy mellow character and their mixability. Bacardi has outdistanced all competitors by identifying these flavorful rums with a wide variety of sodas and mixers. In a rum cocktail, you get both lightness and flavor.

Puerto Rican Rums

The sad colonial history of the tiny island of Puerto Rico chronicles the ravaging of the population by disease. Slaves from Africa repopulated the island providing labor for growing sugarcane and other farming enterprises. Though rum is also produced stateside, over 70 percent of American sugarcane originates on the islands. The production begins in huge fermenters, capable of holding up to 20,000 gallons which require a brief thirty-six hours to produce a 7 percent alcohol wash. The distillate is taken from continuous stills at a rather high proof, from 160° to 180° proof, to eliminate the majority of the congeners.

*Huge fermenters where the sugarcane mo-
lasses is converted to alcoholic wash for distillation at Bacardi.*

Aging for Puerto Rican type rums occurs in uncharred oak barrels up to four years. Since rum retains high esters and acidity, only a minimum tannin exchange is necessary. Often charcoal-filtered, the spirits are rectified with a touch of caramel coloring and reduced to 80° proof for bottling. The white labels on bottles generally indicate two-year-old spirits with the silver labels indicating those of greater age. Whether light or dark in hue, those marked Puerto Rican have the light, airy fragrance and the soft finish so popular in today's market.

MEDIUM LIGHT RUMS

Virgin Island Rum

With their rums of a slightly heavier body than those of Puerto Rico, the Virgin Islands claim the first plantings in the new world at Saint Croix and also the dubious distinction of providing much of the pirate shelter during colonial times. These islands were purchased by the United States in 1917. The rum industry, abandoned during Prohibition, resumed production in 1933. While there is some Cruzan rum produced today, the industry never recovered its former prominence.

Haitian Rums

Another in the group of medium-bodied distillates from molasses are those from French Haiti. These *rhums,* as they are called, utilize the French cognac-type pot stills, involving two separate runs through the stills.

A local favorite taken from but a single run through the pot still is called *clairin.* Retaining both the heads and the tails, clairin is akin to the "white lightnin" of the Kentucky hills moonshiner and is thought to have special voodoo powers to ward off evil spirits, though perhaps one itself!

Martinique Rums

Another rum in the medium-bodied style, also French, comes from Martinique. *Rhum Martiniques* derive from a wash of equal parts of molasses and pure cane juice. The soils, yeast, and production in pot stills yield five times the taste congeners as are contained in Puerto Rican rums.

Other Medium Rums

Other islands producing similarly pungent rums include the French Guadeloupe islands, and yet another major French supplier, Réunion Island, along with Cuba, and Trinidad. Some retain the pot still tradition while others have switched to the patent stills. Of these, Barbados produces a particularly palatable rum rectified with sherry, raisins, Madeira wine, and bitter almonds. Its smoky aroma and taste provide an ideal contrast to the lighter Puerto Rican types.

HEAVY RUMS

Heavy rums can be classified among the world's most distinctive spirits—mahogany in color, redolent in bouquet and forceful on the palate.

*F*ifteen men on the Dead Man's Chest—
Yo-Ho-Ho and a bottle of rum!
Drink and the devil had done the rest—
Yo-Ho-Ho and a bottle of rum!

R. L. Stevenson

Jamaican Rums

Without doubt, the Jamaicans are determined to keep some vestige of the heritage of "kill-devil." But several distinctive steps are taken in their process to assure the kind of London Dock rums so popular in Britain.

First, only wild, natural yeasts are used, in the manner of Bordeaux wine ferments. Second, the fermenting mash is soured with *dunder,* the spent wash from a previous distillation which contains a richness of congeners and previous yeasts. These materials extend the fermentation period up to three weeks, as compared to the two or three days in the light rum washes. The ferment which emerges is rich in congeners designed to make flavorful spirits. Twice distilled in pot stills and taken, like cognac, at no more than 140° proof, Jamaican rums are heavy by design.

The aging process also adds its stamp to Jamaican rums in that most of them mature in the relatively damp atmosphere of London where they experience a much lower evaporation rate than they would in the heat of the Islands. This damp aging adds more assertive character to the finished product. Following a longer aging period, these rums are blended, rectified, and marketed with a deep, mahogany-like sheen, often as high as 151° proof.

Demerara Rums

Our second full-bodied rum originates not on an island but from Guyana, and is called Demerara after the Demerara River along which it is produced. While decidedly heavier in body and style than Jamaican rums, Demerara uses soured dunder mashes but is distilled in patent stills at a high 180° proof which eliminates many congeners. A number of flavoring agents are involved in rectification, including plums, spices, and raisins.

United States Rums

In Kentucky and many eastern seaboard states, the long tradition of producing rum from blackstrap molasses continues. As in the Jamaican spirits, a long fermentation period of twelve days produces a pungent wash. The key to the heavy character of these rums lies in the use of charred oak barrels for aging, in the bourbon manner. Sold at both 80° and 100° proof, American rum is the most natural of all and a delight.

OTHER WORLD RUMS

Since *saccharum officinarum* originated in the wild reaches of India, beer and spirits made from it proliferated during the centuries of home distillation around the Mediterranean and through the subcontinents to the Orient. The most widely recognized commercial rum today from that vast area comes from Djakarta, the pencil-like island south of Borneo previously named Batavia, from which the rum takes its name, Batavia Arak. A very aromatic and pungent distillate, Batavia is produced from equal parts of rice and molasses, a common combination in the East.

*O*ne finds many companions for food and drink, but in serious business a man's companions are few.

Theognis

MARKETING

The year 1958 marks the beginning of the resurgence of rums, in the American market and particularly light, white rums. Barely topping the 1.2 million cases mark by 1964, five years later sales reached 5,579,208 cases, and then soared to 11,712,629 million cases in 1979. That's a success story!

SUGGESTED RUM TASTING

Rum admits of a wide range in tastes, and the following suggested samples should take you up a remarkably diverse ladder of sensations. Should you reside in an area that stocks rum liquors from other nations, products such as Batavia or other arracks, place them on your tasting list as they will provide new sensations.

TABLE 24.1 Top Ten Markets for Rum 1980 vs. 1981 (750ML Per 100 Persons)

State	1980	1981
District of Columbia	363.3	368.0
New Hampshire	150.7	157.2
Nevada	159.7	154.4
Hawaii	169.1	138.6
New York	123.2	131.7
Maryland	128.4	127.4
Alaska	141.9	113.4
Florida	122.9	111.7
Massachusetts	80.4	97.9
Maine	94.5	97.4
National average	66.9	68.8

Source: Dan Hecht, ed., *The Liquor Handbook* (New York: Gavin-Gobson Associates, Inc., 1982), 259.

TABLE 24.2 Rum Tasting

Spirit	General Style	Suggested Brand
Silver label (Puerto Rican)	Light nose and body, complex taste and easy, short finish	Bacardi
Superior (Puerto Rican) 151° proof	Stronger nose, medium to light body, deeper color, hot flavor of alcohol, sharp finish	Bacardi
Virgin Islands	Rich nose, medium body, strong but pleasant flavor, quick finish	Montego Bay
United States	Strong bouquet, pleasant flavor in medium body, strong finish	Jaquins
Jamaican, original dark	Strong nose leading to sharp, full body, sweet flavor, pungent and long, sharp finish	Myers's Seagram's
Demerara Guyana	Fruity nose, mellow mouth feel, medium body, definite spiciness and hot finish	Lemon Hart
Spiced rum liqueur	Fruity, spicy, soft and mellow	Captain Morgan Seagram's

Americán Whiskey

The history of American whiskey making is better documented than that of many of its spirit predecessors. *American Whiskey* refers primarily to spirits produced within the borders of the United States and Canada though some grain spirits are also produced on the South American continent. The most distinctive of these spirits, at least from the standpoint of pungency, is American bourbon which was declared a distinctive product of the United States by Congress in 1964.

DISTILLING: AN OLD WORLD EXPORT

Cortes probably brought a pot still to Mexico as early as 1518, but it was not until the Dutchman Kieft set up the Staten Island still in 1640 that commercial production was undertaken in the Americas. Within one hundred years, over 100 distilleries operated in New England alone, providing about 8 gallons of rum per year to each of the million and one-half thirsty colonists. In 1807, Boston alone supported forty distillers. Rum dominated the alcohol consumption in America because of the easy availability of molasses until the Molasses Act spurred other spirit production.

The Molasses Act of 1733 failed to curb trading for the less costly French, Spanish and Dutch West Indies rum, sugar and molasses and failed to produce new revenues for a number of important historical reasons. First, there was an insatiable demand for Negro slaves to work in the burgeoning cane fields in the Indies and the New England trading ships transported the slaves in exchange for the molasses. Second, the dissident wave of Irish and Scottish farmers leaving Great Britain and

T'was whiskey that made you shoot at the landlord, and what is worse, t'was whiskey that made you miss.

Doggerel

There are two times when you can never tell what is going to happen. One is when a man takes his first drink; and the other is when a woman takes her latest.

O. Henry

pouring into the colonies eventually enabled Americans to produce sufficient whiskey from local grains, thereby lessening the dependence upon rum and its source materials.

A Sure Source of Revenue

The War of Independence created staggering debts that had to be met by the fledgling American government. Alexander Hamilton assured President Washington that the solution was to follow the example of the Irish and British governments and tax the production of spirits. Like the Irish system, the first liquor tax imposed in 1791 by Congress involved taxing both the operation of a still and its production. An unsolvable problem arose immediately in this cash-short, bartering society.

Early American enterprise.

When Abe Bomberger purchased the Shenk distillery operation in Lebanon County, Pennsylvania, it had been in continuous operation since 1753 when it was founded by Mennonite farmers. The main stillhouse, constructed by Bomberger, is even now in daily use and is the oldest such building on the continent.

The operations at Michter's literally transport the viewer back to the founding days of the American spirit enterprise. These "dona cans" contain strains of brewer's yeast known for two hundred years. Pot still No. 2 was hammered into existence under the guidance of Abe Bomberger who purchased the distillery in 1861, expanding the home operation into a commercial firm.

TABLE 25.1 New York State Distilleries (1810–1860)

Year	Number of Distilleries	Value of Product (In Millions)	Gallons (In Millions)
1810	591	$1.7	2.1
1821	1057	—	—
1825	1129	—	(18.0?)
1835	337	3.0	—
1840	212	—	12.0
1845	221	4.2	—
1850	93	4.7	11.7
1855	88	8.6	—
1860	77	7.7	26.2

Source: From *The Alcoholic Republic: An American Tradition* by W. J. Rorabaugh. Copyright © 1979 by the Oxford University Press Inc., 87. Reprinted by permission.

A thoroughly manly image for good spirits.

Farmers simply had no money, but relied on trade in spirits, hogs, and corn to survive.

The short-lived 1794 Whiskey Rebellion which followed included the tarring and feathering of a few excise collectors and trials in Philadelphia for a few offenders. Thirteen thousand soldiers, a stupendous number for the purpose, were sent to quell the insurgents under Light-Horse Harry Lee. The short-lived rebellion did have two important effects. First, even though it was essentially a failure in terms of revenues collected, the tax did forevermore establish the control of the government over spirits. Second, it pushed some of the disconsolate farmers to seek more westerly land where the federal judges appeared a tad more lenient, and that meant Kentucky. By 1790 the Scotch-Irish who had cleared land and settled western Pennsylvania had over 5,000 loghouse stills in Pennsylvania alone, and one in six farmers engaged in the production of rye whiskey. So the military maneuver was a boon to Pennsylvania distillers because the invading troops had to be provisioned, up to a gill of whiskey per man per day, that very spirit the excise tax threatened to make uneconomical.

By the time, then, that the newly independent nation passed the Embargo Act in 1807 and the slave trade was outlawed the following year, a distilling industry had developed in western Pennsylvania. *Di Dummer Irisher,* "The Dumb Irish," as he was often derisively called, was sitting pretty on the plains with his Monongahela spirits made from native rye. A combination of explosive per capita consumption and generally available and ridiculously low-priced rye spirits is suggested by the number of distilleries in New York state alone within a fifty-year span (see table 25.1).

FEDERAL CONTROL

While the Hamilton-Washington liquor taxes largely failed to raise the hoped-for revenues, they did establish governmental control of alcohol production and sales. Even so, there were long periods in the 1800s when the government operated without any taxes on liquor. Since those taxes now represent the largest single source of federal revenue apart from personal and corporate taxes, there can be little hope for a lessening of such productive levies. Tobacco and alcohol are easy targets!

BOURBON COUNTY

The migration of skilled distillers to the Kentucky territory was gradual but continuous. Over the Wilderness Road from Virginia and through the Cumberland Gap at the edge of Kentucky and Tennessee or down the Shenandoah Valley in Virginia went farmers who sought both relief from tax collectors and the promise of a land of steely blue grass, a land ideal for grains. Underlying what were to become the states of Indiana, Kentucky, and Tennessee, there is a vast shelf of limestone which both filters the water and yields rich deposits of calcium carbonate and phosphate, contributing to the bluegrass and the abundant harvests.

Gerald Carson writes in *The Social History of Bourbon* (1963) that distilling was common in Kentucky as it was in the several states, but that corn was the principal grain in that area toward the end of the eighteenth century and that "in 1775, Nicholas Cresswell, an English traveler, recorded in his diary that he had a drink of whiskey at Leestown . . . the sale of whiskey at retail, by the drink, was being regulated in Kentucky in 1781."

At whatever time distilling first occurred in Bourbon County, Carson reports that by 1811 there were 139 distilleries in Fayette county alone and that the total for the state exceeded 2,000.

THE FOUNDING FATHER MYTH

There is a myth, oft repeated, that a Baptist minister by the name of Elijah Craig invented bourbon full-blown when he

Mini-Chronology of Bourbon's History

1767 Daniel Boone's first trip to Kentucky
1783 Evan Williams corn distillery at Louisville
1789 Elijah Craig supposedly invents bourbon whiskey
1808 Slave trade abolished, reducing rum trade
1811 Two thousand distilleries in Kentucky
1848 *Bourbon* first appears on label
1875 Infamous whiskey ring broken by federal agents
1897 Bottled in Bond Act

1906 Pure Food and Drug Act encourages development of name brands
1936 FAA Act designates what constitutes each type of whiskey
1960 International recognition of bourbon whiskey as a distinct type of spirit, unique to the United States

Source: adapted from Gerald Carson, *The Social History of Bourbon* (New York: Dodd, Mead, & Company, 1963), 231–340.

made rye and corn mash, mixed it with limestone waters, and stored the spirit in charred oak barrels. While harmless, there is not much credibility to the myth, and it is uncertain just how the practice of burning the barrels came about. Some say an electrical storm set afire staves ready for coopering. Others suggest charring the staves became customary because of more pliability or to rid used barrels of fishy or salty flavors.

Crowgey reports in *Kentucky Bourbon* (1971) that no color in the spirits was ever mentioned in the many county fair competitions. Indeed, ample evidence exists that char coloration in spirits toward the end of the century resulted simply from long exposures to wood, although some coopers may intentionally have used the coloration technique. Crowgey does point to an ideal social climate, however, for the development of the industry: ". . . and liquor was relished in all classes of society; among the area's clergymen, regardless of denomination, the typical attitude toward distilling and moderate drinking was one of benevolence."

Consider for a moment the really dominant role that Indian corn held in pioneer America. Corncobs yielded clean, efficient fuel as well as such sundries as bottle stoppers, toys for children, and dependable smoking pipes. Corn husks provided cheap and acceptable mattress fillers. But the most pervasive adaptation of this native plant occurred in the food chain. In *Moonshine* (1971) Esther Kellner reveals its varied role:

> First of all, it provided them with a variety of food: cornbread, corn pone, johnnycake, Indian pudding, roasting ears, mush, popcorn, hominy, succotash, parched corn, dried corn, fresh corncakes, scrapple, stuffing, corn pudding, corn relish, corn soup. . . .
> Corn fed the pigs and chickens, the horse and cow
> Cornbread rewarded the faithful dog.

Corn was king, as in many ways it remains today, at least in the center of the country. But the introduction of the hardy Scotch-Irish immigrant distiller to the wonders of corn created the one truly indigenous spirit, American bourbon whiskey.

Before the turn of the century, wholesale drug companies distributed ardent spirits.

THE TECHNOLOGICAL EXPLOSION

By the turn of the nineteenth century, Kentucky had emerged as the dominant source of whiskey, eclipsing both Pennsylvania and Virginia. The adaptation of new technology as well as the growth in supply of grains produced thirty years of phenomenal overproduction. Of greatest significance was the use of steam as the source of heat in stilling, as it was at once more dependable and more efficient. Production soared from about 1½ gallons to 3 gallons of spirit per bushel of corn. Stills of up to a 40 gallon capacity were producing as much as 1,200 gallons daily.

Several important historical developments occurred because of this superabundance of product. First, by 1830 the

Early hand-blown glass bottles were often decorative.

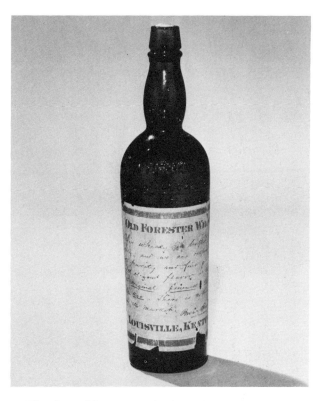

The advent of the automatic bottle machines and the use of government stickers on the necks of bottles brought about the current era of quality assurance. The "old" whiskey within really is!

Y ou say man learnt first to build a fire and then to ferment his liquor. Had he but reversed the process we should have no need of flint and tinder to this day.

H. S. Esquire

Throughout the nineteenth century, whiskey was sold in the barrels in which it was aged as seen in Labrot & Graham's photograph.

price of whiskey had fallen below that of nearly every other potable beverage, vastly encouraging consumption. Second, many producers had to hold their stocks for longer periods and discovered, as the French had with Cognac, that wood aging tempers and mellows the spirits. And, of even greater social significance, the temperance movement gained momentum in the face of the wanton social disorder that cheap whiskey spawned.

The vast majority of the spirits in commerce were raw, crystal white, and unaged. The proof of alcoholic strength was the time-honored method of setting a sample on fire—slow, yellow flames proved weak, adulterated whiskey; slow, iridescent bright blue demonstrated the need for more water, and the familiar steady blue flames indicated the desirable 50 percent level.

Well into the twentieth century, the distillery work force had changed little as evidenced in this shot of the bottling line and the crew at Brown-Forman. However containers shown now are bottles bearing the brand name.

Naturally, the spirits mellowed in that enforced extra period of wood aging in quite a noticeable way. The appellation *old* came into being at this time. Prices for old spirits jumped three or four times above the price for young, raw spirits. By 1870, brand names had emerged and many familiar and still popular labels carry the same designation—Old Forester, Old Crow, Old Fitzgerald, Old Grand Dad, and so on.

Bottled in Bond

In 1897, the federal government passed the Bottled in Bond Act, allowing the producer to delay the excise taxes until the period of maturation had ended. The government sticker on the bottle assured the consumer that the product had truly been aged as opposed to spirits taken from barrels. Many of the barreled spirits were adulterated with cheap whiskey or simply extended with water. The government once again had major impact on the trade by helping to guarantee that brand names were symbols of quality.

Finally, one more technological development occurred in 1903 with the development of the fully automatic glass bottle machines. There was no longer a need to merchandise whiskey or other spirits in barrels, and the bottles assured at least authenticity, if not quality.

So the distinctive American spirit, bourbon whiskey, known and appreciated for its style and pungency worldwide, came into being almost as a child of technology in contrast to the slow historical development of most other potables. Quite unlike the beloved spirits of Ireland, France, and Scotland, bourbon has been both the *bête noir* and the whipping dog of

the American society. For example, in sixteen pages of description of the state of Kentucky, a recent encyclopedia devotes a sum total of three lines to one of that state's most valuable income-producing industries, almost throwing away the information that Kentucky alone produces two-thirds of all American whiskey. The impression given is that they would rather not mention bourbon at all! Remarkably, this same encyclopedia faithfully documents the major agricultural products of the state while omitting any mention of the 50 million gallons of bourbon from grain—a billion dollars or more in revenue.

Of even greater poignancy is William Perrin's commentary in the "History of Bourbon, Scott, Harrison and Nicholas Counties" (in Crowgey [1971]) that only grudgingly acknowledges the obvious:

> That whiskey is a valuable commercial interest in this part of the state, and that the revenues derived from its sale and manufacture is large, is a fact beyond dispute; that it is a foe, bitter and relentless to Christian civilization, is a fact equally palpable. . . . The blue grass region has kept up its reputation for good whiskey, and still makes the best in the world—if the word good may be, without violence, applied to the greatest known evil in existence.

SOURCE MATERIALS

Once again, we begin with the waters. Liquor is mainly water, and few production areas are so blessed as that three state area which rests on massive slabs of limestone. Corn remains the

TABLE 25.2 Types of Whiskey

Type	Description
Neutral spirits	Distilled from any grain or other starch but taken above 190° proof; this category is used as the blending material in whiskey production
Whiskey	Distillate from a fermented mash of grain taken from the still under 190° proof and sold in the bottle no lower than 80° proof
Rye, bourbon, wheat, malt, and rye malt whiskey	From a fermented mash *of a minimum* of 51% of rye, corn, wheat, malted barley grain, or malted rye grain, respectively, and taken from the still *not exceeding* 160° proof
Corn whiskey	From a fermented mash of *not less than* 80% corn grain taken from the still at 160° proof
Straight whiskey	From a fermented mash of grain taken at 160° proof or under and sold at no less than 80° proof following two years aging; includes straight rye, straight bourbon, etc. as defined above
Blended whiskey	A blend containing a minimum of 20% by volume of 100° proof straight whiskey in combination with other whiskeys or neutral spirits and sold at *not less than 80° proof;* also can be blended rye whiskey, blended bourbon whiskey, and so on, according to their definitions
Canadian whisky	From a fermented mash of grains and aged a *minimum of two years* with no requirements for grain percentages or charred cooperage
Light whiskey	From a fermented mash of grain taken from the still *between 160° and 189° proof* and aged in *matured cooperage;* a new category developed in 1968 to allow U.S. distillers to compete with Canadian whisky

Oh, here's yer good Old Whiskey. Drink it down.

Bret Harte

dominant grain in bourbon whiskey because it is plentiful and it provides quick mash and firm body in the distillate. However, in other sections of the United States and Canada, distillers use different mixtures of barley, rye, wheat, and minor grains. Whiskey may be easily classified by the grains involved and by the level of proof taken from the stills.

The distilled spirits industry has had an enormous impact upon American agriculture through the types of grains purchased over the past thirty-six years. There has been a gradual shifting to "other grains" to supplement the more costly corn and barley malts.

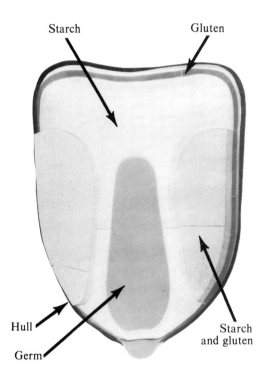

Hybrid corn contains a large amount of starch convertible to maltose.

Table 25.2 outlines the broad definitions for American whiskeys. To avoid off tastes, only the very best of grains are used in production. The slightest defects, molds, or bacteria produce unacceptable spirits that even the mellowing char cannot eradicate. Hybrid corns of the dent variety dominate, as do Polish varieties of barley and rye. The average formula calls for 60 percent corn for body and flavors, about 28 percent rye, and the remainder, barley.

BOURBON PRODUCTION

The steps in producing bourbon apply with much less variation than those in the other spirits. First, the grains are hammered or rolled to a fine consistency for easy sugar conversion. This grist is sifted over screens to clean it of debris and foreign material. Depending upon the grain mixture, as much as 70 percent starchy material is found in the grist when it is introduced into the mash tuns which at times have a capacity of 5,000 gallons. Because of the varying densities, each grain converts to the desired porridge at different heats and times. During this process, the cytase enzymes break down the majority of the starches (particularly cellulose) and diastase enzymes make the maltose sugar conversion. The hot fluid sparged from the mash tun, now called *wort,* is rapidly cooled to a fermenting level of around 70°F.

Large still operations include separate aldehyde columns designed to recapture some measure of pure alcohol from the heavy congeneric flow.

Conventional whisky fermenters, shown here at Walkerville, are 18 feet in diameter and 37 feet in depth with capacities of 48,000 Imperial gallons. These closed fermenters prevent bacterial contamination in the four-day fermentation cycle.

Fermentation

Specially cultured yeasts grow in the laboratories in preparation for the inoculation of the cooled wort. These pampered cultures are designed to convert up to 95 percent of the available sugars into alcohols with just the perfect balance of harmonious congeners—esters, aldehydes, phenolics, and the like.

Yeast cells are so minute that up to 150 million cells fit in a single teaspoon. Once exposed to the wort, they erupt in violent, frenetic growth. The first stage of growth is quite rapid, during which the remaining solids change to sugar. There follows a more patient secondary fermentation dictated by the heat of the fermenter, the type of grains, and the strain of yeast involved. Fully converted, the wort is now called *distiller's beer* and contains from 5 to 7 percent ethyl alcohol.

Sour Mashing

Fermentation is the stage during which sour mashing occurs. In sour mashing, up to 25 percent of the volume is mash stillage or the residue of spent grains from the still. While a much longer period is required to convert soured mash to alcohol, as with the use of dunder in the heavy rums, many advantages for the distiller result from this method. The pH is lowered, protecting against bacterial spoilage, a lighter viscosity occurs and, finally, a pleasant unsour flavor tone results. While *sweet mashing* requires 35 to 50 hours, *sour mashing* will last as long as 90 hours. Because of the practical benefits, most bourbon and other American whiskeys are produced by the sour mashing process, although few bother to claim that distinction on the label.

The most important tool of the baker and the distiller has always been the grindstone. The inscription on this display stone reports that it had been in constant use for fifty-nine years. Sufficient grain to produce 175 million bottles had felt its grinding force.

Distillation

Nearly all domestic spirits utilize sophisticated variations of the continuous still. Various special columns concentrate the fusel oils and aldehydes while selective portions of stillage are separated for treatment as sour mash or cattle feed.

Portions of the distillate flow from different plates from the vaulting still columns. Neutral grains spirits emerge at above 190° proof; some heavy bourbons are taken at as low as 135° proof, but no spirits are taken at lower than 80° proof. At whatever level, the product flows to a cistern room to be cut with distilled or deionized water to 125° proof or less for aging.

No matter where they are produced, distilled spirits need the passage of time in wood barrels to mollify the harvest of congeners. The longer the aging, the milder the spirit.

A cellar master at National Distillers checks new bourbon in brand new barrels.

TABLE 25.3 Congeneric Content of Major Types of Distilled Alcoholic Beverages

Component[a]	American Blended Whiskey	Canadian Blended Whisky	Scotch Blended Whisky	Straight Bourbon Whiskey	Bonded Bourbon Whiskey	Cognac Brandy
Fusel oil	83	58	143	203	195	193
Total acids (as acetic acid)	30	20	15	69	63	36
Esters (as ethyl acetate)	17	14	17	56	43	41
Aldehydes (as acetaldehyde)	2.7	2.9	4.5	6.8	5.4	7.6
Furfural	0.33	0.11	0.11	0.45	0.90	0.67
Total solids	112	97	127	180	159	698
Tannins	21	18	8	52	48	25
Total congeners, wt/vol %	0.116	0.085	0.160	0.292	0.309	0.239

Source: The Encyclopedia of Food Technology by K. Peterson and A. R. Johnson (AVI Publishing Co., P.O. Box 831, Westport, Conn. 06880, 1974).

Note: The above determinations were made according to the official methods of analysis of the Association of Official Agricultural Chemists. Fusel oil was determined by the Komarowsky colorimetric method. Foster D. Snell, Inc.

[a]Grams per 100 liters at 100° proof.

The Bourbon Barrel

The distinction of the charred bourbon barrel cannot be emphasized too strongly. Mandated by law in the definitions of the federal government in 1932, the requirement that bourbon age only in brand new charred wood has ensured forever the uniqueness of the product.

Native American oak, rich in tannin, is cut in varying thicknesses from an eighth to three-quarters of an inch. The entire inside of the barrel, including the lid, receives from 30 to 50 seconds of searing gas flame which creates several char layers. The surface char of nearly pure carbon contributes to the flavors. A second partially burnt level of caramelized wood sugar lends the rich, dark hues to the spirits and the deepest layer of oak yields tannins and vanillin as in wine aging. The barrel containing about 50 gallons weighs up to 400 pounds when filled.

Of course, in so widespread an industry, there are endless variations in ambient air temperature and in the size of the aging warehouses. The average age in wood is four years, with two the minimum. There is a fairly high rate of loss through evaporation, up to 3.5 percent annually which generally increases the alcoholic proofs. An eight-year-old bourbon will lose up to 11 gallons while aging. The longer the aging, the greater the mollifying effect of the various chemicals in the burnt wood with the maximum effective age level believed to be about 12 years.

A chart from the *Encyclopedia of Food Technology* demonstrates both the wide variations between the average and minimum congeners during aging as well as the minute proportions of these congeners in the total volume—about one-tenth of a percent to one-quarter of a percent of the total weight (see table 25.3).

TABLE 25.4 Top Ten Markets for
Straight Whiskeys
1980 vs. 1981
(750ML Per 100 Persons)

State	1980	1981
District of Columbia	384.5	380.0
Nevada	385.3	313.7
Kentucky	258.4	263.1
Oklahoma	242.3	259.5
Virginia	267.5	256.3
Mississippi	264.9	254.2
Arkansas	235.1	228.1
Louisiana	216.2	218.1
Kansas	189.6	212.8
Colorado	216.7	207.7
National average	135.3	131.1

Source: Dan Hecht, ed., *The Liquor Handbook* (New York: Gavin-Gobson Associates, Inc., 1982), 170.

TABLE 25.5 Top Ten Markets for
Blended Whiskeys
1980 vs. 1981
(750ML Per 100 Persons)

State	1980	1981
New Hampshire	370.3	335.7
Alaska	207.2	178.6
Maine	188.7	172.6
Massachusetts	183.3	167.3
Delaware	183.5	162.3
Connecticut	149.9	141.6
New Jersey	147.7	137.6
Michigan	138.9	129.1
Pennsylvania	135.6	127.7
Rhode Island	142.5	124.5
National average	90.0	83.9

Source: Dan Hecht, ed., *The Liquor Handbook* (New York: Gavin-Gobson Associates, Inc., 1982), 183.

Blending

The final familiar step of rectifying and blending provides the bourbon master with choices that rival those available to his peers in Scotland. As many as seventy-five different whiskeys will merge into a single blend in order to maintain a consistency with previous bottlings. Bourbon differs from Scotch and Irish whiskey in that a very large proportion of it is sold and consumed as straight whiskey, the rough equivalent of a single malt Scotch. The big difference is the origin of the bourbon from the rapid continuous stills as opposed to the laborious pot operations for the single malts.

Blends may also be composed of straight whiskeys such as blends of two or more straight bourbons, straight ryes, or straight corn whiskeys. However, most blends are those which contain a minimum of 20 percent up to about 35 percent straight whiskey and the remainder neutral spirits. Sherry and other flavorings may be added up to 2½ percent of the volume. The modern trend to lightness in spirits has begun to favor these lighter blended whiskeys in an attempt to match the lighter Canadian types, as well as the white spirits (see tables 25.4, 25.5, and 25.6). The blends are gently agitated in holding tanks and finally bottled at either 86° or 100° proof with the vast bulk at the lower proofs.

The Pioneer Blender

A word of recognition is due to Sam Bronfman of the Joseph E. Seagram's Company who was ready with great reservoirs of aged, mellowed spirit when repeal of Prohibition finally came. His 7 Crown established the taste norms for a new generation of American drinkers.

TABLE 25.6 Top Ten Markets for
Canadian Whisky
1980 vs. 1981
(750ML Per 100 Persons)

State	1980	1981
South Dakota	382.1	394.0
Nevada	450.5	383.3
North Dakota	372.0	359.9
Alaska	331.4	348.5
New Hampshire	329.0	317.4
Wyoming	280.5	274.4
Montana	235.4	242.0
Washington	237.6	227.6
Vermont	229.3	216.4
Minnesota	233.8	210.0
National average	125.3	123.5

Source: Dan Hecht, ed., *The Liquor Handbook* (New York: Gavin-Gobson Associates, Inc., 1982), 222.

In a biography about Sam Bronfman and his remarkable family enterprise, titled *King of the Castle*, Peter Newman recounts that

what made the Bronfman business boom were some important differences in Sam's approach to the manufacture and marketing of his brands. Instead of selling freshly distilled, unmixed liquors like bourbon or straight rye, the Bronfman brands were well aged and carefully blended. Blending became a Seagram's hallmark.

The magic in Jack Daniel's Tennessee whiskey lies in the carefully prepared and utilized hard maple charcoal. Here, distillery workers observe one of the vats through which the new whiskey is filtered.

*T*here is nothing which has yet been contrived by man by which so much happiness is produced as by a good tavern or inn.

Samuel Johnson

One can hardly give too much credit to Mr. Sam in terms of the educating of the American spirit palate. By the time Seagram's 7 Crown had achieved the pinnacle of case sales in the country in 1947, it was accepted as a standard of sorts, remaining the largest selling spirit for more than a quarter of a century. Parallels to this dominance are difficult to find in any comparable business.

Seagram's began maturing whiskies for the American market as early as 1928 anticipating the eventual repeal of Prohibition. Within two months after their introduction in 1933, Seagram's 5 Crown and 7 Crown commanded a major portion of the United States market. Today the company is without question the largest producer of wines and spirits worldwide with sales in excess of $2.5 billion in twenty-six countries and on four continents. While many people have been involved, this Herculean accomplishment must be credited to the fine and always perceptive leadership of Samuel Bronfman. Anyone with serious interest in the field should read one of the several histories of that ultra-progressive company, now a vast economic enterprise that reaches far beyond vinting and distilling.

A tip of the hat to that stellar figure in the spirit field, a man of the prairies of western Canada who wrote his future largely over the face of the earth.

TENNESSEE WHISKEY

Among the hundreds of labels in the American whiskey market, none possesses greater charm or character than Tennessee sippin' whiskey. The spirit is unique because of an added step in production. The fresh distillate must pass through vats containing 12 solid feet of tightly compacted charcoal before being barreled and aged. Up to that point, it has been conventional bourbon whiskey made from a mash of more than 50 percent corn and taken under 160° proof.

The charcoal utilized comes from local hard maple trees, cut when the sap is down and burned in six-foot-high ricks in the distillery yard. More than ten days transpire before the first impeccable drops begin to appear at the bottom of the charcoal vat with many congeners left behind. The primary producer of Tennessee Whiskey, Jack Daniel, markets it in both Green and Black labels, with the latter being of greater age and higher in alcohol at 90° proof. It is a true delight.

AMERICAN LIGHT WHISKEY

A distinctive category for American producers was created, after years of entreaty, to compete with the light Canadian blends. Introduced for sale in July of 1972, light whiskey differs from its traditional bourbon predecessors in its proximity to the neutral spirit range and in its aging either in used barrels in which the char has lost its major impact or in new uncharred casks. While bourbon must be taken at under 160° proof, light can go as high as 189° proof, just under the absolutely neutral range. Despite the fifty or more labels prepared with diligent care and introduced with fanfare and heavy promotion, the category has so far failed to stem the overwhelming tide of acceptance of the Canadians.

CANADIAN WHISKY

Canadians have been producing fine spirits since colonial times. In fact, the young Canadian industry provided much of the spirit needs of the Revolutionary forces. Like the Scots, they prefer to drop the "e" in their spelling of the word "whiskey." Canadian whisky, without doubt, is the lightest under the whisky label worldwide, is the least expensive to produce, and is, thus, one of the most profitable of all. Logically, Canadians prefer their own to other whiskies, but nearly two-thirds of their entire production is exported, with the United States as the primary customer (see table 25.6). Canada manufactures an impressive 80 million gallons annually, a legacy of the years of prohibition when the industry surreptitiously quenched the thirst of Americans.

A continuous stream of barrels arrives at Walkerville full of aged whisky. The barrels will be emptied and then refilled with new whisky for the journey back to the warehouse. Canadian whisky may be stored in used barrels, effecting great economies for the producers.

To become the lightest whisky, the Canadian distillate is taken from the still at the very high proof of 184°, far above that of their bourbon neighbors to the south. Although the mash must be grain, there are no restrictions as to the formulation as there is with bourbon. Corn is preferred because of its high starch content and ease of sugar conversion, but varying amounts of rye, wheat, and barley are also employed. Strains of these grains that can withstand the cold of Canadian climates have been developed for the industry over the years.

Even more than the higher proof levels, the aging factor, in terms of meeting the trend of softer drinks, favors Canadian whisky. The advantage lies in the use of *used* American whiskey barrels that have lost significant amounts of chemicals in their original aging. Additionally, the distillers save huge amounts of money as the old cooperage is but a fifth of the price of new barrels. This is a considerable factor when one contemplates the extra dollars saved in production that can be devoted to promotion.

Canadian spirits must be aged in wood at least two years, and none can be designated as straight whisky. Therefore, all Canadian whiskies are blends. Rectified up to 2½ percent by volume with cane or fruit spirits, Canadian whisky is sold at 80°, 88.8°, and 100° proof levels. In sum, Canadians are the mellowest of the lot.

The sweep of the Suntory Hakushu fermenting room boggles the mind. Its twenty-four giant, gleaming pot stills are capable of producing 45,000 kiloliters of malt whisky each year. Suntory produced the first Japanese whisky in 1923 and now produces whisky, wine, beer, soda pop and over 200 products through thirty-three subsidiary companies.

OTHER WHISKEYS

Many countries around the globe make products called whiskey, and there are no restrictions on the use of the name as there are with cognac or bourbon. The second largest *consuming* nation, Japan, produces 26 million cases of Scotch-type whisky. Australia, an early market for Scotch export, also makes several brands of whiskey through Distillers Company, Ltd. subsidiaries. Quite a number of small countries like Brazil, Bolivia, Argentina, and Peru import sufficient quantities of single malt Scotch to flavor local grain distillates. The production in all of these countries amounts to a very small fraction of that made in Scotland, Ireland, Great Britain, Canada, and the United States.

In the north of Germany, over 3,000 small distillers produce various brands of *korn* or *kornbranntwein*. Largely the product of rye, corn, and wheat grains, these spirits fall generally into the grain spirit or whiskey category, but many are flavored in the manner of the Dutch gins or the Norwegian or Danish caraway or aquavit liquors. The majority of these korns are consumed locally.

GASAHOL PRODUCTION BY AMERICAN DISTILLERS

Obviously, the American spirit producers have the capacity to manufacture ethanol to meet the growing demand for diluted petroleum known as gasahol. To date, the prohibitive costs of the grain or other starch sources have prevented any large scale movement into this potentially lucrative field. In addition, current techniques of distilling make this conversion to production of gasahol only marginally effective.

Highlights

- Bourbon whiskey must be taken from the still under 160° proof and aged in new, charred oak barrels for a minimum of two years.
- Light American whiskey may be distilled from 160° to 189° proof and aged in new or used barrels without char.
- Canadian whisky is always classified as a blend in the American market although it does not contain straight whiskey as known in the United States and is generally taken at levels above bourbon, up to 185° proof.

- Bottled in Bond is a designation for 100° proof bourbon, aged a minimum of four years, made by one distillery and in one year—but no guarantee about quality is involved.
- Tennessee whiskey is basically a bourbon that is leached through vats of compacted maple charcoal to eliminate congeners before aging.

An announcement by the mammoth firm National Distillers & Chemical Corporation may presage a new era for the industry. The news release claimed that a number of patents had been submitted for a process which would involve continuous fermentation of corn and corn products. The company plans to be in production in 1983 with the capacity to market 50 million gallons of fuel alcohol.

Another project recently announced in Mount Vernon, Washington, foresees the day when the waste product in cheese, known as whey, can be fermented and distilled to the 190° proof level sufficient for a gas additive. Further processing of distilling—and now cheese and other food—wastes has the additional advantage of concentrating the proteins and enriching the remaining stillage for cattle feed.

SUGGESTED AMERICAN WHISKEY TASTING

While the American whiskey industry may be suffering temporarily hard times, the Canadian distillers with their light blends are enjoying strong sales. There is hope that as the American consumer becomes more and more intrigued with character in spirits, as is now occurring in wine and beers, there will be a new and resplendent day for the truly rich and savory native whiskeys.

TABLE 25.7 American Whiskey Tasting

Spirit	General Style	Suggested Brand
Bar whiskey	Light fresh nose, medium to light body, little flavor intensity	Any available
Tennessee whiskey	Attractive aroma, clean, mellow mouth feel, smooth, elegant finish	Jack Daniel (Black Label) Brown-Forman Sourmash
Straight bourbon	Assertive nose, big body, sharp woody taste, long finish	Jim Beam
Straight bourbon	Pleasant bouquet, strong impact on palate, medium body, fine lasting finish	Early Times Brown-Forman
Bottled in Bond	Strong nose, forward and sharp flavor with oaky complexity, long aftertaste	J. W. Dant Schenley
Corn whiskey	Mellow nose, sharp taste but medium body, quick finish	Cornfield
Canadian whisky	Slight nose, easy palate with little complexity, smooth and mellow in finish	Black Velvet Heublein MacNaughton's Schenley
Whiskey liqueur	Floral nose, herby, spicy flavors, lingering finish	Wild Turkey Austin Nichols

Vodka

In his 1957 book, *Wines & Spirits,* Marrison places vodka in the "other" category, saying, "Vodka is made chiefly in Russia, Poland, and Finland from a rye-malt, or sometimes potato starch. It is also made in considerable and increasing quantities in London and the U.S.A." Actually, Heublein had contracted with Gilbey in London to produce vodka in London as early as 1952. Little did Marrison expect the sudden popularity of the distillate a few short years later. This really ancient spirit found new favor on the insentient, citrus-oriented palates of America.

Vodka is really spirit simplicity and for that reason there is no production chart or special terminology. The distillate produced in this country achieves that ultimate—the elimination of all elements of taste and character other than the hospital-like scent of ethyl alcohol diluted with distilled water. Hundreds of years of experimentation with cooling devices, extended columnar stills designed to fraction out the congeners, and endless flavor rectifications coalesced in the one distillate that is, by law, a neutral spirit. The one distillate for which it is necessary to obtain the flavor from the mix! The spirit for the era of coke and orange juice!

MARKETING

Aside from the phenomenal growth of this light and satisfying base for mixed drinks in America, it can be predicted with some certainty that neutral, or nearly neutral, white spirits will continue to occupy a primary position in many countries around the western world.

*V*odka is number one, the Cinderella story of the liquor world. Starting from zero in 1950 when it was not even listed as a separate category, vodka took off like a Russian rocket . . . vodka is currently the largest single selling item in the country and accounts for over 19 percent of the distilled spirits market.

Stan Jones

*W*hen thy neighbor's cheek begins to flush, leave off drinking.

Russian Proverb

Imports of vodka now fluctuate with various promotions and world happenings. A recent disenchantment with the U.S.S.R., for example, seriously diminished what had been a growing market (over 600,000 cases) for their high ticket Stolichnaya, but that gap was rapidly filled with selections from Finland, Turkey, and even China with Tsingtao vodka.

In years to come other sources of imported vodkas could include Poland, where flavored vodkas have been the most popular spirits for over five hundred years, and the rest of the northern European nations.

Heublein recently created a reproduction of the famous Smirnoff de Czar bottle produced originally for Nicholas II.

Modern spirit history was forged by John Martin and Rudolph Kunett, shown in front of a montage of their eminently successful promotion campaigns for Smirnoff Vodka. The foresight of Martin and the imagination of Kunett as advertising manager took what is essentially a bulk product to the top of the sales charts.

A SPIRITED PAST

The first producers of truly white, nearly neutral grain spirits were undoubtedly the Russians and the Poles. Both claim the honor. Ironically, the Smirnoff family originated in Lvov, Poland, although they made their mark in mother Russia. Certainly the name vodka derives from the similar words for water, *voda* and *woda*. White spirits came into being along the giant arc that extended beyond the fringes of the wine culture at the earliest introduction of distillation, in the same areas that avidly produced the *alcool blanc* from native fruit.

Twelfth century Danish and Swedish distillers made akvavit, the Germans made kornbranntwein, and people from the Balkans and the Near and Far East made variations of raki and arrack often including grain, date, palm, and fruit spirits. The Philippines had wine from the nipa palm which produced an *aguardiente de nipa*. In the foothills of India the *Mahua* tree has flowers heavy with fructose. During the phylloxera plague flowers from these trees were shipped to France for fermentation and distillation. The floral substitute for cognac, alas, smelled like mice! These myriad white, hot distillates were progenitors of a sort, but none achieved the purity of that produced in Russia and Poland.

> No ladies are to get drunk upon any pretext whatsoever, nor shall any gentlemen be drunk before 9 o'clock.
> **Catherine I of Russia**

Little Water

The Russians first called their native spirits *zhizenniz voda*, the familiar "water of life" common in other languages. By the fourteenth century, there was a *vodnyi vinnyi* or grape-water spirit, and the term *woda* alone was common in Polish and Czechoslovakian references to drinking.

While not unique, the Poles through all recorded time have tended to flavor their spirits as well as their wines. Favorite flavoring agents, to no surprise, included cinnamon, aniseed, peach stones, and yes, even gold flecks in *zolta woda!*

Heublein's unique charcoal tanks are used for processing vodka.

The clear vodka spirit we know today undoubtedly came to life in 1810 in a St. Petersburg pharmaceutical laboratory under the guidance of a chemist named Andrey Albanov. Experimenting with the leaching potential of charcoal, he accidentally left a lump near an open bottle of iodiform. True to its nature, the charcoal absorbed the fumes. Eight years later, Pëtr Smirnoff used charcoal as a filtering agent for white grain spirits. The result was a spirit nearly devoid of congeners, one which was clean and adaptable.

The Smirnoff firm flavored many of its spirits with honey, lemon, cayenne pepper, and herbs, which were popular at the time. When the Bolsheviks gained control of the nation in 1917 and the distilling industry in 1925, the heir Vladimir Smirnoff went into exile in Paris. Down on his luck, Vladimir sold the family rights to the prestigious spirit to Rudolph Kunetchansky who, in turn, emigrated to the United States with his grant.

After changing his name to Kunett, he began the thankless production of vodka in 1934, following Prohibition. Struggling along without financial resources for market penetration, he finally captured the interest of John Martin, president of a food conglomerate called Heublein, Inc. A Heublein brochure, "The Smirnoff Story" by Thomas Fleming reports that he told Martin, "I'm ready to sell the U.S. rights to Smirnoff to anyone who'll give me $14,000 and a job." The rest is pleasant corporate history, as the pair finally gained world rights to the Smirnoff name in 1947. This giant in the field also produces two other vodkas, Relska and Popov.

A final credit belongs to the proprietor of the Los Angeles Cock 'N Bull Restaurant. In 1948 finding his establishment with an oversupply of the ginger beer he manufactured, he mixed it with vodka and lime juice to create a cocktail dubbed the Moscow Mule. A friend's copper factory supplied the imaginative and attractive copper mugs. The Sunset Boulevard cocktail worked its way up the coast and across the country, aiding and abetting the vodka revolution.

MATERIALS AND PRODUCTION

Vodka may be produced from any source, but the vast majority of the spirit comes from a grain base. American producers have found that potato, vegetable, and fruit spirits cling resolutely to their source fragrances and tastes. In Russia, a wide variety of materials is still used, depending upon which materials are the least expensive. In Belorussia, potatoes dominate; in the Ukraine, most vodka comes from molasses and in the Russian federation of nations grains provide the base. Stolichnaya and Moskovsbaya are Russian export labels.

The taking of the distillates above the 190° proof neutral level is common with vodka makers around the globe. However, the real common denominator with vodka is the charcoal filtration. Many different charcoals work, including hickory, oak, and cherry, each chosen because of its availability and cost. The Poles use vegetable charcoal. It is nearly impossible to remove every trace of congeners so there is considerable variation in the methods of filtration. One giant British firm, Gordon's, claims a secret process involving fifteen filtrations!

The Polish continue their practice, begun in the eleventh century, of flavoring the resulting spirits, particularly with a form of buffalo grass, marketing it with a few strands still in the bottle. Similarly, some discernible taste value comes through in the Russian vodkas now sold in America. However, all of these imports remain, in the broad sense, tasteless and odorless!

Finlandia claims uniqueness in its rectifying waters which come from 10,000-year-old glaciers in Finland. Even the United States offers a unique vodka called Silverado. Produced from California grapes and rectified to austerity, the spirit after two years of aging still carries a pleasant, unusual grapey tone.

Highlights

- Vodka, by definition, must be a neutral spirit in American production, without character, taste, or aroma.
- Vodka production features clean, charcoal filtering to remove any vestige of congeneric character.

- Vodka originated in Russia and Poland where its many variations still dominate liquor consumption, including many flavored fruit and nut varieties.
- Vodka, lacking dominant flavor, is a perfect cocktail mixer where the mix, and not the spirit, is the desired taste.

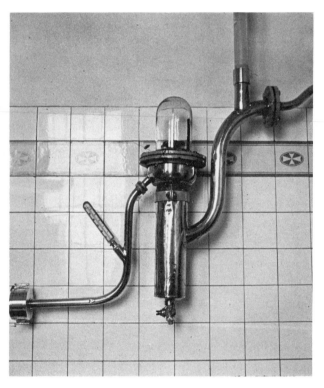

Though Danes have been producing a nearly neutral white spirit from both grain and potatoes for nearly four hundred years, today's Akvavit from Aalborg is typical of the Scandinavian favorite drink. Each potato has sufficient starch for a single shot of the chilled and often flavored versions. Aalborg alone manufactures over ten types of potato spirits, using the flavored caraway as well as dill, coriander, bog myrtle, fennel, angelica and cinnamon. The pictures show Aalborg's ultra-modern two-column stills with draff recovery units looking like boilers in front. The small spirit safe allows monitoring of the flow of neutral spirit, as well as its temperature just below, on the way to the taxing tanks.

FLAVORED VODKAS

Although a flavored vodka is almost a contradiction in terms, eastern Europe abounds with variations of the flavored vodkas similar to the flavored brandies mentioned earlier. More correctly, these are flavored spirits that extend the tradition of warm, fruit-flavored punches and liqueurs. Generally they are compounded with the flavoring agents or the vodka is directly infused into fruit mashes, which often require additional sugar. Citrus fruits, honey, and apples dominate as flavors. Seldom found in export, these flavored spirits are largely local drinks, not designed for long life or travel. Poland produces as much as 50 million liters of flavored vodkas annually, including such exotic flavors as green walnuts and rowanberries.

SUGGESTED VODKA TASTING

With no disrespect to the most popular category in the American spirit market of the day, the tasting for vodka will reveal little because the nuances between American and import vodkas are so infinitesimal as to be easily missed. However, the category provides, as a consequence, the perfect spirit for those who really like the mix.

*I*t is the Russian's joy to drink; we cannot do without it.

The Primary Chronicle

*T*he first glass sticks in the throat. The second glass flies down like a hawk. After the third, they are like tiny birds.

Tolstoy, Anna Karenina

TABLE 26.1 Top Ten Markets for Vodka 1980 vs. 1981 (750ML Per 100 Persons)

State	1980	1981
District of Columbia	734.4	729.9
Nevada	700.2	638.3
New Hampshire	456.1	464.9
Florida	320.4	294.9
California	278.5	285.8
South Carolina	281.4	283.9
Delaware	263.9	269.7
Maryland	278.8	264.9
Vermont	264.2	264.1
Hawaii	291.9	257.3
National average	193.1	193.1

Source: Dan Hecht, ed., *The Liquor Handbook* (New York: Gavin-Gobson Associates, Inc., 1982), 243.

TABLE 26.2 Vodka Tasting

Spirit	General Style	Suggested Brand
American, 80° proof	Medicinal nose, clean, sharp flavor on palate, rapid finish	Smirnoff Heublein
American, 100° proof	Medicinal nose, hot alcohol impact, light body, and rapid finish	Prince Alexis
Finnish	Slight nose, light body, clean taste and finish	Finlandia
Turkish	Odd aroma, light body, clean taste with hint of vegetation	Izmira
Liqueur	Minty, herbaceous nose and flavors with citrus and anise tones	Tava Heublein
Lime flavored	Strong lime character and medium sweet	Arrow Heublein
Danish	Light nose but hint of caraway follows in the taste, light body	Akvavit Aalborg

351

Canned and Bottled Cocktails

*T*hrough the study of the many and diverse alcohols considered in this book, a constant theme asserts itself. People treasure exciting or individualistic tastes in the alcohols they consume. In this sense, cocktails have endured from the earliest flavorings of those flat and brackish Aegean vintages. The *pimentia* of the Dark Ages, the *ratafia* and liqueurs that softened and mellowed the originally crude spirits, the intensity of regionally flavored vodkas; and the slings, punches, shrubs of colonial America; and more recently, the vaulting popularity of the Harvey Wallbanger, Tequila Sunrise and the Piña Colado—all, one and all, brimming with luscious, sugary sweet finishes—one and all prove the quintessential cliché about drinking: people talk dry but drink sweet!

The reality of historical uncertainty must now be completely evident to the reader. Not even for this category of alcoholic beverages do we know—with historical certainty—the time or place of birth. The word "cocktail" is, therefore, "explained by" multiple myths. One pleasant example attributes the word to an Irish lass named Betsy Flanagan who served Continental Army officers punches in crockery mugs with cocktail feathers painted on them. Her punches became known, therefore, as cocktails.

A second source attributes the word "cocktail" to an exchange between Boswell and Dr. Johnson when the latter was given a gin-spiked drink. Johnson commented that it reminded him of "cocked tail horses," those of mixed breed. Another claim is that the word "cocktail" derives from the spiked brews called "cock-ales" because they were served at the cock fights in Britain.

As early as 1768, "gin sling" appeared in the language about drinking in America; the drink often contained rum and

I have made it a rule never to drink by daylight, and to never refuse a drink after dark.

H. L. Mencken

sugared water as well as gin and perhaps had a topping of cinnamon. In 1789, the term *anti-fogmatic* appeared, meaning the same as the "hair-of-the-dog-that-bit-me," a sure cure for the foggy morning after. In 1806, the term changed slightly to *phlegmcutter,* perhaps in recognition of a double duty. The *eye-opener* is recorded by 1818, and the straightforward *fogcutter* in 1833. Finally, the *highball* is attributed to trainmasters who grabbed a quick whiskey and water from those high signal arms at train crossings.

Francesca White in *Cheers* repeats the charming contents of a letter from Mark Twain to his wife while he was in England.

Livy my darling, I want you to be sure to have in the bathroom when I arrive, a bottle of Scotch whisky, a lemon, some crushed sugar and a bottle of Angostura bitters. Ever since I have been in London I have taken in a wine glass what is called a cocktail (made with these ingredients) before breakfast, before dinner and just before going to bed. . . . To it I attribute the fact that up to this day my digestion has been wonderful . . . simply perfect.

Since Dionysus blithe and young inspire
old Hellas air
And beat the muses at their game, "with
vine leaves in his hair";
Since Wotan quaffed oblivion to
Nibelungen gold,
And Thor beside the icy fjord drank
thunder-bolts of gold;
Since Omar in the Persian bowl forgot the
fires of hell
And wondered what the vintners buy so
rare as that they sell—
What potion have the gods bestowed to life
the thoughts afar
Like that seductive cocktail they sell across
the bar?

Perhaps it's made of whiskey and perhaps
it's made of gin;
Perhaps there's orange bitters and a lemon
peel within;
Perhaps it's called Martini and perhaps it's
called, again,
The name that spread Manhattan's fame
among the sons of men;
Perhaps you like it garnished with what
thinking men avoid—
The little blushing cherry that is made of
celluloid;
But be these matters as they may, a *cher
confrère* you are
If you admire the cocktail they pass across
the bar.

"The Great American Cocktail"
Anonymous (c. 1910)

Terms

anhydrous alcohol Pure spirits (or 200° proof) from which all salts and substances have been chemically removed.

bead The bubbles which form at the surface of a spirit around the rim, used to judge congeneric content.

bonded warehouse Storage under federal supervision on untaxed and aging spirits.

bottled in bond Four-year-old whiskey, bottled at 100° proof, and the product of a single distillery.

char The burned inner lining of whiskey-aging barrels that contributes to the character by chemical interaction.

cistern The receiving tank for new whiskey in the distillery.

corn sugar A common name for dextrose.

distillers' beer The alcoholic beer ready for distillation.

doubler Usually a pot still for redistillation of first runs.

excise tax Federal tax imposed on the proof spirit after aging.

high wines The spirits taken from a second distillation.

moonshine Spirit produced illegally and without federal taxation.

neutral spirits Those taken from the still above 190° proof.

prohibition The period between 16 January 1920 and 5 December 1933.

proof gallon A gallon of fluid that is half ethyl alcohol.

low wines The first run saved for redistilling, also called singlings.

sour mash The predominant bourbon mashing technique, involving some percentage of spent beer from distillations.

spent beer The stillage or residual matter from distillation.

strip stamp The revenue stamp placed on the top of the taxed bottle.

tied house A retail establishment under the control of a brewer or distiller, now illegal in the United States.

354

As neat as tins and just as convenient, cans are now in widespread use for cocktails and even wines.

*H*umanity i love you because
when you're hard up you pawn your
intelligence to buy a drink . . .

e.e. cummings

The halcyon days of the cocktail were yet to come. Whatever else Prohibition proved, it did assure that the cocktail, with its juice, sugar, spice, and everything nice, was a sure way to get rotten whiskey down the throat.

CANNED AND BOTTLED

The emergence of this class of already prepared alcoholic beverages was inevitable, and it meets the general demand for convenience packaging of food and drink (see table 27.1). Despite several recessionary periods during the past decade, bottled and, particularly, canned cocktails have demonstrated steady market increases (see tables 27.2 and 27.3).

TABLE 27.1 Average Caloric Content of Cocktails

Cocktail	Total Cal/ Serving	Cocktail	Total Cal/ Serving
Alexander	236	Mint julep	200
Bloody Mary	217	Old Fashioned	155
Bronx	119	Planter's punch	216
Cuba libre	211	Rum Collins	207
Daiquiri	167	Screwdriver	227
Eggnog	219	Sherry flip	187
Gimlet	148	Sidecar	182
Gin fizz	221	Stinger	181
Grasshopper	272	Tom and Jerry	218
Manhattan (dry)	126	Tom Collins	217
Martini (2:1)	119	Whiskey sour	163
Martini (8:1)	143	Zombie	549
Marguerita	146		

Source: Reproduced with permission from Leake, C. D., and Silverman, M.: ALCOHOL BEVERAGES IN CLINICAL MEDICINE. Copyright © 1966 by Year Book Medical Publishers, Inc., Chicago.

Note: The caloric values of these cocktails are based on what are believed to be widely used recipes and may vary according to special formulas employed. In most examples, the total quantity includes about 2 oz of distilled spirits. For these calculations, it is assumed that the distilled spirits are used at alcohol concentrations most frequently dispensed in the United States: 86-proof whiskey, gin and vodka; 80-proof brandy and most rums.

TABLE 27.2 Ranking of the Top Twenty Drinks Used by Famous Bars, Restaurants, and Nitespots

Rank	Recipe	Major Product Used
1	Martini	Gin or vodka
2	Bloody Mary	Vodka
3	Sour	Bourbon or blended whiskey
4	Manhattan	Bourbon or blended whiskey
5	Screwdriver	Vodka
6	Gin 'N Tonic	Gin
7	Tom Collins	Gin
8	Margarita	Tequila
9	Daiquiri	Rum
10	Old-Fashioned	Bourbon or blended whiskey
11	Gimlet	Gin or vodka
12	Black Russian	Vodka & coffee liqueur
13	Tequila Sunrise	Tequila
14	Pina Colada	Rum
15	Bacardi	Rum
16	Rum 'N Cola	Rum
17	Rob Roy	Scotch whisky
18	Sombrero	Coffee liqueur
19	Harvey Wallbanger	Vodka & Galliano liqueur
20	Stinger	Brandy & Creme de menthe liqueur

Source: Dan Hecht, ed., *The Liquor Handbook* (New York: Gavin-Gobson Associates, Inc., 1980), 286.

SUGGESTED COCKTAILS TASTING

Once again, the tasting possibilities are enormous because the American consumer now often finds it more convenient to buy prepackaged cocktails in preference to ingredients and equipment. The following list provides a varied selection from the most popular types. The slogan of Cocktails For Two sums it up: THE BEST COCKTAILS YOU NEVER MIXED.

TABLE 27.3 Top Ten Markets for Prepared Cocktails 1980 vs. 1981 (750ML Per 100 Persons)

State	1980	1981
Alaska	52.7	55.0
New Hampshire	51.9	50.2
California	44.9	41.4
Nevada	43.6	37.8
Delaware	37.5	35.9
Maryland	41.4	33.5
New Mexico	37.9	31.8
District of Columbia	36.4	30.5
Hawaii	30.0	27.9
Rhode Island	33.7	27.0
National average	20.0	18.3

Source: Dan Hecht, ed., *The Liquor Handbook* (New York: Gavin-Gobson Associates, Inc., 1982), 285.

TABLE 27.4 Cocktails Tasting

Spirit	General Style	Suggested Brand
Margarita (tequila)	Thin and pleasingly tart	Cocktails For Two
Hereford Cow (vodka)	Mellow and dairy creamy	Heublein
Black Russian (vodka)	Mellow coffee, rich	Cocktails For Two
Extra Dry Martini (gin)	Mellow	Club Cocktails
Manhattan (bourbon)	Medium sweet and saucy	Club Cocktails
Brass Monkey (vodka and rum)	Thin but satisfying	Heublein
Scotch Sour	Aromatic	Cocktails For Two
Bloody Mary (vodka)	Tangy tomato and worcestershire	Cocktails for Two
Screwdriver (vodka)	Orange juice, that's it	

Tequila 28

Our last major distillate may well have been one of the first to have been produced in the Americas, but it is, without doubt, the final to gain currency as a popular drink outside of Central and South America. In fact, strictly speaking, it remains a unique product like cognac, both originating from small, delimited areas of the world. *Tequilana weber* grows in a small, forty-mile area in Mexico. Tequila City is at the center, its name meaning "hill of lava." The spirit has been called tequila since about 1910.

SHROUDED IN HISTORY

There is no written record of the first production of the distillate of the agave or the mezcal, but pulque, its beer base, was produced from various of the agave plants in ancient times. Emerson, in *Beverages Past and Present* (1908), draws on Frederick A. Ober's *Travels in Mexico* for a record of its use in the early sixteenth century.

> When the Spaniards first came here, in 1519, the native Mexicans had the *maguey,* of which they made almost as many uses as the South-Sea islander does of the coco-palm, namely, a hundred. It is said that there are thirty-three species of this plant growing on the broad plains. The celebrated Mexican naturalist Senor Ignacio Plazquez, professor of Natural History in the State College, Puebla, enumerates . . . more than the above number. . . . the majority of them will produce *pulque,* and the various beverages obtained from the

There is a superior variety of mescal produced near Guadalajara and called of the village in which it is made "Tequila" (pronounced Tekela); this costs more and is sent to the city of Mexico and elsewhere, as something very choice to present to one's friends. I took one drink of it under the supposition that it was anisette, or some other light liquor, swallowing about an ounce, druggists' measure, before I smelled the burning flesh as the lightning descended my throat.

Col. Albert S. Evans, c. 1900

maguey. Twenty-two are enumerated which yield *aguamiel,* or honey-water, and of this number six produce the finest liquor or *pulque fino*.

Ober declares that "this beverage, *pulque,* has been so long in use on the Mexican table-land that its origin is involved in the obscurity of fable. . . . The Aztecs gave it the names of *neutli* and *octli,* while the plant, itself, the *maguey,* was called *metl.*" This rude beer, now as then, ferments in ten to fifteen days into a fragrant, low-alcohol brew, a favorite throughout Mexico, accounting for about a quarter of all the alcohol consumed there.

Terms

agave The generic name for the many types of plants the sap of which is fermented and distilled.

aguamiel The sap or juice of the plant—"honey water."

aguardiente The spirit distilled from the pulque or beer made from aguamiel.

anejo The word for tequila aged at least one year.

DGN The Mexican bureau responsible for certification of tequilas—Direccion General de Normas.

jima The harvest.

jimador The man who does the harvesting.

maguey The Spanish name for the plant.

mezcal Spirit produced from any abundant agaves other than *tequilana weber* (or *mezcal azul*).

mezcal azul The blue-leaved variety used for tequila.

pina The pineapple-looking heart of the mature plant containing the aguamiel.

pulque The beer fermented from the agave, in its natural state popular for thousands of years.

tequila That distillate taken from the *tequilana weber amaryllidacaeae* in a restricted geographic zone and distilled according to restrictions.

tequilero One who produces the spirit.

The native use of this abundant plant of the Amarillydaceae family was similar to the use of maize by the Indians and the American colonists; every usable part seems to have been used. Manuscripts were a fine paper produced from the pulp of maguey leaves. Both twine and tough ropes came from the fibers and sewing needles from the stickers. Many peasant homes had dried leaves for roof thatching and gutters.

Through the centuries of Spanish influence, this *agave aguardiente* became practically a tool of domination. During the nineteenth century, tequila from central Mexico emerged as the finest of the fine. In *Jones' Complete Barguide* (1977) Stan Jones discusses this period in tequila's history.

> During the 19th century, the mezcal produced in the relatively obscure town of Tequila was achieving particular acclaim. It was extracted from *one* species of the agave; *agave tequilana,* known also as *mezcal azul* ("blue mescal") or blue maguey because of its blue-green metallic looking leaves. By 1873, sixteen distilleries had sprung up in Tequila, a small town located in Jalisco, Mexico . . . In 1893 "mescal brandy" from Tequila was presented with an award at the Chicago World's Fair. Other awards were given to "Tequila wine" in San Antonio in 1910 . . . Some Tequila manufacturers still print the words "mescal de Tequila" or "aguardiente de agave" on their labels.

Adaptation to the market in the United States was not swift, even with the considerable Hispanic populations in the Southwest. The awareness and popularity of tequila was enormously enhanced by the national tour of Mick Jagger's Rolling Stones group who popularized it by singing about the Tequila Sunrise cocktail.

According to Jones, "In 1972, Tequila imports had increased almost 100 percent to 1.6 million gallons and two years later increased [another] 162 percent to 4.3 million gallons." This was truly a new alcohol phenomenon since the consuming

This mural at Tequila Sauza depicts production in the nineteenth century with mule power at the pina crusher.

population for 60 percent of those gallons was estimated as being between 18 and 34. Finally, there was a spirit for the young and the beautiful!

SOURCE MATERIALS

The spiny-leaved plant was named *agave* by a Swedish botanist, but it is just as often called by its Spanish name, *maguey,* which means "admirable" in Greek! Over 400 known types of agave have been catalogued, and they bloom in cycles that range from eight to twenty-five years—hence, it is confusingly called the century plant. In terms of agriculture, the plants are delights since they require little care during maturation. Select

The agave thrives in arid soils; it actually rots where there is too much water. These plants will require up to ten years to mature.

The agave farmer seldom faces the crop failures that grain spirit producers experience. Often spaces between the three-foot rows are planted to other crops during the early years. Here a jimadore *chops away the swordlike leaves to reveal the ripe pina.*

types are grown for mezcal and tequila. Mezcal is largely a regional drink, of such power and potency as to confound the average American palate. Many of the import bottles of mezcal contain genuine agave worms, once a source of considerable protein in the native diet, now a promotional novelty.

However, Farb and Armelagos in *Consuming Passions* (1980) present a rather charming defense of the use of such crawling things as sources of human energy.

> The repugnance of modern North Americans and Europeans toward the eating of insects obscures the large proportion of protein they must have supplied for early humans, and still supply for some American Indians and groups in Africa and the Near East. Grasshoppers . . . are an exceptionally nutritious food. Merely a handful provides the daily allowance of vitamin A, as well as protein, carbohydrate, and fat.

The authors conclude that modern societies that shun such protein sources as land crabs, termites, and the agave worm, ironically choose the cousins who live in the water: ". . . other kinds of invertebrates: clams, mussels, oysters, snails, squid,

and especially the lobsters, crabs, and shrimp that are more closely related to insects." Think of that when you squirm at the worm in your next bottle of mezcal!

GROWING THE TEQUILANA

As mentioned earlier, the agave is a superlative plant in that it grows well with little care and almost without flaws. It survives comfortably during droughts. Its only natural enemies are assiduously controlled, as Gorman and Alba report in *The Tequila Book* (1978):

> There could be a bad year due to bugs—two types plague the agaves. One is the "mariposa," a worm that eats into the agave heart; the other is the "piojo arenoso," which is like a louse, millions adhering to the leaves near the heart. To capture the former, the tequileros hire schoolboys to spear the mariposa when they come out to take the early morning sun. To combat the latter, the tips of the pencas (leaves) are trimmed during the 5th or 6th year.

361

Mature pinas weigh up to 150 pounds each and require heavy equipment for handling. The giant fruit is halved and quartered in preparation for cooking that dissolves the sugars from the fiber.

The propagation of the agave tequilana is accomplished by drying out the onion-size seedlike sprouts at the base of the growing plant. This type is about two-thirds the size of the mescal types. Twice yearly, areas are cleared for neat rows of new plants—3 feet apart, providing room for corn, peanuts, or soybean cultivation during early years of agave growth. According to Gorman and Alba:

> At almost any given time, more than 100 million tequila agaves, of varying ages, are under cultivation in this sanctioned territory. Individual Mexican citizens may own up to 200 hectares, or almost 500 acres, of agave land. One hectare can accommodate between 2,500 and 3,000 plants, so Mexicans can have between 500,000 and 600,000 plants on their private properties.

Qualifying growers are awarded a DGN number, *Direccion General de Normas*. These independent merchants cultivate as many as 435 million plants, largely around Tequila, a small, sleepy town of 17,000.

Every tenth to twelfth year, a new batch of mature five-to-six-feet tall plants, is ready for harvesting. Local workers called *jimadores* slash away the foliage to reveal the heart or *pina* which weighs from 80 to 130 lbs. and resembles a huge pineapple. About 20,000 metric tons are harvested annually and trucked to Tequila.

TEQUILA PRODUCTION

The *pina* hearts are quartered and steamed in huge ovens. Steaming releases the sugar-rich core as in the processing of sugarcane. This steaming converts the inulin ($C_6H_{10}O_5$) to

These giant pressure cookers reduce the cooking time to just a day compared to three days needed in conventional stone ovens. The pinas emerge as soft, pumpkinlike hearts ready for the shredder and roller.

monosaccharides that are fermentable, while diverting another offensive chemical *mieles amargas* which is separated and discarded before fermentation. Modern ovens require but a day to accomplish this task, rendering soft, mushy, pumpkin-like hearts that are sent through a shredder and then a rolling mill. Finally, the syrup-like extract called *aguamiel* emerges. The remaining strips are sparged with hot water, and this final fluid is combined with the free run to get approximately 9 percent sugar in the wash.

It is at the fermentation stage that ingenuity stretches the aguamiel to produce approximately twice the amount of tequila. A *piloncillo* of brown cane sugar is added up to 49

Stainless steel has generally replaced older cement or copper fermenters. No more than seventy-two hours is involved in the rapid fermentation.

Tequila must be distilled in pot stills, many of which are copper and reminiscent of early American units. The spirit must be twice distilled and taken from the second run at no more than 110° proof.

percent of the total wash. As long as 51 percent originates as aguamiel from the *tequilana weber,* the distillate may be called tequila. Since it is already a spirit of such marked pungency, little character is lost from the addition of the sugar. The fermentation proceeds for about forty-two hours, yielding distilling material up to 4.5 percent alcohol. Some tequila batches employ 100 percent aguamiel, and others are sour-mashed with still residues, but the majority employ brown sugar piloncillo.

Pot Stilling Required

Like cognac, the spirit called tequila must be twice distilled. The old pot stills hold about 30 gallons of wash and are of simple construction. The first run is called *ordinario,* and it emerges from the still at a very low 28° to 40° proof assuring enough congeners to provide the desired taste. However, the second run also emerges at a relatively low level of around 106° to 110° proof, among the lowest of any spirit studied. Compare it, for instance, to American brandy taken at a maximum of 170° proof. That's what makes tequila, tequila!

The spirit is then charcoal-filtered in the Tennessee whiskey manner to ameliorate the harshest congeners, and most is then bottled for immediate sale. However, most tequila for the United States is exported in tank cars for bottling in this country. In Mexico, it is usually sold at 96° proof but for the United States market it is generally cut to 80° proof. A small percentage of the production is wood aged up to six months, and an even smaller proportion for six years. Look for the *anejo* on the label for the latter.

Wine is a mocker, strong drink is raging: and whosoever is deceived thereby is not wise.

Proverbs, Chapter 20

MEZCAL

Mezcal constitutes a class of one. There exists no other distillate so singular, and it must approximate the Biblical sage's admonition for "strong drink raging." It is made from the Dumpling agave, or *Laphophora Williamsi* that matures widely in Mexico and in the southwestern United States. The spelling with "z" is preferred because of possible confusion with mescal, the tiny, button-like tops of another cactus variety which contain the hallucinogenic mescaline. Chemists have located minute traces of this chemical in mezcal, but not in concentrations that would induce highs, other than those associated with our old favorite, ethyl alcohol.

Extremely high in fusel oils, mezcal projects an herbaceous, weed-like taste and aroma quite unlike any spirit or brew in the preceding pages. Fermentation often occurs with the juice and fibers in the mash, and the distillation requires but one run through pot stills to a very low and pungent 100° proof. Be assured that developing an appetite for mezcal requires one to have a stout heart and an adventurous palate.

Highlights

- Although four hundred varieties of the agave are found in Mexico and South America, only the *Tequilana Weber*, or the blue agave, may be used in tequila.
- All tequila must be produced in the small area surrounding the town of Tequila where the plant is native.

- Tequila is double distilled in pot stills and charcoal filtered before bottling.
- Mezcal is a distillate from the Dumpling agave which is very pungent and congeneric.

Some portion of tequila is placed in the familiar fifty-gallon barrels for aging up to seven years. However, the majority of the product is shipped in bulk to the United States for bottling or is bottled immediately for domestic sale. Mexican tequila is often marketed up to 98° proof.

TEQUILA SALES

As indicated earlier, tequila has enjoyed stunning sales in recent years largely due to the interest of the young in tequila-based cocktails, as well as in the general growth in the Mexican food restaurant industry in the United States (see table 28.2). While this growth is expected to continue, the natural limitation of the source materials will prevent the spirit from rising high on the total sales charts.

TABLE 28.1 Analysis of Mezcal Head (Not Steamed)

Components	Percentage
Moisture	62
Total solids	38
Fiber	11
Inulin	20.0
Ash	2.5
pH	5.5

Source: The Encyclopedia of Food Technology by K. Peterson and A. R. Johnson. (AVI Publishing Co., P.O. Box 831, Westport, Conn. 06880, 1974), 11.

TABLE 28.2 Top Ten Markets for Tequila 1980 vs. 1981 (750ML Per 100 Persons)

State	1980	1981
Nevada	86.7	83.1
Alaska	61.2	75.1
California	48.2	47.4
Colorado	43.7	46.5
Arizona	40.3	39.2
New Mexico	40.5	38.5
Texas	31.6	34.3
Wyoming	31.4	31.5
Hawaii	33.4	31.4
Washington	31.6	31.3
National average	15.9	16.9

Source: Dan Hecht, ed., *The Liquor Handbook* (New York: Gavin-Gobson Associates, Inc., 1982), 253.

Tequila is marketed in three classes: the white or silver sold as it comes from the stills; the gold or amber styles that have seen some wood; and a small proportion that sells as liqueurs, such as *crème de tequila* which has an almond base.

Fifty producers now distill around 4.2 million gallons annually. Tequila is popular in Mexico, and producers now are making efforts to upgrade the purchasing public into the *anejo* or aged bottles. Popular brands include triple distilled Herradura; Cuervo, imported by Heublein; and Sauza, number one worldwide. Sauza is exported to forty-three counties and has one bottling of five years in wood called Commemorativo.

SUGGESTED TEQUILA TASTING

Tequila, in all of spiritdom, possesses one of the unique and, without a doubt, confounding taste components. Reminiscent of metallic oiliness, however not unpleasant, the liquor has charmed and captivated the youth of America. The stunning contrast in this tasting lies between the tequila exported to the United States and that experienced as the fiery young and full strength mezcal.

TABLE 28.3 Tequila Tasting

Spirit	General Style	Suggested Brand
Especial (bottled in the U.S.)	Flowery bouquet, medium body, hint of sweetness, lingering finish	Cuervo Heublein
Gold	Flowery nose, deeper color and strong herbaceous flavor, lingering finish	Sauza
Mezcal	Overpowering fusel oil nose, intense, sharp metallic flavor medium body	Monte Alban Barton Brands
Liqueur	Definite tequila nose, thin, medium body, quite sweet and true fruit flavor, quick finish	Fresa Valida
Canned Cocktail	Syrupy, citrus-sweet flavor	Tequila Sunrise

Suggested Readings

Crowgey, Henry G. *Kentucky Bourbon.* Lexington, Ky.: The University Press of Kentucky, 1971.
  Colorful and anecdotal history of the product and its principal state.

Farb, Peter; and Armelagos, George. *Consuming Passions: The Anthropology of Eating.* Boston: Houghton Mifflin Co., 1980.
  Delightful and easily read survey of what we have eaten through the centuries, and why.

Getz, Oscar. *Whiskey: An American Pictorial History.* New York: David McKay Co., 1978.
  All about America's native distillation, liberally laced with historical documentation.

Gorman, Marion; and de Alba, Felipe P. *The Tequila Book.* Chicago: Contemporary Books, Inc., 1978.
  Concise but complete explanation of tequila processing with 150 pages of recipes.

Jones, Stan. *Jones' Complete Barguide.* Los Angeles: Barguide Enterprises, 1977.
  Excellent background on all types of spirits and the largest collection of drink recipes imaginable!

Lewis, Jack. *Official Liquor Buyers' Guide.* Los Angeles: Holloway House Publishing Co., 1969.
  The basics in paperback with unique brand references.

Mario, Thomas. *Playboy's Host and Bar Book.* Chicago: Playboy Press, 1971.
  A good fundamental bar book with essays on each alcohol and recipes.

de Rasor, Roberto, ed. *Alcohol Distiller's Manual For Gasahol and Spirits.* San Antonio: Dona Carolina Distillers, 1980.
  Technical manual for distillers of spirits and gasahol.

Epilogue

You may recall that the first quote in this book was from Chandler Washburn's fascinating *Primitive Drinking* (1961):

> There is hardly any such thing as a thorough study of a society which presents a more or less complete picture of the meaning, uses and functions of alcoholic beverages within that society.

That worthwhile objective lies far beyond the scope of this work and the abilities of its author. But, this book has attempted to place into some reasonable perspective where we are in the United States today in terms of what alcohols we consume and how they are made.

It is enough that there emerges from these pages some growing recognition of the distinction between abuse and the debilitating disease of alcoholism and the truly temperate drinking that it is our responsibility as alcohol consumers to promote. At a time when medical research gives evidence of breakthroughs in the chemistry of alcohol addiction, and when the social forces such as Mothers Against Drunk Driving justifiably press for reforms which will prevent the carnage that too often results from the combination of alcohol and machinery, it is also the time to keep our wits about us and to evaluate the whole, along with the parts, of the problem.

For, drink we always have and quite probably always will. Let us close then with the gentle wisdom of Brillat-Savarin who repeats this song from *Travels of the Young Anacharsis:*

> Let us drink, and praise Bacchus,
>
> Bacchus who delights in our dances, who revels in our songs to him, who wipes out hatred and envy, and all our disappointments. He is the true father of entrancing Loves, and of seductive Graces.
>
> So let us love, let us drink, let us praise Bacchus.
>
> The future has yet to come, the present will soon be past, our one instant of existence is in the instant of our ecstasy.
>
> So let us love, let us drink, let us praise Bacchus.
>
> Made wiser by our madnesses, and richer by our pleasures, let us grind beneath our heels the world and its futile grandeurs; and in the sweet intoxication which such moments make flood through our souls.
>
> Let us drink, and let us praise Bacchus.

Works Cited

Acton, Bryan, and Peter Duncan. *Making Mead.* Andover, England: "Amateur Winemaker," 1978.

Ade, George. *The Old Time Saloon: Not Wet—Not Dry, Just History.* New York: R. Long and R. R. Smith, Inc., 1931.

Allen, H. Warner. *A History of Wine.* London: Faber and Faber Ltd., 1961.

American Wine Society. "Sensory Identification of Wine Constituents." Royal Oak, Mich.: American Wine Society.

Amerine, Maynard A., and Vernon L. Singleton. *Wine: An Introduction for Americans.* Berkeley: University of California Press, 1968.

"The Ancient Art of Distillation." *Chemistry* (March 1968):22.

Baron, Stanley. *Brewed in America: A History of Beer and Ale in the United States.* Boston: Little, Brown & Co., 1962.

Beebe-Center, J. G. "Standards for Use of the Gust Scale." *Journal of Psychology* 28 (1949):417.

The Beverage Analyst (June 1980):18.

Brandy Advisory Board of California. *America's Brandyland.* California: Brandy Advisory Board of California, 1977.

Braudel, Fernand. *The Structures of Everyday Life: The Limits of the Possible.* New York: Harper & Row, Publishers Inc., 1981.

Brillat-Savarin, Jean Anthelme. *The Physiology of Taste or Meditations on Transcendental Gastronomy.* Translated by M. F. K. Fisher. New York: Harcourt Brace Jovanovich, Inc., 1949.

Broadbent, Michael. *Wine Tasting.* 6th ed. London: Christie Wine Publications, 1979.

Brothwell, Donald, and Patricia Brothwell. *Food in Antiquity.* London: Thames & Hudson, Ltd., 1969.

Brown, John Hull. *Early American Beverages.* Rutland, Vt.: Charles E. Tuttle Co., Inc., 1966.

Carson, Gerald. *The Social History of Bourbon.* New York: Dodd, Mead & Co., 1963.

Cattell, Hudson, and Miller, Lee Stauffer. *The Wines of the East: The Hybrids.* Lancaster, Pa.: L & H Photojournalism, 1978.

———. *The Wines of the East: Native American Grapes.* Lancaster, Pa.: L & H Photojournalism, 1980.

Chafetz, Morris, M.D. *Why Drinking Can Be Good For You.* New York: Stein and Day Publishers, 1976.

Cochran, Thomas C. *The Pabst Brewing Co.: The History of an American Business.* New York: New York University Press, 1948.

Cohen, Sidney, M.D. *The Drug Dilemma.* New York: McGraw-Hill Book Co., 1969.

Cooper, Derek. *Guide to the Whiskies of Scotland.* New York: Cornerstone Library, 1979.

Crowgey, Henry G. *Kentucky Bourbon.* Lexington, Ky.: The University Press of Kentucky, 1971.

The Dimensions of the Affluent Market: 1982 Survey of Adults and Markets of Influence. New York: Monroe Medelsohn Research, Inc., 1982.

Distilled Spirits Council of the United States. *DISCUS Facts Book 1979.* Washington, D.C.: Distilled Spirits Council of the United States, Inc., 1980.

The Drug Abuse Council. *The Facts About "Drug Abuse."* New York: The Free Press, 1980.

Emboden, William. *Narcotic Plants.* New York: Collier Books, 1979.

Emerson, Edward. *Beverages Past and Present.* 2 vols. New York: G. P. Putnam's Sons, 1908.

Farb, Peter, and George Armelagos. *Consuming Passions: The Anthropology of Eating.* Boston: Houghton Mifflin Co., 1980.

Fleming, Alice. *Alcohol, The Delightful Poison.* New York: Dell Publishing Co., Inc., 1975.

Fleming Thomas. *The Smirnoff Story.* Farmington, Conn.: Heublein, Inc.

Forbes, Robert James. *Short History of the Art of Distillation: From the Beginnings up to the Death of Collier Blumenthal.* Leiden, Holland: Brill, 1948.

Ford, Gene. *The ABC'S of Wine, Brew and Spirits.* Seattle: Murray Publishing Co., 1980.

Furnas, J. C. *The Life and Times of the Late Demon Rum.* New York: G. P. Putnam's Sons, 1965.

The Gallup Poll. Statistics released August 19, 1979.

The Gallup Poll. Statistics released September 30, 1982.

Geldard, Frank A. *The Human Senses.* New York: John Wiley & Sons, Inc., 1972.

Getz, Oscar. *Whiskey: An American Pictorial History.* New York: David McKay Co., Inc., 1978.

Gorman, Marion, and Felipe P. de Alba. *The Tequila Book.* Chicago: Contemporary Books, Inc., 1978.

Greeley, Andrew, William C. McCready, and Gary Thiesen. *Ethnic Drinking Subcultures.* New York: Praeger Publishers, 1979.

Green, Bernard, ed. *The Timetables of History.* New York: Simon & Schuster, Inc., 1975.

Greenberg, L. A. *What the Body Does with Alcohol.* Popular Pamphlets on Alcohol Problems, No. 4. New Brunswick, N.J.: Rutgers Center of Alcohol Studies, 1955.

Guilliermond, Alexandre. *The Yeasts.* Translated and revised by Fred Wilbur Tanner. New York: John Wiley & Sons, Inc., 1920.

Hallgarten, Peter A. *Spirits and Liqueurs.* London: Faber and Faber Ltd., 1979.

Hannum, Hurst, and Robert S. Blumberg. *Brandies and Liqueurs of the World.* Garden City, N.Y.: Doubleday & Co., Inc., 1976.

Harrison, Brian. *Drink and the Victorians: The Temperance Question in England, 1815–1872.* London: Faber and Faber Ltd., 1971.

Hecht, Dan, ed. *The Liquor Handbook.* New York: Gavin-Gobson Associates, Inc., 1980.

Hecht, Dan, ed. *The Liquor Handbook.* New York: Gavin-Gobson Associates, Inc., 1982.

Hind, H. Lloyd. *Brewing Science and Practice.* New York: John Wiley & Sons, Inc., 1943.

Horton, Donald. "The Functions of Alcohol in Primitive Societies: A Cross-Culture Study." *Quarterly Journal of Studies on Alcohol* (September 1943): 199–320.

Hunter, Beatrice Trum. *Fact/Book on Fermented Foods and Beverages, An Old Tradition.* New Canaan, Conn.: Keats Publishing, Inc., 1973.

———. *Fact/Book on Yogurt, Kefir and Other Milk Cultures.* New Canaan, Conn.: Keats Publishing, Inc., 1973.

IMPACT. (April 1, 1982):36.

IMPACT. (April 15, 1982):9.

IMPACT. (Oct. 1, 1982):1.

IMPACT. (Oct. 15, 1982):10.

IMPACT. (Nov. 1, 1982):10.

IMPACT. (Dec. 1, 1982):8.

Jackisch, Philips F. *Wine Blending.* Royal Oak, Mich.: The American Wine Society, 1979.

Jackson, Michael, ed. *The World Guide to Beer.* Englewood Cliffs, N.J.: Prentice-Hall, Inc., 1977.

Johnson, Hugh. *The World Atlas of Wine.* New York: Simon & Schuster, Inc., 1971.

Jones, Stan. *Jones' Complete Barguide.* Los Angeles: Barguide Enterprises, 1977.

Kasimatis, A. N., Bruce E. Bearden, and Keith Bowers. *Wine and Grape Varieties in the North Coast Countries of California.* Division of Agricultural Sciences, University of California. Richmond, Calif.: Agricultural Sciences Publications, 1977.

Kasimatis, Amand N., L. Peter Christensen, Don Alurisi, and James J. Kissler. *Wine Grape Varieties in the San Joaquin Valley.* Division of Agricultural Sciences, University of California. Berkeley, Calif.: Agricultural Sciences Publications, 1980.

Kellner, Esther. *Moonshine: Its History and Folklore.* New York: Weathervane Books, 1971.

Kobler, John. *Ardent Spirits, The Rise and Fall of Prohibition.* Greenwich, Conn.: Fawcett Books, 1973.

Lamb, Richard B., and Ernest G. Mittelberger. *In Celebration of Wine and Life.* San Francisco: The Wine Appreciation Guild, 1980.

Leake, Chauncey D., and Milton Silverman. *Alcoholic Beverages in Clinical Medicine.* Chicago: Year Book Medical Publications, Inc., 1966.

Lehrer, Adriene. "We Drank, We Talked, and a Good Time Was Had by All." *Semiotica* 23 (March 4, 1978):243–78.

Lender, Mark Edward, and James Kirby Martin. *Drinking in America: A History.* New York: The Free Press, 1982.

Lichine, Alexis. *Encyclopedia of Wines and Spirits.* New York: Alfred A. Knopf, Inc., 1969.

Liqueurs and Brandies. Louisville, Ky.: Evan Lucas Bols Distilling Company.

Longmate, Norman. *The Waterdrinkers, A History of Temperance.* London: Hamish Hamilton, Ltd., 1968.

Lord, Tony. *The World Guide to Spirits, Aperitifs and Cocktails.* New York: Sovereign Books, 1979.

Louis, J. C., and Harvey Z. Yazijian. *The Cola Wars.* New York: Everest House, 1980.

Lucia, Salvatore Pablo, M.D. *Wine and Your Well-Being.* New York: Popular Library, 1971.

McGuire, E. B. *Irish Whiskey.* Dublin: Gill and Macmillan, 1973.

McKinley, A. P. "Ancient Experience with Intoxicating Drinks: Nonclassical Peoples." *Quarterly Journal of Studies on Alcohol* (December 1948), 388–420.

Marcus, Irving H. *How to Test and Improve Your Wine Judging Ability.* 2d ed. Berkeley, Calif.: Wine Publications, 1974.

Marrison, L. W. *Wines and Spirits.* Great Britain: Penguin Books, 1970.

Marshall, Mac, ed. *Beliefs, Behaviors, and Alcoholic Beverages: A Cross-Cultural Survey.* Ann Arbor: The University of Michigan Press, 1979.

Mead, William Edward. *The English Medieval Feast.* Boston: Houghton Mifflin Co., 1931.

Mishara, Brian L., and Robert Kastenbaum. *Alcohol and Old Age.* New York: Grune and Stratton, Inc., 1980.

Montana Beverage News (December 1982):17.

Monterey Vineyard Winemaker Notes, p. 2.

Morewood, Samuel. *A Philosophical and Statistical History of the Inventions and Customs of Ancient and Modern Nations in the Manufacture and Use of Inebriating Liquors.* Dublin: Wilborn, Curry, Jan, and Co., 1838.

National Alcoholic Beverage Control Association Newsletter (August 1980).

Nelson, Richard R. *Pleasure, Enjoyment and Quality.* Royal Oak, Mich.: The American Wine Society, 1980.

Newman, Peter. *King of the Castle.* New York: Atheneum, 1979.

North, Robert, and Richard Orange, Jr. *Teenage Drinking: The #1 Drug Threat to Young People Today.* New York: Collier Books, 1980.

Patrick, Clarence. *Alcohol, Culture and Society.* Durham, N.C.: Duke University Press, 1952.

Peterson, K., and A. R. Johnson. *The Encyclopedia of Food Technology.* Westport, Conn.: AVI Publishing Co., 1974.

Ray, Cyril. *Cognac.* New York: Stein and Day Publishers, 1974.

Robertson, James D. *The Connoisseur's Guide to Beer.* Aurora, Ill.: Carolina House Publishers, Inc., 1982.

Robertson, James D. *The Great American Beer Book.* New York: Warner Books, Inc., 1980.

Robotti, Peter F., and Frances D. Robotti. *Key to Gracious Living, Wines and Spirits.* Englewood Cliffs, N.J.: Prentice-Hall, 1972.

Rogers, Harold. "Leading Wineries and Grape Buyers." *Western Fruit Grower.*

Rorabaugh, W. J. *The Alcoholic Republic: An American Tradition.* New York: Oxford University Press, Inc., 1979.

Ross, James Bruce, and Mary Martin McLaughlin, eds. *The Portable Medieval Reader.* New York: The Viking Press, 1949.

Roueché, Berton. *Alcohol: The Neutral Spirit.* New York: Berkley Publishing Corp., 1960.

Royce, James E. *Alcohol Problems and Alcoholism.* New York: The Free Press, 1981.

Sadoun, Roland, G. Lolli, and M. Silverman. *Drinking in French Culture.* New Brunswick, N.J.: Rutgers Center of Alcohol Studies, 1965.

Scherratt, Andrew, ed. *Cambridge Encyclopedia of Archaeology.* New York: Crown Publishers, Inc., 1980.

Scholten, Paul, M.D. "Why the Doctor Prescribes Wine." Address to the Society of Medical Friends of Wine, San Francisco, June, 1980.

Seltman, Charles. *Wine in the Ancient World.* Boston: Routledge and Kegan Paul, 1957.

Seward, Desmond. *Monks and Wine.* New York: Crown Publishers, Inc., 1979.

Shearer, Robert J., M.D. *Manual on Alcoholism.* 3d rev. ed. Chicago: American Medical Association, 1973.

Sinclair, Andrew. *Era of Excess: A Social History of the Prohibition Movement.* New York: Harper & Row Publishers, Inc., 1964.

Stateways. (September/October 1981):46.

Stepto, Robert, M.D. "Clinical Uses of Wine." *New Physician* (January 1980).

Tannahill, Reay. *Food in History.* New York: Stein and Day Publishers, 1973.

Timberlake, James H. *Prohibition and the Progressive Movement, 1900–1920.* Cambridge: Harvard University Press, 1963.

U.S. Department of Health, Education, and Welfare. *Third Special Report to Congress on Alcohol and Health.* Washington: Government Printing Office, 1978.

Urdang, Laurence, ed. *The Timetables of American History.* New York: Simon & Schuster, Inc., 1981.

de la Vega, Garcilaso. *The Incas.* New York: The Orion Press, 1961.

Vintage. (June 1974):18.

Wagner, Philip. "The East's Now Wine Industry." *Wines and Vines: The Authoritative Voice of the Wine Industry* (March 1979):24–26.

Wagner, Philip M. *Grapes Into Wine.* New York: Alfred A. Knopf, Inc., 1981.

Washburne, Chandler. *Primitive Drinking: A Study of the Uses and Functions of Alcohol in Preliterate Societies.* New York: College and University Press Publishers, 1961.

Weiner, Michael A. *The Taster's Guide to Beer: Brews and Breweries of the World.* London: Collier Macmillan Publishers, 1977.

Weiss, H. B. *The History of Applejack.* Trenton, N.J.: New Jersey Agricultural Society, 1954.

White, Francesca. *Cheers.* New York: Paddington Press Ltd., 1940.

Credits

Index

Alcohols not listed may be found under the type of drink, e.g., madeira is under dessert wines. The reader is also directed to terms lists within appropriate chapters, e.g., *varietal* is listed in Chapter 9: Still Wines.

W

water, importance of
  for brews, 210, 292
  for spirits, 335, 338, 349
whiskey, America, 333–43, 345
  accidental aging of, 336–38
  classifications of, 338, 342, 343
  history of, 333–38
  production methods, 338, 339–41
  source materials, 338–39
  tasting procedures, 345
  and taxation, 50, 70, 335
  technology and production, 51, 336, 337, 338
  Tennessee vs. Kentucky, 70, 335, 338, 343
whiskey, Ireland, 71, 281–87
  history of, 243, 281–83
  marketing merger, 72, 286
  oldest licensed distillery, 286, 289
  production methods, 281–82, 283, 285
  source materials, 281–82, 283
  tasting procedures, 287
  taxes and controls, 282–83
Whiskey Rebellion, 70, 333–35
whisky, Canada, 72, 343–44
  production methods, 343–44
  sales trends, 343, 345
  source materials, 344
  tasting procedures, 345
whisky, Scotland, 289–99
  blends vs. single malt, 291, 294, 295–98
  first licensed maltster, 291
  marketing merger, 296
  production methods, 291–95
    use of peat to dry malt, 292–93

sales trends, 291, 296, 298
  source materials, 291–93
  tasting procedures, 299
white fruit spirits, 46, 67, 176, 275–79
  vs. flavored brandies, 278
  production methods, 276–79
  sales trends, 278
  source materials, 275–76
    high cost, 275
    limited supplies, 275–76
  tasting procedures, 278–79
Willard, Frances
  leader of temperance movement, 57
William III (King of England) and Mary II
  "Act Encouraging Distilling . . ."
    led to high gin consumption, 48, 69, 317
  trade duties
    led to accidental aging of cognac, 132, 258
wine
  absorption rate, 25–26
  beverage of moderation, 25, 90
  beverage of privilege, 10, 43, 201
  blending of, 136–37
  food and therapeutic value of, 24–25, 47, 171
  mention of, in holy books, 40, 77, 165
  non-alcoholic and "pop," 171, 191
wine acids, 33, 115–18, 121, 127
wine brotherhoods and professional societies, 92
wine concentrate (süssreserve), 106, 133
wine consumption
  annual per capita, in the U.S., 89–90, 102, 109, 207

vs. beer consumption, 78, 102, 207
  vs. spirit consumption, 239
wine corks, 70, 79, 133–34, 136, 153. See *also* pilferproof caps
winemakers, 161, 177, 262
wine marketing, 79, 90, 93
wine production. See also *individual types*
  in America, 70, 82, 86–87, 90–91, 127, 132, 136–37
  in Europe, 71, 77, 88, 90
wine-tasting procedures, 139–51
wormwood, 188
wort (fermentable fluid), 212–16, 339

Y

yeasts, 210–12
  action of, 111, 115, 212, 216, 243
  aerobic (flor), 176, 178, 179
  anaerobic, 114
  for brews, 202, 210
    bottom-fermented, 211, 216
    top-fermented, 114, 198, 211, 216
  cultivated *(var. ellipsoideus)*, 114, 127, 210–11, 216
  in secondary fermentation
    of American whiskey, 340
    of brews, 216
    of sherry, 179
    of sparkling wine, 157
    of still wine, 111, 121, 127
  wild, 114, 123, 165, 176, 178, 210–11, 330

Z

zymase (enzyme), 115